RHETORICALVISIONS

Wendy S. HESFORD · Brenda Jo BRUEGGEMANN

RHETORICALVISIONS

Reading and Writing in a Visual Culture

ASSOCIATE EDITORS

Susan Delagrange
Rebecca Dingo
W. Ben McCorkle

ASSISTANT EDITORS

Kelly Bradbury
Amy Mecklenburg-Faenger
James Fredal
Theresa A. Kulbaga
Deneese Owen
David Ploskonka
Andy Scahill
Edgar Singleton
Anne-Marie Schuler
Kate White
Wendy Wolters Hinshaw

PEARSON
Prentice Hall

Upper Saddle River, New Jersey 07458

Library of Congress Cataloging-in-Publication Data

Hesford, Wendy S.
    Rhetorical visions : reading and writing in a visual culture / Wendy S. Hesford and
Brenda Jo Brueggemann.
        p. cm.
    Includes bibliographical references and index.
    ISBN 0-13-177345-3
1. College readers.   2. English language—Rhetoric—Problems, exercises, etc.   3. Report
writing—Problems, exercises, etc.   4. Visual communication.   I. Brueggemann, Brenda Jo.
II. Title.
    PE1417.H465 2007
    808'.0427—dc22

                                                                              2006026029

Editorial Director: Leah Jewell
Senior Acquisitions Editor: Brad Potthoff
Editorial Assistant: Megan Dubrowski
VP/Director, Production and Manufacturing:
    Barbara Kittle
Production Assistant: Marlene Gassler
Editor in Chief of Development: Rochelle Diogenes
Associate Director, Development: Alexis P. Walker
Development Editor: Stephanie Pelkowski Carpenter
Senior Media Editor: Christian Lee
VP/Director, Marketing: Brandy Dawson
Senior Marketing Manager: Windley Morley
Marketing Assistant: Kimberly Caldwell
Text Permissions Specialist: Kathleen Karcher
Copyeditor: Kathy Whittier
Manufacturing Manager: Nick Sklitsis
Assistant Manufacturing Manager: Mary Ann Gloriande
Creative Design Director: Leslie Osher

Art Director, Interior and Cover Design: Kathryn Foot
Image Resource Center Director: Melinda Patelli
Rights and Permissions Manager: Zina Arabia
Visual Research Manager: Beth Brenzel
Image Permissions Coordinator: Richard Rodrigues/
    Cynthia Vincenti
Photo Researcher: Sheila Norman
Cover Visual Research and Permissions Manager: Karen
    Sanatar
Cover Photo: Watching *Bwana Devil* in 3-D at the
    Paramount Theater, Hollywood, CA, ca. 1952.
    Courtesy of Time Life Pictures/Getty Images
Full-Service Project Management: Karen Berry/Pine
    Tree Composition, Inc.
Composition: Pine Tree Composition, Inc.
Printer/Binder: Quebecor World Color Printing
Cover Printer: Phoenix Color Corp.
Text Type Face: 10/12 New Baskerville

Credits and acknowledgments borrowed from other sources and reproduced, with permission, in this textbook appear
on pages 611–614.

Pearson Education LTD, London
Pearson Education Singapore, Pte. Ltd.
Pearson Education, Canada, Ltd
Pearson Education–Japan
Pearson Education Australia PTY, Limited

Pearson Education North Asia Ltd
Pearson Educación de Mexico, S.A. de C.V.
Pearson Education Malaysia, Pte. Ltd.
Pearson Education, Upper Saddle River,
    New Jersey

10 9 8 7 6 5 4 3 2 1
ISBN 0-13-177345-3

CONTENTS

CHAPTER 3

FAMILIAL GAZES: Reworking the Family Album   56

 KEY RHETORICAL CONCEPTS
memory
description
interpretation
narrative

CHAPTER 6

CONSUMER GAZES: Made in the USA?   368

 KEY RHETORICAL CONCEPTS

the appeals:
logos
pathos
ethos

Critical Frame
Consumer Appeal   369
Logic, Ethics, and Emotion in Ads   371
Consuming College   373

CHAPTER 7

DOCUMENTARY GAZES: Representing History   466

genre
kairos

Critical Frame

Readings

CHAPTER 8

DOING RESEARCH   570

APPENDIX A

CONVERSATIONS ACROSS SECTIONS: Assignment Sequences   599

CONTENTS

FAMILY

HUMAN RIGHTS AND SOCIAL JUSTICE

POPULAR CULTURE

BUSINESS AND LABOR POLITICS

PREFACE

OUR STUDENTS HAVE ALWAYS BROUGHT PASSION AND A SIGNIFICANT AMOUNT OF rhetorical savvy into our classrooms. But when presented with the challenge of developing academic writing using visual and verbal texts, we found that students needed a framework, a set of rhetorical concepts and strategies. *Rhetorical Visions* is designed to tap into the considerable rhetorical awareness our students already possess, particularly with regard to visual culture, and to help them put their insights into words in well-crafted academic papers and projects. In order to exercise their analytical reading and writing skills, *Rhetorical Visions* provides occasions for students to explore and apply key rhetorical concepts such as narrative, description, interpretation, genre, context, rhetorical appeals (*ethos, logos, pathos*), memory, and *kairos,* among others, to the analysis of print and non-print texts.

The reading and writing assignments offered in this book are designed to enable students to move from passive observation or surface description of a text to an engaged analysis of its rhetorical functions. The assignments encourage students to move beyond the binary configurations and the limitations of agree/disagree and pro/con modes of persuasion, asking them instead to explore questions such as these:

- What kinds of stories does the text tell?
- How does the context in which we encounter the text shape how we interpret it?
- What rhetorical appeals are discernible? How do they function?
- Does the text appeal to a viewer's emotions? If so, how? To what end?
- How are images used (if at all)? How do words and images function together?
- Does the text represent a particular genre? How might genre conventions and expectations shape its interpretation?

Why rhetorical *visions*? It's become commonplace these days to assert that our culture is increasingly, or predominantly, a visual culture. New technologies and the new media in large part informed by these technologies mean that students need to cope with visuals in new ways—they need to learn both to make sense of them and to deploy them with increasing sophistication. At the same time, we as teachers need to take ever more seriously the importance of visuals as means, modes, and objects of learning.

Yet one might argue that our (Western) culture has always been a visual one. The classical Greek art of rhetoric—of persuading and presenting and speaking to an audience—was caught up, at the outset, with a dense interweaving of the visual and the verbal. The Greek root for theory—*thereo*—translates into our verb "to see." To theorize in the mind is to "see" in the mind's eye; the goal of theory was to see "all in one glance," all the elements that go into making up a whole, along with their proper relations.

In short, because of the rhetorical roots that the visual and verbal share, and because rhetoric itself is a flexible and powerful tool for both creating and analyzing texts, *Rhetorical Visions* takes rhetoric as its background and frame, and visual texts as a significant object of investigation.

Of course, the "visions" that we refer to in our title do not exclude traditional verbal texts. In fact, as we explain in our first chapter, "rhetorical vision" can best be understood as a metaphor—a description of "the emotional, ethical, or logical responses shared with other members of the audience" encountering a text. The notion of the **gaze** is similarly employed not only to describe the acts of "looking" that occur both *within* and *around* (or *at*) an image, but also, more generally, to describe the particular "way of seeing" that any text can impose upon its viewers, using various rhetorical (persuasive) strategies. Thus, the object of the book becomes at base a discovery of shared cultural context—importantly, but not exclusively, visual.

The Arrangement of *Rhetorical Visions*

The Rhetorical Chapters

Rhetorical Visions bookends its five thematic chapters with three chapters on rhetorical analysis, writing, and research; these opening and closing chapters aim to develop students' analytical reading and writing skills as they explore the complex and often ambiguous and/or contradictory meanings embedded in visual and verbal texts. Together, Chapters 1, 2, and 8 offer a comprehensive guide to engaging, analyzing, and creating texts in a variety of ways: through personal reflection, examination of public texts, historical analysis, field work, advocacy, and creative approaches.

Chapter 1 demonstrates methods of rhetorical analysis and introduces the fundamental relationship between the visual and the rhetorical. Rather than arguing that visual culture supplants the verbal or written text, we address the interdependencies between the visual and verbal, and emphasize strategies that can be used to analyze either kind of text. To read a text rhetorically, for instance, we highlight three sites of analysis: 1) the compositional elements of the text itself; 2) the historical and cultural context of its production; and 3) the historical and cultural context of its reception.

Throughout the introductory chapters, student samples illustrate and reinforce ways of understanding and creating text. Chapter 2's essay and map describing one student's experience growing up in suburban Detroit, for instance, work with that chapter's theme of map-making and representation as persuasive acts. This sample student work demonstrates how to draw on the key rhetorical concepts of *identification* and *difference*.

Chapter 8, "Doing Research," presents methods for working with primary and secondary sources, along with step-by-step guidance in preparing an annotated bibliography, research prospectus, and research paper. The student work in this chapter focuses on the analysis of "kissing" as a representational trend.

The Readings Chapters

Critical Frames

Each of the five thematic chapters is introduced by an introductory section titled "Critical Frame." These frames introduce key rhetorical concepts (KRCs), with some historical background on their use, emergence, and significance. The relationship of each KRC to writing is demonstrated in explanatory boxes that give students practice working with that concept. These introductory critical frames also explicitly address how particular rhetorical concepts can be mobilized toward particular analytical ends. Each critical frame features a specific visual image (or images) selected because it exemplifies the key concepts of the section.

Readings

Each thematic chapter then offers a range of texts that employ different expressions of a particular theme. A mix of visual and verbal, and classic and contemporary texts, the selections are also characterized by generic diversity; essays and articles are grouped with ads, poetry, family photos, news photos, short fiction, and letters. These texts, taken together, aim to break down simple pro/con binaries by offering multiple points of view.

Discussion and Reading Questions

Each reading selection is followed by prompts that will lead students to question, challenge, describe, and analyze representational patterns. These prompts are organized in three interrelated parts:

Re-readings/conversations with the text: These questions are designed to help engage an active reading process and to find ways to re-enter the text from different angles, from repeated engagement, and from reflective thought. Reading and discussion questions draw on the major themes of the section and function as precursors to the writing assignments.

Re-writing and re-seeing: Many of these writing prompts seek to engage, analyze, and even create visual texts in a variety of ways: through personal reflection, through examination of public texts, through historical analysis, through field work, through action and advocacy, and through creative response.

Intertext prompts ask students to compare texts across sections or to extend a line of thought or analytical approach introduced elsewhere.

Chapter 3: Familial Gazes: Reworking the Family Album

Key Rhetorical Concepts: *memory narrative description interpretation*

The first thematic chapter introduces the concept of the familial gaze and the role of texts, verbal and visual, in shaping perceptions of the family. In this section, we go beyond individual texts to explore broader cultural practices that shape representations of the family as a unit.

Chapter 4: National Gazes: Witnessing Nations

Key Rhetorical Concepts: *context   metonymy   metaphor*

This chapter explores archives and memorials to consider the intersections among texts and institutional practices and agendas. The Critical Frame for this chapter encourages us to think in particular about how commemorative photographs re-circulate in new contexts and how they are made meaningful via rhetorical strategies employing metaphor and metonymy. The essays in this chapter explore the intersections of institutional memory and personal memory in national memorial sites such as the Holocaust Museum and the Vietnam Memorial, and also in personal sites, such as one artist's personal photo-archive of the 9/11 events in New York City.

Chapter 5: Traveling Gazes: Shaping Mobile Identities

Key Rhetorical Concepts: *identification   difference*

This chapter focuses on the act of looking as one of social regulation—of inclusion and exclusion, identification and difference. Its texts examine the tourist industry and globalization of media in order to understand how tourism, information technologies, and Western cultural ideals impose themselves upon non-Western cultures, even as these cultures adapt and transform those processes.

Chapter 6: Consumer Gazes: Made in the USA?

Key Rhetorical Concepts: *the appeals: logos   pathos   ethos*

This chapter treats the massive appeal of material consumption, alongside the powerful forces of media, in shaping our rhetorical visions as U.S. consumers. Essays, images, short stories, and poems discuss athletic shoes, Walt Disney, the modern corporate university, Barbie dolls, sweatshop labor, class-based consumption, and non-mainstream products and lifestyles.

Chapter 7: Documentary Gazes: Representing History

Key Rhetorical Concepts: *genre   kairos*

This chapter focuses on documentary representations of "real" events and experiences. Selections focus on a range of documentary media, such as documentary photography, documentary film, news reports, and reality television, which play on our expectations, including the expectation that what is represented conveys truth. Students are invited to explore the blurred lines between fiction and non-fiction and between what is real or unreal by looking at how certain representations convey only partial, and therefore limited, views.

Assignment Sequences

Four assignment sequences appear at the end of *Rhetorical Visions*. Each sequence brings together selections and themes from two or more readings chapters, encouraging students to make connections across chapters while applying and testing out critical concepts and arguments through a series of assignments.

Useful Ancillaries

Ancillaries for *Rhetorical Visions* were created alongside the primary text to provide students and teachers with additional resources for their classes.

Instructor's Manual for *Rhetorical Visions*

The *Instructor's Manual* provides an opportunity for teachers of composition to address the complex pedagogical questions that arise when integrating visual texts into first-year writing and writing-intensive courses, and to help them redesign their courses in ways that reflect an understanding of these complexities and that position rhetoric, namely rhetorical analysis, at the center of the composition classroom. The manual is available upon adoption and can be obtained through your local Prentice Hall representative.

Web Site (www.prenhall.com/hesford)

The accompanying Web site offers essential materials for instructors and students, extending the printed text's scope in terms both of content and pedagogy. Specifically, the *Rhetorical Visions* companion Web site offers the following:

- Resources on the Web: a useful compilation of annotated links keyed to each selection and cluster, leading students to image archives, online museums, e-zines, blogs, and other sites that encourage further reading, writing, and thinking about the complex world of visual culture.
- Additional images, complete with apparatus, and at least one complete Web assignment for each reading in *Rhetorical Visions*.
- Reading the Web: information on searching the Web and evaluating Web sites using the criteria of credibility, reliability, currency, completeness, and usability.
- Writing **for** the Web: a primer on hypertext and Web design, with an emphasis on the rhetorical situation; tips for insuring universal access that meets ADA guidelines; assignments accompanying each cluster for writing and designing projects in a variety of online environments.
- Writing **with** the Web: a guide to citing Web sources, dealing with the ephemeral nature of some Web sites, and understanding Web accessibility.

Acknowledgments

We want to thank all of the assistant and associate editors (listed on the title page) to *Rhetorical Visions* for their critical engagement with the pedagogical questions and challenges at the heart of this project. We are grateful to them for their commitment, patience, and willingness to rethink reading selections and revise assignment prompts. We would also like to acknowledge the influence of the pedagogical vision of Christine Farris and John Schilb at Indiana University, whose curricular work prompted us to reimagine the research paper in first-year writing. Heartfelt thanks to Jill Stephen and David Rosenwasser for the inspirational "Writing Analytically." Thanks also to Wendy Kozol for her work at the early stages and conceptual formation of this project, and whose scholarship continued to inform our approach to visual culture.

Steph Carpenter has provided skilled editorial support throughout the process of bringing this manuscript to publication; her rich, friendly, yet firm readings and responses to our drafts, as well as her willingness just to meet us in electronic space and generate new ideas or alternatives with us there, have left an imprint on every page of this book. We also thank Alexis Walker for critical editorial interventions as we neared completion. Also at Prentice Hall, we'd like to thank Brad Potthoff, Senior Editor; Windley Morley, Senior Marketing Manager; Tara Culliney and Megan Dubrowski, Editorial Assistants; Leah Jewell, Editorial Director; Melissa Casciano, Assistant Editor; and Kathryn Foot, Art Director.

We'd like to thank the many instructors across the country who reviewed the manuscript for this text at various stages and provided invaluable advice for revising it: Christine Abbot, Northern Illinois University; Jim Addison, Western Carolina University; Jonathan Alexander, University of Cincinnati; Norjuan Q. Austin, Stephen F. Austin University; Justin Bain, Westminster College; Gary Bennett, Santa Ana College; Glen Bessonette, Southern Utah University; Patricia Burdette, Ohio State University; David Clay, Canada College; Clark Draney, College of Southern Idaho; Bryan Duncan, University of Oregon; Jefferson Hancock, Cabrillo College; Matthew Hartman, Ball State University; Hal Hellwig, Idaho State University; Charles A. Hill, University of Wisconsin; Catherine Hobbs, University of Oklahoma; Xiaozhao Huang, University of North Dakota; Glenn Hutchinson, University of North Carolina–Charlotte; Mary-Colleen Jenkins, Shoreline Community College; Martha Kruse, University of Nebraska; Jon K. Lindsay, Southern Polytechnic State University; Jamie Armin Mejia, Texas State University–San Marcos; Ailish Hopper Meisner, Goucher College; Robert E. Meyer, DePaul University; Adrielle Anna Mitchell, Nazareth College of Rochester; Patricia A. Moody, Syracuse University; Berwyn Moore, Gannon University; Samantha A. Morgan-Curtis, Tennessee State University; Beverly Neiderman, Kent State University; Suzanne Elizabeth O'Hop, Northland Pioneer College; Dara Perales, Mira Costa College; Jason A. Pierce, Mars Hill College; Deborah Rard, California State University–Hayward; Wylene Rholetter, Auburn University; Jeff Rice, Wayne State University; Patricia C. Roby, University of Wisconsin; Gardner Rogers, University of Illinois; Liz Rohan, University of Michigan; Rebecca Fine Romanow, University of Massachusetts; Barbara Schiffler, Augusta State University; Myra Seaman, College of Charleston; Jason Snart, College of DuPage; Corinne Taff, Fontbonne University; Deborah Coxwell Teague, Florida State University; Cyndi White, University of Miami; Lisa M. Wilson, Winona State University; Kenneth Womack, Penn State Altoona; and Tracy Zank, California State University–Northridge.

Finally, thanks to Matthew Cariello and Jim Fredal and our children, who provided personal support and sacrificed far too many family hours to enable us to work on this project and who make our writing and teaching meaningful every day.

RHETORICALVISIONS

INTRODUCTION
Rhetorical Visions

It is better to be looked over than to be over-looked.
–MAE WEST

Here's looking at you, kid.
–HUMPHREY BOGART IN *CASABLANCA*

HAVE YOU EVER GONE TO A MOVIE WITH A GROUP OF PEOPLE AND FELT that, because of the circumstances (the time, the place, the nature of the film), you were part of a community? Perhaps you took in the first midnight screening of a film that's been "hyped" in the media? Maybe you and your friends—all fans of the original *Star Wars*—have flocked to the sequels (or prequels) of that film? Or you may have participated in the communal rituals of (re)screening a classic film like *The Rocky Horror Picture Show* or *The Wizard of Oz*. You might have found yourself screaming, holding your breath, crying, or cheering in response to the movie—along with others in the theater—even though there were no live performers to receive these responses.

At the same time, you undoubtedly have individual responses to movies in these situations. While you're watching, you might think, for example, about the plot, the acting, and the look of the film, and how they compare to those of other movies you've seen. Perhaps you identify with certain characters onscreen—you might feel that you understand their motives, their emotions, their ethical positions, and even their sense of logic.

All of your responses to the movie—emotional and intellectual, individual and communal—are actually responses to *rhetoric*. The emotional, ethical, or logical responses you share with other members of the audience constitute a shared *rhetorical vision*. Most of us are not used to thinking of a movie as "rhetoric." For many of us, the terms "rhetoric" and "rhetorical vision" are new. But both are useful concepts for helping us understand the world around us and how we respond to it.

Rhetoric: All the Available Means of Persuasion

The word "rhetoric" often carries negative associations: most of us have heard expressions like "It's just rhetoric" or "That's nothing but rhetoric," meaning "It's all talk and no substance," or what's said is not related to "truth" in any way. But while rhetoric doesn't automatically or always equal truth, it's also never "nothing." In fact, whether expressing truth, lies, or something in between, rhetoric always communicates something.

Rhetoric is the art of persuasion. In order to persuade somebody, rhetorician Kenneth Burke tells us, you have to "talk his [*sic*] language by speech, gesture, tonality, order, image, attitude, idea, identifying your ways with his." Rhetoric is often presented as a triangular act of communication:

- A speaker/writer/producer (the **rhetor**) makes up one point or angle of the triangle.
- The listener/reader/viewer (the **audience**) forms the second angle.
- What is being communicated between rhetor and audience (the **text**) makes up the third.

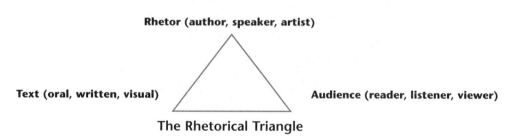

Rhetor (author, speaker, artist)

Text (oral, written, visual)   **Audience (reader, listener, viewer)**

The Rhetorical Triangle

When analyzing a text for its meaning—in other words, when attempting to read it *rhetorically*—it's often helpful to think in terms of the rhetorical triangle. However, the analysis of texts is hardly ever straightforward. The meaning of a text can always change as that text is interpreted by different audiences. There is never any guarantee that different audiences at different times and under different circumstances will perceive it in the same way.

For example, consider for a moment the J.R. Eyerman photograph of a 1950s-era audience watching the film *Bwana Devil* (Figure 1.1).[1] *Bwana Devil*, written, produced,

Figure 1.1   Watching *Bwana Devil* in 3D at the Paramount Theatre, Hollywood, CA. 1952.
Courtesy of Time Life Pictures/Getty Images.

and directed by Arch Oboler, is a 1952 low-budget film about man-eating lions of the Tsavo region in Kenya. It was the first feature-length film in three dimensions to use the advanced polarization 3D systems that required two projectors like those used today in IMAX theatres.

The Eyerman photo originally appeared in *Life* magazine in 1952. Given this information, if we were to consider the photo as a text, we might conclude that the rhetor is the photographer (Eyerman), while readers of *Life* magazine in 1952 are its audience.

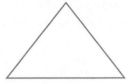

Rhetor: Eyerman (photographer)

Text:
The photo of moviegoers with 3D glasses

Audience: Readers of *Life* in 1952

Of course, the photo as you see it before you today is not in *Life* magazine, and it's not 1952. Your response to the photo is doubtless very different from the response of its original audience. You are, nevertheless, an audience for the photo as it appears in this textbook. Another possibility for the corners of the rhetorical triangle, then, might be as follows:

Rhetor: Eyerman (photographer)

Text: The photo of the moviegoers with 3D glasses

Audience: Readers of this textbook

In changing one corner of the triangle, we must reconsider the others as well, and we must always keep in mind that the meaning of the text can shift with each shift in perspective.

Traditionally, rhetoric has referred to persuasive language. Today, however, the term has entered broader usage and includes other forms of persuasive communication. For example, we use the term **visual rhetoric** to describe how images persuade and argue. Just as we would analyze a speech—its language, structure, tone, etc.—in order to understand how it attempts to persuade, we analyze images in order to understand their effect on viewers. To better understand the Eyerman photo, for example, we would want to study the way the image is set up and laid out—in other words, we would perform a compositional analysis of the image.

Compositional analysis requires that viewers both describe and explain what they see. For example, imagine you were to describe the Eyerman photo to someone who had not seen it. What can you say about the angle of the moviegoers' gaze and the expressions on their faces? What about the spatial organization—the arrangement of objects within the image? What seems to be the main focus of the image—that is, what appears at its center? (Note that if the Eyerman photo were in color, you would also want to consider hue, which refers to the density and intensity of a color.)

As the rhetorical triangle implies, however, understanding rhetoric does not simply require analysis of the composition of the text; it requires understanding the context within which the text was produced, as well as understanding the context of its reception by its audience.

Understanding Rhetorical Context

The first step in reading rhetorically is to identify each element of the rhetorical triangle (rhetor, audience, and text), as we discussed above. The next step is to consider fully how particular **contexts** (the historical, cultural, political, and other environments) influence each element of the rhetorical triangle. All aspects of the rhetorical triangle, including context, are interrelated, interdependent, and informed by each other, as we will see when we examine the context surrounding the rhetor, audience, and text of the Eyerman photograph.

For our purposes, let's choose one set of rhetorical relationships for our context analysis (in other words, one related set of points on the triangle):

Rhetor: Eyerman (photographer)

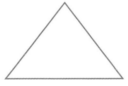

Text:
The photo of the moviegoers with 3D glasses   **Audience:** Readers of this textbook

Rhetor

Because a rhetor attempts to convey a subject matter in a particular way, that rhetoric relies on various means of persuasion. Aristotle claimed that there were three ways of persuading, using the rhetor's own character (*ethos*), appealing to an audience's emotions (*pathos*), and appealing to reason and logic (*logos*). Thus, one strategy in understanding the context of the rhetor is to consider the rhetor's character. In ancient rhetoric, character encompassed the rhetor's patterns of behavior, self-discipline, moral convictions, and reputation. J.R. Eyerman's reputation was built upon his work at *Life* magazine. He was known in the 1950s, as he is now, as one of the prominent photographers of the twentieth century. This image of the audience watching *Bwana Devil* is as well-known as it is, in part, because of Eyerman's reputation and its place within his larger body of work.

Second, in examining the "rhetor" point of the triangle, we might explore the relation between the rhetor and his subject. In composing the image, what message does Eyerman convey? What might it mean that the image situates the photographer as if he were looking down at the subjects in the theater? When examining the rhetor's point of view, we are inevitably considering how the rhetor (in this case the photographer) approaches his or her subject as well as how the rhetor addresses or imagines his or her audience. Like most *Life* magazine photographs, this image was in part intended to record a unique U.S. cultural moment, namely to portray the postwar 1950s as a time of technological advancement and prosperity. At the same time, the photographer's elevated perspective and the oblique angle at which the shot is taken suggest the photographer's particular perspective on the scene. How would you characterize this perspective?

Audience

As audience, we, like Eyerman, look down on the moviegoers in the photo. What relationships between viewer (you) and viewed (the moviegoers) does this photographic angle indicate to you? Consider, for example, whether the point of view invites you to *join* or to *judge,* smile *with* or *at,* look *with* or *upon* the moviegoers. Does the angle of your viewing guide you more toward identification with or distance from this particular community? The original audience for this photography—readers of *Life* magazine in the 1950s, more specifically white middle-class readers—would presumably identify with the audience depicted in the photograph. To what degree do you identify with them? And with the photographer?

Text

Relevant context about the subject of the photo—a particular group of 1950s' moviegoers—involves both the historical moment in which they were photographed and the publication in which their image was originally produced. After the country recovered from decades of international economic crisis and war in the 1940s, *Life* magazine turned in the 1950s to U.S. social life and began featuring photography that predominantly displayed the ordinary domestic life of Americans and the ideals of the white, middle-class family, which were represented as the social norm.

If we focus on the moviegoers as the subject of the photo, we see that all moviegoers are white; the women wear hats, and most of the men are in tailored suits, attire suitable for a social event among the middle or upper classes in that era. The 3D cardboard glasses are, at this time, symbols of technological progress. Thus, this image presents a mix of this "new" technology with leisure. How would you describe the expressions on the moviegoers' faces? Given the historic context for this subject, how would you explain these expressions? What might the photo express that explains its original publication, as well as its enduring interest as a cultural document?

Rhetorical Analysis: A Summation

The primary goal of this book is to introduce you to rhetorical analysis as a method that can help you both analyze and create a range of texts—visual and verbal. To that end, we offer the following summation of the method modeled in the preceding pages:

READING RHETORICALLY

THE RHETORICAL TRIANGLE: THREE SITES OF CONTEXTUAL ANALYSIS

Our reading of visual images, as well as other kinds of texts, suggests that they are more than what immediately "meets the eye" because they are shaped by *context*. To read a text rhetorically, then, is to examine it in "triangulation":

1. The historical and cultural contexts from which the text emerged and in which the **rhetor** created it.
2. The historical and cultural contexts in which it was and is seen and/or read— the context surrounding **audience.**
3. The **message/text** itself, and how historical and cultural contexts shape the way a particular theme or subject is presented.

Reading Rhetors in Context

Exploring the cultural and historical factors that inform the rhetor's point of view, as well as speculating on the presumed or known purpose or intent of its creation, would be part of this angle of rhetorical reading. Research into the technologies that produced the text/image and the conventions employed in producing it can also be helpful in understanding the rhetor's representation of the subject.

Reading Audiences in Context

Considering how viewers or audiences respond involves thinking about, on the one hand, the historical and cultural contexts in which the image or text was produced and, on the other hand, the cultural and historical contexts in which it has been or is presently viewed or read. For example, technological advances, historical hindsight, and shifting cultural relationships among those depicted in the text, as well as between those being seen and those doing the looking, all affect how viewers interpret and receive a text.

Reading Texts in Context

Reading texts in context involves asking how particular historical and cultural contexts shape the representation of the subject/text: the content, symbols, format (in images, e.g., hue), organization, and focal points. This information also will aid in your analysis of the rhetor's point of view.

The Political Power of Rhetoric

The kind of analysis of the Eyerman photograph we outlined above can be applied to more overtly persuasive kinds of texts as well, such as advertisements, political campaigns, and government propaganda. Visual images in particular often carry powerful political messages that can create a particular *rhetorical vision.*

As we saw in the opening section of this chapter, a *rhetorical vision* refers to a shared understanding or perception of reality. Rhetorical visions can be shared among small groups and large groups, and they can even function in ways that unify a nation. The 2001 State of the Union address that President George W. Bush delivered to the nation nine days after the attacks on the World Trade Center and Pentagon is a powerful example of an attempt to shape a national rhetorical vision. In this speech, the President rhetorically unifies the nation through his use of the collective pronoun "we," through testimony about one victim, and through reference to national symbols and shared symbolic practices.

> In the normal course of events, presidents come to this chamber to report on the state of the union. Tonight, no such report is needed. It has already been delivered by the American people.
>
> We have seen it in the courage of passengers who rushed terrorists to save others on the ground, passengers like an exceptional man named Todd Beamer. Please help me to welcome his wife, Lisa Beamer, here tonight.
>
> We have seen the state of our union in the endurance of rescuers working past exhaustion. We have seen the unfurling of flags, the lighting of candles, and the giving of blood, the saying of prayers—in English, Hebrew, and Arabic. We have seen the decency of a loving and giving people, who have made the grief of strangers their own.

The ways we talk about ourselves, our culture, and our nation often follow certain patterns; we tell stories, or **narratives,** about what happened in the past and what is happening presently. One of many national narratives, for instance, that surfaced post–9-11 was one of increased U.S. vulnerability; another concerned national resilience. Individual perceptions are in part shaped by these larger cultural and national narratives.

An example of the power of images in creating a national rhetorical vision can be seen in World War II propaganda. Consider the image below (Figure 1.2).

Here ten Japanese American women are seated around a picnic table in Utah in 1943, sewing patches and stars onto an American flag. This image promotes a vision shared, presumably, by mainstream consumers of the image in that era: that U.S. democracy—specifically, the ideal of the melting pot—works. Though ethnically identified with Japan, a country with which the United States was at war, the women are presented, Betsy Ross–like, as being just as patriotic as other Americans.

Yet these particular women were photographed at the Central Utah Relocation Center, one of several internment camps established by the U.S. government during

Figure 1.2 The sewing class teachers at Topaz making the Service Flag.

Central Utah Relocation Center, Topaz, Utah, 23 April 1943. (No. 210-G-4B-716, Russell Bankson, Central File, RG 210, NACP.) Courtesy of the National Archives and Records Administration.

World War II. After the bombing of Pearl Harbor, the U.S. Department of Justice imposed a federal regulation that closed the borders to all persons of Japanese ancestry. The Treasury Department followed by freezing the assets of Japanese Americans in the United States, and, in February 1942, with Executive Order 9066, President Roosevelt authorized the evacuation of anyone of Japanese descent from the Pacific Coast. Japanese American families were relocated, dispossessed of their homes and most material belongings, and moved to internment camps. The U.S. government established the War Relocation Authority (WRA) to oversee the camps.

As part of public relations efforts, WRA photographers took positive images of the camps—images of happy children in school scenes, of common domestic life, of leisure activities (dances, drama performances, sports, games)—all of which falsely signaled to the U.S. public, as historian Wendy Kozol notes in her essay on representations of Japanese American internment camps, that these were not prison camps.[2] WRA images of Japanese American internment camps efface some of the starker realities of life in these camps, which included lack of fresh food, poor sanitation, and other factors that led to humiliation and the disruption of social and familial life. Thus, when considering the rhetorical vision that an image conveys, we need to consider what kinds of stories the images tell and what (and whose) stories are rendered invisible or inaudible.

Images like these are examples of propaganda. **Propaganda** is material that has been deliberately designed to express a particular rhetorical vision that one person or group wants another person or group to adopt; propaganda is thus ideologically driven. **Ideology** is a term that refers to a pattern or set of ideas, values, assumptions, and beliefs that shapes and permeates a society, culture, or group, and that is made to seem "natural" or objectively "factual." As an example of government propaganda, the WRA image demonstrates the importance of identifying who controls the production and distribution of images and other texts, how the subject is selected and presented, and to whom the text is distributed. In other words, the image demonstrates the importance of identifying rhetor, text, and audience.

As another example of propaganda, consider this famous image taken in Beijing, China in 1989 (Figure 1.3). To most viewers in the United States, the

Figure 1.3   Chinese student stopping tanks at Tiananmen Square, Beijing, 1989.
Courtesy of Jeff Widener/AP Wide World Photos.

image of a Chinese student stopping tanks at Tiananmen Square seems to have an obvious message—it represents the courageous resistance of an individual in the face of tyranny. Because democratic principles and ideals of freedom of expression and the right to protest the government are core American values, the image had and has particular resonance for many U.S. viewers. However, for the government-controlled media within China, which closed down TV and radio stations and banned reporting during this period, the photograph has been used as evidence of military restraint in the face of social unrest. Thus the same powerful image can convey very different messages, depending on who interprets it and for what purpose(s).

One of the assumptions of *Rhetorical Visions* is that viewers and readers are not passive receptacles. Images in particular may have a narcotic affect on some viewers some of the time. But they need not. To say that images have persuasive rhetorical power is not to imply that consumers of it are powerless to resist it, or that powerful images cannot challenge or unsettle dominant points of view.

The Rhetorical Gaze

The common definition of **gaze** is to stare, or to fix the eyes in a steady intent look. But in studies of visual rhetoric, the gaze more generally refers to the acts of "looking" that occur both within and around (or at) an image: who is looking, how they are looking, why they are looking, where they are looking, and who/what is being looked *at*. The gaze also refers to the particular "way of seeing" that an image can impose upon its viewers, using various rhetorical (persuasive) strategies.

Identification, a process by which we come to feel a relationship to a person, a group, an idea, a belief, or even a worldview, is one key rhetorical strategy used by those who create persuasive texts—verbal or visual—to attempt to align an audience with the text's overall message. Identification is a strategy closely aligned with the concept of the gaze, so it is often discussed in the context of visual texts. Filmmakers, for example, use identification to "fix" the gaze of an audience and attempt to align viewers with certain characters or with the film's overall message. It has been said, for example, that an audience's ability to identify in some way with Tom Hanks's portrayal of the character Forrest Gump is in large part what made that film so successful. Certainly, the film is enhanced in part by the character's sympathetic "innocence"; perhaps more importantly, the movie's soundtrack and its integration of footage of famous scenes and people from the 1960s and 1970s allows the audience to identify with the film's story by reliving or remembering specific points in history. Seeing Forrest shake hands with President Nixon, for example, is a scene you likely recognize as familiar because you've seen similar footage, even if you were born after Nixon left office.

As you'll discover in later chapters, we can identify many different types of gazes that in turn reveal different expectations for the relationship between the viewer and what is viewed. Laura Mulvey, a prominent film scholar, uses identification to help explain the concept of the **male gaze,** in which the viewer identifies with the male point of view and male desires: Mulvey's claim is that movies are made with the male viewer in mind. In her research, Mulvey analyzes how camera movements are determined by or follow male heroes and how camera angles assume the male protagonist's position and the male point of view. In Mulvey's analysis, women are positioned as images to be looked at and men are active, those doing the looking. In this way, the viewer comes to identify with the male movie hero.

In paintings, we see similar patterns, as John Berger notes in his seminal book *Ways of Seeing.* Berger notes that women are often depicted in classical paintings as maternal figures or sexual objects. In paintings such as the one below (Figure 1.4) men gaze upon female figures as possessions.

As we've said, the concept of the gaze is a useful one for analyzing visual rhetoric. Because the gaze is so central to visual rhetoric, images that ask us to look at others who are themselves looked at or looking are especially useful for exploring rhetorical significance.

Let's look at a contemporary example: an image of young Afghan girls watching UN workers unloading ballot kits for an historic democratic election in October 2004 (Figure 1.5).

This photograph, taken by an Associated Press photographer and appearing on the front page of *The Columbus Dispatch,* a local paper in Columbus, Ohio, depicts a

Figure 1.4 Peter Paul Rubens (1577–1640), *Judgement of Paris.*
Courtesy of Scala/Art Resource.

Figure 1.5 Afghan girls looking at UN workers, October 2004.

Courtesy of Emilio Morenatti/AP.

collective act of looking. To what degree are we encouraged to identify with the girls pictured? What difference would it make if the UN forces were also included in this image? Presumably, many viewers in the United States will identify with the Afghan girls in sharing the promise of democracy. The expressions on the Afghan girls' faces and their body language, however, suggest a response that is at once hopeful and skeptical. Thus, their gaze both invokes and questions a shared rhetorical vision that presumes the coming of democracy.

You might try out the concepts and methods we have been working with so far on either of the two "looking at others looking" images below: first, identify the "points" on the rhetorical triangle (who or what is the rhetor, audience, subject?), then think about context, using the summary on p. 7 as a guide. Also consider: Who or what groups do you think are being addressed in these images? Do the images presume that audiences will identify with the subjects? How might a viewer's identity or social position alter his or her interpretations of the images? How would you characterize the subjects' gaze(s)? Do you notice similarities or difference among their gazes?

The first image (Figure 1.6) is taken from the July 16, 1969, launch of the moon-bound Apollo 11 at the Kennedy Space Center; former President Lyndon B. Johnson and Ladybird Johnson are among the onlookers here who seem to be "saluting

Figure 1.6   "We have liftoff," July 16, 1969. NASA.
Courtesy of Getty Images.

the space age" in the act of shading their eyes from the Florida sun. The second is from September 11, 2001, and the fall of the World Trade Center Towers (Figure 1.7).

"Rules" about who can look and at whom are called into question by images such as "What you lookn at?" (Figure 1.8). As this image suggests, men, too, can be objects of the gaze. But the inscription of the question "What you lookn at?" onto the image itself gets in the way of the **objectifying** gaze (a gaze that positions people as mere objects) by giving black men the ability to "talk back" to viewers. One might say that this image assumes that some viewers will identify with the subjects represented and that others will position themselves as different. In other words, the rhetorical appeal of this image will vary from viewer to viewer, from one context to another. Some viewers will identify with the subject, and others will see themselves as the object of the black male gaze.

Figure 1.7   People in front of New York's St. Patrick's Cathedral react with horror as they look down Fifth Avenue toward the World Trade Center towers after planes crashed into their upper floors. September 11, 2001.

Courtesy of AP Photo/Maity Lederhandler.

At the same time, images such as "We Are Not a Minority" (Figure 1.9) make us consider who can claim or impose certain identities and on whom. The mural, first painted in 1978 by artists from the Chicano Park struggle in San Diego, features a large image of Ernesto "Che" Guevara, a leader in the revolutionary movement of Cuba in the early 1960s. (You may have been introduced to Che Guevara through Walter Salle's film *The Motorcycle Diaries,* which is based on Guevara's journal of his travels across South America with a friend in 1951–1952.) Reading this mural rhetorically requires that we take into consideration how its geographical location and the historical context in which it was produced shape its message and projected audience. This mural is located in the Estrada Courts housing project in East Los Angeles; therefore, Mexican American residents of the housing projects

Figure 1.8   "What You Lookn At?"
Courtesy of Pat Ward Williams.

Figure 1.9   Congreso de Artistas Chicanos en Aztlán (CACA; Mario Torero, Mano Lima, Tomás "Coyote" Castaneda, and Balazo). *We Are Not a Minority,* 1978, mural. Estrada Courts Housing Project, East Los Angeles.

Courtesy of the artist: Mario Torero.

were the initial target audience. With this slogan, "We are not a minority!!," Che Guevara urged Mexican Americans to assert their identity, rather than to succumb to stereotypes of Mexican Americans as second-class, marginalized citizens. This mural is just one example of thousands of contemporary Chicano paintings throughout the Southwest and Midwest United States, which have come to represent the collective efforts of Mexican American communities toward national self-definition.[3]

Identification and Difference

So far, we've begun to explore the concept of identification. Rhetorician Kenneth Burke has noted that identification often occurs alongside, and is actually built upon, difference. The coexistence of identification and difference, of recognition and misrecognition, is one of the foundational dynamics of the gaze.

Rhetors focus on difference for various purposes. Strategies of disidentification are often used to resist **normalizing gazes**—that is, gazes that classify individuals according to accepted standards and values—or to present alternative identities and therefore to prompt new identifications. Think about the common cover images of popular men's and women's magazines, such as *Sports Illustrated,* which almost invariably represent only fit and healthy bodies. Then consider Figure 1.10 below of Aimee Mullins, a paralympic athlete who holds world records in 110 m, 200 m, and the long jump. Mullins was born without fibulas and had both legs amputated below the knee when she was 1 year old in order for her to walk and not use a wheelchair. In what ways does this image work against popular expectations about sports figures or athletic ability? In what ways does it resemble more conventional representations of athletes (as opposed to "special" athletes)?

Similarly, the fashion shot of Mullins (see Figure 1.11) challenges common perceptions about fashion and what constitutes fashionable beauty. This image is part of a fashion shoot in which people with disabilities appear as models.

There's an interesting tension in this image. On the one hand, the image challenges normalizing gazes that would exclude the disabled body from fashion and beauty advertisements. And yet, the image also seems to promote a rhetorical vision that considers Mullins "different" and even "exotic." Hence this image, like that of Mullins sprinting, emphasizes "difference," but at the same time tries to expand our perspective about who might be considered a "fashion model."

Figure 1.10   Aimee Mullins of the USA competing in the 100 m race during the Paralympics at Olympic Stadium in Atlanta, Georgia, August 1996.

Courtesy of Phil Cole/Allsport/Getty Images.

Figure 1.11   Aimee Mullins fashion shot.

Image by Nick Knight. "Fashion-able." Aimee Mullins, "Dazed & Confused, September 1998."

Like Aimee Mullins's fashion shot, Matuschka's "Picture Prevention" poster (see Figure 1.12), turns the normalizing gaze back on itself. In this image, Matuschka, an ex-fashion model and now photographer and breast cancer art activist, wears a plaster cast of her torso after breast surgery. The viewer's eye (some might say trained, in our culture, to gaze from the male perspective) first recognizes the classical statuesque nude, an iconic image, and moves almost automatically to the level of the naked breast—where it is confronted by a camera. This confrontation, this gaze back at the viewer from the level and "eye" of the model's (now absent) breast, encourages viewers to question their own viewing practices, and more particularly to consider how we, as a culture, commonly imagine health and beauty.

The camera now actually gazes at us, while the subject in the image does not. To what extent, and on what points, could you argue that the "Picture Prevention" poster presents a rhetorical vision of both identification and difference?

Matuschka's image, like the Mullins images, encourages us to participate in already dominant ways of looking, but then also asks us to "look against the grain"—to skew or spin our rhetorical vision. In other words, the image works within an established rhetorical frame, but at the same time persuades viewers to break out of typical frames of interpretation.

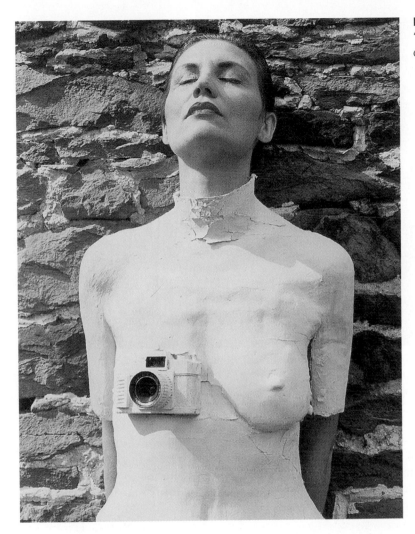

Figure 1.12   Matuschka's "Picture Prevention" poster.
Courtesy of Matuschka.

Like women, Native Americans have long been positioned as objects of a dominant cultural gaze. In other words, they are frequently gazed upon but rarely positioned as onlookers themselves. Figure 1.13 reproduces stereotypical images of Native Americans. Yet here, one of the Native Americans literally breaks through the frame of the television. Like the images of Mullin and Matuschka, this image at once situates Native Americans within a conventional framework, while at the same time suggesting that the viewer question the narrow, static, or fixed identities often ascribed to Native Americans.

We hope that you will remember this image as you work your way through this book and encounter other texts. It is important to examine how and why images

Figure 1.13   Native Americans breaking out of TV frame. Hulleah Tsinhnahjinnie, "Oklahoma: The Unedited Version."

Courtesy of Hulleah Tsinhnahjinnie.

work as they do within the constraints of stereotypes and convention. Yet, in your interpretation of all texts, you must go further, breaking out of that frame to examine the larger historical and cultural contexts surrounding the image, thereby opening space for an alternative, more complex, or more expansive rhetorical vision.

NOTES

1. These man-eating lions of Tsavo are in the Field Museum of Natural History in Chicago, where they have been on display since 1928. Allegedly, the museum acquired the lions from Colonel Patterson, who killed the lions and had their skins made into rugs. The film is partly based on Colonel Patterson's book about his experiences in East Africa on the construction of the Mombasa Railroad.
2. Wendy Kozol, "Relocating Citizenship in Photographs of Japanese Americans during World War II," *Haunting Violations: Feminist Criticism and the Crisis of the "Real"*, eds. Wendy S. Hesford and Wendy Kozol (Urbana: University of Illinois Press, 2001) 217–250.
3. Marcos Sanchez-Tranquilino, "Murales Del Movimiento: Chicano Murals and the Discourses of Art and Americanization," *Signs from the Heart: California Chicano Murals,* eds. Eva Sperling Cockcroft and Holly Barnet-Sanchez (Venice: Social and Public Art Resource Center; Albuquerque: U of NMP, 1999) 93.

*The maps we grow up with, the places we iden-
tify with and feel safe in, the places we avoid
and fear, get imprinted on our minds, and we
carry them with us like miniature road maps,
teaching us about how to interact with the world.*

–JIM SANDERSON

W E READ AND WRITE TO PARTICIPATE—TO PARTICIPATE IN THE
expression of our own ideals and ideas, to participate in a
conversation with others, and to participate in communities. As Chapter 1 explained, we also read and write to
persuade and to be persuaded. We participate and persuade, of course,
not only through our reading and writing of written texts, but also
through the "reading"—that is, the viewing—and "writing"—the creation—of visual texts.

For example, when we look at a map, we are looking at a representation of the world that reflects particular historical and cultural points of
view. If we are persuaded to identify with these points of view, either consciously or not, we take part in a rhetorical vision. One of the best examples of the power of a shared rhetorical vision is found in the Mercator
projection of the world. The Mercator map (Figure 2.1) was designed in
1569 by Gerardus Mercator, a Belgian mathematician.

It was, until the 1980s, the map seen most often hanging on school-
room walls. After hundreds of years of the Mercator projection's domination in schoolrooms and textbooks in America (and elsewhere), most of
us now recognize it readily as "*the* map of the world" and we may often

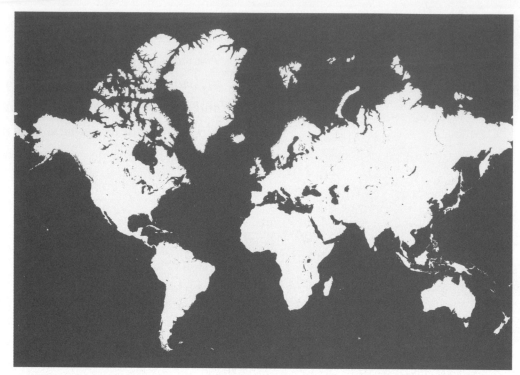

Figure 2.1 Mercator map

find other representations strange, even confusing. In other words, in reading this map, we have participated in a shared rhetorical vision of the world.

Yet the Mercator map is grossly inaccurate in its distortion of the sizes and shapes of the land masses it represents as they are flattened in two dimensions. Often called "the Greenland problem" by cartographers, the little land mass of Greenland projects as large as both Africa, whose land mass is actually fourteen times larger, and South America, with a land mass eight times larger. Antarctica also appears oversized on the Mercator projection, and North America and Europe inaccurately dominate the Mercator space in comparison to the land masses in the southern hemisphere.

These distortions arise, in fact, from the map's original purpose—that is, from the rhetoric of its initial design. The first Mercator map claimed that it was a "new and more complete representation of the terrestrial globe *properly adapted for its use in navigation* [emphasis added]." The Mercator map, though in some respects clearly inaccurate, was nevertheless popular because of the way it laid out so well on flat surfaces and because, using its convenient layout of latitudinal and longitudinal straight lines, navigators on trade routes could easily plot a "true" direction with a compass and a line drawn between the starting and ending points of a destination.

If rhetorical visions are ones that promote particular shared emotional, ethical, or logical responses, what kinds of responses does this "properly adapted" Mercator map encourage? One possibility is that it asserts and assures the dominance of Europe in colonial navigation and trade routes. As Arizona State University professor Alberto Ríos suggests on his Web site,

> This [oversizing of the northern hemisphere in the Mercator projection map] was convenient, psychologically and practically, through the eras of colonial domination when most of the world powers were European. It suited them to maintain an image of the world with Europe at the center and looking much larger than it really was.[1]

Even if colonial relations don't consciously matter to you when you "read" this map, the lasting persuasive effect of the Mercator map in our own shared sense of how the world appears to us must matter: It allows us to talk about, imagine, and place ourselves as individuals and as communities in that world.

Only when we see alternative maps, like the three reproduced below, do we realize that the Mercator map is *a* map of the world, not *the* map of the world. What do these alternative maps persuade you to believe about the world?

The NASA map (Figure 2.2) illustrates global city lights, and so speaks to such things as light pollution, population density, economic development, and energy consumption. The map in Figure 2.3, the so-called "Upside-Down" map, is printed with the South Pole at the top. (Yes, we think of North as "up," but this orientation

Figure 2.2 "Earth at Night," NASA. Original caption released with image: "Global city lights. The Eastern U.S., Europe, and Japan are brightly lit by their cities, while the interiors of Africa, Asia, Australia, and South America remain (for now) dark and lightly populated."

Image by Craig Mayhew and Robert Simmon, NASA GSFC, based on data from the Defense Meteorological Satellite Program. Courtesy of NASA/Jet Propulsion Laboratory.

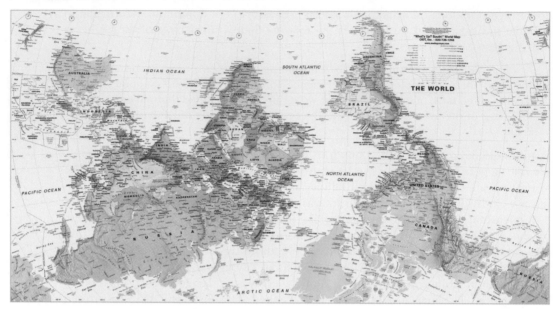

Figure 2.3   Upside-Down map.
© 2005 www.odt.org.

is only a map-making convention.) The Peters Projection Map (Figure 2.4) accurately shows the relative sizes of countries and continents, and thus demonstrates the economic, political, and demographic distortions of the Mercator map. Taken together, these varying visual images of our world raise interesting questions about the power of representation.

Using the three sites of contextual analysis introduced in the previous chapter (page 7), ask yourself the questions about these maps presented in the box on page 30.

In fact, the visual–rhetorical task of mapmaking is fraught at every turn with the problem of distortions and the elusive nature of "accurate" visual portrayals of the world. As the homepage for the Peters Projections maps (http://www.petersmap .com/) proclaims:

> The earth is round. The challenge of any world map is to represent a round earth on a flat surface. There are literally thousands of map projections. Each has certain strengths and corresponding weaknesses. Choosing among them is an exercise in values clarification: you have to decide what's important to you. That is generally determined by the way you intend to use the map.

As this explanation suggests, mapmakers don't simply "draw the world"; they actively select and create one type of visual representation among many, one world among many, one that (the mapmaker hopes) will resonate with and persuade those who view and use it. In this way, the mapmaker and map create a common picture—a shared rhetorical vision—of the viewers' world and their place in it.

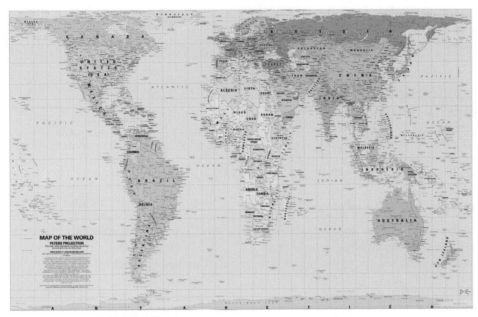

Figure 2.4   Peters Projection Map.
© 2005 Akademische Verlagsanstalt.

Rhetorical Visions asks you to work both like mapmakers and like mapreaders. We will be asking you both to analyze and create a range of texts and images that, like maps, construct a shared vision of the world. All along, we will be encouraging you to see the way you read, write, and create texts as arising out of participation in a rhetorical community.

This kind of analysis may, at first, be a little disorienting. Indeed, you may sometimes feel as if your world has been turned upside down, as some of your more familiar and long-learned "maps" for reading and writing are challenged by some alternatives. Reading and writing based on rhetorical principles—that is, on the interactive relationships among the author and the audience and the text—can sometimes unsettle our more familiar ways of knowing and seeing. In rhetorical analysis, things are no longer just right or wrong, up or down, black or white, left or right. Ideas and beliefs that once seemed obvious are thrown into doubt, and notions that seemed impossible start to seem reasonable. In other words, the map can get pretty messy.

Analysis and Genesis: Twin Rhetorical Acts

But a messy map can also be an exciting map, for the mess can indicate that things are happening. Your task will be to make sense of the mess: to analyze both the obvious and the impossible, the familiar and the strange, so that you can generate new

READING RHETORICALLY

Reading Texts in Context

- What is the significance of the varying scale and size of certain countries and continents?
- Which geographical regions occupy center stage in these particular maps? How and why are certain things "at center"?
- What seems to be the goal, purpose, or main point of this map?

Reading Rhetors in Context

- Whose point of view do the maps represent? Whose vision is made dominant, important, invisible, or marginal?
- What can you tell about the map's creator based on the map itself?

Reading Audiences in Context

- For whom does the map seem designed? Whom does it seem to assume as its primary readers?
  - Is this map in any way about you? Do you see yourself represented in this map?

texts. These new texts will express your view of the world and your place in it, and they will invite others to share the worldview—the rhetorical vision—that you are working to create.

Rhetorical analysis and the genesis or creation of rhetorical texts are both built upon the idea that *how* one frames an issue is as crucial to the meaning conveyed as *what* one says. In other words, form and content influence each other. For this reason, *Rhetorical Visions* asks you to focus not just on what writers say (their topics/subjects) but also on how they say it (their methods, styles, and forms).

Form and Content: The "How" and "What" of Rhetorical Analysis

As an example of the close rhetorical relationship between form and content, between the how and the what of a text, consider once again the NASA "earth at night" map (Figure 2.2 on page 27). The explanation of the map on the NASA Web page that contains this image tells us:

This is what the Earth looks like at night. Can you find your favorite country or city? Surprisingly, city lights make this task quite possible. Human-made lights highlight particularly developed or populated areas of the Earth's surface, including the seaboards of Europe, the eastern United States, and Japan. Many large cities are located near rivers or oceans so that they can exchange goods cheaply by boat. Particularly dark areas include the central parts of South America, Africa, Asia, and Australia. The above image is actually a composite of hundreds of pictures made by the orbiting DMSP satellites. (http://antwrp.gsfc.nasa.gov/apod/ap001127.html)

The NASA map, then, is formed from a composite of actual pictures created via space technology and then patched together in order to simulate one unified global image. The Mercator map, by contrast, is a mathematical drawing created by one person that conveniently lays the world flat and allows it to be plotted in seemingly equal longitudinal and latitudinal spaces. These different forms of mapping correspond to significant differences in their content. Population density and urban space, along with the evidence of human intervention (in its representation of "human-made lights") are made the subject of the NASA map while the Mercator map's content is driven by navigation and trade. The following simple table may help you understand the ways in which form and content contribute to the overall message.

	NASA MAP	MERCATOR MAP
FORM	• Satellite (computer-generated) images patched together (by human design) • Primarily available/viewed online	• Human-generated drawing (on paper) that lays the world flat • Popular reproduction in school textbooks and classroom walls
CONTENT	• Shows such features as population density, light pollution, available electricity, developed/undeveloped areas, rural/urban areas, bodies of water within and surrounding land • Designed by NASA, U.S. government organization	• Shows latitude and longitude (primarily for navigation of ship trade routes in sixteenth-century colonial world) • Designed by Gerardus Mercator as Court Cosmographer for Duke Wilhelm of Cleve

Yet the two maps are also in some ways similar, even though they were created nearly 430 years apart. For while the Mercator projection was explicitly linked to the need to successfully navigate (via water primarily) and establish trade routes, the NASA map also emphasizes trade, development, and economic exchange: "Many large cities," it notes, "are located near rivers or oceans so that they can exchange goods cheaply by boat."

What is more, both maps offer evidence of distortions. The NASA map has what we might think of as the "India problem," akin to the "Greenland problem" of the Mercator map. For while the population and trade density of India is significant in any "view" of the contemporary world, we note that the light density of India in NASA's "projection" roughly equals that of, say, Kansas in the center of the United States. Thus, the NASA map represents perhaps some parts of the world more "accurately" than the Mercator map, while it distorts others.

In fact, this potential for distortion is why most maps are often termed "projections"—as a way of indicating that they are not, and cannot, in fact, represent the reality of the thing they map. What they do represent depends in large part on the projector (the mapmaker, or the rhetor) and the audience of the projection (those who will read and use the map). As projections then, maps are essentially rhetorical. What we don't see in them—or are not encouraged to see—is just as important as what we do see, and are encouraged to see.

In fact, no text is free of the problem of framing, shaping, and thus in some sense distorting the world it portrays; every text necessarily emphasizes some features and ignores others. By considering the form and content together, you can see just how this effect is achieved.

KRCs: Tools of Rhetorical Analysis

To help you with the messy business of writing and reading rhetorically in a visual world, we offer **key rhetorical concepts** (KRCs) throughout this book. These KRCs, derived from the study of rhetoric in ancient Greece, will provide tools—much like a lens or a compass, or even a map—for analyzing the texts you read and for generating your own.

Because they're so significant for rhetorical analysis, we'll begin here by considering two KRCs, metaphor and identification. **Metaphor** refers to the process of comparing something simple, familiar, or well-known to something more complex or unfamiliar, in order to enhance or shape our understanding of it. If, for example, we say the electorate was "polarized" during an election, we are using the image of a magnet to suggest how deeply divided the population is over the issues or candidates in any particular election. In doing so, we tie an abstract concept to something more concrete. However, while metaphors can help bring some concepts or ideas into sharp focus, they can also lead to distortion. For example, while "polarization" might be used metaphorically to clarify the (seemingly) extreme split of votes on an issue, the implication that there are only two poles in the first place distorts the reality of the many voters whose positions really stood somewhere between those poles.

As we saw in Chapter 1, the rhetorical concept of **identification** refers to a process by which we come to feel a relationship to a person, a group, an idea, a belief, or even a worldview. For example, we may identify with a candidate who speaks in a dialect or accent similar to ours, even if he or she says things we disagree with. Or we might identify with people in other regions of the country, people we have never met, on the basis of a shared belief (in scientology, for example) or common group membership (e.g., in the NRA or the Catholic church).

Metaphor and identification often work together. Metaphors can stimulate and help to maintain people's identification with a group or cause. So it is that the simple image of a cross—functioning as a metaphor for a complex set of beliefs—unifies millions of Christians around the globe. Flags and slogans can work in much the same way.

Maps, too, can function metaphorically to assert identification (and differentiation, the opposite of identification). A world political map will show the United States as one color to distinguish it from other nations, and thus encourage U.S. citizens to identify with each other and differentiate themselves from citizens of other countries. A U.S. political map functions similarly, but often at the state, or sometimes regional, level. The maps that show election results provide an interesting series of examples demonstrating how metaphor and identification work together.

Most of us are familiar with the red state/blue state phenomenon that comes from showing the U.S. map divided by states whose electoral votes were predominantly (or unanimously) Republican or Democratic (Figure 2.5). Depicting political affiliation or beliefs through the metaphor of primary colors (red and blue) helps to show clearly and simply how each state's electors cast their votes. And such a map encourages us to identify with others on the basis of party affiliation. Of course, it highlights this one factor at the expense of many others. It portrays and thus constructs the United States as composed of two different types of people and two different kinds of states; it polarizes the national spectrum and ignores all the invisible or blended colors in between.

Further, more subtly perhaps, the use of these two primary colors can color the way we respond to what they represent. What does the color red represent and how

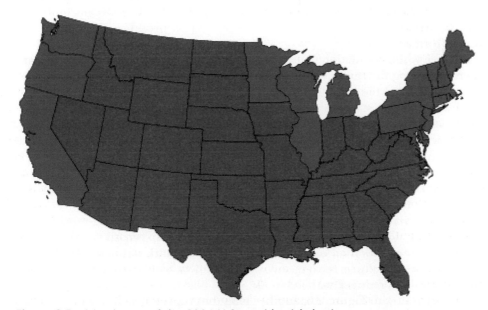

Figure 2.5 Map image of the 2004 U.S. presidential election.

Courtesy of Michael Gastner, Cosma Shalizi, and Mark Newman, www.cscs.umich.edu/~crshalizi/election/.

does it influence our understanding of the political views associated with it? What does it mean to think of certain states as "red" and others as "blue"? What mental, emotional, and situational connections do these colors have for us?

Red is one of the most visible colors of the spectrum; red shades stand out to the human eye more intensely than other colors of the same saturation. Red is often coded as the color of blood, of love, and of the heart. Red is the color of emotion, a hot and sometimes angry color. We often use terms like "redneck," "red-blooded," and "seeing red."

Associations with blue are various, but usually quite distinct from our associations with red. To be "blue" is to be depressed and pessimistic. Yet blue also suggests the ocean and the unclouded sky; it is the color of paint most often recommended to create a sense of calm in a room. Blue is usually classed as a cool color, the color of water and ice, and as such, it can suggest cool logic as opposed to the red heat of emotion. When applied to blood, blue suggests elitism: "blueblood" is a metaphor for people who come from old money; "bluestockings" are highly intellectual (and, conventionally, often spinsterish) women.

Apart from what it literally designates, then—that certain states' electoral votes went to the Republicans, certain to the Democrats—the map also functions rhetorically. Analyzing it rhetorically, we might ask, for example, what to make of the fact that red occupies the center of the map—the rural "heartland" of the country? This position meshes well, of course, with red's metaphoric associations with heart and blood, while it might seem appropriate that blue—the color of water and oceans—is pushed to the country's margins. How we spin these associations, however, depends on our rhetorical purpose in analyzing the map. The marginal position of the blue states could be framed as out of the mainstream (and hence elitist or irrelevant); or it could be conceived of as proud, or independent, or noncomformist.

Further, while population density is not represented on this particular map, most Americans recognize that it is large urban areas (Los Angeles, Chicago, Detroit, New York, Boston, and the Washington, DC corridor) that make the marginal states so blue. Thus, the blue states come to be identified with large cities and everything associated with large cities: high crime rates, pollution, overcrowding, and rude behavior, on the one hand; cultural sophistication, on the other. By contrast, the red states get identified with small-town and rural life, where people leave their doors unlocked at night, wave to passersby, and where children address adults as "sir" or "ma'am"— yet also where provincial attitudes and values hold sway, and nonconformity is not tolerated. None of these characterizations is entirely accurate, of course, but the metaphorical nature of this simplified two-color map can encourage such generalizations. Thus, not only does the red states/blue states map record the electoral vote of a particular presidential election, it also seems to mark out and take sides on a national divide in culture: retro vs. metro, Christian vs. secular, rural vs. urban, heartland vs. coastline, redneck vs. blueblood.

Let's turn now to Figure 2.6, another map that represents election results based on party affiliation. This one does so in a different form, and this alteration in form,

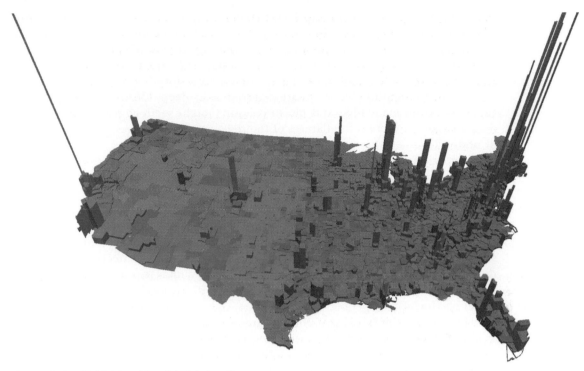

Figure 2.6 "2004 Presidential Election."
Courtesy of Robert J. Vanderbei, Princeton University.

how the results are projected onto the page, necessarily alters what we take from the map, in several important ways. First, the mapmakers in this red/blue state projection use three dimensions, rather than two: The illusion of height or depth is given through shading and perspective in order to reveal population density (voters per square mile), so that the volume of a column represents the total number of voters in an area. Second, the mapmakers here use not simply red or blue, but also shades of purple, in order to reveal the percentage of the population that voted for one party or the other. The addition of these two additional dimensions—height/depth and shading—make this map seem more complex and data-rich than the red/blue map.

　　　Is it, however, necessarily truer than the other map? Most of us would answer, at least at first blush, that it isn't truer—it simply emphasizes different variables, to different effect. It is, however, interesting to note that this second map does complicate the conclusions that the first map seemed to encourage. Where the earlier map showed large swaths of red rimmed by edges of blue, this map is studded with tall blue and purple towers—virtual skylines, as it were—surrounding flat patches of red.

Thus, not only does this map reveal a far smaller proportion of pure red, the red that is shown appears flat and shallow in comparison with the columns of blue. To return to our analysis of metaphors, we might note that metaphors of flatness and shallowness are most often used negatively when contrasted with height and depth; for example, we often call uninteresting characters in a story flat or shallow while the intelligent, thoughtful characters are referred to as deep. On the other hand, the spikiness of the many blue and bluish columns might seem aggressive and intimidating to some, whereas the flatness of the red areas could suggest stability and lack of pretension.

What might we then conclude based on the rhetorical use of metaphor and identification in these two maps? If one map uses color metaphorically to encourage one pattern or kind of identification, the other map uses both color and depth to encourage another form of identification. Both maps can be said to be accurate in some way, yet both emphasize elements and features that will appeal to one group of viewers over another (depending on, among other things, whether viewers see coastal states as extreme in their political views, or as "complex" and "deep," and whether they see midwestern states as the heart of the country, or as "simple" and "shallow."). Through identification and metaphor, both maps encourage a shared rhetorical vision of who "we the people" really are.

Throughout this book, you'll have numerous opportunities to apply KRCs such as identification and metaphor in your examination of rhetoric.

Writing Rhetorical Texts

The creation of a text—whether it is intended to be seen, written/read, or spoken/heard—also constitutes rhetoric, as texts generally ask intended audiences to participate in a vision, idea, or belief expressed by the author.

Aristotle defined rhetoric as "the art of discovering all the available means of persuasion." The five traditional **rhetorical canons,** or parts of the rhetorical process, were *invention, arrangement, style, memory,* and *delivery.* No part of the canon was intended to stand apart from the others; all overlapped and often circled back on each other during the analytical and generative processes. But the focus on discovering the material or ideas for the speech in the standard definition of rhetoric ensured that one part of the traditional five-part canon—**invention**—assumed a central, if not foundational, role. Invention's key role in the process can be discerned in most contemporary textbooks or handbooks or lessons about writing or speaking: Typically such guides begin by asking us to use such techniques as brainstorming, freewriting, or clustering to generate multiple possible topics or multiple possible approaches to a topic we have already chosen. This initial dwelling in multiplicity and possibilities is the essence of invention.

Invention

Whether you're writing a five-page paper or creating a less conventional rhetorical text, you'll start with invention. Let's say, for example, that your assignment is to create a map of your college. First you will want to consider *all the available means* of creating such a map. A famous author once observed that for a map to include every detail of terrain and structure that a land contained, it would have to be as big as the land itself. Thus, necessarily, maps have to be selective about what they include. As you make these considerations, you should ask yourself questions such as those on page 38, questions that take into account each of the three corners of the rhetorical triangle. In other words: How many ways can you invent this map?

Arrangement

After invention, you'll need to give some thought to **arrangement**—that is, to your text's structure or organization. Consider the arrangement of your map. In some ways, the process of invention will begin again here while it also builds upon things you have discovered from your initial invention. Your arrangement of this map—your ordering of the information your map will contain—will significantly shape how your reader responds to, acts upon, or uses your map. While this ordering may seem obvious—"I'll just put things where they really are," you might be saying to yourself—we hope that our review of maps and their many forms illustrates how the arrangement of content (land masses, trade routes, political borders, directions, etc.) shapes quite literally how the map looks and what it conveys.

In this mapmaking exercise, your chosen arrangement will impress both a visual and a narrative structure on your map, influencing not only how it is read, but also why it is read, and exactly what gets read (or not) in it. We discussed narrative briefly in Chapter 1; here we'd like to emphasize **narrative** as the kind of storytelling that tries to capture what has happened (in the past) and what is (in the present), while it also reaches for reframing the future. Narrative, like mapmaking, is often a projective act.

As an example of the projective and narrative structure of maps, consider how most maps now are portrayed from a "God's eye" view (looking directly down upon its subject). Yet this view is not the only perspective available. You might think about how the map might look if viewed from a more "human" angle. What might a lower (closer) point of view reveal that an overhead perspective conceals?

Your questions in considering the arrangement of your map might look like the ones on page 39. It could well be that this process of considering the arrangement possibilities for your map will send you back to invention, to discover and select a different kind of map than the one you had already settled upon. Again, the rhetorical process is almost always **recursive**—folding and looping back on itself, sometimes adding to what is also there, sometimes erasing what has been done so far in order to build anew.

WRITING RHETORICALLY

Text-Centered Invention

- Are there existing models you want to work from or do you want your map to be entirely of your own making?
- What will constitute the center or primary angle of your college map? What will the scale be?
- How exhaustive or limited should your map be?
- How will your college map compare to—or contrast with—other college maps? A town map or neighborhood map? A high school map?
- How large or small do you want the map and its area of focus to be?
- What thing(s) do you want your college map most to highlight, convey, emphasize, or downplay? What will be its key features?
- What are the various ways you can demonstrate those key features? (colors? a key or legend? scale? symbols or icons?)
- What time (of day, year, era, etc.) will your map represent? Will it matter for your purposes?
- What will be found at "up"? At "down"?
- What kind of format(s) are available to you for displaying your college map?
- What materials will you use to create your physical map?
- What are the possible styles and tones (such as cartoonish, scientific, business-like) your map can take?

Rhetor-Centered Invention

- What elements or "places" on or around your college will/should/can you portray (and not portray)? What can you do to inform yourself of these places?
- Where will *you* be located in your map—either directly or indirectly? Will this be, for example, the map according to (only) you? Or will it be a map according to you as a representative of some community or group (a map according to a small-town, rural student; a map according to a young woman; a map according to a nontraditional student; a map according to a young Republican, etc.)? What should the map reveal about you as its creator?
- What are the most memorable features of your college that you want to focus on?

Audience-Centered Invention

- Who will the likely audience be for your map?
  - What will your map-reading audience most want the map to show them?
    - How will any of your attempts to address the questions in the "text" invention prompts above be affected by whom you imagine or know your audience will be?

WRITING RHETORICALLY

Text-Centered Arrangement

- What should be at the visual, narrative, and thematic center and margins of your college map?
- How will scale/size affect the visual and narrative arrangement of the map?
- How will colors contribute to your arrangement?
- Will the map account in any way for the historical or chronological narrative of your college as part of its arrangement?

Rhetor-Centered Arrangement

- What will be the viewpoint of the map? From directly above (God's eye view) or from a lower angle?
- How does what you know (or don't know), or what you want most to convey about this place, affect the way you will arrange your map?
- Where will you locate yourself (your own knowledge or identity in relation to the college) as you consider your arrangement for this map?

Audience-Centered Arrangement

- Should there be a specific or dominant visual/narrative path or movement that guides the mapreader through the map?
- How does the likely or intended audience for the map reflect the arrangement you want to use?
- Will there be a legend that guides the mapreader through the visual/narrative arrangement of your map? What will that legend include/exclude?

Style

Style, the third rhetorical canon, is also bound up with invention and arrangement. Style is all about the way you express your material and argument; therefore, style is about the form of your expression and ideas. Style has traditionally focused upon clarity, correctness, and ornamentation. Maps, for example, are valued for being clear (easy to read), correct (accurate), and even well-ornamented (visually appealing). Not surprisingly, questions about style overlap with and enrich questions we've asked about invention and arrangement.

- What kind of style, slant, or tone do you want your map to carry? (text)
- Do you want it (and you, then, as its maker) to appear scientific, well-balanced, well-informed, naïve, silly, flippant, ironic, odd, sporty, scholarly, social, studious, enthusiastic, or circumspect about your college or any of the features about your institution that might appear on your map? (text/rhetor)
- What features, arrangements, elements can help you create a certain kind of map style? (text)

Stylistically—and thus, rhetorically and visually—it matters, for example, whether you choose to use bright neon colors or light pastels within your map; what you make of boundaries, grids, lines, shapes, and sizes on your map; how thick or sparse you make the legend that accompanies your map; how you choose and use font styles; what and how you label items on your map; whether you use figures of any sort and, if so, what kinds of figures you use—cartoon characters, stick figures, highly stylized clips, artistic elements, etc.

Memory

Memory, the fourth rhetorical canon, was originally represented in techniques for memorizing speeches at a time when literacy was rare and even speeches that were written down were meant to be performed. More recently, the canon of memory has attended not just to the process of memorizing, but to the process of making memorable, as well, since we are generally persuaded and influenced only by what we can remember. How do texts grab hold of the memory of audiences and spectators? What makes something memorable and what do we find worth remembering? Of course, memory intersects at many points with the other canons of rhetoric; how memorable a text is depends largely on what is said (invention), and especially on how it is said (arrangement and style). What can you do to make your map memorable?

Delivery

Because the final canon, **delivery,** originally attended to matters of voice, pronunciation, facial expression, and gesture, it might seem out of place in a discussion about sources that appear on the printed page. Yet delivery has recently been revived as a useful concept, particularly in the study of visual and graphic design (the use of white space, page layout, font style, and the like), and with the rise of the Internet and webpages, where design layout concerns not just one, but many pages, and not just text and color, but images, streaming video, and audio used across many linked pages. You will have already considered some of these elements of page design under the other canons (as we've been saying, they all overlap). Now imagine that your map will be part of a student-designed website of the university, with informational text, other maps, images, sound, and links to other pages. How might you want to use the features of the main site in order to enhance the effectiveness of your map? What other materials might you want to include on your map webpage? What links might you place on the page to encourage your audience to use it?

Explication and Analysis

Once you have generated a map yourself, you might share it with your entire class or in small groups. No doubt, the differences and similarities you will find among your map and those of your classmates will be interesting—even perhaps amazing—to you. Afterwards, in order to explore further what you have learned in the exercise, we suggest you write a brief explication and analysis paper.

Instructions for Explication and Analysis Paper

- Begin with a brief **explication** (explanation) of your map-creating process in your paper. You might look back at the text/rhetor/audience-centered questions for invention, arrangement, and style and recall how you worked to address these in your creation of this particular map.
- Analyze your map using the prompts from Chapter 1, "Reading Rhetorically: The Rhetorical Triangle" (see page 7).
- Identify the shared rhetorical vision that your map shows—that is, the most prominent story the map tells or the most prominent purpose or point it makes. Illustrate, via examples, how your map shows that shared rhetorical vision.
- Consider what an alternate map that "talks back" to your own map might look like. In what ways would this alternate map expose your own map's ideology, its rhetorical visions, its assumptions, etc.?
- Compare and contrast your map to any of your classmates' maps or the one that follows if it will help you accomplish any of the four prompts above.

Sample Project: The Making of a Map

Making My Map of Detroit

(notes)

I lived four miles north of 8 mile (on 12 mile). If you're from Detroit, you get used to talking about everything by the mile roads. There's actually almost nothing there but houses, schools, and strip malls. The occasional hospital or office complex. We lived in Warren ("Borin") near Sterling Heights ("Sterile Whites"). By the time I was in high school, there was pretty much nothing there that interested me at all.

8 mile road is the biggest map or boundary marker that I remember; it separates Detroit from the northern suburbs. It pretty much also separates blacks and whites, at least that's how I was taught. I was not allowed to go south of 8 mile by myself, according to my dad. For us, Detroit was like this

> Why? Will you go into this explanation in your paper?

scary place where blacks lived that you didn't want to get caught in, and I'm pretty sure that most blacks didn't want to get caught in the white suburbs either. We had a black family move into Warren once when I lived there, but that was like a rumor and I'm pretty sure they didn't stay there long. I sure never saw them.

> Can you use this observation to make claims about identification and difference? Perhaps how we learn about identification boundaries?

It feels funny that I say I'm "from Detroit"--when people ask, that's where I say I am from--even though I didn't actually live in Detroit and wasn't even allowed to go there (even though I did). Sometimes, if people know the area, I say I am from Warren, but saying this would be meaningless to most people aren't from Michigan or the Detroit area anyway.

> So how do we define where we are from?

Hamtramck is ok, cause its all Polish and kind of an island within the city. I could show that by a different color or something. We're German, so we would tell jokes about the Polish, but really they were considered to be alright, Catholic and all that. My uncle is pure polish and he tells the most jokes of anyone.

> Why the shift suddenly here to Hamtramck and "Polish"—shifting out of the black/white boundaries suddenly? How does this space figure in your overall map?

Downtown was interesting to me in high school because there was the cultural center, the Institute of Arts with the murals by the Hispanic painter, something Rivera--those were very interesting. Also there is Greektown: great place to go out with dates and stuff, get some flaming cheese, spanakopita, and ouzo, and also Fisher Theater, Tiger Stadium, and all that. My dad wouldn't let me go down there unless we were going to a ballgame with my uncles and cousins in my uncle's big van from his restaurant. My Mom was pretty liberal so she would let me take the bug (VW) and drive downtown and not tell my dad. So downtown is like another separate island.

The area in the northwest of my map are where Sylvan lake and Cass lake are: great for fishing with friends and family on the weekends. Wake up at 5 o'clock in the morning, put in some good music, and drive out there with cash and lunch.

The Zoo was fun when we were kids. After a while we got bored with it, so I probably won't even show it, since I haven't gone for years.

Boblo Island has to be on my map, along with a little bit of Windsor, which you have to visit at least once to get a Canadian souvenir or whatever. Canada was always part of growing up in Detroit, especially since we got Canadian television, half of which was in French. Boblo is actually a Canadian island but we think of it as part of Detroit cause the Bob-lo boats leave from downtown.

The western and southern suburbs are just gray, because we never went there, they are just more white suburbs.

I should also designate the auto center somehow. GM, Chrysler, and Ford were all around us, huge centers with huge parking lots. The Tech Center (GM, I think) was a mile from our house, and it had a strip mall across from it that we would go to for frozen cokes. Cars were a big deal. There's even a restaurant made up of old cars cut open with like, bench seats facing each other inside and a table. I took a girlfriend there once.

There is also Metro Beach on 16 mile (metro parkway). If you're a senior, and it's a nice spring day, and you want to skip school with some friends, then you're probably going to go to Metro Beach. Probably the nicest, biggest beach we knew about at the time (locally, at least).

I could also mark out the rich parts of town, Grosse Point, Grosse Point Isle, Grosse Point Farms, Grosse Point Woods, or whatever, I can't remember the names of all of them, but they're bunched together in the southeast, by the river. I guess rich people like to live by the water.

Then there's Ann Arbor, out to the West, which was important because my mom and all my sisters have gone to UM and we all rooted for the Wolverines, so I could show that somehow. I'm the only non UM "student" in my family.

That's about it, except for Houghton lake up north, where we would go once a year hunting with my dad's friend who had a cabin on the lake. They would also have ice-fishing camps up there in the winter, but I never went.

> How huge? How can you show or relate this hugeness in your map and your paper? When I read this I think of aerial maps, and the large empty grey spaces that such big parking lots can create on a map.

> Why? How can you show this on a map?

> Is water a defining characteristic of identification and difference?

Jim, these map notes are wonderfully rich and detailed—I can almost picture the map already! As you begin to think about what issues, elements, or areas you want to focus on in your paper, you will probably find some parts of your map "fading." I don't think you can write a good cohesive essay and reasonably use ALL this material on your map! You have several possible avenues for your thesis development. I think as you actually begin now to DRAW your map you will begin to notice that certain features/issues become even more outstanding to you. Pay attention to those for possible theses for your paper.

My Map of Detroit

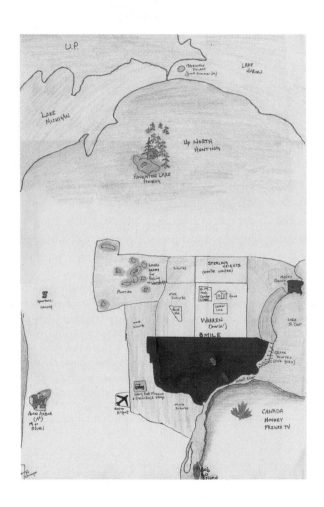

Thesis (drafts):

- 8 mile is an important boundary in Detroit between blacks and whites.
- Growing up we were segregated along 8 mile but didn't really realize it.
- Drawing a map of my hometown made me realize how segregated we were growing up, even though we didn't realize it then.
- My map isn't just about race but about all the boundaries that separated us off from other people, like rich people in Grosse Pointe, too. Though we didn't separate from them so much as vice versa, I guess. But that's how life is. Maybe its about how thinking about and even drawing those boundaries can help us to see how they shaped our beliefs and attitudes growing up.
- 8 mile as a metaphor for separation and distance, ignorance, and therefore racism. How the "8 Miles" in our minds make us identify with people who live in "approved" areas and disidentify with people who live in "prohibited" areas.
- There's also the thing about how boring and dead life in Warren was for teenagers, at least for me. I got more interest from the edges of the map: Metro Beach, Boblo Island, Ann Arbor Football, and Houghton lake are all around the edge of the map, and even places like downtown Detroit (cultural center), Pontiac lake, and Greenfield Village and the Zoo are on the edges of the city rather than in the middle of it. Hmmm. Not sure what to say about that. Thing about the 8 Mile boundary is that I probably wouldn't have done much down there anyways even if I was allowed to, and when I was allowed (by my Mom) I just went to a few select "cultural" places that was mostly whites. So I guess I didn't really do much to challenge the segregation.

Your thesis statements draw upon your interest in the segregation of Detroit, and how this segregation is hidden. You have hit on a significant idea here. Push it further as you redraft your theses. Your thesis statements so far concentrate upon statements of fact, rather than a potential focus for your paper. Think back to our lesson on generating a thesis from ideas. Think

---

Margin notes:

This is clearly generated from the ideas within your notes. However, this is a statement of fact—hard to build a paper around it. Push this idea a little further. Why is it significant?

Again, this is a statement of fact. Why is it significant that Detroit's segregation is hidden to those that live there? What defines this segregation and how is it hidden? Why is that important?

Interesting that in the process of drawing this map you came to realize something new about your "hometown." What's more important: the idea (Detroit's segregation) or the action (drawing the map)?

The multiple possibilities of the boundaries that you express here seem most promising to me—they link in nicely to *identification and difference* (KRCs).

Wow—this is very insightful and promising.

I wonder if this isn't a place or way to move toward an "ending" for your paper—since it stays connected to the "boundary" and map idea but also moves "outward" a little from your original idea?

about discovering a question that needs to be explained and about connecting elements and explaining their significance.

Be sure, too, to think about how any of your notes and your map can be analyzed and discussed in terms of any of the KRCs we've covered so far. You will also want to be sure to tie this into a few of the readings and discussions we've had in class.

Finally, you'll need to think now about how you are going to ORGANIZE your notes into a full paper—where to start and finish on your "map" and how to logically move (travel!) from place to place.

Paper: Draft #1

Jim Sanderson

Since the popularity of Eminem (aka Marshall Mathers, aka Slim Shady), 8 Mile has become a well known landmark in America. Since I was born and raised on "the other side" of 8 Mile, I decided to draw my map and write about being a white suburban kid who always knew about 8 Mile and was never allowed to cross it.

Drawing maps can help us to see who we are and how we think, by showing us where we go and what we see. My map of Detroit made me realize how much my upbringing was defined by racial segregation. But 8 Mile road is more than just a road that marks the boundary of Detroit and its northern suburbs, it is also a metaphor for all the boundaries that we grow up with and that make us segregate from others who are different from us.

I can start by telling a story that came up with the map-making. I was 18, a senior in high school, it was spring, and I had a girlfriend. My mom had an old Volkswagen Beetle. I was taking a Humanities course that asked us to write about some artwork. I thought it would be fun to go down to the Institute of Arts to write about some paintings there, like the big Diego Rivera murals, and then we could go out to eat afterwards in Greektown. My girlfriend was in the class, too, so I asked her to go and we made it a date. When I asked my mom to borrow the car, she said "You want to go where? I don't know what your father is going to say about that." Then she paused for a minute, like she was thinking and said, "You can go, but you'd better not tell your father. We'll just say you're working on a homework assignment at the library," and she made me promise to go to the library, too, while I was gone . . . the downtown Detroit library, not our local Warren branch.

It never occurred to me at the time that my Dad wouldn't want me to go to Detroit. People always talked about the muggings and locking your car doors if you have to drive through, but I thought that was only about the bad areas, or only at night, or only for people who couldn't handle themselves. I hadn't ever asked to go there by myself before, so it never came up.

One of your first tasks will be to find a fitting title for your whole paper, Jim—something that captures the idea of your thesis.

Great popular culture tie-in and attention-gathering opening.

Here you are concentrating upon the action rather than the ideas that were generated from it. Think about your audience. What information is important to them? Are they also interested in drawing maps? Probably not—more important is what came from the experience.

Good thesis! Nice that you draw in the KRC of metaphor here. (But aren't you also writing about identification/difference?) I like how you make this paper larger than just the Detroit of your growing up years.

Suggestion: combine these two paragraphs, concentrating on making smoother transitions to your thesis and into the story. How are these ideas connected? Articulate the connections for the reader.

What is the significance of this story? How is it related to your thesis? Make these connections clear for the reader.

What a wonderful descriptive paragraph! I wonder if you couldn't make a more critical connection, though, with any of the readings we've discussed or with any of the KRCs?

Concentrates on action, not ideas. You really must start thinking about how to draw your audience into your ideas, and away from your thought process.

What a wonderful transition into "the moral of your story" (the reason for your careful description). Very nice.

Nice literary reference. What defines these places though? You are on to something here, but you should think about how to connect this to larger cultural ideas.

You repeat this "funny thing" phrase twice and it isn't very effective (or funny?) by the second time.

Again, I'm not sure you have made this segregation clear for a larger audience. Think about how these cultural boundaries are set up, and why. How might this be different from another city? Why is this difference important?

Just recently, I decided to take 8 Mile on my way home from college. It was slower than the freeway, and a little bit out of the way, but I had never really even seen this legendary boundary that I wasn't supposed to cross. 8 Mile was wide, busy, and bright with neon. There were pawn shops, restaurants, peep shows, car lots, store fronts with bars on the windows. And there were lots of people. Some standing, some walking, or just standing in groups on street corners, talking. They were all black. Some shouting at each other, crossing the road jaywalking against the lights, or laughing. I was a little nervous--it was dark by the time I got there--even though I didn't really have anything to fear. The traffic was as heavy at 10:00 at night as it might have been during rush hour. Pimped out Caddis and hopping low riders. I was used to cruising Gratiot in my friends remodeled 'Cuda, but this was different. These weren't people I felt comfortable around, especially in my old little bug.

I haven't thought about moments like that till I made this map, and realized that virtually the entire city, the city that I say I'm from, is a dark splotch in my memory. I don't really know anything about it. I know about the Zoo, Greenfield Village, the town of historic buildings and shops that Henry Ford assembled. We would watch the weavers and blacksmiths when we went in the summer, saw the Wright Brothers bicycle shop, and bought souvenirs and orange push-ups with our allowance money. I knew about Hamtramck because my Uncle was Polish, told Polish jokes, and talked to me like a grown-up when I was little. "Get a job that helps people, drink good whiskey, and don't smoke cheap cigars," he advised. Later I knew about the cultural center. I went to the Institute of Arts, the Library, and Greektown on weekend evenings with friends. All those things were south of 8 Mile, like islands in the heart of the darkness.

So the funny thing isn't that I never traveled around in Detroit or knew much about it. There really wasn't any reason for me to go there for the most part. The funny thing is that I never really thought about that fact that everyone in Warren was white, everyone in Detroit was black (or so I was raised to believe) and that we were actually learning about segregation and Jim Crow in social studies as though it were all over, or occurring somewhere else. It amazes me now that I never thought about how much segregation was a part of my everyday life. [How much my attitude towards blacks was shaped by my sheer ignorance of them individually and as a group.] So not only was I ignorant about the people who live in "my" city (Detroit, Rock City!), I was ignorant about my own ignorance. That's just amazing to me now.

This is a fragment sentence, Jim. Can you rework it to stand as a complete sentence on its own?

I wonder if you could discuss this ignorance/ coming to awareness in terms of identification and difference?

So what? That wasn't my fault. Just because I didn't live next door to blacks doesn't make me racist. Blacks never came to live next door to us, either, and if they did I wouldn't have cared, so it works both ways. Plus, I like lots of Black athletes and hip-hop artists, Chris Rock and Dave Chapelle, Wesley Snipes, and Beyonce Knowles, and that speed skater in the Winter Olympics.

But then I think of a basketball game that I went to in high school. Our team, was pretty good that year, and we went to regionals. The game we lost was to a black team in an all black school. The stands looked like my map: white on one side and black on the other. And I'm sort of embarrassed now by how we acted and how I felt. I was more afraid of this team than other white teams, I was more convinced that they would play dirty and use fouls to get the edge. The refs were black, too, so there you go. What do you expect? One lousy call after another, of course, since they all look after one another. I remember how red and flushed our players were. Theirs, you could hardly tell what they were feeling, but you could sure hear their fans, loud and obnoxious. By the end of the close game, the tension was bad and I thought for a minute that a fight would break out, but it didn't.

Where are these schools? How do they relate to the ideas in your map? How does this push your thesis further? Make those connections clear to your reader.

Everything about that game was different because they were black. Everything we said about that game afterwards was easy to say because our ignorance was filled by stereotypes. Everything that happened depended upon a situation where none of "their kind" ever went to our school, and none of "our kind" ever went to their school. We hated them and they probably hated us (and especially loved beating us) purely because of where we lived, because of 8 Mile road, and because of the stories we were told about what we should be afraid of.

This basketball game story is VERY compelling and seems very important—but it does waltz a long way around your map, doesn't it? How can you make this story anchor back more in your map (or any of our readings or the KRCs)?

The other side of it is that I really didn't get along with most of the kids in my high school. I wasn't a jock, a stoner, a rich kid, or a geek. Since I like to read and got good grades, I guess I was a brain, but it seemed there weren't many others that I knew there that I was friends with. But

I still identified with these people that I didn't really get along with at all, and disidentified with people that I might have gotten along with (some of them at least, there had to have been black "brains" at the school), but just didn't know, feared, and therefore hated. I always talked about how much I hated Warren and wanted to live someplace more vibrant, with more culture, but I never thought about the place that I said I was from but was never allowed to go.

> What a resonant and powerful ending line! Wow. Now if you could make some critical connections, this essay would be quite remarkable, Jim.

Jim, I hear resonances of several of the essays from the Traveling Gazes set here in your essay—esp. at the end. You could make this an even better critical essay now in your final draft by weaving some of that material in. The essay that most comes to mind is Hockenberry's "Walking with the Kurds." But others in this unit (as well as the national and family gazes unit) will surely connect to your own thesis, maps, and powerful argument.

And although you don't need to force it into this draft, there are all those other places on the map that seemed to figure so strongly in your notes (and in the map you have drawn) that DON'T get taken up here because it becomes all about white/black boundaries. I wonder . . . I just wonder . . . if drawing in Hamtramck and the "Polish" factor a little more wouldn't help further articulate the racial/ethnic boundaries of Detroit? You don't HAVE TO pull in that little red zig-zag (of Hamtramck) in your final draft . . . but it does seem very compelling to me as I look at your map and your notes. . . .

In all, a very strong draft that just needs some critical buffing. As you move toward revising this draft, think about your audience and the ideas you are trying to articulate to them. Concentrate more about the critical ideas and articulating your thesis than on just moving through from one thought to another. How do your ideas connect to something larger about cultural boundaries than just the invisible lines in Detroit?

Keep going and push your ideas further!

Sanderson 1

Jim R. Sanderson

Professor Brueggemann

Rhetoric 101

5 March 2006

8 Mile: The Boundary of Discovery

Since the popularity of Eminem (a.k.a. Marshall Mathers, a.k.a. Slim Shady), 8 Mile, one of the many Detroit mile roads, has become a well-known landmark in America. But for those who live in Detroit, 8 Mile also is a boundary marker that separates the city of Detroit from the northern suburbs, and the blacks from the whites. When I was growing up in the suburbs, Detroit was a scary and foreign place where we were not allowed to go. Now I know that 8 Mile is not just a road that marks the boundary of Detroit and its northern suburbs; it is also a metaphor for all the boundaries that we grow up with and that make us different from those who looked different from us.

As I got older, when I was a senior in high school, Detroit seemed like an oasis from the boring suburbs, filled with fun places to go like the Institute of Arts, Greek town, Fisher Theater, and Tiger Stadium. But outside these tourist spots, Detroit was still taboo, a place where my dad wouldn't let me go. In "From 'A Small Place,'" Jamaica Kincaid talks about tourists, what they like to see (the brilliant sun, the beautiful beach, the local cuisine) and what they ignore (the lack of a sewage system, the crumbling library, and corruption). Detroit was also a kind of tourist destination that suburban kids could selectively identify with (the cultural centers) and ignore (everything else). But unlike the tourists in Kincaid's Antigua who feel welcome in a place where they are not, we knew we weren't welcome on Detroit city streets any more than we wanted blacks in our neighborhood.

The spring of my senior year, I was taking a Humanities course that asked us to write about a painting. I thought it would be fun to cruise down to the Institute of Arts to write about some paintings there, like the big Diego Rivera murals, and then go out to eat afterwards. My girlfriend was in the class too, so I asked her to go and we made it a date. But when I asked my mom to borrow her car, a Volkswagen Bug, she said, "You want to go where? I don't know what your father is going to say about that." Then she paused for a minute, like she

The introduction now focuses on the ideas that the author wishes to express, rather than on the act of making the map.

The first few sentences lead nicely into the thesis.

Paper now uses a transition into the story.

was thinking, and said, "You can go, but you'd better not tell your father. We'll just say you're working on a homework assignment at the library," and she made me promise to go to the library, too, while I was gone. Not our local Warren branch, but the downtown library, so that I didn't make a liar out of her. It never occurred to me that my dad wouldn't let me go to the Institute of Art. I knew Detroit was bad, but this was different. People always talked about the muggings and locking your car doors as you drove through, but I thought that the cultural center was different, it wasn't really Detroit, even. I hadn't ever asked to go there before, so it never came up. I now realize though that even though my mother allowed me to take her car, it was only because I was going to a select few "cultural" places, places that she thought might be good for me, mostly white places: the Institute of Arts, the library, Greektown fit into the permissible places for white kids to go and get cultured and have fun, in ways that the rest of the city was not.

That was the last time I drove through Detroit until recently, when I decided to travel 8 Mile on my way home from college. It was slower than the freeway, and a little bit out of the way, but I had never really even seen this famous boundary that I wasn't supposed to cross. 8 Mile was wide, busy, and bright with neon. There were pawn shops, restaurants, peep shows, car lots, store fronts with barred windows. And there were lots of people, lots of blacks: some walking, some standing in groups on street corners, talking, some shouting at each other, crossing the road, jaywalking against the lights, or laughing. Driving in the dark, I was a little nervous, even though I didn't really have anything to fear. Immediately I was conscious of the difference between me and the people that surrounded me. I was used to cruising Gratiot with my friend's remodeled 'Cuda. But here on 8 Mile, pimped out Caddis and hopping lowriders sped down the street, creating a flow of traffic, even at 10:00 at night, as heavy as during rush hour. These weren't people I felt comfortable around, especially in my old little bug. It was more than just the cars, though; it was the clothes, the shops, and the music. Where Warren, my hometown in the suburbs, was filled with familiar side streets and lawns, 8 Mile stretched before me with lights, sounds, and colors that were foreign.

But aside from that roadside tour and the trips downtown, the entire city of Detroit, the city that I say I'm from, is a dark splotch in my mind. I don't really

---

Sidebar annotations:

Writer moves toward an analysis of the events described in the narrative, rather than letting the narrative speak for itself.

Writer concludes the paragraph with a critical connection, describing the boundaries of identification and difference.

The writer concentrates on the ideas he is presenting to the reader, concentrating on the "dark splotch" in his mind, rather than on the map itself.

Sanderson 3

know anything about it. I know about the Zoo and about Greenfield Village, the town of historic buildings and shops that Henry Ford assembled. We would watch the blacksmith when we went in the summer, saw the Wright Brother's bicycle shop, and bought souvenirs and orange push-ups to eat. I know about Hamtramck because my uncle was Polish, told Polish jokes, and talked to me like a grown up when I was little. "Get a job that helps people, drink good whiskey, and don't smoke cheap cigars," he would say. Later, I learned about the cultural center: the Institute of Arts, the Library, and Greek town. All those things were in Detroit but permissible, like islands in the heart of darkness.

Like many other places in America, what separated these "good" areas from other parts of the city, the ones we ignored and never traveled to, was whether or not I was supposed to identify with the people and culture there. Arts, sports, music, and cultural food were part of how I saw myself and my family; musicians playing in smoky bars, jobless men hanging around on street corners, and pawn shops framed by liquor stores and check-advance offices were not. The places I didn't go were poor and dirty. But the funny thing isn't that I never traveled around in Detroit or knew much about it.

After all, there really wasn't any reason for me to go there. I was raised knowing that everything I needed was in Warren, which was white, and nothing was in Detroit, which was black. Blacks were something you saw on the news or on TV comedies, not something that I thought about otherwise. In fact in school, we were learning about segregation and Jim Crow laws in the South after Reconstruction, as if the fight for Civil Rights was over, or as if racial separation was something that occurred in the past or somewhere else, the old South. The funny thing is that I never thought about how much segregation was a part of my everyday life, and how my attitude toward blacks was shaped by my sheer ignorance of them individually and as a group. I guess I was like the tourists in Antigua that Jamaica Kincaid refers to in "A Small Place," totally ignorant of the natives they saw. Not only was I ignorant about the people who lived in "my" city (Detroit, Rock City!), I was ignorant about my own ignorance and how easy it would have been to learn. The city was just a void to me, and so were the people that lived there, a void that I replaced with my own ideas of "my" Detroit.

Notice how the ethnic identification seems to complicate, if not blur, the black/white boundaries that the writer establishes elsewhere in the paper.

The writer makes a larger connection, speaking of Detroit as representative of other places in America. In doing so, he asks the readers to make connections to their hometowns.

Paragraph focuses on the aspects of culture that create boundaries of identification and difference.

Paragraph concludes by drawing larger connections to American culture and questions of racism.

But there is another part of me that says, "So what? That wasn't my fault that I didn't grow up around a bunch of black kids." Just because I didn't drive through Detroit in some lame attempt to make black friends doesn't make me a racist. Blacks never came to our neighborhood either, so it works both ways. People shouldn't be blamed for what they don't know about. Plus I do know about lots of black athletes and musicians and comedians like Chris Rock and Dave Chapelle and Queen Latifah, or Wesley Snipes and Beyonce Knowles, and that one speed skater in the Winter Olympics.

But then I think of that basketball play-off game in high school. Our team was pretty good that year, and we went to regionals, and we had to play a team from the city: a *black* team from an all black school. The stands looked like the two sides of 8 Mile--white on one side and black on the other. And I'm sort of embarrassed now by how we acted and how I felt. I was more afraid of this team than other teams we played. I was more suspicious that they would play dirty and use cheap fouls to get ahead. The refs were black, too, so there you go. What do you expect? One lousy call after another. I remember how flushed and frustrated our players were. Theirs were laughing and hollering at each other, and their fans were loud and obnoxious. By the end of the close game, the tension was bad, and I thought a fight would break out, but it didn't

Everything about that game was different because they were black. Everything we said about the game was easy to say because we already didn't trust them. Everything that happened happened because none of "those kids" ever went to our school and none of "us" went to theirs. We hated them, and they probably hated us (and loved beating us), just like the Antiguans hated the tourists, purely because of where we lived, because of 8 Mile road, and because of the stories we were told about what we should be afraid of.

The other funny thing about all of this is that I really didn't even like most of the kids at my school. I wasn't a jock, or a prep, or a stoner, or a geek. Since I like to read and got good grades, I guess I was a brain, but I didn't exactly have a lot of friends there and was mostly ignored by all the popular kids. But I still identified with these people that I didn't get along with, and dis-identified with other people that I might have gotten along with (some of them must have been "brains" who liked goofing around with electronic equipment), but didn't know and therefore didn't like. I always talked about Warren as a place I hated and Detroit as the place where I was from, but it's pretty clear to me now that I was mostly talking out of ignorance, still living across the 8 Mile in my mind.

NOTE

1. See www.public.asu.edu/~aarios/resourcebank/maps/page10.html.

FAMILIAL GAZES
Reworking the Family Album

> *Secrets haunt our memory-stories, giving them pattern and shape. Family secrets are the other side of the family's public face, of the stories families tell themselves, and the world, about themselves.*
>
> –ANNETTE KUHN, *FAMILY SECRETS: ACTS OF MEMORY AND IMAGINATION*

KEY RHETORICAL CONCEPTS

memory   description   interpretation   narrative

Archives and Familial Gazes

FLIP THROUGH A FAMILY ALBUM. WHAT PATTERNS DO YOU NOTICE? ARE certain types of occasions or events represented more than others? Family photographs, scrapbooks, and photo albums function for many Americans as **family archives,** that is, as places to record significant rites of passage, such as births, marriages, and graduations. To **archive** something is to place or store an artifact in an area, or to transfer an artifact to a lower level in the hierarchy of memories (*Oxford English Dictionary,* 2nd ed, 1989). The archiving of family images is not a neutral process, but one in which certain experiences or memories are valued over others. Certain memories or members of the family may be excluded from the family's self-presentation. For example, upwardly mobile families may chose not to archive images of their roots in lower-middle-class neighborhoods. Such exclusions tell as much about the family's sense of itself as do the inclusions.

When we speak of **familial gazes,** we're talking about the ways in which common notions of family provide a lens through which families see and understand themselves. Family albums and scrapbooks often tell stories about a family's class and social status. Assumptions about age, femininity, masculinity, racial differences, disability, and other aspects of identity can be discerned through an analysis of family photographs. For example, baby pictures ritualize generational memories of innocence and youth. As Shawn Michelle Smith points out, "baby pictures remain highly valued commodities in contemporary culture. . . . the family photograph albums that protect these images are nearly sacred records."[1]

Family albums create visual narratives and themes, and, for this reason, they can become contested sites of representation, where particular family members may "struggle for control of the image, narrative, and memory."[2] When family photographs are removed from the familial context, they often take on different cultural meanings. We use the term **memory** therefore to refer not only to individual memories but also to broader familial, cultural, or national memories and processes of remembrance. For instance, family photographs left at commemorative national sites such as the Vietnam Memorial take on additional personal and public meanings.[3]

This unit invites you to use family photographs as a basis for telling stories and to use description as well as cultural and historical interpretation in a critical analysis of such photographs.

Reading Family Photographs: Moving from Description to Interpretation

To **describe** something—to offer basic information about its content and form—is an essential part of understanding it. When you describe a family photograph, you will probably start with statements about its subject matter. You might discuss the formal elements of the photograph, such as its composition, point of view or angle of vision, hue (or the tonal range of black and white images), scale, proportion, and the emphasis or subordination of particular subjects or objects. (See, for example, questions for "Reading Rhetorically" on page 30.) Your descriptions might highlight the historical period and social milieu of the photograph. For example, when looking at a family photo, you might ask yourself: Is the photograph one of a formal occasion like a wedding, or a casual picnic at the grandparents? What are the people in the photograph wearing? How is the relationship of the people in the photograph reflected in their composition and positioning?

Descriptions are not, however, merely neutral observations; they are not value-free. Rather, they reflect the worldview and social position of the looker. In other words, **interpretation** is an inevitable part of description. Descriptions, like family albums themselves, have the power to include as well as exclude certain meanings; a writer may highlight certain observations over others. Photographers make choices about how to capture an image and present it to an audience. When writing about family photographs, therefore, we are faced with the challenge of interpreting what appear to be straightforward realistic images.

Figure 3.1 Portrait of Edward William Trevenan, c. 1910

For example, the family photograph in Figure 3.1 denotes (shows) Wendy Hesford's great-grandfather sitting in a small room next to a young black male; but to our eyes it connotes (suggests, implies), by virtue of the composition alone, the subordination of the young black man to the older white man. Take a look. Do you agree? Why, or why not?[4]

In addition, family stories or narratives, which impose order on events and experiences, shape our reading of family photographs. Rarely do we see family photographs without some accompanying arrangement and narrative, which is most readily identifiable by the placement of photographs in family albums or scrapbooks. Even if a family does not compose temporal narratives, but perhaps randomly places family photographs in a box in the kitchen cabinet, narratives often accompany individual family photographs.

Indeed, family photographs and verbal narratives (the stories that accompany the photographs) frame each other. The back-and-forth exchange between these visual images and the narratives that accompany them provides clues to the values that characterize the family. Thus family photographs, like family narratives, can be analyzed for what they convey about a family's identity and its sense of itself in the world. As Annette Kuhn tells us in one of the reading selections in this chapter, these narratives—what she calls "memory-stories"—also contain secrets.

Critical Frame

AND WRITING

Memory, one of the five classical canons of rhetorical study, has always been linked to writing. Ancient philosophers regarded memory as the basis for or foundation of the other canons.

The earliest method for remembering was said to have been discovered in ancient Greece quite by accident when a writing school burned down. The fire had been so intense that when the grieving parents came to collect their children, none could be visually identified. But an instructor, by recalling the place of each student in the room, was able to identify each of the student's remains. This incident, whether factual or not, became set as a process for remembering a speech: Speakers would first imagine a room furnished with objects; each object would correspond to one point to be made in the speech, so that by arranging the objects around the room in the correct order, speakers could then "walk" through their speeches, covering each point as they "saw" those objects in their mind's eye.

Yet while writing was often referred to as a memory aid in classical times, the ancient Greek philosopher Plato also denounced writing not as a tool of remembering, but rather as one of forgetting. He argued in *The Phaedrus* that once we store knowledge in writing, we will no longer bother to store it up in our own minds. Instead of writing things down to remember them, Plato strongly believed that writing things down would, in fact, make us forget them—that writing would make our memories lazy.

Ekphrasis, or "bringing-before-the-eyes," was one of the original elementary exercises (the *progymnasmata*) used in the ancient rhetorical schools. It was addressed by Aristotle in his treatise on the art of rhetoric. *Ekphrasis* was originally a rhetorical exercise involving the description of a painting: The student was asked to bring a certain painting "before the eyes" of others by creating a translation, or a verbal copy, of the visual image. Thus, this primary rhetorical exercise from the ancient Greco-Roman schools tightly triangulated the acts of memory, writing/speaking, and the visual.

In contemporary times, advertising often makes the most of this visual–verbal–memory triangulation. The immensely successful "Got Milk?" advertising campaign, for example, has welded, for many of us, the memorable image of milk mustaches placed on all sorts of popular heroes and heroines (from media stars to sports figures to political leaders) to that catchy questioning verbal phrase, "Got Milk?" What is more, this welding is said to have revived sagging sales in milk at a time when milk had largely come to be seen as a kids-only drink.

Examples ■■■

❶ In "Photograph of My Parents" from Maxine Hong Kingston's *The Woman Warrior,* the visual–verbal bond forged (yet also made unsure) through memory appears when Kingston notes:

> There are no snapshots of my mother. In two small portraits, however, there is a black thumbprint on her forehead, as if someone had inked in bangs, as if someone had marked her.
> "Mother, did bangs come into fashion after you had the picture taken?" One time she said yes. Another time when I asked, "Why do you have fingerprints on your forehead?" she said, "Your First Uncle did that." I disliked the unsureness in her voice.

❷ Likewise, bell hooks blends visual moments from the past, captured in photographs, with more extended verbal memories in her essay "In Our Glory: Photography and Black Life." Commenting on a snapshot of herself as a child in a costume leads her into further memories:

> I loved this snapshot of myself because it was the only image available to me that gave me a sense of presence, of girlhood beauty and capacity for pleasure. It was an image of myself I could genuinely like. At that stage of my life I was crazy about Westerns, about cowboys and Indians. . . . I grew up needing this image, cherishing it—my one reminder that there was a precious little girl inside me able to know and express joy. I took this photograph with me on a visit to the house of my father's cousin, Schuyler. . . .

Exercise ■■■

● First, draw or create a visual map of an early place in your life: a room (your bedroom, kitchen, living room as a kid), your family's first house, your childhood neighborhood, the town you grew up in, etc. Then describe the scene that emerges in memory from the map you have sketched.

Critical Frame

There are six major categories that can help you in considering the narratives in family photographs. These include **characters, actions, setting, temporal relations, audience,** and **point of view.**

- **Setting:** What settings or scenes are depicted by family photographs? Do certain settings seem to appear more than others?
- **Character:** Who are the main characters in the photographs? What are the traits of the characters? Do these traits change over the course of the family album?
- **Actions/Events:** In what actions do the characters engage? Are family members or friends depicted having fun? In ceremonies? Engaged in other kinds of activities?
- **Point of View:** From whose point of view are the photographs taken?
- **Temporal Relations:** Do the events depicted by the photographs occur in a brief period of time or over many years?
- **Audience:** Who do you think the photographer and/or the person responsible for putting together the family album envisioned as his or her audience?

Families operate like a community of interpreters. For instance, sometimes one family member might function as a "corrector," who claims authority over both the ordering and interpretation of family photographs. "No," this person might say, "that's not what happened," or "You're reading too much into a single photograph." While we might all see the same details of a photograph, we will not all have the same reading. Narrative variations, however, tell as much about the familial representation as do the images themselves. We thus use the term **relational narratives** to highlight how narratives are shaped by the contexts in which they are created, spoken, heard, or read. Think about the role of family albums or particular photographs in your own family.

- What do family photographs say or narrate about the family in general?
- What photographs are a part of an unofficial or official history of your family?
- What social and cultural values shape your family's visual representation of itself?
- What is the relationship between certain photographs and the stories that accompany them?
- How do these stories change depending upon who is telling them? How have these stories changed over the years?
- If you are from a family that does not place particular value on family photographs, what are some of the alternative ways your family images itself?

What Is Seen

The family photograph we saw on page 59 (Figure 3.1) was once prominently displayed on the fireplace mantel of Wendy Hesford's parents' home, along with other pictures of rites of passage and family rituals: engagements, marriages, school graduations, and the sacred family heirloom, a large, black, leather-bound Holy Bible, with pressed family birth announcements and obituaries crumbling between its pages. The portrait is of her maternal great grandfather, Edward William Trevenan, who left his wife Amelia and their five children in Cornwall, England, in 1910 to work as a Supervisor of Operations at one of the gold mines in Johannesburg, South Africa.

Although this photograph had been present in her house for most of her life, Wendy had never taken the time to really think about it until recently. One of the first details that we notice about the photograph is that Trevenan, probably in his mid-thirties, is seated in a small room on a simple wooden chair. The other furnishings are well-worn and merely functional: two low cots, a small wooden table, two battered steamer trunks. The floorboards are rough and paint is peeling off the walls. Edward is wearing black leather shoes, dark cuffed pants, a button-down shirt (without a collar), and what he would have called "braces" to hold his pants up. He has rolled his shirt sleeves up to his elbows, which are placed casually on the chair back and the table top. His legs are comfortably crossed before him, and his black leather shoes shine in the camera's light. His appearance suggests a sense of control over his domain, such as it is.

On the table are what appear to be the necessities of an English workingman's life at the turn of the century: two tobacco pipes, two brushes (one for shoes, one for hair), a pot of ink with a pen stuck in it, a tin canister, several bottles, and some papers (letters home?). The walls, too, are covered with "civilizing" touches: a pocket watch and chain hanging where a clock might be kept at home, a felt pin cushion (identifiable as such only because Trevanan's daughter still has the memento), and pictures from magazines.

A young black man sits on the edge of a steamer trunk in front of Trevenan. Trevenan's eyes look neither at the camera nor at anything within the frame of the picture, but gaze out, over, and beyond the visual field; the black youth, on the other hand, looks directly into the camera. He is dressed in baggy plaid pants that end above the knee, a plain long sleeve shirt, and thin-soled white shoes. His clothes do not fit well. The pants are clearly too large, gathered at the waist by a thick black belt; his shirt is too small and rises up his back. Upon his head sits a misshapen felt hat turned up in the front, and on his feet he wears scuffed white boots.

What Is Not Seen

This description of the photograph of Trevenan and his unnamed companion may appear fairly straightforward and objective. Since all descriptive acts are far from neutral, however, what we've left out is as important as what we've left in. For instance, we highlighted certain details and rejected or ignored others. Neither the photograph nor our description depict the struggles that Edward's wife Amelia must have faced in raising five children on her own or what must have been her conflicting emotions over her husband's stay in South Africa, which lasted over eighteen months. The historical context of the photograph includes the dangerous working conditions in the mines, the black workers' resistance to these conditions, as expressed in riots, strikes, and work stoppages, and the brutal suppression of such resistance by those in power. What is not seen is as much a part of the context of the photograph as what is seen.

If we think for a moment about our interpretation of the photograph thus far, we can see some evidence of how interpretations are shaped by the interpreter's relationship to those represented. Take a look again at the caption of the photo. This description (written by Wendy, but following family practice in referring to the image) reinforces the great grandfather's position of privilege in several ways. Labeling the image a "portrait" confers a certain dignity to the photo (it's a "study," rather than a casual snapshot) and places Trevenan squarely at its center (since portraits are often of a single figure, and this one is described as "Portrait of . . .

AND WRITING

description

Cicero, who was famed as the greatest speaker in all of ancient Rome, once said that in a speech, the speaker should not describe events so that the audience sees them vividly and clearly. Instead, he argued, the speaker should describe those events so that it becomes impossible for the audience *not* to see them. In teaching young students about persuasive speaking and writing, Cicero (who was also a lawyer) encouraged his students to conjure the event before the eyes of the jury, like so many magicians. This is (and was), of course, impossible. Words are not things but rather, only representations of things. No word, or words, can precisely duplicate the looks, sounds, textures, tastes, or smells of things, much less perfectly recreate people or entire events. Try, for example, to describe the taste of your favorite food, or the face of someone you love. It's impossible to do it perfectly, so that your listener experiences it as you do.

But we still do try to describe these things. The more words we use, and the more specific and detailed these words are, the closer our **description** comes to seeming real. So, for example, we don't write just "He was really, really angry," but we write instead: "His big, fat, bulbous nose was flaming crimson and spittle flew out from between his cursing, accursed teeth as he verbally flayed the disheveled waitress alive for serving the steak medium instead of medium rare." Or something like that.

Description can bring a scene or a character "to life," making the person or the event distinct, memorable, and even "real" for your reader. Description can give a verbal (written) representation a strong visual (or other sensory) impact. The power that description has in making writing more specific, more robust, more visual, and more memorable is why writing teachers are often so fond of saying (and writing in the margins of their students' papers), "Don't tell—show!"

Example ■■■

● The opening of Maxine Hong Kingston's "Photograph of My Parents" illustrates the power of careful description, especially when visual detail is supplemented with other sensory details:

Once in a long while, four times so far for me, my mother brings out the metal tube that holds her medical diploma. On the tube are gold circles crossed by seven red lines each—"joy" ideographs in abstract. There are also little flowers that look like gears for a gold machine. According to the scraps of labels with Chinese and American addresses, stamps, and postmarks, the family airmailed the can from Hong Kong in 1950. It got crushed in the middle, and whoever tried to peel the labels off stopped because the red and gold paint came off too, leaving silver scratches that rust. Somebody tried to pry the end off before discovering that the tube pulls apart. When I open it, the smell of China flies out, a thousand-year-old bat flying heavy-headed out of Chinese caverns where bats are as white as dust, a smell that comes from long ago, far back in the brain.

Exercises ▪▪▪

1 In small groups, generate a list of some commonplace things—people, events, or objects. For example: a teacher, a lawyer, wedding, a first day of school, the first day in this particular class, a potato, a lemon, etc. Then work as individuals to write *specific* descriptions of any of these items/events. Compare the descriptions you generate and discuss the different ways you do (or don't) use certain kinds of visual, or other sensory, details to make these things come to life.

2 First, write a one-line, unembellished sentence that (barely) describes a "family" you know from popular culture, history, the media, etc. (You are free to extend or develop your own definition of "family" in this exercise.) Exchange this one-line stock description with a partner. Now write TWO detailed descriptions of a page or so each: one description in which you show more (via details) about the family you first described, and the second description to show more (again, via details) about the family your partner described. You may or may not have a sense of the identity of the family your partner has described for you. This is okay. The point is to build these characters more vividly via description.

Trevenan"). Similarly, not naming the second man in the photo—or, indeed, referring to him at all—ensures that the viewer's attention will stay focused on Trevenan (who is identified by not just one but three proper names). The very caption assigned to the photograph is an interpretive act. Contrary to what one might at first think, what seems to be mere description or reportage is laced with cultural meanings.

Reading Contexts

Linking Family Stories with Family Photographs

What was your first impression of the relationship between the two subjects in the photograph? How do you interpret the young black man's gaze back at the camera? To what degree might the commanding, "masterly" view of the older white man be seen as the equivalent of the colonial looking out over his dominion—that is, as a visual statement of control or privilege? One might say that the young black male is positioned as an object to be surveyed and regulated, while Trevenan's posture refuses the camera's surveillant gaze.

Reading this photograph is like entering a space wherein the visual and verbal narratives of past and present generations collide. Despite the distance that separates us from the historical and social location of this photograph, the passage of the "portrait" from one generation to the next (it has traveled from South Africa to England to the United States) indicates a lingering commitment to a sense of history.

There is perhaps no way to interpret the photograph without recognizing the "relational network that composes all family pictures."[5] As we've said, the fact that the young black man was never named in the narrative of this picture that was passed down through the Hesford family is telling. Not only is his name unknown, but there is no definitive way of identifying his language or place of origin. One might argue that this lack is itself a vestige of "colonial" attitudes. The process of naming and leaving unnamed is one way in which one group or culture subordinates another.

Over time—most likely after the sweeping civil rights reforms of the 1960s—family members created a myth of a friendship between the two men, as they were uncomfortable with the master/servant aspect of the photo. Wendy's mother inherited the photograph and the story of their friendship. In the late 1970s, she displayed the photograph on the fireplace mantel in the family's newly purchased four-bedroom colonial home in a largely white New England. Throughout the 1980s, the photograph was part of a collection of portraits on the mantel. However, in the early 1990s, with the increasing attention to race relations in the United States (Rodney King, L.A. riots), the photograph disappeared to the basement. This "deauthorization" of the photograph as a family heirloom is telling. When the photograph disappeared, so, too, did the stories that accompanied it. These images were replaced by new idealized images of family rites of passages and achievements (graduations, marriages) that reflect currently acceptable cultural values and beliefs.

Critical Frame

Popular Images of the American Family

The movement of the Trevenan photograph from one country and one generation to another, and from one room to another, highlights how family narratives (visual and verbal) are shaped by and collide with particular cultural and historical contexts. Family images and narratives also have meaning(s) outside of the context of the family; we can see frequent struggles for control of familial images and narratives in popular culture. Within the national news media, photographic images of families become part of a national rhetorical vision.

Consider Figure 3.2 below, sponsored by the Council on American-Islamic Relations. This image appeared in the *New York Times* on March 19, 2003, at the onset of the war with Iraq.

That this image appeared after the attacks on the United States on September 11, 2001, and just prior to the onset of the war with Iraq is important. What significance would you say the timing of this image had on its audience? Might we understand the

Figure 3.2   Portrait of Islamic family.

Courtesy of the Council on American-Islamic Relations.

image as a call for tolerance at a time of national crisis? To what degree might this image have been seen as an example of U.S. patriotism?

The concept of family and the association of certain kinds of family with the American ideal have changed over time. In the post–World War II years, for example, traditional gender roles, particularly images that linked women with the domestic sphere and men with the public sphere of politics and action, were the norm. Family television shows like *Leave it to Beaver* (Figure 3.3) and *Father Knows Best,* which portrayed the idealized nuclear family, were the epitome of 1950s and early 1960s family drama. On *Leave it to Beaver,* Ward Cleaver, the head of the household, came home from the office to an immaculate house and a hot meal prepared by his well-coiffed wife, June.

Compare these early portrayals of the U.S. middle-class family with those depicted on television today. In what ways do television families reflect—or serve as a model for—their audience? In what ways do current programs challenge and reinforce the social norms of the day?

Figure 3.3   American actors (clockwise, from left) Tony Dow, Hugh Beaumont, Jerry Mathers, and Barbara Billingsley pose together in a 1957 promotional portrait for the television series *Leave It to Beaver.*

Courtesy of Getty Images.

The reality television program *The Osbournes* (Figure 3.4) demonstrates the social and cultural forces that work against traditional notions of family and family relations. The television program rebels against traditional notions of the family, at least at first sight. Ozzy Osbourne, former singer in British hard-rock band Black Sabbath, was legendary as an off-the-wall performer, usually dangerously drugged or drunk on stage. However, in the MTV reality television series, Ozzy and his family in their multimillion-dollar mansion are depicted ironically, as the "soul of normalcy." Is the

Figure 3.4 The Osbournes pose in their living room in a 2002 promotional portrait for *The Osbournes.*

Courtesy of Getty Images.

memory description interpretation narrative

AND WRITING

interpretation

When we engage in **interpretation,** we are both *finding* and *creating* meaning in artifacts or language. That is, while we might like to think that we are searching for just what it was that the creator (author, artist, speaker, etc.) meant when he or she said, wrote, or did this, we are also actually *creating* our own new meaning from the artifact or language before us. Thus, when we interpret, we are also making value judgments. What's more, we interpret images and texts based on our own experiences, our personal and collective history, our mood, the age in which we live, and a host of other factors. A story that seems serious and sad to me may be ridiculous to you.

Imagine that you are walking on a path in the woods and encounter two sticks neatly laid across each other in an "X" pattern. This pattern may or may not mean something to you, depending upon your readiness and ability to interpret it. Perhaps you did not even notice the sticks and stepped on them, thereby destroying the pattern. Perhaps you noticed them and smiled at the interesting way nature sometimes works. Perhaps you saw them and immediately began an extended reverie about yourself as a woodsman from the past, reading the signs left for you by a partner who had traveled this path a day before you. Perhaps you saw them and dropped down on your knees, digging wildly with your hands to unearth the treasure that should be buried beneath the "X." Perhaps you gathered them up to take back to your campsite as kindling for the evening campfire. Perhaps you interpreted the "X" in yet another way?

Interpretation is really about figuring out what "X" means, as well as aiming to understand why something is worth recording, recalling, remembering, and writing about at all. Interpretation answers the "so what?" question; thus, it stands behind most critical college-level writing.

Examples ■■■

❶   In Annette Kuhn's critical essay "Remembrance," she works through several interpretations of a detail—her mother's written caption that accompanies a family picture. In her several layers of interpretation she tells us, for example:

Critical Frame

What I am telling you—"my own story"—about this picture is itself changeable. In each re-enactment, each re-staging of this family drama, details get added and dropped, the story fleshes out, new connections are made, emotional tones—puzzlement, anger, sadness—fluctuate.

. . . Another, and more disturbing, reading of my mother's inscription is available, however . . .

. . . In the first reading, my mother writes herself into the picture by claiming the right to define the memories evoked by it; and by omission and commission negates my father's involvement in both the photograph and the family.

❷ Writing about how visual/photographic representations of "black folk . . . within the culture of apartheid" were interpreted by those (black folk) who were being represented, bell hooks tells us about the variability of interpretation in the essay "In Our Glory: Photography and Black Life":

We saw ourselves represented in these images not as caricatures, cartoon-like figures; we were there in full diversity of body, being, and expression, multidimensional. Reflecting the way black folks looked at themselves in those private spaces, where those ways of looking were not being overseen by a white colonizing eye, a white supremacist gaze, these images created ruptures in our experience of the visual.

Exercises ▨■▨

❶ Go on with that "X." . . . How many other things might those two sticks in the woods mean?

❷ Bring in several interesting images or photographs of family interactions from your own collection or from magazines, newspapers, etc. Remove any captions accompanying them. In small groups, pass around the images while everyone writes a paragraph of interpretation for each one. When each of you has four to five paragraphs on four to five images, stop and share your interpretations with each other. Also share a discussion about how and why your interpretations of various images are alike or unlike.

AND WRITING

narrative

In ancient Greece, forgetting was called *lethe* (from the name of the river that the dead crossed into Hades), while *aletheia* (or "unforgotten") was the word for truth. Because nothing is easier to remember than a good story, the most important truths in the ancient world were set down in stories, most famously in epic poetry. Many cultures have preserved their way of life through storytelling, particularly in stories of gods, heroes, and ancestors whose deeds established the central beliefs of the people. Specifically national stories are proliferated to inform and educate citizens not only about cultural or historic heroes, but also about national and cultural virtues (as, for example, in the story of George Washington and the cherry tree).

On an individual and familial level, too, the power of **narrative** is significant: We often "remember" moments of our childhood not through our own memory of the experience, but because the event has been narrated to us by parents or other significant figures in our early life. As no doubt we've all experienced, the telling of a story from the past can powerfully recreate the event in the present. This is why when someone can't remember, for example, what they had for dinner last night, they can still often remember an entire story told or read to them as a child.

Example ■■■

● In her critical essay "Remembrance," Annette Kuhn makes evident the connection between verbal narration and family photos when she claims:

formerly out-of-control rock star truly a Ward Cleaver for our times? Has our culture changed that much? If so, in what way(s)?

Memory and Interpretation

Chicana artist Kathy Vargas creates images that invite viewers to question the relationship between remembrance and interpretation. In one of her art pieces, "My Alamo"—the "Shrine of Texas Liberty"—she creates a photomontage of family photographs, cultural artifacts, and texts (Figure 3.5). Vargas urges us as viewers to wander through

Here, then, is one more story: about a family album; about the kinds of tales (and the kinds of families) family albums construct; and about how my photograph was put to use once upon a time, and still survived to be used today, again and again.

Family photographs are quite often deployed—shown, talked about—in series: pictures get displayed one after another, their selection and ordering as meaningful as the pictures themselves. The whole, the series, constructs a family story in some respects like a classical narrative—linear, chronological. . . .

Exercises ▪■■

❶ As a class or in small groups, decide upon a general *kind* of story that you all want to (re)tell. For example, you could all tell stories about the first word you said, the first time you read or wrote your name, your first day of school, your first love, your first well-remembered embarrassing moment, or even where you were and what you were doing when _____ happened (where the event is likely to be one that others will have some memory of). Or, you could choose together to tell stories about some hero or local/regional/national myth with which you are all familiar. No matter what kind of story you agree on, it must be a story that *was first told to you*. Now: Tell (write) a story about this story that was once told to you. Once you have all drafted these stories, share them with each other, paying particular attention to the way the stories vary, in terms of details, ordering, inclusion/exclusion of events, etc.

❷ Bring in several photographs of you and/or your family, or clip several images of family scenes from magazines or web sites. Exchange these images with a partner or a small group. Now arrange the images you received from your partner as if they were in a photo album, and write a brief narrative about them.

this landscape of private and public memories and to consider whose memories and experiences get enshrined into history.

As in the writing and telling of stories, pieces of memory inevitably go missing. Memories are lost and narratives are reconfigured. Like hand shadows on a wall, memories and the stories they tell are never exactly the same shape twice.

NOTES

1. Shawn Michelle Smith, *American Archives: Gender, Race, and Class in Visual Culture* (Princeton: Princeton UP, 1999) 113.

Figure 3.5   Kathy Vargas, "My Alamo," 1995. Series #2A, hand colored gelatin silver print; 20" x 16".

Courtesy of Kathy Vargas/University of the Incarnate Word.

2. Marianne Hirsch, ed., *The Familial Gaze* (Hanover and London: UP of New England, 1999) xii.

3. Bill Roorbach, *Writing Life Stories* (Cinncinnati: Story Press, 1998) 21, 24.

4. An earlier and longer version of Wendy Hesford's discussion of this family photograph appeared in her book *Framing Identities: Autobiography and the Politics of Pedagogy* (Minneapolis: U of MN P, 1999).

5. Marianne Hirsch, *Family Frames: Photography, Narrative, and Postmemory* (Cambridge: Harvard UP, 1997) 3.

Photograph of My Parents

MAXINE HONG KINGSTON

In examining photographs that would seem to indicate happy moments in the lives of her mother and father, *MAXINE HONG KINGSTON* instead chooses to disclose painful memories surrounding them. The course of this short but vivid remembrance leads Kingston to make astute observations about the differences between the cultural settings in which her parents grew up: Her father's happy-go-lucky American past stands in marked contrast to the painful, oppressive life led by her mother in China. This selection is taken from Kingston's acclaimed memoir *The Woman Warrior* (1976). Kingston is the author of numerous books, including *China Men* (1980) and *The Fifth Book of Peace* (2003).

Once in a long while, four times so far for me, my mother brings out the metal tube that holds her medical diploma. On the tube are gold circles crossed with seven red lines each—"joy" ideographs in abstract. There are also little flowers that look like gears for a gold machine. According to the scraps of labels with Chinese and American addresses, stamps, and postmarks, the family airmailed the can from Hong Kong in 1950. It got crushed in the middle, and whoever tried to peel the labels off stopped because the red and gold paint came off too, leaving silver scratches that rust. Somebody tried to pry the end off before discovering that the tube pulls apart. When I open it, the smell of China flies out, a thousand-year-old bat flying heavy-headed out of the Chinese caverns where bats are as white as dust, a smell that comes from long ago, far back in the brain. Crates from Canton, Hong Kong, Singapore, and Taiwan have that smell too, only stronger because they are more recently come from the Chinese.

Inside the can are three scrolls, one inside another. The largest says that in the twenty-third year of the National Republic, the To Keung School of Midwifery, where she has had two years of instruction and Hospital Practice, awards its Diploma to my mother, who has shown through oral and written examination her Proficiency in Midwifery, Pediatrics, Gynecology, "Medecine," "Surgary," Therapeutics, Ophthalmology, Bacteriology, Dermatology, Nursing, and Bandage. This document has eight stamps on it: one, the school's English and Chinese names embossed together in a circle; one, as the Chinese enumerate, a stork and a big baby in lavender ink; one, the school's Chinese seal; one, an orangish paper stamp pasted in the border design; one, the red seal of Dr. Wu Pak-liang, M.D., Lyon, Berlin, president and "Ex-assistant étranger à la clinique chirugicale et d'accouchement de l'université de Lyon"; one, the red seal of Dean Woo Yin-kam, M.D.; one, my mother's seal, her chop mark larger than the president's and the dean's; and one, the number 1279 on the back. Dean Woo's signature is followed by "(Hackett)." I read in a history book that Hackett Medical College for Women at Canton was founded in the nineteenth century by European women doctors.

The school seal has been pressed over a photograph of my mother at the age of thirty-seven. The diploma gives her age as twenty-seven. She looks younger than I do, her eyebrows are thicker, her lips fuller. Her naturally curly hair is parted on the left, one wavy wisp tendrilling off to the right. She wears a scholar's white gown, and she is not thinking about her appearance. She stares straight ahead as if she could see me and past me to her grandchildren and grandchildren's grandchildren. She has spacy eyes, as all people recently from Asia have. Her eyes do not focus on the camera. My mother is not smiling; Chinese do not smile for photographs. Their faces command relatives in foreign lands—"Send money"—and posterity forever—"Put food in front of this picture." My mother does not understand Chinese-American snapshots. "What are you laughing at?" she asks.

The second scroll is a long narrow photograph of the graduating class with the school officials seated in front. I picked out my mother immediately. Her face is exactly her own, though forty years younger. She is so familiar, I can only tell whether or not she is pretty or happy or smart by comparing her to the other women. For this formal group picture she straightened her hair with oil to make a chin-length bob like the others'. On the other women, strangers, I can recognize a curled lip, a sidelong glance, pinched shoulders. My mother is not soft; the girl with the small nose and dimpled underlip is soft. My mother is not humorous, not like the girl at the end who lifts her mocking chin to pose like Girl Graduate. My mother does not have smiling eyes; the old woman teacher (Dean Woo?) in front crinkles happily, and the one faculty member in the western suit smiles westernly. Most of the graduates are girls whose faces have not yet formed; my mother's face will not change anymore, except to age. She is intelligent, alert, pretty. I can't tell if she's happy.

5   The graduates seem to have been looking elsewhere when they pinned the rose, zinnia, or chrysanthemum on their precise black dresses. One thin girl wears hers in the middle of her chest. A few have a flower over a left or a right nipple. My mother put hers, a chrysanthemum, below her left breast. Chinese dresses at that time were dartless, cut as if women did not have breasts; these young doctors, unaccustomed to decorations, may have seen their chests as black expanses with no reference points for flowers. Perhaps they couldn't shorten that far gaze that lasts only a few years after a Chinese emigrates. In this picture too my mother's eyes are big with

what they held—reaches of oceans beyond China, land beyond oceans. Most emigrants learn the barbarians' directness—how to gather themselves and stare rudely into talking faces as if trying to catch lies. In America my mother has eyes as strong as boulders, never once skittering off a face, but she has not learned to place decorations and phonograph needles, nor has she stopped seeing land on the other side of the oceans. Now her eyes include the relatives in China, as they once included my father smiling and smiling in his many western outfits, a different one for each photograph that he sent from America.

He and his friends took pictures of one another in bathing suits at Coney Island beach; the salt wind from the Atlantic blowing their hair. He's the one in the middle with his arms about the necks of his buddies. They pose in the cockpit of a biplane, on a motorcycle, and on a lawn beside the "Keep Off the Grass" sign. They are always laughing. My father, white shirt sleeves rolled up, smiles in front of a wall of clean laundry. In the spring he wears a new straw hat, cocked at a Fred Astaire angle. He steps out, dancing down the stairs, one foot forward, one back, a hand in his pocket. He wrote to her about the American custom of stomping on straw hats come fall. "If you want to save your hat for next year," he said, "you have to put it away early, or else when you're riding the subway or walking along Fifth Avenue, any stranger can snatch it off your head and put his foot through it. That's the way they celebrate the change of seasons here." In the winter he wears a gray felt hat with his gray overcoat. He is sitting on a rock in Central Park. In one snapshot he is not smiling; someone took it when he was studying, blurred in the glare of the desk lamp.

There are no snapshots of my mother. In two small portraits, however, there is a black thumbprint on her forehead, as if someone had inked in bangs, as if someone had marked her.

"Mother, did bangs come into fashion after you had the picture taken?" One time she said yes. Another time when I asked, "Why do you have fingerprints on your forehead?" she said, "Your First Uncle did that." I disliked the unsureness in her voice.

The last scroll has columns of Chinese words. The only English is "Department of Health, Canton," imprinted on my mother's face, the same photograph as on the diploma. I keep looking to see whether she was afraid. Year after year my father did not come home or send for her. Their two children had been dead for ten years. If he did not return soon, there would be no more children. ("They were three and two years old, a boy and a girl. They could talk already.") My father did send money regularly, though, and she had nobody to spend it on but herself. She bought good clothes and shoes. Then she decided to use the money for becoming a doctor. She did not leave for Canton immediately after the children died. In China there was time to complete feelings. As my father had done, my mother left the village by ship. There was a sea bird painted on the ship to protect it against shipwreck and winds. She was in luck. The following ship was boarded by river pirates, who kidnapped every passenger, even old ladies. "Sixty dollars for an old lady" was what the bandits used to say. "I sailed alone," she says, "to the capital of the entire province." She took a brown leather suitcase and a seabag stuffed with two quilts.

Re-reading/Conversations with the Text

1. Re-read "Photograph of My Parents" and pay particular attention to the various "looks" Kingston mentions. What role do the eyes play? List these "looks" and also note how Kingston chooses to describe them. Why do you think she makes these distinctions? What reasons can you cite from the text to explain these differences?

2. Although this excerpt is rather short, it offers some telling characterizations of the differences between native Chinese and Chinese American cultures. Working in pairs, create a profile for each of these cultural sketches drawn by Kingston. What techniques does she use to describe each culture and to distinguish one culture from another? Based on the text, what do you gather are Kingston's attitudes toward each culture?

3. One commonality among many of the photographs Kingston views is that they have been altered in some way—the stamps and seals on the medical diploma and photograph, the thumbprint over Kingston's mother's hair. What do these alterations indicate about the relationships among family members, men and women, and about institutions in Chinese culture? How (if at all) are family photographs altered in your family? Does a certain family member compose family albums or "touch up" the photographs in any way? How do these alterations shape the meanings of particular photographs?

Re-seeing and Re-writing

1. Choose one family photograph, a series of related photographs, or a home video with which to work. First, ask yourself whether the photographs you

have chosen are part of an unofficial history of a family. In what ways, for example, does the family album represent the family members and their everyday lives? More specifically, does the photograph represent an *idealized* image of your family, yourself, or particular family members? As Kingston does in her essay, try to move between description of the family photographs and the family's interpretation of them, in order to convey the role of photography in constructing a sense of familial history and identity.

The following are additional questions to consider in developing your analysis of the visual arguments put forth by the photographs:

- What kinds of events are recorded? How might these events shape the family's image of itself?
- What is missing from the albums? For example, what pictures might have been taken but never were? What events or people were not recorded? In other words, what is invisible within the family archives?
- What do these photographs tell you about the ways in which particular people in the family (e.g., the women, young boys) are positioned in the family and/or the world? What social and cultural values and ideas shape the family's visual representation of itself?
- In what ways do these photographs prompt you to reconsider your "self-history"?

2. Review the descriptions Kingston gives of the photographs of her parents and describe how she looks at each photo. Then, as an experiment in point of view, write a narrative that tells the story about each parent based on Kingston's description. You might want to compose the narrative in the first person, as if you were speaking from the point of view of one of her parents.

Throughout several of the essays in this unit, the process of picture-taking is analyzed. Look at the essays by hooks, Kingston, Kuhn, and/or Hirsch. Recall and record the way each author explains various reasons that photos are taken. What similarities and differences do you notice? What might account for the differences? Why do *you* think photos are taken?

In Our Glory: Photography and Black Life

BELL HOOKS

It's likely that we consider the pictures placed in our homes as intimate depictions of our friends and families meant for private consumption; we don't generally consider the impact these images might have on a larger community. For *BELL HOOKS*, the display of photographs in the domestic spaces of African Americans constitutes a political act, one in which visual representations of black culture are made semi-public, while the dominant culture is often reluctant to show such images. The often-outspoken hooks is the author of a number of articles and books dealing with the political dimensions of race, gender, and class, including *Ain't I a Woman? Black Women and Feminism* (1981), *Teaching to Transgress: Education as the Practice of Freedom* (1994), and *Art on My Mind: Visual Politics* (1995), from which this excerpt is taken.

Veodis Watkins, 1949
Photographer: unknown (Courtesy bell hooks)

Always a daddy's girl. I was not surprised that my sister V. became a lesbian, or that her lovers were always white women. Her worship of daddy and her passion for whiteness appeared to affirm a movement away from black womanhood, and of course, that image of the woman we did not want to become—our mother. The only family photograph V. displays in her house is a picture of our dad, looking young with a mustache. His dark skin mingling with the shadows in the photograph. All of which is highlighted by the white T-shirt he wears.

In this snapshot he is standing by a pool table. The look on his face confident, seductive, cool—a look we rarely saw growing up. I have no idea who took the picture, only that it pleases me to imagine that he cared for them—deeply. There is such boldness, such fierce openness in the way he faces the camera. This snapshot was taken before marriage, before us, his seven children, before our presence in his life forced him to leave behind the carefree masculine identity this pose conveys.

The fact that my sister V. possesses this image of our dad, one that I had never seen before, merely affirms their romance, the bond between the two of them. They had the dreamed-about closeness between father and daughter, or so it seemed. Her possession of the snapshot confirms this, is an acknowledgment that she is allowed to know—yes, even to possess—that private life he had always kept to himself. When we were children, he refused to answer our questions about who he was, how did he act, what did he do and feel before us? It was as though he did not want to remember or share that part of himself, that remembering hurt. Standing before this snapshot, I come closer to the cold, distant, dark man who is my father, closer than I can ever come in real life. Not always able to love him there, I am sure I can love this version of him, the snapshot. I give it a title: *in his glory*.

Before leaving my sister's place, I plead with her to make a copy of this picture for my birthday. It does not come, even though she says she will. For Christmas, then. It's on the way. I surmise that my passion for it surprises her, makes her hesitate. Always rivals in childhood—she winning, the possessor of Dad's affection—she wonders whether to give that up, whether she is ready to share. She hesitates to give me the man in the snapshot. After all, had he wanted me to see him this way, "in his glory," he would have given me a picture.

5   My younger sister G. calls. For Christmas, V. has sent her a "horrible photograph" of Dad.

There is outrage in her voice as she says, "It's disgusting. He's not even wearing a shirt, just an old white undershirt." G. keeps repeating, "I don't know why she has sent this picture to me." She has no difficulty promising to give me her copy if mine does not arrive. Her lack of interest in the photograph saddens me. When she was the age our dad is in the picture she looked just like him. She had his beauty then—that same shine of glory and pride. Is this the face of herself that she has forgotten, does not want to be reminded of, because time has taken such glory away? Unable to fathom how she can not be drawn to this picture, I ponder what this image suggests to her that she cannot tolerate: a grown black man having a good time, playing a game, having a drink maybe, enjoying himself without the company of women.

Although my sisters and I look at this snapshot and see the same man, we do not see him in the same way. Our "reading" and experience of this image is shaped by our relationship to him, to the world of childhood and the images that make our life what it is now. I want to rescue and preserve this image of our father, not let it be forgotten. It allows me to understand him, provides a way for me to know him that makes it possible to love him again and against past all the other images, the ones that stand in the way of love.

Such is the power of the photograph, of the image, that it can give back and take away, that it can bind. This snapshot of Veodis Watkins, our father, sometimes called Ned or Leakey in his younger days, gives me a space for intimacy between the image and myself, between me and Dad. I am captivated, seduced by it, the way other images have caught and held me, embraced me like arms that would not let go.

Struggling in childhood with the image of myself as unworthy of love, I could not see myself beyond all the received images, which simply reinforced my sense of unworthiness. Those ways of seeing myself came from voices of authority. The place where I could see myself, beyond the imposed image, was in the realm of the snapshot. I am most real to myself in snapshots—there I see an image I can love.

My favorite childhood snapshot then and now shows me in costume, masquerading. And long after it had disappeared I continued to long for it and to grieve. I loved this snapshot of myself because it was the only image available to me that gave me a sense of presence, of girlhood beauty and capacity for pleasure. It was an image of myself I could genuinely like. At that stage of my life I was crazy about Westerns, about cowboys and Indians. The camera captures me in my cowgirl outfit, white ruffled blouse, vest, fringed skirt, my one gun and my boots. In this image, I became all that I wanted to be in my imagination.

10   For a moment suspended in this image: I am a cowgirl. There is a look of heavenly joy on my face. I grew up needing this image, cherishing it—my one reminder that there was a precious little girl inside me able to know and express joy. I took this photograph with me on a visit to the house of my father's cousin, Schuyler.

His was a home where art and the image mattered. No wonder, then, that I wanted to share my "best" image. Making my first big journey away from home, from a small town to my first big city, I needed the security of this image. I packed it carefully. I wanted Lovie, cousin Schuyler's wife, to see me "in my glory." I remember giving her the snapshot for safekeeping; only, when it was time for me to return home it could not be found. This was for me a terrible loss, an irreconcilable grief. Gone was the image of myself I could love. Losing that snapshot, I lost the proof of my worthiness—that I had ever been a bright-eyed child capable of wonder, the proof that there was a "me of me."

The image in this snapshot has lingered in my mind's eye for years. It has lingered there to remind of the power of snapshots, of the image. As I slowly work on a book of essays titled *Art on My Mind,* I think about the place of art in black life, connections between the social construction of black identity, the impact of race and class, and the presence in black life of an inarticulate but ever-present visual aesthetic governing our relationship to images, to the process of image making. I return to the snapshot as a starting point to consider the place of the visual in black life—the importance of photography.

Cameras gave to black folks, irrespective of our class, a means by which we could participate fully in the production of images. Hence it is essential that any theoretical discussion of the relationship of black life to the visual, to art making, make photography central. Access and mass appeal have historically made photography a powerful location for the construction of an oppositional black aesthetic. In the world before racial integration, there was a constant struggle on the part of black folks to create a counter-hegemonic world of images that would stand as visual resistance, challenging racist images. All colonized and subjugated people who, by way of resistance, create an oppositional subculture within the framework of domination, recognize that the field of representation (how we see ourselves, how others see us) is a site of ongoing struggle.

The history of black liberation movements in the United States could be characterized as a struggle over images as much as it has also been a struggle for rights, for equal access. To many reformist black civil rights activists, who believed that desegregation would offer the humanizing context that would challenge and change white supremacy, the issue of representation—control over images—was never as important as equal access. As time has progressed, and the face of white supremacy has not changed, reformist and radical blacks alike are more likely to agree that the field of representation remains a crucial realm of struggle, as important as the question of equal access, if not more so. Significantly, Roger Wilkins emphasizes this point in his recent essay "White Out" (published in the November 1992 issue of *Mother Jones*). Wilkins comments:

In those innocent days, before desegregation had really been tried, before the New Frontier and the Great Society, many of us blacks had lovely, naïve hopes for integration. . . . In our naïveté, we believed that the power to segregate was the greatest power that had been wielded against us. It turned out that our expectations were wrong. The greatest power turned out to be what it had always been: the power to define reality where blacks are concerned and to manage perceptions and therefore arrange politics and culture to reinforce those definitions.

15   Though our politics differ, Wilkins' observations mirror my insistence, in the opening essay of *Black Looks: Race and Representation,* that black people have made few, if any, revolutionary interventions in the arena of representations.

In part, racial desegregation, equal access, offered a vision of racial progress that, however limited, led many black people to be less vigilant about the question of representation. Concurrently, contemporary commodification of blackness creates a market context wherein conventional, even stereotypical, modes of representing blackness may receive the greatest reward. This leads to a cultural context in which images that would subvert the status quo are harder to produce. There is no "perceived market" for them. Nor should it surprise us that the erosion of oppositional black subcultures (many of which have been destroyed in the desegregation process) has deprived us of those sites of radical resistance where we have had primary control over representation. Significantly, nationalist black freedom movements were often only concerned with questions of "good" and "bad" imagery and did not promote a more expansive cultural understanding of the *politics* of representation. Instead they promoted notions of essence and identity that ultimately restricted and confined black image production.

No wonder, then, that racial integration has created a crisis in black life, signaled by the utter loss of critical vigilance in the arena of image making—by our being stuck in endless debate over good and bad imagery. The aftermath of this crisis has been devastating in that it has led to a relinquishment of collective black interest in the production of images. Photography began to have less significance in black life as a means—private or public—by which an oppositional standpoint could be asserted, a mode of seeing different from that of the dominant culture. Everyday black folks began to see themselves as not having a major role to play in the production of images.

To reverse this trend we must begin to talk about the significance of black image production in daily life prior to racial integration. When we concentrate on photography, then, we make it possible to see the walls of photographs in black homes as a critical intervention, a disruption of white control of black images.

Most southern black folks grew up in a context where snapshots and the more stylized photographs taken by professional photographers were the easiest images to produce. Significantly, displaying those images in everyday life was as central as making them. The walls and walls of images in southern black homes were sites of resistance. They constituted private, black-owned and -operated, gallery space where images could be displayed, shown to friends and strangers. These walls were a space where, in the midst of segregation, the hardship of apartheid, dehumanization could be countered. Images could be critically considered, subjects positioned according to individual desire.

Growing up inside these walls, many of us   20 did not, at the time, regard them as important or valuable. Increasingly, as black folks live in a world so technologically advanced that it is possible for images to be produced and reproduced instantly, it is even harder for some of us to emotionally contextualize the significance of the camera in black life during the years of racial apartheid. The sites of contestation were not *out there,* in the world of white power, they were *within* segregated black life. Since no "white" galleries displayed images of black people created by black folks, spaces had to be made within diverse black communities. Across class, black folks struggled with the issue of representation. Significantly, issues of representation were linked with the issue of documentation, hence the importance of photography. The camera was the central instrument by which blacks could disprove representations of us created by white folks. The degrading images of blackness that emerged from racist white imaginations and circulated widely in the dominant culture (on salt shakers, cookie jars, pancake boxes) could be countered by "true-to-life" images. When the psychohistory of a people is marked by ongoing loss, when entire histories are denied, hidden, erased, documentation may become an obsession. The camera must have seemed a magical instrument to many of the displaced and marginalized groups trying to create new destinies in the Americas. More than any other image-making tool, it offered African Americans disempowered in white culture a way to empower ourselves through representation. For black folks, the camera provided a means to document a reality that could, if necessary, be packed, stored, moved from place to place. It was documentation that could be shared, passed around. And ultimately, these images, the worlds they recorded, could be hidden, to be discovered at another time. Had the camera been there when slavery ended, it could have provided images that would have helped folks searching for lost kin and loved ones. It would have been a powerful took of cultural recovery. Half a century later, the generations of black folks emerging from such a history of loss became passionately obsessed with cameras. Elderly black people developed a cultural passion for the camera, for the images it produced, because it offered a way to contain memories, to overcome loss, to keep history.

Though rarely articulated as such, the camera became in black life a political instrument, a way to resist misrepresentation as well as a means by which alternative images could be produced. Photography was more fascinating to masses of black folks than other forms of image making because it offered the possibility of immediate intervention, useful in the production of counter-hegemonic representations even as it was also an instrument of pleasure. Producing images with the camera allowed black folks to combine image making in resistance struggle with a pleasurable experience. Taking pictures was fun!

Growing up in the fifties, I was somewhat awed and frightened at times by our extended family's emphasis on picture taking. Whether it was the images of the dead as they lay serene, beautiful, and still in open caskets, or the endless portraits of newborns, every wall and corner of my grandparents' (and most everybody else's) home was lined with photographs. When I was younger I never linked this obsession with images of self-representation to our history as a domestically colonized and subjugated people.

My perspective on picture taking was more informed by the way the process was tied to patriarchy in our household. Our father was definitely the "picture takin' man." For a long time cameras were both mysterious and off-limits for the rest of us. As the only one in the family who had access to the equipment, who could learn how to make the process work, he exerted control over our image. In charge of capturing our family history with the camera, he called and took the shots. We constantly were lined up for picture taking, and it was years before our household could experience this as an enjoyable activity, before anyone else could be behind the camera. Before then, picture taking was serious business. I hated it. I hated posing. I hated cameras. I hated the images they produced. When I stopped living at home, I refused to be captured by anyone's camera. I did not long to document my life, the changes, the presence of different places, people, and so on. I wanted to leave no trace. I wanted there to be no walls in my life that would, like gigantic maps, chart my journey. I wanted to stand outside history.

That was twenty years ago. Now that I am passionately involved with thinking critically about black people and representation, I can confess that those walls of photographs empowered me, and that I feel their absence in my life. Right now, I long for those walls, those curatorial spaces in the home that express our will to make and display images.

25   Sarah Oldham, my mother's mother, was a keeper of walls. Throughout our childhood, visits to her house were like trips to a gallery or museum—experiences we did not have because of racial segregation. We would stand before the walls of images and learn the importance of the arrangement, why a certain photo was placed here and not there. The walls were fundamentally different from photo albums. Rather than shutting images away, where they could be seen only by request, the walls were a public announcement of the primacy of the image, the joy of image making. To enter black homes in my childhood was to enter a world that valued the visual, that asserted our collective will to participate in a non-institutionalized curatorial process.

For black folks constructing our identities within the culture of apartheid, these walls were essential to the process of decolonization. Contrary to colonizing socialization, internalized racism, they announced our visual complexity. We saw ourselves represented in these images not as caricatures, cartoon-like figures; we were there in full diversity of body, being, and expression, multidimensional. Reflecting the way black folks looked at themselves in those private spaces, where those ways of looking were not being overseen by a white colonizing eye, a white supremacist gaze, these images created ruptures in our experience of the visual. They challenged both white perceptions of blackness and that realm of black-produced image making that reflected internalized racism. Many of

these images demanded that we look at ourselves with new eyes, that we create oppositional standards of evaluation. As we looked at black skin in snapshots, the techniques for lightening skin which professional photographers often used when shooting black images were suddenly exposed as a colonizing aesthetic. Photographs taken in everyday life, snapshots in particular, rebelled against all of those photographic practices that reinscribed colonial ways of looking and capturing the images of the black "other." Shot spontaneously, without any notion of remaking black bodies in the image of whiteness, snapshots posed a challenge to black viewers. Unlike photographs constructed so that black images would appear as the embodiment of colonizing fantasies, these snapshots gave us a way to see ourselves, a sense of how we looked when we were not "wearing the mask," when we were not attempting to perfect the image for a white supremacist gaze.

Although most black folks did not articulate a desire to look at images of themselves that did not resemble or please white folks' ideas about us, or that did not frame us within an image of racial hierarchies, that need was expressed through our passionate engagement with informal photographic practices. Creating pictorial genealogies was the means by which one could ensure against the losses of the past. They were a way to sustain ties. As children, we learned who our ancestors were by endless narratives told to us as we stood in front of pictures.

In many black homes, photographs—particularly snapshots—were also central to the creation of "altars." These commemorative places paid homage to absent loved ones. Snapshots or professional portraits were placed in specific settings so that a relationship with the dead could be continued. Poignantly describing this use of the image in her most recent novel, *Jazz*, Toni Morrison writes:

> . . . a dead girl's face has become a necessary thing for their nights. They each take turns to

throw off the bedcovers, rise up from the sagging mattress and tiptoe over cold linoleum into the parlor to gaze at what seems like the only living presence in the house: the photograph of a bold, unsmiling girl staring from the mantelpiece. If the tiptoer is Joe Trace, driven by loneliness from his wife's side, then the face stares at him without hope or regret and it is the absence of accusation that wakes him from his sleep hungry for her company. No finger points. Her lips don't turn down in judgement. Her face is calm, generous and sweet. But if the tiptoer is Violet the photograph is not that at all. The girl's face looks greedy, haughty and very lazy. The cream-at-the-top-of-the-milkpail face of someone who will never work for anything, someone who picks up things lying on other people's dressers and is not embarrassed when found out. It is the face of a sneak who glides over to your sink to rinse the fork you have laid by your place. An inward face—whatever it sees is its own self. You are there, it says, because I am looking at you.

I quote this passage at length because it describes the kind of relationship to photographic images that has not been acknowledged in critical discussions of black folks' relationship to the visual. When I first read these sentences I was reminded of the passionate way we related to photographs when I was a child. Fictively dramatizing the way a photograph can have a "living presence," Morrison offers a description that mirrors the way many black folks rooted in southern traditions used and use, pictures. They were and remain a mediation between the living and the dead.

30   To create a palimpsest of black folks' relation to the visual in segregated black life, we need to follow each trace, not fall into the trap of thinking that if something was not openly discussed, or if talked about and not recorded, that it lacks significance and meaning. Those pictorial genealogies that Sarah Oldham, my mother's mother, constructed on her walls were essential to our sense of self and identity as a family. They provided a necessary narrative, a way for us to enter history without words. When words entered, they did so in order to make the images live. Many older black folks who cherished pictures were not literate. The images were crucial documentation, there to sustain and affirm oral memory. This was especially true for my grandmother, who did not read or write. I focus especially on her walls because I know that, as an artist (she was an excellent quiltmaker), she positioned the photos with the same care that she laid out her quilts.

The walls of pictures were indeed maps guiding us through diverse journeys. Seeking to recover strands of oppositional worldviews that were a part of black folks' historical relationship to the visual, to the process of image making, many black folks are once again looking to photography to make the connection. Contemporary African America artist Emma Amos also maps our journeys when she mixes photography with painting to make connections between past and present. Amos uses snapshots inherited from an elder uncle who took pictures for a living. In one piece, Amos paints a map of the United States and identifies diasporic African presences as well as particular Native American communities with black kin, using a family image to mark each spot.

Drawing from the past, from those walls of images I grew up with, I gather snapshots and lay them out, to see what narratives the images tell, what they say without words. I search these images to see if there are imprints waiting to be seen, recognized, and read. Together, a black male friend and I lay out the snapshots of his boyhood, to see when he began to lose a certain openness, to discern at what age he began to shut down, to close himself away. Through these images, he hopes to find a way back to the self he once was. We are awed by what our snapshots reveal, what they enable us to remember.

The word *remember* (*re-member*) evokes the coming together of severed parts, fragments becoming a whole. Photography has been, and is, central to that aspect of decolonization that calls us back to the past and offers a way to reclaim and renew life-affirming bonds. Using these images, we connect ourselves to a recuperative, redemptive memory that enables us to construct radical identities, images of ourselves that transcend the limits of the colonizing eye.

Re-reading/Conversations with the Text

1. hooks compares the walls of pictures found in the homes of her relatives to a photo gallery; she describes these walls as "curatorial spaces in the home that express our will to make and display images." What does hooks gain in making this comparison? How might hooks's comparison complicate the presentation of photos in actual museum spaces? How might the comparison redefine the way we think about representations of African Americans in popular culture?

2. At the end of this piece, hooks emphasizes the importance of "re-membering," the putting "together of severed parts, fragments becoming a whole" through photography. She concludes that by "[u]sing . . . images, we connect ourselves to a recuperative, redemptive memory that enables us to construct radical identities, images of ourselves that transcend the limits of the colonizing eye." Reread hooks's essay, paying close attention to how she interacts with and describes her own photographs. What does she choose to write about? How does she "remember" and "re-member" her photographs? What aspects of hooks's identity seem to inform her reading?

3. For hooks, a specific picture of her father "gives a space for intimacy between the image" and herself. Why is this so? What does the photo represent for her? First, examine and then describe how she represents this photo. How does hooks use her critical eye when examining the photograph of her father, and what narrative emerges from her description? Second, consider how her sister "G" describes and remembers the same photograph. What narrative emerges from "G's" description? How does hooks account for radically different reactions to the same photograph?

Re-seeing and Re-writing

1. This assignment asks you to investigate your own photographs as a site for re-membering and assembling the fragments of memory. Recall significant childhood pictures from memory or look at the collections of photographs in your own house/dorm room. Analyze these pictures in a manner similar to the one used by hooks, paying attention to any thematic or representational patterns in your photos. What narratives begin to emerge as a result of this particular type of rereading, and how are these interpretations informed by your present identity or location? How do these narratives contribute to or resist dominant narratives about the family?

2. hooks places great importance on the camera as a means for recording the history of an oppressed people. She remarks, "Elderly black people developed a cultural passion for the camera, for the images it produced, because it offered a way to contain memories, to overcome loss, to keep history." This assignment asks you to identify and analyze several different ways we document history, keeping in mind the various strategies and mediums for documentation (museums, photography, personal narratives, and Web sites are a few of these). In doing so, address the following questions: Who documents or "authors" history? What is the social and cultural position of those documentarians? Whose history, or which history, gets documented? Ultimately, who is the audience for these histories?

Intertext

Throughout several of the essays in this unit, the process of picture-taking is analyzed. Look back at the essays by hooks, Kingston, and/or Hirsch. What themes, narratives, or interpretations, if any, do you see missing from this cluster of articles? Do you find one essay more persuasive than another? Why or why not? In answering the above question, you might consider the relationship between descriptive and interpretative passages, between evidence and analytical claims.

The Visible Cripple (Scars and Other Disfiguring Displays Included)

MARK JEFFREYS

MARK JEFFREYS was raised in New Jersey in a large, multiethnic, multiply abled family of genetic, adopted, and foster children. He started his adult life in a career as a junior executive for a large insurance firm, but left the corporate world to eventually become a professor of English at the University of Alabama at Birmingham. Currently, Jeffreys is an associate professor of Integrated Studies and Behavioral Science at Utah Valley State College and is working on earning a second doctorate degree, this time in human evolutionary ecology, from the anthropology department at the University of Utah. He has published work on genetics, cultural evolution, disability, and science fiction films.

One of the defining difficulties for disability studies scholars is going to be a grappling with ideas and experiences of physicality in a historical moment of constructivism.

–David T. Mitchell and Sharon L. Snyder

. . . At the seam where body joins culture, every construction of the body begins and ends. On the efforts of cultures to hide that seam, every oppression depends. Jim, my brother, has no legs. Jim has wheels. Jim has both wheels and legs. Jim has neither wheels nor legs. All this is true.

Jim was born without legs, none at all, in Seoul, South Korea, in 1967 and left in a basket at the door of an orphanage. When my parents were contacted about adopting him, it was because they had already adopted a Korean girl. Furthermore, not only was my mother a registered nurse but my father himself had an unusual genetic condition, osteogenesis imperfecta, aka brittle-bone disease, which had also been passed on to one of his children, me. The adoption agency must have reasoned that such a family might be uniquely willing and qualified to adopt a congenital double amputee. In any

case, they were eager to get him adopted, as he was already four years old and in Korea would have been multiply stigmatized as disabled, an orphan, and a Eurasian.

They had to make sure, however, that we knew not just who but what we were adopting. They sent us the usual winsome portrait photos of Jim (then Kim Byung Chul) but also pictures of his naked bottom, in stark black and white, taken from multiple angles, like mug shots. We sat around the kitchen table one day when I was eight and looked at them. The pictures seemed sinister to me, alien. I had never seen any human body portrayed like that before, and the high contrast of the prints and the Korean lettering on the back only emphasized their harsh otherness. But I was fascinated by the croissant-shaped button of smooth flesh that capped one buttock and by the single baby toe, complete with toenail, that capped the other. His otherwise unremarkable body had been neatly tied off at the hips.

Garland-Thomson employs the term "extraordinary bodies" to include all "the related perceptions of corporeal otherness we think of variously as 'monstrosity,' 'mutilation,' 'deformation,' 'crippledness,' or 'physical disability'." That was how my brother was first presented to me: a documented body, ordinary enough in most respects and utterly healthy but, in that one direction, extraordinary. Obviously, his body had been textualized, pathologized. The pictures were meant to contain its extraordinariness by their unblinking, comprehensive documentation, reducing what was "wrong" with him to authoritative illustrations, as if to say, You see, this is how it is, we have hidden nothing, this is the whole truth of it, "Only this, and nothing more."

5   I have an educational toy stuck on a shelf in my office, a partially assembled plastic anatomic model, one of those kits that have been marketed for decades as the Visible Man and the Visible Woman. The appeal of the toy is that it standardizes the internal, biological reality of the human body and renders it visible and accessible through a removable, translucent outer shell. The shell itself is stamped with the normative features of a young white adult. In some sense, those first photographs presented my brother as the Visible Cripple, a presentation enhanced by numerous X rays taken soon after his arrival in the States, revealing a complete pelvic bone but no hips, only the tiny floating bones of the single small toe. The reality of his extraordinary body, once seen and seen through, was no longer mysterious but understood, and once understood, manipulatable.

No sooner had my parents completed the medical surveys of the reality of my brother's extraordinariness than they began to think how best to conceal it. The decision of the adults, including my father in his wheelchair, was that

to mainstream Jim as much as possible necessarily meant making him appear as normal as possible. Before long the family was making regular road trips to Delaware to have Jim fitted by the DuPont prosthetic specialists. Jim hated those trips, as all his siblings did, but he most hated the times when he was left with the doctors over a weekend or a week. I hated the boredom of the place, the smell of the prosthetics, all the things that reminded me of the hospitals my own traumas took me to from time to time. And what was accomplished by all this effort, alienation, and expenditure? The most inappropriate and useless deception possible, my brother marooned on stilts. Culture was doing its damnedest to construct his body as it pleased, and my parents were doing their damnedest to appease the demands of culture by making their boy as unobtrusive in his difference as possible.

What strikes me now as awful about all this was not that culture constructed us. Culture *could* take my brother's healthy, nimble leglessness and make it into a dark comedy of monstrosity, a nearly immobilized boy-cyborg, one-half flesh, one-half mechanism. But if culture was as omnipotent as constructivist theory would have it, and the body was entirely culture's fiction, then culture could have also succeeded in erasing the difference it could not tolerate. Instead, Jim's body, and Jim, resisted. Well enough to talk about making our culture accommodate physical difference; but only in acknowledging that there is some physical reality beyond culture can that accommodation be reached. The refusal to make such an acknowledgment can only result in betraying and torturing the body in a futile attempt to erase it.

Jim made constant requests, every birthday and Christmas and anytime in between, for action figures, macho dolls with guns and biceps and articulated limbs. When he got them, he pried off all their macho legs. Stripping the camouflage pants, he figured out how the rubberband device concealed in the torso hooked up the swiveling hips, or he discovered that this particular doll had simpler joints that could be unscrewed or popped loose. Either way, he eventually pulled off the legs. He has since told me that he simply couldn't relate to the legs. His fantasy was to have enormously powerful arms, but the legs, far from enhancing the fantasy, destroyed it. Culture could offer him guns and biceps, but the experience of legs was literally unimaginable and therefore unassimilable.

I can't remember whether he ever tried to put back on the soldiers' pants, and neither, he says, can he. He himself wore shorts with the leg holes sewn shut, at least when he wasn't swaying precariously in his custom-fitted bucket atop his latest pair of DuPont artificial legs, all their straps and plastics cloaked in slacks, the idea being to make him look as standardized as possible, even though the contraption imprisoned him.

10   He was much more comfortable in his wheelchair, of course, but our parents, once again including our wheelchair-using father, insisted that he learn to walk. He had to wear the legs to school, as I recall, until he went to public high school, where the long hallways and tight schedule demanded the wheel-chair's speed. He recently told me that Mom tried to insist he use his legs at school, arguing that all the time, money, and practice put into acquiring an upright posture would be wasted otherwise. Jim held firm, and the compromise, apparently, was that he could go to school in his chair for his safety and convenience but that he would have to wear the legs while sitting in the chair. Thus the true, dissembling purpose of the legs becomes clear. In his freshman year, few classmates knew he had no legs. Only when he joined the wrestling team did the reality of his body become obvious. Not long after that, he says, he started making friends, began acting like himself, and soon stopped wearing the legs to school altogether.

Even then, he continued to wear the legs for formal occasions. At our sister Alleene's wedding, someone took away his crutches while posing the family portrait. He stands there between us, his four-limbed brothers, shoulder to shoulder for balance, suited and propped like FDR for a publicity still. Except for the ironic perfection of his machine-tooled stance and the slightly odd forward lean of his counterbalancing torso, the illusion is perfect: the invisible cripple.

Not that his was the only illusion in that photograph; it was only one of the more successful. The least successful was probably Dad's. Having never walked without prosthetic support in his life, in the photo Dad stands petrified with pride, dressed in a custom-tailored suit purchased for the purpose, his wheelchair out of sight and my mother's hand clutching his in apparent affection but actually to support him. The pose was foolhardy on two counts. Given a lifetime history of more than a hundred fractures, he knew that he could break a bone just supporting and balancing his own weight, to say nothing about what would happen if he toppled over. And whatever invisibility he thought he was achieving was delusory; if anything, his four-foot-tall inverted triangle shape looks more unusual when upright. It was as if he felt that if he stood still enough, somehow his bodily difference would disappear into the traditional patriarchal role of father of the bride.

Nor did the dissembling end with Dad. The brothers propping Jim up hid their own disabilities. In the picture, Peter, born with spina bifida, stands so that his partial paralysis looks more like a casual, hipster's slouch. Clark, who had polio as a child in Korea, stands in the second row so that his legs cannot be seen. My own brittle bones were at that time supporting me fairly well, so I stand in the front with a smug look on my face, perhaps because I knew I could pass, or perhaps because I had been mischievously teasing Jim about leaning on him and causing the whole house of cards to tumble. Oddly enough, even our able-bodied youngest sister, Alice, who was coincidentally recovering from a broken leg, had her crutches taken from her and stands awkwardly, her weight on her good leg.

The whole arrangement was both mundane and unique. Other families pose with smiles to approximate whatever they believe a normal happy family should look like. They pose to disguise the ordinary, daily frictions of their household. We did too, but we also posed to disguise the ordinary, daily realities of our bodies. We were used to being stared at; we just wanted to look our "best" for such a special occasion. We understood how people look at photographs. We understood that if our disabilities were framed, our disabilities would frame us, and we wanted to exclude them so we wouldn't vanish behind them. But to understand the full nature of our dissembling, we would have had to understand also both the cultural construction of that ideal normality to which we aspired—physical, familial, matrimonial, ritual—and the physical existence that, by being only partially reconstructable, testified to a reality outside that construction. And that's an understanding that disability studies is just beginning to attempt.

15   By the time Jim himself got married, he almost never wore the artificial legs, having completed college and gone to work for years in his chair. Yet, something about the magic of matrimony brought out all the old props once more for his wedding, where I served as best man. During the course of the ritual, both of us literally risked our necks to walk in, climb steps, stand, and descend steps. For reasons I don't at all remember, the charade extended beyond the posing of photographs and became an absurd, utterly unnecessary kind of high-wire act. At one point we both stood with our backs to the congregation, high on a platform, the edge of which was just inches behind our heels, while the minister droned through some laborious homily that neither of us could hear above the buzzing of terror in our ears. Jim was swaying slightly, one of his crutches having again been taken from him, and I was certain that he would lose his balance and grab me, and that we'd both go backward over the edge. I would land with six or seven fractures, and he would sit there looking dazed, half his tuxedoed form in one place, the other half still hanging off the stage.

And what, I asked him years later, was the point of that whole performance? Hadn't Cathy, his bride, fallen in love with him as a man in a wheelchair? Ah, another cultural appeasement was at work: Cathy was unusually tall, and her dream of her wedding ritual demanded that her groom not make her look like a giantess. If Jim got married in his legs, they could stand together in front of the preacher, just as she had always imagined. When Jim told me about this, a comment that Cathy had made later at the reception made better sense to me. Her sister, who was her maid of honor, was even taller than she, as was their brother, the other groomsman, whereas I could barely top five feet. When we readied ourselves to enter the reception hall in pairs, we violated one small tradition for the sake of Cathy's sense of symmetry, and rather than the maid of honor and best man traipsing in together, the maid of honor came in on her brother's arm, led by the shorter bridesmaid on the best man's arm and followed by the bride and her groom. As we walked in, Cathy joked awkwardly, "Here we come, the dwarves, the giants, and the freaks." . . .

Re-reading/Conversations with the Text

1. Describing his brother's resistance to his doctors' attempts to outfit him with state-of-the-art prosthetic legs, Jeffreys adopts an ironic tone meant to explain his brother's (Jim's) animosity:

   > Culture *could* take my brother's healthy, nimble leglessness and make it into a dark comedy of monstrosity, a nearly immobilized boy-cyborg, one-half flesh, one-half mechanism.

   First consider: What makes this statement *ironic?* Alone, or with your class-mates, make a list of technological and/or prosthetic inventions/interventions (implants, additions, enhancements, corrections, replacements, etc.) to the human body. How many can you come up with? Once you have a list, explore these questions further: Who has these? Is there anything you can learn about race, class, gender, and so on by looking at who has (or wants) prosthetics of various kinds? Which prosthetics would you be willing (or even eager?) to have or receive? Explore the limits of how you could imagine technology/prosthetics enhancing/supplementing your own body.

2. Jeffreys describes and narrates his first "encounter" with his soon-to-be adopted brother, Jim, by relating a scene from when he was 8 and his family was sent pictures of Jim. Locate and re-read this portion of his essay, focusing on elements of description. Working in pairs, make a list of the impressions you might remember from encountering a person with a disability and also describe their disability and your reactions to it. Use this passage from Jeffreys' essay as your model.

3. Jeffreys relates a story of how he posed/dressed (or *was* posed/dressed) for his brother Jim's wedding. Locate and reread this portion of his essay and pay particular attention to the "staging" of the photograph. How might the "staging" have been different? Reimagine and discuss the two paragraphs in which he describes the taking of this photograph with a different scenario: What if they had all been just themselves? What would that look like? What would you imagine would have had to change about the traditional staging of a wedding?

Re-seeing and Re-writing

1. Using Jeffreys's essay as a model—especially the passages where he describes his own and his brother's "performances" as "invisible cripple" at weddings and other key events—write an essay in which you describe yourself in a staged event from your own life. Narrate a scene from that event, using detailed description, and then step back out of the scene and analyze what was happening in it—and why—from your present perspective.

2. Much of Jeffreys's essay relies on key photographs of his family—and especially of his brother Jim—to build his analysis of how the "invisible cripple" is con-

structed in our culture. Explore your own family album or any pictures you have of yourself and build a collage—or narrative—of yourself from these photos. Use five to ten photos. Organize and arrange them as you see fit.

Next, write an essay that approaches your collage/narrative in multiple ways:

- By offering a brief *caption* beneath each picture.
- By offering a more *extended description* of each picture somewhere in your essay, analyzing such issues as why the photo was taken; who took it and what the photographer seemed to want to represent of you; and how it conflicts with, compromises, or confirms your own self-image.
- Finally, by offering a *narrative* of what the collage or sequence tells about you, discussing what is erased, left out, made invisible in this series or collage; what is enhanced, illuminated, brought to the foreground; and what someone else—someone who doesn't know you at all—might conclude about you from this series or collage.

Marianne Hirsch, like Jeffreys, argues that photographs help to validate the status quo of a particular culture: both essays focus on photographs that represent an idealized family that shares the values and beliefs of the larger culture. However, what makes up that status quo, and what deviates from it, is markedly different for each writer. Supplying evidence from both texts, describe the different views of what constitutes "the status quo" and its transgression for each writer. Next, consider Marianne Hirsch's focus on *The Family of Man* exhibit. In what ways might Jeffreys' family photo be interpreted as a (non)representative "Family of Man" photo?

Remembrance

ANNETTE KUHN

ANNETTE KUHN uses family photographs to explore how memory shapes the stories we tell about our past. For Kuhn, memory work has a great deal in common with detective work and archaeology, in that all three processes "involve working backwards—searching for clues, deciphering signs and traces, making deductions, patching together reconstructions out of fragments of evidence" (*Family Secrets: Acts of Memory and Imagination,* London: Verso, 1995, 4). Kuhn is the author of numerous books, including *Family Secrets: Acts of Memory and Imagination* (1995); *Cinema, Censorship, and Sexuality* (1988); and *The Power of the Image: Essays on Representation* (1985).

The six-year-old girl in the picture is seated in a fireside chair in the sitting-room of the flat in Chiswick, London, where she lives with her parents, Harry and Betty. It is the early 1950s. Perched on the child's hand, apparently claiming her entire attention, is her pet budgerigar,

Greeny. It might be a winter's evening, for the curtains are drawn and the child is dressed in hand-knitted jumper and cardigan, and woollen skirt.

Much, but not all, of this the reader may observe for herself, though the details of time and place are not in the picture: these are supplied from elsewhere, let us say from a store of childhood memories which might be anybody's, for they are commonplace enough. The description of the photograph could be read as the scene-setting for some subsequent action: one of those plays, perhaps, where the protagonists (already we have four, which ought to be enough) will in a moment animate themselves into the toils of some quite ordinary, yet possibly quite riveting, family melodrama.

All this is true, up to a point. Photographs are evidence, after all. Not that they are to be taken at face value, necessarily, nor that they mirror the real, nor even that a photograph offers any self-evident relationship between itself and what it shows. Simply that a photograph can be material for interpretation—evidence, in that sense: to be solved, like a riddle; read and decoded, like clues left behind at the scene of a crime. Evidence of this sort, though, can conceal, even as it purports to reveal, what it is evidence of. A photograph can certainly throw you off the scent. You will get nowhere, for instance, by taking a magnifying glass to it to get a closer look: you will see only patches of light and dark, an unreadable mesh of grains. The image yields nothing to that sort of scrutiny; it simply disappears.

In order to show what it is evidence of, a photograph must always point you away from itself. Family photographs are supposed to show not so much that we were once there, as how we once were: to evoke memories which might have little or nothing to do with what is actually in the picture. The photograph is a prop, a prompt, a pre-text: it sets the scene for recollection. But if a photograph is somewhat contingent in the process of memory-production, what is the status of the memories actually produced?

Prompted by the photograph, I might recall, say, that the budgie was a gift from Harry to his little girl, Annette; that underneath two layers of knitted wool, the child is probably wearing a liberty bodice; that the room in which the photo was taken was referred to not as the sitting-room but as the lounge, or perhaps occasionally as the drawing-room. Make what you will of these bits of information, true or not. What you make of them will be guided by certain knowledges, though: of child-rearing practices in the 1950s, of fashions in underwear, of the English class system, amongst other things.

What I am saying is: memories evoked by a photo do not simply spring out of the image itself, but are generated in an intertext of discourses that shift between past and present, spectator and image, and between all these and cultural contexts, historical moments. In all this, the image figures largely as a trace, a clue: necessary, but not sufficient, to the activity of meaning-making; always signalling somewhere else. Cultural theory tells us there is little that is really personal or private about either family photographs or the memories they evoke: they can mean only culturally. But the fact that we experience our memories as peculiarly our own sets up a tension between the 'personal' moment of memory and the social moment of making memory, or memorising; and indicates that the processes of making meaning and making memories are characterised by a certain fluidity. Meanings and memories may change with time, be mutually contradictory, may even be an occasion for or an expression of conflict.

On the back of this photograph is written, in my mother's hand: 'Just back from Bournemouth (Convelescent) [*sic*]'. In my own handwriting 'Bournemouth' has been crossed out and replaced with 'Broadstairs', and a note added: 'but I suspect the photo is earlier than this'.

If, as this suggests, a photograph can be the site of conflicting memories, whose memory is to prevail in the family archive? This little dispute between a mother and a daughter points not only to the contingency of memories not attached to, but occasioned by, an image, but also to a scenario of power relations within the family itself. My mother's inscription may be read as a bid to anchor the meaning of a wayward image, and her meaning at some point conflicted with my own reading of the photograph and also irritated me enough to provoke a (somewhat restrained) retort. As it turns out, my mother and I might well both have been 'off' in our memories, but in a way this doesn't matter. The disagreement is symptomatic in itself, in that it foregrounds a mother-daughter relationship to the exclusion of something else. The photograph and the inscriptions point to this 'something else' only in what they leave out. What happens, then, if we take absences, silences, as evidence?

The absent presence in this little drama of remembering is my father. He is not in the picture, you cannot see him. Nor can you see my mother, except in so far as you have been told that she sought to fix the meaning of the image in a particular way, to a particular end. In another sense, however, my father is very much 'in' the picture; so much so that my mother's intervention might be read as a bid to exorcise a presence that disturbed her. The child in the photograph is absorbed with her pet bird, a gift from her father, who also took the picture. The relay of looks—father/daughter/father's gift to daughter—has a trajectory and an endpoint that miss the mother entirely. The picture has nothing to do with her.

10   Here is another story: about taking a photograph indoors at night in the 1950s, on (probably slow) black-and-white film in a 35mm camera. My father knew how to do this and get good results because photography was his job:

he was working at the time as, if you like, an itinerant family photographer; canvassing work by knocking on likely-looking (that is to say, 'respectable' working-class) doors, taking pictures of children in the parents' homes or gardens, and developing and printing them in a rented darkroom. This must have been the last moment of an era when, if people wanted something better than a blurred snapshot from a Box Brownie, they would still commission photographs of their children. The photo of me, no doubt, is the sort of picture Harry Kuhn might have made for any one of his clients.

Stylistically speaking, that is: for at this level the picture eschews the conventions of the family photograph to key, perhaps, into professional codes of studio portraiture; or into the cute-kiddie-with-pet subgenre of amateur photography. The peculiar context of this picture's production lends it very different cultural meanings, however, and imbues it with a kind and an intensity of feeling a professional or hobbyist piece of work would scarcely evoke. In this image, Harry's professional, his worldly, achievements are brought home, into a space where such achievements were contested, or at best irrelevant. In this photograph, my father puts himself there, staking a claim: not just to his own skills, to respect, to autonomy; but to the child herself. In this picture, then, Harry makes the child his own daughter. Later on, my mother would assert that this was not so, that Harry Kuhn was not my father.

Thus can a simple photograph figure in, and its showing set the scene for the telling of, a family drama—each of whose protagonists might tell a different tale, or change their own story at every retelling. What I am telling you—'my own story'—about this picture is itself changeable. In each re-enactment, each re-staging of this family drama, details get added and dropped, the story fleshes out, new connections are made, emotional tones—puzzlement, anger, sadness—fluctuate.

Take my mother's caption to the picture—I don't know when it was written—and my own alteration and footnote, added because I believed she had misremembered a key event of my childhood. At eight years old (two years, that is, after the picture was taken) I was sent off to a convalescent home in Broadstairs, Kent, after a bad bout of pneumonia and a spell in hospital. The adult Annette took the apparent errors of time and place in her mother's caption (by no means an isolated instance) as yet another manifestation of obsessive (and usually 'bad') remembering; as an attempt by her mother to force others' memories into line with her own, however off-the-wall these might be. A capricious piece of power-play, if you like, but—given the transparent inaccuracy of the details—easily enough seen through.

Another, and more disturbing, reading of my mother's inscription is available, however: possibly the biographical details are correct after all, but refer not to me, the ostensible subject of the picture, but to my mother herself. Around the time the photograph was taken, she had suffered an injury at her job as a bus conductor, and been sent by London Transport to convalesce at the seaside. Is this perhaps the event to which the caption refers? If so, my mother is pinning the moment of a photograph of her daughter to an event in her own life.

15   In the first reading, my mother writes herself into the picture by claiming the right to define the memories evoked by it; and by omission and commission negates my father's involvement in both the photograph and the family. In the second reading, my own involvement as well as my father's is negated, as the caption constitutes a central place for the writer herself in a scenario from which she is so clearly excluded: my mother thereby sets herself up as both enunciator of, and main character in, the family drama.

The intensity of feeling attaching to these stories greatly exceeds the overt content of the tales of dissension and deception in the family I seem to have unearthed: utter rage at my mother's egomaniac powermongering; sadness at the nullification of my father's stake in the picture/the family; joy in the possibility of remembering his nurturing me; grief over his loss of power and over my loss of him, for I was soon to become, in effect, my mother's property. My use of this photograph as a piece of evidence, a clue—as material for interpretation—is an attempt, then, to instate and enact if not exactly a father's, then certainly a daughter's, version of a family drama.

A photograph bearing a huge burden of meaning and of feeling, this one—to use Roland Barthes's term—*pierces* me. It seems to utter a truth that goes beyond the *studium,* the evidential, however intricately coded. My desire is that the little girl in the picture be the child as she is looked at, as she is seen, by her father. A friend who has not heard these stories looks at the picture, and says: There is a poignancy about her absorption with her pet; she looks lovable with her floppy hair ribbons and warm woollen clothing. Perhaps Harry Kuhn, in giving the child the gift of a living creature, and even more so in the act of making this photograph, affirms not merely a dubious paternity, but also that he loves this child. This photograph, I want to believe, is speaking a relation that excludes her, resists—perhaps finally transcends—my mother's attempt to colonise its meaning.

The stories, the memories, shift. There is a struggle over who is to have the last word—me; my father, the father who figures in my desire; my mother, the monstrous mother of my fantasy. With only one of the characters still alive to tell the tale, there is unlikely ever to be a last word, as the struggle over the past continues in the present. The struggle is now, the past is made in the present. Family photographs may affect to show us our past, but what we do with them—how we use them—is really about today, not yesterday. These traces of our former lives are pressed into service in a never-ending process of making, remaking, making sense of, our selves—now. There can be no last word about my photograph, about any photograph.

Here, then, is one more story: about a family album; about the kinds of tales (and the kinds of families) family albums construct; and about how my photograph was put to use once upon a time, and still survives to be used today, again and again.

20 Family photographs are quite often deployed—shown, talked about—in series: pictures get displayed one after another, their selection and ordering as meaningful as the pictures themselves. The whole, the series, constructs a family story in some respects like a classical narrative—linear, chronological; though the cyclical repetition of climactic moments—births, christenings, weddings, holidays (if not deaths)—is more characteristic of the open-ended narrative form of soap opera than of the closure of classical narrative. In the process of using—producing, selecting, ordering, displaying—photographs, the family is actually in process of making itself.

The family album is one moment in the cultural construction of family; and it is no coincidence that the conventions of the family album—what goes in and how it is arranged—are, culturally speaking, rather circumscribed. However, if the family album produces the family, produces particular forms of family in particular ways, there is always room for manoeuvre within this, as within any other, genre. People will make use of the 'rules' of the family album in their own ways.

The one and only family album in my family is a case in point. It was made by me at the age of eight, when I collected together some snapshots with a few studio portraits and some of my father's relatively professional efforts, stuck them in an album (whose cover, significantly, sports the legend: 'Memory Lane'), and captioned them. Even at such an early age, I obviously knew all about the proper conventions of the family album: photos of myself, my parents, and a few of other relatives and of friends are all set out in chronological order—starting with a picture of me at six months old in the classic tummy-on-the-rug pose.

The eight-year-old Annette clearly 'knew', too, what a family album is for. If she was putting together her 'own' history, this sought to be a history of a family as much as of an individual; or rather, of an individual in a family. The history constructed is also an expression of a lack, and of a desire to put things right. What is being made, made up for, by the work of the album is the 'real' family that the child's parents could not make: this particular family story starts not with a wedding, but with a baby. The album's project is to position that baby, that child, the maker, within a family: to provide itself/herself with a family. Giving herself the central role in the story told by the album, the child also gives herself a family: not only positioning herself within a family, but actually bringing it into being—authoring it, parenting it.

Now, as I tell this story, I can set an interpretation of an eight-year-old girl's preoccupation with photographs alongside a reading, today, of a picture that figures in the collection she put together—a portrait of the same child, a couple of years younger, raptly involved with the pet bird perched in her hand. My mother's reading of that portrait is at odds not only with my present understanding(s) of it but also with the little girl's account, in the photograph album she made, of herself and of the family she wanted.

Whilst my 'Memory Lane' album contains a 25 number of photographs of me as a baby and a toddler with my father, there are few early pictures of me with my mother. There is no way of knowing whether this is because no pictures of me with my mother were actually made, or whether it is because certain images were selected for the album in preference over others. Whatever the explanation, the outcome is that, in a child's first years, a father-daughter relationship is foregrounded at the expense of that between a mother and daughter. Just as Harry's photograph of Annette excludes Betty, so too does the family album marginalise her. Or at least seems to try to: my mother does make more frequent appearances in its later pages, though still not often with me. Both these observations speak of conflict: between my father and my mother over me; between my mother and me over the 'truth' of the past. In all these struggles, my project was to make myself into my father's daughter. My mother's project—in an ironic twist of the ocdipal triangle—was to cast herself as my only begetter. Not, however, with complete success: had her story carried the day, you would not now be reading minc.

My stories are made in a tension between past and present. I have said that a child's making a family album was an expression of, and an attempt to come to terms with, fears and desires; to deal with a knowledge that could not be spoken. These silences, these repressions, are written into the album, into the process of its making, and into actual photographs. All the evidence points in the same direction: something in the family was not right, conflicts were afoot, conflicts a little girl could not really understand, but at some level knew about and wanted to resolve. Solving the puzzle and acknowledging *in the present* the effects *in the past* of a disturbance in the family must be the necessary conditions of a retelling of the family story in its proper order.

As clues are scrutinised and pieces fitted together, a coherent story starts to emerge from the seeming contingency and chaos of a past hinted at by these fragments—a photograph, a photograph album, some memories. A coherent story not only absorbs the listener, but—being a moment in the production of self—satisfies the teller as well, for the moment at least.

Family photographs are about memory and memories: that is, they are about stories of a past, shared (both stories and past) by a group of people that in the moment of sharing produces itself as a family. But family photography is an industry, too, and the makers of the various paraphernalia of family photography—cameras, film, processing, albums to keep the pictures in—all have a stake in our memories. The memories promised by the family photography industry are characterised by pleasure and held-off closure—happy beginnings, happy middles, and no endings to all the family stories. In the way of these things, the promises point towards the future: our memories, our stories, *will* be. They *will* be shared, they *will* be happy—the tone of the seduction is quite imperious. With the right equipment to hand, we will make our own memories, capture all those moments we will some day want to treasure, call to mind, tell stories about.

The promise is of a brighter past in the future, if we only seize the chance today to consume the raw materials of our tomorrow's memories. This past-in-the-future, this nostalgia-in-prospect, always hooks into, seeks to produce, desires hingeing on a particular kind of story—a family story with its own forms of plenitude. The subject position publicly offered is, if not quite personal (consumption is, after all, a social activity), always in the 'private' realm of household and family. All this is familiar enough to the cultural commentator. But the discourses of consumerism form just one part of a bigger picture, one moment in a longer—and probably more interesting—story about the uses of family photography.

Desire is an odd thing. If it can be called upon, even if it can be harnessed to consumption, it can also be unruly and many-sided. It can run behind, or ahead of, the better past tomorrow promised by the family photography industry; it can run somewhere else entirely; it can, perhaps, not run at all. When we look at how family photographs may be used—at what people can do with them once they have them—past and present and the tension between them insert themselves into an equation weighted a little too much towards a certain sort of future. This can stir things up, confuse matters—possibly productively. Just as there is more than one way of making photographs, so there is more than one way of making photographs, so there is more than one way of using them. If, however commonplace, my pictures and my stories are not everybody's, my uses of the one, and my method of arriving at the other, could well be.

My thanks to students in the Autobiography and Female Identity class at the City Lit, London, 1987–8; to the University of Glasgow Photographic Unit; to Ann Game for discussion and comments; and to Jo Spence and Rosy Martin for their example.

Re-reading/Conversations with the Text

1. Reread Kuhn's essay, noting how she moves from description to interpretation. Highlight each descriptive passage with one color and the interpretive (analytical) passages with another. How would you describe the relationship between description and interpretation in this essay? Are the analytical moves supported by description?

2. In this essay, Kuhn's analysis suggests a family drama and struggle over the meaning of certain photographs and memories. How would you describe this family drama?

3. Kuhn notes that "the absent presence in this little drama of remembering is my father." What does she seem to mean by the phrase "absent presence"? How can a memory be understood as absent and present at the same time?

Re-seeing and Re-writing

1. This assignment invites you to work with an early childhood photograph of yourself and to consider what it reveals and/or conceals about family relations. For example, Kuhn argues that family photographs "set the scene for recollection." What memories does your childhood image prompt? Is there a caption? If so, who wrote the caption and how does it "frame" how viewers see and interpret the photograph? In order to understand the family photograph as a personal and social moment of making meaning, as does Kuhn, you might need to do a little research on child-rearing practices at the time the image was taken. What do you need to know about the historical context within which the photograph was taken in order to generate a cultural analysis?

2. Kuhn argues that family photography is an "industry . . . and the makers of various paraphernalia of family photography—cameras, film, processing, albums to keep the pictures in—all have a stake in our memories." This assignment asks you to analyze the commodification of family memories by gathering advertisements for paraphernalia of family photography and home video. Make ten observations about the advertisements you've collected. Consider

how the relationship between family and technologies are construed. What does the advertisement seem to sell—the technology, and/or a particular image of the family?

Intertext

1. This assignment invites you to compare how Kuhn in "Remembrance" and hooks in "In Our Glory: Photography and Black Life" situate themselves in their essays. How do they come across as narrators and interpreters of family photographs? Is there a level of self-reflexivity in their essays? In other words, do Kuhn and hooks contemplate the value of their own interpretations? In what ways are their depictions of the family drama—familial relationships—similar or different? What social or cultural factors might account for these similarities or differences?

2. Compare the descriptions that Kuhn and Kingston give of family photographs and how each author depicts the family drama. What interpretative strategies or methods of analysis might account for the similarities and/or differences? Is the structure of the two essays similar or different?

No Snapshots in the Attic:
A Granddaughter's Search for a Cherokee Past

C O N N I E   M A Y   F O W L E R

CONNIE MAY FOWLER's essay focuses on the art of storytelling and the profound ways in which such stories shape our understanding of our familial past. In a pursuit to understand her paternal grandmother's erasure of her Native American identity, Fowler discovers the historical and familial significance of storytelling, as well as the important ways in which these stories are shaped by cultural forces. Fowler's story challenges the dominant focus on documentation and "facts" and instead privileges oral histories. Connie May Fowler is the author of a memoir, *When Katie Wakes* (2002), and five novels, including *Sugar Cage* (1992), *Before Women Had Wings* (1996), and *Remembering Blue* (2000).

For as long as anyone can remember, poverty has crawled all over the hearts of my family, contributing to a long tradition of premature deaths and a lifetime of stories stymied behind the mute lips of the dead. The survivors have been left without any tangible signs that evoke the past: no photographs or diaries, no wedding bands or wooden nickels.

This absence of a record seems remarkable to me since our bloodline is diverse: Cherokee, Irish, German, French; you would think that at least a few people would have had the impulse to offer future generations a few concrete clues as to who they were. But no; our attics are empty. Up among the cob-webs and dormer-filtered light you will find not a single home-made quilt, not one musty packet of love letters.

Lack of hard evidence of a familial past seems unnatural to me, but I have developed a theory. I believe that my relatives, Indians and Europeans alike, couldn't waste free time on preserving a baby's first bootee. There were simply too many tales to tell about each other, living and dead, for them to be bothered by objects that would only clutter our homes and our minds.

The first time I noticed this compulsion to rid ourselves of handed-down possessions was in the summer of my eighth year when my mother decided to fix the front screen door, which was coming off its hinges. As she rummaged through a junk drawer for a screwdriver, she came upon a dog-eared photograph of her father. He stood in front of a shack, staring into the camera as though he could see through the lens and into the eyes of the photographer. "Oh, that old picture," my mother said disdainfully. "Nothing but a dust catcher." She tossed the photo in the trash, pulled up a chair, lit a cigarette and told me about how her Appalachian-born daddy could charm wild animals out of the woods by standing on his front porch and singing to them.

The idea that my family had time only for survival and storytelling takes on special significance when I think of my grandmother, my father's mother, Oneida Hunter May, a Cherokee who married a white man. Hers was a life cloaked in irony and sadness, yet 30 years after she died her personal history continues to suggest that spinning tales is a particularly honest and noble activity.

Throughout her adult life, the only time Oneida Hunter May felt free enough to claim her own heritage was in the stories she told her

5

children. At all other times, publicly and privately, she declared herself white. As both a writer and a granddaughter, I have been haunted by her decision to excise her Indian heart and I have struggled to understand it. Of course, her story would work its way into my fiction, but how it did and what I would learn about the truth of cultural and familial rumors when they contradict the truth of our official histories would change the way I see the world, the way I write, and how and whom I trust.

Until I became an adult this is what I accepted as true about my grandmother: She was a Cherokee Indian who married a South Carolinian named John May. Early in the marriage they moved to St. Augustine, Fla. They had three children, two boys and a girl. Shortly after moving to Florida, John May abandoned his wife and children. The family believed he joined the circus. (When I was a child my family's yearly pilgrimage to the Greatest Show on Earth took on special significance as I imagined that my grandfather was the lion tamer or the high-wire artist.) Grandmama May was short and round. While she was straightforward with the family about her Indian ancestry, she avoided instilling in us a shred of Native American culture or custom. Through the use of pale powder and rouge, she lightened her skin. Her cracker-box house on the wrong side of the tracks was filled with colorful miniature glass animals and hats and boots, all stolen from tourist shops downtown. According to my father, she was "run out of town on a rail" more than once because of the stealing, and she even spent time in the city jail. Her laughter was raucous. She tended to pick me up by putting her hands under my armpits, which hurt, and it seemed as if every time I saw her she pinched my cheeks, which also hurt. My grandmother mispronounced words and her syntax was jumbled. I've since realized that her strange grammar patterns and elocution were the results of having no formal education and of speaking in a language that was not her native tongue.

For me, growing up was marked not only by a gradual loss of innocence but by the loss of the storytellers in my life: grandparents, aunts and uncles, parents. With them went my ability to believe and know simple truths, to accept the face value of things without needless wrestling. As the cynicism of adulthood took hold, I began to doubt the family stories about my grandmother and I even decided my recollections were warped by time and the fuzzy judgment of childhood, and that the stories were based on oral tradition rooted in hearsay. What is this ephemeral recitation of our lives anyway? A hodgepodge of alleged fact, myth and legend made all the more unreliable because it goes unchecked by impartial inquiry. After all, don't scholars dismiss oral histories as anecdotal evidence?

I told myself I was far too smart to put much stock in my family's Homeric impulses. In choosing to use my grandmother's life as a stepping-off point for a new novel; I decided that everything I knew as a child was probably exaggerated at best and false at worst. I craved empirical evidence, irrefutable facts; I turned to government archives.

I began my inquiry by obtaining a copy of my grandmother's death certificate. I hoped it would provide me with details that would lead to a trail back to her early life and even to her birth. The document contained the following data: Oneida Marie Hunter May was born Aug. 14, 1901, in Dillon, S.C. She died June 8, 1963, of diabetes. But from there her history was reduced to no comment. Line 13, father's name: five black dashes. Line 14, mother's maiden name: five dashes. Line 16, Social Security number: none. The most chilling, however, because it was a lie, was line 6, color or race: white.

Her son, my uncle J. W., was listed as the "informant." Perhaps he thought he was honoring her by perpetuating her longstanding public falsehood. Perhaps, despite what he knew, he considered himself white—and therefore so was she. Perhaps in this small Southern town he was embarrassed or frightened to admit his true bloodline. Did he really not know his grandparents' names? Or did he fear the names would suggest his Indian lineage? Whether his answers were prompted by lack of knowledge or a desire to be evasive, the result was that the "facts" of the death certificate were suspect. The information recorded for posterity amounted to a whitewash. The son gave answers he could live with, which is what his mother had done, answers that satisfied a xenophobic society.

Thinking that perhaps I had started at the wrong end of the quest, I went in search of her birth certificate. I contacted the proper office in South Carolina and gave the clerk what meager information I had. I realized that without a Social Security number, my chances of locating such a document were slim, but I thought that in its thirst for data the government might have tracked Indian births. "No, I'm sorry," I was told over the phone by the clerk who had been kind enough to try an alphabetical search. "South Carolina didn't keep detailed files on Indians back then. You could try the Cherokees, but I don't think it will help. In those days they weren't keeping good records either."

I was beginning to understand how thoroughly a person can vanish and how—without memory and folklore—one can be doomed to oblivion. But I pursued history, and I changed my focus to Florida. I began reading accounts of St. Augustine's Indian population in the last century, hoping to gain insight into my grandmother's experience. There is not a great amount of documentation, and most of what does exist was written by long-dead Roman Catholic missionaries and Army generals, sources whose objectivity was compromised by their theological and military mandates. Nevertheless, I stumbled on an 1877 report by Harriet Beecher Stowe about the incarceration of Plains Indians at Castillo de San Marcos (then called Fort Marion) at the mouth of the St. Augustine harbor.

During their imprisonment, which lasted from 1875 to 1878, the Indians were forced to abandon their homes, religions, languages, their dress and all other cultural elements that white society deemed "savage"—a term used with alarming frequency in writings of the time. Calling the Indians in their pre-Christian state "untamable," "wild" and "more like grim goblins than human beings," Stowe apparently approved of what they became in the fort: Scripture-citing, broken-spirited Indians dressed like their tormentors, United States soldiers. She writes, "Might not the money now constantly spent on armies, forts and frontiers be better invested in educating young men who shall return and teach their people to live like civilized beings?"

The written record, I was discovering, was fabulous in its distortion, and helpful in its unabashedness. It reflected not so much truth or historical accuracy as the attitudes of the writers.

The most obvious evidence of the unreliable nature of history is the cultural litany set down in tourist brochures and abstracted onto brass plaques in parks and on roadsides across America. My family has lived for three generations in St. Augustine, "The Oldest Continuously Inhabited City in America. Founded in 1565." What this proclamation leaves out is everything that preceded the town's European founding. Like my uncle's carefully edited account of my grandmother's life, St. Augustine's official version amounts to historical genocide because it wipes away all traces of the activities and contributions of a specific race. For hundreds of years this spit of land between two rivers and the sea was the thriving village of Seloy, home to the Timucuan Indians. But while still aboard a ship, before ever stepping onto the white and coral-colored shores of the "New World," Pedro Menéndez renamed Seloy in honor of the patron saint of his birthplace. Then he claimed this new St. Augustine and all of "La Florida" to be the property of Spain; the Timucuans and

15

their culture had been obliterated by a man at sea gazing at their land.

These distinctions between European facts and Indian facts are not trivial. The manipulation of our past is an attempt, unconscious or not, to stomp out evidence of the success and value of other cultures. My grandmother's decision to deny her heritage was fueled by the fear of what would happen to her if she admitted to being an Indian and by the belief that there was something inherently inferior about her people. And the falsehoods and omissions she lived by affected not just her; her descendants face a personal and historical incompleteness.

But when the official chronicles are composed of dashes and distortions and you still hunger for the truth, what do you do? For me, the answer was to let my writer's instincts take over. I slipped inside my grandmother's skin and tried to sort out her motives and her pain. I imagined her birth and what her mother and father might have looked like. I gave them names, Nightwater and Billy. I called the character inspired by my grandmother Sparrow Hunter. She would bear a daughter, Oneida. And it would be Oneida's offspring, Sadie Hunter, who would uncover the stories that revealed the truth.

But I needed to know how a young Indian woman with three babies to feed survives after she's been abandoned in a 1920's tourist town that promoted as its main attraction an ancient and massive fort that had served as a prison for Comanches, Kiowas, Seminoles, Apaches, Cheyennes, Arapaho, Caddos and others. The writer-granddaughter listened to her blood-born voices and heard the answers. Her grandmother made up a birthplace and tried to forget her native tongue. She stayed out of the sun because she tanned easily, and she bought the palest foundations and powders available. She re-created herself. For her children and grandchildren never to be called "Injun" or "savage" must have been one of her most per-sistent hopes. And what bitter irony it must have been that her children obeyed and took on the heritage of the man who had deserted them. I was discovering that my novel would be far better served if I stopped digging for dates and numbers and instead strove to understand my grandmother's pain.

My research had another effect, one far more important than causing me to question our written record. It pushed me forward along the circle, inching me back to where I had started: the oral history. My family has relentlessly nurtured its oral tradition as though instinctively each of us knew that our attics would be empty for generations but our memory-fed imaginations could be filled to overbrimming with our tales of each other. And certainly, while the stories are grandiose and often tall, I decided they are no more slanted than what is fed to us in textbooks.

I have come to view my family's oral history as beautifully double-edged, for in fiction—oral or written—there is a desire to reveal the truth, and that desire betrays my grandmother's public lie. It is in the stories shared on our beloved windy porches and at our wide-planked pine tables, under the glare of naked moth-swept light bulbs, that the truth and the betrayal reside. Had my grandmother not felt compelled to remember her life before John May stepped into it and to relate to little Henry and J. W. and Mary Alice what times were like in South Carolina in the early 1900's for a dirt-poor Indian girl, then a precious link to her past and ours would have been lost forever. And while she raised her children to think of themselves as solely white, she couldn't keep secret who she really was.

Those must have been wondrous moments when she tossed aside the mask of the liar to take up the cloak of the storyteller. It was a transformation rooted in our deepest past, for she transcended her ordinary state and for a brief time became a shaman, a holy person who

20

through reflection, confession and interpretation offered to her children an opportunity to become members of the family of humankind, the family that traces its history not through DNA and documents but through the follies and triumphs, the struggles and desires of one another. So I turn to where the greatest measure of truth exists: the stories shared between mother and child, sister and brother, passed around the table like a platter of hot biscuits and gravy and consumed with hungry fervor.

My attempt to write about my grandmother's life was slow and often agonizing. But turning a tangle of information and inspiration into a novel and into a facet of the truth that would shine was the process of becoming a child again, of rediscovering the innocence of faith, of accepting as true what I have always known. I had to believe in the storyteller and her stories again.

The novel my grandmother inspired is fiction, for sure, but it reinforces the paradox that most writers, editors and readers know: fiction is often truer than nonfiction. A society knows itself most clearly not through the allegedly neutral news media or government propaganda or historical records but through the biased eyes of the artist, the writer. When that vision is tempered by heaven and hell, by an honesty of the intellect and gut, it allows the reader and viewer to safely enter worlds of brutal truth, confrontation and redemption. It allows the public as both voyeur and safely distanced participant to say, "Aha! I know that man. I know that woman. Their struggles, their temptations, their betrayals, their triumphs are mine."

25 One of my favorite relatives was Aunt Emily, J.W.'s wife. I saw her the night of my father's death in 1966 and—because my aunt and uncle divorced and because my father's death was a catastrophic event that blew my family apart—I did not see her again until 1992. She was first in line for the hometown book signing of my debut novel, "Sugar Cage." We had a tearful and happy reunion, and before she left she said, "I remember the day you were born and how happy I was that you were named for your Grandmother Oneida."

I looked at her stupidly for a moment, not understanding what she was saying. Then it dawned on me that she misunderstood my middle name because we pronounced Oneida as though it rhymed with Anita. "Oh no," I told her. "My name is Connie Anita." Aunt Emily smiled and said, "Sweetheart, the nurse wrote it down wrong on your birth certificate. All of us except for your grandmother got a big laugh out of the mistake. But believe me, it's what your parents said: you're Connie Oneida."

I loved that moment, for it was a confirmation of the integrity of our oral histories and the frailties of our official ones. As I go forward with a writing life, I accept that my creative umbilical cord is attached to my ancestors. And to their stories. I've decided to allow their reflective revelations to define me in some measure. And I have decided not to bemoan my family's bare attics and photo albums, because as long as we can find the time to sit on our porches or in front of our word processors and continue the tradition of handing down stories, I believe we will flourish as Indians, high-wire artists, animal charmers and writers all. And the truth will survive. It may be obscured occasionally by the overblown or sublime, but at least it will still be there, giving form to our words and fueling our compulsion to tell the tale.

Re-reading/Conversations with the Text

1. What does the "absence of record" mean in Fowler's search for her familial past? How is this lack of photographs or diaries significant? How does it relate to the role of storytelling in her family? What connections does the author make among storytelling, history, and cultural identity?

2. Describe the evolution of Fowler's point of view about the role and authenticity of the art of oral storytelling. Why, for example, did she turn to government archives to understand her familial past? What experiences or observations lead her to change her view of documented narratives as objective evidence to a view of these narratives as interpretations, shaped by culture, history, language, and religion?

3. What does Fowler mean when she states that "fiction is often truer than nonfiction"? What spaces does fiction allow Fowler to occupy that historical documents do not?

Re-seeing and Re-writing

1. Many families create a sense of the past by collecting family heirlooms, such as quilts, antique furniture, books, and family albums. For many, collecting such items is more than an act of nostalgia; it is a way to shape the experiences of generations to come. This writing option invites you to create a multilayered memoir, a text that includes both print and nonprint artifacts, to create a sense of your familial past. What objects have been passed down from one generation to another in your family? What is the significance of such objects, and for whom? Perhaps, like Fowler, there are no photographs, diaries, wedding bands, or wooden nickels in your attic. If this is the case, how have you or particular family members achieved or constructed a sense of the past?

2. Fowler discusses the "unreliable nature of history [and] the cultural litany set down in tourist brochures and abstracted onto brass plaques in parks and on roadsides across America." To illustrate her point, she describes the erasure of the historical presence of Timucuan Indians in St. Augustine, Florida. She notes, for example, that the plaque that marks the town "as The Oldest Continuously Inhabited City in America. Founded in 1565," leaves out the village of Seloy, home to Timucuan Indians, who lived in the town before its European founding. In what ways does this historical erasure of the region's Native American Indian past parallel her grandmother's urge to assimilate?

 Intertext

Consider the ways in which cultural and historical context contributes to the different interpretations about the role of photography in hooks's and Fowler's essays, and how these interpretations are related to official written or visual records. How does hooks support her argument that photos taken by African Americans enable a counter-narrative to images in white photographs? How does the absence of photographs—and the family's own disdain of them— open a space for Fowler's counternarrative of orality? How do their individual and cultural contexts affect the conclusions that the two authors reach about the value of photography?

La Familia

DOROTHY AND THOMAS HOOBLER

DOROTHY AND THOMAS HOOBLER are the authors of over sixty books, including the award-winning American Family Album series. The following essay is excerpted from *The Mexican American Family Album* (1994), a collection of testimonies, interviews, diary entries, scrapbook pages, and photographs that document the multi-faceted Mexican American experience in the United States. This essay is a collection of interviews from Mexican Americans about their personal family memories.

The Romero family at the funeral of an infant in Tucson, Arizona, in 1890.
Courtesy of Arizona Historical Society/Tucson AHS #64313.

Ramiro Quintero's parents went to Texas after the Mexican Revolution, which had destroyed their *estancia* (large farm). Born in the United States, Quintero recalled in 1989 the family life of his childhood.

Our family's always been close. Comin' up, the biggest thing was discipline. The worst thing you could do was bring the folks *una queja* from a neighbor. A *queja* is basically a gripe or a complaint. "Your son broke a limb off my tree," or broke my window, or kicked the chicken. That would tear it. You'd get a whuppin' or a scoldin' or something. The way my dad would punish us is work. Every day he went to work he had chores for brothers or sisters to do. . . .

If it's ten o'clock at night you'd finish it. There was always discipline and control over the family. That was the main thing, discipline and control. They were not whoopers or hollerers or screamers. They just spoke one time and that was it. The father was the breadwinner, the father was in charge of the whole house, what he said went, and the mother went along with him. There was no room for discussion. He was the boss and he never was wrong. No matter how wrong he could be, he still was right and that was the way of life. He kept real control of the family. He knew where everybody was at,

and the later you came in at night the earlier you would get up the next day to go to work. You sure would, yes sir. Kept up on everyone, stayed on top of everything. . . .

We didn't always have new clothes, but we had plenty to eat. How my father did it, I don't know. He was a horse trader. He'd trade chickens into the hogs. There might have been three or four hogs today an' he might have thirty or forty tomorrow. He learned the value of the dollar quick, and he understood the value of things.

Jacinta Carranza and her husband Simón Salazar Carranza had eight children. Simón worked for the railroad. As an old woman, Jacinta recalled her role as a mother.

I have never worked outside the home. My husband didn't want me to work—he said it wasn't necessary. He said that he supported me so that I could care for the children. And that is how I have spent my life—caring for my children. Even after my husband died in 1953, I did not leave the house to work. I worked right here— washing, ironing, cooking—and my children went to work to help out. I always loved my children very much—I never wanted to be apart from them because I worried that something might happen to them. They were always at my side. . . . I taught my daughters how to embroi-

der, and I kept my sons sweeping and raking up the yard. . . .

When my children were little I always used to   5
tell them that they could not go to the movies if they did not go to Mass. So they would take their baths and get dressed and go to Mass and then I would let them go to the movies. I have always been religious and have had a lot of faith. I am especially devoted to the Virgen de Guadalupe, and she has been good to me and taken care of me and my children and protected us from harm. I prayed to her while my sons were in the Korean War and she brought them home safely.

Children were expected to show respect for their elders. Often, they were served their food after the adults had eaten. A Mexican woman from south Texas recalls an experience when, as a child, she complained:

All my relatives sat down to eat before us children. My mother had fixed chicken *mole* [spiced chicken stew], *frijoles*, rice, salad and fried potatoes. When the adults finished eating, she called us children to come in and eat. We sat down, and I realized that there was no fried potatoes

left. That was my favorite dish. I made a fuss, complaining out loud that people had left nothing for us to eat. My mother almost died of embarrassment. She took the people to the other room and told me, "I am going to fix you now." Then she started peeling a mountain of potatoes right there and to fry them. She made a pile of fried potatoes and put them in front of me saying, "Now you are going to eat everything so that never again you complain about not having what to eat." I started eating but soon was full, and there was still a lot of potatoes to eat. I cried saying I couldn't eat anymore, and she simply said, "Go on eating, you are going to eat every single one of those potatoes." I begged my brothers to come help me eat, but she wouldn't let them do that either. Never again I complained about food in front of other people. My lesson was well taught.

> Although the man was generally in charge in the Mexican home, sometimes there was a more equal sharing of authority. A woman in southern Texas looked back on the relationship of her parents, who lived on a ranch around 1910.

My mother *mandaba en la casa* [was the boss of the house], but decisions were made by both her and my father. If my father wanted to sell all the maíz or a cow, he first consulted with my mother. Of course, not all the couples around there were the same. There were some husbands who would lock the food in a compartment that only they could open. When the wife needed some food she'd have to ask him to open the compartment. A woman's life was very hard. We had little freedom and a lot of work. We had no horses, for instance, so we depended on the men for transportation. But it wasn't like that with my mama and papa. They were good to each other.

Family portraits decorate the wall of this Mexican American farm family's home in Santa Maria, Texas.
Courtesy of the Library of Congress.

The Mexican American novelist Victor Villaseñor, in his book *Rain of Gold,* told the history of three generations of his family, ending with his parents' marriage. In researching the book, Villaseñor interviewed many of his relatives.

For myself, my biggest personal regret is that I never met my grandmother, Doña Margarita. She died two years before I was born. My father told me that he saw her only days before her death, shuffling down a dirt road in Corona, California, with the sunlight coming down on her through the tree branches. She was almost ninety years old, and he saw her walking along, doing a little quick-footed dance, singing about how happy she was because she'd tricked a little dog and he hadn't been able to bite her again.

My father said that tears came to his eyes, seeing how his mother—a little bundle of dried-out Indian bones—could bring such joy, such happiness, to her life over any little thing. "She was the richest human on earth, I tell you," said my father to me. "She knew the secret to living, and that secret is to be happy . . . happy no

Rose Acevez Aguirre with her children David (the infant) and Blanca. The photograph was taken in a studio in San Gabriel, California, in 1911. The oceanfront scene is a painted backdrop.
Courtesy of Los Angeles Public Library (LAPL).

matter what, happy as the birds that sing in the treetops, happy as she came shuffling down that lonely dirt road, stopping now and then to do a little dance."

10   But . . . I did get to meet my mother's mother, Doña Guadalupe, and I was able to sit on her lap and have her rock me back and forth and tell me about the early days of La Lluvia when the gold had rained down the mountainsides and the wild lilies had filled the canyon with "heavenly fragrance." . . .

And I'm proud to say that I was able to finish the book before my father died. He was able to read it and see how I'd portrayed his loved ones, especially his mother. And on the last night of my father's life, I stayed with him, and his last words to me were, "I'm going to see *mi mama,* and I'm so proud of you, *mi hijito,* that you got her right in our book." He took my right hand in both of his, squeezing it, stroking it. "For she was a great woman," he said to me, "the greatest, just like your own mother!" And he hugged and kissed me goodbye.

I put him to bed, and he died in his sleep at the age of 86 or 84, depending on which relative I ask. All his life he'd been so strong and sure and confident and he died the same way. It wasn't that he had lost the will to live; no, he'd gained the will to die. For, I'd asked him, "Papa, aren't you afraid?"

"Of what?" he'd said in his deep, powerful voice. "Of death? Of course not. To fear death is to insult life!"

ELSIE CHAVEZ CHILTON was born in Las Cruces, New Mexico, around 1915. Her parents had arrived from Mexico some years before. In 1983, Chilton recalled her childhood.

We had a big house. At that time, since the town was so sparsely populated, they built a house on each corner of the block so each block had only two houses. There was a vastness of brush, mesquite bushes, lizards and what have you. So we weren't crowded or close. . . .

15   We used to have a big dormitory room in our house for the five boys in our family. There were two of us girls. The boys would go out, I guess you would call it grubbing, for something to burn in the stove they had in their big room. They would get those mesquite roots, or tires or whatever else they could find and burn it in the big stove. We would have a roaring fire for a while and we were too hot. Then when the fire went out we would be cold again. Sometimes we would bundle up and go outside and play to keep warm. Mother would get up real early and go down to the *leniero* [the man who sold wood] for wood for the stove in the kitchen. For a quarter she would get a tub full of wood and then she would have a nice warm fire going by the time we got up to dress. When we got out of school the sun would be shining and it wouldn't be so cold.

The Spanish word *compadre* can be translated as "close friend," but the relationship of a *compadre* is deeper than that. A *compadre* is a protector and guide. The most common way for a Mexican American to become a *compadre* is to sponsor a friend's child at its baptism. The person who does this is linked not only to the child but to its parents as well. One Mexican American explained the relationship in detail.

A compadre means a lot. It's something real, it means a lot. When you make a compadre you have to respect him and he has to respect you. Compadres help each other; you can't talk about him, and he can't talk about you. For example, if you tell someone that your compadre is drinking too much then he may go over and tell your compadre that you were talking about him. Then your compadre will come to you and ask why you are talking about him. Then you may get into an argument and maybe you won't talk to each other after that. You shouldn't run around with the girls in front of him because of respect. You should try to show off that you're a nice man, and that you were chosen because you are a nice man.

Like you take Francisco, for example. He's a good friend of mine, but he wouldn't be good for a compadre. What I mean is that he comes into the house and jokes with me and my wife, he cusses around us, he doesn't respect us. He wouldn't be good for a compadre, but he's a good friend. . . .

When you choose a compadre, you have to call him *Sir* in a way. You say *Usted* [the polite, respectful form of "you"]. When you see him on the street, you can't go rushing up to him

An elderly Mexican American man in a south Texas town recalled one of the traditional methods of courtship:

It used to be that when a boy's father went to the home of the girl to ask her father for his daughter's hand that the girl's father would say: "Well, I don't know. I'll tell you what. Send your boy over to my house for two months and we'll see how he works. We'll see what we can expect from that young man!" Then the father of the boy would agree to do this. But he would tell the father of the girl that he, also, wished to see how the girl behaved and what kind of a worker she was. He suggested that the girl come to his house for two months. That way there was an exchange [*intercambio*].

The girl would get up at three in the morning and see what kind of condition the *nixtamal* [tortilla dough] was in, and she would set the fire, bake the *tortillas,* and tidy up the place. At her family's home the boy would be working himself to death; he would be walking in from the fields with a load of sweet cane over one shoulder, and a load of corn on the other shoulder. People knew how to work and keep house then! After two months, when the parents had seen how well the children were able to work, they would give them permission to wed.

and yelling, "Hey, you—come here!" If you know him real well, you address him by Sir. . . . Even if he is younger than you are, you address him nicely.

Sometimes a young man would use a friend or other relative as a *portador*—an intermediary to approach the parents of the woman he wished to marry. One Mexican American in south Texas, returning from World War II, decided to marry his girlfriend.

She wanted to go off with me, but I . . . went and told my father that I wanted to get married and told him that I might *robar* [elope with] my bride. But he told me: "No, son; you must play it straight. . . ." So that same week I got hold of two older men. I gave them each ten dollars. . . . They went to her house, and I went over to the Rincón bar to drink some beer. I was very nervous.

20   After a while they came over to the Rincón and sat down. . . . They said that the parents of the girl had told them to come back in eight days, and that's a sign that they approve of the marriage. If they had told them to come back in fifteen days for an answer, then it would have meant that they disapproved of the marriage.

I was very happy about the whole thing. In eight days I went over with my parents to make the first of the visits. While we were there, I told them that I was prepared to give her twenty dollars each week so that she could tell how I would support her. But she said, "No. Don't give me any money. Save the money and we'll go on a honeymoon instead." And that was all right with her parents; so when we got married we went to Monterrey and had a wonderful time!

A woman makes tortillas in her home near Taos, New Mexico, in the 1930s.
Courtesy of the Library of Congress.

Rose Reyes Pitts is a third-generation Mexican American. Her father's grandmother came to Edinburg, Texas, many years ago. Even so, as Reyes Pitts recalled, the spirit of *machismo* was still alive in her family.

My dad is very *mexicano*, very macho. In fact, even though I have a good relationship with him now, we never really communicated when I was growing up. It never bothered me, because I was so close to my mom. She always smoothed things out. I never realized it then, but now it sort of hurts my feelings. My father never really talked to me. If he wanted me to do something,

Artemio Duarte, Jr., and his grandfather, Lauro Torres, in front of the family home on Del Amo Boulevard in Los Angeles. Artemio's father built the house himself.
Courtesy of Los Angeles Public Library (LAPL).

At a party, a blind-folded girl swings at the piñata overhead. Filled with candy or toys, the piñata will release its prizes when broken.*

Courtesy of Lawrence Migdale/Pix.

he would tell my mother and, my mother would tell me. When I married things got better; he had a little more respect for me; he talked to me. And since I've been a mother we've got along great.

My dad does all the men things. He barbecues, he keeps the yard perfect, keeps the cars. Of course he never changed a diaper. I can't even imagine that—I mean, I can't imagine being married to a man who would not help feed your child or change her diaper.

He always gives my mother a lot of credit though. He says she's the leader in the family, the one who's kept us all together, the smart one. And she is. She handles the household, pays all the bills, knows about the insurance and finances. He doesn't want to know about it. Even though he's real *macho,* she controls what happens, the important things. She really is in control of my father.

*The original photo used in the Hooblers' essay was not available. This image is a close approximation.—W.H. & B.J.B.

A family of Mexican immigrants in San Diego, CA, 1941.*
Courtesy of Library of Congress.

A birthday party for Lulu Moreno in Los Angeles. She is the smallest girl, getting plenty of help blowing out the candles on her cake.
Courtesy of Los Angeles Public Library (LAPL).

*The original photo used in the Hooblers' essay was not available. This image is a close approximation.—W.H. & B.J.B.

Re-reading/Conversations with the Text

1. Each of the interview excerpts included in this section addresses recollections of Mexican American family life. Do you notice any trends in the kinds of memories that are represented in these interviews? Do these excerpts work together to give the reader a coherent sense of family life? If so, how? Also consider the result of placing these excerpts in close proximity to one another.

2. One of the issues that many of these excerpts address is the question of gender roles in the family context, especially the relationship between husband and wife. Re-read the essay and think about the different kinds of gender roles represented in the excerpts. How are traditional gender roles described? How are nontraditional roles described? How do these representations of gender affect the ways in which the interviewees recall their family life?

3. Examine the images that appear alongside the text. What kinds of events are represented in the images? How do the images relate to the issues presented in the text? How do the images affect the way you interpret the interviews? Conversely, how does the text affect the way you interpret the images?

Re-seeing and Re-writing

1. This assignment asks you to create a document about your own family that is similar in structure to the one you just read. Interview two or three adult family members about their memories of their relationships to other family members. Compile the interviews into a document and think about what overarching issues and themes regarding family life and familial relationships appear in these interviews. Then, choose photographs from your family album that best coincide with or represent those issues and themes. Finally, write an essay in which you analyze and interpret the document that you have created and discuss the connections between family and the issues that your document raises.

2. Many of the interview excerpts are about the speaker's relationship to another person in the family. Choose one of the excerpts, and in a short essay about the same event or relationship, adopt the persona of the family member that the speaker writes about. Then, write a response in which you analyze how point of view affects the interpretation of the event or relationship.

Intertext

In the interview excerpt from Victor Villaseñor, he recalls his relationships to his grandmothers and discusses the function of storytelling, through both Doña Guadalupe's stories and his own book about his family. Compare and contrast the significance of storytelling in Villaseñor's excerpt and Connie May Fowler's essay. How does each writer represent storytelling? What is its significance in family life? How does it help future generations understand their origins?

The Portrait

TOMÁS RIVERA

A Texas native and the son of Mexican American migrant farmers, *TOMÁS RIVERA* enjoyed success as an award-winning writer and as a university-level administrator. Rivera's story, which appears in his book . . . *And the Earth Did Not Devour Him* [. . . *y no se lo tragó la tierra*] (1987), describes an anonymous narrator's encounter with a dishonest portrait salesman. Rivera explores the significance of photography and its relationship to the migrant farmer experience. Rivera's work includes *The Harvest, The Searchers,* and a volume of collected poetry entitled *Always and Other Poems.*

The portrait salesmen were just waiting for the people to return from up north before coming from San Antonio. They came down to water. They knew that the people had money, and that was the reason why, as father used to say, they came down in droves. Their suitcases were full of samples. They always wore white shirts and ties, that way they looked more important and the people believed everything they said and welcomed them into their homes without a second thought. I think that secretly they wished that their children would someday grow up to be like that. Anyway, they came and walked along the dusty streets loaded down with their suitcases full of samples.

I remember once I was at the house of one of my father's friends when one of these salesmen arrived. I also remember that that particular one seemed a little frightened and timid. Don Mateo asked him to come in because he wanted to do business.

"Good afternoon, sir; look, I would like to explain something new that we have this year."

"Let's see, let's see."

5   "Well, look, give us a picture, any picture you have, and we will not only enlarge it, but also frame it in wood, with wood inlays, one might say three dimensional."

"Yes, but what's the reason for that?"

"So he'll look as though he were alive. Like this, look. Let me show you this one. What do you think? Doesn't he look lifelike, as though he were alive?"

"Yes, you're right. Look, vieja. This one looks great. You know, we wanted to enlarge some pictures. But that must cost a lot, right?"

"Not at all; you know, it costs about the same. Of course it takes more time."

"Well, alright, let's see. How much does it   10 cost?"

"For just thirty dollars we'll have it inlaid for you. One this size."

"Damn, it's expensive. Didn't you say it didn't cost too much more? Can one take it on payments?"

"You know, we have another manager and he wants everything in cash. The thing is that it's excellent workmanship. We'll make him look like real. Inlaid, like this. Look, what do you think? Beautiful job, isn't it? We'll bring it back to you all finished within a month. You just tell us the color of his clothes, and we'll be back with it before you know it, all finished, frame and all. You wouldn't believe it, but not much more than a month. But, as I told you, this man who is the manager now wants cash. He's very demanding, even with us."

"But it's much too expensive."

"Well, yes. But it's excellent work. Don't tell   15 me you've seen pictures inlaid with wood before?"

"No. You're right. What do you say, vieja?"

"Well, I like it very much. Why don't we have one made? And if it turns out all right

. . . Chuy's picture. May his soul rest in peace. It's the only one we have of him. We took it before he went to Korea. My poor son; we never saw him again. Look, here is his picture. Do you think you can have it inlaid to make him look lifelike?"

"And why not? You know, we've made many dressed in soldier's uniform. Inlaid they're more than pictures. Yes, why not? You just tell me what size you want it, and if you want a square or a round frame. What do you say? How shall I write it up?"

"What do you say, vieja? Shall we have it made like this?"

"I told you what I want. I'd like to have my son's picture inlaid like this and in color."

"Alright, write it down. But take good care of the picture for us because it's the only one we have of our son grown up. He promised to send us one all dressed up as a soldier, with the American and Mexican flags crossed above his head. But as soon as he arrived over there we received a letter telling us that he was missing in action. So take good care of it."

"Don't worry. We're responsible people. We know very well what a sacrifice it is for everyone. Don't worry. You'll see how pretty it'll look when we bring it back. What do you say, shall we give him a navy blue suit?"

"But he's not wearing a uniform in the picture."

"Yes, however, it's just a matter of fixing it up with a little wood. Look at this one. He didn't have a uniform, but we gave him one. So, what do you say? Shall we give him a navy blue uniform?"

"Alright."

"And don't worry about the picture."

All that day the portrait salesmen travelled from one street to another filling their suitcases with pictures. At the end, a great number of people had ordered that kind of enlargement.

"It's about time to get our portraits, don't you think?"

"I think so, but the workmanship is excellent. That takes longer. Those people do excellent work. Did you notice how lifelike the pictures were?"

"Yes, you're right. They do excellent work. No one can deny that. But remember, it's been more than a month since they came through here."

"Yes, but they were picking up pictures all day along the little towns from here to San Antonio, that's for sure. So they probably took a little longer."

"That's right, that's right."

Two more weeks went by before the whole matter became clear, when some very heavy rains came down and some children who were playing in one of the tunnels that led to the dump found a sack full of wet, dissolving pictures. What identified them as pictures was the fact that there were many of them, all the same size, and the faces could almost be made out. Everyone understood immediately. Don Mateo became so angry that he left for San Antonio in search of the man who had tricked them.

"Well, you know, I stayed at Esteban's house. And every day I went out with him to sell vegetables at the market. I helped him in everything. I hoped to meet up with that particular man one fine day. After being there for a few days, I started going out to the different barrios and I learned many things that way. I didn't care so much about the money, what concerned me was my wife's crying, since it was the only picture of Chuy that we had. And even though we found it in the sack along with the other pictures, it was completely destroyed, as you can imagine."

"Yes, but how did you find him?"

"Well, you see, to make a long story short, he turned up at the vegetable stand one day. He stood right there in front of us and bought some vegetables. He seemed to recognize me. Of course I recognized him, because when one is harboring anger one doesn't forget faces. And right there and then I grabbed him. The poor man couldn't even say anything. He was really scared. All I said was that I wanted my son's picture, inlaid, and that he'd better do it or he'd get it. I went with him to where he lived. And right there I made him get to work. The poor man didn't even know where to begin. He had to do it all from memory."

"And how did he do it?"

"I don't know. But I think that a person is capable of doing anything out of fear. Three days later he brought me the finished portrait, just as you see it there close to the Virgin on the table. What do you think? How does my son look?"

"Well, quite frankly I don't remember what Chuy looked like anymore. But more and more he was beginning to resemble you, right?"

"Yes. I think so. That's what everyone tells me now. That Chuy resembled me more and more, and that he was beginning to look like me. There's the portrait. One might say we're one and the same." 40

Re-reading/Conversations with the Text

1. In Rivera's story, there are a number of references to clothing and the ways in which people are dressed. At the beginning of the essay, for example, there is a description of the portrait salesman's clothing. In addition, when the salesman attempts to convince Don Mateo to purchase an enlargement, the salesman offers to alter the image so that Chuy will appear to be wearing a military uniform. How does the uniform function in terms of preserving Chuy's memory? What is the significance of these references to clothing? How does clothing alter the characters' interpretations of each other?

2. The portrait salesman seems to be engaged in the act of selling memories. Think about the potential significance of this act. What kinds of memories is he selling? How does he try to market his product to the family? How is memory constructed as a commodity that can be sold? What is the significance of Don Mateo's insistence that he receive a finished product from the salesman? What does this reveal about the function of memory in this story?

3. At the end of the story, the narrator and Don Mateo discuss the finished portrait. The narrator admits to not being able to remember what Chuy looked like except that Chuy was beginning to resemble Don Mateo, and Don Mateo agrees. The story concludes when Don Mateo says about Chuy "we're one and the same." What does he mean when he says this? Does this tell the reader something about Chuy? If so, what? How might we understand this statement in light of the fact that the portrait salesman constructed the portrait from memory? Why might it be significant that it is the portrait salesman's memory that must be relied upon to create the portrait?

Re-seeing and Re-writing

1. This prompt asks you to examine and analyze Web sites advertising professional family photography. Locate two or three Web sites that advertise these services and look carefully at the images and text that are on the sites. How do the Web sites represent the idea of family portraits? What do the Web sites suggest customers will receive from posing for family portraits? How is the

process of preserving family memories represented on the sites? What patterns do you see in the images on the sites? What kinds of families are represented? What kinds of families are absent from the sites? What notions of family are reinforced by these images?

2. In Rivera's story, the portrait salesman must construct Chuy's portrait from memory. As an exercise in exploring the function of memory and its relationship to photography, write a detailed description of a family photograph that is important to you. Do not look at the photograph, but instead, describe it from memory. After you have done this, go to the photograph itself and note the similarities and differences between your description and the actual photograph. Write an essay explaining the significance of those similarities and differences.

Intertext

One interesting parallel between Maxine Hong Kingston's essay and Rivera's story is that both narrators use images of family members posing for the camera to come to various interpretations of family relationships, identity, and culture. Compare and contrast Kingston and Rivera's essays in terms of how they represent the process of interpreting photographs. What conclusions do the narrators draw? How do the writers represent the importance of the photographs to their families? How do their cultural contexts, such as race, class, and gender, affect the way they represent the importance of photography?

Images from *Written in Memory: Portraits of the Holocaust*

J E F F R E Y   W O L I N

JEFFREY WOLIN's series of photographs from *Written in Memory: Portraits of the Holocaust* (1997) addresses the issue of the creative nature of memory and how we construct past experience. *Written in Memory* is a collaborative effort with over fifty Holocaust survivors and families. Wolin began each session by videotaping the survivor's stories prior to creating an individual portrait with a still camera. Excerpts from each survivor's testimony are included as part of the background of the image. Wolin is a professor of photography at Indiana University. He has received visual artist fellowships from the National Endowment for the Arts and Guggenheim Memorial Fellowship, among other institutions. His photographs have been exhibited and acquired by numerous museums, including the Museum of Modern Art in New York.

Rena Grynblat, born 1926, Warsaw, Poland

Jeffrey A. Wolin, *Written in Memory*. San Francisco: Chronicle Books, 1997.

...ther. They gave us one loaf of bread, period. And that had to last - but we didn't know for how long it had to last. People were dying in the train left and right. Next to me was a Jewish doctor from Vienna and he was dying and it was real dark on the train. He kept on making noises. We were maybe the fourth row from the front and there were German soldiers with guns sitting in front of us. One of them said, ... started to talk and nothing came out. Not a word. 'Quiet. Quiet!' But he wasn't quiet because now I think ... I tried for maybe ten minutes. And I never he was unconscious. With his rifle the German start- ... told them why... I became a real workaholic. -ed to beat us. He beat me horrible. As a matter ... I constantly worked day and night, day of fact I couldn't speak for a whole week. Nothing ... and night, day and night. Then when would come out. After he beat me the German shot ... I was 44 I had a heart attack. I the guy and he was dead. The body, of course, stayed ... had delivered 92 babies that month. 92 there all along. As a matter of fact I sat on him be- ... deliveries! All our effort is to make -cause it was more comfortable to sit on him than on ... sure the mothers and babies are well the floor. I still have the aftereffects of that beating. And ... and healthy. On the other hand the when I get tense I cannot talk. Years later I became ... Germans killed millions of president of my hospital's medical staff and ... children like nothing. chief of obstetrics at St. Margaret's ... You tell me. hospital. I remember one day ... Is there a there were arguments back ... God?" and forth among exec- -tive committee members. The. discussion became heated. And

Jacob Schwartz, born 1928, Sofiendorf, Czechoslovakia
Jeffrey A. Wolin, *Written in Memory.* San Francisco: Chronicle Books, 1997.

They took me to work in the quarry at Mauthausen. Oh, that was bad. You had to go down stone steps, way down I don't know how many stone steps, real steep, rocks all over and you were barefoot too. You pick up a rock — you go up all those stone steps and walk all the way to the camp which was a few miles and put the stone down. In the meantime the SS is all around you. If you took too big a stone you won't make it. If you take a little stone they beat you — they make you run to the fence and I witnessed that many times. They started to scream, beat you and say, 'Run!' Everyone knew if you run to the fence you're dead because from the watchtowers they will shoot you and besides the fence is electrified. They beat you so hard you're practically dead anyway. So the biggest dilemma was what kind of rock to take... They took a group of us and they sent us by train to Linz II, a satellite camp of Mauthausen, for labor at Hermann Göring Works. The conditions were really bad at Linz II. The longer we were there the worse it got. Hunger — that was the main thing. With every step you tried to economize your energy. If I was walking I tried to figure out what is the shortest way. One step less — everything was an effort. I could hardly walk, I was so weak from hunger... I saw people — I witnessed this: can you imagine eating a raw dead rat? Naturally they died. They would have died anyway. Some of the Polish and Russian prisoners once in a while were able to get packages from home, so they used to go pick them up. And on the way to the barracks the other prisoners would attack them and get away. So they came after me — I saw it. They attacked him and there was granulated sugar there in one package and it spilled into the mud. And after they left I picked up that sugar with the mud and I ate it. There was mud and sugar mixed. That's as far as I went personally."

Henryk Werdinger, born 1923, Boryslaw, Poland
Jeffrey A. Wolin, *Written in Memory*. San Francisco: Chronicle Books, 1997.

Re-reading/Conversations with the Text

1. What stories do these photographs tell? What emotional response do they elicit?

2. For each photo, describe the facial expression on the subject of the image. How would you describe the subject's gaze at the camera or viewer? In what ways do these photographs invite or repel us as viewers?

3. What is the relationship between the written texts (survivors' testimonies as told to the photographer) and the visual portraits? Do the portraits and written texts complement each other? In what ways does the written text become photographic and the photograph a narrative?

Re-seeing and Re-writing

In her work on the children of Holocaust survivors, Marianne Hirsch puts forth the notion of "postmemory," which she uses to describe a kind of "secondary witnessing" brought about by the children's identification with their parent(s). However, "identification with the victim or witness of trauma," Hirsch argues, is "modulated by an admission of an unbridgeable distance separating the participant from the one born after" (*Extremities,* eds. Nancy Miller and Jason Tougaw, Urbana: U of IP, 2002, 8). What do Wolin's images suggest about the relation between the past and the present? How do these images and/or written texts depict the family and/or the nation?

Reframing the Human Family Romance

MARIANNE HIRSCH

Cameras and videorecorders have become one of the family's primary instruments of representation, or, as *MARIANNE HIRSCH* argues, the "primary means by which a family's story is told" (*The Familial Gaze,* xi). These family stories, Hirsch argues, are not formed in a social vacuum, but rather they respond to cultural and national mythologies of family life. In this essay, excerpted from *Family Frames: Photography, Narrative, and Postmemory* (1997), Hirsch considers the mythologies that Americans have inherited and how certain configurations of the family are associated with the American ideal. Hirsch is professor of English and professor of comparative literature at Columbia University.

The family is an image we seek so desperately.

—E. Ethelbert Miller

The people in the audience looked at the pictures, and the people in the pictures looked back at them. They recognized each other. A Japanese poet has said that, when you look into a mirror, you do not see your reflection, your reflection sees you.

—Edward Steichen

Guests

On February 3, 1993, the sports page of the *New York Times* featured a touching human interest story, "Riddick Bowe Has Family in Scarsdale": "They remembered him as a laughing boy, sweet and bright, who graced their home for two weeks one summer. And then he came back into their lives as the heavy-weight champion of the world." It seems that in the summer of 1975 the Goldstein family hosted a 7-year-old African-American child from Brooklyn in their Scarsdale home through the Fresh Air Fund. Eighteen years later, when they recognized his name on television and in the newspaper, they contacted him. The reunion revolved around a familiar ritual: perusing the family photograph album. "We gave him

a few photographs of himself, and this was something I never realized about our middle class values, but he just didn't have many photos from his childhood. He looked at one photo and he said, 'Gee, that looks just like my daughter.' "[1]

The Goldsteins identify the impetus for participating in the Fresh Air Fund as the "sixties ideals" they hope never to lose, and the article celebrates their generosity, quoting the world's heavyweight champion's memories of "seeing lots of trees" and finding a family who was "very nice" to him: "Being a little kid, you don't hear much about racism. You figure everyone's the same."

Although I live in Vermont among a lot of trees, I have never participated in the Fresh Air

Fund, but I can identify with the Goldsteins' "sixties ideals." Thus, in the aftermath of the Gulf War with its images of Iraqi children hurt by American bombings, my family "adopted" a Bolivian child through an international organization. The advertisement to which we responded featured a photograph of a little Indian girl with beautiful sad eyes, and informed us that for only $60 per quarter, we could make a real difference in a child's life somewhere in the world, a world we saw as profoundly endangered by American military technology. We didn't know much about the particular organization we chose, but their multi-purpose approach to international aid—combining personal sponsorship with family and community assistance—was appealing.

On the form we received, we checked that we wanted to support a male child of our 8-year-old son Gabriel's age, intending to encourage in him fraternal feelings of identification transcending the borders of class and nationality. We chose a Bolivian child for the same reasons—we had recently visited Bolivia with Gabriel; his father Leo was born in Bolivia and has some childhood photos that depict him playing with Aymara age-mates; we knew Spanish, and the landscape of our "foster child's" surroundings would be familiar. Remembering how shocked Gabriel had been when he saw abandoned boys his age roaming through La Paz trying to earn a living by shining shoes, we knew it would not be difficult to get him interested in a "foster brother."

5 When we received the name, address, and photograph of Secundino Callisaya, from the Altiplano above La Paz, we immediately wrote in Gabriel's name in Spanish about our family, Gabriel, his school and interests, and we included a picture of Gabriel and his brothers, Oliver and Alex. The response soon followed. The polite letter in awkward English, translated (from Spanish? Aymara?) and typed by a member of the organization's Bolivian office, told us about Secundino's life on the Altiplano, his

family and his school, and assured us that Secundino's mother and his much-older brother both worked very hard. Our subsequent contact has remained similarly mediated, including the quarterly reports about improvements that our dollars are making possible in the Altiplano clean-water plan, in the local clinic and immunization programs, and in the Callisaya household. Gabriel has remained interested in Secundino and would have liked a more direct and informative correspondence.

I have begun to understand the determining role of the mediating organization with its ready-made communication kits. But I have been unable to let go of my ambivalence and discomfort with the philanthropic role I am playing, nor of my questions about whether our modest contribution actually benefits Secundino and his community. Thus, when a personalized letter subsequently arrived asking us to adopt another child—a beautiful 5-year-old Indian boy whose glossy photograph, staring intently at its addressee, was included in the envelope—I politely, though painfully, declined.

What does this gesture of "adopting" a disadvantaged child into the middle-class nuclear family and its family album mean—the Goldsteins' impulse to become a Fresh Air Fund host family and mine to participate in the international sponsorship program? What ideologies underlie it and why do they appear so suspect to me? And how can photographs help us to read the complex feelings and motivations determining these experiences?

Looking closely at the Goldsteins' photographs reproduced on the *New York Times* page I find a more complicated narrative than the upbeat human interest story suggests. The four slightly overlapping pictures on the page display, in fact, some of the same, perhaps inevitable, failures of connection that have characterized Gabriel's relationship with Secundino (Figures 1–4). The first shows the smiling African-American boy posing in a back yard on a bicycle. It is a counter-illustration to

Sandy Goldstein's story about Riddick's very first ride on a bike, when he ran into a fence, leaving dents in her son's bike and the fence. According to the article, the accident left Michael "slightly ticked off" to this day. But what happened to Riddick, I want to ask?

The other pictures focus on the two boys: "If racism isn't taught," Bowe is quoted as saying, "you're just a black kid and a white kid together," and the pictures seem to illustrate just that. But do they? In the second picture, taken at the zoo and featuring fences and bars, the two boys are looking at a peacock. But while the young guest politely looks at the bird, the host child climbs on the fence and faces the camera, thus subtly asserting his centrality in the family image. The third photograph is the only one in which the two boys stand close to each other: their legs are far apart though their upper bodies lean into the center of the image, as though they had been told to pose together. But a subtle competition dictates this pose as well: Michael puts his right hand on the garden hose which is positioned between the two arms with which Riddick hugs his own waist—perhaps indicating that the guest has no claim on this household object? In the last image Michael sits on a bike, smiling brightly at the camera; Riddick looks down at the picnic table, his hands just barely holding on to the handlebars of a bicycle, perhaps illustrating his memory in the article that "when I left, for the first time in my life, I cried."

As I study these pictures probably more attentively than any of the participants themselves would, it seems to me that the desire to believe that "everybody's the same" is quickly qualified for the young Riddick. These photographs, after all, until very recently graced only the Goldsteins' album and constructed their memories, not Riddick Bowe's. I wonder, therefore, what layers of feeling are suppressed beneath the drawing of a smiley face that the adult Bowe gave to Michael Goldstein: "Bowe signed a magazine cover to Michael 'from your old buddy Riddick' and he drew one of those

10

Figure 1   Courtesy of the Goldstein family.

Figure 2   Courtesy of the Goldstein family.

Figure 3   Courtesy of the Goldstein family.

Figure 4   Courtesy of the Goldstein family.

smiley faces. The Goldsteins got a kick out of a large man who hits people for a living drawing a smiley face."

But could my skeptical reading of these photographs be dictated by the same "middle-class values" which left Sandy Goldstein so surprised at the absence of photos in the history of an inner-city child? Could the awkwardness that I see in the poses be explained more simply by Riddick's unfamiliarity with photographic conventions and the codes of posing, codes which the young Michael seems to have mastered so well? Only the first photograph of Riddick, in fact, corresponds to the conventions of the family album: a smiling boy, central in the frame, displaying one of the necessary accoutrements of middle-class childhood, the bicycle. Having to share the frame with a child of longer-standing training in these conventions would then make his pictures more hesitant and tenuous, his return look in them less direct. Sitting on the bike, Riddick can look out at the camera and the viewer, but, lacking any visible posses-

sions in the later photographs, he looks down: there is no available look for the temporary guest from the inner-city neighborhood, no easy space for integration into the middle-class Scarsdale family album and family romance.

I find it equally difficult to read Secundino's look in the photographs which were no doubt taken by the organization's officer. Secundino, standing in front of a whitewashed wall, unsmiling, his arms hanging down, stares out quite intently at an unknown world beyond the camera lens. In another image, standing next to his smiling mother in front of a building that could not be his own house, he has no distinct space of his own. He does not look into the lens; his look does not engage us, the return look it invites is not familial, not identificatory, but neither is it disidentificatory or anti-affiliative. There may be a shared desire to relate familially, but no obvious way to do so. Even if our family albums were up to date, I doubt that we would have remembered to include Secundino's picture.

The conventions of family photography, with its mutuality of confirming looks that construct a set of familial roles and hierarchies, reinforce the power of the notion of "family." The pervasiveness of these conventions opens the family image and album to the possibility of broad-based identification and affiliation I have already discussed. Paradoxically, however, these very same conventions and practices can also support the antidemocratic aspects of photography, drawing borders around a circumscribed group and strengthening its power to include and thus also to exclude. It is not simply a question of class: box cameras have been available to working-class families throughout much of this century, as the work of Jo Spence and Valerie Walkerdine and the texts of many working-class writers and photographers attest. It is that representational conventions consolidate family and group identity—with its dreams, fantasies, and aspirations—whatever the particular group might be. In the case of the Goldsteins' pictures and mine, they admit the outsider but visibly as a temporary guest. Through his marginal presence and through his subtle difference, he helps to delineate the central group with its elaborate systems of representation, from which he is, and to some extent remains, excluded. Or, if he is admitted into the particular bourgeois family romance of the family album in the mid- to late-twentieth-century United States, it is to support the ideologies that undergird it, that is, as the desiring other, fantasizing that "everyone's the same," and thus supporting the dominant desire to veil inequality and exclusion.

How does the family album represent otherness? How much diversity can it accommodate, and how does that negotiation between difference and identity shift at different historical moments? Through certain common strategies, attributable to the powerful idea of "family," the family album, in our historical moment particularly, can transform difference into specular mirroring in order to include children like Riddick Bowe and Secundino Callisaya and to promote the fantasy that "everyone's the same." But this transformation is never uncomplicated, for the family album does not forget to reassert its boundaries of difference at certain strategic moments. The structure of the family album and of the familial gaze—the affiliative and specular looks it constructs—can suggest what happens when, in this way, diversity is reconfigured as familiality. It can expose the relationship between family photography and the ideological structures of—in this case—the American family romance with its ever shifting meanings.

The Human Family

If one instrument helped construct and perpetuate the ideology which links the notion of universal humanity to the idea of familiality, it is the camera and its by-products, the photographic image and the family album. Jo Spence and Patricia Holland go so far as to claim that "Cameras and film have been developed with the family in mind."[2] Pierre Bourdieu has demonstrated the integral connection between the ever-spreading practice of photography and the ideology of the modern family: "photographic practice only exists and subsists for most of the time by virtue of its *family function* or rather by the function conferred upon it by the family group, namely that of solemnizing and immortalizing the high points of family life, . . . of reinforcing the integration of the family group by reasserting the sense that it has both of itself and of its unity."[3]

But the widely accepted sense of photography as a "natural language"—a 1989 Kodak advertisement claimed, for example, that "150 years ago a language was invented that everyone understood"—helped to extend photography's familial gaze beyond the nuclear family's domestic domain and to endow it with vaster and more global ambitions. Thus photography could support an expanded notion of a *human* family, a liberal ideology of universalism that has remained powerful throughout the post–World War II period and that is exhibited on a very small scale in the Goldsteins' family album and in the strategies used by many charitable organizations.

In thinking about how the ideology of the family and the technology of photography support and reinforce each other during this historical moment, I began to wonder about how family albums treat images of "others."[4] Thus I came to look at a rather unusual set of "family pictures," those of the 1955 Museum of Modern Art exhibition *The Family of Man,* curated by Edward Steichen, then the Director of Photography at MOMA. It is no coincidence that the first "blockbuster" museum exhibit should connect family with photography, or that it should superimpose familiality with universality. *The Family of Man* attracted 270,000 visitors to MOMA in its first fifteen weeks, more visitors than any other exhibit had seen until that time. Following the show at MOMA, the 503 images from 68 countries then toured 37 countries in six separate editions. The equally successful book, deliberately produced in inexpensive editions (one cost one dollar) could be found in most middle-class American living rooms in the 1950s and 1960s. Many treasure this book even now. As Steichen claims in his introduction, his exhibit "is the most ambitious and challenging project photography has ever attempted . . . It was conceived as a mirror of the universal elements and emotions in the everydayness of life—as a mirror of the essential oneness of mankind throughout the world."[5] Steichen and his assistant Wayne Miller chose the 503 photographs from among 2 million which were sent to New York "from every corner of the earth . . . from individuals, collections and files." The 273 photographers were "amateurs and professionals, famed and unknown."

Several ambitious ideas and generous impulses underlie Steichen's conception of the exhibit. In his autobiography, *A Life in Photography,* Steichen links it directly to his own war experience as an aerial photographer in World War I and a naval photographer in the Pacific in World War II, and to his attempt to use photography as an instrument with which to prevent war. After organizing three exhibitions of war photos at MOMA—the last on the Korean War—he felt he had failed. "Although I had presented war in all its grimness in the three exhibitions, . . . I had not incited people into taking open and united action against war itself . . . I came to the conclusion that I had been working from a negative approach, that what was needed was a positive statement on what a wonderful thing life was, how marvelous people were, and, above all, how alike people were in all parts of the world."[6] Stressing what one of Steichen's assistants called the "universal brotherhood of man," the *Family of Man* exhibit allowed him to envision the power of the medium in a new way: "Photography can be a moving force in the world as I saw it in the war. It can lift individuals as subjects from the humdrum and turn them into symbols of universal humanity," the assistant quotes him saying.[7]

Photographic images could thus represent the universality of human experience and, because of the particular qualities of the medium as Steichen saw it—its "natural" communicative abilities and its powerful illusion of unmediated and "truthful" representation—they could be effective instruments of that universality as well. In an article published in *Daedalus* in 1960, Steichen stresses that possibility: "Long before the birth of a word language the caveman communicated by visual images. The invention of photography gave visual communication its most simple, direct, universal language." It may have been to stress this universal form of communication, often also attributed to music, that Steichen chose the image of the Peruvian Indian boy joyfully playing the flute as the emblem of the exhibit to punctuate its sequence at many intervals and to serve as the cover illustration of the book. Steichen's claim for the universal comprehensibility of the photographs seemed to be corroborated in the response enjoyed by the *Family of Man* exhibit: "The audiences not only understand this visual presentation, they also participate in it, and identify themselves with the images."[8]

20   In the aftermath of World War II and the Korean War, in view of an escalating Cold War and an increasing nuclear threat, and in the midst of growing movements of national liberation and decolonization, the invocation of human universality had the force of a powerful political statement, particularly emerging from the United States. To demonstrate an overriding human equality was to reinvoke Enlightenment notions of a universal brotherhood that directly contradicted all-too-recent Nazi ideologies of racial hierarchy which denied humanity to the greater part of the earth's population. The exhibition was an attempt to assert close human bonds across increasing political divisions between East and West, capitalism and communism, colonizers and colonized, rich and poor.

Appealing to the most compelling aspects of American liberalism, *The Family of Man* used the camera, the museum, and the book as tools of change aligned to political institutions such as the United Nations, which is itself prominently featured in the exhibit, "determined to reaffirm faith in fundamental human rights, in the dignity and worth of the human person, in the equal rights of men and women and of nations large and small" (184).

If today the familial humanism of Steichen's *Family of Man* appears naive in its too easy erasure of particularity and difference, we must remember the political context in which difference had so recently been used as a justification for genocide. Today, in the aftermath of the Cold War, the hopes of decolonization have shattered against the rise of new forms of racism and persecution. The memory of the Holocaust has become a postmemory. As American and Western European intellectuals continue to search for a usable discourse of commonality and difference and for forceful roles for the United States and Europe in a shifting global map, new humanisms and universalisms and new invocations of Enlightenment values are emerging. New photographic exhibits repeat the strategies Steichen made so successful. The familial photographic representations of *The Family of Man* might provide a measure of the contradictory grounds for this renewed interest in humanistic discourses.[9]

The key to *The Family of Man*'s appeal lies in the familial gaze it focuses on the global sphere with the aim of revealing points of intersection between familial relation, on the one hand, and cross-racial and cross-national interaction, on the other. A familial gaze can transform diversity into specular mirroring and can reshape global issues into domestic concerns.[10] It can undo the seemingly irreconcilable differences between Spiegelman's mice, cats, and pigs, revealing these diverse creatures with competing interests to all be equally and interrelatedly "human" instead.

The familial gaze emerges out of the elements of family photography. The illusion that photographs simply record a preexisting external reality, the fact that still photographs freeze particular moments in time, and the ambiguity that results from the still picture's absent context all help to perpetuate a mythology of the family as stable and united, static and monolithic. The photograph's perceived transparency and universal comprehensibility, combined with its pervasive presence within family life, at least in the West, enable Steichen to promote a liberal humanist agenda based on familiality. The positivist modes of reading that photography engendered, moreover, serve further to disguise the exhibit's intricate ideological constructedness. Thereby the exhibit and, with it, the institution of the museum itself, is encoded within the realm of everyday life. Inasmuch as it could be photographically recorded and disseminated, universal humanity can thus be normalized and made available as "real." On the level of representation itself, then, domesticity and transparency subsume the layered contradictions inherent in aesthetics and politics.

25   To use the notion of family as its primary instrument of universalization, *The Family of Man* needs to represent an image of familial relations that would be widely recognizable, applicable, and exportable. In Alan Sekula's terms, it "universalizes the bourgeois nuclear family, suggesting a globalized, utopian family album, a family romance imposed on every corner of the earth."[11] In doing so, it follows and popularizes the prevalent familial theories of the 1950s—Talcott Parson's structural functionalism and Claude Lévi-Strauss's universalized incest taboo. Parsons universalizes the nuclear family as the most advanced and, in his terms, differentiated and progressive of familial organizations, based on strict gender divisions into male instrumentality and female expressiveness. One could argue that Steichen follows Parsons in promoting the patriarchal bourgeois nuclear family as the norm and standard against which other arrangements are measured. And one could see, as well, a reflection of Lévi-Strauss's structural anthropology. The incest taboo, Lévi-Strauss's universalized Oedipus complex, as well as the system of reciprocal exchanges of women, and the universally present relations of consanguinity, alliance, and descent, demonstrate the characteristics of the modern nuclear family to be structurally equivalent to other arrangements rather than specific to industrial capitalism.

Sekula usefully invokes the Freudian notion of the family romance to underscore Steichen's universalization of one prevalent familial model. Freud's "family romance" is a shared individual fantasy of mythic origin: the child's dream of parental omnipotence and infallibility which, when shattered, becomes the fantasy of replacing the father with a different, a richer and more noble one, in Freud's terms, a king or emperor.[12] This is more than a sexual fantasy encouraging oedipal desire: it is also a fantasy of class aspiration, an economic fantasy of enrichment. The family romance is primarily a narrative structure, making narrative space for the ways in which the family becomes a locus for intersecting dreams of sexual fulfillment, property, and social status. Located in childhood, it reveals a point where public and private, social and psychological structures can collapse within one another. Photographs enable us to locate some of these fantasy structures in the visual and to read, through the monocular lens determining the image's structure, the circumscribed direction that fantasy takes.

The Family of Man disseminates the fantasies of Steichen and his contemporaries, located in a specific space and time and articulated from a particular viewpoint. It can be read as a narrative of the idealization of the bourgeois nuclear family and its social, psychological, and economic foundations. Including the culturally and economically "other" in the exhibit undergirds the power of the exhibit's author and organizer as both the subject and the object of his own fantasy. Victor Burgin's 1990 digital work "Family Romances" invokes Steichen's *Family of Man* in just this spirit:

> Identification with the perfect parents in an international arena underlies the 1955 photographic exhibition *The Family of Man*. Prevalent opinion in the United States during the immediate post-war years saw the country as being in a tutelary position of benevolent authority towards the rest of the world. Appropriately, the particular version of 'the family' which this exhibition projected into every part of the globe was the domestic ideal of the Eisenhower years.[13]

In the conception of Steichen's exhibit, the family functions as an idealized haven of potential protection from discord and war. At the same time the family becomes an instrument of political intervention: in its role of fragile space itself in need of protection from the dangers of global politics, it attempts to act as an effective sphere of influence and transformation. If Art Spiegelman uses family pictures to reveal the ironies of this familial mythology in the face of war and genocide, on the one hand, and the family's own Oedipal psychodramas, on the other, Steichen tries to revive this same traditional familial mythos as a means of positive political action. But can it still be workable "after such knowledge"?

The Familial Gaze

Steichen's "family album" progresses thematically from love and marriage, to birth, childhood, adolescence and courtship, adulthood, and branches out to consider aspects of adult life, such as work, dancing, singing, eating, religion, death and mourning, war, loneliness, politics and justice. It returns to childhood at the end, opening out toward new beginnings. While some of the images conform to the conventions of familial snapshot photography, others are more akin to ethnographic photography, documentary photography, and art photography. Steichen's album, moreover, does not just have the function Bourdieu associates with the family album, that of "solemnizing and immortalizing the high points of family life" (*Photography,* 19). Although "happy" and poignant images predominate, there are also pictures of hunger, begging, war, loneliness, and grief, even a few images of domestic discord. Steichen does not attempt to suppress the underside of his "universal brotherhood." If this is a family album, it is clearly one that stretches the limits of the genre, not least because of the diverse cultures and physiognomies it includes: couples from France and the USA kiss or marry next to couples from Japan, Czechoslovakia, India, Sweden, and Mexico; children from India, South Africa, Botswana, Austria, and the USA play near one another; farmers from Iran, Indonesia, Japan, China, Italy, Ireland, and the USA till the land in the same exhibit space.

In his exhibit Steichen had to create an identificatory, familial look which would effect the affiliative mutuality and specularity to which he aspired: "They recognized each other." He had to suture his viewers into images most of which are bound to diverge radically from their own self-representations and their own habitual processes of recognition. The spectatorial look invited by the exhibit and album had to be able to transform a global space of vast differences and competing interests into a domestic space structured by likeness and specularity.

It is my argument that the family is in itself traversed and constituted by a series of "familial" looks that place different individuals into familial relation within a field of vision. When I visually engage with others familially, when I look through my family's albums, I enter a network of looks that dictate affiliative feelings, positive or negative feelings of recognition that can span miles and generations: I "recognize" my great-grandmother because I am told that she is an ancestor, not because she is otherwise in any way similar or identifiable to me. It is the context of the album that creates the relationship, not necessarily any preexistent sign. And when I look at her picture, I feel as though she also recognizes me. We share a familial visual field in which we see even as we are seen. When Barthes finds the winter-garden photograph, he knows his mother and also wants to be known by her. When Artie looks at Richieu's picture, he both sees and wants to be seen, desiring thus to bridge an unbridgeable distance and to undo the effects of death and separation. As Steichen puts it, "in corroboration of the words of a Japanese poet, 'When you look into a mirror, you do not see your reflection, your reflection sees you.' "

When Barthes omits the winter-garden photo of his mother from his book, he delineates the boundaries of the familial look and excludes his readers from it. Steichen tries an opposite strategy: he subsumes a complex set of intersecting gazes and looks under an overarching affiliative look of familiality. The subjects photographed look at one another within the picture and at the photographer who looks at them, and the reader and museum visitor observe this interaction, usually through the photographer's lens and perspective.[14] In *The Family of Man* these looks are mediated by enormous cultural, economic, gender, and racial differences, and by the institutional gazes of ethnography, anthropology, tourism, journalism, or art photography. But, in Steichen's conception, they are also mediated by a familial gaze of mutual recognition which is meant to override these alienating forces dividing subject from object. What specific strategies and principles of selection did Steichen devise in order to further and expand this transcendent recognition, investing it with global proportions? How does his human family metaphor work and what can it tell us about the family's representational frames?

Reading the exhibit, we can identify several predominant strategies, strategies that allow us not only to understand the workings of *The Family of Man* but to explore, as well, some of the more troubling aspects of familial looking: individualization, naturalization, decontextualization, differentiation within identification, and the universalization of one hegemonic familial organization. Some of these strategies have been identified and virulently criticized by commentators at various moments since the exhibit enjoyed its monumental success. These critiques, in themselves—most notably by Roland Barthes in the 1950s, Edmundo Desnoes in the 1960s, and Alan Sekula in the late 1970s—form an integral part of the story of *The Family of Man*. In looking at what makes Steichen's vision work so powerfully for his audiences, one inevitably encounters, as well, the problematic strategies he used, and these critical readings inform my reading of Steichen's exhibit. Interestingly, however, the 1980s and 1990s have given rise to more recuperative and sympathetic readings such as Eric J. Sandeen's effort to "recover some of that founding power"—perhaps an echo of the new humanisms of this, our, moment.[15]

The specularity that Steichen envisioned—to produce the sense that "everybody's the same"—had to occur on the level of the individual and of relations among individuals, and, in fact, the album's images are predominantly limited to individuals and couples, removed from their social, political, and economic context. Thus, the album begins with a series of couples of diverse origin, hugging and kissing, in various poses of erotic attachment.

Robert Doisneau's famous picture is emblematic, I believe, for the entire album (Figure 5). The picture is clearly taken in Paris on the banks of the Seine. In the foreground a small child stands on a bench looking left, beyond the frame; a policeman stands in the center, looking at a woman sitting on a bench at frame right. She contemplates, quite intently, a kissing couple barely visible through the bars of the fence that divides the two planes of the photograph, because they are standing behind the three central figures on a lower level of the park. The kiss completely absorbs them, but evades the authoritative gaze of the policeman and that of the child. Only the woman sees them, whether judgmentally, longingly, or approvingly, we don't know. The kiss occurs on a different visual plane, outside the space of the social, challenging the nuclear family structure that dominates the foreground, with its mother, father, and child figures. These seemingly "private" candid images, which give the erroneous impression of occurring outside of the space of the camera's surveillance or intrusion, make the position of the camera inherently ambiguous and contradictory. Love conquers all, love attracts our spectatorial look, deflecting our attention from the public life depicted in the rest of the image. Global, legal, and social issues are addressed on the individual and the familial

Figure 5   *Galant Vert Square,* by Robert Doisneau, c. 1945.

Courtesy of the Los Angeles County Museum of Art, Gift of anonymous donor, Los Angeles, AC 199.233.60. Photograph copyright © 2005 Museum Associates/LACMA.

levels: the background of the image moves into the foreground and absorbs our look. Like the woman, we conspire with the couple against the policeman. Eroticizing the social with her/our desire, we arrive at Steichen's "brotherhood": a seemingly singular, individual connection, forging familial ties, across private/public divides.[16]

The fantasy that structures the entire exhibit is this fantasy of the hug and the kiss with which it starts, the fantasy that global, legal, and social problems might be resolved as we hug, kiss, and make up. The primary unit of interaction in Steichen's family is the couple: heterosexual courting or married couples, two children play-

ing, two women talking, two men working together. "We two form a multitude" is the recurring phrase that runs over several pages depicting a diverse series of couples. But we must consider that the many couples, enacting this friendship and marriage fantasy throughout the album, are all, with the exception of one image of two young boys, heterosexual and of the same race or ethnicity: no chances are taken in this familial solution to global strife.

To consolidate the individual affiliation and identification between the people in the audience and the people in the pictures, the exhibit invokes nature over culture, thus diminishing, if not erasing, pronounced differences due to culture and history, and also thus naturalizing and sentimentalizing the institution of the family. Roland Barthes points this out in one of the most scathing of his *Mythologies* devoted to the Paris showing of "La Grande Famille des hommes" in 1956: "This myth of the human 'condition' rests on a very old mystification, which always consists in placing Nature at the bottom of History."[17] The exhibit is framed by majestic images of sky, stars, and oceans, risking that the important distinction between "nature" and "human nature," between the biological and the social/psychological will be blurred. Thus, within this frame viewers experience human "nature" as pervasive, as common to all, as undifferentiated, like the ocean and the sky. To place human life on the level of nature, Steichen needs to tease out the most fundamental elements of human ritual, recognizable and acceptable to everyone in their sameness and repetition as universal.

The strong emphasis on nature and its broad definition, covering human nature as well, carries the risk that events represented in the album will be ascribed to human nature, thus erasing historical agency. For example, viewers might attribute the images of hunger, deportation, devastated cities, war, and violent death, as well as the images of strife within the family, to a constant human nature. And if the album indeed implies that war is as natural and as universal as kissing and singing, then it might also appear to be as inevitable, directly contradicting Steichen's explicit purpose of invoking universality to prevent war. The risk, for example, is that viewers might read the large transparency of the H-bomb explosion which took up an entire room at the end of the exhibition as "natural."

Could it be that agency and political change, clearly among Steichen's primary goals, are actually antithetical to the familial look the album fosters, a look based on the elevation of nature over culture and history, and that, in fact, Steichen's means do not ultimately support his ends? If the exhibit expresses a wish or desire, a utopian aspiration on Steichen's part, thus encouraging intervention to make his utopia a reality, he may well be hampered by the indexical and iconic aspects of photography, by the fact that photographs tend to be read as mimetic representations of what is rather than as wishful constructions of what might be.

Perhaps the most troubling aspect of *The Family of Man* is the decontextualized exhibition of the images. Although the country of origin is provided on each photograph, they are not dated, which gives the impression of synchrony, the antithesis of the possibility of change—Matthew Brady's civil war image is next to images of World War II, for example. If this juxtaposition is meant to emphasize a reassuringly unchanging continuity in family relations and human nature to support the universality of the album it also serves to underscore the perpetuity of hunger and war. If this repetition and continuity are inherent in the recognition of the familial look, they also directly contradict the possibility of intervention and transformation, especially because this familial look represses its disidentifications and the specificity of its temporal and geographical location, and thus further isolates itself from agency.

By radically de- and recontextualizing the images, Steichen exerts strong authorial control over the reading process, invoking and cultivating an affiliative look that underscores similarity and relationship, even as it ultimately represses agency and change. As Barthes concludes: "I rather fear that the final justification of all this Adamism is to give to the immobility of the world the alibi of a 'wisdom' and a 'lyricism' which only make the gestures of man look eternal the better to defuse them" (*Mythologies*, 102).

Even granting that Steichen's strategies of individualization, naturalization, and decontex-

40

Figure 6   Courtesy of Vito Fiorenza/the Museum of Modern Art, New York.

tualization serve the larger purpose of constructing an effective familial spectatorial gaze, however, I look at some of the album's pages and, where I should see specularity, I begin to see subtle differences. Even as the family album is enlarged to include diversity, a centrally North American gaze asserts reassuring limits. Let us consider, for example, the images of four extended families consciously posing as units for the camera (Figures 6–9). They are all rural farming families and thus similar to one another. But while the Sicilian and the U.S. family are shown in indoor settings, the Japanese and Botswanan families are outdoors. And only the members of the U.S. family, though agricultural, participate in a tradition of representation: they are surrounded by family portraits that grace their walls. Such a subtle play with difference within identity might serve on the one hand to establish the specularity desired—*the Bushmen have families like us they are farmers like us*—even as it confirms, on the other, Western museum-visitors in their own distinct identity: *We, unlike them, have our distinct domestic spaces, we have pictures on our walls.* From this insight only a small step leads to the next—*We*

can admit their picture into our album, onto our coffee table without threat, because their difference has been acknowledged. They do not threaten to invade our space; they can become like us, but we don't have to become like them.

The exhibit and the album shape an ultimately reassuring dissimilarity even within their overriding universalizing frame, assuring the implied European and the European-American viewer that their humanism is, in

Figure 7   Courtesy of Carl Mydans/Time Life Pictures/Getty Images.

Figure 8   Courtesy of Nat Farbman/Time Life Pictures/Getty Images.

Etienne Balibar's terms, a "humanism of differences" and not a "humanism of identity" or of "absolute civic equality."[18] Two photographs of mothers, each with two small children, illustrate this (Figures 10, 11). In the picture taken by Wayne Miller in the USA, a young white mother is lying on a bed looking into space, just past the little girl to her right, who is cradling a small baby. The three figures form a closed and close triangle: their bodies are interconnected in the traditional iconography of Madonna with children. The camera is clearly a familiar object that does not intrude on the intimacy of the scene: it should not surprise us to learn that this is a picture of the photographer's wife and children. Maternity is sentimentalized in the softness of the pose and the light, and is seen to pass down from mother to daughter-apprentice. The figures are comfort-

ably settled in a protected domestic space and iconographic representation that both seem to disguise the mother's distracted unfocused look, the absence of a visual interaction between her and her children.

An entirely different image also from the USA is Consuelo Kanaga's best-known

Figure 9   Courtesy of Nina Leen/Time Life Pictures/Getty Images.

photograph and Steichen's favorite in the entire exhibit. Photographed from a very low angle, it depicts a tall and very thin black woman standing in front of a white brick wall, resting one arm on a small boy at her right side while a little girl stands to her left. The three figures look not at each other but at the camera. The woman is wearing a much-too-small sweater with two safety pins in front, and a scarf tied into a turban. The children are healthy-looking and cleanly though poorly dressed. Their looks are intent but not easily readable: the mother looks tired and resigned to a tough life, the children look confrontational, perhaps suspicious or curious, maybe intrigued by the large camera and the itinerant white woman who came into their community to take pictures. In spite of the

protective gesture with which the mother holds the children close to her, there is no warmth or comfort in this picture, no domesticity or circularity. The three figures are more directly engaged with the intrusive photographer than with one another.

Whereas Miller's image fits into a long-standing tradition of mother-child representation—from Leonardo, Raphael, and del Sarto—Kanaga's echoes the ethnographic iconography of the 1930s images of the Farm Security Administration, amply represented in other parts of the exhibit. Maternity and mother-child relations are very different for these two families. Perhaps, then, we are not all the same just because we all—culturally—share maternity and childhood. The Cuban writer

45

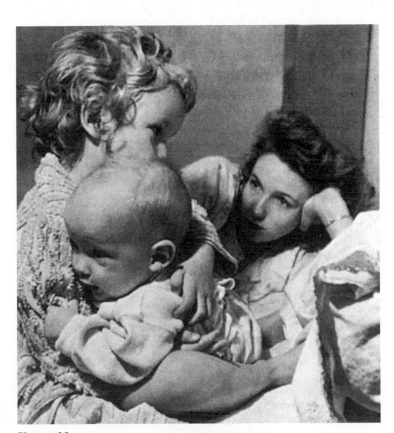

Figure 10 Courtesy of Wayne Miller/Magnum Photos.

Edmundo Desnoes, revealing some of his own cultural prejudices, writes in 1967 of the "visual lies," such as this one, which structure *The Family of Man:* "an indigenous New Guinea couple is hugging next to couples from Italy, North America and France; love in the jungle and in ignorance is not the same as in civilization and among commodities."[19] Roland Barthes's comment is even more biting: "But why not ask the parents of Emmet Till, the young Negro assassinated by the Whites, what *they* think of *The Great Family of Man?* . . . It will never be fair to confuse in a purely gestural identity the colonial and the Western worker (let us also ask the North African workers of the Goutte d'Or district in Paris what they think of *The Great Family of Man)*" (*Mythologies,* 101–102).

But is not the establishment of difference, albeit unconscious, as essential to the exhibit's success as the cultivation of similarity? Does not the African-American mother in her very contrast, in her external unspecified location, confirm the white mother in her domesticity and specificity? That contrast is necessary to the European-American museum visitor's look, a look which must mix a mirroring recognition with a sense of distinct identity. Barthes and Desnoes object by invoking the excluded look of Emmet Till's parents or of the guest-worker from the Goutte d'Or. As left-wing intellectuals, they are trained to perceive the omissions that Steichen's strategies disguise. Contrary to what Steichen might have desired, the look that is cultivated in *The Family of Man* is the look of the middle-class European and European-American museumgoer. If it is a familial look, then it illustrates how the familial look operates in relation to disidentification as well as identification, how it invokes alterity as well as identity, how it insists on drawing up boundaries that ultimately enclose it.

Steichen inadvertently admits this in one of his most ambiguous narratives about foreign showings of the exhibit: "On the final day of the exhibition [in Guatemala City], several thousand Indians from the hills of Guatemala came on foot or mule back to see it. An American visitor said it was like a religious experience to see these barefoot country people who could not read or write walk silently through the exhibition gravely studying each picture with rapt attention" (*A Life in Photography,* ch. 13). If this is "like a religious experience," it is clearly that of the American visitor and not the Guatemalan Indians. For him it would confirm the fact that even though he could read and write and they could not, photographic images offered a shared medium of communication. But what did the Indian visitors see? Did they recognize themselves, did they recognize their similarity to the European subjects, or the European subjects' similarity to them? Did they enjoy seeing themselves as represented by others, a decentered and therefore potentially illuminating look?

The images themselves would make that difficult, for even though South American native populations are represented along with many other non-Western subjects, those images are overwhelmingly attributed to European and American photographers and originate in journals or photographic services such as *Life, Magnum,* or *Rapho Guillumette.* In the photographs' original contexts of production, the camera gazes tended to belong to European and American photographers who created images from their own perspectives, mostly for their own viewers. For example, we see Guatemala through Lisa Larsen's image published in *Life* (p. 29), Cuba through Eve Arnold of *Magnum* (p. 31), Botswana through Nat Farbman of *Life* (p. 35), and South Africa through Constance Stuart of *Black Star* (p. 34). There are exceptions: most of the Russian photographs are from the Soviet service *Sovfoto;* many Mexican images are by Mexican photographer Alvarez-Bravo; and the Polish images are by Roman Vishniac. Still, 163 of 273 photographers are from the United States and approximately 88 of the 503 pictures originated in *Life* magazine. Just as Steichen self-confirmingly

Figure 11   *She Is a Tree of Life to Them,* by Consuelo Kanaga, 1950.

Courtesy of the Brooklyn Museum, gift of Wallace B. Putnam from the estate of Consuelo Kanaga, 82.65.2250.

quotes the line of "a Japanese poet" but does not name him or her, so the exhibit's images grant a more developed subjectivity to the Western subject and viewer.

Even if the Guatemalan Indians might enjoy seeing themselves as they are seen by others, they could not help noticing the power differentials, and the overwhelming control of the medium exercised by a specifically located European or European-American gaze. How are we to imagine these encounters between the photographers and their subjects? What kinds of power and economic relationships does the exhibition's familial discourse suppress? I thought about this when, in 1995, I visited the Isla del Sol on Lake Titicaca between Bolivia and Peru. As we tourists disembarked for a brief visit of the island and a climb to the spring that is said to be the source of Inca civilization, we were accosted by a group of native women and children eager to sell us inexpensive hand-made souvenirs: woven bracelets and hair ribbons, flowers and herbs. It was clear that this isolated population depended on the tourists for their livelihood. An economy of dollars, Bolivianos, and pesos had developed there with tourists acting as money changers as well as consumers. But visits seemed to be infrequent and, that day, the tourists were tired from their long trips over the mountains and were unwilling participants in the exchange. As a last resort many of the local women, dressed in the colorful dresses and the bowler hats of the Andes, brought up another suggestion: "Fotografia! fotografia! con niño! un dolar." "Take my picture, with my baby, for a dollar."

50   In selling their own image along with other souvenirs, the women on the Isla del Sol expose the economic underpinnings of a relationship the tourists wish to perceive as mutual. The women expose the inequities that the tourist industry and the ideologies of *The Family of Man* try to disguise. When North American or European visitors, whether ordinary tourists or art photographers, come into a context like the Isla del Sol and the local inhabitants become flat images to be shown off in albums or exhibited in museums they will never see, then the relationship between photographer and model becomes a relationship of unequal exchange which must be compensated, financially or otherwise. The women of the Isla del Sol know something that the producers of *The Family of Man* and many generations of tourists have wished to forget. And Steichen's exhibit works powerfully to disguise this knowledge. [. . .]

Looking Back

If *The Family of Man* is, in Alan Sekula's terms, a "guidebook for the collapse of the political into the familial" ("The Traffic in Photographs," 95), the camera, the family picture, and the family album are effective instruments of this collapse. The appeal of large-scale exhibits and coffee-table books such as *The Family of Man* has never waned. Several new such books have appeared in the 1990s, for example, the expensive *The Circle of Life: Rituals from the Human Family Album*, edited by David Cohen (1991), with images of rites of passage from different cultures throughout the world. The rationale for this book, uncannily reminiscent of Steichen, is articulated through the words of the anthropologist Barbara Myerhoff: "Given the fragmented, complex, and disorderly nature of human experience, rites of passage are more important than ever to orient and motivate us during life crises" (142). More recently, the United Nations Population Fund sponsored *Material World: A Global Family Portrait*, edited by Peter Menzel, featuring a series of images of families from around the world depicted with all of their material possessions spread out all around them.[20] The book's inside cover reproduces currency bills from many countries signaling that the global family is differentiated economically and that, indeed, money will shape the images and their content. The text reproduces statements by the different photographers, outsiders who selected the families in different countries and spent a few days with them in their homes to take these unusual pictures of people and things. Although *Material World* is a great deal more self-conscious about the complex factors shaping global interactions than *The Family of Man* and although its images are carefully contextualized and historicized, it still fundamentally seems to hold to a notion of a universal humanity, suggesting that if we only had the same amount of money we might all be the same. Its very format—the large-scale global exhibit based on individual families representing their individual countries and enacting cross-cultural relationships—disallows any deeper political or ideological analysis.

No simple notion of a "human family" can hold in the 1990s. Even the new universalism of theorists like Tzvetan Todorov wishes to find the "universality of the human race" through a systematic scrutiny of particularities, not in a simple specularity. Todorov's integrationism, like Jürgen Habermas's Enlightenment humanist community, does not erase otherness and power, but wishes to respond with ideals of civility and mutuality, a recognition of fundamentally shared values and a model of responsible citizenship.[21] In this spirit, the family still serves as an operative unit of these new humanisms and universalisms.

Notes

1. George Vecxey, "Riddick Bowe Has Family in Scarsdale," *New York Times* (Feb. 3, 1993): B7.
2. Jo Spence and Patricia Holland, eds., *Family Snaps: The Meanings of Domestic Photography* (London: Virago, 1991), p. 4.
3. Pierre Bourdieu, *Photography: A Middle-Brow Art,* trans. Shaun Whiteside (Stanford: Stanford University Press, 1990), p. 19.
4. Laura Wexler's "Seeing Sentiment: Photography, Race, and the Innocent Eye," in Elizabeth Abel, Helene Moglen, and Barbara Smith, eds., *Female Subjects in Black and White: Race, Feminism, Psychoanalysis* (Berkeley: University of California Press, 1997), examines this issue in turn-of-the-century photography.
5. Edward Steichen, *The Family of Man* (New York: Museum of Modern Art, 1955), pp. 4, 5.
6. Edward Steichen, *A Life in Photography* (New York: Doubleday, 1966), ch. 13.
7. Rita Sylvan with Avis Berman, "Edward Steichen, A Memoir, the Making of *The Family of Man,"* *Connoisseur* 218 (Feb. 1988): 121.
8. Rpt. in Nathan Lyons, ed., *Photographers on Photography: A Critical Anthology* (Englewood Cliffs, N.J.: Prentice Hall, 1966), p. 107.
9. For an excellent discussion of the persistence of universalism see the special issue of *Differences* 7, no. 1 (Spring 1995), entitled "Universalism."
10. Kaja Silverman's distinction between idiopathic and heteropathic identification provides a useful model for this process, though the familial gaze adds another dimension to the notion of identification. To admit the other into one's familial image offers different and broader possibilities from admitting the other into one's image of self. The latter process, as Silverman shows, is most often incorporative and cannibalistic, ideopathic. But the former, especially if based on the connection between familiality and humanity, is no less problematic. The question of this chapter is whether the familial gaze can allow for a truly heteropathic nonappropriative form of affiliation. See Kaja Silverman, *The Threshold of the Visible World* (New York, Routledge, 1996), esp. ch. 1.
11. Alan Sekula, "The Traffic in Photographs," in *Photography Against the Grain: Essays and Photo Works, 1973–1983* (Halifax: Press of Nova Scotia College of Art and Design, 1984), p. 89.

12. Sigmund Freud, "Family Romances" ("Der Familienroman der Neurotiker," 1908), in *The Standard Edition of the Complete Works of Sigmund Freud,* ed. James Strachey, 24 vols. (London: Hogarth, 1953–1974), vol. 9, pp. 237–241.

13. Victor Burgin, "Family Romance," in Lucien Taylor, ed., *Visualizing Theory: Selected Essays from V.A.R., 1990–1994* (New York: Routledge, 1994), pp. 452, 453.

14. In his "Looking at Photographs," Victor Burgin defines "four basic types of look in the photograph: the look of the camera as it photographs the 'pro-photographic' event; the look of the viewer as he or she looks at the photograph; the 'intra-diegetic' looks exchanged between people (actors) depicted in the photograph (and/or looks from actors toward objects); and the look the actor may direct at the camera" Victor Burgin, "Looking at Photographs," in *Thinking Photography* (London: Macmillan, 1982), p. 148. See also Catherine Lutz and Jane Collin's "The Photograph as an Intersection of Gazes," in their *Reading National Geographic* (Chicago: University of Chicago Press, 1993), pp. 187–216.

15. Echoing Steichen's own motivations, Sandeen concludes his introduction thus: "As I sit before my computer screen in the summer of 1994, Yugoslavia is devouring itself in ethnic and religious warfare. To think of humankind as one, in these circumstances, may not be an unhealthy exercise." *Picturing an Exhibition: "The Family of Man" and 1950's America* (Albuquerque: University of New Mexico Press, 1995). Sandeen's reading, however, is closely contextualized and thus does distance itself from Steichen's easy universalism. Sandeen also points out the difficulty of reading Steichen's exhibit, which, in effect, has disappeared. Using, as I do, the book and installation phonographs as well as published contemporary accounts, is less than an ideal solution. Sandeen spent years trying to reconstruct the exhibit itself, through conversations with Steichen's assistant Wayne Miller. It is no wonder he feels as close to it as he does.

16. The spontaneity of this photograph is called into question by the recent suits brought against Doisneau which reveal that many of his kissing couples might have been actors hired by him to stage the street kissing scenes.

17. Roland Barthes, *Mythologies,* trans. Annette Lavers (New York: Hill and Wang, 1972), p. 101.

18. Etienne Balibar, "Racism and Nationalism," in Etienne Balibar and Immanuel Wallerstein, eds., *Race, Nation, Class: Ambiguous Identities* (London: Verso, 1991), pp. 63, 64.

19. Edmundo Desnoes, *Punto de Vista* (Havana: Instituto de Libro, 1967), pp. 82, 83 (my translation). See also Julia Lesage's trans., "The Photographic Image of Underdevelopment," *Jump Cut* 33 (Feb. 1988): 69–81.

20. David Cohen, ed., *The Circle of Life: Rituals from the Human Family Album* (New York: HarperCollins, 1991); Peter Menzel, ed., *Material World: A Global Family Portrait* (San Francisco: Sierra Club, 1994).

21. Christian Boltanski, *Menschlich* (Köln: Thouet Verlag, 1994).

Re-reading/Conversations with the Text

1. Hirsch's essay asks to what extent the family photo album is able to accommodate diversity, and to what extent it subsumes otherness into "the fantasy that 'everyone's the same.' " Reread the essay, marking passages (and images) that address this question. In particular, is *The Family of Man* exhibit able to accommodate diversity and difference? How do the conventions of family photography enable and/or constrain the representation of otherness?

2. Hirsch identifies three strategies used by *The Family of Man* exhibit to connect family photographs to the political concept of human rights: individuation, naturalization, and decontextualization. Re-examine three of the images included with this essay: Robert Doisneau's picture of a kissing couple in Paris, Wayne Miller's photo of a white American mother gazing at her children, and Consuelo Kanaga's image of an African American mother with her arms around her children. Consider the ways in which each image participates in—or problematizes—the three strategies identified by Hirsch.

3. Hirsch's interpretation of *The Family of Man* exhibit indicates a strong tendency to universalize the nuclear Western family, in effect positioning it as the "natural" model. According to Hirsch, what is this model of family like? What current cultural narratives about families (or "the family") can you find that perform a function similar to the one Hirsch characterizes?

Re-seeing and Re-writing

1. As Hirsch describes *The Family of Man* exhibit, she lists a catalog of various factors that might inform how one looks at the images: "[T]hese looks are mediated by enormous cultural, economic, gender, and racial differences, and by the institutional gazes of ethnography, anthropology, tourism, journalism, or art photography." After selecting a family photograph from a recent issue of *National Geographic* or supplied by your instructor, choose three of these different types of gazes through which to read the photo. Compose three paragraphs in which you offer different interpretations of the image, and comment on how your reading changes with each way of looking.

2. Choose a memorable family picture about which to write. Compose two separate, page-long descriptions of plausible narratives contained in the photograph. Shape one description so that it emulates a romantic and idealized family mythos and embellish the other description to provide an alternative interpretation. The purpose of this writing assignment is to encourage you to think about the various (and often contradictory) possibilities of reading a text, acknowledging in the process how these different interpretations can be plausible. What makes a reading "true" in this sense often depends on factors that exist outside of the image itself—the reader's attitude toward the text, the array of associations he or she makes with it, and so on.

In describing *The Family of Man* exhibition, Hirsch identifies the collapse of the political into the familial as one of the collection's central themes. In other words, she argues that the exhibit displaces political struggles onto the familial realm, and that by conforming to conventions of the "universal" family photograph, it erases cultural and historical differences. In what ways are representations of the family political, according to Hirsch? How is this theme also approached by bell hooks in "In Our Glory."

"Looking at Them Asleep" and "I Go Back to May 1937"

SHARON OLDS

David Leavitt has described **SHARON OLDS**'s poetry as exhibiting "lyrical acuity which is both purifying and redemptive. She sees description as a means to catharsis, and the result is impossible to forget" (www.albany.edu/writers_inst/olds.html). Currently, Olds is a professor at New York University, and she is one of the founding members of NYU's creative writing program for the disabled at Goldwater Hospital in NYC. Olds's focus in her poetry frequently reveals the complexity of everyday living—often with her family as the subject.

Looking at Them Asleep

When I come home late at night and go in to kiss the children,
I see my girl with her arm curled around her head,
her face deep in unconsciousness—so
deeply centered she is in her dark self,
5   her mouth slightly puffed like one sated but
slightly pouted like one who hasn't had enough,
her eyes so closed you would think they have rolled the
iris around to face the back of her head,
the eyeball marble-naked under that
10   thick satisfied desiring lid,
she lies on her back in abandon and sealed completion,
and the son in his room, oh the son he is sideways in his bed,
one knee up as if he is climbing
sharp stairs up into the night,
15   and under his thin quivering eyelids you
know his eyes are wide open and
staring and glazed, the blue in them so
anxious and crystally in all this darkness, and his
mouth is open, he is breathing hard from the climb
20   and panting a bit, his brow is crumpled
and pale, his long fingers curved,
his hand open, and in the center of each hand
the dry dirty boyish palm
resting like a cookie. I look at him in his
25   quest, the thin muscles of his arms
passionate and tense, I look at her with her
face like the face of a snake who has swallowed a deer,
content, content—and I know if I wake her she'll
smile and turn her face toward me though
30   half asleep and open her eyes and I
know if I wake him he'll jerk and say Don't and sit

up and stare about him in blue
unrecognition, oh my Lord how I
know these two. When love comes to me and says
35   What do you know, I say This girl, this boy.

I Go Back to May 1937

I see them standing at the formal gates of their colleges,
I see my father strolling out
under the ochre sandstone arch, the
red tiles glinting like bent
5   plates of blood behind his head, I
see my mother with a few light books at her hip
standing at the pillar made of tiny bricks with the
wrought-iron gate still open behind her, its
sword-tips black in the May air,
10   they are about to graduate, they are about to get married,
they are kids, they are dumb, all they know is they are
innocent, they would never hurt anybody.
I want to go up to them and say Stop,
don't do it—she's the wrong woman,
15   he's the wrong man, you are going to do things
you cannot imagine you would ever do,
you are going to do bad things to children,
you are going to suffer in ways you never heard of,
you are going to want to die. I want to go
20   up to them there in the late May sunlight and say it,
her hungry pretty blank face turning to me,
her pitiful beautiful untouched body,
his arrogant handsome blind face turning to me,
his pitiful beautiful untouched body,
25   but I don't do it. I want to live. I
take them up like the male and female
paper dolls and bang them together
at the hips like chips of flint as if to
strike sparks from them, I say
30   Do what you are going to do, and I will tell about it.

Re-reading/Conversations with the Text

1. The parent-focused poem "I Go Back to May 1937" is obviously focused on memory. Less obviously, the poem about her children ("Looking at Them Asleep") is also centered on memory. Discuss the way Sharon Olds calls upon and uses memory in these two poems.

2. Both of these poems are centered on seeing/looking. Go back and read each poem carefully and underline or highlight any reference to either. Is the "looking" that goes on in the poems always literal, or is it sometimes also metaphorical or figurative and less direct?

3. What is the narrative behind each poem? Retell each poem in a few summary lines to see if you can capture the basic narrative. Next, consider the way that Olds highlights, enhances, transforms, and accentuates the narrative. Make a list of devices that she uses to expand upon the narrative behind each poem.

Re-seeing/Re-writing

1. Build a double-sided biography of a person: Locate in your own family album, or the family album of someone else (online, etc.), a person represented in the middle generation—as both parent and child. Write a biographical narrative of that person. Uncover and reconstruct that person's story in the family from that "between" space. If possible, use an interview with that person and actual photos from both directions of his or her life (as parent and as child) to organize your biography. You may also use official records and stories from others to build your account.

2. Conduct research around poets who have written about their parents or their children. You might try popular song lyrics, as well. Choose one or two poems you find particularly interesting and write an essay about the way this other poet represents parents or children, as compared or contrasted to the way Sharon Olds does in these two poems. In your analysis, focus on the way the two poets use their memory and storytelling capabilities (narrative) in the poems.

Intertext

Both Sharon Olds's poems and Mark Jeffreys's essay are characterized by careful details as well as significant absences. Write a comparative essay that addresses how each work presents family details while also shadowing/hiding absences. What is the function of "absence" (or what is not said or present) in each work?

Research Prompts
FAMILIAL GAZES

Option #1:

Families and Reality Television

This option asks you to choose several episodes of a reality television show that focuses on families or family issues. Analyze the representations of family and family life as they are exhibited in your chosen episodes. To whom do these shows appeal? Whose stories (narratives) are prioritized? Whose experiences do such stories represent? Whose stories are not represented? What conceptions of family are presented to the audience? How do these shows challenge or reinforce "traditional" notions of family? What cultural or historical factors might contribute to the visibility and acceptability of certain depictions of the family? How do your secondary sources account for these kinds of shows? What trends within the themes of family and family life do critics discuss in regards to your primary text(s)? How do critics analyze the families in your primary texts in terms of larger social issues or concerns? How does your analysis extend, complicate, or challenge the secondary readings?

Option #2:

Political Campaign Rhetoric and Families

This option asks you to analyze the rhetoric of political advertisements that address the issues surrounding families and education. To what kinds of audience do these advertisements appeal? Whose stories (narratives) are represented? Whose stories are not represented? How do these advertisements define family values? How do the candidates use the rhetoric of family values? To what degree do these advertisements reinforce "traditional" notions of family? How do these advertisements complicate or extend "traditional" notions of family? What cultural, historical, and/or political factors might contribute to the visibility and acceptability of certain depictions of families within the campaign? How do your secondary sources answer these questions (or questions like them)? Do these secondary sources rely more upon description or interpretation of the ads? How does your own analysis extend, complicate, or challenge the secondary readings?

Option #3:

Rhetorical Analysis of Family-Focused Web Sites

This option asks you to choose and analyze several of the Web sites that focus on families and/or issues surrounding families. For example, you could examine Web sites that address the issues surrounding adoption, foster families, single parenting, gay/lesbian parenting, etc. What kinds of terminology do the Web sites use to represent families? How do the Web sites define family values? To what degree do these Web sites reinforce "traditional" notions of family? How do these Web sites complicate or extend "traditional" notions of family? What are the consequences of these complications and extensions? Whose stories (narratives) are represented? Whose stories are not represented? What cultural, historical, and/or political factors might contribute to the visibility and acceptability of certain depictions of families within the organization and its materials? How do your secondary sources answer these questions (or questions like them)? Do these secondary sources rely more upon description or interpretation of the sites? How does your own analysis extend, complicate, or challenge the secondary readings?

NATIONAL GAZES
Witnessing Nations

The photographs that move from personal and familial contexts into public arenas . . . are restless images, changing meaning and moving onward, asking us to pay attention to the stories, both declarative and secretive, that they tell.

–MARITA STURKEN

KEY RHETORICAL CONCEPTS

context   metaphor   metonymy

Critical Intersections: Familial and National Gazes

I N THE PREVIOUS CHAPTER, WE INTRODUCED THE CONCEPT OF **FAMILIAL GAZES** as "lenses through which families see and understand themselves." We examined the multiple meanings of family photographs and family photo albums in order to see how certain memories and narratives are highlighted and others are obscured. This chapter looks at how certain national memories and narratives are prioritized in images, but also at the way(s) in which familial and national memories intersect. Consider, for example, the use of family photographs and personal possessions in national acts of commemoration, such as those left at the Oklahoma City Memorial. Such photos take on a public and even national function; they become part of an imagined collective *national gaze* and memory (see Figures 4.1 and 4.2 below).

Or consider "The Tower of Faces" located at the center of the U.S. Holocaust Memorial Museum (see Figure 4.3). This is a collection of several hundred sepia-toned photographs of people who lived in the

Critical Frame

159

Figure 4.1 Oklahoma City National Memorial at night.

Courtesy of Steve Liss/Corbis Sigma.

Lithuanian shtetl of Ejszyszki, which was destroyed by a mobile Nazi unit in 1941, leaving no survivors. In this example, ordinary portraits of individuals, groups, and family rituals come to represent Jewish prewar life, a life that was all but obliterated. When we look at these images of family rituals and rites of passage, we can be reminded of our own family albums and of our own attempts to create and preserve memories. "The Tower of Faces" thus encourages a familial gaze as it prompts museum visitors to identify with the images; but the images, and the museum more broadly, also prompt a **national gaze**—an imagined, collective lens through which the nation is seen and understood by its members and that creates and/or presumes a sense of national identity and belonging. In doing so, the exhibit brings out the powerful intersections between familial and national gazes "as media of mourning."[1]

One might argue that the U.S. Holocaust Memorial Museum's location adjacent to the National Mall in Washington, DC, alongside other prominent national memorials, positions Holocaust memory squarely within the U.S. national gaze. But, as James Young argues in his essay "Memory and the Politics of Identity,"[2] the museum also creates a rhetorical vision that masks the history of racial and ethnic discrimination in the United States. As Young suggests, visitors may identify with many of the seemingly ordinary family photos in "The Tower of Faces," but they do not often imagine themselves as potential victims in the present day—indeed, they are encouraged instead to imagine themselves as belonging to a nation of liberators, a nation

Figure 4.2 A stuffed toy sits on one of the small chairs at the Oklahoma City National Memorial, which has 168 chairs representing each of the victims of the 1995 bombing of the federal building.

Courtesy of Jeff Mitchell/Reuters/Corbis Images.

that, in fighting and winning World War II, saved many other families just like the ones represented in the photographs.

As this example shows, national images, like family photographs, acquire meaning in context. We use the term **context** here to refer to both the *spatial* locations (architectural structures, cityscapes, landscapes, and so on) and the *temporal* locations (certain moments in time) in which images appear.

This unit asks you to consider the prominence of visual images in U.S. commemorative practices, as well as the role of memorials and monuments in the (self-)portrayal of the United States as a nation. In addition, this unit encourages you to explore ways in which memorials function as metaphors. Literally, a **metaphor** is a

Figure 4.3 "The Tower of Faces." Sunlight illuminates a wall of photographs in the interior of the United States Holocaust Memorial Museum in Washington, DC.
Courtesy of Pete Souza/Liaison/Getty Images.

word or object used in place of another, suggesting a likeness between the two. The term metaphor derives from the Greek *meta-pherein,* which means to carry from one place to another, or to transfer. As we'll see below, the twin beams of light that shone as a memorial for the World Trade Center were visual metaphors. The Tribute in Lights, as it was called, also served a metonymic function. **Metonymy** refers to the process wherein an image or object—such as a beam—stands in for a larger concept. The key rhetorical concepts in this unit, *context, metaphor,* and *metonymy,* can help you to understand the national and cultural work that memorials do.

The Rhetorical Work of Memorials

U.S. war memorials, the AIDS quilt, the FDR Memorial, the Oklahoma City Memorial, the U.S. Holocaust Memorial Museum, and the Tribute in Lights memorial function to create a national rhetorical vision. Since they are designed and approved by individuals or committees on behalf of the nation, memorials make concrete certain collectively shared interpretations or representations of events or people. Interestingly, the concept of "nation" is itself a contested rhetorical and political terrain. Historian Benedict Anderson, for example, claims that nations are imagined communities, because "members of even the smallest nation will never know most of their fellow-members, meet them, or even hear of them, yet in the minds of each lives the image of their communion."[3] In this imagined community, national identities are formed around memorials.

The controversies examined in several essays in this section illustrate how memorials and the process of creating them can foster divisions among the public and disrupt their sense of national identity. In the article "Slave Site for a Symbol of Freedom," for example, historians and local Philadelphia residents argue that the new pavilion for the Liberty Bell—a symbol of freedom—does not sufficiently address the history of slavery at the site, where George Washington lived during his presidency and where his slaves worked. Such controversies show that memorials create a particular sense of history and affirm particular national gazes, which render visible some national memories, yet hide others. For example, some have argued that the abstract Vietnam Veterans Memorial represents the nation's ambivalence toward the Vietnam War, especially in contrast to the more concrete, heroic depictions of soldiers in surrounding war memorials.

Others defend the abstraction of the Vietnam Veterans Memorial as fostering an interactive and rhetorical quality: Visitors play an active and direct role in commemoration, often tracing names of the deceased onto paper for safe-keeping and/or leaving family photographs, memorabilia, or flowers on the site while gazing at their own shadow reflected in the granite slab. Similarly, the new Franklin Delano Roosevelt Memorial invites a participatory and rhetorical role. Visitors to the open-air "four-room" space of the FDR Memorial often directly interact with the various statues placed in those rooms: standing behind to push FDR in his wheelchair at the memorial's entrance; posing at the foot of FDR's robe in the final large statue; petting his memorialized dog, Fala; standing in the Depression-era food line along with the five other statues there; posing arm in arm with the statue of Eleanor Roosevelt. Visitors also rub their hands across the numerous inscriptions of things FDR said, which are scattered throughout the memorial, or dip hands or feet into the many pools of cascading or still waters.

The FDR Memorial and the Vietnam Veterans Memorial represent "transformations of memorials from classic . . . edifices that suggest ancient sites of worship to a more decentered and interactive public space."[4] Whether memorials reflect a classic edifice or envision a more participatory public space, the meanings of commemorative sites are passed down from one generation to the next through national traditions and rituals.[5] Therefore, this chapter invites you to consider questions such as:

- What memories are made visible—or invisible—by particular memorials?
- To what degree are national memorials shaped by the historical period (the temporal context) in which they were constructed? To what degree are they shaped by the setting (the spatial context) in which they appear?
- Who has access to which memorials and under what circumstances?
- How are certain memorials used politically or religiously in the community? In other words, what role do particular memorials play in current history?
- To what degree do national memorials remember for us and thereby enable us to forget?

Critical Frame

AND WRITING

context

"Location, location, location": No doubt you've heard this old realtor's saw (an ironic answer to "What are the three most important selling points for any piece of property?"). In persuasive (rhetorical) writing, we might say something similar: *Context* can be everything. The **context** (history, time, space, location, genre, situation) in which a piece of writing is produced, as well as the context in which it is received, can make all the difference in how it is read, received, understood, and acted upon. Comedians, for example, depend on contextual knowledge to make their punch lines work: A joke isn't a joke unless you understand the situation, or the context, that makes it funny in the first place.

Building a bridge to connect reader and writer (or speaker and audience) is just as tricky as delivering successful comedy. When a writer sits down to write, no matter how hard she might try, it is sometimes difficult for her to imagine the various audiences who might come to read her work. She might imagine an "ideal" audience— one she puts in her head as the best possible reader to receive her words. But that "ideal" audience may, in fact, not be anything like the "real" audience that does receive it. If you have to write a paper and you know that four or five of your classmates will be reading and responding to it, do you write it with only them in mind? Or do you forget about them and focus only on trying to understand, persuade, and please your teacher? Is there another audience who consititutes part—or the whole— of your "ideal" audience?

Understanding context, especially in writing that aims to be persuasive, is like a challenging game—there are rules, to be sure, but the possibilities that arise with different players at different skill levels and with different strategies and backgrounds are evershifting. Context might well be the crux of rhetoric, since it sits squarely in every corner of the rhetorical triangle—expressing variations in text, audience, and rhetor (speaker or writer) alike.

Critical Frame

- In what ways do personal/familial memories become part of public memory?
- What imagined community is reflected in any given memorial or monument— and in our gaze at, and interaction with, it?
- What metaphors do certain memorials create? How does the connection between metaphor and this memorial make our own memory stronger or different?
- What structures or symbolic elements of a memorial or monument stand in for larger concepts? That is, what parts (or whole) of a memorial are metonymic?

● In Marita Sturken's essay "The Image as Memorial," she evokes the term *context* to describe the way that events, location, people, and the placement of photographs helps us to make meaning of an image. In fact, Sturken suggests that it is the context of an image that can jar our memories and move us emotionally:

> It can be argued that the most poignant of photographs are those that were created within personal or familial contexts yet have since acquired a cultural, legal, or historical status. These images seem innocent and unsuspecting in retrospect—the casual image of a place that will later be destroyed, the framing of a group of friends, one of whom will soon be dead, the hauntingly informal images of the soon-to-be victims of war.

Exercises ■ ■ ■

1 Make a list of the most important issues surrounding you. What are the hotly contested subjects in the communities in which you live (your hometown, state, nation, college, dorm, or family)? Compare your list to that of several of your classmates. Where do your lists converge (compare) and diverge (differ)? How might the various contexts in which you and your classmates live, work, and play account for these similarities or differences?

2 Imagine that you did very poorly in one of your classes during your freshman year. You want to invoke the "freshman forgiveness rule" (which many colleges have in place so that students can have that grade erased and "try again" without any penalty or notice on their overall academic record). Write a brief letter (a paragraph or so) to each of the following people in which you explain your reason(s) for pleading "freshman forgiveness" in the case of class X:

- Your parents or other family members
- One of your closest friends (at college or from home)
- Your academic advisor at X college where the course has been taken
- The instructor in the course for which you will be asking "forgiveness"

What are the spatial and temporal contexts that lend these elements their metonymic function?

When we analyze commemorative practices at times of national emergency or crisis, we can gain a sense of the prominence of visual imagery in prompting certain national gazes. The initial disbelief experienced by many Americans in response to the September 11, 2001, terrorist attacks illustrates the complex role of visual representations in shaping cultural and national meanings. Pictorial representations, especially family

Critical Frame

Figure 4.4   Missing person posters in Manhattan, September 13, 2001.

Courtesy of Orjan Ellingvag/Corbis Sygma.

photographs, played a formative role in shaping the public's view of Ground Zero. Family and friends of victims of the World Trade Center attacks posted family photographs on telephone poles, street lampposts, and windows (see Figure 4.4). Just days after the attacks, American news media produced stories about now fatherless babies born on or soon after September 11, 2001. Familial narratives of loss turned out to be a central focus in the nation's struggle to come to terms with such a catastrophic event.

Picturing the Nation's Wounds

The Tribute in Lights memorial, which rose above the lower Manhattan sky for one month during 2002, illuminated the memory of those lost on September 11, 2001. The Tribute in Lights, which returned on the 2003 and 2004 anniversaries of September 11, consisted of twin pillars of light created by 88 searchlights and 616,000 watts of power (see Figures 4.5 and 4.6). Although the memorial itself was designed to be temporary, the transient image has not faded but has become part of the national memory.

Cliff Wassmann, one photographer whose images of the memorial have often been reproduced, describes the twin beams of light as memorializing "a turning point in the painful process that started on September 11, 2001" and serving as both

Figure 4.5 Tribute in Light shines on September 11.

Courtesy of Shannon Stapleton/Reuters/ Corbis Images.

"a defiant gesture and spiritual recognition of the lives lost." The "towers" of light flip the switch, as it were, turning loss into hope, sadness into defiance. Wassmann himself writes in a descriptive essay of how he shot the Tribute in Lights on the last night the beams were on:

It was about 1:00 AM by the time I got to that location again. The lights of the bridge sparkled and reflected in the water below. And where the twin towers once stood the twin beams rose silently in the sky. A few people milled about but soon

Critical Frame

Figure 4.6 Two beams shine in New York City on March 11, 2002, as a tribute to the six-month anniversary of the terrorist attack.

Courtesy of David Drapking/Image Direct/Getty Images.

left as . . . rain started falling. I was about to leave too when something magic began to happen in the sky. The mist in the air gave the lights something to illuminate and they began to glow brightly. And fast-moving low clouds passed through the beams creating various shapes that quickly appeared and disappeared. For a fleeting moment while my camera shutter was open, a faint heart-shaped spot formed on the clouds over the city. . . .

While the Towers of Light are not planned to be part of whatever permanent memorial is ultimately built on the site, they will forever be remembered as the turning point in the painful process that started on September 11, 2001. During wartime, cities were told to turn down the lights and what does New York do? It sets up the brightest lights in the country, a beacon that could be seen from 20 miles away! It was, at once, a defiant gesture and spiritual recognition of the lives lost. And we will remember.[6]

Reading Contexts through Metaphor and Metonymy

As "twin beams," "twin pillars," and "twin towers," the two columns of light are a metaphor for the actual towers of the World Trade Center. They evoke all the positive associations we have with a beam of light—warmth, brightness, and hope—and so might be considered a straightforward nostalgic and patriotic image. Yet the beams of light also recognize the temporary nature of all structures. The memorial is, like the twin towers themselves, powerful but not everlasting. The towers' steel beams could not withstand the 1000-degree temperatures generated from the crash and so they fell, their beams folding back to earth, just as the memorial's beams of light reached for the sky for a month but then were darkened, only to reappear each year on the anniversary of the tragedy. Unlike permanent structures such as the Lincoln Memorial, the Tribute in Lights introduced the concepts of temporality and transiency into the memorial. The Tribute in Lights thus reflected collective aspirations, as well as national fears.

The Tribute in Lights also serves a metonymic function, projecting a national rhetorical vision of unity and identity at a time of crisis and loss. The Tribute represents all that the World Trade Center represented—wealth, capitalism, superior technology—as well as all that it had come to stand for post-9/11—great loss, profound grief, but also resilence. Thus the Tribute in Lights memorial points to past achievements and links them to present events, such as the call to rebuild the U.S. economy.

Indeed, many of the memorials we discuss in this section rely upon metaphors and metonyms to frame our understanding of national memory. Consider Figure 4.7, "Young woman looking at pictures of missing people." Here, the image is of a single mourner at one of the many displays that sprang up spontaneously after the September 11, 2001, attacks. What metonymic and/or metaphorical functions does this photograph serve?

Remembrance: Rituals and Collective Identification

A single image can both evoke individual action and cement our cultural collective consciousness. This dual process, like mortar and brick, builds the house of rhetoric. The use of twin beams in the Tribute in Lights memorial points not only to the actual structure of the twin towers, but also to the images of bare steel beams that dominate the post-9-11 "aftermath" photos. Consider, for example, the memorial service held for the "death of the structure" itself (Figure 4.8) at the moment when the last beam was pulled from the World Trade Center site on May 30, 2002.

Critical Frame

AND WRITING

metaphor

The term *metaphor* comes from the compounding of *meta,* meaning "beyond or over," and *pherein,* meaning "to carry." Metaphors carry us beyond or over ideas and meanings we already have. Metaphor was of major importance for Aristotle, who spent more time considering it in several of his treatises than he did any other rhetorical trope or strategy. Metaphor's central place in language use, creative expression, and rhetoric looms large in almost any text on rhetoric or literature (especially poetry) that you might care to pull down from a shelf today. In fact, metaphor may well be, as author Bill Roorbach suggests, "the elemental condition of language" since "comparison is the basic gesture of the human mind."[7]

We make metaphors by comparing an idea, sensory impression, or object with which we are already familiar to an object or idea that is not so familiar—or, in reverse, by taking something familiar to us and making it interesting all over again through a unique new comparison. Metaphors work, declares Aristotle, because they give us pleasure: "because metaphors help us to learn new things, and learning is naturally pleasurable to humans."[8] In truth, we can hardly write (or write well) without making metaphors. We compare—and thus, splice together—two unlike images, sensory impressions, or objects in order to create a new way of thinking about something. Watson and Crick's famous "double helix" figure for DNA is, in fact, only a metaphoric model to help us understand (and associate) something that was, especially when they created it, beyond easy comprehension.

Metaphor has a particular strong emotional appeal (*pathos*) because it most often uses concrete sensory impressions or objects. This is why, for example, even though we may not know all the specific sequences that can (and do) take place to create DNA within that so-called "double helix," we can see an image of the double-helix figure and immediately now associate it with "DNA."

Examples ■■■

1   In "The Kind of People Who Make Good Americans," Wendy Kozol analyzes how the post–World War II suburban family became a metaphor for U.S. national identity and the "American Dream." She looks for example, at how images in *Life* magazine help to demonstrate this metaphor:

> Although they represented an ideal, labeled as such by the generic [picture title] "The American," the people who posed for this picture were not actors. *Life* presents Dale and Gladys Welling, the "real" family who recently bought one of these dream houses, as evidence of actual families

Critical Frame

170

living the American Dream. In this way, the magazine legitimizes its association of the American economy with a particular social group by individualizing representation.

❷ In "The Rusted Iron Curtain," Robert Kaplan employs the visual image of a curtain
as a metaphor for the border between Mexico and the United States. Although
Kaplan describes an *actual* iron curtain, made of rusted metal from the first Persian Gulf War and standing on one part of the border, he also uses the curtain as
a metaphor for how the United States sees—or rather, how it *doesn't* see—Mexico. The curtain cuts the land sharply into two countries *and* into two socioeconomic zones. As Kaplan describes these two curtained sides:

> I checked into a hotel and then walked toward the border, where I saw two
> boys kick a soccer ball made of rags until one of them kicked the ball onto
> a scrap metal roof. When the ball failed to roll back down, the boys walked
> away. . . .
>   Walking back from the border I saw neat squares and rectangle roofs of
> houses on the American side, where it was obvious that every joint fit and
> that every part was standardized, in contrast to the amateurish and
> inspired constructions all around me.

Exercises ▪ ▪ ▪

❶ This Nation Is . . .

Create a list of metaphors for nations. You might start with our own nation. With what
objects or sensory impressions can the United States be compared or associated? (Don't
be afraid to be creative and adventurous here.) Also pick a few other nations you know
about (a little or a lot) and create a few metaphors for them as well. Share these lists (or
create them together) with your classmates.

❷ Metaphor Profile

Think about metaphors you may have known—comparisons that have been made in
your everyday life. Create a list of your own "commonplace metaphors." Survey your
own educational, familial, peer/friend, regional, local, cultural, and national backgrounds: What associations or comparisons between X and Y might have been made in
these various backgrounds?

You might think, for example, of the music you have known—what metaphors are
made in its lyrics or titles? You can also turn to other media—visual and print texts
around you—to find these metaphors. Compile a list of them—a kind of "metaphor
profile." Share these profiles with group members or classmates. Note the ones that
seem familiar to all or most of you (as a class or group) but also the ones that seem very
particular to or for you (as an individual).

Figure 4.7   Young woman looking at pictures of missing people, September 18, 2001.
Courtesy of Kai Pfaffenbach/Getty Images Inc.—Hulton Archive Photos.

The photograph on the front page of *The New York Times* depicts this 18-wheel truck, bearing a 58-ton steel column and draped in black cloth and an American flag. As it drives across a bridge-like structure that spans the pit of Ground Zero, hundreds of police officers and firefighters line the bridge and salute. The text accompanying the photo characterizes the scene as follows:

> But at 10:29 yesterday morning, after the tolling of bells and in the presence of thousands, silence took its proper place. A corner of the city became still, as a stretcher bearing the weight of no body was carried out of the swept-clean pit where the twin towers once stood, followed by a truck carting a 58-ton steel column—the last symbolic remnant of what was.[9]

U.S. culture's dominant ritual for the burial and memorial of heroes is reenacted in this scene. The photo captures those elements: the salute of "relatives" and officials, the black cloth over a coffin-like structure, an American flag draped over that, the one hearse-like vehicle bearing the "body," and the raw, silent seriousness of the scene. Carrying the last beam of the twin towers is a way of mourning for a structure that represented a significant part of U.S. national and economic identity.

There is no shortage of beam-filled images in relation to September 11, 2001. For example, in Figure 4.9, a single fireman is photographed staring up at an

Figure 4.8   A flatbed truck hauls the last steel girder from the Ground Zero site, May 30, 2002.

AND WRITING

metonymy

Metonymy is a metaphor that folds back in on itself. Where metaphor tends to reach for a connection to an object or idea outside or beyond the thing itself, metonymy lets a *part* of the thing stand in for the whole. Thus, metonymy is a metaphor where two things already do have some kind of relation to each other. In ancient Greek, the term *metonymy* translates as "altered name." Thus, "the White House" can come to stand in for "the President" or for "the U.S. government." Finally, metonyms acquire power through repetition. For example, the metonym "crown" stands in for the larger concept of kingship, as in "the crown rules." For this association to exist, the crown must be repeatedly associated with the king. Similarly, in order for the World Trade Center, metaphorically represented by the Tribute in Lights, to function as a metonym, particular associations must be established and repeated over time, so that the World Trade Center comes to stand in for "U.S. economic superiority" or, more specifically, U.S. capitalism.

Some of our most potent, provocative, and long-lasting symbols in personal, familial, national and cultural relationships are metonymic: The Tomb of the Unknown Soldier stands in for all of our wars and lost soldiers; a heart-shaped necklace given between friends, lovers, or family members stands in for "love"; the "mother ring," built from the birthstones of all her children, represents family bonds; a diamond (ring, necklace, earrings) stands in for love and commitment; the flag and the eagle represent the United States; and the peace symbol (especially when included with anything tie-dyed) represents the 1960s counterculture.

Examples ■ ■ ■

❶ In Aurora Levins Morales' poem "Child of the Americas," the speaker describes herself in several parts. Yet, as we discover at the end of the poem, each part is actually representative of the whole person.

For example, the speaker explains:

> I speak English with passion: it's the tongue of my consciousness,
> a flashing knife blade of crystal, my tool, my craft.
> I am Caribeña, island grown. Spanish is in my flesh,
> ripples from my tongue, lodges in my hips:
> the language of garlic and mangoes,
> the singing in my poetry, the flying gestures of my hands.

And then the speaker concludes:

> I am new. History made me. My first language was spanglish.
> I was born at the crossroads
> and I am whole.

❷ In Diana Taylor's essay "Lost in the Field of Vision," she begins by describing the events of 9-11. However, her essay's focus quickly changes when photographs of the fallen towers are banned. In the banning of such photographs, the towers come to be metonyms: They characterize the whole of the United States—and perhaps the nation's moment of weakness—and the absence of their image demonstrates the nation's loss. As Taylor describes this metonymic move:

> The signifying objects [the twin towers] gone, we had access only to photos of the objects. Instantly, it seemed, newly minted organizations produced glossy journals, passing as weeklies, to circulate the permitted images, the permissible stories. Bylines, photo credits, and authenticating sources disappeared.

Exercises ▧■■

❶ Metonymic Me

What are the metonyms of your family, your town, your school, your state, your culture, your nation? What *parts* of these entities, locations, objects, and times are used to represent the *whole?* Make a list of these for yourself. What parts is your (personal) metonymic whole made up of? Compare this metonymic whole to that of others in your class and consider where you part from (and come together with) them.

❷ Making a Metonymic Person or Place

Design (in words) a memorial or monument. Be creative. Make certain that *parts* of it represent something larger.

Or, create a series of metonyms for (fictional or real) *Citizen X*. You might base your construction on an actual person you know, or you may choose to have him or her be entirely fictional. Whatever your choice, the goal is the same: to create a metonymic profile of the various *parts* of things that stand in for the larger local, regional, ethnic, racial, gendered, class-based, age-anchored, national, educational, familial, and other identities and relationships of your character. For example, say I decide that I want to make a metonym for Citizen Kansas: His neck is red, his speech is plain, he wears Lee or Levi jeans, shops at Sears, has Sunday dinner (following church) at the Golden Corral, owns a pickup truck, plays George Strait and Reba McEntire on his CD player, drinks Coors beer, waves at strangers on the highway as they come into his sight, has a Skoal can circle worn on the back pocket of his jeans, and wears Tony Llama boots with the slight odor of cow or pig manure on them. Each one of these seemingly "simple" assigned characteristics rests on a larger understanding of something "whole" about this person that is connected to a larger (admittedly stereotypical) representation of locations, regions, cultures, behaviors, and values. Go ahead, then: make your metonym.

Figure 4.9 A firefighter pauses to look at the flag flying atop the last remaining beam from the collapsed south tower of the World Trade Center, April 3, 2002.

Courtesy of Kathy Willens/AP.

American flag (now also a metonymic image of 9-11), which has been placed on top of that last beam.

The broken beams of the towers—metonymically standing in for the shattering of the American spirit after 9-11—are everywhere in the photo essays that memorialize, testify, and narrate September 11 and beyond. There is, for example, the now-

Figure 4.10 Three New York City firefighters raise an American flag at the site of the World Trade Center.

Courtesy of Ricky Flores/The Journal News/Corbis Images.

famous image that has emerged as one of September 11's most iconic, in which firefighters raise the American flag over the World Trade Center rubble (Figure 4.10), thereby carrying our consciousness back to the Iwo Jima Memorial (Figure 4.11), itself based on journalist Joe Rosenthal's photograph capturing a symbolic moment following a key battle in World War II.

In the background of the Ground Zero image are the ubiquitous beams of the fallen towers. The broken beams represent a shattering, a jagged hole in U.S. national memory. Yet this sense of loss has often been juxtaposed with the more hopeful metaphor of beams of light, as represented in the Tribute of Lights, and in

Critical Frame

Figure 4.11   Iwo Jima Memorial, Arlington, VA.

such photos as the one below, of the entrance to the subway station at the World Trade Center (Figure 4.12).

Figure 4.12 blends the broken, almost violent rubble of beams and debris with the softer, hopeful quality of beams of light, which are diffused through the dust and which illuminate an entrance. Our gaze is directed both toward the pain and loss represented in those hard, shattered edges, as well as toward the possibility of a new day, and perhaps a new way.

Figure 4.12 Entrance to the subway station at the World Trade Center, post-9/11.

Courtesy of Susan Meiselas/Magnum Photos, Inc.

Critical Frame

Figure 4.13 International 9-11 memorial in Bangladesh.

Courtesy of Rafiqur Rahman/Reuters/Corbis Images.

Across the country—indeed across the globe (see Figure 4.13)—after September 11, people gathered for candlelight vigils, creating multiple and collective "beams" of memory. More often than not, these lighted ceremonies also featured the American flag, and in doing so, they bound our memories together in a national, near-unified rhetorical vision.

NOTES

1. Marianne Hirsch, *Family Frames: Photography, Narrative, and Postmemory* (Cambridge, MA: Harvard UP, 1997) 256.
2. James Young, *The Texture of Memory: Holocaust Memorials and Meaning* (New Haven: Yale UP, 1993).
3. Benedict Anderson, *Imagined Communities: Reflections on the Origin and Spread of Nationalism,* rev. ed. (London: Verso, 1991) 6.

Critical Frame

4. Rosemarie Garland-Thomson, "The FDR Memorial: Who Speaks from the Wheelchair," *Chronicle of Higher Education*, 26 Jan. 2001: 2.

5. James Young, *The Texture of Memory: Holocaust Memorials and Meaning* (New Haven and London: Yale UP, 1993) xii.

6. Cliff Wassmann, "America's New Sacred Site," *Mysterious Places: Ancient Civilizations, Modern Mysteries*, 20 Aug. 2005 <www.mysteriousplaces.com/ny.html>.

7. William Roorbach, *Writing Life Stories* (Story Press, 1998) 125–26.

8. Aristotle, *On Rhetoric: A Theory of Civic Discourse*. trans. George Kennedy (New York: Oxford UP, 1991).

9. Dan Barry, "End to Awful Task," *New York Times*, 31 May 2002: 1.

Slave Site for a Symbol of Freedom

DINITIA SMITH

There's an old adage stating that history is written by the winners—in other words, those in power. "Slave Site for a Symbol of Freedom," an article in the April 20, 2002 *New York Times,* reports on one attempt to challenge such a history. By looking at the controversy surrounding the National Park Service's development of a Liberty Bell Pavilion on a former site of slaves' quarters, *DINITIA SMITH*'s article raises questions about the types of memories, beliefs, and values that get sanctioned in the creation of memorials and monuments, as well as those that are often silenced or diminished. Dinitia Smith is an Emmy award-winning journalist for the *New York Times* who has written articles on topics ranging from copyright law to arts and entertainment and African American culture.

The National Park Service's plans to showcase the Liberty Bell next year in a new $9 million pavilion in Philadelphia have come under attack from historians and local residents, who have accused the Park Service of trying to cover up a less noble element of American history on the same spot: the existence of slave quarters.

The pavilion, to be called the Liberty Bell Center, is part of an ambitious $300 million redesign of Independence National Historic Park. It will be located partly on the former site of the Robert Morris house, where George Washington lived during his presidency and where his slaves slept, ate and worked.

The loose-knit coalition of historians, led by Gary B. Nash, an expert on the American Revolution and Philadelphia history, and the Independence Hall Association, a citizens' group, have asked the Park Service to present a complete explanation of the Morris house's history in the area outside the new center, including a full-size floor plan outlined in stone, a description of the mansion and first-person accounts from the 18th century. They are also asking that the exhibition inside depict slavery more extensively.

The Park Service has refused, saying an elaborate floor plan and detailed information out-

doors would be confusing for visitors, although earlier this month it did agree to add an additional interpretive panel to the exhibition planned for the interior of the new center. That panel will be "an examination of the institution of slavery, focusing on its 18th-century Philadelphia context," according to a summary provided by the Park Service.

Those proposals are inadequate, say the historians, who sent a detailed letter this week to Martha B. Aikens, the superintendent of the park, requesting a meeting with her.

"What we are talking about is historical memory," said Mr. Nash, a professor of history at the University of California at Los Angeles, who pointed out that it was abolitionists who made the Liberty Bell a symbol of the nation's freedom. "You either cure historical amnesia, or you perpetuate it. This is a wonderful example of trying to perpetuate historical amnesia."

The dispute, which was first reported in The Philadelphia Inquirer, began when Edward Lawler Jr., a local scholar, researched the Morris mansion, which stood at 190 High Street, on the south side of what is today Market Street, one block from Independence Hall.

He said he spent three years delving into original records on the house. "I decided not to trust anything," Mr. Lawler said, that had been written about the mansion before.

At the Library of Congress, he found a copy of a 1785 ground plan of the mansion. He also discovered letters between Washington and his secretary, Tobias Lear, in which they discussed building an extension to the smokehouse for stable slaves.

10   Mr. Lawler said Washington maintained eight or nine slaves in the house. In 1780 Pennsylvania enacted a law providing for gradual emancipation; it permitted residents of other states living in Pennsylvania to keep slaves. Washington gradually replaced his own slaves with German indentured servants.

Mr. Lawler said he notified the Park Service of his findings a year ago. In January, he published them in the Pennsylvania Magazine of History and Biography, the scholarly journal of the Historical Society of Pennsylvania.

The Robert Morris house, named for the Philadelphia financier who owned it, was where Washington stayed when he presided over the drafting of the Constitution in 1787, and it later served as the executive mansion of the United States from 1790 to 1800. Slaves waited on visiting dignitaries at official functions there during Washington's residence, in addition to caring for the personal needs of the president and his family. Martha Washington's personal slave, Oney Judge, escaped from the house in 1796, as the Washingtons were eating dinner. Washington's prized cook, Hercules, fled in 1797.

After Washington left the house, President John Adams, who was opposed to slavery, moved in. (Benedict Arnold also once lived there and began his treasonous correspondence with the British in the house in 1779). When Adams moved out in 1800, the building was turned into a hotel. The hotel was not a success, and in 1832 it was gutted, leaving only the side walls and foundation standing. The walls were demolished in 1951 to create Independence Mall.

A public toilet now stands on the site, with a small plaque commemorating the house. The Park Service plans to tear down the toilet, mark the site of the house and install a new interpretive panel outside. Future visitors to the Liberty Bell Center will cross more than 140 feet of what was once the president's house, including the slave quarters.

15   The Liberty Bell is now housed in a glass pavilion a few steps from where the new center will stand.

The fight over how to depict the tragic intersection of slavery and freedom at the heart of the nation's founding is just the latest instance of historians and others challenging the way national monuments interpret and represent history.

"So much of our history is buried," Mr. Nash said. "Millions who went through Monticello would never have known that Jefferson, after his wife died and his daughters grew up, was living as a single white man in a sea of black slaves, let alone that he had sired a child by Sally Hemmings."

The same silence is to be found in Colonial Williamsburg, Mr. Nash said. "It is one of the most visited of all historical sites," he observed. "They have changed their interpretive line greatly in the last 20 years. From the 1930's well into the 80's, it was a story of whites in Williamsburg. But African-Americans represented 50 percent of the population."

Phil Sheridan, a Park Service spokesman, said Ms. Aikens declined to be interviewed about the new center. But in a letter to the Independence Hall Association last October, she wrote that a detailed floor plan would "create a design dissonance" between the new center and the area outside, "potentially causing confusion for visitors."

20   Ms. Aikens has said that a fuller interpretation of slavery will be offered at the Deshler-Morris House in Germantown, where Washington also lived. Located in another part of the park, it has had relatively few visitors.

Some of the historians have also protested that the Morris house location has not been completely excavated. Park Service archaeologists have excavated five of nine sites there.

"At this point there is nothing there that could be clearly tied to distinctive African-American cultural practices," Mr. Sheridan said. He said further digging would destroy the archaeological sites.

Mr. Nash, the author of *First City: Philadelphia and the Forging of Historical Memory* (University of Pennsylvania Press, 2002), complained in a telephone interview that "this fascinating history is being relegated to this plasticized wayside panel outside the building."

The additional panel that the Park Service has agreed to install inside the center, Mr. Nash said, "speaks mostly to the achievement of American independence and the devotion to the ideal of freedom thereafter."

"This does not address the braided historical relationship between freedom and slavery," he continued, "how interdependent they were and how the freedom of some was built upon the unfreedom of others."

Mr. Nash said the symbolic importance of Washington's slave quarters could not be overestimated. After Oney Judge escaped to Portsmouth, N.H., he said, "life was hard for her as a free black." He continued: "She was always poor. But at the end of her life, she said one hour of freedom was worth it all because freedom was so precious to her."

"There are other liberty bells," Mr. Nash added. "There are the bells the slaves' masters made rebellious slaves wear that would ring if they tried to run away. These are stories a mature democracy that is the most visible in the world should not be burying." 25

Re-reading/Conversations with the Text

1. Memorials often have a didactic function in that they offer particular national narratives and arguments about what we "should" believe or remember. Memorials may presume a coherent national "we," but they also create divisions in the national "we." What divisions in the national "we" characterize the disputes over the plans of the National Park Service to showcase the Liberty Bell?

2. How can a memorial perpetuate historical amnesia? According to local residents and scholars cited in the article, what are the cultural and political implications of such acts of historical forgetting?

3. How does Smith structure her essay? To what degree and in what ways does she craft her argument to reflect the values of a particular audience and cultural or historical context?

Re-seeing and Re-writing

1. This assignment asks you to research other memory sites that commemorate the emancipation of slaves or represent slavery as an institution in the United States. You might consider memorials such as the Freedmen's Memorial to Abraham Lincoln (http://www.culturaltourismdc.org). Analyze the visual argument that the memorial presents. Where is the memorial located and how does its geographical context shape its meaning? How does the memorial imagine

its audience? Does the memorial invite a particular sensory response? Who is gazing at whom? Is it meant to persuade viewers to remember certain historical events and forget others? What power relationships are configured through the visual placement of particular subjects or objects?

2. This assignment asks you to locate a memory site that depicts gender, race, and/or class struggles and achievements in the United States. You might consider, for example, the Civil Rights Memorial that Maya Lin created for the Southern Poverty Law Center (http://www.splcenter.org/center/crmc/civil .jsp). To complete this assignment, you will need to do some research. First, consider the stories and images depicted. Next, find out all you can about the production (design, creation, financial backing, etc.) of the memory site and its reception (the public's response). How was the site described in local newspapers? Has the site received local and/or national attention? Have disputes arisen with regard to the site? If so, what positions characterize these disputes? If not, why do you think the public was so eager to accept the memory or narrative the site offered? Did/do particular social, political, or economic factors shape the reception? How might past reactions contrast with contemporary viewers' reactions?

 Intertext

This assignment asks you to create an *anti*-memorial that tells a story different from the one depicted by an existing national memorial. You may create a sculpture, a digital text or Web site, or a performance. Before you create your anti-memorial, however, you must first describe and analyze the memorial to which you intend to create an alternative. Describe the initial site and pay particular attention to the national narratives that it offers or experiences that it renders invisible or inaudible. As you create your anti-memorial, consider the relationship between the visual and verbal elements. Do the visual and verbal elements complement or contradict each other? Will the anti-memorial invite a participatory role from viewers? Also consider the political context and geographical location and how the anti-memorial will interact with surrounding structures. Your anti-memorial should be accompanied by a reflective essay in which you describe your intentions as its maker, the historical memories you hope it will foster, and your hopes for its public reception.

The Image as Memorial

MARITA STURKEN

In this essay, MARITA STURKEN draws provocative parallels between the Vietnam Memorial, the AIDS quilt, and photographs of missing children in order to connect the concept of "lost innocence" with personal and national remembering. The complicated relationship between cultural and national memory that she proposes is a heuristic that can be applied to other national memorials like the World Trade Center, and also to personal memory sites like family photo albums. Sturken is a professor in the Department of Culture and Communication at New York University, where she teaches cultural studies, visual culture, and technology and new media. Her publications include Tangled Memories: The Vietnam War, The AIDS Epidemic, and The Politics of Remembering (1997) and Practices of Looking: An Introduction to Visual Culture (2001) and the forthcoming Tourists of History.

The personal photograph is an object of complex emotional and cultural meaning, an artifact used to conjure memory, nostalgia, and contemplation. The photograph of personal value is a talisman, in which the past is often perceived to reside so that it can be reexperienced. It evokes both memory and loss, both a trace of life and the prospect of death. Yet, while the photograph may be perceived as a container for memory, it is not inhabited by memory so much as it produces it; it is a mechanism through which the past can be constructed and situated within the present. Images have the capacity to create, interfere with, and trouble the memories we hold as individuals and as a culture. They lend shape to personal stories and truth claims, and function as technologies of memory, producing both memory and forgetting.

A photograph does not in itself state its status as personal or cultural. Yet, the photograph plays an important function in the relationship of personal memory, cultural memory, and history precisely because of the ways in which images can move from one realm to the next. If we regard personal memory as the memories that remain solely within personal and familial contexts, separate from a public sharing of

memory, and history as a form of sanctioned narratives of the past, cultural memory can be seen as memory that is shared outside of formal historical discourse, yet is imbued with cultural meaning. As technologies of memory, photographs play a primary role in the traffic between personal memory, cultural memory, and history. When personal memories are shared and exchanged in contexts distinct from history making, they form a kind of collective memory, either as interventions into or resistance to official history. Cultural objects, photographs among them, often move from personal memory to cultural memory to history and back. Hence, a historical photograph has the capacity to affect the personal memory of an historical survivor, and a personal image can often acquire cultural meaning or historical meaning. This is increasingly the case with the proliferation of personal images in the form of videotapes, where, for instance, the amateur image taken by George Holliday of the beating of Rodney King acquired historical meaning when it was shown on national television and became the catalyst for the Los Angeles uprising. At the same time, survivors of historical events often report that, after time, they cannot sort out what is personal memory, what the memories of others, and what derived from the images of the news media and popular culture. Hence, the public image, often marked as historical, can change and produce personal memories as well. Indeed, rather than positing memory and history as oppositional, as they are often described, we should consider them to be entangled, each pulling forms from the other.

It can be argued that the most poignant of photographs are those that were created within personal or familial contexts yet have since acquired a cultural, legal, or historical status. These images seem innocent and unsuspecting in retrospect—the casual image of a place that will later be destroyed, the framing of a group of friends, one of whom will soon be dead, the hauntingly informal images of the soon-to-be victims of war. Unlike the official images of war victims that were created by the Nazis or the Cambodians who systematically catalogued the soon-to-be dead, the informal and personal images that acquire historical status speak to a moment captured by the photographic camera that is totally separate from the weight it will come to bear. These images thus present a compelling prior innocence to which they offer a partial and enticing kind of retrieval. At the same time, they can be hauntingly tragic in their evocation of loss.

In this paper, I would like specifically to examine several contexts in which personal and family photographs journey into realms of cultural memory and acquire new meanings: the photographs left at the Vietnam Veterans Memorial in Washington, D.C., the personal pictures sewn into the AIDS Memorial Quilt, and the images of missing children disseminated on supermarket flyers, grocery bags, and television detective shows. In these three contexts, the images function both to memorialize their subjects and to speak to imagined audiences, though often with divergent purposes. Each is a particular form of address that reveals aspects of trauma in late-twentieth-century American culture, the trauma of untimely

death, in particular those who died young and tragic deaths, and the trauma of the lost child. In the case of the memorial and the quilt, images are primarily viewed as forms of memory, and in the case of the missing children, they are used as law enforcement forms of identification. Yet they all demonstrate the fluid capacity of the image to change cultural status and, more important, the malleability of the personal images that acquire cultural status. All are fraught with the weighted meaning of the family in contemporary American culture. The images I will discuss here are deployed for a number of personal and public agendas—among others, to memorialize the dead, to speak for and against the participation of the United States in the Vietnam War, to celebrate gay identity, to support families who have lost someone to AIDS, to refuse to mourn, to act as identification in criminal investigations, and finally to ask viewers to participate in searching for missing children among their neighbors. These agendas address viewers in different roles—as mourners, citizens, family members, and concerned observers. Each testifies to the traffic across the boundaries between public and private realms.

The Vietnam Veterans Memorial and the Image as Monument

Late-twentieth-century American culture has witnessed an unprecedented interest in the building of memorials. At a time when critics of postmodernism have labeled it antihistorical, it seems in fact that postmodern culture is preoccupied with the question of memory, and national culture has produced an increasing number of memorials to war and to figures of the past. This process began with the construction of the Vietnam Veterans Memorial on the Mall in Washington, D.C., in 1982, which then prompted the building of the memorials to Korean War veterans, American women soldiers, the civil rights movement, President

5

Franklin D. Roosevelt, and the veterans of World War II. This process of memorialization also extended to the ongoing creation of the AIDS Memorial Quilt, which was begun in San Francisco in 1987 and which is periodically exhibited in its entirety on the Washington Mall.

Why are we as a nation so preoccupied with memory on the eve of the millennium? American culture is constantly referred to as a culture of amnesia, a nation with little sense of history, a society that identifies with the future rather than the past. Yet the relentless memorializing of the 1980s and 1990s reveals the fundamental role that national memory plays in the politics of the present.

In the early 1980s, Roland Barthes wrote: "Earlier societies managed so that memory, the substitute for life, was eternal and that at least the thing which spoke Death should itself be immortal: this was the Monument. But by making the (mortal) Photograph in the general and somehow natural witness of 'what has been,' modern society has renounced the Monument."[1] Barthes argued that the photograph had superseded the monument and memorial. Like others, he saw the emergence of photography as signaling the end of the monument, replacing it with the image technologies of memory. Yet, how could Barthes have foreseen, from his perspective on modernism and the photograph, the excessive memorialization taking place in Euro-American culture today? It seems, rather, that the contemporary photograph has not replaced the monument so much as it is demanded in its presence.

This can be seen through the interaction of visitors at the Vietnam Veterans Memorial. Since it was built in 1982, the memorial has become a kind of national shrine. Unlike any other place on the Washington Mall or in the nation's capital, it invites a participatory interaction. As the most visited site in the nation's central tourist region, it has acquired a unique status as the place at which people feel they can speak to the nation in some form. The low,

black walls of the memorial, sunken into the landscape, break the commemorative codes of the Mall; as such, they inspire contemplation and invite visitors to ritualistic forms of action. People may touch the engraved space of the names, make rubbings of names to take away with them, or leave objects at the base of the long black granite walls. These experiences of emotional engagement with the memorial have provided the material for innumerable coffee-table books of photographs in which the pain of a nation is enacted and rememorialized again.

Originally, when people began leaving letters, photographs, and objects at the memorial, the National Park Service classified them as "lost and found." Then, officials realized the artifacts had been left there intentionally and began to save them. There are now over forty thousand objects that have been left at the memorial, which are housed in a government archive and some of which are exhibited at the Smithsonian. These range from the expected (combat boots and military insignia) to the extraordinary (a Harley-Davidson motorcycle), to the evocative and poignant, objects long carried and finally let go, such as the wedding ring of a dead Vietnamese soldier, a pair of Vietnamese sandals, or a can of C-rations. More and more objects concerning contemporary controversies that are the focus of marches on Washington have also been left at the memorial. Hence, talismans regarding the Gulf War, the abortion debate, and the gay rights movement have been left there as a form of speech. However, a significant number of the artifacts left at the memorial are compellingly cryptic, ambiguous, and mysterious. It is clear that many of the stories behind these objects will not be told, because they were left at the memorial not to explain anything to its audience, but to speak directly to the dead.

Family and personal photographs proliferate among these objects, where they assert particular strands of memory. While many images of men at war have been left as tributes, there

10

have also been many images that presumably represent the war dead in their youth, in times of prior innocence before they became first soldiers and then casualties. What inspires this kind of interaction at the memorial? The Vietnam Veterans Memorial is unique in its foregrounding of the loss of an individual in war. Its listing of names of those who died in the war, in chronological order of when they were killed, has produced a very rich and complex discourse of memory. The names, by virtue of their multiplicity, situate the memorial within the multiple strands of cultural memory. For many visitors, this has the effect of imagining the widening circle of pain and grief that extends out from each to family and friends, imagining in effect the multitude of people who continue to be directly affected by the war. Despite the fact that the listing of names allows for a reclamation of codes of heroism and sacrifice in the nationalistic context of the Washington Mall, in its foregrounding of the individual over the collective the memorial is a powerful antiwar statement about the tragic and futile loss of so many lives.

The personal photographs at the memorial testify to the previous aliveness of the war dead. As images of states of prior innocence—the soldier as a child, the family gathering before the tragic loss of a family member, the now long-absent father hugging a child—these images demand an acknowledgment of the insanity of the priorities of war. Each seems to ask: How could this life, so simple and important in its ordinary experience of the everyday, have been worth sacrificing? How could a war—many would argue, in particular, this war—have warranted this price? Placed in the context of the memorial, these photographs condemn the act of war simply in the contrast between their ordinariness and their presence at a memorial to war dead. They personalize the names, give them flesh, faces, and family connections, and in so doing they speak to the incomprehensibility and irrationality of war.

The memorial is perceived by many of the families and friends of the war dead to be a kind of living memorial, where the dead are located and can be spoken to, hence where, by implication, they can hear and respond. This means that many of the photographs that have been left at the memorial chronicle the continuing lives of those who have been left behind. These images, of grandchildren and family rituals, allow the living to feel that the dead can witness the continuity of life and its rites of passage. In one, a frame that contains an image of a fetal sonogram, is accompanied by a note, which reads:

> Happy Father's Day, Dad! Here are the first two images of your first grandchild. I don't know if it's a boy or a girl. If the baby is a boy—he'll be named after you. Dad, this child will know you—Just how I have grown to know and love you, even though the last time I saw you I was only 4 months old. I love you daddy, your daughter Jeannette. (Sgt. Eddie E. Chervony, 55E 6)

The sonogram "photograph," which is now the requisite first image in the baby album, is presented here as a form of connection and witnessing, a means of speaking to the absent father.

The names on the memorial act as surrogates for the bodies of the Vietnam War dead, and visitors to the memorial often make rubbings of names to carry away with them. Yet the presence of the photographs, letters, and objects attest as well to the incompleteness of the names. It is as if the names present the individual so powerfully inscribed in death that they demand the presence of photographs to bring the dead alive. What is, after all, a name marked in stone but a name that is irrevocably inscribed within a narrative of remembrance? What does it mean to read a name? On one hand, it signals the life of the individual in war, on the other hand, it is a shallow evocation of their presence. Judith Butler writes, "But do names really 'open' us to an intersubjective ground, or are they simply so many ruins which designate a history irrevocably lost? Do these names really signify for us the fullness of the lives that were lost, or are they so many tokens of what we cannot know, enigmas, inscrutable and silent?"[2] The need to bring photographs and objects to the Vietnam Veterans Memorial and to leave them for others to witness indicates the need to memorialize the dead with images, stories, details, and specifics, precisely because of the way in which the name provides only an empty shell of remembrance.

By nature of its placement within the nationalistic context of the Washington Mall, the Vietnam Veterans Memorial constructs a narrative that foregrounds the loss of 58,196 American lives over those of the three million Vietnamese who died in the war. Yet one of the most compelling photographs that was left at the memorial is an image that speaks not to the dead whose names are listed on the wall, but to a dead Vietcong soldier. It is a worn, hand-colored image of a Vietnamese man, dressed in a military uniform, with a young girl beside him, both seriously regarding the camera. The note that accompanies it reads:

> Dear Sir, For twenty-two years I have carried your picture in my wallet. I was only eighteen years old that day that we faced one another on that trail in Chu Lai, Vietnam. Why you didn't take my life I'll never know. You stared at me for so long, armed with your AK-47, and yet you did not fire. Forgive me for taking your life, I was reacting the way I was trained, to kill V.C. . . . So many times over the years I have stared at your picture and your daughter, I suspect. Each time my heart and guts burn with the pain of guilt. I have two daughters myself now . . . Above all else, I can now respect the importance that life held for you. I suppose that is why I am able to be here today . . . It is time for me to continue the life process and release my pain and guilt. Forgive me, Sir.[3]

As we read these lines, the photograph, with its crumpled image and faded color, evokes many

narratives—the act of placing it within one's military uniform and carrying it into combat as a talisman of good luck, the scene in which it is taken from the dead man who carried it, the years it was kept and continued to haunt, the ways in which it most likely continues to haunt in its absence. The letter is deeply contradictory, both moving and troubling. I am moved by the evocation of guilt and helplessness in this note, yet disturbed by the impulse that resulted in its eventual arrival at the memorial. What does it mean to take a photograph from the dead body of someone one has just killed? Is it an act of remorse or a further violation? The photograph pulls from another place and another life a set of enigmatic and ultimately unknowable stories, each charged with loss. Where is that little girl now, did she survive the

Photograph left at the Vietnam Veterans Memorial.
Courtesy of Claudio Vasquez–Turner Publishing, Inc. Courtesy Vietnam Veterans Memorial Collection, Museum Resource Center, National Park Service/National Capital Region.

war or is she also memorialized here? Why did her father hesitate?

15   Above all, the photograph contains a startling view into a moment of prior innocence—how could they have known in that moment not only the fate of the father but the eventual trajectory of the image itself: that it would be carried for many years by the father's murderer, left at a memorial in Washington, D.C., that commemorates not the Vietnamese but the American dead, held in an archive by the United States government, and photographed for a coffee-table book of that collection, purchased by middle-class Americans? Indeed, its trajectory continues. In the summer of 1997, Richard Luttrell, the veteran who left the photograph at the memorial, contacted the embassy and received a letter from the dead man's son, who had identified his father in the photograph with the help of relatives. At the time that I write this, he is planning to travel to Vietnam to return the photograph to the family.[4]

These unanswered questions occur in the movement of photographs across the boundaries of personal and cultural memory. The photographs at the memorial change status several times, from personal and family images, often placed in family albums, to images that are meant to be shared by the audience at the memorial. Often, as is the case with this image, this means an attempt to bear witness to one's pain and a need to ask forgiveness at a site where the dead are perceived to be present (even the dead who are not named on the wall). Once placed at the memorial, these photographs acquire the status of cultural objects and shift from personal to cultural memory. When they are subsequently placed in the archive, they acquire the status of historical artifacts. Those that are exhibited in the Smithsonian are also described as artistic artifacts and assigned authorship, where possible, by curators and writers. Awarded authorship and secured within a historical archive, where they are treated as precious objects and held only by

gloved hands, these photographs and objects are pulled from cultural memory, a realm in which they are meant to be shared and to participate in the memories of others, and reinscribed in official narratives. Yet the majority of the objects and images that have been left at the memorial are either unexplained or, like these images, powerfully evocative of untold stories. Many are compelling in their anonymity and ambiguity. Their refusal to tell all their stories and their impulse to speak directly to the dead, rather than to the memorial's audience, continues to work in tension with the narratives of history.

The AIDS Quilt: Reclaiming the Bodies of the Dead

Like the Vietnam Veterans Memorial, the AIDS Memorial Quilt memorializes by naming the dead and presenting their images. The quilt, which now consists of more than forty thousand panels, each three by six feet, is a collectively produced, grass-roots project in which lovers, friends, families, and concerned strangers make panels in tribute to those who have died of AIDS. Quilt panels have been created from an enormous variety of materials, ranging from cloth, clothing, stuffed animals, cowboy boots, wedding rings, letters, and feather boas to photographs and cremation ashes. In their attempts to symbolically evoke aspects of the lives of the dead, many makers of quilt panels resort to highly literal forms: a scrub tunic for a doctor, scissors for a hairdresser, or a crib cover for an infant. Other panels are anticommemorative in their gestures, deploying humor, anger, and an aesthetics of antimourning. Because quilt panels allow for a hyperindividualization of the dead and because the aesthetics of the quilt is often vibrant and irreverent, it is often perceived as a testimony not to death but to lives lived.

Like the memorial, the quilt memorializes primarily through naming the dead, yet this

The AIDS Quilt, Washington, D.C., October 1996.

Courtesy of Ron Edmonds/AP Wide World Photos.

naming is individualized through the testimony, objects, and photographs embedded within the quilt. In many ways, the quilt presents a conversation with the dead, in which questions are asked, testimony provided, and entreaties presented, all with the implication that the dead are located within the quilt and can witness and listen from there. The voices of the quilt speak to an imagined audience, often perceived as either the community of people affected by AIDS or as a naïve and uninformed audience that needs to be educated as to the value of the lives lost.

Personal photographs take many forms in the quilt. They are often sewn into panels or screened onto cloth. This sometimes gives pan-els the quality of fabric photo albums, which depict the absent person in many different places and states of being. Photographs are clearly perceived in the quilt to offer not only the trace of the dead person as alive but also concrete testimony to his or her existence. They are a primary means by which the quilt provides evidence of the human loss of the AIDS epidemic. Because the quilt responds to the fear that the AIDS dead will be forgotten, their lives less valued and their loss less mourned than that of other dead, quilt panels often testify simply to the fact that these people existed—they lived, loved, and felt pain; their lives were tragically cut short. Personal photographs affirm this existence.

To evoke lives lived, the quilt often attempts to render present the bodies of the dead. Each panel corresponds approximately to the size of a body or coffin, and many quilt panels conjure the absent bodies of the dead through a variety of likenesses—as outlines of the frame of someone's body or empty articles of clothing that echo the body that once filled them. Here, photographs are used almost exclusively to establish the dead as youthful, healthy, and alive. The representation of bodies in the quilt must be seen in the context of the discourse on bodies of the AIDS epidemic itself. One of the distinguishing features of AIDS is the aging effect of the opportunistic infections that ultimately cause death. These diseases waste away once-strong bodies to skeletal frames, making those in the advanced stages of AIDS appear to be decades older than they are. Theirs have been, in particular in the beginning of the epidemic, bodies that were coded as contaminating and untouchable. Through the fabric and tactile quality of the quilt itself, these bodies are retrieved as warm, touchable, loving, and erotic. In photographs, the dead are presented as vigorous and healthy, bodies that emanate sexuality and energy. These images seek to restore these bodies to their pre-AIDS status and retrieve some of their dignity.

20

These are images that convey, like the images left at the memorial, a profound sense of prior innocence. In a panel for Bill Bell, who died in 1984, a series of casual photographs frame a swatch of Japanese fabric. Here, smiling while costumed at a party, eating dinner, sitting in Golden Gate Park, he conveys a sense of the profoundly irretrievable everydayness of his life. His friend Paul Harman's panel frames a series of casual snapshots with elaborate fabric and two cats guarding the image of the Golden Gate Bridge. Many quilt panels evoke this sense of a tragically produced photo album, its images chosen in an attempt to convey the facets of a life now gone. These images function as icons, along with the symbols of places visited and professions pursued, of the pleasure of life before the presence of death. In this context, the casual aspects of their snapshot qualities convey a terrible sadness.

The photographs in AIDS quilt panels testify to previous states of being, to lives lived before AIDS entered the gay community and the lives of the AIDS dead. Many are highly nostalgic images, which defiantly reclaim the exuberant hedonism of the 1970s gay community before AIDS devastated it and irrevocably changed its status. These photographs of young, healthy men thus inevitably became political statements that refuse to apologize, regret, or moralize. They achieve a kind of poignancy through their lack of awareness of what will come, representing a time when the onslaught of AIDS was unimaginable.

Photographs in the quilt not only retrieve a time of prior innocence but also reaffirm connections to those who are still living. Many of the most moving quilt panels have been made by families and contain within them family photographs. Removed from the context of a family album, these images acquire political status in the quilt. While it can be implicated in many of the divisions between the communities affected by AIDS, the AIDS quilt has succeeded in fostering new communities across

lines of sexuality, race, and class. Many stories surround the quilt of strangers meeting and coming together to mourn the dead and celebrate their lives. The numerous stories of alienation, rejection, and discrimination, of lovers excluded by families or names removed from panels, are balanced by moving stories of the construction of an AIDS-affected community unified in loss. They speak directly to the stereotype of young gay men as inevitably estranged from their families and the popular refusal to acknowledge the kinds of extended families that are constructed within the gay community. The discourse of gays as existing outside of the notion of family in the context of AIDS has been so extreme that the term *family* has often been equated with being HIV-negative. This was most evident in 1986 with the passage of a bill that legalized the creation of designated-donor pools that would allow families to donate blood within the family to prevent transmission of HIV, implying that families are inherently HIV-negative and those who are HIV-positive remain outside family structures.[5]

This larger context renders the presence of family photographs within the quilt a politically charged statement about the capacity of families to love and care for the sick and dying, to work against homophobia, and to participate in the work of gay and lesbian communities. Like the teddy bears that proliferate in the quilt (and at the memorial), family photographs of the dead also suggest not only how young many of them were (there are many children memorialized in the quilt, however most of the dead represented in it were young men when they died), but also a desire to revisit a time when they were unmarked by tragedy, as they now inevitably are.

The mix of simplicity and complexity of many quilt panels attests to the difficulty of summarizing and representing a life. Indeed, the presence of photographs both at the memorial and in the quilt testifies to the fact that the names are not enough. The names act as surrogates for the bodies of the dead, yet they remain incomplete. The photographs within the memorial and the quilt are attempts to fill these empty names with individual significance. Yet these memorials also demonstrate the inability of the photograph to conjure the dead: while these images attempt to make the dead present, they testify to the profound incommensurability between the dead and the living. Ultimately, it is contestable whether these images can conjure in any sense the presence of the dead. Photographs have been used since their invention to signify a trace of the absent one, yet their complex relationship to contemporary memorials might, indeed, suggest that this capacity is profoundly limited. Perhaps we need to consider the ways in which the desire to build so many memorials in the late twentieth century constitutes a recognition of the incompleteness of the image (the same image that Barthes believed signaled the end of the monument) to provide rituals of remembrance and make present those who are absent.

Images of Mortality: Photographs of Missing Children

Images that move through the realms of personal memory, cultural memory, and history cross the porous boundaries between the private and public arenas. When the images left at the Vietnam Veterans Memorial or incorporated into the AIDS Memorial Quilt acquire cultural and historical status, they function as public memorials for the dead. These photographs have been transferred from personal to cultural memory with the aim of speaking to a larger audience about the impact and resonances of a life. But what of the photograph that unintentionally acquires cultural status? I would like to turn finally to the meaning of the images of missing children, which have proliferated in American culture in the 1980s and 1990s. These personal photographs, like those of the memorial and the quilt, have acquired

specific cultural meanings. Unlike those images, they are awarded legal and investigative status. Yet, because of their status as photographs, they also function, despite their intended role, as image memorials.

Photographs of missing children greet us throughout our daily lives, in advertising flyers, on grocery bags and milk cartons, on the Internet, and on investigative television shows. They ask us to register the face of the missing child in order to scan the faces around us and offer identification. They ask us, "Have You Seen Me?" and demand that we respond by looking at them.[6] The context in which these images are produced indicates as much about American culture in the 1990s as the AIDS Memorial Quilt evokes of the 1980s and the Vietnam Veterans Memorial of the 1960s and 1970s. The contemporary concern about the numbers of missing children is part of a larger context in which discourses of popular culture, fears about the state of childhood, and accusations of sexual abuse have produced a collective hysteria about the abuse of children and the experience of childhood.[7] It is worth noting, for instance, that many of children whose images are circulated as missing children have either run away from home or have been "abducted" by one of their parents in a custody battle.[8] This is an enormous topic, which I will not attempt to address here, but I would like to examine the ways in which the cultural status of these family photographs can have unintended effects.

Photographs have long been analyzed as objects of death. In its freezing of time in an instant, and its capacity to carry the image of the dead forward in time, the photograph renders a mortality to its subject. A photograph represents the what-has-been, awarding to its subject the quality of being of the past—once a photograph is taken, its moment is situated in the past, unlike the video image, for instance, which can operate in the present. This quality allows the photograph to function as a means of

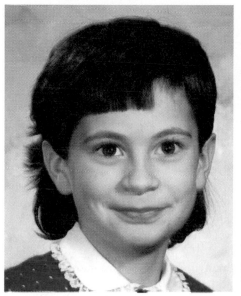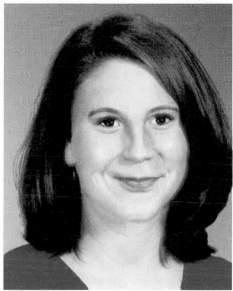

Detail from direct mail flyer with "age progression" photograph of a missing child.
Courtesy of AP Wide World Photos.

retrieval from the past, but it also gives the photograph an aura of death. Its stillness produces a sense of finality, and allows the photograph to be, in Eduardo Cadava's words, "the uncanny tomb of our memory."[9]

The photographs of missing children are highly self-conscious in their status as the what-has-been. Because we understand that these are photographs of children, people whose appearances can change dramatically in a relatively short period of time, these images often entreat us to note immediately the date on which the child was reported missing, and to look again at the photograph to gauge its pastness. After all, we know that it represents a child who no longer looks like this. These images are often computer-enhanced for "age progression" in attempts to update the children's images for better identification. Who is this child who is asking us if we have seen him or her, a virtual child who may or may not resemble the real child who may or may not be out there some-

where? This computer enhancement gives these images the quality of time slipping quickly away, rapidly erasing the original face and morphing it into another, older, perhaps more awkward visage.

This use of the "age-progressed" photograph, which falls into the realm of the more low-tech police sketch in terms of witnessing, has taken on the kind of narrative of wonder once reserved for the photograph itself. The traditional wonder at what the photograph can represent of the absent is replaced by the "gee whiz" response to the capacity of technology to predict the aging process of child to teenager. This can be, under examination, profoundly unnerving. I recently received an image flyer of Jacob Wetterling, who has been missing since 1989. In his photograph, the eleven-year-old Jacob smiles innocently for the camera. In the age-progressed image ("sponsored by the ADVO Tampa Sales office") he has morphed into a teenager, yet with the exact same smile.

30

The image is uncannily convincing, yet, like many digital images, disturbing in its lack of referent. Is Jacob alive? Does he look like this?

Both the computer-enhanced images and the photographs that demand our gaze register a poignant and desperate grasp of the past, one that appears to be quickly slipping away. Like the photographs at the memorial and in the quilt, these are images coded with prior innocence, terribly ordinary pictures of childhood faces, smiling at the camera. In the context of a querying milk carton; they intend to shock and provoke us. The ordinariness of the image asks, how could such a seemingly average child be gone? Where is this child? We are not meant to look beyond the question to the potential problems of the narrative, although those images that feature the parent who is with the child disrupt this poignancy dramatically.

The photographs of missing children speak directly to us as citizens. They ask us to engage with them not as personal images, snapshots of the past, but rather as participants in an investigation. Citizenship is defined through these images as the active surveillance of one's neighbors, always on the lookout for suspicious groupings of individuals and potential missing children under cover. These images speak a belief in the capacity of the casual family photograph to function as a form of identification and evidence in a search. They state that the child is retrievable through the photograph and that the photograph can aid in the reclamation of the family. Hence, the family image is deployed to make the country feel safe in the knowledge that the highly disruptive narrative of the missing child can be contained through technology—specifically the technologies of photography and digital computer enhancement. I do not mean to say that the stories of children who have been kidnapped are not deeply tragic and troubling. But the photograph of the missing child who is a runaway or with an angry parent also entreats us to respond with uncritical outrage. The photo-

graph that prompts its viewer to feel anger about a missing child yet safe about the means to recover that child cannot accommodate the narrative of the child who left the family by choice or design, and who may actually be better off away from it.

The narrative of technological comfort is sharply evident in the photographs that form a part of the success stories of missing children searches. The National Center for Missing & Exploited Children (NCMEC) runs an online database and website in which the complex technological status of these images becomes evident.[10] The website and database are allied with television shows such as *Unsolved Mysteries* and *America's Most Wanted* and the ADVO direct mail and supermarket campaigns in a complex web of nonprofit, commercial, and government interests. In one of NCMEC's online success stories, the recovery of three children, Hans, Heather, and Laurel Holmgren, is declared as the "direct result" of the age-progressed image of Heather, which was seen by a neighbor. However, other parts of the story begin to seep into the narrative, since it is revealed that the "abductor" who was arrested "within 45 minutes" was her "abductor father," whose photograph was also distributed. The story of this "abduction" is entirely unclear and unrevealed—who was searching for these children and why is their father now a criminal? Allowed to remain intact in this narrative of success, however, is the notion of allied technologies of surveillance which can be used to offer the public a sense of safety and security.

These photographs of missing children, whether enhanced or not, often can have effects other than their intended role as identifiers. Because of the phenomenological relationship of photographs to the what-has-been, these images often convey a sense of finality and irretrievability, not queries of hope and investigative optimism but image memorials. These children who ask us to search for them look, in fact, already gone, marked by the mortality of thc image. They appear arrested in a previous time, unable to grow older. They offer moments of prior innocence that proclaim the end of that innocence. The computer enhancement only makes the problem worse, creating instead virtual images of the child who never was—by implication, the child who never will be. If this child is unreachable (by contemporary standards this means unphotographable) then his or her replacement with a morphed image signals only a kind of technological death knell. Hence, contrary to their intent to incite the reader to recognize and identify them nearby, these images seem to suggest the hopelessness of the search, the child as already lost. This unintended effect can also circle back again to the discourse of the threat to childhood that produces the anxiety about the missing child in the first place. If the child is already missing and irretrievable, then forces must be mustered to find him or her, indeed to retrieve childhood itself in a nostalgic state.

35   If thcse images signify a lost past and, hence, a kind of memorial, what kind of memorial is this? The images of missing children reach us through a variety of commodified contexts—flyers with coupons, grocery bags, milk cartons, television. Indeed, we see them almost exclusively in the context of commerce. They share cultural meaning with the increased number of electronic memorials—website tributes and memorial pages, for instance. In what ways do they ask us to shift from the mode of the consumer to the consumer-citizen to the citizen-investigator to the witness to memory?

The Public/Private Image

These family and personal images demonstrate the paradoxical cultural role of the photograph—both a testimony to the lives of those who are absent and an object that in itself renders mortality. Their proliferation in cultural arenas speaks not only of the technological development that has allowed for greater access to the production of public images, but also to an erosion of the realm of the private. Once released into public arenas, these images can operate as free-floating signifiers, open to diverse meanings and available to many different political agendas. They retain the status of personal, but their shifting meanings are evidence not only of the malleability of the image but also the fraught role played by the family as a signifier in contemporary politics. As snapshots, they are replete with the public meanings of the personal lives they depict.

Indeed, the capacity of these images to carry their poignancy into realms of cultural meaning indicates the ways in which the notion of a private realm separate from the public has always been a fallacy. For the so-called private moments that they depict are, of course, already coded with social meanings about youth, childhood, marriage, family, and the ideologies of American culture.

The photographs that move from personal and familial contexts into public arenas, from family photograph albums to public memorials such as the Vietnam Veterans Memorial and the AIDS Memorial Quilt, from picture frames set on bureaus to missing children mailers and milk cartons, function as forms of speech in the face of cultural traumas. These photographs are offered up as testimony, hopeful evidence to the humanity once embodied by their subjects, proclamations of prior innocence, and often desperate cries for those who are absent, missing, or dead. They speak to a national public in ways that ask it to be both empathetic and vigilant. As they are pulled from personal memory into cultural memory and public discourse, they symbolize many of the hopes, fears, and desires that circulate through concepts of the family and the nation. In their ordinariness, they demand an attention to the small details and casual meanings of daily life. They are restless images, changing meaning and moving onward, asking us to pay attention to the stories, both declarative and secretive, that they tell.

NOTES

1. Roland Barthes, *Camera Lucida: Reflections on Photography,* trans. Richard Howard (New York and Wang, 1981), 93.

2. Judith Butler, "Review Essay: Spirit in Ashes," *History and Theory* 27, no. 1 (1988): 69.

3. This photograph and letter are included in Thomas Allen, *Offerings at the Wall: Artifacts from the Vietnam Veterans Memorial Collection* (Atlanta: Turner Publishing, 1995), 52–53. People who have left mementos at the memorial can contact the archive at NPS/MRCE, Box 435, Glenn Dale, MD 20769.

4. Identification of the picture was also aided by the fact that it has the name and place of the photographic studio on the back. There has been some controversy generated in Vietnam around the image. After Luttrell announced his intention to return the photo, an article published in Vietnam stated that it was a case of misidentification. The young girl in the picture remains unidentified. Associated Press, "Letter Ends Anguish of Vet's Vietnam 'Kill,'" *Newark Star-Ledger,* Aug. 19, 1997, and telephone interview with Richard Luttrell by author, Oct. 8, 1997.

5. See Jan Grover, "AIDS: Keywords," in *AIDS: Cultural Activism/Cultural Analysis,* ed. Douglas Crimp (Cambridge, Mass.: MIT Press, 1988), 23.

6. Marilyn Ivy analyzes the paradoxical aspects of this speaking position on the advertising flyers, which read "ADVO Asks . . . Have You Seen Me?" in which ADVO the company speaks to the recipient, but the child asks the question. See Marilyn Ivy, "Have You Seen Me? Recovering the Inner Child in Late Twentieth-Century America," *Social Text* 37 (Winter 1993): 227–52.

7. I have written more extensively about contemporary concerns about recovered memories of child abuse in "The Remembering of Forgetting: Recovered Memory Syndrome as Cultural Memory," *Social Text* (Spring 1999). See also Anne Higonnet's essay in this volume.

8. See Ivy, 231.

9. Eduardo Cadava, "Words of Light: Theses on the Photography of History," *Diacritics* (Fall/Winter 1992): 92.

10. See http://www.missingkids.com.

Re-reading/Conversations with the Text

1. In this essay, Sturken analyzes the significance of personal photographs left at the Vietnam Memorial, sewn into the AIDS quilt, and printed on milk cartons and grocery bags. While most of these photographs were originally taken to commemorate a significant personal event—a birthday, a holiday, a graduation—their display in a public space invests them with new meanings. Private photographs from the past become public exhibits in an ongoing cultural experience of grief and memory and finally become inscribed in the historical record. Sturken says these photos "form a kind of collective memory." As you re-read, jot down the personal, cultural, and historical contexts of photographs incorporated into the Vietnam Memorial, the AIDS quilt, and missing

children notices, and note how the context (Memorial, quilt, milk carton) changes the meaning of the photographs. Pick one photograph mentioned in the essay and explain how it affects the cultural and/or historical meaning of the site where it appears and, conversely, how the meaning of the photograph may be changed by the site where it appears.

2. According to Sturken, many of the personal photographs left at the Vietnam Memorial, sewn into the AIDS quilt, and printed on milk cartons point to a particular context, time, and state of "prior innocence." They depict children before they went off to war, or contracted AIDS, or disappeared from their family homes. Yet there are significant differences between the meaning of "prior innocence" in the photos of those who are memorialized in the Vietnam Memorial and the AIDS quilt, and the meaning of "prior innocence" in the photos of missing children on milk cartons and "America's Most Wanted." As you re-read, list the different ways in which Sturken uses the concept of "innocence" and how these uses reflect the personal, cultural, and historical contexts in which the photographs appear.

3. Sturken notes that many things besides photographs are left at the Vietnam memorial and incorporated into the AIDS quilt, including letters, teddy bears, wedding rings, and articles of clothing. For example, a Harley-Davidson motorcycle was left at the Vietnam Memorial, perhaps a tribute to a passionate enthusiast. These objects frequently exemplify aspects of culture that we value—childhood, relationships, work, hobbies—and as Sturken points out, are "often perceived as a testimony not to death but to lives lived." Imagine that you have an opportunity to leave a small collection of photographs and objects about yourself in a public place, a testimony to a "life being lived." What would you choose, and why? Do any of your choices serve as metaphors of some kind? How would you say these objects reflect U.S. cultural values, or the context in which you live? In what ways might they resist or oppose mainstream values and beliefs, and why?

Re-seeing and Re-writing

1. While most of the photographs to which Sturken refers were originally taken to commemorate a significant personal event—a birthday, a holiday, a graduation—their display in a public space invests them with new cultural and historical meanings. Sometimes these new meanings are overtly political. One effect of the photographs incorporated into the AIDS quilt, for example, is to humanize the victims of AIDS and solicit support for AIDS research. Other groups and individuals have displayed photographs of their loved ones in public contexts that give those photos new cultural and political meanings. In Argentina, the Asociación Madres de Plaza de Mayo demonstrated against the repressive government by displaying photographs of Los Desaparecidos (the disappeared), their missing family members and loved ones. After the September 11th attack on the World Trade Center, many distraught relatives and

friends placed photographs and descriptions of missing people on walls and windows near the site. Use Sturken's concepts and terms to analyze one of these spontaneous memorials, or another memorial of your own choosing.

2. "The Image as Memorial" discusses how personal images have been incorporated into public memorials to create a "collective memory" that both offers a testimony to those lost and affirms the trauma of war, AIDS, and violence against children. The Internet has provided a new public venue for individuals and groups to participate in cultural contexts of memory and testimony. Find a website that uses photographs of individuals as part of its public message and discuss how it supports or negates Sturken's interpretation of "participatory interaction" with public events. You can find some good examples at the Smithsonian American Memory site (http://memory.loc.gov), or you can look for an example of your own to analyze.

Sturken argues that personal and family photographs take on different meanings in various national and cultural contexts and are "deployed for a number of personal and public agendas. . . . These agendas address viewers in different roles—as mourners, citizens, family members, and concerned observers. Each testifies to the traffic across the boundaries of public and private realms." This essay option invites you to read Diana Taylor's essay through the lens of Sturken. To what degree are the boundaries between the public and the private, and between other boundaries, such as the international and national, blurred in representations of the September 11, 2001, attacks on the World Trade Center?

Lost in the Field of Vision: Witnessing September 11

D I A N A   T A Y L O R

In the wake of the terrorist attacks on September 11, 2001, media coverage of the event was saturated with photographs and video footage from private citizens who happened to be in the vicinity with their cameras. This collision of professional and amateur media is explored in *DIANA TAYLOR*'s "Lost in the Field of Vision: Witnessing September 11." In it, Taylor argues that this practice of amateur photography should be taken seriously as a means of conveying information and knowledge within our society, just as seriously as the information generated by established media entities, government, or other professional organizations. Taylor's essay was originally included as a chapter in her 2003 book *The Archive and the Repertoire: Cultural History and Performance in the Americas,* which provides an alternative history of the Americas based on political demonstrations, theatrical arts, and documentary practices.

When I saw the north tower of the World Trade Center in flames, about five minutes after the first plane hit, I thought, "God, it's going to take a lot of time and money to fix that." A small community of watchers gathered in the street. Two women recounted that they had heard the low-flying plane zoom by, then saw it slice into the building. Others joined us. It was a freakishly beautiful day. We stretched closer to hear what others were saying. The women told their story again. Again, we listened. "Are people trapped inside?" it finally occurred to us to ask. Groups formed, dissolved, reformed. I headed home, using my cell phone to contact my family. No signal. Traffic stopped. Then the second plane. Another explosion. Outside of my building, more people. The building manager's wife worked in one of the towers; she was there now, he told us, as we stared dumbfounded down the street at the flames. Even then we didn't start talking about deliberate terrorist attacks. That happened only after word of the Pentagon and Pennsylvania filtered onto the street. We stood transfixed, watching, witnesses without a narrative, part of a tragic chorus that stumbled onto the wrong set. The city stopped. The phones were dead, cars vanished, stores closed.

Like many others, I went inside to turn on the television, trying to find sense in what I was seeing. I could not assimilate it, either live or on TV. As in sports stadium, I watched both at the same time. The large windows framed a surreal and mostly silent scene. The wind was blowing toward Brooklyn, so the smell and smoke had not yet started to leak inside. From the twenty-ninth floor of my NYU housing, a mile or so north of the WTC, I couldn't see people. I'd turn to the television and see the running, the screaming, the collage of frantic yet nonetheless contained images of disaster on the screen. Giuliani was talking, news anchors were talking, foreign correspondents were talking. Then I'd run back to the window. I took a photograph, not knowing why exactly, and started taping the CNN broadcast: TV, window, photo, TV, window, photo, back and forth, my options limited to a back-and-forth, trying to contain and grasp what was happening. Should I go get my daughter? Was she better off at school, a mile uptown, or here? Back and forth, back and forth. I went to get my daughter.

The mood on the street had changed. We were in full crisis mode—the city, still and suddenly stark, in shock. Stunned, people wandered around the streets looking for loved ones. Yet everything was quiet except for the persistent wails of ambulances, fire trucks, police cars.

As we walked back, Marina and I wanted to do something, do anything. We tried to give blood at St. Vincent's, but the line was hours long.

5   We went home and looked out the window. It was eerie not seeing people. The catastrophe, one could believe for a second perhaps, was about planes and towers, about loss of property rather than loss of life. This looked like one of those surgical strikes that the U.S. military claims to have perfected. Our aviation technology and terror tactics turned against us. Our Hollywood scenarios live—complete with towering infernos and raging sirens—just down the street. Collateral damage, reconfigured. I wondered if my inability to make sense of what I was seeing had been conditioned by the dominance of this virtual repertoire of images, characters, plotlines. I had seen it all before on computer and television monitors. Did this blinding signal the failure of the live as a means of knowing? Or the triumph of what George Yúdice calls the "Military Industrial Media Complex," more commonly known as "entertainment," that has rendered the live one more reiteration? I turned on the TV.

On TV, a narrative sequence was beginning to emerge; people spoke of the attack, the response, "the world reacts," victimization, evil, revenge. But the linear plotline too had little to do with what we were seeing. The images, repeated again and again, froze the moment of impact. Television's multiframes simultaneously conveyed and controlled the crisis: in one tight box, a speaker delivered an opinion; in another, frantic videos taken with handheld cameras caught the panic that I couldn't see from my window. On the bottom of the screen, the information loop also kept repeating, freezing time. The time of the first attack, 8:46 A.M., the time of the second, 9:02 A.M. . . . The loop caught the movement and

the stasis of the phenomenon, the obsessive coming back to that one fixed moment. Then the frames shifted again: now a steady Giuliani dominated the foreground, pushing havoc into the tight background box. I ran back to the window.

The Towers smoldered silently in the distance, waves of smoke stuck in the too blue sky. Time itself seemed to have stopped, conjured into fixity perhaps by the TV's invocation of the first strike, then the second. It looked as if the Towers would just keep standing there, smoldering. More photos. Seeing through the lens extended the reach and holding power of my vision. Aware that a historical event was overtaking my capacity to understand it, I too wanted to contain the moment and freeze it for later: TV, window, photo, TV, window, photo, back and forth. Each click of my camera was my own pause/hold, as I entered into the suspended rhythm of the present. The archival impulse prompted me to save the images to understand them at some future time. One day I would write about it, I told myself, even as I considered taking out my journal and writing about it *now.* But I couldn't. I put the *now* away for later. I envisioned the moment from the post*now*, what I would do with it from a safe distance, sorting through the neat, glossy 4×6 images of disaster. Like the TV's *now*, mine was already a repeat, a retrospective as I projected myself into the future, looking back. Photography, at this moment, was paradoxically both action and anti-action, performance and antiperformance, a doing, a click, in the face of the impossibility of doing, about the need to stop everything until I could get a hold of it. I took another photo and thought I really should be writing down the time of each click. But I couldn't do that either. The failures of the archive linked again to the failures of the live. I went back to the TV, my options limited to a back-and-forth. On TV, I heard that the south tower had fallen. I rushed back to the window. I couldn't believe I hadn't seen it live.

The Towers gone, seeing took on a different charge. The TV obsessively repeated images, itself trapped in the traumatic loop. A few newly heroic protagonists, like Giuliani, emerged from the rubble to cordon off the catastrophe, trying to limit it to "ground zero." Almost immediately, he ordered a media blackout at the site. Only designated images would circulate, only professionals allowed to photograph. The signifying objects gone, we had access only to photos of the objects. Instantly, it seemed, newly minted organizations produced glossy journals, passing as weeklies, to circulate the permitted images, the permissible stories. Bylines, photo credits, and authenticating sources disappeared. Unsigned testimonials invoked, yet hid, the seeing "I." Specifics gave way to the ubiquitous footer "God Bless America." Media as vehicle of consumerism partly surrendered to its other, only somewhat less apparent mode: media as delivery system for state ideology.

In spite of all attempts at containability, the catastrophe spread. The attack we had witnessed was now being called a war, albeit a "different kind of war." CNN came up with a logo and a title: the flag toward the bottom left-hand corner, and just under that, "America's New War." The world was suddenly reshuffled into those who stood by "us" and those who turned against "us." Giuliani, live on TV, spoke of the "tragedy that we're all undergoing right now" and said that his "heart goes out to all the innocent victims." Yet even that first day, when people were walking around in shock, anxious that further devastation might follow, he assured a nervous country that "people in New York City can demonstrate our resolve and our support for all the people viciously attacked today by going about their lives." The "our" immediately shifted into the "their." The roles already assigned: the heroes (Giuliani, the firefighters, etc.), the victims (those who had been "viciously attacked"), and those of us who were neither but who struggled to get on with our lives. As

bad as the fear, perhaps, was the physical sensation of being close to the site. We inhaled the Towers, smelled them, tasted them in our mouths, rubbed them from our teary eyes, crunched them with our feet as we walked through the streets. Many people were displaced following the evacuation of lower Manhattan and looking for places to sleep. Was that what Giuliani meant by "going on with our lives"? Giuliani and Bush Jr. soon spelled it out: stay out of the way, buy theatre tickets, eat at restaurants, fly on planes. In a parody of the language of sacrifice that accompanies war, Bush Jr. recognized the sacrifice demanded of us: we were to wait patiently in lines at airports and ballparks, knowing it was for a greater good. If this was a tragedy, we were not recognized as participants. The role of witness, as responsible, ethical, participant rather than spectator to crisis, collapsed in the rubble of talk of victims, heroes, and the rest of us. Even though officials invoked the inclusive "we" to refer to the attack and "our" determination to fight back, there was no place for us, no participation that could conceivably be meaningful.

To *do* something, I kept taking photos, though now mostly photos of photos. I also met regularly with three close friends who were also thinking about photography in relation to September 11: photographer Lorie Novak, cultural theorist Marianne Hirsch, folklorist and performance studies scholar Barbara Kirshenblatt-Gimblett. Speaking about the need to photograph with them made up for what the photos could not communicate in themselves, a recognition, perhaps, that taking a photograph was in itself an act of interlocution, a need to make sense and communicate. It was a way of assessing whether we had all seen the same things, or if our takes on the events—apparently so similar in the photos that we had a hard time remembering who took which—were in fact quite different. Our views had perhaps little connection with the viewfinder—the seeing, again, dislocated from the knowing. Marianne

10

felt uncomfortable about photographing, as if we were further violating the victimized. I felt that the only way I could cope was by photographing, piecing together my own narrative.

The media's inundation of the must-see covered the tensions around the political mustn't-see. The immediate talk about who had *seen* what when (the Towers, the planes), suddenly complicated by the who *knew* what when (FBI, sources close to the White House). If anything, the more we saw the images circulating in the media, the less we had access to. For one thing, too much was going on backstage, out of public view. For another, the intensely mediatized seeing became a form of social blinding: percepticide, a form of killing or numbing through the senses. Our very eyes used against us.

Lost in the field of vision. I think it wasn't until a few days later that some of us started developing hero envy, some trauma envy.

For days, all we saw were images of heroic men in uniform rushing to ground zero. In this time of national bodybuilding, a *New York Times* article on September 12 stated that "the coming days will require [Bush] to master the image of sturdy authority and presidential strength." The photos that followed showed all the determination and polish of the revitalized mise-en-scéne. The front-page photo on the *New York Times* on September 13 shows an army of men amid a sea of debris. On September 15, it's Giuliani, Bush, and Fire Commissioner Von Essen looking at the wounded site with grim courage. "Bush tells the military to 'get ready,'" says the *New York Times* headline of September 16. The front cover of *Time* magazine's special issue of September 24 depicts Bush standing on the ruins, holding the U.S. flag resolutely over his head with his right hand. *U.S. News and World Report* that same week shows a firefighter hanging an enormous flag high over the eerie remains of the crumbled towers.

Women were noticeably absent that first week, except for the front cover of the *New Republic,* which featured a woman, well, a symbolic woman. The Statue of Liberty holds her burning beacon high with her right hand; the tall towers lit up behind her. On her body, the words "It happened here." Should the instant feminization of loss surprise us? Or the masculinist rush to save the day? Soon images of weeping widows and women in burkhas appeared in the media, strengthening "our" national resolve. It is interesting how quickly the official scenario of active men rescuing vulnerable women got reactivated. For an event labeled "unprecedented," "singular," a watershed that changed everything forever, it is clear how little the logic of justification had changed and how much it relied on gendering self and other. The attacks immediately triggered the same old scenario drawn from a repertoire of frontier lore: evil barbarians, threatened damsels protected by heroic males. Wanted: Dead or Alive.

Arts and sports fully engaged in the patriotic and militaristic spectacle. The Concert for the City of New York that October, highlighting artists such as Paul McCartney, the Rolling Stones, and the Who (to name a few), paraded police officers, firefighters, emergency and rescue workers, along with dozens of uniformed athletes to perform the heroics of the hitherto ordinary. Male bonding was not only okay again but sanctified. A handful of women appeared among the sea of uniforms. From our seats, we could feel the craving for protagonism on the part of the audience. Many of us had dutifully accepted our non-heroic roles by taking out our credit cards and paying to participate. The 800-number for contributions flashed on the screens around the stage, addressing the intended audience sitting at home watching TV rather than those of us physically there. We, the live, served as an enthusiastic background for the real show taking place in the public arena, a show of national unity and directionality that by-passed the public itself. As in the political arena, where daily polls tracked the growing support for war, our role was to sit back and

15

clap. Sports clamored to get in the act. The Mets' first game after September 11 included a ceremony featuring uniformed men and flags in honor of those who had contributed to the rescue efforts. So, of course, did the Yankees'. Moments of silence and other commemorative acts froze us again in that forever time, September 11.

So what about us, the nonheroes who were not allowed to play, who were trying to do what the Mayor asked of us, that is, get on with our lives? At Tisch School of the Arts, some students lamented that they had chosen to pursue arts rather than medicine. At Bellevue Hospital, I heard a doctor say he was sorry he'd gone into medicine rather than rescue work.

But there was a competing spectacle on the streets. The entire surface of lower Manhattan was wrapped in images of the missing—the missing towers, the missing people.

The loss of the Towers triggered a phantom limb phenomenon: the more people recognized the lack, the more they felt the presence of the absence.

Never had the Towers been so visible. Photos, postcards, T-shirts, banners, and street art immediately hit the streets, performing the existence of what no longer was physically there. Their ghostly presence, by definition repetition, like Derrida's revenant, filled the vacuum. Instead of their ontology, we can think about their hauntology. At this moment, in New York, we were haunted.

The smiling faces of the missing also haunted. They were everywhere, but they were nowhere to be found: 8 × 10 Xerox and laser fliers taped on street-lamps, at bus stops, on mailboxes and hospital walls; theirs were the only happy faces in the city. The photos multiplied endlessly, making the absence of those in them more palpable. From the fliers, it looked as if the people in them came from every imaginable background and part of the world. Most were young. All were "legal" immigrants or citizens. Families of undocumented workers who worked in the Towers did not dare display their photos—yet one more disappearance. Mexicans would sometimes simply

Someone drew the towers and inserted them where the Towers once stood, Brooklyn. September 2001.

Photo by Lorie Novak. Copyright © 2001 by Lorie Novak, www.lorienovak.com.

The first Mets game after September 11.
Photos by Diana Taylor.

post an anonymous Virgen de Guadalupe to show that their loved one belonged among the missing.

The photographs of the missing were recent: a man holding his newborn, a joyous family gathering with an arrow pointing to the lost person, a woman proudly holding up the fish she'd caught. The photos now had an entirely different function; we, the passersby, are begged to recognize and help locate the missing. In a sudden reversal, the relatively inanimate and flimsy photograph had outlasted its more "permanent" subject: the living person, the towering buildings.

On or around the photographs, someone had added text to convey something not in the photos themselves. The captions all note exact positions: "Last seen 85th floor, WTC 2." As with the September 11 crisis in general, the emphasis was on *where* people were. All but the essential particularities vanished, leaving the where, the when. The photos, as Barbara Kirshenblatt-Gimblett noted, conveyed hope; the captions anticipated the worst. They painfully mixed the intimate and forensic. They included physical descriptions as well as identifying body marks, envisioning that the loved ones, though, it was hoped, alive, would not be able to identify or speak for themselves. Sometimes the possible scenarios were explicitly spelled out. If you have any Jane Does please call. . . . Maybe the loved one was wandering around in shock? Sometimes, the captions imagined a body lying unconscious, exposed to the medical gaze: mole on back of thigh, heart-shaped tattoo on pelvic area, appendectomy scar. Family members made the rounds with stacks of fliers—St. Vincent's, Bellevue, the VA—taping the fliers on all available surfaces as they went.

As opposed to the language of heroism, the fliers avoided the gendered pitfalls. Lorie Novak notes that men were identified as fathers, husbands, and brothers as often as women were described as executives, managers, and office assistants. Family photos included the missing in a wide variety of poses—fishing, holding children, cutting the birthday cake—few of them conventionally gendered. Both male and female photos and captions showed the loving perspective of a family member, intimately connected to that lost body.

The walls near Bellevue and St. Vincent's were called the Wall of Prayers and the Wall of Hope and Remembrance. On Wednesday, September 12, and Thursday the 13th, the areas were filled with family members searching for loved ones, pasting up fliers.

City officials couldn't use the photos; they asked family members to bring in toothbrushes, cigarette butts, and hair clippings. Recognition in this day and age has more to do with DNA than with body marks and photography.

But the photographs fulfilled an enormous public function: they involved us, the non-heroes, non-victims, in the search, in the hope, in the mourning. They enabled acts of transfer: the missing were now "ours," and New York City suddenly part of "America."

After the rain on Thursday and Friday, the fliers were covered with plastic sheets, shrouds for the victims, protection against further damage. The photos occupied the space of the missing bodies.

The "missing" signs turned into memorials: "In Loving Memory of . . ." Tiny shrines emerged, with messages, poems, photos, religious passages, flowers, stuffed bears, and children's drawings. People arrived with cameras, ready to memorialize in their own ways. Television cameras clogged the passageways.

The *New York Times* had started running portraits of the missing on September 15 as "Snapshots of Their Lives," a section that became "Portraits of Grief" after hope of the "lives" was gone.

Soon, the missing were officially declared dead. In October, the government handed small mahogany urns to the families of the

From the fliers, it looked as if the people in them came from every imaginable background and part of the world. Most were young. The undocumented victims disappeared from the walls much as they had disappeared from the Towers.

Photos by Diana Taylor.

Bellevue Hospital's Wall of Prayers.
Photo by Diana Taylor.

victims, each one containing debris from the site. Although there were some strong parallels with countries such as Argentina, where victims were also pawns of terrorist violence and their bodies never found, the U.S. government wanted no "disappeared." Photographs of the victims' faces, unlike in the case of Argentina, have not been used in pro- or antimilitary demonstrations or to bring a performance claim against any individual, party, or political platform. This is not to say that financial claims have not been made on behalf of the victims. References to them continue to permeate our daily lives, but these have not involved the photographs. Somehow, the images remained particularized, cordoned off, a testimony to lives, now lost.

Loved ones used photographs to create portals for their dead. Tiny shrines, adorned with teddy bears and flowers, became the point of contact where the living went to communicate recent events with those no longer here to witness them. Somebody left a sonogram of their unborn child; someone else took a recent photo of the newborn baby to show the missing father. A son wrote a message to his dead mother. These sites became privileged conduits between here and there.

But where did the rest of us fit? And what was our role in this event, so often referred to as a tragedy? Because of the time lag between the first hit and the fall of the second tower, September 11 was an event that produced a huge number of eyewitnesses. The attack had also inscribed our positions. Everyone started their description by stating where they were; what they had seen. Yet it was clear from early on that "we" had no neat place in all of this. A photograph published in the *New York Times* the day after the attack had already converted witnesses into spectators. The caption read: "Spectators walking through debris from the World Trade Center." Those of us who lived here were deterritorialized, not just by the events but by official pronouncements that turned us into tourists, walking through.

People responded as citizens, however, wanting to help by giving blood or volunteering. But the city could not cope with the outpour of

New York City suddenly became part of "America."

The plastic shrouds for the victims' photographs protected them against further damage.

Photos by Diana Taylor.

public participation. There were very few survivors in the hospitals, which already had more than enough blood. When the fliers of the missing started appearing we were interpolated as potential heroes: PLEASE HELP!!! some fliers begged. The new spatial inscriptions asked us to interact with the city in a different way, as actors in the public space and not merely passive recipients or consumers. Many people responded by turning themselves into the embodiment of unity and national fervor, wearing flags on jackets, as headscarves, as T-shirts; FDNY and NYPD baseball caps magically appeared on every street corner. Immigrants and people of color knew they would be targeted as terrorists and preemptively protected themselves behind the American flag. Artists, like mural artist Chico, offered their homage by painting walls and erecting shrines throughout the city. Public interventions in the parks gave people a place to participate actively and put forward their views about the escalating war talk and ethnic tensions. Thousands of people gathered daily in Union Square (among other places), turning every inch into a shrine, a protest, a performance event. This live interaction showed a far greater range of opinion than the TV coverage did, and soon the media stopped referring to this show of popular opinion.

Politicians hurried to interpret this show of civil activity in specific ways. Senator Lewis, who sits on the Senate Appropriations Committee, claimed he got the bellicose message of "the American people" behind these demonstrations: they're being patient, but they're not going to wait forever. Nonetheless, the show of activity made many officials nervous. Giuliani ordered the Park Service to take away the flowers, posters, candles, and other offerings, claiming that, after the rain, they made the city look dirty. Why would tourists visit a dirty city?

35   Many people participated by taking photographs. Inundated in images, we created our own. Thousands upon thousands of photographs flooded the public sphere, some

highly professional and aesthetically compelling, but many more of them like mine, undistinguished and indistinguishable snapshots of the Towers, the fliers, the memorials. Photography was evidence, proof not so much of the existence of the object of the photograph but of our own existence. We, the backgrounded participants in this drama, were nonetheless *there*. In photography, some of us found an act of unity of sorts: we were all focused on the same thing, we were all framing what we saw from our position. Photography was also democratic: we could all point and shoot. Taking photos, for some, surely represented an effort to gain access, to gain understanding, both officially denied. It allowed people like me to formulate our own take in response to those circulated through the media. Maybe, too, it allowed us to confine disaster to pocket-size dimensions, 4 × 6s and 8 × 10s. It was a way of doing *something* when it seemed that nothing could be done. At the same time, photo taking has become a cultural habit, a way of documenting without necessarily seeing, a way of entering into the structured frame of visibility: pointing, shooting, and posing. Two students recounted, with utter disbelief and self-disgust, that they had posed, smiling at the camera, with the burning towers behind them.

A gallery in SoHo offered space to *This Is New York*, an exhibit that understood the democratizing and testimonial role of photography in a time of social crisis by anonymously displaying all the photos submitted in relation to September 11. Those by famous professionals hung clipped to clotheslines next to those by everyone else.

Signs went up prohibiting photography near ground zero, which had been turned simultaneously into a battle zone, a crime scene, "a tragedy site," and a sacred site. The Mayor accused us of "gawking."

What I most remember of the months following September 11 is all about seeing, about the failure to understand what I was seeing with

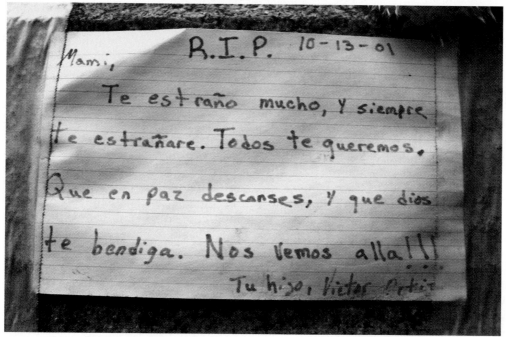

Memorial shrines and portals for the dead.
Photos by Lorie Novak.

(*left*) A photograph published in the *New York Times* the day after the attack had already converted witnesses into spectators. The caption reads: "Spectators walking through debris from the World Trade Center."
Photo by Justin Lane for the *New York Times*.

(*below*) New Yorkers started interacting with the city in a different way, as active participants in a crisis.
Photo by Diana Taylor.

A man reading the inscription on a mural by Chico, Lower East Side, New York City.
Photo by Diana Taylor.

my own eyes, to make sense of the images in the media, and the downright prohibition of seeing and knowing imposed by the government. It wasn't just ground zero and popular protest that was blocked out. Coverage of the U.S. attacks on Afghanistan was highly censored; surveillance was turned back on the public at home. The group Americans for Victory over Terrorism (AVOT) urged people to "support democratic patriotism when it is questioned; and take to task those groups and individuals who fundamentally misunderstand the nature of the war we are facing." University professors and public intellectuals critical of the war efforts were silenced and, at times, lost their jobs. Ashcroft announced that our democratic system made us vulnerable to the enemy. Like our airplanes and popular entertainment, our democracy had turned against us.

In the midst of this crackdown on dissent, we hear that "we" are indeed also actors in this tragedy, also victims of trauma. Victimization has been expanded to include not only "those who were viciously attacked" but an increasing number of others affected by the attacks. The *New York Times* included a small brochure inside the paper several times, *New York Needs Us Strong: Coping after Sept. 11,* that outlined the stress and trauma affecting "those who saw it happen from the street, or from their window, or over and over again on television." Funded by Project Liberty: Feel Free to Feel Better, the brochure adds that the disaster seems uncontainable: "Unlike other disasters that seem to have an end, the attacks on New York and Washington have been followed by other disturbing events, including the threat of bio-terrorism." The anxiety, detachment, forgetfulness, and lack of concentration that the brochure links to the crisis are, of course, common symptoms of trauma. But what, I wonder, are the political ramifications of such a public discourse of vic-

Drawing by Marina Manheimer-Taylor. The writing on the flag reads: "bigotry/hate crimes/discrimination."
Photo by Diana Taylor.

Local mural artists, like Chico from the Lower East Side, offered their homage.
Photo by Diana Taylor.

timhood in the face of the United States' expanding, and undefined, war against terrorism? Many of us have experienced trauma and struggled to regain some sense of balance in the face of accelerated global violence after September 11, but we might find more enabling models than the one put forth by Project Liberty. The Mothers of the Plaza de Mayo, to go back to Argentina for a moment, coped with their grief through the weekly, ritualized protest against the government. Women in Black meet weekly to protest and mourn the loss of life in the Middle East. Yet, amid talk of anxiety and detachment, we have been slow to mobilize against the escalating politics of violence, largely perpetuated by the U.S. government. Where is our ethical engagement?

40   If this is a tragedy, whose tragedy? As an aesthetic category, tragedy turns around the challenge of containment. Can Oedipus curb the tide of devastation that has wrecked Thebes? Hamlet's inability to act decisively leads to generalized death and the loss of the kingdom. Yet, tragedy is not just *about* containment, it functions as a structure of containment. Tragedy cuts catastrophe down to size. It orders events into comprehensible scenarios. Aristotle specifies that tragic events are of a certain magnitude, carry serious implications, and have an air of inevitability about them; protagonists have a "defined moral character," and the plot leads to recognition in the tragic hero as well as the spectator. Most theories of tragedy identify the hero as committing a huge mistake, related to a tragic flaw or hubris. The massive potential for destruction depicted in tragedy is contained by the form itself, for tragedy delivers the devastation in a miniaturized and "complete" package, neatly organized with a beginning, middle, and end. Ultimately, tragedy assures us, the crisis will be resolved and balance restored. The fear and pity we, as spectators, feel will be purified by the action.

The events of September 11, however, make me think that we're looking at not only a different kind of war but a different kind of tragedy. When people refer to "the tragedy," they usually are referring to the unexpected fall of the mighty, to that awesome spectacle of pity and fear so brilliantly executed by the suicide pilots and so efficiently delivered nationally and globally by the U.S. media. They refer to the hijacked planes and the thousands of victims, to Bush Jr., hastily recast as a leader with a definable moral character, gearing up to set time right. Tragedy also allows us to stress the exceptional and isolated nature of the catastrophe and dovetails neatly with the language of the "unprecedented" and "watershed" occurrence. The catastrophe was certainly tragic in the vernacular sense, and the term offers us a vocabulary for fear and sorrow. Yet, I think that using *tragedy* in its aesthetic connotation not only structures the events but also blinds us to other ways of thinking about them.

Take tragedy's organizational timetable: beginning, middle, and end. Did the tragic action really start on September 11? Some might argue that we were hijacked long before, maybe starting in fall 2000, when the elections were pulled off course. Important items on the national agenda; such as improving education and health care, went up in smoke. The victims from that catastrophe remain uncounted, although they are certainly identified. New victims are created daily: antiterrorist legislation, anti-immigrant sentiment, racial profiling, and unaccountable military tribunals seep into our social system even as corporate welfare packages wind their way through the Congress. Others might point out that we have been on a seemingly inevitable collision course with Islamic oil-producing nations for decades. Should the civilian losses they have sustained figure among the victims? What about their trauma? As for the ending, nothing seems certain except that it won't be speedy, make sense, or bring purification and release.

And if this is a tragedy, who is the tragic hero? Bush Jr., as the representative of the United States, cannot take on the role because that would entail assuming a position of recognition and self-indictment. "Fearful and pitiable happenings," as Aristotle notes, involve a change "from good fortune to bad, and not thanks to wickedness but because of some mistake of great weight and consequence, by a man such as we have described" (38–39). Rather than owning that many of the events leading to September 11 resulted from a mistaken politics of great weight and consequences, however, the administration has stressed that this is about "good" fighting "evil." The struggle, moreover, lacks the linear directionality of tragedy. The war, too, is a revenant, a haunting: in simple terms, it's a replay of an earlier Bush war. More subtly, it's a recycling of Manifest Destiny ideology that justifies ("our") annihilating "evil" under the banner of righteousness. The victims lost in the World Trade Center, on the other hand, can't be the heroes unless we can pinpoint their tragic stature, their mistake, their recognition.

The events of September 11 become tragedy through claims to universality. The U.S. government and the media present it as a limit case, as "incommensurable," the greatest, worst, most unimaginable and unspeakable crisis ever. Commentators tend to place limit cases at the outer edges of intelligibility, at the very boundaries of representation. We can talk about them only in the language of exceptionalism. Limit cases are paradigmatic. They signal models to which many disparate issues can be related, but only by illustration. However, it is clear to most commentators outside the United States that the attacks, though criminal, were in no way exceptional. For many Latin Americans, for example, September 11 was all too familiar. State terrorism and antistate terrorism vie for public control through escalating attacks on the civilian population, whether it's the bombing of buildings or the silencing of dissent. Talk of ground

The "live" performances, installations, and protests showed a far greater range of opinion than the TV coverage did.

Photos by Diana Taylor.

Towers for peace, towers for war . . .
Photos by Diana Taylor.

zero, moreover, illuminates what it most seeks to hide: that "ground zero" originally referred to Hiroshima and Nagasaki, the two sites bombed by U.S. nuclear forces that killed between one hundred thousand and three hundred thousand innocent people. The government's performance of innocence and Giuliani's cordoning off of the site urge the public to forget historical precedence. So, instead of the language of exceptionalism, there is a political argument to be made against the discourse of incommensurability. The language of tragedy and limit cases works against broader emancipatory politics because it detaches events, refusing to see connections and larger frameworks. Insulated claims to protagonism and universality work at odds with

coalition building that enables cross-event understanding.

Finally, none of the tragic events seems destined to occasion recognition or insight in the spectators. On the contrary: September 11 created a revealing paradox. This is an event that banished and blinded the witnesses, even as it created them. Will purification and release come from participating in polls asking whether we support war efforts? What insights can we salvage from the rubble?

During the final phases of the cleanup, ground zero was open for viewing. The massive rubble that was the World Trade Center took on a life of its own. The twisted steel and pulverized concrete reminded us that the event was "real." Now that all that has been cleared away, the

45

Signs went up prohibiting photography near ground zero.
Photos by Diana Taylor.

People on the World Trade Center viewing platform.
Photo by Diana Taylor.

fenced-in display of sacralized remains provides the authenticating materiality that animates the resuscitations and sustains the performance of retribution. The Towers live. This moment of postdisappearance functions politically; the endless revisualizations of the Towers will continue to motivate foreign and domestic policy. City officials and business advocates balance the demands of tourism with those of commercial real estate. Sixteen acres in lower Manhattan are too valuable to remain sacred for long. But the 7,700 viewers who visit the site daily need to have something to commemorate. The negotiations demand yet more shifts in language and the creative concentration of the aura in one discrete place.

A few weeks before the final cleanup, I walked down to the site, stood in line for a ticket, waited hours for my assigned time, snaked through the viewing platform with dozens of other people. I took a photograph. There was nothing to see.

Debris from the World Trade Center, on display on the viewing platform.
Photo by Diana Taylor.

Ground zero. There was nothing to see.
Photo by Diana Taylor.

Re-reading/Conversations with the Text

1. "Lost in the Field of Vision" begins with the author's reflection on her thoughts and actions during the September 11 World Trade Center attacks. Re-read the first few paragraphs of the essay and compare Taylor's personal account of the event to your own experiences on that day. What were your initial thoughts and feelings? What specific words, images, or metaphors associated with the event resonate for you? How did the various news media affect your reaction to the events?

2. Taylor claims that two main categories of people emerged in the days and weeks following September 11: heroes and nonheroes. According to Taylor, how are these categories characterized? Who belongs in each category? What are their major distinctions? What language and/or imagery are used in describing and depicting each group? Are particular metaphors or metonymic relations at work in Taylor's description and interpretation of representations of the attacks? Do you agree with her categorization? Why or why not?

3. As the events of September 11 unfolded, Taylor admits that one of her first instincts was to document the tragedy with her camera. Re-read paragraph seven. Explain Taylor's motivation for wanting to photograph the towers. What specific emotions or thoughts compelled her to take such actions? Why would she choose to witness the events through a camera rather than experiencing the event "live" or unfiltered by a camera lens?

Re-seeing and Re-writing

1. "Lost in the Field of Vision" presents us with two very distinct types of images. On the one hand, Taylor focuses on images produced and distributed by "regular" people, who created their own posters and makeshift memorials in the wake of September 11. These types of images stand in marked contrast to another class of images described by Taylor: the "professional" imagery produced by news organizations and government officials. For this assignment, compare the visual compositions of these two classes of images. As you write your analysis, consider whether and how the two types of images depict different contexts, have different looks and/or purposes, and evoke different reactions in those who see them.

2. Taylor explores the tension between (or at least competing ideas about) people's perceived right to see and the state's control or regulation of what is seen. According to Taylor, how does this occur with respect to the events surrounding September 11 and government officials' attempts to provide the public with "sanctioned" images? Think of other events in recent history for which a similar power dynamic (or censorship) is present. Create an image portfolio with accompanying captions to depict the tension over the control of sight between citizens and the state. You might compare, for example, images associated with September 11 and the most recent war with Iraq. What notable

shifts in tone, character, choice of subject, or persuasive strategies do you notice as you examine these two sets of images? How do certain words and terms (e.g., "hero," "sacrifice") take on different connotations depending on the immediate context in which they're placed?

Intertext

One of the key rhetorical concepts for this section is "context," or the outside events, conditions, and belief systems that have some influence on a specific text. For this assignment, you are to conduct a contextual analysis of two memorial events. Both Diana Taylor's "Lost in the Field of Vision" and Dinitia Smith's "Slave Site for a Symbol of Freedom" deal in part with memorials—for the victims of the September 11 attacks and the victims of the institution of slavery, respectively. First, in what ways do the memorials substantially differ from one another, be it in form, medium, tone, duration, or meaning? Second, how have the differing contexts affected the eventual outcome of the memorials in question?

Four Images from the FDR Archives

Born in 1882, Franklin Delano Roosevelt was the Democratic nominee for Vice President in 1920, at the remarkably young age of 38. Then, as the official White House biography explains it:

> In the summer of 1921, when he was 39, disaster hit—he was stricken with poliomyelitis. Demonstrating indomitable courage, he fought to regain the use of his legs, particularly through swimming. At the 1924 Democratic Convention he dramatically appeared on crutches to nominate Alfred E. Smith as "the Happy Warrior." In 1928 Roosevelt became Governor of New York. (http://www.whitehouse.gov/history/presidents/fr32.html).

Although FDR never again walked unaided—either by crutches, a wheelchair, or the physical support of others—he was elected President of the United States in 1932. He went on to serve an unprecedented four terms in office. He is noted for setting in motion the New Deal, the Social Security system, and the United Nations—and for leading the nation into World War II in response to the attack on Pearl Harbor. He died shortly into his fourth term, in April 1945, while in Warm Springs, Georgia (site of the Polio Foundation and the warm springs bath that he frequented).

All of the public photos and appearances of FDR were carefully orchestrated to cloak his disability. (See Hugh Henry Gallagher's historical account, *FDR's Splendid Deception: The Moving Story of Roosevelt's Massive Disability and the Intense Efforts to Conceal It from the Public,* New York: Dodd, Mead 1985.) In the official FDR photo archives, however, many photos exist of him in primarily family interactions. These images make his disability slightly more evident, while they also point out other interesting sociocultural dynamics of the era.

FDR with Dr. MacDonald and his valet, 1924.
Courtesy of Picture History.

FDR, Eleanor, and Missy LeHand (Roosevelt's secretary) in Hyde Park, 1930.

Franklin and Eleanor Roosevelt, 1933.
Courtesy of Picture Desk, Inc./Kobal Collection.

FDR with Fala and Ruthie Bie, Top Cottage, 1941.
Courtesy of Margaret Suckley/Franklin D. Roosevelt Library.

Re-reading/Conversations with the Text

1. The first image, "FDR with Dr. MacDonald and his valet," is from 1924, three years after FDR contracted polio. Read this image in context—paying special consideration to the era of the photograph, the 1920s—with an attempt to describe the photo to someone who has never seen it. Attend especially to the triangulated relationship between the three men, describing their clothing, their postures, their expressions, and their gaze in relation to the camera/photographer. What details from the background also add to a description of the scene? How might you compare your description and reading of this photograph to the one Wendy Hesford offers of her great-grandfather and his valet (see pp. 59–67)?

2. The second image is taken in FDR's hometown, Hyde Park, New York; the year is 1930, two years before he was elected President and nine years after he contracted polio. Focus first on reading this photograph in terms of where its center is: Who gazes directly at the camera; who is background, and who is foreground? Do you think FDR intended this photo to be taken? Why or why not? Finally, compare this photo to the one from 1924: What is similar and what is different about the images?

3. The third image, "Franklin and Eleanor Roosevelt," is from 1933; it was often used as an official press photo for the President and First Lady during his first term in office. What is remarkable and unremarkable about this photo? Does it fit the expectations you have of official portraits of the President and First Lady? How does this photograph serve metaphorically and metonymically as an official presidential image?

4. The final image, "FDR with Fala and Ruthie Bie, Top Cottage," is taken in 1941, shortly after the start of FDR's third term. This image shows the President with his famous dog, Fala (also memorialized in bronze at the FDR Memorial) and his granddaughter. This photo is one of the most popular photos of FDR, sold as postcards in the tourist shop at the FDR Memorial and serving as the feature image for the cover of Hugh Henry Gallagher's *FDR's Splendid Deception.* What elements of this photo make it seem similar to and different from the other three photos? How does this photo "fit" in the FDR family album? How, too, does it "fit" in the FDR national (public) album? What elements of the photograph find echos in other national symbols/metaphors?

Re-seeing and Re-writing

1. Visit the New Deal online archives at http://newdeal.feri.org/library/l_14.htm and view the other eight (8) photos included along with these four. Try arranging them in some order of your own and then writing a "national album" narrative of FDR based on these twelve images. Aim for two pages of narrative. You need not do further extensive historical background research on FDR in general or these images in particular, although you are certainly welcome to

fill in your album with further context. Then present your arranged album and narrative to your classmates (or a group of your classmates) in an oral report, explaining your arrangement and your accompanying exposition to them. When you have all finished presenting, write another page reflecting on the various arrangements and their rhetorical significance.

2. Visit another presidential photo archive (online or from published photo essays or historical books about that president). Write an analytical paper in which you consider the balance of public and "private" images offered there. What stories and scenes (e.g., people often photographed with, places often photographed in, emotional states and expressions captured) come through in patterns in the series of images? What stories and scenes seem left out?

You can find some presidential biographies and photos via a White House–sponsored site: http://www.whitehouse.gov/history/presidents/.

"The Kind of People Who Make Good Americans": Nationalism and *Life*'s Family Ideal

WENDY KOZOL

In *Life's America: Family and Nation in Postwar Photojournalism* (1994), from which this essay is drawn, **WENDY KOZOL** explores the visual portrayal of familial and domestic life in the years following World War II. Her project focuses on photo-essays in *Life* magazine, one of the most popular U.S. magazines in the twentieth century. Kozol is most interested in the narratives that the photo-essays tell about social hierarchies of race, class, gender, and ethnicity. Kozol is an Associate Professor of Gender and Women's Studies at Oberlin College in Ohio. She has published articles in academic journals such as *Signs* and *Genders,* and is the editor (with Wendy Hesford) of *Haunting Violations: Feminist Criticism and the Crisis of the "Real"'* (2001) and *Just Advocacy? Women's Human Rights, Transnational Feminisms, and the Politics of Representation* (2005). She has appeared on local Cleveland television to discuss *Life* magazine and its ongoing popularity.

> *In fact, within the very narrow range of family products, more than gardening or cake-making . . . photography affirms the continuity and integration of the domestic group, and reaffirms it by giving it expression.*
>
> —PIERRE BOURDIEU, *PHOTOGRAPHY: A MIDDLE-BROW ART,* 1990

> *Nation-ness is assimilated to skin-colour, gender, parentage and birth-era—all those things one can not help. And in those "natural ties" one senses what one might call "the beauty of the* gemeinschaft.*" To put it another way, precisely because such ties are not chosen, they have about them a halo of disinterestedness.*
>
> —BENEDICT ANDERSON, *IMAGINED COMMUNITIES,* 1991

Life's January 5, 1953, cover photograph (Figure 1) depicts a woman kneeling with her arms around two blond girls who are leaning on a window sill. Behind them, a man in a business suit holds a toddler seated on the crosspiece of the window frame. Looking out of a large window, this neatly groomed white family smiles at the camera. The frame connotes a domestic setting, yet the building is clearly unfinished without any glass in the frame. By itself, this picture does not provide information about the specific type of house, but read alongside *Life*'s numerous photographs of suburbia in stories about news events, architectural designs, and the Modern Living section of the magazine, the frame easily suggests a middle-class domicile. Underneath the window frame, the caption states: "Family Buys 'Best $15,000 House.'" The cost of the house confirms a reading of the family as middle class, and the unfinished building suggests progress, a future that appears bright for this family. On a yellow banner cutting diag-

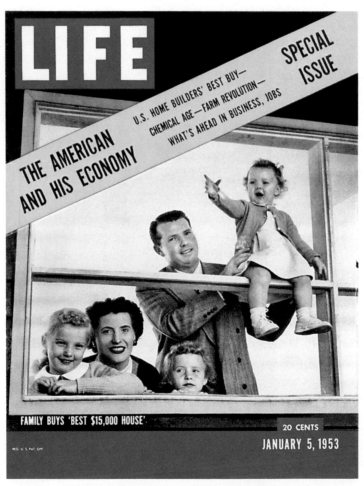

Figure 1. Cover of *Life* Magazine, January 5, 1953.
Courtesy of Getty Images/Time Life Pictures.

onally across the page, the headline connects this vision of familial intimacy to the newsworthy concerns of postwar America as it announces the topic of this special issue: "The American and His Economy."

Domesticity lies at the heart of photographer Nina Leen's portrait of middle-class suburban living, and in that sense it serves as a representative artifact of its time. In the postwar years, middle-class Americans increasingly turned toward the privatized world of home and children. Direct federal spending on highway construction and innovative home loan and taxation policies supported business efforts to create unprecedented opportunities for these Americans to inhabit single-family, detached suburban houses. At the same time, an ascendant ideology of domesticity based on strictly divided gender roles pervaded American life, involving such areas as hiring decisions in industry and child-rearing practices. These policies and ideals reshaped the contours of domestic life, encouraging a privatism isolated from broader community activities. Appropriately enough, the cover photograph for "The American and His Economy" underscores that turn to privatization with a visual representation containing no references to the outside world. Moreover, the composition repeats the gender divisions basic to postwar domestic ideology through the man standing above his kneeling wife and children. *Life* makes these connections between middle-class status and patriarchy explicit in the title that labels the economy "his"; her role apparently is only one of support. News images like the one of this family privileged heteroexist ideals of domesticity through photographic realism, visually inscribing culturally assigned gender roles. The woman's supportive embrace encodes her maternal responsibilities; the man's looming protectiveness identifies him as the patriarchal breadwinner. In turning the camera's gaze to the family to represent the American economy, *Life* visualizes postwar prosperity as a white, middle-class familial experience.

This celebratory cover photograph, so reminiscent of advertisements, creates a visual mystery through the unfinished building that encourages the reader to turn to the interior essay to solve. The photograph introduces a story titled "$15,000 'Trade Secrets' House," about a collaborative project in which the building industry pooled its resources to produce a design for a "good looking, skillfully engineered $15,000 house." The article shows color plates of model homes, design plans, and the various stages of building this suburban, three-bedroom house. Although they represented an ideal, labeled as such by the generic "The American," the people who posed for this picture were not actors. *Life* presents Dale and Gladys Welling, the "real" family who recently bought one of these dream houses, as evidence of actual families living the American Dream. In this way, the magazine legitimizes its association of the American economy with a particular social group by individualizing the representation.

Despite the economic prosperity celebrated in this portrait, the 1940s and 1950s were a time of instability and unease. A severe housing shortage, labor unrest, McCarthyism, and the Korean War confronted postwar Americans. In addition, major technological developments in transportation and communications systems altered Americans' perceptions of themselves and their worlds. People were on the move, migrating from east to west, south to north, rural to urban, and urban to suburban. Locating "The American" in a suburban home visually narrates a pattern of migration out of urban centers experienced by many white Americans after the war. During the 1950s, 64 percent of the nation's population growth occurred in the suburbs. As Steven Mintz and Susan Kellogg write, "Suburbanization reinforced the family orientation of postwar society."[1]

Migration, of course, took on different meanings for people of color moving from rural poverty into urban slums than for the seven   5 million white Americans moving from inner cities to the outlying suburbs. Between 1950 and 1970, five million African Americans, largely from the South, moved into central cities.[2] In addition, millions of immigrants facing poverty and unemployment at home came to the United States during this period, often through recruitment programs designed to supply cheap labor for agriculture and other industries. For instance, more than four million Mexican workers immigrated through the *Braceros* program. New arrivals to urban areas frequently confronted racial discrimination, low wages, a lack of health care, and other social dislocations.[3] The extremely varied consequences of mobility during the postwar years created upheavals in people's economic, political, and social lives, further contributing to the anxieties and tensions of the period. The special issue addresses white mobility but ignores this other story of migration. By visually excluding people of color who were physically barred from moving into the suburbs, the issue reproduces a discourse of racism. Moreover, when *Life* depicted the city, it was portrayed either as a place of danger and crime, or as a boomtown that exemplified economic prosperity. Rarely did the magazine show families living in cities, except if they were impoverished or in crisis. In the special issue, the only pictures of cities depict urban skylines without people.

In pictures like "The American and His Economy," *Life*'s figuration of the family, including the absences, reinforced racial, class, and gender differences that in turn had profound consequences for the magazine's representation of the nation. David Halberstam argues that *Time* was the most political magazine of the Luce publishing empire. "*Life* was different, less political, more open; it was more dependent upon pictures and thus more tied to events themselves rather than to interpretation of events. . . . *Life,* by its dependence upon photography, made itself closer to the human heartbeat."[4] Halberstam narrowly conceptualizes

political representation in terms that retain a faith in photographs' ability to represent events transparently, events that he conceives as sharing a single heartbeat. But photographs are mediated signs that contain politically significant messages. This is especially true because politics involves more than battles to control the government; it is also the exercise of power in symbolic and practical activities of everyday life. As John Hartley and Martin Montgomery note, "The news is active in the *politics* of sense-making, even when the stories concern matters not usually understood as political."[5] In structuring ways of understanding the world, *Life*'s family portraits played an important political role in establishing, promoting, and reproducing hegemonic social relations.

In the postwar years, *Life* solidified a photojournalistic formula that relied on images of the middle-class family to represent a national culture. Nationalism, a powerful but contradictory cultural force that shapes social identities, can construct a popular or democratic arena of shared interests and objectives. The concept of nation, however, typically relies on historically determined geographical, cultural, and conceptual distinctions. These distinctions too often are based on exclusionary assumptions of ethnic or racial superiority.[6] In the service of the nation-state, nationalism can offer "a privileged narrative perspective on the nation ('the people') and thus justifies its own capacity to narrate its story."[7] This does not mean that nationalism is a form of false consciousness. Instead, as Benedict Anderson argues, "Communities are to be distinguished, not by their falsity/genuineness, but by the style in which they are imagined." Anderson further argues that the nation is imagined because "members of even the smallest nation will never know most of their fellow-members, meet them, or even hear them, yet in the minds of each lives the image of their communion." National ideals may be arbitrary, but their power lies in their appeal to human needs for identity, order, and immortality. In this regard, people imagine the nation as a *community* "because, regardless of the actual inequality and exploitation that may prevail in each, the nation is always conceived as a deep, horizontal comradeship."[8] Moreover, Anderson observes that the nation appears, like the family, as "the domain of disinterested love and solidarity."[9]

I find Anderson's formulation that communities are defined by "the style in which they are imagined" useful for interpreting the power of media like *Life* to envision nationhood. His term "style" refers to representation and, more particularly, to the politics of representations that construct national identity. Examining the origins of nationalism, Anderson argues that the advent of print capitalism, especially the novel and the newspaper, "provided the technical means for 're-presenting' the *kind* of imagined community that is the nation."[10] Through reading, people could "imagine" shared experiences with thousands of other readers they would never meet. Print literacy may have supported the emergence of the concept of nation, but visual mass media have even greater capacities to visualize social norms and differences that form national identities. The mass media have the power to break down geographical and cultural barriers to connect viewers to other individuals who appear to share their concerns. In so doing, as Eric Hobsbawm points out, the mass media have the ability to make "national symbols part of the life of every individual, and thus to break down the divisions between the private and local spheres in which most citizens normally lived, and the public and national one."[11]

Life, for instance, claims a transcendent nationhood by presenting Dale Welling as "The American" who loves his family. Yet, there is nothing disinterested or neutral in this portrait. Closer inspection reveals how racial, class, gender, and sexual differences encoded in photoessays forge the boundaries of national identity. The concept of imagined communities provides

a way of understanding how photojournalism encodes the multiple consciousnesses that coexist and contradict each other, for even as they depend on and reinforce traditions and conventions, photo essays reveal the tensions and struggles to define the nation. As Stuart Hall points out, the nation is always at stake when culture is invoked because nationalism is one of the identities advanced or displaced in any cultural utterance.[12] In the hegemonic struggle to define and assert a national identity in the postwar years, *Life* vigorously promoted a vision of the American nation through pictures of nuclear families surrounded by consumer products in suburban homes. The association between family and nation formed the justification not only for the Cold War but for social relations in both intimate personal and national public arenas. *Life*'s nonfictional news status, especially its photographs, enhanced the cultural legitimacy of this narrative. In the midst of many social changes in American society, *Life*'s special gift was to make change seem traditional by locating the tensions of an unfamiliar world within the seemingly familiar and nonthreatening orbit of the "happy" nuclear family.

. . .

Family Portraits

In the early postwar years, news reports . . . about boomtowns and successful businessmen visualized the "reality" of prosperity. In so doing, these reports also established the characteristics of *Life*'s family ideal. For instance, "U.S. Success Story 1938–1946," from the September 23, 1946, issue, examines the economic boom in the automobile industry by focusing on one successful auto dealer, Romy Hammes from Kankakee, Illinois.[13]

Life sent its staff photographer Bernard Hoffman back to Kankakee to do a follow-up to an article published in 1938 on economic conditions in the auto industry. In contrast to 1938, when Hammes was only moderately well off, in

10

1946 he was an extremely successful businessman who owned dealerships in two cities and had expanded into real estate. Hoffman depicts the dealer selling cars, looking over architectural plans, and selling real estate. The accompanying text underscores his representative status, explaining that "Romy was no isolated example. In other Kankakees were other Romys. The man who used to work a gasoline pump now ran the filling station. His boss now had three stations and was dickering for a fourth. In America the dream was still there for those who believed it strongly enough to roll up their sleeves." This statement discounts the social benefits or disadvantages of education, class, and ethnic status as it praises the self-made Hammes, and all the men like him, who climb the mythic ladder of success. In this way, *Life* represents the United States as a classless society of opportunity. Hammes's representative status makes his, and thus the United States', prosperity common. In addition, the choice of an auto dealer to illustrate American economic conditions aligns corporate capitalism, in this case the automobile industry, with the nation. In the postwar period, the magazine repeatedly credited modern corporations with bringing affluence to the nation.[14]

This portrait of corporate America depends on masculine ideals by representing men as the ones rolling up their sleeves for success. In contrast, photographs confine women exclusively to the home. Hoffman's photographs depict separate worlds of work, occupied solely by men, and home, occupied by the nuclear family. The final two-page spread begins with a headline "Romy the Man Loves His Family and His Community." The text describes community involvement in domestic terms, commenting that Hammes "has a simple, homey ideal of service both to his customers and his community. . . . These same homey ideals permeate Romy's family life." Despite textual assertions of Hammes's community involvement, the photoessay includes no pictures of the community, only photographs of his family. *Life* represents a

privatized vision of the United States in which community has no visual place.

. . .

Rather than represent community, *Life* visualizes the breadwinner ethic by measuring the success of the businessman in familial terms. The breadwinner ethos was articulated in a variety of postwar discourses, including psychoanalytic arguments about male and female roles and sociological treatises by David Riesman, William Whyte, and others.[15] This ethos carried with it the expectation "that required men to grow up, marry and support their wives."[16] Hoffman represents Hammes's success as a breadwinner through photographs of domestic possessions, such as his home and vacation cottage. One picture shows Hammes with his family seated in their boat on a lake (Figure 2). The photograph displays the family as evidence, like the boat, of the businessman's prosperity.[17] Patriarchy and affluence are mutually reinforced through the image of the Father as caretaker of his family and possessions.

Hoffman's photographs of Romy Hammes and his family are characteristic of the magazine's attention to individual personalities, or what Luce referred to as "the little people." Realistic photographs construct an apparently seamless narrative about the "normal life" of representative families. A humorous essay on the Beat poets at the end of the fifties uses distinctive contrasts to identify the boundaries of this normative culture. "Squaresville U.S.A. vs. Beatsville," from September 1959, upholds middle-class ideals as it ridicules social differences.[18] *Life* describes Hutchinson, Kansas, as "the personification of traditionally accepted American virtues—a stable, prosperous community, given to conservatism but full of get-up-and-go." In contrast, the text characterizes Venice, California, as throbbing "with the rebellion of the beatnik, who ridicules U.S. society as 'square.'" Comparing suburbs, aligned with American virtues, to the decadence of Venice foregrounds

15

the physical association of the family ideal with a specific location.

The top half of a two-page spread, with the headline "A Happy Home in Kansas," shows a family looking at a photo album and watching television in a comfortable suburban home. The photographs visually elevate consumer habits to a standard of virtue, the happy home. In contrast, underneath a headline announcing "Hip Family's Cool Pad," the photograph depicts a bearded man lying on a mattress on the floor with another man seated on a box. A barefoot woman stands in the center of the room holding a baby. In contrast to industrious men like Dale Welling and Romy Hammes, who stand and display their families and possessions, the Beat men lie on the floor, not working and not wearing suits, while the mother stands above them. Through humor and ridicule, *Life* visually privileges middle-class suburban values defined in terms of place, dress, language, and social relations.

Figure 2. Courtesy of Bernard Hoffman/Time Life Pictures/Getty Images.

The ordinariness of *Life*'s representative, middle-class families celebrated a single cultural standard for domestic life. Articles on politicians, celebrities, and other famous people similarly focused on family life to demonstrate their ordinary status. The magazine's coverage of male politicians included ubiquitous photographs of homes, wives, and children which connote values such as stability and responsibility, important characteristics associated with the right to rule.[19] Pictures of adoring wives and children provided an aura of moral legitimacy for male politicians by presenting the imperatives of politics and statecraft as logical and natural extensions of domestic roles.

No one exemplified *Life*'s consensus America more than Dwight D. Eisenhower. Throughout the postwar period, the magazine praised this leader first as the war hero and later as the president. Eisenhower represented stability and order as the patriarch who led the Allies to victory in World War II and concluded a peace in Korea. Calling him a patriarch is appropriate, for *Life* exploited this grandfatherly image in numerous pictures of him with his young grandchildren. Moreover, photographs of him with his wife in family settings frequently underscored the connections between his political and domestic roles. The February 2, 1953, issue on Eisenhower's inauguration relied on domesticity to depict one of the most significant moments in American politics—the transfer of power from one administration to the next.[20] A full-page photograph shows President and Mrs. Eisenhower waving to the camera as they enter "their new home" at the White House. On the facing page, Mr. and Mrs. Truman similarly wave to the camera as they enter their "old home" in Independence, Missouri. . . .

In general, portraits of politicians and their families conformed to ideals of middleclass domesticity. Politicians were especially important in *Life* because they represented social and political authority through which they conferred legitimacy onto "everyday values." For instance, a February 13, 1950, news story about Truman's vice president, Alben Barkley, and his new bride reports on the lifestyle of this recently married couple who were popular among Washington's social elite.[21] Although the Barkleys' associations and celebrity status clearly show them not to be members of the middle class, *Life* champions the ideals of middle-class domesticity in photographs of the couple. Scenes depicting "everyday life" include a picture of Mrs. Barkley, still in her nightclothes, at the door saying goodbye to her husband who carries a briefcase as he "leaves for the Senate."

Photographer Hank Walker's concluding picture of the Barkleys in their kitchen visually constructs the gender divisions essential to *Life*'s ideology of domesticity (Figure 3). Mrs. Barkley, wearing an apron, washes dishes while her husband leans against the sink next to her. Walker emphasizes domesticity by placing a chair with a dish towel draped over it at the picture plane, making it the first thing the viewer sees. There is a sense of informality in this seemingly unposed portrait, especially in the figures whose faces appear in profile, apparently oblivious to the camera, deep in conversation. Walker tightly crops the sides to focus attention on the couple in the middle ground while the kitchen wall cuts off depth in the background. The photograph's realism encourages a reading of this as an intimate scene of a couple cleaning up after dinner. Visualizing these famous people through traditional gender roles makes the roles themselves seem natural, normal, and inevitable. Moreover, the headline, "On the Maid's Night Out, Veep Presides over Dishwashing," conflates political and domestic languages, which reinforces the mutuality of political and patriarchal authority. The text anchors these conventional gender ideals by explaining that the vice president urges his wife to let the dishes dry in the rack, "but like any bride proud of her new things, she sees the chore through and carefully puts them away." The statement "like any bride" not only associates her with stereotypes of the housewife but implies that there is an automatic connection leading from female gender to bride to housewife. In stories like this one, *Life* envisioned American politicians as breadwinners with wives who care for the home. Two women who wrote letters to the editor underscore the Barkleys' typicality by commenting on the old-fashioned sink. One of them writes that "I view my old sink with new respect. It's just like the Veep's." Such comments imply a community of readers who share the same social space as politicians. The

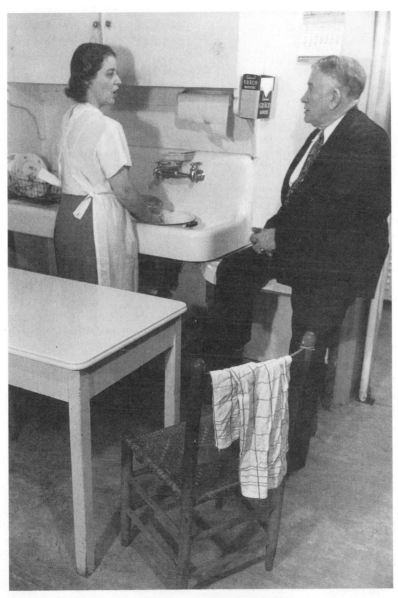

Figure 3.   Courtesy of Hank Walker/Time Life Pictures/Getty Images.

one male letter calls attention to conventional gender divisions in which women presumably rule in the home. He comments that "Mrs. Barkley has laid the drying cloth out on a chair right in front of the Veep. Yet he sits there and 'presides.' I couldn't get away with that in my home!"[22] The published letters assume, like the article, the naturalness of historically specific gender relations in part by ignoring the active role of the camera.

Idealized pictures of women in domestic settings during the postwar period were particularly important in light of changing paid-work opportunities for women. Although women's participation in the paid labor force continued to rise, segregation in low-paying, gender-specific jobs reversed many of the gains made by women during World War II. Employers, unions, and government officials alike endorsed the downgrading of job skills for female workers. "Family wage" arguments that presented men exclusively as breadwinners and women as wives first and workers second justified a variety of discriminatory labor policies, including mass firings of women workers with seniority at the end of the war to make room for returning veterans. Other forms of assistance for male workers at women's expense included skilled apprenticeship and job training programs reserved exclusively for men and indirect government and business subsidies to male workers through homeloan and education programs tied to military service.[23] *Life* supported these trends by promoting a domestic ideology that ignored the diversity of circumstances facing working women. It also precluded options and alternative social roles for those women who did their primary work at home. Although advertisements presented this ideology relentlessly, news stories like the feature on the Barkleys provided seemingly factual evidence justifying these ideals.

Life vociferously promoted patriarchal gender divisions in such articles as a December 1956 essay by Robert Coughlan that blamed divorce on the breakdown of these divisions.[24]

The writer relies on the authority of psychoanalytic and scientific discourses to characterize the sexual act in terms of aggressive masculine actions and passive female ones. Divorce results from a breakdown in these natural relations. Coughlan singles out working women for blame because when they leave the domestic sphere they become more aggressive while men become more passive and lose their natural masculine drives. This argument is similar to the theories espoused by sociologist Talcott Parsons, who promoted the nuclear family as a transhistorical ideal, associating this family form with evolutionary processes of modernization and claiming that patriarchal gender roles are universal and progressive.[25] *Life* promoted a similar ideology in its editorials and articles as well as in pictures like the one of the vice president's wife washing dishes. Photographic realism, moreover, has the visual power to circumscribe women's social roles within a domestic world.

Domesticity governed media portraits of men's responsibilities as much as it shaped depictions of women. During this period, men's role as breadwinners expanded beyond expectations that they be providers; social critics, psychologists, and others in the popular media urged fathers to participate more actively in family life. Fatherhood became a defining characteristic of masculinity and maturity. Television viewers, for instance, rarely saw sitcom fathers working, as these characters traded in public identities for participation in domestic life.[26] Similarly, a 1958 news story on Vice President Richard Nixon and his family used expensive color photographs to depict Nixon as the involved father playing with his children.[27] Hank Walker poses Nixon sitting with his family in the backyard, and playing with his daughters in a tree house. Walker creates an informality similar to that in his portrait of the Barkleys. He has the Nixons ignore the camera, which implies that this is an everyday scene upon which the photographer has stumbled. In one photograph, the vice president sits at his desk in shirtsleeves next to his daughter Julie in pajamas as they laugh at a recording she made on his dictaphone. Silly antics of childhood turn Nixon's political responsibilities into a job that supports his family. The text also emphasizes the family's desire for privacy to give "the girls a chance to grow up the way their father would like them to." Visual images display the pleasures and joys of domestic privacy with no references to the outside world.[28]

25   *Life* participated in a postwar culture that repeatedly focused on domesticity. Books and magazines gave endless advice to parents about everything from raising families to home improvements. In broadcasting as well, both advertisements and domestic sitcoms effectively integrated familial values with the values of consumer society. Comedies like "Father Knows Best," "The Donna Reed Show," and "Leave It to Beaver," showcased ideal domestic homes in which mothers cared for the home and fathers solved their children's problems. As early as 1948, television advertisers and designers directed marketing strategies toward the middle class. To encourage middle-class consumption advertisers masked class heterogeneity through an image of the nuclear family as natural and ahistorical.[29]

Moreover, throughout the period, intellectuals, popular writers, and politicians advocated domesticity in similarly nationalistic terms. The most famous photography exhibition of postwar America, "The Family of Man," first exhibited in 1955, similarly promoted family photography in what Allan Sekula terms a "celebration of the power of the mass media to represent the whole world in familiar and intimate terms." According to Edward Steichen, who was curator of the show, by 1960, over seven million people in twenty-eight countries had seen the exhibition. This traveling show promoted American democracy by presenting the bourgeois family as universal in this "globalized utopian family album."[30]

In retrospect *Life*'s attention to the family in news stories, like other forms of popular culture, appears to be powerful evidence for a national consensus about the family in postwar America. In an age of unprecedented family formation—with marriage and childbirth occurring more frequently and earlier than at any time in the preceding three decades—the centrality of family images in news stories seems natural, even obvious. But the connection between state power and family form celebrated in *Life*'s photo-essays was neither natural nor inevitable. Rather it was the product of ideological contestations brought on by changes in American social life. *Life*'s photo-essays featuring representative families engaged in dialogue with social forces, urging readers to connect a family ideal with national imperatives.

A Nation of Families

. . .

Life's almost obsessive attention to the nuclear family in stories about social issues such as housing, labor crises, and the economy demonstrates how strategies of legitimation aligned national imperatives with domestic ideals. These strategies often relied on a rhetoric of democracy. Like the World War II appeals that borrowed heavily from a small-town ideal, *Life*'s postwar pictorial record borrowed from the rhetoric of wartime emergency by linking the family to moral obligations and patriotic behavior. Specifically, narratives about postwar social, political, and economic situations tried to legitimate consumption by making it a matter of obligation to the family and the state.

Life appealed to middle-class Americans by connecting a vision of nuclear families owning their own homes and experiencing upward mobility with national ideals. As illustrated by the presidential transfer of power and the photographic representations of the Barkleys' and the Nixons' domestic bliss, the home was a prominent symbol in *Life*'s portrait of America. In its Modern Living and Design sections, *Life* featured model suburban homes as the new architectural ideal. Merging editorial and advertising material in these sections, *Life* promoted a vision of the United States as a nation of middle-class homeowners. Luce wrote in 1946 that "it is the first job of Modern Living to show how the multiplicity of goods in an industrial age can be used with relatively better rather than relatively worse taste."[31] News stories supported this consumer aesthetic by reporting on developments in suburban living. The January 5, 1953, issue "The American and His Economy," for instance, begins with a news story on the latest developments in suburban housing design.[32] Color plates show landscaped exteriors and the interior decor of houses with three bedrooms, 1½ baths, a fireplace, and an open floor plan. Photographic realism demonstrates the popularity of suburbia through representations of young married couples with small children standing outside their new homes in Ohio, Louisiana, Colorado, Pennsylvania, Texas, and Indiana. Pictures of real families represented middle-class Americans from different regions as participants in a shared American Dream.

30   Housing, however, was not just a symbol of prosperity and domestic bliss in postwar America, it was also a source of tension and conflict. According to the National Housing Agency, at least 3.5 million new houses were needed in 1946 just to provide veterans with decent housing, yet there was only enough material and labor to build 460,000 units. In addition, the influx of people of color from rural areas to industrial centers resulted in a severe housing crisis in inner cities. Poor people who were most in need of government intervention in the housing crisis faced the racially discriminatory policies of both private landlords and government agencies, as well as limited job prospects and inflated rents and grocery bills.[33] Although the National Housing Act of 1949 established "the goal of a decent home and a suitable living environment for every American family," little progress was made in alleviating this problem. By 1964, only 550,000 of the 810,000 low-cost dwelling units promised by the Act had been completed.[34]

Instead, the federal government supported suburbanization through such programs as the FHA and VA mortgage guarantees.[35] With these government guarantees, buyers could secure mortgages at low interest rates and with small down payments, making it cheaper to buy than to rent. As taxes went up, the homeowner deduction became more important, creating an added subsidy for homeownership and an added penalty for renters. In this way, the government subsidized the move into the suburbs of millions of white Americans. Starting in 1956, federal government investments in interstate highway construction projects encouraged the use of private automobiles over public transportation and furthered suburban growth. At the same time, redlining policies and the refusal to fund renovation projects on older houses in the cities precluded poor people and people of color from participating in these social developments.[36]

Throughout the postwar years, *Life*'s news coverage of housing rarely discussed apartment buildings or urban renovation as possible solutions. Photographs of Americans living in trailers and Quonset huts, and doubling up in apartments, visualized the housing shortage, but the only solution the magazine showed was the single-family house. Photographs supplied the visual evidence for the claim that all Americans demanded suburban housing, but only white nuclear families were shown in their new suburban homes or standing in long lines to purchase these houses.

Although social crises challenged *Life*'s claims of consensus, the magazine's representational strategies worked to contain such threats. Ideology played a part not only in the proposed solution to the problem, but in how the narrative represented the problem. In December 1945, as the United States faced potential crises in unemployment, inflation, and housing during reconversion, *Life* featured a big news story titled "The Great Housing Shortage."[37] Housing was a serious problem for a nation whose cen-

Figure 4.   Courtesy of Tony Linck/Time Life Pictures/Getty Images.

tral myth of the American Dream included home ownership.

A prominent full-page photograph shows two navy officers and their families sharing an apartment (Figure 4). In the foreground, an officer sits on a couch reading a newspaper. At his feet, a young boy lies on the floor while next to the man a baby sleeps in a bassinet. In an armchair in the middle distance a woman sits holding another baby. The other officer and another woman stand in the background in front of dry-ing laundry. The composition accentuates the cramped conditions of seven people in two rooms through tight framing that cuts off any view into the rest of the apartment. The adult figures line up in a diagonal that emphasizes the sharply receding perspective. This diagonal encourages the eye to move quickly from the foreground to the background, further under-scoring the small dimensions of the apartment.

Life's focus on military personnel was signif-icant first because the housing crisis intensified

35

with demobilization. Moreover, *Life* depicts navy officers who fought a war for democracy living under such "un-American" conditions. *Life*'s readers knew this was un-American because they had been shown numerous images of what was American. The cramped conditions and the laundry recall photographs of working-class tenements where tenants hung laundry between the buildings. This association casts the housing problem and solution in class terms whereby apartments are part of the problem that deprives these officers of their "natural" right to own a single-family home. *Life* locates democracy and nationhood as the stakes involved in the housing crisis by focusing on the military who were equated with patriotism.

After visualizing the crisis through the officers' apartment, *Life* presents statistics and graphs to document the problem. Such graphs provide empirical evidence to legitimize *Life*'s claims; they also indicate change through time, thereby suggesting the temporary nature of the crisis and the potential for future progress. The photo-essay also features single-family model homes in different price ranges and ignores altogether the more economical apartment solution. *Life* negates class differences by featuring different types of houses as choices instead of examining the conditions and options for people at different economic levels. In its penchant for narrative closure, *Life* ends with a picture of a factory making parts for prefabricated houses. This was the privileged solution offered by *Life* at the dawn of the housing boom. In a letter to the editor responding to this report, Congressman Wright Patman insisted on the government's responsibility to ensure "that our scarce supply of building materials is channeled to the most worthy type of projects."[38] Letters like this one, and others from business leaders, praised the article without specifying what constituted a worthy type of project. Such praise legitimated the building industry and *Life*'s favored solution, the single-family home.

Advertisements also reinforced the ideal of suburbia since they featured only white families in suburban dwellings. Two pages before the news story, a Plymouth ad depicts a single-family house on a snowy night. A family of four looks out of a bay window at a sign on their garage that reads "Reserved for Our New Plymouth." On the page opposite the opening page of the article, an ad for Prudential Life Insurance titled "Bless This House," shows a family of four admiring a Christmas tree. The text emphasizes the importance of the home for the family's financial security. Both advertisements and news reports make explicit associations between domesticity and class through an emphasis on single-family suburban homes.

Life's reporting on political and social problems emphasized middle-class concerns by encouraging readers to identify with an ideology that equated democracy with capitalism through ideals of suburban home ownership. The consequences of this strategy are most evident in news coverage of class conflict where *Life* repositioned workers' actions as threats to democracy, not critiques of capitalist inequalities. One of the greatest fears at the conclusion of World War II was that the country would return to the desperate conditions of the thirties. This fear seemed warranted when, along with inflation and unemployment, conflicts between labor and management escalated in the immediate postwar years. Unions and corporations attempted to rationalize labor relations in ways that often ignored or hurt workers' interests. Workers registered their anger and frustration in wildcat strikes, insisting not just on wage increases but on control over the work place.[39] Prior to World War II, *Life* had strongly opposed unionism. Although it remained an avowedly conservative journal, its editors now accepted the trend toward union involvement in corporate management, even praising successful contract negotiations. What it would not tolerate were disruptions of the economy. *Life* often represented strikes through photographs of empty warehouses and idled factories that surely must have resonated with middle-class readers' pictorial memories of the Depression. Rather than looking at the faces of workers, *Life*'s readers saw pictures of empty warehouses that illustrated how work stoppages affected the middle class. The crucial question became whether middle-class Americans would be deprived of consumer goods; rarely did writers analyze the causes of strikes. In this way, *Life*'s news coverage of labor conflicts often deflected the politics of class struggle by focusing on the bourgeois family as the location for the successful resolution of social discord.

The June 3, 1946, big news story, "The Great Train Strike," angrily denounces a nationwide work stoppage by railroad workers because it asked too much of Americans.[40] According to *Life*, although Americans accept that "working-men had a constitutional right to organize, negotiate and, if necessary, strike, to improve their working conditions," when strikes threaten the quality of life, the "United States" loses its temper. The text establishes social boundaries here by distinguishing Americans who are patient, and the United States that loses its temper, from the workers who test this patience. . . .

A letter written by a housewife from Connecticut forms the centerpiece of the story. Instead of placing it in the letters section, *Life* prominently displays it in the photo-essay, printed in large typewritten letters offset by a thick gray border. Betty Knowles Hunt, a housewife and mother, condemns strikers for paralyzing the country and "killing our prestige abroad." She also criticizes the government for jeopardizing democracy by placing the public welfare in the hands of pressure groups. Who, she asks, "will save Democracy for America and the World?" . . . This letter invokes both democracy and domesticity to legitimize the hierarchical inequalities of capitalism.

I should be scrubbing the kitchen, mending the stockings, weeding the flower beds, and planning the dinner. Much of my time and energy has been spent in trying to teach my three little minorities that their private interests will often conflict, but that they must learn to sacrifice in the larger interest of our family as a whole. For what am I preparing them? Is it of any value to teach them Democracy at home, while our government in Washington fails to teach its minorities to sacrifice and work together for the common American good?[41]

Hunt establishes an us–them relationship by comparing "our family" and "our government" with working-class "minorities." Moreover, she trivializes working-class people's political efforts by equating her children with workers when she refers to them both as minorities. Hunt patronizingly represents labor activists as children to be taught by their parent, the government.[42]

Hunt represents this social crisis in terms of the family, which aligns middle-class interests with the state in opposition to the working class, which threatens social stability. The prominence of the letter privileges a bourgeois ideal of the family that in turn regulates knowledge about the political society. The discursive frame controls how readers understand this crisis as well as casts the working class outside the bourgeois norm. When she condemns workers for stepping outside of normative boundaries, Hunt defines national identity in terms of social conventions of respectability.[43]

Hunt also defines democracy in familial terms as a matter of working together for the common good (of economic prosperity), just as children must put aside their "private interests" for the sake of the family. The letter legitimizes capitalist structures by displacing political critiques of the system in favor of family concerns. In addition, Hunt represents workers' demands for self-determination as private interests of lesser value than the needs of (dominant)

America. Indeed, the text presents class struggle not merely as a threat to a generalized social welfare but more specifically as a threat to the home. Not all readers accepted Hunt's claims. One of two letters to the editor critical of her position appropriated the same rhetoric, arguing that "the people also include a tremendous amount of union families. They're American too, Mrs. Hunt."[44] This response demonstrates both that texts are open to various interpretations and that domestic iconography is available to alternative perspectives. *Life*'s decision to highlight Hunt's letter, however, like the four letters praising her position, indicates the power of editorial manipulation to impose an ideological direction on the news coverage.

Framing the train strike as both an economic and a family crisis conforms to *Life*'s larger discursive attempt to align the middle-class family with the capitalist economy. Here, photographs visualized the danger to capitalism through idled factories. Elsewhere, *Life* connected the health of the political economy with a particular social class through photographs of families enjoying the postwar economic boom. Far from being subtle, the magazine repeatedly stated both in editorials and in news coverage of economic issues that it was Americans' patriotic responsibility to consume in order to keep demand high and the economy prosperous. Popular media like *Life* played an important role in promoting the consumer spending and government economic policies that helped bring about the preconditions for an unprecedented rise in the American standard of living that lasted until the 1960s.

The American economy underwent radical changes after the war. Government and business leaders sought to control the instabilities endemic to capitalism by regulating the economic structure. The federal government implemented Keynesian theories of economic stimulation by pumping vast sums into the economy to ensure the relative stability of the postwar boom. The federal budget rose from $38 billion in 1947 to $77 billion in 1960, with the most significant increases in military spending: the Defense Department budget climbed from $14.3 billion to $49.3 billion between 1950 and 1953 but did not decline after the Korean War. Structural modifications to welfare, social security, and unemployment compensation policies further protected the economy from major upheavals. Increasing centralization of the state accompanied the centralization of private multinational corporations. These corporations developed foreign markets where raw materials, cheap labor, and new investment opportunities stimulated American economic hegemony while foreign countries still labored under reconstruction efforts.[45]

Consumer spending, stimulated by suburban growth and demands for housing, appliances, automobiles, and shopping malls, also fueled the postwar boom. After fifteen years of economic crisis and war, Americans in 1945 were ready to spend, urged on by consumption ideologies promoted by the mass media. Between 1946 and 1950, manufacturers sold 21.4 million automobiles and over 20 million refrigerators.[46] The boom continued throughout the 1950s, despite several recessions and inflation. In 1955, for instance, automobile dealers sold almost 8 million new cars, and the housing industry initiated 1.6 million new housing units.[47] The government subsidized these remarkable postwar consumer habits through federally financed loan programs like those offered by the FHA and the GI Bill, which enabled more than 7.6 million veterans to go to college and 1.3 million to secure home loans. Banks also extended credit to middle-class Americans for mortgages, cars, and other large purchases.[48]

The boom, however, was not without social and economic costs: the government never fully controlled inflation, and unemployment went up and down throughout the 1950s. Even more significant was the failure to change social hierarchies despite this general affluence. As Marty

45

Jezer points out, income distribution remained static: "Whatever the method of computation, the evidence is clear that though everyone except the hardcore poor gained during this period, the rich tended to get richer, the middle class tended to stay in its place, and the poor, relative to everyone else, were left further and further behind."[49] *Life,* like the government and private corporations, did not so much ignore social differences as argue that productivity would raise everyone to a higher level of affluence.[50] This ideal of productivity pervaded the magazine's vision of social progress.

As part of a national corporation with its own direct political and economic interests, and as an institution with responsibilities to its investors and advertisers, *Life* supported government and business efforts to maintain a stable economy and political consensus. Toward that end, *Life* often cajoled its readers to be civic minded by spending more money. In a May 5, 1947, article entitled "U.S. Tackles the Price Problem," *Life* linked the ideal suburban family to the state by making the family accountable for economic prosperity.[51] The article ends with a two-page spread on Ted and Jeanne Hemeke and their three children. The headline specifically associates consumption with civic responsibility: "Family Status Must Improve: It Should Buy More for Itself to Better the Living of Others." The editors use a popular photo-essay formula of a before-and-after narrative. The Hemekes appear first in their present home, an old frame house, then visiting a new suburban house. The text explains the latter as the vision of the future, "what life should be like in the U.S. by 1960."

In the foreground of the first picture, Ted Hemeke, having just returned from work, stands with his back to the camera holding a child's hand. The photographer's perspective encourages the viewer to identify with Hemeke's vision by putting us in his shoes. Following his gaze, we look past the foreground figures toward the house, observing the weeds and the grassless lawn as well as the poorly maintained house next door. In the background, Jeanne Hemeke stands in the doorway holding one child while another child sits on a barrel next to her. The other picture on this page shows Jeanne Hemeke using a large shovel to scoop coal into a "dirty coal furnace next to [the] stove" while her baby daughter sits on the floor nearby. This shot emphasizes the antiquated facilities of the old house as well as the woman's hard work.

On the facing page, two photographs parallel the ones on the previous page in composition, size, and layout. The first picture again shows the Hemekes in front of a house (Figure 5). This time, however, the wife stands in the doorway of a modern ranch-style house. By repeating the action of Ted Hemeke walking into the scene from the street, the visual narrative suggests that once again he is arriving home from work. Although the text explains that the Hemekes are visiting a model house, repeating the composition encourages a reading of economic progress from the old house to the new one. The Hemekes' attire underscores this narrative of upward mobility. In the first scene, Ted Hemeke wears heavy boots and a work jacket. His daughter does not wear a coat or socks. Here, he wears a suit and his daughter has on a coat, hat, socks, and dress shoes. The daughter in the background no longer sits on a barrel but rides a tricycle.

The second photograph of the alternative vision shows Jeanne Hemeke again in the kitchen but this time in a modern kitchen with gingham curtains and shiny new appliances. She stands at a counter with her hands on an electric beater, as if she were baking; behind her a kettle gleams on a gas stove. The baby no longer sits on the floor dangerously close to the furnace but plays with a toy in a high chair that has a bottle of milk on the tray. Visually, if not in actuality, Jeanne Hemeke and her family have attained these middle-class accouterments. The realistic *mise en scène* (for this is a staged performance by two different photographers)

Figure 5.   Courtesy of Al Fenn/Time Life Pictures/Getty Images.

reinforces a reading that this woman is cooking in her own new kitchen. Here, domesticity constructs conventional gender roles by positioning the woman in the private space of the home. Moreover, placing her in a modern kitchen with new appliances, a composition frequently used in advertisements, objectifies her as an ideal consumer. Her husband, on the other hand, occupies space in the outside public world, signified by the sidewalk and the narrative journey from work. Visually and textually, *Life* presents a vision of America that characterizes people like the Hemekes through conventional gender identities and material possessions.

As with photo-essays on Romy Hammes and other representative families, here too *Life*

locates the consumer ideal in the physical space of the suburbs, an isolated space in which no one else appears on the sidewalk. Thus, the magazine's vision of the nation integrates the ideals of social progress with ideologies of consumption and the private realm of domesticity. Indeed, the article claims that families have civic responsibilities based on their roles as consumers. At the conclusion of the story on the Hemekes, *Life* cites a Twentieth Century Fund projection study on the economy in 1960, stating that:

To achieve a health and decency standard for everyone by 1960 each U.S. family should acquire, in addition to a pleasant roof over its head, a vacuum cleaner, washing machine, stove, electric iron, refrigerator, telephone, electric toaster and such miscellaneous household supplies as matching dishes, silverware, cooking utensils, tools, cleaning materials, stationery and postage stamps.

This prescriptive message presents a list of consumer goods as the minimum that families have not only the right to expect but the duty to acquire in order that everyone attain a decent standard of living. Concluding a story on inflation at a time when many still worried about an economic collapse, *Life's* visual mediation of these fears takes on great ideological significance. In linking the family to the political economy, *Life* creates a portrait of the nation that legitimizes the social order by connecting moral authority to familial consumption.

In stories about people like the Hemekes, *Life* denied class distinctions when it pointed to consumption as evidence of upward mobility. Instead, the uniform domesticity that pervades photo-essays like this one offered a portrait of a national community of families with shared concerns. The political consequences of this nationalism are especially apparent in stories that explicitly linked domesticity to anti-Communist rhetoric. *Life* often supported the political tensions of the Cold War by contrasting the oppressive Communist state with the opportunities and freedoms of American families. For example, the January 1957 photo-essay on the Hungarian Csillag family recreates the deeply familiar story about progress through the layout. . . .

Pictures of the Csillags settled in the United States combine domesticity and consumption to represent what the American nation offers these refugees. Three large photographs on a two-page spread offer evidence of that success by showing the Csillags standing in front of a table laden with food, having just arrived home from the grocery store.[52] The first photograph shows the Csillags with American relatives unpacking groceries. In the second photograph, a relative demonstrates how to use a tis-sue. In the third photograph, the adults are all laughing as Pal Csillag tries one. The Hungarians' awe at the consumer products destabilizes the norm of American consumption in order to foreground it as evidence of national ideals. The focus on consumption exemplifies the magazine's frequent Cold War strategy to contrast communism with American capitalism, assured that such comparisons easily demonstrated which culture was superior. The Csillags join an imagined community of families that defines social conventions in terms of gender divisions and political action in terms of Americans' consumer habits. The text underscores this position through unsubtle contrasts between the United States and the impoverished conditions of the Communist system the Csillags left behind. This narrative of immigrant assimilation submerges ethnicity as the Csillags become, as in Nixon's comment, the "kind of people who make good Americans" through the products they consume. Perhaps more than any other national narrative, this narrative of the successful immigrant enjoying the riches of capitalism embodies the American Dream.

Within the context of other media representations of the family, *Life's* images of domesticity must be read as participating in the ongoing constructions of national social and political ideals in postwar America. The family's importance lies not only in its economic value in reproducing and maintaining the labor force or as a channel for socializing children, but equally important, in its role in reproducing cultural values.[53] *Life's* narrative promoted the reproduction of a particular set of values and norms that formed a national culture around the dominant middle class.

Creating *Life*'s Audience

Life's narrative about consensus America did not merely reflect the trends of the baby boom or middle-class affluence. Instead, *Life* actively constructed meanings for its readers. This has significance for a postwar American society that was more heterogeneous than is typically imagined by stereotypes of postwar suburbanites, who were in fact a mixed group including returning GIs, second-generation immigrants, and working-class people.[54] Although the majority of *Life*'s readers were middle-class professionals, the letters to the editor indicate a degree of diversity among the magazine's audience. For instance, in response to the article on the internment of Japanese Americans at Tule Lake, a Nisei man used patriotic rhetoric to condemn "American fascists and race-baiters."[55] Similarly, a woman responding to a news article on a strike at a Detroit GM plant in 1946 identified with the striker, explaining that her husband was also on strike and therefore they could no longer afford her subscription.[56] Many in this heterogeneous group may have felt insecure about their place in the American Dream. Even 1950s television demonstrated more social diversity; not all shows were middle-class family comedies, especially in the early days, with shows like "The Goldbergs," "The Honeymooners," and "Amos 'n' Andy." What united these shows, however, was a capitalist ethos that typically resolved problems of work, family, and politics through consumption.[57] Similarly, *Life*'s news reports worked to convince its readers just then moving into the suburbs that they too belonged to "America." An America, that is, that was upwardly mobile and consumer oriented.

Life's focus on the middle-class family occurred at a time when Americans were reorganizing social relations into nuclear families. Documentary photography, historically aligned with reform movements, had previously turned the camera's gaze on groups with lower status than the middle-class audiences viewing these images. *Life*'s contribution to photojournalism was to turn the camera's gaze on the middle class in an effort to mirror the readers' world. Readers saw in *Life* an optimistic vision of American society, which, they were told, was a reflection of their lives as homeowners. *Life*'s

photo-essays invited viewers to make connections between a single family form and national interests through identification with signs of domesticity.[58] Realistic photographs of the family visualized socially constructed relationships, such as that between the breadwinner and housewife, in concrete and seemingly unmediated ways. Stories about individuals directed attention away from the political meanings embedded in representation by encouraging viewers to relate emotionally to the people in the news.[59] Like the letter writers who recognized their old sinks, readers frequently wrote in with pictures or stories that resembled the ones published in the magazine, fostering a climate that urged people to recognize the similarities.

Life addressed these readers through representational strategies in which seamless narratives present the working-class Hemekes, or even the Hungarian Csillags, as families just like other Americans. In this way, the photo-essay hails the reader into the signifying spaces of national identity, a space severely circumscribed by the patriarchal and racist ideals of domesticity. Underlying the clear anti-Communist message in the Csillag story, for instance, is a didacticism common in *Life:* both photographs and texts demonstrate "the kind of people who make good Americans." . . .

In studying news stories that constructed an ideal of nationhood, it is also crucial to acknowledge who is left out of that ideal. In stories about representative Americans, ethnic differences were typically limited to Europeans, like the Hungarian Csillags. In contrast, people of color, including Latinos and Native Americans, appeared as representative of social problems but never to signify the American Dream. Moreover, some social groups, like Asian Americans after the close of the internment camps, were rarely seen. The one major exception was African Americans and their struggle for civil rights.

The elderly were also notably absent from *Life*'s narrative of postwar family life. Suburban dwellers, at least in the pages of *Life*, did not live with elderly parents, much less aunts, uncles, or friends. When *Life* represented elderly people, it was typically in association with specific problems or issues. A June 1950 article on pension programs represents the elderly since they are the major recipients of these programs.[60] Photographs from a retirement settlement in St. Petersburg, Florida, include a group playing shuffleboard and an elderly couple smiling outside their cottage. In contrast, the final full-page picture depicts an old man in a county poorhouse. Seated on a wrought-iron bed showing signs of rusting, the man's unshaven face looks at the camera. Strong light from the window highlights his clenched hands while leaving his face in shadow. The text reassuringly notes that the surge in retirement plans will mean an "increasing scarcity of pictures of pathetic misery like that on the opposite page," yet the painful and disturbing photograph undermines any comfortable solution claimed by the text. The article praises retirement towns because the elderly there "entertain themselves, are a burden to nobody and best of all maintain the independence so cherished by old folks." The "nobody" evidently refers to the family relations who are not discussed.

This story, which contains no photographs of children or relatives, identifies both the problem and the solution as socially and politically distinct from the ideals of domesticity. *Life*'s first major treatment of aging, a July 1959 special series "Old Age," begins with an article titled "In a Dutiful Family Trials with Mother."[61] Unlike the earlier photo-essay, here the editors present aging as a problem for the family. Cornell Capa's photographs narrate the story of an elderly woman living with her son and his family. In one picture, Capa captures the situation through a grainy close-up shot of the daughter-in-law and a friend laughing at the kitchen table in a scene of intimacy and informality. The mother sits in profile in the background, spatially isolated and excluded from the conversa-

tion. Other pictures reveal cramped conditions, and two full-page pictures feature an emotional confrontation between the mother and her daughter-in-law. Most significant, in this first extensive report on the elderly, *Life* characterizes them as a problem that invades the family home.

Life's coverage of the elderly may have been limited, but homosexuality was beyond the representational limits of the magazine for most of the period. Postwar persecution of homosexuality and the homophobic currents in anti-Communist rhetoric are well documented, but in *Life* the denial of sexual difference, rather than an attempt to condemn it, was most prominent.[62] Homophobic rhetoric permeated the magazine, as did the heterosexual imperative that shaped its representation of social life. The limited visibility of different social and racial groups clearly shaped the news discourse to produce an extremely narrow portrait of "the kind of people who make good Americans."

For *Life* magazine, the task of constructing a unified nation out of a diverse polity depended on news presentations that advanced the twin ideologies of consumption and domesticity not just as goals of the nation-state but as the fulfillment of the democratic aspirations of the people in the nation. The family was a primary site through which *Life* hailed its audience as part of that unified nation. It is incorrect to assume, however, that there was a priori an audience of nuclear families for the magazine to address. Audiences are not typically unified but, rather, disorganized and disparate communities. Media producers, however, need to imagine an audience because communication is a dialogic process oriented "toward an addressee."[63] In other words, a text has to address a reader, however that reader is imagined. *Life* envisioned its readers to be midwestern, middle class, not very sophisticated, and definitely not intellectual. It is clear, moreover, from the forms of address in the photo-essays that *Life* conceptualized its readers as family members and as consumers. Seeking empirical evidence for these assumptions about its readers, the magazine's demographic studies determined the composition of its audience through extensive questionnaires on the age, gender, number in the family, and income level of its readers.[64] *Life* used demographic information to attract advertisers, as well as to shape its own discourse for a perceived audience. Nonetheless, common wisdom in the publishing industry until the 1960s insisted that magazines amass the broadest possible circulation.[65] Thus, *Life*'s vision both responded to a perceived middle-class audience, and yet sought to make a widely accessible product.

In constructing images to appeal to a mass audience, *Life* presented an ideal with which it encouraged its readers to identify. This does not mean that *Life* created nuclear families, for many Americans in these years lived in family forms resembling *Life*'s families. Yet, even these people lived complex and multiply constructed lives, and their identification with a specific ideological position, religion, political party, or ethnic group varied according to the context. Recognizing oneself as belonging to a nuclear family, therefore, comes about in the active process of reading and viewing. *Life* urged its readers to identify with domesticity by focusing on the nuclear family as the representational ideal of American culture. As a form of representation, the nuclear family works so well because it blurs commercialism and consumer identity with seemingly voluntary ties of intimacy and affection.

. . .

NOTES

1. Steven Mintz and Susan Kellogg, *Domestic Revolutions: A Social History of American Family Life* (New York: Free Press, 1988), 184.

2. John H. Mollenkopf, *The Contested City* (Princeton, N.J.: Princeton University Press, 1983), 28.

3. Juan Ramon Garcia, *Operation Wetback: The Mass Deportation of Mexican Undocumented Workers in 1954* (Westport, Conn.: Greenwood Press, 1980), 23–36; Teresa L. Amott and Julie A. Matthaei, *Race, Gender, and Work: A Multicultural Economic History of Women in the Untied States* (Boston: South End Press, 1991), 79–80, 274–279.

4. David Halberstam, *The Powers That Be* (New York: Alfred A. Knopf, 1979), 60.

5. John Hartley and Martin Montgomery, "Representations and Relations: Ideology and Power in Press and TV News," in *Discourse and Communication: New Approaches to the Analysis of Mass Media Discourse and Communication,* ed. Teun A. van Dijk (Berlin: Walter de Gruyter, 1985), 260.

6. Among the growing theoretical literature on nationalism, see Anthony D. Smith, *The Ethnic Origins of Nations* (Oxford: Basil Blackwell, 1986); E. J. Hobsbawm, *Nations and Nationalism since 1780: Programme, Myth, Reality* (Cambridge: Cambridge University Press, 1990); and Benedict Anderson, *Imagined Communities: Reflections on the Origin and Spread of Nationalism,* rev. ed. (London: Verso, 1991).

7. Mary Layoun, "Telling Spaces: Palestinian Women and the Engendering of National Narratives," in *Nationalisms and Sexualities,* ed. Andrew Parker et al. (New York: Routledge, 1992), 411.

8. Anderson, *Imagined Communities,* 6–7; he argues that nationalism is not an ideology, but rather, that concepts of nation, like those of gender or kinship, are neither inherently reactionary or progressive. Eve Kosofsky Sedgwick similarly defines nationalism as an "underlying dimension of modern social functioning that could then be organized in a near-infinite number of different and even contradictory ways"; see "Nationalisms and Sexualities in the Age of Wilde," in *Nationalisms and Sexualities,* 238.

9. Anderson, *Imagined Communities,* 25.

10. Hobsbawm, *Nations and Nationalism,* 142.

11. Anderson, *Imagined Communities,* 144.

12. Stuart Hall, "Toad in the Garden: Thatcherism among the Theorists," in *Marxism and the Interpretation of Culture,* ed. Cary Nelson and Lawrence Grossberg (Urbana: University of Illinois Press, 1988), 35–73, esp. 58.

13. "U.S. Success Story 1938–1946: Auto Dealer Romy Hammes, Whom 'Life' Looked at in 1938, Is Now Going Like a House Afire," *Life,* September 23, 1946, 29–35.

14. *Life* was not alone in equating the automotive industry with the nation's economy. In what has become one of the most famous clichés of the period, Eisenhower's Secretary of Defense Charles Wilson testified before Congress that "what was good for our country was good for General Motors, and vice versa"; quoted in John Patrick Diggins, *The Proud Decades: America in War and Peace, 1941–1960* (New York: W.W. Norton, 1988), 130. See Larry May, "Introduction," in *Recasting America: Culture and Politics in the Age of Cold War,* ed. L. May (Chicago: University of Chicago Press, 1989), 5, for a discussion of the shift in postwar nationalistic rhetoric from an antimonopolistic to procorporate position.

15. See, e.g., David Riesman, *The Lonely Crowd: A Study of the Changing American Character* (New Haven: Yale University Press, 1950); William H. Whyte, *The Organization Man* (New York: Simon and Schuster, 1956); and Ferdinand Lundberg and Marynia F. Farnham, Modern Woman: The Lost Sex (New York: Harper and Bros., 1947).

16. Barbara Ehrenreich, *The Hearts of Men: American Dreams and the Flight from Commitment* (New York: Anchor, 1983), 11.

17. See Julia Hirsch, *Family Photographs: Content, Meaning, and Effect* (New York: Oxford University Press, 1981), 21, for a discussion of the visual convention of representing the family as a possession.

18. *Life,* September 21, 1959, 31–37.

19. Hirsch, *Family Photographs,* 101, 120.

20. "It Couldn't Have Happened Anyplace Else in the World," *Life,* February 2, 1953, 14–23.

21. "New Leaders, New Zeal: Take 'Old' Out of G.O.P.," *Life,* July 21, 1952, 14–27.

22. "Letters to the Editor," *Life,* March 6, 1950, 4.

23. Hartmann, *Home Front and Beyond,* 66–70.

24. Robert Coughlan, "Changing Roles in Modern Marriage: Studying Causes of Our Disturbing Divorce Rate, Psychiatrists Note Wives Who Are Not Feminine Enough and Husbands Not Truly Male," *Life,* December 24, 1956, 108–118. Throughout this period *Life* often pointed to divorce as evidence of a crisis in the family despite statistics that revealed the 1950s to have the lowest divorce rate in the century.

25. Mary P. Ryan, *Womanhood in America: From Colonial Times to the Present,* 3d ed. (New York: Franklin Watts, 1983), 260–261.

26. For discussion of postwar cultural attitudes toward fathers, see Elaine Tyler May, *Homeward Bound: American Families in the Cold War Era* (New York: Basic Books, 1988), 145–149; and Ehrenreich, Hearts of Men, chap 2. Margaret Marsh, "From Separation to Togetherness: The Social Construction of Domestic Space in American Suburbs, 1840–1915," *Journal of American History* 76, 2 (September 1989): 506–527, argues that by the late nineteenth century, the suburban ideal had recast domesticity. Previously an ideal defined by women and the family, domesticity in its new version emphasized family togetherness, including men. For discussions of 1950s television representations of the family see, e.g., Mary Beth Haralovich, "Sitcoms and Suburbs: Positioning the 1950s Homemaker," *Quarterly Review of Film and Video* 11, 1 (1989): 61–83; and Spigel, *Make Room for TV.*

27. "The Nixons in Their Backyard," *Life,* September 22, 2958, 43–46.

28. The color photographs and Nixon's status as Vice President would appear to give him a cultural advantage over John Kennedy (anticipating the 1960 election) in this staunchly Republican magazine. News stories about politicians, however, used the same format regardless of party affiliation. In fact, even as a junior senator, Kennedy's charms, good looks, and young family made him a frequent subject of sympathetic photo essays in *Life.*

29. Haralovich, "Sitcoms and Suburbs"; and Lynn Spigel, "Installing the Television Set: Popular Discourses on Television and Domestic Space, 1948–1955," *Camera Obscura* 16 (January 1988): 11–46.

30. Allan Sekula, "The Traffic in Photographs," in *Modernism and Modernity,* ed. Benjamin H. D. Buchloch, Serge Guilbaut, and David Solkin (Halifax: Press of Nova Scotia College of Art and Design, 1983), 136–143.

31. Quoted in Wainwright, *Great American Magazine,* 165; see Clifford E. Clark, "Ranch-House Suburbia: Ideals and Realities," in *Recasting America,* 171–191, for a discussion of how suburban architecture represented cultural ideals.

32. "$15,000 'Trade Secrets' House," *Life,* January 5, 1953, 8–15.

33. Jackson, *Crabgrass Frontier,* 209–218.

34. Marty Jezer, *The Dark Ages: Life in the United States 1945–1960* (Boston: South End Press, 1982), 179.

35. Mollenkopf, *Contested City,* 41.

36. Jackson, *Crabgrass Frontier,* 190–245.

37. *Life,* December 17, 1945, 27–35.

38. "Letters to the Editor," *Life,* January 7, 1946 , 6.

39. George Lipsitz, *Class and Culture in Cold War America: "A Rainbow at Midnight"* (South Hadley, Mass.: Bergin and Garvey, 1982).

40. "The Great Train Strike: Railroad Shutdown Brings Wrath of People Down on All U.S. Labor," *Life,* June 3, 1946, 27–33.

41. Ibid., 32.

42. *Life* also uses this strategy on the first page of the essay when the writer quotes a dentist from Des Moines who said, "Labor is like a kid who gets too much money from his parents."

43. Hunt's attention to proper behavior is reminiscent of the relationship between respectability and nationalism that developed in conjunction with the rise of the bourgeoisie in modern Europe. See George L. Mosse, *Nationalism and Sexuality: Respectability and Abnormal Sexuality in Modern Europe* (New York: Howard Fettig, 1985), 8–9, who argues that respectability played a crucial role for the middle class by distinguishing it from both the aristocracy and lower classes, as well as providing stability amid the upheavals of industrialization and modernization.

44. "Letters to the Editor," *Life*, June 24, 1946, 6.

45. Jezer, *Dark Ages*, 119–122; Douglas F. Dowd, *The Twisted Dream: Capitalist Development in the United States since 1776* (Cambridge, Mass.: Winthrop, 1974), 65–75, 105–107.

46. Hartmann, *Home Front and Beyond*, 8.

47. Jezer, *Dark Ages*, 120.

48. Hartmann, *Home Front and Beyond*, 7–8.

49. Jezer, *Dark Ages*, 203.

50. Charles S. Maier, "The Politics of Productivity: Foundations of American International Economic Policy after World War II," *International Organization* 31, 4 (1977): 607–633.

51. *Life*, May 5, 1947, 27–33.

52. In an excellent discussion of Tom Wesselman's Pop Art images of "the economy of domesticity," Cecile Whiting analyzes an image that bears a resemblance to these pictures in their display of consumer goods on the kitchen table; see "Pop Art Domesticated: Class and Taste in Tom Wesselman's Collages," *Genders* 13 (Spring 1992): 43–72.

53. See Judith Williamson, *Consuming Passions: The Dynamics of Popular Culture* (London: Marion Boyars, 1986), 115–116, who discusses the family in relation to Gramsci's concept of political and civil society, arguing that the family participates in both sectors.

54. Jezer, *Dark Ages*, 192–193.

55. "Letters to the Editor," *Life*, April 10, 1944, 4.

56. Ibid., *Life*, February 11, 1946, 4.

57. George Lipsitz, "The Meaning of Memory: Family, Class, and Ethnicity in Early Network Television," *Time Passages: Collective Memory and American Popular Culture* (Minneapolis: University of Minnesota Press, 1990), 39–75.

58. This reading of how photographs secure identification derives from Judith Williamson's *Decoding Advertisements: Ideology and Meaning in Advertisements* (London: Marion Boyars, 1978), 44–45. She argues that advertisements work by combining unrelated signifiers, like a product and an actress, leaving the readers to make meaningful connections between the two. Thus, the advertisement draws the reader into the space of the signified so that the reader identifies with the message.

59. John Fiske, *Television Culture* (New York: Routledge, 1987), 169.

60. "GM Paces the U.S. Pension Parade," *Life*, June 5, 1950, 21–25.

61. The article appeared in *Life*, July 13, 1959, 16–25, as part of a series of articles titled "Old Age: Personal Crisis, U.S. Problem." The title indicates the perspective the magazine took on this topic.

62. See Lee Edelman, "Tearooms and Sympathy, or, The Epistemology of the Water Closet," in *Nationalisms and Sexualities*, 263–284, for an excellent discussion of

Cold War attacks on homosexuality and the role of the media in promoting virulent homophobia. He examines *Life*'s first photo-essay on gays and lesbians, "Homosexuality in America,"which appeared on June 26, 1964, 66–80.

63. John Hartley, "Invisible Fictions: Television Audiences, Paedocracy, Pleasure," in *Television Studies: Textual Analysis,* ed. Gary Burns and Robert J. Thompson (New York: Praeger, 1989), 223–243; see also Horace M. Newcomb, "On the Dialogic Aspects of Mass Communication," *Critical Studies in Mass Communications* 1 (1984): 34–50.

64. See, e.g., *Life Study of Consumer Expenditures,* vol. 1–6, conducted for *Life* by Alfred Politz Research, Inc. (New York: Time Inc., 1957).

65. Curtis Prendergast, *The World of Time Inc.: The Intimate History of a Changing Enterprise,* vol. 3: 1960–1980 (New York: Atheneum, 1986), 53–54.

Re-reading/Conversations with the Text

1. Re-read Kozol's essay, noting how she moves from description to analysis. How would you describe the relationship between description and analysis in this essay? Are the analytical moves supported by description? What constitutes evidence in this essay?

2. How does Kozol define the concept of "nationalism" in this essay? To what extent does she embrace or critique Benedict Anderson's notion of the nation as an imagined community? Is our use of the key rhetorical concept "context" synonymous with Kozol's conception of the nation? According to Kozol, what is the role of print media in supporting particular concepts of the nation?

3. Kozol argues that *Life* magazine's depiction of economic prosperity in the 1940s and 1950s covered up the unease and instability of the time. According to Kozol, what were some of the instabilities that *Life* concealed? How does Kozol account for these absences?

Re-seeing and Re-writing

1. According to Kozol, *Life* in the 1940s and 1950s depicted idealized images of middle-class domesticity and traditional gender roles. Kozol argues that the magazine represented "postwar prosperity as a white middle-class familial experience." This assignment asks you to locate recent issues of *Life* in your college or local library and to analyze the images of domesticity and gender found there. Do similar patterns characterize the photo essays today? Do you find similar connections between representations of middle-class status and traditional gender roles? How would you describe the similarities and/or differences?

2. This assignment invites you to create your own photo essay that counters or reveals the limited vision and/or bias of *Life*'s depiction of the U.S. family in the 1940s and 1950s. In order to create a counter vision, perhaps one that is more inclusive, you'll need to do a little archival work of your own. Go to your local

or college library and research the status of the family in the 1940s and 1950s in the United States. Consider, for example, the millions of immigrants who came to the United States during this time. Create a photo essay that offers social commentary on these exclusions.

Intertext

In Kozol's essay, she begins with Benedict Anderson's concept of "imagined communities." Anderson argues that the nation appears, like the family, as "the domain of disinterested love and solidarity." Consider Kozol's use of Anderson's concept of how communities are imagined as you re-read Robert Kaplan's "The Rusted Iron Curtain." Do you notice similarities in their explanations of how communities are imagined or created?

Child of the Americas

A U R O R A   L E V I N S   M O R A L E S

AURORA LEVINS MORALES is a poet, community historian, and activist, who writes from the perspective of a Puerto Rican and Jewish feminist. Among Levins Morales' most recent books are *Remedios: Stories of Earth and Iron from the History of Puertorriqueñas* (1998), and *Telling to Live: Latina Feminist Testimonios* (2001). In the poem below, Morales considers how identity and difference shape the concept and experience of citizenship.

I am a child of the Americas,
a light-skinned mestiza of the Caribbean,
a child of many diaspora, born into this continent at a crossroads.

I am a U.S. Puerto Rican Jew,
5   a product of the ghettos of New York I have never known.
An immigrant and the daughter and granddaughter of immigrants.
I speak English with passion: it's the tongue of my consciousness,
a flashing knife blade of crystal, my tool, my craft.
I am Caribeña, island grown. Spanish is in my flesh,
10   ripples from my tongue, lodges in my hips:
the language of garlic and mangoes,
the singing in my poetry, the flying gestures of my hands.
I am of Latinoamerica, rooted in the history of my continent:
I speak from that body.

15   I am not african. Africa is in me, but I cannot return.
I am not taína. Taîno is in me, but there is no way back.
I am not european. Europe lives in me, but I have no home there.

I am new. History made me. My first language was spanglish.
I was born at the crossroads
20   and I am whole.

Re-reading/Conversations with the Text

1. Throughout her poem, Morales employs several metaphors. Re-read the poem and highlight these metaphors. What is the function of each metaphor? How does each one provide meaning in the poem?

2. Unlike traditional essays, poems do not contain thesis statements. However, in "Child of the Americas" there seems to be an implicit argument. Re-read the poem and note specific locations where Morales puts forth an argument.

Next, working in pairs, restate Morales' argument as though you were describing it to somebody who has not read the poem.

3. What is the rhetorical function of repetition in the poem? Does the repetition of "I am" and "I am not" enable readers to embrace the narrator's stance and vision? Or does it seem to position the reader at a distance from the narrator?

Re-seeing and Re-writing

1. Conduct research about poets who write about their intersecting identities—whether in terms of ethnic background, social status, public/private roles, or other topics. Choose two poets who are particularly interesting to you. Next, write an essay comparing/contrasting these poets and Morales. In your analysis, focus on the way the three poets use metaphor and context in their poems in order to represent shifting identities or identities in conflict.

2. The concept of diasporatic communities refers to the voluntary or involuntary dispersal of a people from their traditional homeland. There are numerous diasporatic communities throughout the United States. This assignment asks you to research one of these communities and to locate where it has settled. Create a "map" (a literal or figurative map) of this community. You might consider how ethnic or national identities are shaped by local contexts or politics. Be prepared to share your map with the your class and to discuss the multiple and intersecting identities diasporatic communities embrace.

Intertext

Morales describes "being at the crossroads" in her poem and yet being "whole." In contrast, Kaplan in "The Rusted Iron Curtain" describes Mexico and the United States as being split and separated by a (literal and metaphoric) iron curtain. Why do you think each author uses these distinct metaphors?

The Rusted Iron Curtain

ROBERT KAPLAN

"The Rusted Iron Curtain" is taken from a series of articles that *ROBERT KAPLAN* wrote for *Atlantic Monthly,* a journal to which he is a contributing editor. In the article, Kaplan describes two towns on the border of Mexico and Arizona and the movement there among geographical and cultural boundaries. Kaplan is the author of several books, including *Balkan Ghosts: A Journey Through History* (1993) and *An Empire's Wilderness: Travels into America's Future* (1998). As one reviewer put it, "reading Robert D. Kaplan, the master of writing about globalization's dark side, is like putting on a pair of glasses you didn't know you needed. From the static and overflow of information about world events, layers of crisp, dazzling insight emerge. The rocky landscape of political crisis and conflict suddenly yields patterns, trends and meaning" (Laura Rozen, http://dir.salon.com/people/bc/2001/04/17/kaplan/index.html).

What we call "the border" has always been a wild and unstable swath of desert, hundreds of miles wide— a region that the Aztecs, cruel as they were, could not control, that the Apaches brutalized in eighteenth-and nineteenth-century raids, and where U.S. soldiers unsuccessfully chased the bandit revolutionary Pancho Villa.

My bus came around a low rise, and a long, narrow belt of factories and shanties stretched out almost to the horizon between brown hills studded with juniper and sagebrush. This was the border town of Nogales, a crowded warren of distempered stucco façades spray-painted with swastikas and graffiti, of broken plastic-and-neon signs, of garish wall drawings of the Flintstones and other television icons. Among the façades were the industrial *maquiladora* plants I had heard about—plants that attract blue-collar workers from throughout Mexico, who assemble American-made parts into products exported to the United States.

Not all the workers find jobs, and the migration has spawned shantytowns and violent crime, drug and alcohol abuse, class conflict, and the breakup of families. Both rape and car accidents are more common in the north than in the rest of Mexico. More than 2,000 companies opened factories in this region from the late sixties to the midnineties, resulting in what the American Medical Association has labeled a "cesspool" of polluted air, contaminated groundwater and surface water, unsanitary waste dumps, and other health and environmental problems associated with uncontrolled urban growth. The abandonment of subsistence farming by workers in search of better-paying manufacturing jobs is a latter-day gold rush— ugly upheaval and bright promise—but on a vast scale and likely to be permanent.

Many of our microwave ovens, televisions, VCRs, toasters, toys, and everyday clothes are made by Mexican laborers in border towns like this one. They earn three to five dollars a day— not an hour but a day!—and as Charles Bowden, an expert and writer on Mexico and the U.S. Southwest, notes, they work in conditions that are often dangerous because of pollution and toxic chemicals. American consumers are now in a tight political and economic relationship with Third World workers. This close relationship is also oligarchic, and not much different from that between the citizens of ancient Athens or Rome and their slaves.

5   I checked into a hotel and then walked toward the border, where I watched two boys kick a soccer ball made of rags until one of them kicked the ball onto a scrap-metal roof. When the ball failed to roll back down, the boys walked away. I saw a group of teenagers with hair cut in punk styles and dyed primary colors, wearing expensive leather belts, winter ski hats, and summer shorts—anything they could get their hands on. Their expressions were untamed. A hundred yards from the border began a concentration of scrap-metal storefronts, offering every manner of souvenir and after-hours activity, including off-track betting.

Here were crowds of destitute people reeking of alcohol. Edward Gibbon wrote in *The History of the Decline and Fall of the Roman Empire* that the fifth-century Goths "imbibed the vices, without imitating the arts and institutions, of civilised [Roman] society." What I saw at the border is nothing new.

The actual border, on International Street, was at the time of my visit a twelve-foot-high, darkly rusted iron curtain, constructed by the American authorities from scraps of metal that the U.S. Army used in the Persian Gulf War. (It has since been partly replaced by a new wall.) Walking back from the border I saw the neat

In Nogales, looking into Mexico, Feb. 23, 2001.
Courtesy of Monica Almeida/The New York Times.

squares and rectangular roofs of houses high on the hills of the American side, where it was obvious that every joint fit and that every part was standardized, in contrast to the amateurish and inspired constructions all around me.

Though here, in the middle of a city, the border looked forbidding, out in the desert it ebbs to a few strands of barbed wire, which work to keep only cattle from migrating. Along the narrow Rio Grande in Texas, where there is no fence at all, or any natural obstruction, no mountain range or wide, surging river, the border is highly penetrable. The military radar used by U.S. border guards is like a penlight in a dark forest, as William Langewiesche has written (see "The Border," May and June, 1992, *Atlantic*). An artificial, purely legal construct, the border has for several centuries been an unruly and politically ambiguous "brown zone" where civilizations—Spanish and Anglo, Athapaskan-speaking Indians from the Arctic and Aztecan Indians from southern Mexico—mingle.

The factors that have kept Mexico at bay—drug profits and the wages of illegal aliens—stem from the very activities that Washington claims it wants to stop. Without the drug trade and illegal migration the United States would face what it has always feared: a real revolution in Mexico and true chaos on the border. To deprive Mexico of its largest sources of income would hasten the collapse of its already weak central authority. Indeed, by supporting the Mexican economy, America's appetite for marijuana and cocaine protects against a further flood of immigrants from a contiguous, troubled, and ever more populous Third World country.

The unpalatable truth about Mexico is its intractability—the intractability of an ancient "hydraulic" civilization, like Egypt's, China's, and India's, in which the need to build great water and earth works (Mexico has both canal systems and pyramids) led to a vast, bureaucratic tyranny. Centuries of what Karl Marx called "oriental despotism" have imprinted the political culture, despite the influence of a great demo-

cratic civilization to the north. And it is not clear that our influence on Mexico is beneficial. Our appetite for drugs may be turning this ancient non-Western civilization into an amoral yet dynamic beast of the twenty-first century.

Meanwhile, integration proceeds irreversibly. Vectors of binationhood have emerged between Phoenix and Guaymas, Tucson and Los Mochis, Dallas and Chihuahua City, in which prosperous Mexicans and Americans commute back and forth by air. North America's geographic destiny may be no longer east to west but one in which the arbitrary lines separating us from Mexico and Canada disappear, even as relations between the East Coast and Europe, the West Coast and Asia, and the Southwest and Mexico all intensify. Is our border with Mexico like the Great Wall of China—a barrier built in the desert to keep out Turkic tribesmen which, as Gibbon wrote, held "a conspicuous place in the map of the world" but "never contributed to the safety" of the Chinese?

"Ambos Nogales"

I had crossed the Berlin Wall several times during the Communist era. I had crossed the border from Iraq to Iran illegally, with Kurdish rebels. I had crossed from Jordan to Israel and from Pakistan to India in the 1970s, and from Greek Cyprus to Turkish Cyprus in the 1980s. In 1983, coming from Damascus, I had walked up to within a few yards of the first Israeli soldier in the demilitarized zone on the Golan Heights. But never in my life had I experienced such a sudden transition as when I crossed from Nogales, Sonora, to Nogales, Arizona.

Surrounded by beggars on the broken sidewalk of Mexican Nogales, I stared at Old Glory snapping in the breeze over two white McDonald's-like arches, which marked the international crossing point. Cars waited in inspection lanes. To the left of the car lanes was the pedestrian crossing point, in a small building constructed by the U.S. government. Merely by touching the door handle one entered a new physical world.

The solidly constructed handle with its high-quality metal, the clean glass, and the precise manner in which the room's ceramic tiles were fitted—each the same millimetric distance from the next—seemed a marvel to me after the chaos of Mexican construction. There were only two other people in the room: an immigration official, who checked identification documents before their owners passed through a metal detector; and a customs official, who stood by the luggage x-ray machine. They were both quiet. In government enclosures of that size in Mexico and other places in the Third World, I remembered crowds of officials and hangers-on engaged in animated discussion while sipping tea or coffee. Looking at the car lanes, I saw how few people there were to garrison the border station and yet how efficiently it ran.

I gave the immigration official my U.S. passport. She glanced up at me and asked how long I had been in Mexico. I told her several weeks. She asked, "Why so long?" I explained that I was a journalist. She handed back my passport. With her eyes she motioned me through the metal detector. The customs official did not ask me to put my rucksack through the machine. U.S. Customs works on "profiles," and I evidently did not look suspect. Less than sixty seconds after walking through the glass doors on the Mexico side, I entered the United States.

15   The billboards, sidewalks, traffic markers, telephone cables, and so on all appeared straight, and all the curves and angles uniform. The standardization made for a cold and alienating landscape after what I had grown used to in Mexico. The store logos were made of expensive polymers rather than cheap plastic. I heard no metal rattling in the wind. The cars were the same makes I had seen in Mexico, but *oh*, were they different: no chewed-up, rusted bodies, no cracked windshields held together by black tape, no good-luck charms hanging inside the windshields, no noise from broken mufflers.

The taxi I entered had shock absorbers. The neutral gray upholstery was not ripped or shredded. The meter printed out receipts. As I sank into the soft upholstery for the ride to the hotel, I felt as though I had entered a protective, ordered bubble—not just the taxi but this whole new place.

The Plaza Hotel in Nogales, Sonora, and the Americana Hotel in Nogales, Arizona, both charged $50 for a single room. But the Mexican hotel, only two years old, was already falling apart—doors didn't close properly, paint was cracking, walls were beginning to stain. The American hotel was a quarter century old and in excellent condition, from the fresh paint to the latest-model fixtures. The air-conditioning was quiet, not clanking loudly as in the hotel across the border. There was no mold or peeling paint in the swimming pool outside my window. The tap water was potable. Was the developed world, I wondered, defined not by its riches but by maintenance?

As I walked around Nogales, Arizona, I saw a way of doing things, different from Mexico's, that had created material wealth. This was not a matter of Anglo culture per se, since 95 percent of the population of Nogales, Arizona, is Spanish-speaking and of Mexican descent. Rather, it was a matter of the national culture of the United States, which that day in Nogales seemed to me sufficiently robust to absorb other races, ethnicities, and languages without losing its distinctiveness.

The people I saw on the street were in most instances speaking Spanish, but they might as well have been speaking English. Whether it was the quality of their clothes, the purposeful stride that indicated they were going somewhere rather than just hanging out, the absence of hand movements when they talked, or the impersonal and mechanical friendliness of their voices when I asked directions, they seemed to me thoroughly modern compared with the Spanish-speakers over in Sonora. The sterility, dullness, and predictability I observed on the American side of the border—every building part in its place—were signs of economic efficiency.

20 Though the term *"ambos Nogales"* ("both Nogaleses") asserts a common identity, the differences between the two towns are basic. Nogales, Arizona, has only 21,000 residents, a fairly precise figure; nobody in Nogales, Sonora, has any idea how many people live there—the official figure is 138,000, but I heard unofficial ones as high as 300,000. Here the streets were quiet and spotless, with far fewer people and cars than in Mexico. Distances, as a consequence, seemed vast. Taxis did not prowl the streets, and thus I was truly stranded without a car. I had reached a part of the earth where business is not conducted in public, so street life was sparse.

When the English and other Northern European settlers with their bourgeois values swept across this mainly uninhabited land, they swept away the past; technology and the use of capital have determined everything since. Because subsequent immigrants sought opportunity, the effect of periodic waves of immigration has been to erase the past again and again, replacing one technology with another. Economic efficiency, as these streets in Nogales, Arizona, proclaimed, is everything in America. Liberals

may warn against social Darwinism, but the replacement of obsolete technology and the jobs and social patterns that go with it are what our history has always been about, and immigrants want it that way. For them it means liberation: the chance to succeed or fail, and to be judged purely on their talents and energy and good fortune.

In Mexico the post offices looked as if they had just been vacated, with papers askew and furniture missing. In Nogales, Arizona, the Spanish voices in the post office were the last thing I noticed; what struck me immediately was the evenly stacked printed forms, the big wall clock that worked, the bulletin board with community advertisements in neat columns, the people waiting quietly in line, and a policeman standing slightly hunched over in the corner, carefully going through his paperwork, unlike the leering, swaggering policemen I had seen in Mexico.

The silent streets of Nogales, Arizona, with their display of noncoercive order and industriousness, cast the United States in a different light not only from Mexico but from many of the other countries I had seen in my travels. Nogales, Arizona, demonstrated just how insulated America has been—thus far, at least.

Re-reading/Conversations with the Text

1. In this essay, Robert Kaplan compares the border between Nogales, Sonora (Mexico), and Nogales, Arizona (U.S.) with the "iron curtain"—a term used to describe the border between communist Europe and western Europe until 1989. How, according the Kaplan, are these borders similar and different? What does the literal and metaphoric "iron curtain" between the United States and Mexico separate?

2. Describe Kaplan's writing style. Do you think his style is effective? Are you persuaded by his use of detail in his close comparisons of Nogales, Sonora, and Nogales, Arizona? Kaplan's article does not have a distinct thesis statement; if you were to write one for him, what would it be?

3. Working in groups of two or three, make a list of the differences Kaplan describes between the two towns: Divide one page in half, putting the details about the Arizona town on one side and the Sonora town on the other. What

dominant themes emerge from this list? If you were to write Kaplan's essay yourself, would you have organized it differently? If so, why? Be prepared to share your findings and reasoning with your classmates.

Re-seeing and Re-writing

1. Kaplan is a journalist. Imagine that a major magazine has critiqued his essay arguing that the use of personal experience alone does not make a persuasive story. Now, imagine that you are Kaplan's assistant, and he has asked you to help him. Your task is to research other border towns along the Mexican/U.S. border and then write an editorial-style essay. Specifically, you are to come up with some intriguing statistics, a brief history of the border areas, and some personal stories and images to represent the relationship between U.S. towns and Mexican towns. Feel free to draw on Kaplan's observations in making your own claims.

2. Often, when we think about borders, we imagine the borders between two nations. However, there are probably borders that exist in your own community; for example, a line between ethnic neighborhoods, straight and gay neighborhoods, poor and wealthy neighborhoods, frat row and campus "ghetto," etc. Find a border that exists in your community. Once you have identified your border, take some time to explore it. Make a list of your observations from each side of the border. What are some similarities and differences between the two spaces? Produce a first-person narrative that describes, analyzes, and articulates the significance of your border.

In the essay "Lost in the Field of Vision," Diana Taylor witnesses the events of 9/11 from her home in Manhattan. Like Kaplan, Taylor observes the events from several "border" locations: the border between TV and the "real" scene outside her window; the border between the World Trade Center site and the zone where onlookers were required to stand; and the evoked border between the missing and found. Are there any similarities among the authors' writing styles, observations, and/or modes of witnessing? If so, what are they? What are the dominant differences? What makes one essay more successful than the other?

Champion of the World

MAYA ANGELOU

MAYA ANGELOU, born in 1928 and raised in segregated Arkansas, is an author, poet, playwright, director, and civil rights activist. However, she is probably best known for her poetry and her autobiographical writing. In 1993, she was asked to read a poem at Bill Clinton's inauguration, and her poetry collection *Just Give Me a Cool Drink of Water 'Fore I Die* (1971) was nominated for the Pulitzer Prize. In "Champion of the World," excerpted from her autobiography *I Know Why the Caged Bird Sings* (1969), Angelou recreates the impact of Joe Louis's monumental victory on her immediate community of family and neighbors, as well as on African Americans in general.

The last inch of space was filled, yet people continued to wedge themselves along the walls of the Store. Uncle Willie had turned the radio up to its last notch so that youngsters on the porch wouldn't miss a word. Women sat on kitchen chairs, dining-room chairs, stools, and upturned wooden boxes. Small children and babies perched on every lap available and men leaned on the shelves or on each other.

The apprehensive mood was shot through with shafts of gaiety, as a black sky is streaked with lightning.

"I ain't worried 'bout this fight. Joe's gonna whip that cracker like it's open season."

"He gone whip him till that white boy call him Momma."

5 At last the talking finished and the string-along songs about razor blades were over and the fight began.

"A quick jab to the head." In the Store the crowd grunted. "A left to the head and a right and another left." One of the listeners cackled like a hen and was quieted.

"They're in a clinch, Louis is trying to fight his way out."

Some bitter comedian on the porch said, "That white man don't mind hugging that niggah now, I betcha."

"The referee is moving in to break them up, but Louis finally pushed the contender away and it's an uppercut to the chin. The contender is hanging on, now he's backing away. Louis catches him with a short left to the jaw."

A tide of murmuring assent poured out the door and into the yard. 10

"Another left and another left. Louis is saving that mighty right . . ." The mutter in the Store had grown into a baby roar and it was pierced by the clang of a bell and the announcer's "That's the bell for round three, ladies and gentlemen."

As I pushed my way into the Store I wondered if the announcer gave any thought to the fact that he was addressing as "ladies and gentlemen" all the Negroes around the world who sat sweating and praying, glued to their "Master's voice."

There were only a few calls for RC Colas, Dr Peppers, and Hires root beer. The real festivities would begin after the fight. Then even the old Christian ladies who taught their children and tried themselves to practice turning the other cheek would buy soft drinks, and if the Brown Bomber's victory was a particularly bloody one they would order peanut patties and Baby Ruths also.

Bailey and I laid the coins on top of the cash register. Uncle Willie didn't allow us to ring up sales during a fight. It was too noisy and might shake up the atmosphere. When the gong rang for the next round we pushed through the near-sacred quiet to the herd of children outside.

15   "He's got Louis against the ropes and now it's a left to the body and a right to the ribs. Another right to the body, it looks like it was low . . . Yes, ladies and gentlemen, the referee is signaling but the contender keeps raining the blows on Louis. It's another to the body, and it looks like Louis is going down."

My race groaned. It was our people falling. It was another lynching, yet another Black man hanging on a tree. One more woman ambushed and raped. A Black boy whipped and maimed. It was hounds on the trail of a man running through slimy swamps. It was a white woman slapping her maid for being forgetful.

The men in the Store stood away from the walls and at attention. Women greedily clutched the babes on their laps while on the porch the shufflings and smiles, flirtings and pinching of a few minutes before were gone. This might be the end of the world. If Joe lost we were back in slavery and beyond help. It would all be true, the accusations that we were lower types of human beings. Only a little higher than apes. True that we were stupid and ugly and lazy and dirty and, unlucky and worst of all, that God Himself hated us and ordained us to be hewers of wood and drawers of water, forever and ever, world without end.

We didn't breathe. We didn't hope. We waited.

"He's off the ropes, ladies and gentlemen. He's moving towards the center of the ring." There was no time to be relieved. The worst might still happen.

20   "And now it looks like Joe is mad. He's caught Carnera with a left hook to the head and a right to the head. It's a left jab to the body and another left to the head. There's a left cross and a right to the head. The contender's right eye is bleeding and he can't seem to keep his block up. Louis is penetrating every block. The referee is moving in, but Louis sends a left to the body and it's an uppercut to the chin and the contender is dropping. He's on the canvas, ladies and gentlemen."

Babies slid to the floor as women stood up and men leaned toward the radio.

"Here's the referee. He's counting. One, two, three, four, five, six, seven . . . Is the contender trying to get up again?"

All the men in the store shouted, "NO."

"—eight, nine, ten." There were a few sounds from the audience, but they seemed to be holding themselves in against tremendous pressure.

"The fight is all over, ladies and gentlemen.   25 Let's get the microphone over to the referee . . . Here he is. He's got the Brown Bomber's hand, he's holding it up . . . Here he is . . ."

Then the voice, husky and familiar, came to wash over us—"The winnah, and still heavyweight champeen of the world . . . Joe Louis."

Champion of the world. A Black boy. Some Black mother's son. He was the strongest man in the world. People drank Coca-Colas like ambrosia and ate candy bars like Christmas. Some of the men went behind the Store and poured white lightning in their soft-drink bottles, and a few of the bigger boys followed them. Those who were not chased away came back blowing their breath in front of themselves like proud smokers.

It would take an hour or more before the people would leave the Store and head for home. Those who lived too far had made arrangements to stay in town. It wouldn't do for a Black man and his family to be caught on a lonely country road on a night when Joe Louis had proved that we were the strongest people in the world.

Re-reading/Conversations with the Text

1. The introduction to this chapter defined national gazes as "an imagined, collective lens . . . which creates and/or presumes a sense of national identity and belonging." In what ways does Angelou show how the African American community imagined their "belonging" in 1930s' America? What passages in her account illustrate how other people may have seen African Americans?

2. The introduction to this chapter also defined the terms *metaphor* and *metonymy,* both of which are types of symbolic substitutions. How does Joe Louis work metaphorically and/or metonymically for the audience listening to the broadcast? What elements of Louis's character become symbolic? With which aspects of Louis do the African Americans in Angelou's narrative identify?

3. How does Angelou structure her narrative? To what degree and in what ways does she craft her argument to reflect the values of a particular audience and cultural or historical context? How would the rhetorical effect of this piece have been different if it had been written as, say, a formal academic essay? Or as a newspaper article?

Re-seeing and Re-writing

1. For this assignment, research and find images of memorials to Joe Louis constructed in Detroit (one designed by Robert Graham in 1986 and one by Ed Hamilton in 1987). Write an essay in which you compare the vision of Louis contained in Angelou's narrative and the ones imagined by the designers of these memorials. What elements has each person chosen to remember and translate into stone and/or text? What elements of symbolism do you see in these memorials and to what extent are they similar to the metonymic or metaphoric use of Louis in Angelou's text? Finally, consider the extent to which a narrative or autobiography can be considered a memorial. How does Angelou's personal memory of the Joe Louis fight get translated into a cultural memory? In what ways might her narrative be similar to/different from a memorial?

2. Angelou's essay suggests that sports figures can become iconic representations of entire communities. Do some research on the web about other famous sports icons in the twentieth and twenty-first centuries, such as Tiger Woods, Martina Navratilova, or Jesse Owens. In what ways have they come to represent certain communities? What aspects of their characters become symbolic and what do they symbolize? To what extent does context affect how different people identify with these sports figures?

Intertext

Sturken argues that personal and family photographs take on different meanings in various national and cultural contexts and are "deployed for a number
of personal and public agendas. . . . These agendas address viewers in different roles—as mourners, citizens, family members, and concerned observers.
Each testifies to the traffic across the boundaries of public and private realms."
This essay option invites you to read Angelou's narrative through the lens of
Sturken. To what extent does Angelou's autobiography (personal memory)
become a community memory as well? What roles does her narrative invite
readers to play: that is, what does she ask readers to think or do in response to
her story? What personal and public agendas are (or can be) deployed through
autobiography? Why might these agendas have been particularly relevant to
the time period in which her autobiography was published (the late 1960s)?

Research Prompts
NATIONAL GAZES: Witnessing Nations

**context
metaphor
metonym**

Option #1:

Analyzing Commemorative Photography

Browse through post-9/11 photography publications, such as *One Nation* (Time/Life Books), *A Nation Challenged: A Visual History of 9/11 and Its Aftermath* (*The New York Times*), or *Life* magazine's *Year in Pictures: 2001*. Analyze the representational patterns implicit in the collection, with particular attention to the stories that the images tell and the contexts they depict.

1. **Heroes and Victims:** Are certain visual patterns used to convey the experiences of victims and/or heroes? What stories do these images tell? To whom might these stories appeal? Do these stories reinforce traditional gender roles? Are certain groups represented as more heroic than others? What geographical contexts are depicted and what is their rhetorical appeal? What metaphoric or metonymic relationships are established or hinted at? What insights do your secondary sources enable you to make about these conceptions and patterns? How does your analysis of the photographs (as primary texts) extend, complicate, or challenge the claims made by the secondary sources?

2. **The Family as Nation:** To what degree and in what ways were media representations of the "attack on America" and its aftermath shaped by traditional notions of the "family"? Do certain images construe the nation as a type of extended family? If so, in what ways does this conception of the nation speak to its potential attraction for certain individuals or groups in our culture? What is the rhetorical appeal of certain familial depictions of the "nation"? What metaphoric or metonymic relationships are established or hinted at? What insights do the secondary sources enable you to make about these patterns? How does your analysis of the photographs extend, complicate, or challenge the claims made by the authors of the secondary sources that you've chosen?

Option #2:

Analyzing Political Campaigns

This prompt invites you to examine public speeches and political campaigns. You could choose to analyze campaign websites, posters and buttons, television, radio, or newspaper ads, campaign speeches, and so on. Focus on a particular political campaign or series of related speeches. What representational trends do you notice? How do the campaigns position themselves in relation to their opponents? What historical contexts, events and narratives (stories) come up repeatedly in the campaign? What is the appeal of such stories and on what occasions and in what contexts do they seem to emerge? How do audience and/or context affect which historical events or narratives are referred to or how they are represented? How does invoking history shape the perception and representation of current issues and events?

The following sites might help you get started:

History Channel: Speech Archives: The Words that Moved the World
http://www.historychannel.com/speeches/archive1.html
The American Museum of the Moving Image—The Living Room Candidate: Presidential campaign commercials, 1952–2004
http://livingroomcandidate.movingimage.us/index.php
Picture History: Campaign materials
http://www.picturehistory.com/find/c/262/mcms.html

Option #3:

Analyzing Online Archives: National Identities and History

This option asks you to analyze images from online archives (some sample sites are listed below). Identify a category of analysis that interests you, such as race, class, gender, or sexuality, or a genre that interests you, such as war propaganda, and then browse through the archives searching for images that speak to that category. Then write an essay in which you analyze the patterns and trends among the photographs according to your selected category. Consider the narratives about national identity that these images tell. How have images been grouped together within the archive? How do the images and/or text (including captions) define national identity, and for what purposes? What values do the images associate with certain nations and why? Do the images tell certain stories at the expense of others? Whose? Who is excluded or marginalized? What insights do your secondary sources enable you to make about these conceptions and patterns? How does your analysis extend, refute, or challenge the claims made by the secondary readings?

Library of Congress: The American Memory Project Digital Archives
http://memory.loc.gov
Smithsonian Institute for American History: Virtual Exhibits
http://americanhistory.si.edu/ve/index.htm
The National Archives Online exhibit: The Powers of Persuasion: Poster Art from WWI
http://www.archives.gov/exhibit_hall/powers_of_persuasion/powers_of_persuasion_home.html
WWII posters archive
http://www.evansville1st.com/war_post.htm
Images from the United States Holocaust Memorial Museum
http://www.ushmm.org
American History—Public Domain Images
http://www.princetonol.com/groups/iad/lessons/middle/histlink.htm
National Archives and Records Administration
http://www.archives.gov/exhibit_hall/

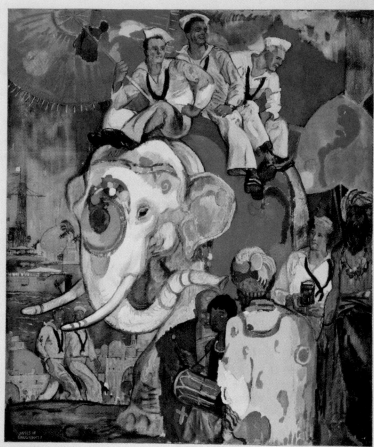

Every native of every place is a potential tourist, and every tourist is a native of somewhere.

–JAMAICA KINCAID

identification   difference

Identifying Tourists and Tourism

WHY DO PEOPLE TRAVEL? WE TRAVEL TO GET AWAY FROM IT ALL, yet we also travel to be a part of it all. We acquire things—perspectives, material goods, a different sense of ourselves—when we become tourists, yet we also abandon things—worries and workday stress, our usual wardrobes, our neighbors and pets, even our "home" identities. We associate with the place we travel to, while we dissociate from the place we travel from. In the act of traveling, we hope to find our identities, yet at the same time be(come) different. Tourism, it seems, is caught up in interesting contradictions.

Both the visual lure of tourism—creating the desire for us to go here, go there, go anywhere—and the visual records we create of the tour (through postcards, photos, and souvenirs) are based on a double-sided rhetoric involving *identification* and *difference*. Through tourism we come to identify with others, but, if we believe the popular ideas in

Critical Frame

tourism rhetoric, we also come to find ourselves as well. Tourism draws us in by making difference exotic and attractive, capitalizing on our eagerness to be or become something different or "other," while also keeping difference familiar enough to keep us grounded. In this unit, through a critical tour of *traveling gazes, tourism,* and *global rhetorics,* we will explore this seemingly contradictory relationship between identification and difference.

The tourist industry creates a desire in us for escape, difference, and mobility. But just who is this "we" to whom tourism appeals? Like the term *travel,* tourism most often refers to a voluntary leisure pursuit; obviously, this pursuit offers a sharp distinction from the experience of the refugee and the migrant worker. This distinction raises one of the key questions we explore in this unit: who has the means and the power to move from one place to another as a tourist?

Consider, for example, the two images below (Figures 5.1 and 5.2), taken from tourist postcards on sale in a small gift shop in the Tucson, Arizona, airport.

Each of these images was taken around the turn of the last century and represents Native American life at that time; the captions, however, are more recent.

Figure 5.1   Description from the back of the postcard: "This picturesque canyon scene shows a Navajo woman sitting on her knees to weave a rug. It took many weeks' work to finish a rug of this size. Note the tree branches used to make the loom. Photographed ca. 1905 by Edward S. Curtis."

Courtesy of the Library of Congress.

454

Figure 5.2   Description from the back of the postcard: "Mollie Juana, Pima, lived on the Salt River Reservation. Pima women usually wore their hair loose, with long bangs cut to shade the eyes from the bright desert light. Mollie Juana is wearing white clay on her face and hair. The design has no special significance. Photographed ca. 1880 by Henry Buehman."

Critical Frame

What is significant, even controversial, about these images is their representation, over a century later, as tourist commodities in an early twenty-first-century southwestern airport. Alongside shot glasses, coffee mugs, and key chains—most of them styled with Native American–associated images such as Kokopelli, lizards, a Zuni fetish bear replica, cacti, and rattlesnakes—were these images from the distant past. Featuring photographs by a turn-of-the-century southwestern tourist, the postcards capitalize on the "otherness" of the subjects represented, but also attempt to have today's Tucson tourist identify with the characters and scenes in the images.

For example, as viewers of "The Blanket Weaver" (Figure 5.1), we are drawn in to the distant scene—distant in both camera perspective and actual years from our own lives—as we gaze over the shoulder of the blanket weaver. We watch her, yet she does not see us. The description on the reverse side of the postcard encourages us to see the scene as "picturesque" and to "note the tree branches used to make the loom"— almost like a placard in an art museum that points out certain features of a painting before us, or like an anthropological description of a "primitive" culture. The image presumes a gaze from above or from outside—a traveling gaze that depicts difference and a commanding view that affords us access to colonized peoples and their lands.

We use the term **traveling gaze** to refer to the ways in which individuals, groups, institutions, and disciplines (e.g., anthropology, sociology, and business) employ the rhetorical strategies of identification and difference to depict the movement(s) of peoples, cultures, languages, goods, and knowledge from one place to another. The attraction of traveling gazes is the ability to enter rhetorically into another place, lifestyle, or cultural moment and to participate voyeuristically, while imagining that the natives and native landscape go unchanged, unaware of our presence.

Tourists often have the commanding view and are given the power to look. But we also need to be careful not to overly generalize the experience of "the tourist," as if there were no differences among tourists. Native Americans are not always objects of the outsider's gaze; contemporary Native Americans visiting Tucson, for example, might see themselves in a very different relation to "The Blanket Weaver." As Jamaica Kincaid puts it in "A Small Place," "every native is a potential tourist." Like Kincaid, we view the term *tourist* as an identification based on action, rather than on some presumably "natural" identity. In other words, those who practice tourism are tourists.

In contrast to "The Blanket Weaver," in which both the native and the landscape are objects of the tourist's gaze, the 1880 photo of a Pima girl, "Mollie Juana" (Figure 5.2), gazes directly at us. We see that she wears her bangs long and her hair loose (hardly the fashion of white American women in the 1880s), and her face and hair are painted with lines and dots. These face markings are exotically different; in fact, they are perhaps the element that most draws our eye to the photo in the first place—yet they are declared, on the back of the postcard, to have "no special significance." Tourists are therefore assured that her markings are "safe," that is, witholding no hidden meanings. We can also see that she not only poses in a Western chair, but her dress—with dots and capped sleeves—is identifiably familiar. As viewers of the image, we are thus able to both identify with the Pima girl and recognize her difference from us.

Troubling Binaries

There are a number of ways to think about the contrasting cultural references in the two Tucson postcards. One way is to consider, like rhetorician Kenneth Burke, that all acts of identification are in fact predicated upon difference. The mixed cultural styles and dress in "Mollie Juana" might be interpreted as the Pima girl's consumption of Western products, and therefore her acceptance of, and identification with, Western values. On the other hand, they might be seen as transforming Western cultural styles and dress, presenting a more fluid understanding of identity and cultural difference. In both instances, identification and difference intermingle.

Identification and difference are not really binary opposites, though they are often used as if they were. Rather, they are relational terms, which encompass a wide spectrum of power relations. Consider, for example, how the binary racial categories *Native American/white* and *black/white* exclude many groups and assume that whiteness is the category against which all other identities are defined. What a binary understanding of identification and difference misses is that individuals can occupy more than one identity position, and that identities can also be mis-recognized. We need, therefore, to consider the complexity of categories of identity.

Of course, to say that identities are complex, mobile, and shifting is not to dismiss the significance of identity markers in political, legal, and social realms. For instance, the history of how Native Americans in the United States have been defined highlights the serious consequences of identity categories and the role of the federal government in determining just who is "Indian." The 1887 Dawes Allotment Act distinguished between "full-bloods" and "mixed bloods" among Cherokee and related tribal groups in order to determine eligibility for allotment lands. As a result, many "mixed bloods" were denied land. More recently, such identifications have been linked to consumption. The 1990 Indian Arts and Crafts Act is intended to promote the development of Native American art through federal recognition and certification of Indian artists by tribe. But, as some critics have argued, the Act promotes censorship and criminalizes those who are "noncertified" Native American artists, including the non-federally recognized.

The Economics of Tourism

Tourism is tied up in the ebb and flow of global and local economies. Not only does the tourism industry encourage us to spend our paid vacations in efforts to become or to know "the other," but it also enters us into a complex economic relationship with those "others" as our traveling gazes come to both support and undermine their local economies and cultures.

Take Hawai'i as an example. Native Hawai'ian Haunani-Kay Trask has written in *From a Native Daughter: Colonialism and Sovereignty in Hawai'i* that the relationship between tourists' desires and the political and economic realities of daily lives for most native Hawai'ians is destructive at best: "Tourists flock to my Native land for escape, but they are escaping into a state of mind while participating in the destruction of a host people in a Native place."

Transnational corporations, Trask argues, alongside other economic, educational, and governmental powers, promote tourism as a boon to the local economy and (thus) an obviously good thing. For example, in a brief history of how tourism "saved" the natives from martial law and labor abuses (a result of changes in sugar and pineapple industries after World War II), the "Let's Go Hawai'i" Web site chronicles "the growth of tourism" as a positive force, concluding that "by the 1970s, tourism had a firm position as the state's top industry, surpassing the military." Trask emphasizes that the "tourist infrastructure" of Hawai'i is bent on perpetuating the rhetorical vision, in place since the close of World War II, of Hawai'i as the "American Paradise" and native Hawai'ians as "natural" hosts and hostesses for travelers. Indeed, in a widely reproduced vintage poster (Figure 5.3), a smiling hula dancer shimmies atop the Hawai'ian Islands, beckoning travelers to come to "The Islands of Paradise." The alluring dancer, clearly the focal point of the image, towers over the island and its natural resources and exists solely for the visual pleasure of tourists. And the lush flora and fauna at the dancer's feet portray Hawai'i as an undisturbed garden of Eden rather than an environmental and economic trouble spot.

The "firm position" of Hawai'ian tourism celebrated by the "Let's Go Hawai'i" Web site is maintained through the rhetorical work of both identification and difference. As scholar Jane Desmond has recently written, the organized development of tourism in a place like Hawai'i springs from the "Euro-American fascination with things 'exotic'"[1]—but not too exotic. But the traveling gaze has had a profound impact on the Hawai'ian islands and natives, and the welcome mat of the "American Paradise" is wearing thin. Writing recently in *Fragile Paradise: The Impact of Tourism on Maui, 1959–2000*, Mansel Blackford concludes with a sum of the deleterious effects of tourism on Maui: a devastating environmental impact, acrimonious disputes over land and water rights, a cost of living that is nearly 36 percent higher than on the mainland; high unemployment rates and employment that is often not sustainable for whole families, and a reduction of the diversity of industry options on the islands. And when tourism declines—as it did in the mid-1990s—the economy can all but collapse. In 1996, for example, business failures on the Hawai'ian Islands were an astonishing 47 percent, compared with 1 percent on the mainland that year, according to Blackford.

Multinational corporations, of course, are heavily invested in the tourism industry. United Airlines, for example, owns not only the path to Hawai'i (by dominating the airline travel options) but much of the destination itself, since it also owns the majority of the islands' major hotels and resorts and is one of the state's largest employers. In order to keep themselves solvent, corporations like United must seek to (re)stimulate the rhetoric promoting the "American Paradise." So much can depend on the gaze of a traveler.

Far and Away Places

Sometimes products or artifacts that are associated with a certain place can satisfy our traveling gaze and our desire to be or know that "other." Gift shops and the fashion industry, for example, often help us to identify with a place—visually supplementing, or even supplanting, our travel.

AND **WRITING**

We identify because we differ. One of the key rhetoricians of the twentieth century, Kenneth Burke, named **identification** as the central concept in his own theories about persuasion. In Burke's influential book, *A Rhetoric of Motives* (1969), he describes our drive for identification as inherently biological: Because we are born physically distinct and separate, Burke claims, we aim to establish areas of intersection and communion with each other—points in common among our interests, activities, opinions, values, and experiences. What is more, we find these intersections primarily through symbols, in writing, speaking, and creating images. For example, when a hopeful presidential candidate journeys to Iowa farm country for his bid in the opening primary caucus and he begins his speech there with a line such as "I was a farm boy myself," he is using rhetoric to identify with his audience.

Identification works powerfully through visual means. Consider the remarkably successful "Got Milk?" campaign, which used the milk mustache on adult celebrities to identify its product with the innocence and simple pleasures of childhood. Even those who don't drink milk can appreciate the power of such a campaign.

Examples ■■■

❶ In the beginning of John Hockenberry's essay, "Walking with the Kurds," he sees himself as very different from the refugees around him: He is on a donkey's back, he is blond, he is American, and he is well-fed. However, as the trip (and essay) continues, Hockenberry begins to identify more with those around him:

> As time went on I ceased even to look like an American journalist. Anonymity intensified the feeling of who I was, where I had come from, and how my own body worked, or didn't. As an American I had no right to be afraid here, I thought. I was safe and distinct from this horror. As a human being I had no way to separate myself from the river of Kurdish flesh making its way toward the valley. In my own invisible way, I was as close to death as they were. As a paraplegic, I was inside a membrane of unspoken physical adversity.

❷ In Lisa Nakamura's essay "Where Do You Want to Go Today?" she demonstrates how computer companies use familiar American slogans alongside "exotic" places

Critical Frame

to suggest that computers will help to make foreign countries and people accessible. The placement of the familiar American slogans next to less familiar foreign places helps establish identification. Nakamura goes on to examine an IBM ad, which demonstrates the power of identification:

> The gap between exotic Otherness of the image and the familiarity of its American rhetoric can be read as more than an attempt at humor, however. IBM, whose slogan "Solution for a Small Planet" is contained in an icon button in the lower left hand side of the image, is literally putting these incongruous words in the Other's mouth, thus demonstrating the hegemonic power of its "high-speed information network" to make the planet smaller by causing everyone to speak the *same* language—computer speak.

Exercises ▨▪▨

❶ Musical (Visual) Mind-Meld

Music is one of the most powerful tools of identification in our modern day culture; in addition to the melody, it often works effectively through incorporating both the "visual" (videos) and the verbal (lyrics). For this exercise, make a list of ten or so songs you identify with for some reason or another. Then, do one of the following:

- Share that list in small groups and generate notes on what kind of identifications and points of commonality (values, experiences, etc.) any of you might have over any songs on your shared lists. Write a brief paper to the other members of the class in which you describe the identifications your group members found through one or several of the songs.
- In small groups, imagine and script the elements of a music video for a song you all identify with (do not use a music video already created). Create a script for the music video that you believe would help the rest of the class members also identify with you as they listened to this song.

❷ Image Identification

Bring in four or five images that you want to use to help create some identification/association among members of your class. These images might be ones that are fairly well known that you think others will recognize, or images of common events (high school prom pictures, holiday gatherings) that might bring out shared associations. Share your images in small groups and have the other group members write quick associative paragraphs (or even just phrases) about each of the images.

What souvenirs link you to a place you have been? What objects anchor you to travel you have never (or not yet?) taken, but that encourage you to identify with that place or its people, its culture, its landscape? Many of us could open a drawer at home and pull out objects that are associated with specific places we have visited. Many of us, when we travel, buy ornaments and accessories in airports and local shops. Travel itself is a form of "accessory" for people who have the economic means to tour. For some of us, tourism is an ornament with which to adorn ourselves.

In fact, the marketing of travel often goes hand in hand with the marketing of fashion. It is not unusual to find a feature spread in a contemporary fashion magazine that will take as its theme a certain destination. The material we wear can, marketers would have us believe, transport us to—and identify us with—some far and away place. For example, the December 2002 issue of *Marie Claire,* a women's fashion and beauty magazine, features a nine-page spread on "Far and Away Pieces." In this spread, the pieces of clothing promise escape for the winter-weary to exotic (and warm) places—to Peru and Chile, specifically. "Escape from winter basics with a spicy mix of exotic prints and textures," the subtitle beckons.

The two-page centerfold of this fashion spread (Figure 5.4) features a young woman posed with five seemingly native children, three llamas, and one parrot. The model has dark hair and complexion, like the children she poses with. She also echos

Figure 5.4   "Far and Away Places," *Marie Claire,* December 2002.
Courtesy of Matt Albiani.

the children with her bright red dress, since they too are all covered in bright multi-colored jackets, ponchos, and hats (presumably their "native" wear), most likely made from the wool of llamas like the ones they hold on frayed ropes.

Their shoes, however—four dust-covered pairs of sandals and one worn pair of sneakers—stand in stark contrast to the substantially heeled, knee-high leather boots the model wears (at $420 a pair). Differences, then, are emerging, this time economic. The model's brocaded leather knee-length coat marks her as a traveler, not only because of its different appearance but surely also because of its cost ($1,525). The natives do not accessorize (at least not in this image), but the model's earrings weigh in at $3,650 a pair. All told, her outfit—complete with a leather hat that is the "model's own"—would cost $8,020. In developing countries such as Chile and Peru, where the average annual income is approximately $5,000 (Chile) and $1,980 (Peru) per adult citizen, the model's real-life distance from the children of the high Andes is more than just a matter of geography. While her traveling gaze, and presumably our own, can consume their culture, they can most likely never consume ours.

Whatever our desires, and however our traveling gazes might aim to fulfill those desires, one thing is certain: Images attract tourists and images travel. Like the century-old Native American postcard images meant to appeal to contemporary tourists to Tucson, photographic representations of a location, its people, its attractions, and its food can help create a sense of identification and comfort, as well as engender a sense of difference and a desire to know more about that place. The visual representations of a place can lure us to enter the site and become a part of the photographic landscape ourselves.

Touring Differently

While images of the U.S. Southwest, Hawai'i, and developing countries inspire us to travel there for escape and for fun, the tourist industry has also developed several alternatives to traditional forms of tourism. These "educational tours" promise meaningful travel, a chance not just to see a faraway place but to learn about it and to connect with the people who live there. For example, Global Exchange, an international human rights organization, offers "Reality Tours" that provide "hands-on opportunities to explore the crucial issues facing the world and examine how the U.S.'s economic and foreign policies impact other countries" (www.globalexchange .org/tours/). For a fee, individuals or groups can experience a "Reality Tour" of Brazil, Ireland, Zimbabwe, Vietnam, or one of numerous other countries connected to the United States through global economic or foreign policy.

Global Exchange's Reality Tours, then, connect tourism and travel to educational and humanitarian interests. Like traditional tourism, Reality Tours relies on a rhetoric of identification and difference to convince people to undertake travel. The organization promises, for example, connection (identification) with human beings across the globe as well as education about specific cultural and national places and peoples (difference). Moreover, visual representations featured on their Web site evoke both identification and difference by depicting "others" while offering meaningful ways in which tourists can make a positive difference in their lives.

Critical Frame

AND WRITING

difference

Identification and difference operate almost as mirrored, twin images of each other. In fact, creating difference can be just as effective as creating identification in an effort to persuade. Even as it has aimed to establish identification with its potential consumers, advertising, for example, has long capitalized on establishing difference—difference from other products, and even difference from a former version of its own product. (It seems that household products are almost always "new" and "improved" versions of their former incarnations.)

Popular media also rely heavily on difference, while clinging to identification. When one kind of TV show becomes popular, for example, numerous close (but not completely identical) clones of that show appear quickly: "Queer Eye for the Straight Guy" becomes "Queer Eye for the Straight Girl"; the medical drama "ER" spawns a half dozen similar shows, including a half-hour sitcom, "Scrubs." Finally, travel destinations must draw upon some familiarity (identification) in order to woo tourists, but they must also work hard to establish their unique advantage over all other destinations.

Whether in popular entertainment or consumer advertising, the power of difference, rubbing right alongside the power of identification, is made manifest largely through a blend of visual and verbal rhetorical strategies. The "new" and "improved" version of a product must in most cases retain brand identification, but also look different, with a change in packaging, a new size/shape, new odor, and so on. In the travel industry, the tourist shops must stock the ubiquitous tourist t-shirts for purposes of easy identification; they also aim, however, to offer some "unique" product that travelers can carry home with them in order, ironically, to identify with that particular place.

Examples ■■■

1 In the essay "The Photograph as an Intersection of Gazes," Catherine Lutz and Jane Collins's argument depends upon differentiating between the representation of Western and non-Western subjects in *National Geographic.* In discussing the non-Western person, they note, for example,

The photograph and the non-Western person share two fundamental attributes in the culturally tutored experience of most Americans; they are objects at which we look. The photograph has this quality because it is usually intended as a thing of either beauty or documentary interest and surveillance. Non-Westerners draw a look, rather than inattention or interaction, to the extent that their difference or foreignness defines them as noteworthy or yet distant. A look is necessary to cross the span created by the perception of difference, a perception which initially, of course, also involves looking.

❷ One of the key rhetorical devices that activist, scholar, and writer Haunani-Kay Trask employs is difference. For example, in Trask's five opening paragraphs she uses the pronouns "us," "our," and "we" to define native Hawai'ians as being distinctly different from mainland "Americans."

For us, native self-government has always been preferable to American foreign government. No matter what Americans believe, most of us in the colonies do not feel grateful that our country was stolen along with our citizenship, our lands, and our independent place among the family of nations. We are not happy natives.

Exercises ▪▪▪

❶ Pronoun Power

Although they seem so small, pronouns such as *I, me, we, you, they, us, he/she, his, hers, theirs* wield great power in establishing both identification and difference. First, discuss with your classmates how you believe each of the pronouns listed above adds to, or detracts from, a sense of identification or difference. Then, take a piece of persuasive prose—an op-ed in your local newspaper, the text from an advertisement, a speech from a politician, a travel brochure, a flyer posted around campus, etc.—and analyze its use of pronouns, with an eye to their function in establishing identification and/or difference.

❷ Difference Sells

Create an advertisement for a new product or place—for example, a new kind of Barbie doll, a fabulous laundry soap just for college students, a sitcom about dorm life, or a new destination for spring break. Think carefully about what strategies of identification and differentiation will help you "sell" your product. Your advertisement should include both visual and verbal material.

Figure 5.5   Refugees at the Abushouk camp in Darfur, Sudan, Saturday, July 31, 2004.
Courtesy of Guillaume Bonn/The New York Times.

As Global Exchange reminds us, tourism and travel are not equally available to everyone. Other forms of mobility—immigration, for example, or displacement—circulate people, goods, and ideas around the globe, often without such feel-good effects. Images of displacement, common in the news and in human rights activism, can encourage viewers to adjust their traveling gazes. Figure 5.5, for example, depicts refugees from Sudan, a site of significant contemporary conflict.

The refugees in this image look directly at the camera, returning the viewer's gaze. Their faces betray suffering, but they also appear dignified, their gazes steady. Their native dress and the violent circumstances surrounding their refugee status evoke our difference from them; instead of a rosy, paradisal picture of exotic difference, this image offers a gritty, devastating view of "otherness," as well as a somber view of coerced global mobility. At the same time, the women's expressions appeal to our common humanity. This moving photo reminds us of all the forces, local and global, cultural and individual, that are present when we look at an image of another.

NOTE

1. Jane Desmond, *Staging Tourism: Bodies on Display from Waikiki to Sea World* (Chicago: U Chicago P, 1999) 37.

TRAVEL POEMS

ELIZABETH BISHOP, ADRIENNE RICH

Born in Worcester, Massachusetts, *ELIZABETH BISHOP* wrote barely 100 poems in her lifetime, but was known as a "poet's poet" for the subtle precision of her work; her good friend, the poet Robert Lowell, praised her "commanding genius for picking up the unnoticed," and her poetry is filled with descriptions and impressions of her surroundings. She was well-traveled and lived in Brazil with her companion Lota Soares for many years.

ADRIENNE RICH is the author of a score of books of poetry and several nonfiction collections. Recipient of the National Book Award and a MacArthur fellowship, she lives and writes in northern California. Rich, considered a key figure in twentieth-century feminist poetry, frequently explores issues of social and domestic injustice and dwells, as Rhonda Pettit notes, on the "points where private lives and public acts intersect."

Questions of Travel

ELIZABETH BISHOP

There are too many waterfalls here; the crowded streams
hurry too rapidly down to the sea,
and the pressure of so many clouds on the mountaintops
makes them spill over the sides in soft slow-motion,
5   turning to waterfalls under our very eyes.
—For if those streaks, those mile-long, shiny, tearstains,
aren't waterfalls yet,
in a quick age or so, as ages go here,
they probably will be.
10   But if the streams and clouds keep travelling, travelling,
the mountains look like the hulls of capsized ships,
slime-hung and barnacled.

Think of the long trip home.
Should we have stayed at home and thought of here?
15   Where should we be today?
Is it right to be watching strangers in a play
in this strangest of theatres?
What childishness is it that while there's a breath of life
in our bodies, we are determined to rush
20   to see the sun the other way around?
The tiniest green hummingbird in the world?

To stare at some inexplicable old stonework,
inexplicable and impenetrable,
at any view,
25   instantly seen and always, always delightful?
Oh, must we dream our dreams
and have them, too?
And have we room
for one more folded sunset, still quite warm?

30   But surely it would have been a pity
not to have seen the trees along this road,
really exaggerated in their beauty,
not to have seen them gesturing
like noble pantomimists, robed in pink.
35   —Not to have had to stop for gas and heard
the sad, two-noted, wooden tune
of disparate wooden clogs
carelessly clacking over
a grease-stained filling-station floor.
40   (In another country the clogs would all be tested.
Each pair there would have identical pitch.)
—A pity not to have heard
the other, less primitive music of the fat brown bird
who sings above the broken gasoline pump
45   in a bamboo church of Jesuit baroque:
three towers, five silver crosses.
—Yes, a pity not to have pondered,
blurr'dly and inconclusively,
on what connection can exist for centuries
50   between the crudest wooden footwear
and, careful and finicky,
the whittled fantasies of wooden cages.
—Never to have studied history in
the weak calligraphy of songbirds' cages.
55   —And never to have had to listen to rain
so much like politicians' speeches:
two hours of unrelenting oratory
and then a sudden golden silence
in which the traveller takes a notebook, writes:

60   *"Is it lack of imagination that makes us come*
to imagined places, not just stay at home?
Or could Pascal have been not entirely right
about just sitting quietly in one's room?

65
Continent, city, country, society:
the choice is never wide and never free.
And here, or there . . . No. Should we have stayed at home,
wherever that may be?"

An Atlas of the Difficult World

ADRIENNE RICH

What homage will be paid to a beauty built to last
from inside out, executing the blueprints of resistance and mercy
drawn up in childhood, in that little girl, round-faced with clenched fists,
    already acquainted with mourning
in the creased snapshot you gave me? What homage will be paid to beauty
5   that insists on speaking truth, knows the two are not always the same,
beauty that won't deny, is itself an eye, will not rest under contemplation?
Those low long clouds we were driving under a month ago in New Mexico, clouds
    an arm's reach away
were beautiful and we spoke of it but I didn't speak then
of your beauty at the wheel beside me, dark head steady, eyes drinking the spaces
10 of crimson, indigo, Indian distance, Indian presence,
your spirit's gaze informing your body, impatient to mark what's possible, impatient
    to mark
what's lost, deliberately destroyed, can never any way be returned,
your back arched against all icons, simulations, dead letters
your woman's hands turning the wheel or working with shears, torque wrench,
    knives, with salt pork, onions, ink and fire
15 your providing sensate hands, your hands of oak and silk, of blackberry juice
    and drums
—I speak of them now.

(FOR M.)

Re-reading/Conversations with the Texts

1. Before you read, inventory your own experiences with travel. What expectations did you have? What pleasures or fears do you associate with your experiences? After you read, brainstorm with a partner the contrasts between your
   experiences and expectations and those depicted by Bishop and Rich.

2. Bishop and Rich each create a palpable tension between coming and going,
   leaving and staying. Rich paints urban vignettes of isolated individuals, while
   Bishop describes a single journey caught between the familiar and the strange,
   between home and away. Considering each poem individually, what is the

cumulative effect of the images they call up? How does each poet invoke sight and light, seeing and being seen, to heighten this effect?

3. Rich describes a scene of intimate traveling in which she addresses her companion directly ("your beauty at the wheel beside me"); Bishop, on the other hand, uses the more intimate "we." What is the effect of these forms of address on the reader? In what way does each promote or impede the reader's identification with the poet? With the characters in her narrative? How is this identification or differentiation anticipated in the titles, "Questions of Travel" and "An Atlas of a Difficult World"? How is it played out in the imagery?

Re-seeing and Re-writing

1. Family photographs are most often taken as records of celebratory occasions— birthdays, weddings, graduations. Both of these selections attend to details of the everyday that are rarely captured in photographs—driving, working in the kitchen, a birdcage on a rusty gasoline pump. Create a collage using images of the everyday. You could take your own photographs over a 24-hour period, or use clippings from magazines or images from the internet (try www .fotolog.com). Write a narrative to accompany your collage. Then imagine that you are from a culture unfamiliar with the artifacts and customs depicted in your images. Write a second narrative that reimagines the story told by these images from an "outsider" perspective.

2. Plan a documentary based on the worlds depicted by Rich and Bishop. Working in two groups, choose photographs, paintings, sketches, or other images to accompany the lines of each poem. Put your documentaries together in a PowerPoint or Flash presentation. Pay particular attention to how choices of font, text color, and other elements work visually with the images to contribute to the meaning of your presentation.

Intertext

In *A Small Place,* Jamaica Kincaid draws vivid word-pictures of her homeland of Antigua. Kincaid, Rich, and Bishop each reinterpret travel and tourism within the framework of ordinary daily life. (In many ways, their work resembles contemporary cultural ethnography.) Rather than writing narratives from places that seem exotic and distant, they each focus on the minutiae of the worlds they know well. What do you think each wants to accomplish with her narrative? Where do they position their readers—within the world they describe? Outside, observing at a distance? Both?

The Photograph as an Intersection of Gazes

CATHERINE LUTZ AND JANE COLLINS

A publication such as *National Geographic* is filled with exotic images of places and people that we might immediately recognize as "others." How often do we consider the ways in which these same images reveal or help create the values and beliefs of our own culture? The cultural studies scholars *CATHERINE LUTZ* and *JANE COLLINS* explore just this issue in "The Photograph as an Intersection of Gazes," a chapter from their 1993 book *Reading National Geographic.* In this excerpt, the authors outline a variety of gazes to which viewers of magazines like *National Geographic* are subject; these gazes work together to create and reinforce complex ideological messages in the text. Such intersections of gazes, one might argue, are at work in virtually any text one might encounter.

> *If photographs are messages, the message is both transparent and mysterious.*
>
> (SUSAN SONTAG, *ON PHOTOGRAPHY*)

All photographs tell stories about looking. In considering the *National Geographic*'s photographs, we have been struck by the variety of looks and looking relations that swirl in and around them. These looks—whether from the photographer, the reader, or the person photographed—are ambiguous, charged with feeling and power, central to the stories (sometimes several and conflicting) that the photo can be said to tell. By examining the "lines of sight" evident in the *Geographic* photograph of the non-Westerner, we become aware that it is not simply a captured view of the *other,* but rather a dynamic site at which many gazes or viewpoints intersect. This intersection creates a complex, multidimensional object; it allows viewers of the photo to negotiate a number of different identities both for themselves and for those pictured; and it is one route by which the photograph threatens to break frame and reveal its social context. We aim here to explore the significance of "gaze" for intercultural relations in the photograph and to present a typology of seven kinds of gaze that can be found in the photograph and its social context: the photographer's gaze (the actual look through the view-finder); the institutional magazine gaze, evident in cropping, picture choice, and captioning; the reader's gaze; the non-Western subject's gaze; the explicit looking done by Westerners who may be framed with locals in the picture; the gaze returned or refracted by the mirrors or cameras that are shown in local hands; and our own academic gaze.

A Multitude of Gazes

Many gazes can be found in every photograph in the *National Geographic*. This is true whether the picture shows an empty landscape; a single person looking straight at the camera; a large group of people, each looking in a different direction but none at the camera; or a person in the distance whose eyes are tiny or out of focus.

In other words, the gaze is not simply the look given by or to a photographed subject. It includes seven kinds of gaze.[1]

The Photographer's Gaze

This gaze, represented by the camera's eye, leaves its clear mark on the structure and content of the photograph. Independently or constrained by others, the photographer takes a position on a rooftop overlooking Khartoum or inside a Ulithian menstrual hut or in front of a funeral parade in Vietnam. Photo subject matter, composition, vantage point (angle or point of view), sharpness and depth of focus, color balance, framing, and other elements of style are the results of the viewing choices made by the photographer or by the invitations or exclusions of those being photographed (Geary 1988).

Susan Sontag argues that photographers are usually profoundly alienated from the people they photograph, and may "feel compelled to put the camera between themselves and whatever is remarkable that they encounter" (1977:10). *Geographic* photographers, despite an

expressed fundamental sympathy with the third world people they meet, confront them across distances of class, race, and sometimes gender. Whether from a fear of these differences or the more primordial (per Lacan) insecurity of the gaze itself, the photographer can often make the choice to insert technique between self and

The gaze of the camera is not always exactly the same as the gaze of the viewer, but in most *Geographic* photographs the former structures the latter in powerful ways. In this August 1976 photograph of a Venezuelan diamond transaction, the viewer is strongly encouraged to share the photographer's interest in the miner rather than in the broker.

Courtesy of Robert Madden/National Geographic Society.

[1]An early typology of the gaze from a colonial and racist perspective is found in Sir Richard Burton's accounts of his African expeditions, during which he felt himself to be the victim of "an ecstasy of curiosity." Wrote Burton: "At last my experience in staring enabled me to categorize the infliction as follows. Firstly is the stare furtive, when the starer would peep and peer under the tent, and its reverse, the open stare. Thirdly is the stare curious or intelligent, which generally was accompanied with irreverent laughter regarding our appearance. Fourthly is the stare stupid, which denoted the hebete incurious savage. The stare discreet is that of Sultans and greatmen; the stare indiscreet at unusual seasons is affected by women and children. Sixthly is the stare flattering—it was exceedingly rare, and equally so was the stare contemptuous. Eighthly is the stare greedy; it was denoted by the eyes restlessly bounding from one object to another, never tired, never satisfied. Ninthly is the stare peremptory and pertinacious, peculiar to crabbed age. The dozen concludes with the stare drunken, the stare fierce or pugnacious, and finally the stare cannibal, which apparently considered us as articles of diet" (Burton in Moorehead 1960:33). One can imagine a similarly hostile categorization of white Westerners staring at exotics over the past centuries.

his or her subjects, as can the social scientist (Devereux 1967).

15   Under most circumstances, the photographer's gaze and the viewer's gaze overlap. The photographer may treat the camera eye as simply a conduit for the reader's look, the "searchlight" (Metz 1985) of his or her vision. Though these two looks can be disentangled, the technology and conventions of photography force the reader to follow that eye and see the world from its position.[2] The implications of this fact can be illustrated with a photo that shows a Venezuelan miner selling the diamonds he has just prospected to a middleman (August 1976). To take his picture, the photographer has stood inside the broker's place of business, shooting out over his back and shoulder to capture the face and hands of the miner as he exchanges his diamonds for cash. The viewer is strongly encouraged to share the photographer's interest in the miner, rather than the broker (whose absent gaze may be more available for substitution with the viewer's than is the miner's), and in fact to identify with the broker from whose relative position the shot has been taken and received. The broker, like the North American reader, stands outside the frontier mining world. Alternative readings of this photograph are, of course, possible; the visibility of the miner's gaze may make identification with him and his precarious position more likely. Ultimately what is important is the question of how a diverse set of readers respond to such points of view in a photograph.

[2]Some contemporary photographers are experimenting with these conventions (in point of view or framing) in an effort to undermine this equation. Victor Burgin, for example, intentionally attempts to break this down by making photographs that are "'occasions for interpretation' rather than . . . 'objects of consumption'" and that thereby require a gaze which more actively produces itself rather than simply accepting the photographer's gaze as its own. While one can question whether any *National Geographic* photograph is ever purely an object of consumption, the distinction alerts us to the possibility that the photographer can encourage or discourage through technique, the relative independence of the viewer's gaze.

The Magazine's Gaze

This is the whole institutional process by which some portion of the photographer's gaze is chosen for use and emphasis. It includes (1) the editor's decision to commission articles on particular locations or issues; (2) the editor's choice of pictures; and (3) the editor's and layout designer's decisions about cropping the picture, arranging it with other photos on the page to bring out the desired meaning, reproducing it in a certain size format to emphasize or downplay its importance, or even altering the picture. The reader, of course, cannot determine whether decisions relating to the last two choices are made by editor or photographer. The magazine's gaze is more evident and accessible in (4) the caption writer's verbal fixing of a vantage on the picture's meaning. This gaze is also multiple and sometimes controversial, given the diverse perspectives and politics of those who work for the *Geographic*.

The Magazine Readers' Gazes

As Barthes has pointed out, the "photograph is not only perceived, received, it is *read,* connected more or less consciously by the public that consumes it to a traditional stock of signs" (1977:19). Independently of what the photographer or the caption writer may intend as the message of the photo, the reader can imagine something else. This fact, which distinguishes the reader's gaze from that of the magazine, led us to investigate the former directly by asking a number of people to look at and interpret our set of photos. Certain elements of composition or content may make it more likely that the reader will resist the photographic gaze and its ideological messages or potentials. These include whatever indicates that a camera (rather than the reader's eye alone) has been at work—jarring, unnatural colors, off-center angles, and obvious photo retouching.

What *National Geographic* subscribers see is not simply what they get (the physical object, the photograph) but what they imagine the world is about before the magazine arrives, what imagining the picture provokes, and what they remember afterwards of the story they make the picture tell or allow it to tell. The reader's gaze, then, has a history and a future, and it is structured by the mental work of inference and imagination, provoked by the picture's inherent ambiguity (Is that woman smiling or smirking? What are those people in the background doing?) and its tunnel vision (What is going on outside the picture frame? What is it, outside the picture, that she is looking at?). Beyond that, the photo permits fantasy ("Those two are in love, in love like I am with Stuart, but they're bored there on the bench, bored like I have been even in love" or "That child. How beautiful. She should be mine to hold and feed.").

The reader's gaze is structured by a large number of cultural elements or models, many more than those used to reason about racial or cultural difference. Cultural models that we have learned help us interpret gestures such as the thrown-back shoulders of an Argentinean cowboy as indicative of confidence, strength, and bravery. Models of gender lead to a reading of a picture of a mother with a child as a natural scenario, and of the pictured relationship as one of loving, relaxed nurturance; alternatively, the scene might have been read as underlaid with tensions and emotional distance, an interpretation that might be more common in societies with high infant mortality. There is, however, not one reader's gaze; each individual looks with his or her own personal, cultural, and political background or set of interests. It has been possible for people to speak of "the [singular] reader" only so long as "the text" is treated as an entity with a single determinate meaning that is simply consumed (Radway 1984) and only so long as the agency, enculturated nature, and diversity of experience of readers are denied.

20   The gaze of the *National Geographic* reader is also structured by photography's technological

form, including a central paradox. On the one hand, photographs allow participation in the non-Western scene through vicarious viewing. On the other, they may also alienate the reader by way of the fact that they create or require a passive viewer and that they frame out much of what an actual viewer of the scene would see, smell, and hear, thereby atomizing and impoverishing experience (Sontag 1977). From another perspective, the photograph has been said (Metz 1985) to necessarily distance the viewer by changing the person photographed into an object—we know our gaze falls on a two-dimensional object—and promoting fantasy. Still, the presumed consent of the other to be photographed can give the viewer the illusion of having some relationship with him or her.

Finally, this gaze is also structured by the context of reading. How and where does the reader go through the magazine—quickly or carefully, alone or with a child? In a less literal sense, the context of reading includes cultural notions about the magazine itself, as high middlebrow, scientific, and pleasurable. Readers' views of what the photograph says about the other must have something to do with the elevated class position they can assume their reading of *National Geographic* indicates. If I the reader am educated and highbrow in contrast to the reader of *People* magazine or the daily newspaper, my gaze may take on the seriousness and appreciative stance a high-class cultural product requires.

The Non-Western Subject's Gaze

There is perhaps no more significant gaze in the photograph than that of its subject. It is how and where the other looks that most determines the differences in the message a photograph can give about intercultural relations. The gaze of the other found in *National Geographic* can be classified into at least four types; she or he can confront the camera, look at something or someone within the picture frame, look off into the distance, or not look at anything at all.

The gaze confronting camera and reader comprises nearly a quarter of the photos that have at least some non-Western locals in them.[3] What does the look into the camera's eye suggest to readers about the photographic subject? A number of possibilities suggest themselves.

The look into the camera must at least suggest acknowledgment of photographer and reader. Film theorists have disagreed about what this look does, some arguing that it short circuits the voyeurism identified as an important component of most photography: there can be no peeping if the other meets our gaze. The gaze can be confrontational: "I see you looking at me, so you cannot steal that look." Others, however, have argued that this look, while acknowledging the viewer, simply implies more open voyeurism: the return gaze does not contest the right of the viewer to look and may in fact be read as the subject's assent to being watched (Metz 1985:800–801).

25   This disagreement hinges on ignoring how the look is returned and on discounting the effects of context inside the frame and in the reader's historically and culturally variable interpretive work. Facial expression is obviously crucial. The local person looks back with a number of different faces, including friendly smiling, hostile glaring, a vacant or indifferent glance, curiosity, or an ambiguous look. Some of these looks, from some kinds of ethnic others, are unsettling, disorienting, and perhaps often avoided. In *National Geographic*'s photos, the return look is, however, usually not a confrontational or challenging one. The smile plays an important role in muting the potentially disruptive, confrontational role of this return gaze. If the other looks back at the camera and smiles, the combination can be read by viewers

as the subject's assent to being surveyed. In 38 percent of the pictures of locals where facial expressions are visible (N = 436), someone is smiling (although not all who smile are looking into the camera), while a higher 55 percent of all pictures in which someone looks back at the camera include one or more smiling figures.

The camera gaze can also establish at least the illusion of intimacy and communication. To the extent that *National Geographic* presents itself as bringing together the corners of the world, the portrait and camera gaze are important routes to those ends. The other is not distanced, but characterized as approachable; the reader can imagine the other is about to speak to him or her. The photographers commonly view the frontal shot as a device for cutting across language barriers and allowing for intercultural communication. The portrait is, in the words of one early *Geographic* photographer, "a collaboration between subject and photographer" (National Geographic Society 1981:22). In published form, of course, the photographed person is still "subjected to an unreturnable gaze" (Tagg 1988:64), in no position to speak.

The magazine's goal of creating intimacy between subject and reader contradicts to some extent its official goal of presenting an unmanipulated, truthful slice of life from another country. Virtually all the photographers and picture editors we spoke with saw the return gaze as problematic and believed that such pictures ought to be used sparingly because they are clearly not candid, and potentially influenced by the photographer. They might also be "almost faking intimacy," one editor said. Another mentioned that the use of direct gaze is also a question of style, suggesting more commercial and less gritty values. The photographer can achieve both the goals of intimacy and invisibility by taking portraits which are not directly frontal, but in which the gaze angles off to the side of the camera.

To face the camera is to permit close examination of the photographed subject, including

---

[3]This figure is based on 438 photographs coded in this way, 24% of which had a subject looking at the camera.

scrutiny of the face and eyes, which are in common-sense parlance the seat of soul—feelings, personality, or character. Frontality is a central technique of a documentary rhetoric in photography (Tagg 1988:189); it sets the stage for either critique or celebration, but in either case evaluation, of the other as a person or type. Editors at the magazine talked about their search for the "compelling face" in selecting photos for the magazine.

Racial, age, and gender differences appear in how often and how exactly the gaze is returned and lend substance to each of these perspectives on the camera gaze. To a statistically significant degree, women look into the camera more than men, children and older people look into the camera more often than other adults, those who appear poor more than those who appear wealthy, those whose skin is very dark more than those who are bronze, those who are bronze more than those whose skin is white, those in native dress more than those in Western garb, those without any tools more than those who are using machinery.[4] Those who are culturally defined as weak—women, children, people of color, the poor, the tribal rather than the modern, those without technology—are more likely to face the camera, the more powerful to be represented looking elsewhere. There is also an intriguing (but not statistically significant) trend toward higher rates of looking at the camera in pictures taken in countries that were perceived as friendly towards the United States.[5]

To look out at the viewer, then, would appear to represent not a confrontation between the West and the rest, but the accessibility of the other. This interpretation is supported by the fact that historically the frontal portrait has been associated with the rougher classes, as the Daumier print points out. Tagg (1988), in a social history of photography, argues that this earlier class-based styling was passed on from portraiture to the emerging use of photography for the documentation and surveillance of the criminal and the insane. Camera gaze is often associated with full frontal posture in the *Geographic;* as such, it is also part of frontality's work as a "code of social inferiority" (Tagg 1988:37). The civilized classes, at least since the nineteenth century, have traditionally been depicted in Western art turning away from the camera and so making themselves less available.[6] The higher-status person may thus be characterized as too absorbed in weighty matters to attend to the photographer's agenda. Facing the camera, in Tagg's terms, "signified the bluntness and 'naturalness' of a culturally unsophisticated class [and had a history which predated photography]" (1988:36).

These class-coded styles of approach and gaze before the camera have continued to have

---

[4]These analyses were based on those photos where gaze was visible, and excluded pictures with a Westerner in the photo. The results were, for gender (N = 360) x^2 = 3.835, df = 1, p < .05; for age (N = 501) x^2 = 13.745, df = 4, p < .01; for wealth (N = 507) x^2 = 12.950, df = 2, p < .01; for skin color (N = 417) x^2 = 8.704, df = 3, p < .05; for dress style (N = 452) x^2 = 12.702, df = 1, p < .001; and for technology (N = 287) x^2 = 4.172, df = 1, p < .05. Discussing these findings in the photography department, we were given the pragmatic explanation that children generally are more fearless in approaching photographers, while men often seem more wary of the camera than women, especially when it is wielded by a male photographer.

[5]In the sample of pictures from Asia in which gaze is ascertainable (N = 179), "friendly" countries (including the PRC after 1975, Taiwan, Hong Kong, South Korea, Japan, and the Philippines) had higher rates of smiling than "unfriendly" or neutral countries (x^2 = 2.101, df = 1, p = .147). Excluding Japan, which may have had a more ambiguous status in American eyes, the relationship between gaze and "friendliness" reaches significance (x^2 = 4.14, df = 1, p < .05).

[6]Tagg (1988) notes that the pose was initially the pragmatic outcome of the technique of the Physionotrace, a popular mechanism used to trace a person's profile from shadow onto a copper plate. When photography took the place of the Physionotrace, no longer requiring profiles, the conventions of associating class with non-frontality continued to have force.

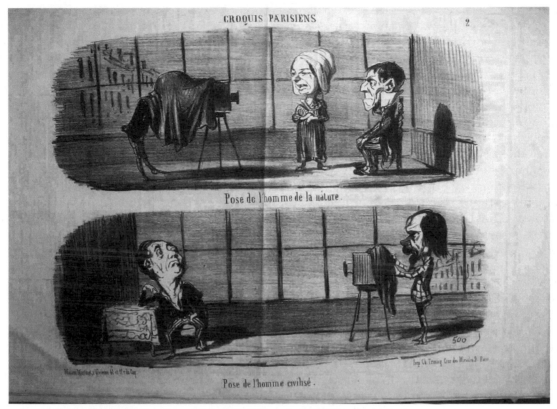

A gaze toward the viewer, in *National Geographic's* photographs, appears to represent the accessibility of the photographic subject. Historically, frontal portraits have been associated with low-class status, as suggested by this 1853 Daumier print, "Pose de l'homme de la nature" and "Pose de l'homme civilisé." Courtesy of www.daumier.org.

force and utility in renderings of the ethnic other. The twist here is that the more civilized quality imparted to the lighter-skinned male in Western dress and to adult exotics who turn away from the camera is only a relative quality. Full civilization still belongs, ideologically, to the Euroamerican.

Whether these categories of people have actually looked at the camera more readily and openly is another matter. If the gaze toward the camera reflected only a lack of familiarity with it, and curiosity, then one would expect rural people to look at the camera more than urban people. This is not the case. One might also expect some change over time, as cameras became more common everywhere, but there is no difference in rate of gaze when the period from 1950 to 1970 is compared with the later period. The heavy editorial hand at the *Geographic* argues that what is at work is a set of unarticulated perceptions about the kinds of non-Westerners who make comfortable and interesting subjects for the magazine. *National Geographic* editors select from a vast array of possible pictures on the basis of some notion about what the social/power relations are between the reader and the particular ethnic subject being photographed. These aesthetic choices are outside explicit politics but encode politics nonetheless. A "good picture" is a picture that makes sense in terms of prevailing ideas about the other, including ideas about accessibility and difference.

In a second form of gaze by the photographed subject, the non-Westerner looks at someone or something evident within the frame. The ideas readers get about who the other is are often read off from this gaze, which is taken as an index of interest, attention, or goals. The Venezuelan prospector who looks at the diamonds as they are being weighed by the buyer is interested in selling, in making money, rather than in the Western viewer or other compatriots. The caption supplies details: "The hard-won money usually flies fast in gambling and merry-making at primitive diamond camps, where riches-to-rags tales abound."

A potential point of interest in our set of photographs is the presence of a Western traveler. In 10 percent of such pictures, at least one local looks into the camera. Yet in 22 percent of the pictures in which only locals appear, someone looks into the camera. To a statistically significant degree, then, the Westerner in the frame draws a look away from those Westerners beyond the camera, suggesting both that these two kinds of Westerners might stand in for each other, as well as indexing the interest they are believed to have for locals.

35   Third, the other's gaze can run off into the distance beyond the frame. This behavior can suggest radically different things about the character of the subject. It might portray either a dreamy, vacant, absent-minded person or a forward-looking, future-oriented, and determined one. . . . Character connotations aside, the out-of-frame look may also have implications for the viewer's identification with the subject, in some sense connecting with the reader outside the frame (Metz 1985:795).

Finally, in many pictures no gaze at all is visible, either because the people in them are tiny figures lost in a landscape or in a sea of others, or because the scene is dark or the person's face covered by a mask or veil. We might read this kind of picture (14 percent of the whole sample) as being about the landscape or activity rather than the people or as communicating a sense of nameless others or group members rather than individuals. While these pictures do not increase in number over the period, there has been a sudden spate of recent covers in which the face or eyes of a non-Western person photographed are partly hidden (November 1979, February 1983, October 1985, August 1987, October 1987, November 1987, July 1988, Feburary 1991, December 1991). Stylistically, *National Geographic* photographers may now have license to experiment with elements of the classical portrait with its full-face view, but the absence of any such shots before 1979 can also be read as a sign of a changing attitude about the possibilities of cross-cultural communication. The covered face can tell a story of a boundary erected, contact broken.

A Direct Western Gaze

In its articles on the non-Western world, the *National Geographic* has frequently included photographs that show a Western traveler in the local setting covered in the piece. During the postwar period, these Western travelers have included adventurers, mountain climbers, and explorers; anthropologists, geographers, botanists, and archaeologists; United States military personnel; tourists; and government officials or functionaries from the United States and Europe, from Prince Philip and Dwight Eisenhower to members of the Peace Corps. These photographs show the Westerners viewing the local landscape from atop a hill, studying an artifact, showing a local tribal person some wonder of Western technology (a photograph, a mirror, or the camera itself), or interacting with a native in conversation, work, or play. The Westerner may stand alone or with associates, but more often is framed in company with one or more locals.

These pictures can have complex effects on viewers, for they represent more explicitly than most the intercultural relations it is thought or hoped obtain between the West and its global neighbors. They may allow identification with the Westerner in the photo and, through that, more interaction with, or imaginary participation in, the photo. Before exploring these possibilities, however, we will speculate on some of the functions these photographs serve in the magazine.

Most obviously, the pictures of Westerners can serve a validating function by proving that the author was *there,* that the account is a first-hand one, brought from the field rather than from library or photographic archives. In this respect the photography sequences in *National Geographic* resemble traditional ethnographic accounts, which are written predominantly in the third person but often include at least one story in the first person that portrays the anthropologist in the field (Marcus and Cushman 1982). For this purpose, it does not matter whether the Westerner stands alone with locals.

40   To serve the function of dramatizing intercultural relations, however, it is helpful to have a local person in the frame. When the Westerner and the other are positioned face-to-face, we can read their relationship and their natures from such features as Goffman (1979) has identified in his study of advertising photography's representation of women and men—their relative height, the leading and guying behaviors found more often in pictured males, the greater emotional expressiveness of the women, and the like.[7] What the Westerners and non-Westerners are doing, the relative vantage points from which they are photographed, and their

facial expressions give other cues to their moral and social characters.

Whether or not the gaze of the two parties is mutual provides a comment on who has the right and/or the need to look at whom. When the reader looks out at the world through this proxy Westerner, does the other look back? Rich implications can emerge from a photo showing two female travelers looking at an Ituri forest man in central Africa (February 1960). Standing in the upper left-hand corner, the two women smile down at the native figure in the lower right foreground. He looks toward the ground in front of them, an ambiguous expression on his face. The lines of their gaze have crossed but do not meet; because of this lack of reciprocity, the women's smiles appear bemused and patronizing. In its lack of reciprocity, this gaze is distinctly colonial. The Westerners do not seek a relationship but are content, even pleased, to view the other as an ethnic object. The composition of the picture, structured by an oblique line running from the women down to the man, shows the Westerners standing over the African; the slope itself can suggest, as Maquet (1986) has pointed out for other visual forms, the idea of *descent* or decline from the one (the Western women) to the other.

A related function of this type of photo lies in the way it prompts the viewer to become self-aware, not just in relation to others but as a viewer, as one who looks or surveys. Mulvey (1985) argues that the gaze in cinema takes three forms—in the camera, in the audience, and in the characters as they look at each other or out at the audience. She says that the first two forms have to be invisible or obscured if the film is to follow realist conventions and bestow on itself the qualities of "reality, obviousness and truth" (1985:816). The viewer who becomes aware of his or her own eye or that of the camera will develop a "distancing awareness" rather than an immediate unconscious involvement. Applying this insight to the *Geographic* photograph, Mulvey

---

[7]Goffman (1979) draws on ethological insights into height and dominance relations when he explains why women are almost always represented as shorter than men in print advertisements. He notes that "so thoroughly is it assumed that differences in size will correlate with differences in social weight that relative size can be routinely used as a means of ensuring that the picture's story will be understandable at a glance" (1979:28).

Photographs in which Western travelers are present encode complete messages about intercultural relations. The non-reciprocal gazes in this February 1960 picture encode distinctly colonial social relations.

Courtesy of Lowell Thomas, Jr./National Geographic Society.

might say that bringing the Western eye into the frame promotes distancing rather than immersion. Alvarado (1979/80) has also argued that such intrusion can reveal contradictions in the social relations of the West and the rest that are otherwise less visible, undermining the authority of the photographer by showing the photo being produced, showing it to be an artifact rather than an unmediated fact.[8]

Photographs in which Westerners appear differ from others because we can be more aware of ourselves as actors in the world. Whether or not Westerners appear in the picture, we *are* there, but in pictures that include a Westerner, we may see ourselves being viewed by the other, and we become conscious of ourselves and relationships. The act of seeing the self being seen is antithetical to the voyeurism which many art critics have identified as intrinsic to most photography and film (Alloula 1986; Burgin 1982; Metz 1985).

This factor might best account for Westerners retreating from the photographs after 1969. Staffers in the photography department said that pictures including authors of articles came to be regarded as outdated and were discontinued. Photographer and writer were no longer to be the stars of the story, we were told, although text continued to be written in the first person. As more and more readers had traveled to exotic locales, the *Geographic* staff realized that the picture of the intrepid traveler no longer looked so intrepid. While the rise in international tourism may have had this effect, other social changes of the late 1960s contributed as well. In 1968 popular American protest against participation in the Vietnam War reached a critical point. Huge antiwar demonstrations, the police riot at the Democratic convention, and

---

[8]The documentary filmmaker Dennis O'Rourke, whose films *Cannibal Tours* and *Half Life: A Parable for the Nuclear Age* explore third-world settings, develops a related argument for the role of reflexivity for the image maker (Lutkehaus 1989). He consistently includes himself in the scene but distinguishes between simple filmmaker self-revelation and rendering the social relations between him and his subjects, including capturing the subject's gaze in such a way as to show his or her complicity with the filmmaker. O'Rourke appears to view the reader's gaze more deterministically (for instance, as "naturally" seeing the complicity in a subject's gaze) than do the theorists considered above.

especially the Viet Cong's success in the Tet offensive convinced many that the American role in Vietnam and, by extension, the third world, would have to be radically reconceptualized. The withdrawal or retreat of American forces came to be seen as inevitable, even though there were many more years of conflict over how, when, and why. American power had come into question for the first time since the end of the World War II. Moreover, the assassinations of Malcolm X and Martin Luther King, and the fire of revolt in urban ghettoes, gave many white people a sense of changing and more threatening relations with people of color within the boundaries of the United States.

45   Most of the non-*Geographic* photos now considered iconic representations of the Vietnam War do not include American soldiers or civilians. The girl who, napalmed, runs down a road towards the camera; the Saigon police chief executing a Viet Cong soldier; the Buddhist monk in process of self-immolation—each of these photographs, frequently reproduced, erases American involvement.

The withdrawal of Americans and other Westerners from the photographs of *National Geographic* may involve a historically similar process. The decolonization process accelerated in 1968 and led Americans (including, one must assume, the editors of *National Geographic*) to see the third world as a more dangerous place, a place where they were no longer welcome to walk and survey as they pleased. The decreasing visibility of Westerners signaled a retreat from a third world seen as a less valuable site for Western achievement, more difficult of access and control. The decolonization process was and is received as a threat to an American view of itself. In Lacan's terms, the other's look could threaten an American sense of self-coherence, and so in this historic moment the Westerner, whose presence in the picture makes it possible for us to see ourselves being seen by that other, withdraws to look from a safer distance, behind the camera.

The Refracted Gaze of the Other: To See Themselves as Others See Them

In a small but nonetheless striking number of *National Geographic* photographs, a native is shown with a camera, a mirror, or mirror equivalent in his or her hands. Take the photograph of two Aivilik men in northern Canada sitting on a rock in animal skin parkas, one smiling and the other pointing a camera out at the landscape (November 1956). Or the picture that shows two Indian women dancing as they watch their image in a large wall mirror. Or the picture of Governor Brown of California on Tonga showing a group of children the Polaroid snapshots he has just taken of them (March 1968).

Mirror and camera are tools of self-reflection and surveillance. Each creates a double of the self, a second figure who can be examined more closely than the original—a double that can also be alienated from the self, taken away, as a photograph can be, to another place. Psychoanalytic theory notes that the infant's look into the mirror is a significant step in ego formation because it permits the child to see itself for the first time as an other. The central role of these two tools in American society—after all, its millions of bathrooms have mirrors as fixtures nearly as important as their toilets—stems at least in part from their self-reflective capacities. For many Americans, self-knowledge is a central life goal; the injunction to "know thyself" is taken seriously.

The mirror most directly suggests the possibility of self-awareness, and Western folktales and literature provide many examples of characters (often animals like Bambi or wild children like Kipling's Mowgli) who come upon the mirrored surface of a lake or stream and for the first time see themselves in a kind of epiphany of newly acquired self-knowledge. Placing the mirror in non-Western hands makes an interesting picture for Western viewers because this theme can interact with the common perception that the non-Western native remains somewhat childlike and cognitively immature. Lack of self-awareness implies a lack of history (E. Wolf 1982); he or she is not without consciousness but is relatively without self-consciousness. The myth is that history and change are primarily characteristic of the West and that self-awareness was brought to the rest of the world by "discovery" and colonization.[9]

50   In the article "Into the Heart of Africa" (August 1956) a magazine staff member on expedition is shown sitting in his Land-Rover, holding open a *National Geographic* magazine to show a native woman a photograph of a woman of her tribe. Here the magazine serves the role of reflecting glass, as the caption tells us: "Platter-lipped woman peers at her look-alike in the mirror of *National Geographic*." The *Geographic* artist smiles as he watches the woman's face closely for signs of self-recognition; the fascination evident in his gaze is in the response of the woman, perhaps the question of how she "likes" her image, her own self. An early version of this type of photo a quarter of a century earlier shows an explorer in pith helmet who, with a triumphant smile, holds up a mirror to a taller native man. He dips his head down to peer into it, and we, the viewers, see not his expression but a redundant caption: "His first mirror: Porter's boy seeing himself as others see him." By contrast with the later photo, the explorer's gaze is not at the African but out toward the

camera, indicating more interest in the camera's reception of this amusing scene than in searching the man's face for clues to his thinking. It also demonstrates the importance of manipulating relative height between races to communicate dominance. In the same genre, a Westerner in safari clothes holds a mirror up to a baboon (May 1955). Here as well, the *Geographic* plays with boundaries between nature and culture. The baboon, like third-world peoples, occupies that boundary in the popular culture of white Westerners (see Haraway 1989); its response to the mirror can only seem humorously inadequate when engaged in the ultimately human and most adult of activities, self-reflection.

The mirror sometimes serves as a device to tell a story about the process of forming national identity. National self-reflection is presumed to accompany development, with the latter term suggesting a process that is both technological and psychosocial. The caption to a 1980 picture of a Tunisian woman looking into a mirror plays with this confusion between individual and nation, between the developing self-awareness of mature adults and historically emergent national identity: "A moment for reflection: Mahbouba Sassi glances in the mirror to tie her headband. A wife and mother in the village of Takrouna, she wears garb still typical of rural women in the region. Step by step, Tunisia has, by any standards, quietly but steadily brought herself into the front rank of developing nations."

Cameras break into the frame of many *National Geographic* photographs. In some, a Westerner is holding the camera, showing a local group the photograph he has just taken of them. Here the camera, like the mirror, shows the native himself. Frequently the picture is handed to children crowding happily around the Western cameraman. Historically it was first the mirror and then the camera that were thought to prove the superiority of the Westerner who invented and controls them (Adas

---

[9]Compare the pictures of natives looking into a mirror with that of an American woman looking into the shiny surface of the airplane she is riveting in the August 1944 issue. It is captioned, "No time to prink [primp] in the mirror-like tail assembly of a Liberator." The issue raised by this caption is not self-knowledge (Western women have this) but female vanity, or rather its transcendence by a woman who, man-like, works in heavy industry during the male labor shortage of World War II. Many of these mirror pictures evoke a tradition in Western art in which Venus or some other female figure gazes into a mirror in a moment of self-absorption. Like those paintings, this photo may operate within the convention that justifies male voyeuristic desire by aligning it with female narcissistic self-involvement" (Snow 1989:38).

A surprising number of *Geographic* photographs feature mirrors and cameras, with Westerners offering third-world peoples glimpses of themselves. In this August 1956 picture, a staff artist in what was then French Equatorial Africa shows a woman "her look-alike."

Courtesy of Volkmar Kurt Wentzel/National Geographic Image Collection.

1989). In many pictures of natives holding a mirror or camera, the magazine plays with what McGrane (1989) identifies with the nineteenth century European mind, the notion "of a low threshold of the miraculous [in the non-Western native], of a seemingly childish lack of restraint" (1989:50).

In other pictures, the native holds the camera. In one sense, this violates the prerogative of the Western surveyor to control the camera, long seen as a form of power. In an analysis of photographs of Middle Eastern women, Graham-Brown (1988) provides evidence that colonial photographers were motivated to keep local subjects "at the lens-end of the camera" and quotes one who, in 1890, complained, "It was a mistake for the first photographer in the Pathan [Afghanistan] country to allow the natives to look at the ground glass screen of the camera. He forgot that a little learning is a dangerous thing" (1988:61). The camera could be given to native subjects only at the risk of giving away that power.

Pictures in *National Geographic* that place the camera in other hands, however, merely suggest that the native's use of the camera is amusing or quaint. A broad smile graces the face of the

This February 1925 photograph is captioned "His first mirror: Porter's boy seeing himself as others see him," suggesting that self-awareness comes with Western contact and technology.

Courtesy of Felix Shay/National Geographic Society.

Aivilik man above who uses the camera lens to view the landscape with a companion. At least one caption suggests that, although the subject goes behind the camera—in 1952 a young African boy looking through the viewfinder—what he looks out at is the imagined self at whom the Western photographer has been looking moments before: "Young Lemba sees others as the photographer sees him."

Such pictures were more common in the 1950s. We can detect a change, as decolonization proceeded, in the simple terms with which the problem is depicted in an amazing photograph from August 1982. It sits on the right-hand side of the page in an article entitled "Paraguay, Paradox of South America." The frame is nearly filled with three foreground figures—a white female tourist standing between an Amerindian woman and man, both in native dress, both bare-chested. The three stand close together in a line, the tourist smiling with her arm on the shoulder of the sober-faced native woman. The tourist and the man, also unsmiling, face off slightly toward the left where a second camera (besides the one snapping the photo for the magazine) takes their picture. The caption asks us to look at the natives as photographic subjects: "Portraits for pay: A tourist poses with members of the Macá Indian tribe on Colonia Juan Belaieff Island in the Paraguay River near Asunción. The Indians charge 80 cents a person each time they pose in a photograph."

55

A rare picture from August 1982 draws attention to the presence of the camera by photographing people being photographed for pay.
Courtesy of O. Louis Mazzatenta/National Geographic Society.

This rare photograph invites us into a contradictory, ambiguous, but, in any case, highly charged scene. It is not a pleasant picture, in contrast with more typical *Geographic* style, because it depicts the act of looking at unwilling subjects, suggesting the voyeurism of the photograph of the exotic, a voyeurism *doubled* by the presence of a second photographer. Further, the picture's ambiguity lies in its suggestion that we are seeing a candid shot of a posed shot, and that we are looking at the other look at us though in fact the Indian gaze is diverted twenty degrees from ours. This unusual structure of gaze draws attention to the commodified nature of the relationship between looker and looked-at. The Indians appear unhappy, even coerced; the tourist satisfied, presumably with her catch. Here too an apparent contradiction—the diverted gaze and its candid appearance suggest that the

National Geographic photographer took this picture without paying, unlike the tourists; the caption suggests otherwise.

The photograph's potentially disturbing message for *National Geographic* readers is muted when one considers that the camera has not succeeded so much in representing the returned gaze of indigenous peoples as it has in taking the distance between Western viewer and non-Western subject one step farther and in drawing attention to the photographer (and the artifice) between them. A symptom of alienation from the act of looking even while attention is drawn to it, this photo may exemplify a principle that Sontag says operates in all photography: "The photographer is supertourist, an extension of the anthropologist, visiting natives and bringing back news of their exotic doings and strange gear. The photographer is always trying to colonize new experiences or find new ways to look at familiar subjects—to fight against boredom. For boredom is just the reverse side of fascination: both depend on being outside rather than inside a situation, and one leads to the other" (1977:42). Avoiding boredom is crucial to retaining readers' interest and therefore membership.

One could also look at the photograph from a 1990 issue on Botswana showing a French television crew—in full camera-and-sound gear and from a distance of a few feet—filming two Dzu Bushmen in hunting gear and authentic dress. The Frenchmen enthusiastically instruct the hunters in stalking posture, and the caption critiques them, noting that they have dressed up the natives (who otherwise wear Western clothing) for the benefit of European consumers. While this photograph is valuable in letting the reader see how images are constructed rather than found, its postmodern peek behind the scenes may also do what Gitlin notes contemporary journalism has done: engaged in a demystifying look at how image makers control the face political candidates put forward, they encourage viewers to be "cognoscenti of their own bamboozlement" (1990a).

Ultimately the magazine itself is a mirror for the historical, cultural, and political-economic contexts of its production and use. That context is reflected in the magazine's images, but not in a simple, reflective way, as either the objectivist myth of the nature of cameras and mirrors or as the Althusserian notion of a "specular, or mirrorlike ideology (in which the subject simply recognizes him- or herself) would have it. It is perhaps more in the form of a rippled lake whose many intersecting lines present a constantly changing and emergent image.

with its family of other cultural representations, its formal and informal schooling in techniques for interpreting both photograph and cultural difference, and its social relations. We read the *National Geographic* with a sense of astonishment, absorption, and wonder, both as children and, in a way that is different only some of the time, as adults. All of the looks embedded in the pictures are ultimately being filtered for you the reader through this, our own gaze. At times during this project, we have looked at the reader of an American magazine who is looking at a photographer's looking at a Western explorer who is looking at a Polynesian child who is looking at the explorer's photographed snapshot of herself moments earlier. While this framing of the seventh look might suggest that it is simply a more convoluted and distanced voyeurism, it can be distinguished from other kinds of readers' gazes, including the voyeuristic and the hierarchic, by both its distinctive intent and the sociological position (white, middle class, female, academic) from which it comes. Its intent is not aesthetic appreciation or formal description, but critique of the images in spite of, because of, and in terms of their pleasures. We aim to make the pictures tell a different story than they were originally meant to tell, one about their makers and readers rather than their subjects.[10] The critique arises out of a desire "to anthropologize the West," as Rabinow (1986) suggests we might, and to denaturalize the images of difference in the magazine in part because those images and the institution which has produced them have historically articulated too easily with the shifting interests and positions of the state. The strong impact of the magazine on popular attitudes suggests

The Academic Spectator

60 | In one sense, this gaze is simply a subtype of the reader's gaze. It emerges out of the same American middle-class experiential matrix

[10]Our interviews with readers show that they do not always ignore the frame but also sometimes see the photograph as an object produced by someone in a concrete social context.

that anthropological teaching or writing purveys images that, even if intended as oppositional (certainly not always the case), may simply be subsumed or bypassed by the *National Geographic* view of the world.

A suspicion of the power of images is inevitable, as they exist in a field more populated with advertising photography than anything else. The image is experienced daily as a sales technique or as a trace of the commodity. That experience is, at least for us and perhaps for other readers, transferred to some degree to the experience of seeing *National Geographic* images.

Our reading of theory has tutored our gaze in distinctive ways, told us how to understand the techniques by which the photographs work, how to find our way to something other than an aesthetic or literal reading, suggesting that we view them as cultural artifacts. It also suggested that we avoid immersion in the many pleasures of the richly colored and exotically peopled photographs, as in Alloula's reading of Algerian colonial period postcards. He notes his analytic need to resist the "aestheticizing temptation" (1986:116) to see beauty in those cards, a position predicated in part on a highly deterministic view of their hegemonic effect. Alternative, more positive views of the political implications of visual pleasure exist, a view which Jameson (1983) and others argue is achieved in part by unlinking a disdain for popular culture products from the issue of pleasure. Validating both seemingly contradictory views, however, would seem to be the fact that the seductiveness of the pictures both captures and instructs us. We are captured by the temptation to view the photographs as more real than the world or at least as a comfortable substitute for it, to imagine at some level a world of basically happy, classless, even noble others in conflict neither

with themselves nor with "us." These and other illusions of the images we have found in part through our own vulnerability to them. The pleasures are also instructive, however. They come from being given views, without having to make our own efforts to get them, of a world different, however slightly, from the American middle-class norm. The considerable beauty with which those lives are portrayed can potentially challenge that norm.

Conclusion

The many looking relations represented in all photographs are at the foundation of the kinds of meaning that can be found or made in them. The multiplicity of looks is at the root of a photo's ambiguity, each gaze potentially suggesting a different way of viewing the scene. Moreover, a visual illiteracy leaves most of us with few resources for understanding or integrating the diverse messages these looks can produce. Multiple gaze is the source of many of the photograph's contradictions, highlighting the gaps (as when some gazes are literally interrupted) and multiple perspectives of each person involved in the complex scene. It is the root of much of the photograph's dynamism as a cultural object, and the place where the analyst can perhaps most productively begin to trace its connections to the wider social world of which it is a part. Through attention to the dynamic nature of these intersecting gazes, the photograph becomes less vulnerable to the charge that it masks or stuffs and mounts the world, freezes the life out of a scene, or violently slices into time. While the gaze of the subject of the photograph may be difficult to find in the heavy crisscrossing traffic of the more privileged gazes of producers and consumers, contemporary stories of contestable power are told there nonetheless.

REFERENCES

Adas, M. (1989). *Machines as the measure of men: Science, technology, and ideologies of western dominance.* Ithaca, NY: Cornell University Press.

Alloula, M. (1986). *The colonial harem.* Minneapolis: University of Minnesota Press.

Alvarado, M. (1979/80). Photographs and narrativity. *Screen education, 29,* 5–17.

Barthes, R.(1977). *Image-music-text.* London: Fontana Press.

Burgin, V. (Ed.). (1982). *Thinking photography.* London: Methuen.

Devereux, G. (1967). *From anxiety to method in behavioral sciences.* Paris: Mouton.

Geary, C. M. (1988). *Images from Bamum: German colonial photography at the court of King Njoya, Cameroon, West Africa, 1902–1915.* Washington, D.C.: Smithsonian Institute.

Goffman, E. (1979). *Gender advertisements.* Cambridge, MA: Harvard University Press.

Graham-Brown, S. (1988). *Images of women: The portrayal of women in photography of the Middle East 1860–1950.* New York: Columbia University Press.

Lutkehaus, N. (1989). Excuse me, everything is not all right: On ethnography, film and representation. *Cultural Anthropology, 4(4),* 422–437.

Marcus, G., & Cushman, D. (1982). Ethnography as text. *Annual review of sociology, 11,* 25–69.

McGrane, B. (1989). *Beyond anthropology: Society and the other.* New York: Columbia University Press.

Metz, C. (1985). Story/discourse: Notes on two kinds of voyeurism. In B. Nichols (Ed.), *Movies and methods* (pp. 543–548). Berkeley: University of California Press.

Moorehead, A. (1960). *White Nile.* New York: Harper.

National Geographic Society. (1981). *Photographer's field guide.* Washington, D.C.: Author.

Rabinow, P. (1986). Representations are social facts: Modernity and postmodernity in anthropology. In J. Clifford & G. Marcus (Eds.), *Writing culture: The poetics and politics of ethnography* (234–261). Berkeley: University of California Press.

Radway, J. (1984). *Reading the romance: Women, patriarchy, and popular literature.* Chapel Hill, NC: University of North Carolina Press.

Snow, E. (1989). Theorizing the male gaze: Some problems. *Representations, 25(1),* 30–41.

Sontag, S. (1977). *On photography.* New York: Farrar, Straus, and Giroux.

Tagg, J. (1988). *The burden of representation.* Amherst, MA: University of Massachusetts Press.

Wolf, E. (1982). *Europe and the people without history.* Berkeley: University of California Press.

Re-reading/Conversations with the Text

1. In this essay, Lutz and Collins carefully examine the patterns of gazes they notice in photographs in the magazine *National Geographic.* They explain that "[b]y examining the 'lines of sight' evident in the *Geographic* photograph of the non-Westerner, we become aware that it is not simply a captured view of the *other,* but rather a dynamic site at which many gazes or viewpoints intersect." How does Lutz and Collins's reading of *National Geographic* photos complicate our consumption of them? What is it that Lutz and Collins want us to see beyond the gaze of the camera?

2. Pointing out the position that the reader of *National Geographic* has in consuming its photographs, Lutz and Collins claim that, "[i]ndependently of what the photographer or the caption writer may intend as the message of the photo, the reader can imagine something else." Reread the essay's section on "The Magazine Readers' Gazes" keeping in mind this section's focus on identification and difference. How does *National Geographic* serve to establish categories of identification and difference along the lines of non-Western/ Western, race, class, and gender? How does consumption of the magazine serve to establish categories of identification and difference between and among citizens of the West? How does the magazine, to some extent, create a sense of community?

3. According to Lutz and Collins, "the photographed person is . . . 'subject to an unreturnable gaze' and in no position to speak." Reread the essay's section on "The Non-Western Subject's Gaze." Working in a small group, discuss what Lutz and Collins note about the characteristics of those who face the camera. Do you think that the subject who faces the camera is never in the "position to speak"? Or do you think that the subject's choice to face the camera does speak to the audience? What messages might such a subject send?

Re-seeing and Re-writing

1. Leaf through some issues of *National Geographic,* or visit the magazine's online photography archive at www.nationalgeographic.com/photography/. Collect ten or more photos that interest you—concentrate on photos from one period of time or organize them according to a central theme or location. Examine the various gazes that are present in the photographs, while noting any predominant patterns. Then choose one particularly compelling image and write three short narratives from the perspective of subject, the camera, and the audience. For the narrative that describes the actions and thoughts of the subject(s), you might contemplate whether the subjects worked to represent themselves as active agents and not passive objects. For the narrative from the perspective of the photographer, you might consider what you imagine the photographer sees or what the photographer imagines his or her audience would like to see. Last, write a narrative that describes what you see in the

photos. Do your narratives differ from each other? If so how? Do your narratives resist the dominant gazes of *National Geographic?*

2. At several points, Lutz and Collins refer to cultural historian and artist Victor Burgin, who challenges the assumption that photographs are objects for passive consumption. Rather, Burgin as a photographer works to make pictures that are "occasions for interpretation." Search online for photographs created by Burgin, and then look at photographs from *National Geographic* that were produced the same year as Burgin's photos. Select two or three photos from each set of images; then list ten or more observations of each photo and compare each list to the other. Describe and analyze the dominant patterns that emerge in each set of images and then describe and analyze the innovative strategies that are used to work against those dominant patterns. Consider whether Burgin is able to complicate the gazes that Lutz and Collins mention. Finally, write a brief one-page essay/proposal to convince an audience of your classmates which photo you think should be on the cover of a new magazine focused on documentary photography. Be sure to explain and justify your recommendation through close analysis of the differences among the photos.

Look at the images present in the Nakamura essay through the gazes presented by Lutz and Collins. How does the reading that Nakamura provides change if we consider the various gazes that Lutz and Collins mention (for example, the photographer's gaze, the magazine's gaze, the reader's gaze, the non-Western subject's gaze)? Are there any productive gazes that Nakamura overlooks in her reading of these images? How might these new gazes be applied to a reading of the advertisements in Nakamura's article?

Images: Travel to India

The first image here is a recruiting poster for the United States Navy created circa 1919. The second is the Internet home page of the Department of Tourism of the Government of Kerala (a state in India).

"Give the World the Once Over in the United States Navy" (recruitment poster). James H. Daugherty for the Press Navy Recruiting Bureau, c. 1919.
Courtesy of the Library of Congress.

Keralatourism.org home page (www.keralatourism.org), accessed May 2006.

Re-reading/Conversations with the Text

Look closely at these documents and make ten or more observations about each one. Analyze both the image (where people are placed, the use of color, perspective, etc.) and the words in each. What rhetorical appeals (*ethos, logos, pathos*) does each use to make travel to India attractive? Consider in particular this section's focus on identification and differentiation. How do the documents use these concepts? What kinds of gazes do the documents themselves represent or encourage in readers?

Re-seeing and Re-writing

Now that you have analyzed the rhetorical appeals of the travel ad, work in groups of three or four and search for ways in which travel to "exotic" and "foreign" countries is marketed to a U.S. audience. Look at different *genres* of travel information. For example, one of you might examine online travel agencies such as travelocity.com, hotwire.com, or expedia.com; another could look at travel magazines; still another could examine Web sites for various countries' travel bureaus or tourist offices. While gathering your information, take note of how travel advertisements utilize both identification and differentiation to lure tourists. Next, discuss your findings with your group and see if there are any dominant patterns that emerge across all genres. Do you notice any pervasive patterns in the representations of the people, culture, leisure activities, accommodations and/or audience/tourist? Keeping these observations in mind, create your own travel brochure that works against the dominant patterns presented in travel ads. Remember: You still want to make travel attractive to a particular audience, so you will need to choose a specific audience in creating your brochure.

Walking with the Kurds

JOHN HOCKENBERRY

"Walking with the Kurds" opens *Moving Violations: War Zones, Wheelchairs and Declarations of Independence* (1995), *JOHN HOCKENBERRY*'s memoir of life as a foreign correspondent. In this essay Hockenberry introduces himself as disabled while he also establishes his prowess as a political thinker and skilled journalist. Hockenberry is currently a correspondent for *Dateline NBC,* where he has earned an Emmy for his broadcast journalism. He has also worked in broadcast news at both National Public Radio and ABC News. His most prominent *Dateline NBC* reports include an hour-long documentary on the lives of three former AT&T employees affected by the company's massive layoffs; a hidden-camera investigation that indicts discrimination facing the disabled community; and his extensive coverage of the circumstances surrounding Princess Diana's death. In 1996, Hockenberry performed "Spokeman," a one-man, off-Broadway show, based on his book. He has also published a novel, *A River Out of Eden* (2001).

There were legs below. Stilts of bone and fur picking around mud and easing up the side of a mountain near the Turkish border with Iraq. Two other legs slapped the sides of the donkey at each step like denim-lined saddlebags. They contained my own leg and hip bones, long the passengers of my body's journeys, and for just as long a theme of my mind's wanderings.

I was on the back of a donkey plodding through the slow, stunned bleed of the Gulf War's grand mal violence. The war was over. It remained only for Desert Storm's aftermath to mop up the historical details wrung out of Iraq. The Kurds were one such detail. It had taken another war, Desert Storm, for the Kurds to unexpectedly emerge from the obscurity they had received as a reward for helping the Allies during the First World War, nearly eight decades before. The Kurds had helped the Allies again this time, but this was just another detail.

In the calculus of victory and defeat echoing through world capitals and in global headlines, in the first moments of Iraq's surrender there were few details, and fewer human faces. The first pictures of the war were taken by weapons; Baghdad, a city of five million, rendered in fuzzy, gun-camera gray. Snapshots of hangars, bridges, roads, and buildings. No people.

We had won. They had lost.

The winners were well known: they were the faces on billboards. The smiling, enticing face of the West, its prosperity and its busy president, Bush, were known to the youngest schoolchild in the Middle East. In the West only one Middle Eastern face was as prominent, the face of the demon who became the vanquished, the singular, ever-present Saddam Hussein. The other losers were invisible. As time went on the war began to bleed the faces of its true victims.

Here on the Turkish border it was an open artery of Kurdish faces, streaming out of Iraq and down mountainsides in Turkey and Iran as the world's latest refugee population. Under cover of surrender and Western backslapping, Saddam Hussein had uprooted the mutinous Kurds and sent them packing under helicopter gunship fire north and east into nations that are neighbors only on the most recent of maps. To the Kurds, the region from northern Iraq to eastern Syria, southeastern Turkey, and western Iran is all one land: Kurdistan. It has been this way for more than one thousand years of warfare and map drawing. So for these Kurdish refugees, border checkpoint traffic jams were just old insults lost in the latest slaughter.

My fists held tight to the saddle and up we went toward the final ridge on the edge of Iraqi Kurdistan. A village called Üzümlü on the Turkish side was the destination. It lay three or more valleys beyond. There, the horizon contained the spilled wreckage of the refugee exodus from inside northern Iraq. Here it was just mountains against the brisk, gray, clouded sky punched through with brilliant patches of blue. Deep below in the valley roared the Zab River, muddy with the melting snowpack's promise of spring.

In March of 1991 the spectacular sky and the brisk air rimmed with intermittent hot alpine sun was a welcome escape from the visa lines and news briefings, SCUD missile attacks and second guessing of Saddam, Bush, and Schwarzkopf that so dominated the business of covering Desert Storm. I watched the sky while everyone else stared at their own feet. Ahead and behind, Kurdish men in black slacks walked with enormous sacks of bread on their backs. Like a line of migrating ants, a parade of white bundles snaked up the mountain on black legs.

Neither the heroic foot-borne relief efforts, anticipation of the horrors ahead, nor the brilliance of the scenery around me struck home as much as the rhythm of the donkey's forelegs beneath my hips. It was walking, that feeling of groping and climbing and floating on stilts that I had not felt for fifteen years. It was a feeling no wheelchair could convey. I had long ago grown to love my own wheels and their special physical grace, and so this clumsy leg walk was not something I missed until the sensation came rushing back through my body from the shoulders of a donkey. Mehmet, a local Kurd and the owner of the donkey, walked ahead holding a harness. I had rented the donkey for the day. I insisted that Mehmet give me a receipt. He was glad to oblige. I submitted it in my expense report to National Public Radio. The first steps I had taken since February 28, 1976, cost thirty American dollars.

It was a personal headline lost in the swirl of news and refugees. I had been in such places before. In my wheelchair I have piled onto trucks and jeeps, hauled myself up and down steps and steep hillsides to use good and bad telephones, to observe riots, a volcano, street fighting in Romania, to interview Yasir Arafat, to spend the night in walk-up apartments on every floor from one to five, to wait out curfews with civilian families, to explore New York's subway, to learn about the first temple of the Israelites, to observe the shelling of Kabul, Afghanistan, to witness the dying children of Somalia. For more than a decade I have experienced harrowing moments of physical intensity in pursuit of a deadline, always keeping pace with the rest of the press corps despite being unable to walk. It is the rule of this particular game that it be conducted without a word of acknowledgment on my part. To call attention to the wheelchair now by writing about it violates that rule. My mind and soul fight any effort to comment or complain, even now, years after the events I write about.

This quiet, slow donkey ride was easily the farthest I had gone, out onto a ledge that was never far from my mind during the fifteen years I had used a wheelchair. It was a frightening edge where physical risks loomed like the echoes of loose stones falling into a bottomless canyon, and the place where I discovered how completely I had lost all memory of the sensation, the rhythm, even the possibility of walking. I held on to the saddle or the donkey's neck. The locking of donkey knees and the heavily damped strokes of each donkey leg finding a cushioned foothold in the cold, soft mud of the Iraqi hillside rippled up my hanging limbs and drove into the bones of my arms. My arms were the sentries holding me in place, doing the job of arms and legs once again, as they had for a decade and a half. Though this was the closest to walking that I had felt in all of that time, the job of my arms could not change. FIRST STEPS IN FIFTEEN YEARS. It was a headline composed and discarded, footnote without essay, ridiculous, like the young blond man on the donkey on the mountain. And it was all perfectly true.

In March 1991 I found myself climbing a hillside where civilization was bulldozing a whole people up onto the mud and snow of a place called "no-man's-land" on maps. It was the end of a very long journey; I had arrived in a place that I could not have imagined. In this soupy outpost, the trucks seemed to have arrived long before the roads. As I watched out taxi windows, I could see that there would come a point where the wheelchair would have to be left behind if I was to make it to the place where early reports said hundreds of thousands of civilians were fleeing Saddam Hussein's terror. Wheels of any kind were out in this terrain. Saddam Hussein had chased the Kurds to the edge of pavement and well beyond. In the pockets of snow, starvation, rock and mud, only legs could travel.

The story of the Kurds had drawn me from a hotel room in Ankara, onto a plane to Istanbul, then on a charter flight to Van, an old Kurdish city once part of the Armenian empire, on a long, boring drive to the village of Hakkari and then a plunge through the boulder strewn mountain trails to the border town of Çukurca. I left my wheelchair with the driver from Van beside the road to Çukurca and climbed onto a tawny-colored, medium-size donkey who accepted without a sound what was a more than ample load. Before we began the steep ascent, I had only the time it took to cross a rope and plank bridge in a perilous state of disrepair to figure out how to keep my mostly paralyzed body on the animal's back. We crossed over the raging waters of the Zab River in the first weeks of the spring thaw and began the slow, steep climb toward Üzümlü.

The bare facts of what had happened in Iraq and Kuwait in the initial aftermath of Desert Storm read like a random shooting in America:

"World outraged as crazed father attacks neighbor then turns guns on family and self." The truth was not as simple. For one thing, Saddam took great pains to make sure that he would not get hurt. Others were neither so lucky, nor did they have much in the way of control over their destiny. The civilians in Baghdad, the Shia of southern Iraq, and the Kurds of the north were all innocent bystanders, caught in the forty day drive-by shooting that was Desert Storm. Unlike the Kurds, I had some control over my destiny, but in pursuit of this slice of Saddam's long, brutal story I took none of his pains to avoid harm. I would get into northern Iraq any way possible. Whatever difficulties I might encounter in being separated from my wheelchair in the open mountainous country across the border, I would deal with then. I had made this calculation many times before in covering the Middle East, or in deciding to do anything out in a world not known for its wheelchair-friendly terrain.

I had often thought of riding a donkey in the mountains of western America as recreation but had never found the time to orchestrate such a break in space and time. As a vacation it had seemed like a lot of bother, but here, for the sake of a story, the impulse to toss my own wheelchair to the wind was as natural as carrying a notebook is to other journalists. Still, that I would find myself here, holding on for dear life, with no sense of what lay ahead and certainly no way to control events from the top of a donkey, was unsettling. Was I supposed to be here, or was I in the way? To Mehmet the donkey man, I was just another paying customer.

Feeling out of place was an old sensation, almost as old as the paralysis in my legs. It was a feeling I had among friends, among strangers, and just as often when completely alone. I worried when I held up a check-out line at the supermarket. I smiled sheepishly at restaurant patrons as I made my way through the narrow spaces between the tables to my

15

own place. My anonymity torn from me, I interrupted conversations, intruding on peaceful diners. Was it their eyes or mine that said I was in the way until proven otherwise? I could go away or push ahead. Where wheelchairs could not venture, people working together inevitably could. Still, the choice of pushing ahead through the obstacles or just going away was always a matter of selecting the lesser of two evils. Going away was always a defeat. Pushing ahead was never a victory, and asking for help always reduced the score.

The staring began with the trickle of refugees near the village. They walked slowly, mostly downhill now, toward Turkey. They looked up from their feet at the passenger on the donkey. The incongruity suggested neither disability nor pity. The first refugees we met were the least affected by their week-long trek and a harrowing three days in the mud and snowy cold of the mountainous border region. They carried sacks and misshapen crates of clothing and provisions looted from their own hastily departed neighborhoods in Mosul, Sulaimaniya, Zakho, Kirkuk, and Erbil. Some of the women raised their eyes, wondering why a perfectly good donkey should be wasted on a blond Westerner who seemed to be so well-fed. One man suggested to the guide that the donkey would be better suited to carrying a sack of bread, or perhaps a dead or sick person. In Arabic and Kurdish, Mehmet told them that I was a reporter come to see Üzümlü, and that I was unable to walk.

I had been anonymous for a moment; now I was unmasked. The faces of these Kurdish refugees became faces of familiar worry and pity, faces that I had spent so much time thanking. Their concern was appreciated, I told them, but misguided in my case. The men and women gathered around and started to warn me of the dangers ahead. "If you cannot walk, why are you here?" they asked. "There is only death here. People are dying everywhere in Üzümlü. Saddam is killing everyone. Why did America not help us?" they asked. "There is no food. You could die."

I responded just as I did when people wanted to push my chair, or hold a door, or hand me something they thought I was looking at on a supermarket shelf. With a workable, relaxed face of self-assured confidence I could dismiss all of these people politely or rudely, but dismiss them I did. "No need to be concerned," I said. "I've got the door. I am fine. I can make it across the street. No problem. I'm not sick. I don't need a push. I'm not with anyone, no." It was habit, not arrogance that caused me to insist: "I'm just fine here on the donkey in the middle of one hundred and fifty thousand starving, war-terrified refugees."

In Üzümlü, flimsy shelters made of sticks and plastic sheets covered people forced to sleep on crusted mud. A dirty graveyard contained the twenty to fifty people who died each night. The yellow, bloodless, milky-eyed corpse of a child lay next to a partially dug grave. Perhaps two hundred thousand people would pass through here on their way to official Turkish refugee camps. The first had come across minefields, and among the initial group to gather around me and Mehmet and the donkey were a man and the gray-skinned unconscious companion on his back. He had an ugly blackened bandage around his waist, and one of his legs was merely a stump. This man would not make it to the Zab River, let alone the medical facility in Hakkari three hours away by car and already overflowing with casualties. His back and leg had absorbed a mine explosion that had halved his brother. The man carrying him looked at me with authority, pointed at his wounded friend, and said: "There is danger here. He cannot walk . . . we have here many who cannot walk. We have enough," he said with muted anger. "Why are you here?"

I got down off the donkey, sat on the ground, and assembled my tape recorder and microphone. The Kurdish refugees wanted to know why I couldn't walk and if the Iraqis had shot me. Gradually they began to talk.

"The helicopters came and we had to leave. I am a teacher," said one. "I am an engineer," said another.

To an outsider, they were only the sick and the well. Otherwise they were differentiated by the time of day they had decided to flee for the border. Those who fled at night were wearing pajamas under overcoats. Those caught during the day had time to don what looked like their entire wardrobes, especially the children, who stood staring and bundled up like overstuffed cloth dolls. Occasionally someone would walk by in just a thin jacket and torn slacks. Such shivering people explained that they were caught away from home running errands when the gunships came.

Mostly they wanted to talk about "Bush." It was in the bitterest of terms that the leader of Desert Storm was evoked on those cold muddy hills. "Bush is liar. Why he not help us?" "We fight Saddam, but why Bush let Saddam fly helicopters?" They said the word "helicopter" with the accent on the third syllable, and spit it out like an expletive. I sat cross-legged beneath a circle of anger, aiming the microphone to catch the shouting voices.

25   At that moment, much of the world I knew was reveling in victory. Two days earlier in a conversation with someone from Washington I had learned of the stellar approval ratings for President Bush. Historic peaks in the nineties, enshrining in statistics the apparently unshakable kingship behind the second sacking of Baghdad in a thousand years. As the Kurds might have said, "The warlord Tamerlane did a better job the first time," in 1253. The wind picked up and rattled the plastic sheeting anchored to stubborn mountain shrubs. The plastic made blurry apparitions of the blank young and very old faces inside. A large man stepped up and grabbed my microphone and began to speak in a hoarse, exhausted voice.

"Why is Saddam alive and we are dead? What is for America democracy? Bush is speaking of freedom and here we are free? You see us. They send you to us. You, who cannot stand? You are American, what is America now? Why are you here?" His words echoed out from the hill and mixed with the sobs and squeals of the refugees. To him my presence was an unsightly metaphor of America itself: able to arrive but unable to stand. I could not escape his metaphor any more than I could get off that mountain by myself. These were the questions. And so they remain.

The day was beginning to fade. It was a four-hour ride back down the mountain and at least another hour to file stories to Washington. It was time to go. Mehmet and I hoisted me up onto the donkey and we started our descent. The Turkish army had begun to airlift soldiers by helicopter to the mountaintop to urge the refugees down from Üzümlü and into a camp at a lower elevation. Later the Kurds would discover that this new camp was actually inside Iraq by a couple of hundred yards, a fact Secretary of State James Baker would learn in a photo op visit to the camp three days later. With its own far less headline-grabbing program of Kurdish oppression in southeastern Turkey, the Turkish government made it clear that it did not want the Iraqi Kurds.

Until the biblical scale of the catastrophe was apparent, the U.S. government was inclined to agree with Turkey. James Baker and George Bush spoke of territorial integrity in regards to the Kurdish issue. There would be no partitioning of Iraq, they said. The Kurds would have to move . . . again. The Turkish soldiers on the mountain pass fired their automatic weapons into the air, herding people like cattle. The narrow trail down to a spit of Iraqi border territory near the Turkish town of Çukurca was soon clogged with Kurds.

Donkey riding was a slow business. Without any abdominal muscles, my spine twisted and folded with each step. To sit up straight was to get a brief respite from the sharp back pains, but it could only be sustained for a few moments. I held the entire weight of my upper body in my wrists, rubbery and cramped from hours of gripping. They collapsed with each stumble and downward slide of the donkey, pressing my face helplessly into the mane of my tireless friend.

30   I hadn't figured that the trip down the mountain would be so much harder than the trip up. With the donkey angled upward during the ascent, my weight was pulled back, and holding on had been a simple clinging maneuver. With the donkey descending and angled downward in something of a controlled slide, I had to maintain my weight on my hands, balancing my shifting hips with sheer arm and wrist muscle. The alternative was to tumble down onto the rocks or into one of the many ravines. The crush of refugees narrowed the options for my sure-footed companion and had the effect of periodically spooking him. Mehmet had begun to tire of the earlier novel challenge of escorting the paraplegic on the donkey, and was dragging on the harness. He was also aware that the trail was in considerable danger of jamming into a pedestrian gridlock of desperate refugees.

The sounds of Turkish gunfire caused the donkey to lurch, and me to hold tighter. The rhythm of the donkey's forelegs was intoxicating; it vibrated mechanically up my arms. My whole frame was suspended like a scarecrow on two sticks locked at the elbows. Beneath me walked people clutching their belongings and hurrying to get to shelter before the sun set. Their heads wound along the trail stretching to the horizon.

All around me children stopped to relieve themselves in an agony of diarrhea. In the very same soil, the muddy foot tracks of people and animals filled with snowmelt and rainwater, and children stooped to drink from the puddles. They stood up, and their lips were ringed with brown mud like the remains of a chocolate milk shake. I had drunk nothing all day and had eaten nothing either.

If I was different from other reporters it was in the hydrogen peroxide I carried along with microphones, notebooks, audio tapes, cassette recorders, and cash. Peroxide was the most important item, especially here. In this remote area soaked in mud and surrounded by human waste, there were limits to sanitation. While the closest most reporters came to contaminating their own bodies was by eating a piece of local bread with unwashed hands, for me it was quite different. I use a catheter. Every four hours, every day, for the past fifteen years I have had to insert a tube to empty my bladder. It is a detail which can remain fairly discreetly hidden in most situations. While the processes demanding filling and emptying remained just as urgent here, this environment was hardly optimal for maintaining the near-sterile conditions necessary for using a catheter safely. To expose the catheter to the elements for even a few seconds was to risk infection as definitively as using a contaminated hypodermic syringe risked introducing hepatitis, or worse, into the blood.

After two days my hands had become utterly filthy, and my tattered gloves were soaked through with every local soil. At a certain point one can feel the collective momentum of a human tragedy. With overwhelming power, biological forces penetrate skin, culture, geography, careers, and deadlines. The Kurdish refugees clawed through the mountain foliage, plowing up a rich loam of conquered humanity. I did not want to become fertilizer.

It was not the first time I had encountered   35 potentially lethal mud in the course of covering a story. To prevent infections in such situations, I adopted a simple if crude strategy of self-denial that had served me well in the past. I would go into something of an emergency-induced body shutdown. Nothing in; nothing out. No food meant no waste. No water meant no parasites and therefore no infection.

In an environment without anything resembling a toilet, the inability to stand, squat, or balance above the ground meant that the simplest of bodily functions was impossible to perform without making a mess well outside the specifications of a person's normal notions of human dignity. In this place, human dignity was hard to fathom and beside the point.

But to lose control meant certain contamination. Aside from preventive deprivation, I could ration the peroxide carefully, avoid food and water, and pop vitamin C tablets to keep the acid content and therefore the antibacterial chemistry of my urine high. There was no room for error out here. The weakness that came with intense thirst and having starved for three days, along with being an equal number of travel days from any kind of hospital, would give infection an absolutely lethal head start.

So whatever my face conveyed to the concerned refugees coming down the mountain, I was no more fine than they were, and I was about as confused as to why I was here in this barely inhabitable edge of two warring nations. The accumulated delirium of the war, the Kurdish refugees, and my own deprivation made a dirgelike dream of the donkey ride. From this perch I was again as tall as I used to be. I could see the tops of heads and the shoulders all around me laden with leather straps tied to overstuffed suitcases. In this position my knees seemed farther away from my face. My feet were fully out of view. I had to strain to see them below the flanks of Mehmet's donkey. My abdomen was stretched by my extended and hanging leg bones. It gave me the impression that my lungs had grown larger. None of these details would have mattered to anyone else sitting on a donkey. To me they were a richly hued garment of memory and sensation long lost. In this wondrous garment I was invisible.

The joy of these sensations stood out in surroundings overrun with terror and death. I was unknown and unseen here. There were no presumptions about my body. All that people could tell, unless they were told otherwise, was that I was well-fed and blond. Beyond this, nothing was given away. As time went on I ceased even to look like an American journalist. Anonymity intensified the feeling of who I was, where I had come from, and how my own body worked, or didn't. As an American I had no right to be afraid here, I thought. I was safe and distinct from this horror. As a human being I had no way to separate myself from the river of Kurdish flesh making its way toward the valley. In my own invisible way, I was as close to death as they were. As a paraplegic, I was inside a membrane of unspoken physical adversity. There was no reason to expect bodies to function in such conditions, and each additional moment of life required a precise physical calculation. Durability of flesh pitted against the external elements. Each transaction final. The limits fully real. There was no room for mistakes.

I was not alone in contemplating those limits. Each dying person knew who he or she was. Each struggling refugee could see how much they had left to wager. The chill of circumstance made the crowd and myself quiet. Energy was conserved. The well-fed Turkish conscripts ahead and behind swaggered and fired their weapons, breaking the collective silence of one hundred thousand people.

Why was I there? It is an imperative of journalists to get the story. It was an imperative of those civilians to make their way off the mountain. There were others. The global imperatives of America to confront Saddam. The imperative of America to go home and beat the drum or lick its wounds. In victory, the United States lifted off from Iraq just as it did from the embassy roof in Saigon in 1975 following defeat in Vietnam. Some Vietnamese clung to the chopper back then. They imagined that despite the circumstances of defeat, the promises of America might be honored elsewhere.

In 1991 those promises seemed hollow and frozen, archived for unborn historians. The Kurds wondered why in victory the Americans would leave them to the wolves more swiftly and

40

surely than the Cambodians and South Viet-namese were abandoned following America's humiliating defeat in Indochina. Aside from the few colorless platitudes thrown their way from Washington, the Kurds had little to do with the business at hand for a triumphant president and his new world. In the anger of the Kurds there was no expectation that America would find their cause worthy, no expectation that their cries would be heard. They had given up on this America without a message and no inter-est in moving hearts and minds in Iraq. This time when the American chopper lifted off, no one would bother to hold on. Walking in the mud seemed the surer course now.

Fifteen years after lying in an intensive care unit in Pennsylvania I was near the summit of a mountain on the Iraqi border. If this was another event in the struggle for independence and tri-umph over physical adversity, what about the people who were dying all around me? Was I here to do something for them, or was it for me?

On a donkey among the Kurds at the end of a dreadful back-lot surgical abortion of a war, the paths of truth and physical independence seemed to diverge. I had no good answer for the Kurdish man who insisted that there were already too many people who could not walk in Üzümlü. Why I had gone to Kurdistan was as complicated a question as why George Bush's army did not in the first weeks after the war. What seemed an unquestionable virtue had become an excuse for doing something in my case, nothing in the president's.

45 During the Gulf War, President Bush spoke a lot about how America could regain its sense of mission, its confidence as a world leader, and declare independence from a burden of history. But in a war against historical burdens, the wider battlefield is blocked from view. There is no place for the identity of the people who are simply fighting to save their own miserable lives, the lives that never made it onto the American gun-camera videos, the lives of those we called the enemy, or the Kurdish friends in Iraq we never even knew we had until many thousands of them were dead.

I was fighting my own burdens. Holding on to the flimsy saddle and feeling each donkey step in my back and in my cramped and throb-bing fingers, I could see that my entire exis-tence had become a mission of never saying no to the physical challenges the world presented to a wheelchair. It was this that had gotten me through a fiery accident and would provide me with a mission upon which I could hang the rest of my life. I had made the decision to get on that donkey when I had gotten out of a hospital bed years before and vowed never to allow the world to push me. I would pull it instead. In Kurdistan I discovered that the world is a much larger place than can be filled by the mission of one man and his wheelchair.

If the Kurds had truly left me alone and gone about the business of only saving them-selves, I would just have died right there, hold-ing my tape recorder. They did not. "I'm fine," I said. There on the mountains between Turkey and Iraq, I had lost my way. It was up to Mehmet, the donkey, and me to find my way back.

In the last valley before the river, the steep trail was teeming with refugees. Just eight hours before it had been deserted and tinged with early spring grass; now each bend had been churned into slippery mud. The donkey was having trouble keeping its footing; Mehmet pulled on the harness as the beast locked knees next to a family pushing a wheelbarrow piled with clothes, utensils, a cassette player, and some toys. The animal would not budge, and Mehmet angrily shoved it and yanked on its tail. The donkey made a spitting noise, moaned, and bolted down a steep slope toward the grass. I held on and twisted as the animal half-tum-bled off the trail.

Trail was a generous description for the steep, narrow switchback that folded three times along the gravelly slope. With tens of thousands of refugees clogging the trail, the hillside began to look like a rickety shelf of old books shaking in an earthquake. Every few minutes rocks from the upper trail would be dislodged by someone's feet and tumble down on people one and two tiers below. Shouts and screams would greet the stones. A shower of debris was kicked up by the feet of my fleeing donkey. He landed in a hillock of grass at the river's bank and began to munch and graze with a resolve that suggested that his paraplegic reporter carrying duties had ended.

50   I had slipped off the donkey's back farther up the hill. With an exhausted smile, I rolled onto my back, clutched my bag of equipment, and stared up at the sky. The refugees made a moving silhouette against the fiery dusk sky, and the rope bridge over the river was now in darkness. The only sounds were the roar of the river and the shouts of refugees who argued with Turkish soldiers attempting to control access to the bridge.

The crowd was trying to storm a flimsy bridge that could withstand perhaps twenty people at a time without collapsing. The sound of Turkish weapons fired into the air peppered the din. My arms and cramped fingers ached. It felt good to lie down in the cold, wet grass. But I needed to cross that bridge to have any chance at all of filing a story. Without a donkey there seemed to be no way to even approach it from my repose on the river's bank. I turned my head and saw the muddy water raging in frosty darkness. There was no chance of swimming the Zab. The water churned its way around the canyon toward the Tigris, Baghdad, and the Persian Gulf hundreds of miles away. The opposite bank was a traffic jam of relief trucks and makeshift camps, as flimsy shelters from Üzümlü were erected once again along the road to Çukurca. Flickering fires and headlights made shadows on the rocks. Prone and unable to walk on the bank of an unswimmable river with a runaway donkey lost in a crowd of one hundred thousand refugees seemed to be as good an excuse as any for missing a deadline.

Mehmet was taking my predicament much more seriously than I was. He had brought back three men, and insisted on carrying me up to the bridge on a blanket. On the boggy riverbank the blanket quickly became saturated, making it difficult to hold with a body inside. They dropped me half a dozen times and eventually gave up. I laughed. Mehmet's crew went back to attend to their own places in the line to cross the bridge.

I lay there reveling in being invisible. My sore arms were stiff. There was a certain joy in just lying quietly in the grass while the river and the people swirled around me. For two years, more or less, I had been a correspondent in the Middle East. For all that time I had stood out as an American or as a journalist with a microphone; for fifteen years I had been scrutinized continuously because of my wheelchair. But for that moment in Kurdistan surrounded by thousands of refugees, covered with mud, without a chair, and lying in the grass, I was utterly, completely anonymous.

Mehmet's attempts to move me had brought us closer to the bridge, and the confusion of the mob was almost overhead. Sheep grazed near my head in the growing darkness. Up on the bridge some members of the international press corps had arrived and were shooting pictures. I recognized two faces, though I couldn't remember which newspaper they worked for. But they looked at the man with the backpack and after a moment recognized me. They must have recalled that I used a wheelchair. They looked around with some alarm. No wheelchair to be seen. I shrugged my shoulders at them. I mouthed the words "I'm fine." I chuckled out loud, and said, "I could use a donkey right about now." Like the slow movement of the moon over the sun during an eclipse, my moment of anonymity was passing.

In the end, Mehmet himself, a cigarette in   55 his mouth, carried me on his back up the slope to the bridge. After a screaming argument with the Turkish officer, he carried me across and put me down next to a family with their belongings spread out by the road.

"I am American," I said when asked by a young Kurdish boy.

"Do you know Chicago?" he asked. "I have a brother in Chicago."

I nodded and tried out some broken Arabic on him to pass the time. As darkness fell, the Kurdish taxi driver from Van who had been taking care of my chair for twelve hours found me in the crowd and joyfully hugged me. He had watched the exodus of his Kurdish compatriots with tears in his eyes, and with alarm had watched all day for me to appear in the crowd.

He brought my wheelchair over and I hoisted myself into it: it felt so good to move and to feel its support beneath my sore shoulders. There were my feet, just below my knees and my lap, right there below my face. Creased since 1976, my six-foot frame folded itself back into a sitting position once again. After only a day I had forgotten what it felt and looked like.

I took a breath and paused for a moment before I rolled toward where the driver had parked his cab. I looked around. There around me, the noise of the refugees quieted. I saw all eyes watching. In their staring gazes I was home. I waved good-bye. I made the deadline.

Re-reading/Conversations with the Text

1. Consider and discuss the functions of the gaze in this essay:

   a. Describe (in your own words but citing passages as necessary) how Hockenberry looks at *them*—the Kurd refugees.

   b. Describe (again in your own words and citing passages) how they look at *him*.

   c. Who stares at whom—when, how, and why?

2. How is Hockenberry's disability revealed to us as readers? When, where, and how does this happen in the essay? Can you recapture how you think you felt/responded when it was first revealed? How is Hockenberry's disability revealed to the refugees? How did they respond? Do you identify with their response? Why or why not?

3. This is very much an essay about identifying the personal with the political. Locate at least two passages/places where Hockenberry makes that connection/identification. Share them in small groups and try to determine why your classmates came up with the same or different ones.

Re-seeing and Re-writing

1. In a rather famous late twentieth-century poem, "Contradictions: Tracking Poems," Adrienne Rich writes:

   > The problem, unstated till now is how
   > To live in a damaged body
   > In a world where pain is meant to be
   >   Gagged
   > Uncured un-grieved-over. The problem is
   > To connect, without hysteria, the pain
   > Of any one's body with the pain of the body's world.

How could you argue that Hockenberry addresses this "problem"? Does he "connect"? Write a one- or two- page response in which you use the lines from Rich's poem to explain Hockenberry's essay.

2. Consider how Hockenberry moves through multiple "identifications" in this essay—with the donkey, with "[his] own burdens," with the refugees, with politics, with his job as a reporter, with the United States, with you, with ———? First, list as many of these identifications as you can, then write a few lines about each, grounding your comments in a passage from the text. (You might do this in groups—first listing possible identifications as a group and then splitting up to write separately about one to three of those identifications.)

Intertext

The danger of exposure plays a big role in both Lutz and Collin's critical examination of *National Geographic* images and Hockenberry's essay. Hockenberry feels "unmasked" when his guide tells Kurdish refugees that he is unable to walk and welcomes the "anonymity" that not being in his wheelchair affords him. Examine how Lutz and Collins utilize identification and difference to discuss physical and racial markers. What is similar about the ways in which Hockenberry and Lutz and Collins set themselves apart from the racial "Others" with whom they come into contact or represent? What is different? What similarity or difference between the two texts strikes you as most significant? Why?

A Small Place

JAMAICA KINCAID

JAMAICA KINCAID, née Elaine Potter Richardson, was born and lived on the British protectorate of Antigua until at 16 she was sent to work as an *au pair* in Westchester, New York. She studied photography at the New School of Social Research and launched her career as a self-taught writer with articles in *Ingenue, Rolling Stone,* and *The New Yorker.* She is the author of *At the Bottom of the River* (1983), *Lucy* (1990), and *The Autobiography of My Mother* (1995), among other novels and nonfiction works.

If you go to Antigua as a tourist, this is what you will see. If you come by aeroplane, you will land at the V. C. Bird International Airport. Vere Cornwall (V. C.) Bird is the Prime Minister of Antigua. You may be the sort of tourist who would wonder why a Prime Minister would want an airport named after him—why not a school, why not a hospital, why not some great public monument? You are a tourist and you have not yet seen a school in Antigua, you have not yet seen the hospital in Antigua, you have not yet seen a public monument in Antigua. As your plane descends to land, you might say, What a beautiful island Antigua is—more beautiful than any of the other islands you have seen, and they were very beautiful, in their way, but they were much too green, much too lush with vegetation, which indicated to you, the tourist, that they got quite a bit of rainfall, and rain is the very thing that you, just now, do not want, for you are thinking of the hard and cold and dark and long days you spent working in North America (or, worse, Europe), earning some money so that you could stay in this place (Antigua) where the sun always shines and where the climate is deliciously hot and dry for the four to ten days you are going to be staying there; and since you are on your holiday, since you are a tourist, the thought of what it might be like for someone who had to live day in, day out in a place that suffers constantly from drought, and so has to watch carefully every drop of fresh water used (while at the same time surrounded by a sea and an ocean—the Caribbean Sea on one side, the Atlantic Ocean on the other), must never cross your mind.

You disembark from your plane. You go through customs. Since you are a tourist, a North American or European—to be frank, white—and not an Antiguan black returning to Antigua from Europe or North America with cardboard boxes of much needed cheap clothes and food for relatives, you move through customs swiftly, you move through customs with ease. Your bags are not searched. You emerge from customs into the hot, clean air: immediately you feel cleansed, immediately you feel blessed (which is to say special); you feel free. You see a man, a taxi driver; you ask him to take you to your destination; he quotes you a price. You immediately think that the price is in the local currency, for you are a tourist and you are familiar with these things (rates of exchange) and you feel even more free, for things seem so cheap, but then your driver ends by saying, "In U.S. currency." You may say, "Hmmmm, do you have a formal sheet that lists official prices and destinations?" Your driver obeys the law and shows you the sheet, and he apologises for the incredible mistake he has made in quoting you a price off the top of his head which is so vastly different (favouring him) from the one listed. You are driven to your hotel by this taxi driver in his taxi, a brand-new Japanese-made vehicle. The road on which you are travelling is a very bad road, very much in need of repair. You are feeling wonderful, so you say, "Oh, what a marvellous change these bad roads are from the splendid highways I am used to in North America." (Or, worse, Europe.) Your driver is reckless; he is a dangerous man who drives in the middle of the road when he thinks no other cars are coming in the opposite direction, passes other cars on blind curves that run uphill, drives at sixty miles an hour on narrow, curving roads when the road sign, a rusting, beat-up thing left over from colonial days, says 40 MPH. This might frighten you (you are on your holiday; you are a tourist); this might excite you (you are on your holiday; you are a tourist), though if you are from New York and take taxis you are used to this style of driving: most of the taxi drivers in New York are from places in the world like this. You are looking out the window (because you want to get your money's worth); you notice that all the cars you see are brand-new, or almost brand-new, and that they are all Japanese-made. There are no American cars in Antigua—no new ones, at any rate; none that were manufactured in the last ten years. You continue to look at the cars and you say to yourself, Why, they look brand-new, but they have an awful sound, like an old car—a very old, dilapidated car. How to account for that? Well, possibly it's because they use leaded gasoline in these brand-new cars whose engines were built to use non-leaded gasoline, but you musn't ask the person driving the car if this is so, because he or she has never heard of unleaded gasoline. You look closely at the car; you see that it's a model of a Japanese car that you might hesitate to buy; it's a model that's very expensive; it's a model that's quite impractical for a person who has to work as hard as you do and who watches every penny you earn so that you can afford this holiday you are on. How do they afford such a car? And do they live in a luxurious house to match such a car? Well, no. You will be surprised, then, to see that most likely the person driving this brand-new car filled with the wrong gas lives in a house that, in comparison, is far beneath the status of

the car; and if you were to ask why you would be told that the banks are encouraged by the government to make loans available for cars, but loans for houses not so easily available; and if you ask again why, you will be told that the two main car dealerships in Antigua are owned in part or outright by ministers in government. Oh, but you are on holiday and the sight of these brand-new cars driven by people who may or may not have really passed their driving test (there was once a scandal about driving licences for sale) would not really stir up these thoughts in you. You pass a building sitting in a sea of dust and you think, It's some latrines for people just passing by, but when you look again you see the building has written on it PIGOTT'S SCHOOL. You pass the hospital, the Holberton Hospital, and how wrong you are not to think about this, for though you are a tourist on your holiday, what if your heart should miss a few beats? What if a blood vessel in your neck should break? What if one of those people driving those brand-new cars filled with the wrong gas fails to pass safely while going uphill on a curve and you are in the car going in the opposite direction? Will you be comforted to know that the hospital is staffed with doctors that no actual Antiguan trusts; that Antiguans always say about the doctors, "I don't want them near me"; that Antiguans refer to them not as doctors but as "the three men" (there are three of them); that when the Minister of Health himself doesn't feel well he takes the first plane to New York to see a real doctor; that if any one of the ministers in government needs medical care he flies to New York to get it?

It's a good thing that you brought your own books with you, for you couldn't just go to the library and borrow some. Antigua used to have a splendid library, but in The Earthquake (everyone talks about it that way—The Earthquake; we Antiguans, for I am one, have a great sense of things, and the more meaningful the thing, the more meaningless we make it) the library building was damaged. This was in 1974, and soon after that a sign was placed on the front of the building saying, THIS BUILDING WAS DAMAGED IN THE EARTHQUAKE OF 1974. REPAIRS ARE PENDING. The sign hangs there, and hangs there more than a decade later, with its unfulfilled promise of repair, and you might see this as a sort of quaintness on the part of these islanders, these people descended from slaves— what a strange, unusual perception of time they have. REPAIRS ARE PENDING, and here it is many years later, but perhaps in a world that is twelve miles long and nine miles wide (the size of Antigua) twelve years and twelve minutes and twelve days are all the same. The library is one of those splendid old buildings from colonial times, and the sign telling of the repairs is a splendid old sign from colonial times. Not very long after The Earthquake Antigua got its independence from Britain, making Antigua a state in its own right, and Antiguans are so proud of this that each year, to mark the day, they go to church and thank God, a British God, for this. But you should not think of the confusion that must lie in all that and you must not think of the damaged library. You have brought your own books with you, and among them is one of those new books about economic history, one of those books explaining how the West (meaning Europe and North America after its conquest and settlement by Europeans) got rich: the West got rich not from the free (free—in this case meaning got-for-nothing) and then undervalued labour, for generations, of the people like me you see walking around you in Antigua but from the ingenuity of small shopkeepers in Sheffield and Yorkshire and Lancashire, or wherever; and what a great part the invention of the wristwatch played in it, for there was nothing noble-minded men could not do when they discovered they could slap time on their wrists just like that (isn't that the last straw; for not only did we have to suffer the unspeakableness of slavery, but the satisfaction to be had from "We made you bastards rich" is taken away, too), and so you needn't let that slightly funny feeling you have from time to time about exploitation, oppression, domination develop into full-fledged unease, discomfort; you could ruin your holiday. They are not responsible for what you have; you owe them nothing; in fact, you did them a big favour, and you can provide one hundred examples. For here you are now, passing by Government House. And here you are now, passing by the Prime Minister's Office and the Parliament Building, and overlooking these, with a splendid view of St. John's Harbour, the American Embassy. If it were not for you, they would not have Government House, and Prime Minister's Office, and Parliament Building and embassy of powerful country. Now you are passing a mansion, an extraordinary house painted the colour of old cow dung, with more aerials and antennas attached to it than you will see even at the American Embassy. The people who live in this house are a merchant family who came to Antigua from the Middle East less than twenty years ago. When this family first came to Antigua, they sold dry goods door to door from suitcases they carried on their backs. Now they own a lot of Antigua; they regularly lend money to the government, they build enormous (for Antigua), ugly (for Antigua), concrete buildings in Antigua's capital, St. John's, which the government then rents for huge sums of money; a member of their family is the Antiguan Ambassador to Syria; Antiguans hate them. Not far from this mansion is another mansion, the home of a drug smuggler. Everybody knows he's a drug smuggler, and if just as you were driving by he stepped out of his door your driver might point him out to you as the notorious person that he is, for this drug smuggler is so rich people say he buys cars in tens—ten of this one, ten of that one—and that he bought a house (another mansion) near Five Islands, contents included, with cash he carried in a suitcase: three hundred and fifty thousand American dollars, and, to the surprise of the seller of the house, lots of American dollars were left over. Overlooking the drug smuggler's mansion is yet another mansion, and leading up to it is the best paved road in all of Antigua—even better than the road that was paved for the Queen's visit in 1985 (when the Queen came, all the roads that she would travel on were paved anew, so that the Queen might have been left with the impression that riding in a car in Antigua was a pleasant experience). In this mansion lives a woman sophisticated people in Antigua call Evita. She is a notorious woman. She's young and beautiful and the girlfriend of somebody very high up in the government. Evita is notorious because her relationship with this high government official has made her the owner of boutiques and property and given her a say in cabinet meetings, and all sorts of other privileges such a relationship would bring a beautiful young woman.

Oh, but by now you are tired of all this looking, and you want to reach your destination—your hotel, your room. You long to refresh yourself; you long to eat some nice lobster, some nice local food. You take a bath, you brush your teeth. You get dressed again; as you get dressed, you look out the window. That water—have you ever seen anything like it? Far out, to the horizon, the colour of the water is navy-blue; nearer, the water is the colour of the North American sky. From there to the shore, the water is pale, silvery, clear, so clear that you can see its pinkish-white sand bottom. Oh, what beauty! Oh, what beauty! You have never seen anything like this. You are so excited. You breathe shallow. You breathe deep. You see a beautiful boy skimming the water, godlike, on a Windsurfer. You see an incredibly unattractive, fat, pastrylike-fleshed woman enjoying a walk on the beautiful sand, with a man, an incredibly unattractive, fat, pastrylike-fleshed man; you see the pleasure they're taking in their surroundings. Still standing, looking out the window, you see yourself lying on the beach, enjoying the amazing sun (a sun so powerful and yet so beautiful, the way it is always overhead as if on permanent guard, ready to stamp out any cloud that dares to darken and so empty rain on you

and ruin your holiday; a sun that is your personal friend). You see yourself taking a walk on that beach, you see yourself meeting new people (only they are new in a very limited way, for they are people just like you). You see yourself eating some delicious, locally grown food. You see yourself, you see yourself . . . You must not wonder what exactly happened to the contents of your lavatory when you flushed it. You must not wonder where your bathwater went when you pulled out the stopper. You must not wonder what happened when you brushed your teeth. Oh, it might all end up in the water you are thinking of taking a swim in; the contents of your lavatory might, just might, graze gently against your ankle as you wade carefree in the water, for you see, in Antigua, there is no proper sewage-disposal system. But the Caribbean Sea is very big and the Atlantic Ocean is even bigger; it would amaze even you to know the number of black slaves this ocean has swallowed up. When you sit down to eat your delicious meal, it's better that you don't know that most of what you are eating came off a plane from Miami. And before it got on a plane in Miami, who knows where it came from? A good guess is that it came from a place like Antigua first, where it was grown dirt-cheap, went to Miami, and came back. There is a world of something in this, but I can't go into it right now.

The thing you have always suspected about yourself the minute you become a tourist is true: A tourist is an ugly human being. You are not an ugly person all the time; you are not an ugly person ordinarily; you are not an ugly person day to day. From day to day, you are a nice person. From day to day, all the people who are supposed to love you on the whole do. From day to day, as you walk down a busy street in the large and modern and prosperous city in which you work and live, dismayed, puzzled (a cliché, but only a cliché can explain you) at how alone you feel in this crowd, how awful it is to go unnoticed, how awful it is to go unloved, even as

5

you are surrounded by more people than you could possibly get to know in a lifetime that lasted for millennia, and then out of the corner of your eye you see someone looking at you and absolute pleasure is written all over that person's face, and then you realise that you are not as revolting a presence as you think you are (for that look just told you so). And so, ordinarily, you are a nice person, an attractive person, a person capable of drawing to yourself the affection of other people (people just like you), a person at home in your own skin (sort of; I mean, in a way; I mean, your dismay and puzzlement are natural to you, because people like you just seem to be like that, and so many of the things people like you find admirable about yourselves—the things you think about, the things you think really define you—seem rooted in these feelings): a person at home in your own house (and all its nice house things), with its nice back yard (and its nice back-yard things), at home on your street, your church, in community activities, your job, at home with your family, your relatives, your friends— you are a whole person. But one day, when you are sitting somewhere, alone in that crowd, and that awful feeling of displacedness comes over you, and really, as an ordinary person you are not well equipped to look too far inward and set yourself aright, because being ordinary is already so taxing, and being ordinary takes all you have out of you, and though the words "I must get away" do not actually pass across your lips, you make a leap from being that nice blob just sitting like a boob in your amniotic sac of the modern experience to being a person visiting heaps of death and ruin and feeling alive and inspired at the sight of it; to being a person lying on some faraway beach, your stilled body stinking and glistening in the sand, looking like something first forgotten, then remembered, then not important enough to go back for; to being a person marvelling at the harmony (ordinarily, what you would say is the backwardness) and the union these other people (and

they are other people) have with nature. And you look at the things they can do with a piece of ordinary cloth, the things they fashion out of cheap, vulgarly colored (to you) twine, the way they squat down over a hole they have made in the ground, the hole itself is something to marvel at, and since you are being an ugly person this ugly but joyful thought will swell inside you: their ancestors were not clever in the way yours were and not ruthless in the way yours were, for then would it not be you who would be in harmony with nature and backwards in that charming way? An ugly thing, that is what you are when you become a tourist, an ugly, empty thing, a stupid thing, a piece of rubbish pausing here and there to gaze at this and taste that, and it will never occur to you that the people who inhabit the place in which you have just paused cannot stand you, that behind their closed doors they laugh at your strangeness (you do not look the way they look); the physical sight of you does not please them; you have bad manners (it is their custom to eat their food with their hands; you try eating their way, you look silly; you try eating the way you always eat, you look silly); they do not like the way you speak (you have an accent); they collapse helpless from laughter, mimicking the way they imagine you must look as you carry out some everyday bodily function. They do not like you. *They do not like me!* That thought never actually occurs to you. Still, you feel a little uneasy. Still, you feel a little foolish. Still, you feel a little out of place. But the banality of your own life is very real to you; it drove you to this extreme, spending your days and your nights in the company of people who despise you, people you do not like really, people you would not want to have as your actual neighbour. And so you must devote yourself to puzzling out how much of what you are told is really, really true (Is ground-up bottle glass in peanut sauce really a delicacy around here, or will it do just what you think ground-up bottle glass will do? Is this rare, multicoloured, snout-mouthed fish really an aphrodisiac, or will it cause you to fall asleep permanently?). Oh, the hard work all of this is, and is it any wonder, then, that on your return home you feel the need of a long rest, so that you can recover from your life as a tourist?

That the native does not like the tourist is not hard to explain. For every native of every place is a potential tourist, and every tourist is a native of somewhere. Every native everywhere lives a life of overwhelming and crushing banality and boredom and desperation and depression, and every deed, good and bad, is an attempt to forget this. Every native would like to find a way out, every native would like a rest, every native would like a tour. But some natives—most natives in the world—cannot go anywhere. They are too poor. They are too poor to go anywhere. They are too poor to escape the reality of their lives; and they are too poor to live properly in the place where they live, which is the very place you, the tourist, want to go—so when the natives see you, the tourist, they envy you, they envy your ability to leave your own banality and boredom, they envy your ability to turn their own banality and boredom into a source of pleasure for yourself.

Re-reading/Conversations with the Text

1. Kincaid draws vivid word-pictures of what "you" will see as a tourist in Antigua—the sun-drenched scenery, the beautiful water, the people in harmony with nature. At the same time, however, she suggests that you, a tourist, might wonder about some of the things you see, like the new but noisy Japanese taxis, or the old "Under Renovation" sign at the library. Furthermore, she says there are things it might be better *not* to think about, like where the waste from your bath and toilet go. As you re-read, consider how Kincaid's direct form of address (to "you" the tourist), and her emphasis on what you should see but should not think about, serve to heighten your sense, as tourist/reader, of yourself being examined and scrutinized. How does this prepare you for Kincaid's shift to discussing how tourists look to Antiguans? What is your reaction to this shift? Do you think your reaction is what Kincaid intended? Why or why not?

2. Kincaid states that "every native of every place is a potential tourist, and every tourist is a native of somewhere." Touring, she claims, is an escape from "a life of overwhelming and crushing banality and boredom and desperation and depression." Re-read this excerpt, taking particular note of Kincaid's contention that the animosity against tourists comes from the fact that the natives, who are too poor to travel, envy them for turning the natives' banality and boredom into pleasure for themselves. Do you agree? Why or why not?

3. Writers establish their *ethos*—their credibility, their authority or right to speak—through various means, including the evidence they present and the standpoint from which they view their topic. How does Jamaica Kincaid establish her ethos in this excerpt? Later in *A Small Place* we learn that Kincaid is a native of Antigua. Does this enhance or reduce her credibility? Why?

Re-seeing and Re-writing

1. Kincaid's style of direct address is unusual; it has the effect of making the reader hyperaware of her identification with or difference from the "tourist" addressed by Kincaid. Re-write several pages of Kincaid's essay in either the first person ("I see . . .") or the third person ("The tourist sees . . ."), and then re-read what you've written. How does your re-writing change your perspective as a reader? Do you identify more with Kincaid? With the tourist? With the Antiguans? Why do you think this is so?

2. This assignment asks you to collect a series of images of Antigua and the West Indies from travel magazines and Internet travel sites. Write an essay that argues that your images support (or contradict) Kincaid's representation of her childhood home. Make sure you refer to specific evidence in the images and the text to buttress your claim. Use your findings to make a 5-minute presentation to the class.

Intertext

Kincaid states: "Every native would like to find a way out, every native would like a rest, every native would like a tour. But some natives—most natives in the world—cannot go anywhere." Re-read Hockenberry's "Walking the with the Kurds" and use Kincaid as your lens to examine his position. Consider, for example, the point at which one Kurdish man angrily tells Hockenberry: "There is danger here . . . we have here many who cannot walk. We have enough. . . . Why are you here?" Are reporters tourists? Why or why not? How does Hockenberry's experience differ from the tourists that Kincaid criticizes in her essay? How is it similar? What would Kincaid say about Hockenberry's position; would she say he is like a tourist in that he is able to leave once he gets the story? How would Hockenberry respond?

Tourist, Stay Home

HAUNANI-KAY TRASK

HAUNANI-KAY TRASK is a professor of Hawai'ian studies at the University of Hawai'i–Manoa and an activist in Hawai'i's self-determination movement—a movement that focuses on Hawai'i's right to secede from the United States. Trask compares the struggles of Hawai'ians to those of other Native Americans; as in "Tourist, Stay Home," her writing tends to focus on the problems that tourism has brought to Hawai'i, paying particular attention to the racial, class, and colonial bases of Hawai'i's economy.

Most Americans have come to believe that Hawai'i is as American as hotdogs and CNN. Worse, they assume that they, too, may make the trip, following the path of the empire into the sweet and sunny land of palm trees and hula-hula girls.

Increasing numbers of us not only oppose this predatory view of my native land and culture, we angrily and resolutely defy it. On January 17, 1993, thousands of Hawai'ians demonstrated against continued American control of our homeland. Marking the 100th anniversary of the overthrow of our native government by U.S. Marines and missionary-descended sugar barons, Hawaiian nationalists demanded recognition of our status as native people with claims to a land base and political self-determination.

For us, native self-government has always been preferable to American foreign government. No matter what Americans believe, most of us in the colonies do not feel grateful that our country was stolen along with our citizenship, our lands, and our independent place among the family of nations. We are not happy natives.

For us, American colonialism has been a violent process—the violence of mass death, the violence of American missionizing, the violence of cultural destruction, the violence of the American military. Through the overthrow and annexation, American control and American citizenship replaced Hawaiian control and Hawaiian citizenship. Our mother—our heritage and our inheritance—was taken from us. We were orphaned in our own land. Such brutal changes in a people's identity, its legal status, its government, its sense of belonging to a nation, are considered among the most serious human-rights violations by the international community today.

As we approach the twenty-first century, the effects of colonization are obvious: outmigration of the poor amounting to a diaspora, institutionalization in the military and prisons, continued land dispossession by the state and Federal governments and multinational corporations, and grotesque commodification of our culture through corporate tourism.

This latest affliction has meant a particularly insidious form of cultural prostitution. Just five hours by plane from California, Hawai'i is a thousand light years away in fantasy. Mostly a state of mind, Hawai'i is the image of escape from the rawness and violence of daily American life. *Hawai'i*—the chord, the image, the sound in the mind—is the fragrance and feel of soft fondness. Above all, Hawai'i is "she," the Western image of the native "female" in her magical allure. And if luck prevails, some of "her" will rub off on you, the visitor.

The predatory reality of tourism is visible everywhere: in garish "Polynesian" revues; commercial ads using Hawaiian dance and language to sell vacations and condominiums; the trampling of sacred *heiau* (temples) and burial grounds as tourist recreation sites. Thus, our world-renowned native dance, the *hula*, has been made ornamental, a form of hotel exotica for the gaping tourist. And Hawaiian women are marketed on posters from Paris to Tokyo promising an unfettered "primitive" sexuality. Far from encouraging cultural revival, as tourist industry apologists contend, tourism has appropriated and prostituted the accomplishments of a resurgent interest in things Hawaiian (the use of replicas of Hawaiian artifacts such as fishing and food complements, capes, helmets, and other symbols of ancient power, to decorate hotels).

As the pimp for the cultural prostitution business, the state of Hawai'i pours millions into the tourist industry, even to the extent of funding a private booster club—the Hawai'i Visitors' Bureau—to the tune of $30 million a year. Radio and television propaganda tells locals "the more you give" to tourism, "the more you get."

What Hawaiians get is population densities as high as Hong Kong in some areas, a housing shortage owing to staggering numbers of migrants from Asia and the continental United States, a soaring crime rate as impoverished locals prey on ostentatiously rich tourists, and environmental crises, including water depletion, that threaten the entire archipelago. Rather than stop the flood, the state is projecting a tidal wave of twelve million tourists by the year 2010. Today, we Hawaiians exist in an occupied country. We are a hostage people, forced to witness and participate in our own collective humiliation as tourist artifacts for the First World.

10   Meanwhile, shiploads and planeloads of American military forces continue to pass through Hawai'i on their way to imperialist wars in Asia and elsewhere. Every major Hawaiian island has lost thousands of acres to military bases, private beaches, and housing areas. On the most populous island of O'ahu, for example, fully 30 per cent of the land is in military hands.

Unlike other native peoples in the United States, we have no separate legal status to control our land-base. We are, by every measure, a colonized people. As a native nation, Hawaiians are no longer self-governing.

Because of these deplorable conditions, and despite the fact that we are less than 20 per cent of the million-and-a-quarter residents of Hawai'i, native Hawaiians have begun to assert our status as a people. Like the Palestinians, the Northern Irish, and the Indians of the Americas, we have started on a path of decolonization.

Beginning with the land struggles in the 1970s, and continuing with occupations, mass protests, and legislative and legal maneuvering in the 1980s and 1990s, Hawaiian resistance has matured into a full-blown nationalist struggle.

The contours of this struggle are both simple and complex. We want to control our own land base, government, and economy. We want to establish a nation-to-nation relationship with the U.S. Government, and with other native nations. We want control over water and other resources on our land base, and we want our human and civil rights acknowledged and protected.

In 1921, Congress set aside 200,000 acres of   15 homesteading lands specifically for Hawaiians. We are fighting for control of these lands, as well as approximately 1.2 million acres of the Kingdom of Hawai'i illegally transferred by the white oligarchy to the United States in 1898. Called the "trust" lands because the Federal and state governments allegedly hold them in "trust" for the Hawaiian people, this land base is currently used for all manner of illegal activities, including airports, military reservations, public schools, parks, and county refuse sites, even private businesses and homes. Because of this long record of abuse, and because nationhood means self-determination and not wardship, Hawaiians are organized and lobbying for return of the "trust" lands to the Hawaiian people.

To this end, we have re-created our own political entity, *Ka Lāhui Hawai'i,* a native initiative for self-government. At our first Constitutional Convention in 1987, we devised a democratic form of government, with a Kai'āina or governor, a legislature and judges, elders, and chief advisory councils. We have made treaties with other native nations, and we have diplomatic representatives in many places. We want recognition as a sovereign people.

Sovereignty, as clearly defined by our citizens in 1987, is "the ability of a people who share a common culture, religion, language, value system, and land base to exercise control over their lands and lives, independent of other nations." We lay claim to the trust lands as the basis of our nation.

While we organized in Hawaiian communities, the state of Hawai'i created an Office of Hawaiian Affairs, or OHA, in 1980. Ostensibly for representation of Hawaiian rights by Hawaiians (the only group allowed to vote for its all-native trustees), OHA was powerless as a mechanism for self-government. It had no control over trust lands, and no statutory strength to prevent abuses of native culture. For the next ten years, OHA supported reparations for the overthrow and forcible annexation to the United States, rather than recognition and restoration of our nationhood.

Because OHA is a state agency beholden to the reigning Democratic Party, it has made no claims for a land base against the state. Arguing that they represented Hawaiians rather than the state, OHA trustees made an agreement with the governor—an unprincipled Hawaiian named John Waihe'e—to settle all ceded lands claims. OHA was to receive over $100 million in 1991, then $8.5 million annually. No lands were to be transferred. They would instead be lost to Hawaiians forever.

20   As a result of humiliating public criticism from the Hawaiian community for OHA's sell-out role in this deal, OHA proposed a kind of quasi-sovereign condition which it would oversee. In direct opposition to the Ka Lāhui model of a "nation-to-nation" relationship with the Federal Government, OHA argued that the governing structure of the Hawaiian nation, landless though it might be, should come under the state of Hawai'i.

There were several problems with this position. OHA was not representative of all Hawaiian communities and never had been, because voting procedures gave too much weight to the most populous island of O'ahu, resulting in a skewed underrepresentation of neighbor island people. Any lands or monies transferred by the Federal Government to OHA would go to the state, not to the Hawaiian people, since OHA was a state agency; this would mean *less,* not more, control by Hawaiians over their future. Giving OHA nation status would be akin to calling the Bureau of Indian Affairs an Indian nation. And finally, state control of Hawaiians, even under an alleged "Office of Hawaiian Affairs," is still wardship, not self-determination.

While the tide of native resistance swelled, a coordinated state strategy emerged. First, Governor Waihe'e came out in favor of a landless model of a "nation-within-a-nation." Speaking as if he invented the concept and never once mentioning Ka Lāhui's leadership, Waihe'e publicly advocated Federal recognition of Hawaiians as a native nation. In his "state of the state" address immediately following the January 17 commemoration, Waihe'e called for Hawaiian sovereignty to be devised by an OHA-led constitutional convention and funded by the state legislature. OHA supported the governor's efforts.

After nearly two decades of organizing, forces for and against sovereignty were clearly drawn: the state of Hawai'i and its Bureau of Indian Affairs clone, the Office of Hawaiian Affairs, supported continued wardship of our people under the tutelage of OHA; Ka Lāhui Hawai'i, a native initiative for self-government, supported self-determination on a definable land base with Federal recognition of our nationhood.

While OHA and the governor submitted legislation mandating the constitutional convention, Ka Lāhui's membership soared to 16,000 enrolled citizens. As the largest sovereignty organization, Ka Lāhui now poses a substantial threat to the legitimacy of OHA. Sensing this danger, and hoping to head off our own efforts in Washington, D.C., Waihe'e traveled to the American capital to float the notion of an OHA-type nation with President Clinton and his Secretary of the Interior. As we pass the midpoint of this centennial year, the state strategy appears to be Federal recognition, but no real "nation-within-a-nation" on the order of the American Indian nations. A land base is out of the question.

25 For Hawaiians, the stakes are high indeed: self-determination, or the yoke of perpetual wardship. In the meantime, marginalization and exploitation of Hawaiians, our culture, and our lands, continues, while corporate tourism thrives on nearly seven million visitors a year (thirty tourists for every native). In the face of Hawaiian resistance, it's still business as usual.

If OHA is successful, the Hawaiian people will be burdened with yet another agency, non-Hawaiian in design and function, set in place to prevent rather than fulfill native autonomy. Historically, the decline of Hawaiians and our culture is directly traceable to land dispossession. Therefore, any attempt to address Hawaiian sovereignty which does not return control of lands to Hawaiians is doomed to fail.

Like agencies created by the Federal government to short-circuit Indian sovereignty, OHA will be a top-down institution whose architects envision an extension of the state of Hawai'i rather than a native initiative to promote self-government.

Elsewhere in the Pacific, native peoples struggle with the same dilemma.

The Maori, like the Hawaiians a minority in their own land, have been dispossessed through conquest and occupation by a foreign white people, and have suffered psychologically from cultural suppression. They, too, have been demanding a form of sovereignty, seeking identity and cultural integrity by returning to their lands. And they have supported Hawaiian resistance, as fellow Polynesians and as fellow colonized people.

30 In Tahiti, a strong independence movement has captured the mayorship of the second-largest city while uniting antinuclear, labor, and native nationalist forces to resist French colonialism. With others in the Pacific, Tahitians have spearheaded the nuclear-free and independent Pacific movements.

Aborigines, Kanaks, East Timorese, and Belauans focus world attention on genocide and military imperialism. And for each of these indigenous peoples, there is the familiar, predictable struggle for self-determination.

If Hawaiians are not alone in the Pacific Basin, our struggle for self-determination is certainly unknown across most of the North American continent, particularly to the hordes of tourists who inundate our beautiful but fragile islands. In this United Nations "Year of Indigenous People," a willful ignorance about native nationhood prevails in the dominant society. Given this, and given the collaborationist politics within colony Hawai'i, whatever successes my people do achieve will be won slowly and at great expense.

For those who might feel a twinge of solidarity with our cause, let me leave this final thought: Don't come to Hawai'i. We don't need any more tourists. If you want to help, pass this message on to your friends.

Re-reading/Conversations with the Text

1. In this essay, Trask's tone seems almost angry. Re-read the essay, paying close attention to the rhetorical appeals Trask uses to set up her authority. Do you think that Trask is successful in getting her audience to identify with her cause? If so, how does she do this? If not, how does she fail? Finally, consider: Does it matter?

2. Trask describes Hawai'i's two worlds, the one that the tourists see and the one that the Hawai'ian natives live every day. Re-read this part of Trask's essay and note the differences she outlines between these two experiences. How do visual representations of Hawai'i function to mask these differences? Why is Trask concerned about how these representations have affected important Hawai'ian traditions?

3. Trask ends her essay by asserting the following: "For those who might feel a twinge of solidarity with our cause, let me leave you with this final thought: Don't come to Hawai'i. We don't need any more tourists." Do you find her final statement persuasive? Would you consider not traveling to Hawai'i based on Trask's essay?

Re-seeing and Re-writing

1. In this essay, Trask presents a side of tourism/touring we do not usually see in popular media. In essence, Trask presents an alternative narrative of tourism. Working in pairs, find a set of travel ads to Hawai'i. First, provide a written analysis of these representations. Next, using digital media, produce alternative images that tell the story of tourism from the perspective of Trask. In order to tell this alternative story, you might need to do some research. Be prepared to share your work with your classmates.

2. Historiography is a form of historical storytelling where the author takes evidence and constructs a possible narrative of an event. This assignment asks you to research the history of Hawai'i and to tell the story of an aspect of this history by creating a documentary film or Web site. You need not represent facts "accurately"; rather, you might exaggerate the story in order to highlight the parts of Hawai'i's history we tend not to be told. Be prepared to share this with your classmates.

Intertext

Trask and Kincaid both have powerful feelings about the tourists who come to their countries, and there are significant similarities in the way they construct the identities of these tourists. Within the similarities you find between Trask and Kincaid, what are the major differences? What are the greatest similarities within their differences? Explore how the context of each author and the audience they write to might have influenced their choices of focus. Finally, are there any benefits to tourism that Trask and Kincaid do not mention?

Los Intersticios: Recasting Moving Selves

EVELYN ALSULTANY

Is it possible to occupy more than one category of identity? To identify as Arab American *and* Latina, Muslim *and* unmarried, Spanish-speaking *and* "American"? In this short essay, *EVELYN ALSULTANY*, a graduate student in Arab American studies at Stanford University, meditates on these complicated questions as she is "read" differently in different places and times. ("Los Intersticios," from the title, translates as "The Interstices"—the in-between spaces.) Alsultany's graduate work focuses on representations of Arab and Muslim Americans after 9/11, but also encompasses sociology, political science, gender studies, and the study of media and technology. Alsultany is the author of numerous scholarly articles and creative pieces and teaches writing and Arab American studies courses at Stanford.

Ethnicity in such a world needs to be recast so that our moving selves can be acknowledged. . . . Who am I? When am I? The questions that are asked in the street, of my identity, mold me. Appearing in the flesh, I am cast afresh, a female of color—skin color, hair texture, clothing, speech, all marking me in ways that I could scarcely have conceived of.

—MEENA ALEXANDER

I'm in a graduate class at the New School in New York City. A white female sits next to me and we begin "friendly" conversation. She asks me where I'm from. I reply that I was born and raised in New York City and return the question. She tells me she is from Ohio and has lived in New York for several years. She continues her inquiry: "Oh . . . well, how about your parents?" (I feel her trying to map me onto her narrow cartography; New York is not a sufficient answer. She analyzes me according to binary axes of sameness and difference. She detects only difference at first glance, and seeks to pigeonhole me. In her framework, my body is marked, excluded, not from this country. A seemingly "friendly" question turns into a claim to land and belonging.) "My father is Iraqi and my mother Cuban," I answer. "How interesting. Are you a U.S. citizen?"

I am waiting for the NYC subway. A man also waiting asks me if I too am Pakistani. I reply that I'm part Iraqi and part Cuban. He asks if I am Muslim, and I reply that I am Muslim. He asks me if I am married, and I tell him I'm not. In cultural camaraderie he leans over and says that he has cousins in Pakistan available for an arranged marriage if my family so desires. (My Cubanness, as well as my own relationship to my cultural identity, evaporates as he assumes that Arab plus Muslim equals arranged marriage. I can identify: he reminds me of my Iraqi relatives and I know he means well.) I tell him that I'm not interested in marriage but thank him for his kindness. (I accept his framework and respond accordingly, avoiding an awkward situation in which he realizes that I am not who he assumes I am, offering him recognition and validation for his [mis]identification.)

I am in a New York City deli waiting for my bagel to toast. The man behind the counter asks if I'm an Arab Muslim (he too is Arab and Muslim). I reply that yes, I am by part of my father. He asks my name, and I say, "Evelyn." In utter disdain, he tells me that I could not possibly be Muslim; if I were truly Muslim I would have a Muslim name. What was I doing with such a name? I reply (after taking a deep breath and telling myself that it's not worth getting upset over) that my Cuban mother named me and that I honor my mother. He points to the fact that I'm wearing lipstick and have not changed my name, which he finds to be completely inappropriate and despicable, and says that I am a reflection of the decay of the Arab Muslim in America.

I'm on an airplane flying from Miami to New York. I'm sitting next to an Ecuadorian man. He asks me where I'm from. I tell him. He asks me if I'm more Arab, Latina, or American, and I state that I'm all of the above. He says that's impossible. I must be more of one ethnicity than another. He determines that I am not really Arab, that I'm more Latina because of the camaraderie he feels in our speaking Spanish.

5   I am in Costa Rica. I walk the streets and my brown skin and dark hair blend in with the multiple shades of brown around me. I love this first-time experience of blending in! I walk into a coffee shop for some café con leche, and my fantasy of belonging is shattered when the woman preparing the coffee asks me where I'm from. I tell her that I was born and raised in New York City by a Cuban mother and an Arab father. She replies, "Que eres una gringa."

I am shocked by the contextuality of identity: that my body is marked as gringa in Costa Rica, as Latina in some U.S. contexts, Arab in others, in some times and spaces not adequately Arab, or Latina, or "American," and in other contexts simply as *other*.

My body becomes marked with meaning as I enter public space. My identity fractures as I experience differing dislocations in multiple contexts. Sometimes people otherize me, sometimes they identify with me. Both situations can be equally problematic. Those who otherize me fail to see a shared humanity and those who identify with me fail to see difference; my Arab or Muslim identity negates my Cuban heritage. Identification signifies belonging or home, and I pretend to be that home for the mistaken person. It's my good deed for the day (I know how precious it can be to find a moment of familiarity with a stranger). The bridge becomes my back as I feign belonging, and I become that vehicle for others, which I desire for myself. Although it is illusory, I do identify with the humanity of the situation—the desire to belong in this world, to be understood. But the frameworks used to (mis)read my body, to disconnect me, wear on me. I try to develop a new identity. What should I try to pass for next time? Perhaps I'll just say I'm Cuban to those who appear to be Arab or South Asian. A friend suggests I say I'm an Italian from Brooklyn. I wonder if I could successfully pass for that. Ethnicity needs to be recast so that our moving selves can be acknowledged.

Notes

I would like to thank Marisol Negrón, Alexandra Lang, María Helena Rueda, Ericka Beckman, Karina Hodoyan, Sara Rondinel, Jessi Aaron, and Cynthia María Paccacerqua for their feedback in our writing seminar at Stanford University with Mary Pratt. I would especially like to thank Mary Pratt for her invaluable feedback, and AnaLouise Keating and Gloria Anzaldúa for their thoughtful editing.

Re-reading/Conversations with the Text

1. "Los Intersticios" is structured as a series of episodic encounters Alsultany has with others. It is not until the penultimate paragraph that she begins to analyze these encounters through the lenses of identification and difference. What is the rhetorical effect of this structure? As you read the piece initially, did you recognize her argument about "moving selves" before you got to her final paragraphs? As you *reread* the essay, can you find passages that illustrate "the contextuality of identity"? Did you find Alsultany's reliance on personal experience more or less convincing than the evidence used in a conventional scholarly argument? Why?

2. Reread "Los Intersticios," marking passages in which others "(mis)read [Alsultany's] body." Working in small groups, make a list of the binaries that inform their (mis)readings of her identity—for example, American/foreigner, Latina/gringa. In what ways do these binaries limit identification and/or difference? Discuss.

3. Alsultany argues that "Sometimes people otherize me, sometimes they identify with me. Both situations can be equally problematic." Reread the essay, looking for evidence from Alsultany's experience that supports this claim. As a class or in small groups, make two lists based on your findings: one list of when and where dis-identification is problematic for her, and one list of when and where identification is "equally problematic." In which contexts (that is, in which times and places) do they become an issue, and why? Discuss.

Re-seeing and Re-writing

1. Think of a time in your life when you were (mis)read by another—when someone either mistakenly identified with you, or mistakenly considered you radically (even completely) different from them. Using Alsultany's essay as a model, write a brief narrative (or series of episodes) about the incident(s), then write a critical analysis of the incident(s). In your analysis, be sure to consider the following: (a) how context (place and time) affected the person's (mis)reading of you; (b) how false binaries informed the person's assumptions about you; and (c) how identification and difference operated in the incident(s). Your goal is to arrive at a sophisticated understanding of what Alsultany calls "moving selves," identities that change according to context.

2. In "Los Intersticios," Alsultany describes her many identities—as woman, Muslim, Arab American, Latina, U.S. citizen. This assignment asks you to consider how these identities overlap and affect each other. You may choose to focus on one pair of identifications in particular (Muslim/woman, for example), or you may examine several pairs of related identifications (Arab/American, Cuban/American, Muslim/American). In your essay, analyze how each identity changes when it is paired with another. Be sure to support your analysis with evidence from Alsultany's essay.

Alsultany ends "Los Intersticios" with a restatement of Meena Alexander's argument in the epigraph: "Ethnicity needs to be recast so that our moving selves can be acknowledged." Many authors in this unit consider ethnicity, identification, and difference in their essays. This assignment invites you to compare and contrast how various authors "recast" ethnicity (or not) in order to acknowledge "moving selves" (or not). Choose one of the following essays to review, in addition to "Los Intersticios": John Hockenberry, "Walking with the Kurds"; Jamaica Kincaid, "A Small Place"; or Haunani-Kay Trask, "Tourist, Go Home." Does each author acknowledge, as Alsultany suggests, "the contextuality of identity"? If not, or if an author's understanding of ethnicity is radically different from Alsultany's, consider why this might be so.

The Fourth of July

A U D R E   L O R D E

AUDRE LORDE was born in New York City of West Indian immigrant parents. She attended Hunter College, spent a year as a student at the National University of Mexico, and upon her return to New York obtained a master's degree from Columbia University. A renowned lesbian poet and essayist, Lorde's work includes *The Cancer Journals* (1980) and *Zami: A New Spelling of My Name* (1982). This excerpt from *Zami*, in which Lorde tells the story of her family's visit to Washington, DC, in 1947, reflects Lorde's concerns with race, racism, national identity, and socioeconomic class. Lorde died in 1992.

The first time I went to Washington, D.C., was on the edge of the summer when I was supposed to stop being a child. At least that's what they said to us all at graduation from the eighth grade. My sister Phyllis graduated at the same time from high school. I don't know what she was supposed to stop being. But as graduation presents for us both, the whole family took a Fourth of July trip to Washington, D.C., the fabled and famous capital of our country.

It was the first time I'd ever been on a railroad train during the day. When I was little, and we used to go to the Connecticut shore, we always went at night on the milk train, because it was cheaper.

Preparations were in the air around our house before school was even over. We packed for a week. There were two very large suitcases that my father carried, and a box filled with food. In fact, my first trip to Washington was a mobile feast; I started eating as soon as we were comfortably ensconced in our seats, and did not stop until somewhere after Philadelphia. I remember it was Philadelphia because I was disappointed not to have passed by the Liberty Bell.

My mother had roasted two chickens and cut them up into dainty bite-size pieces. She packed slices of brown bread and butter and green pepper and carrot sticks. There were little violently yellow iced cakes with scalloped edges called "marigolds," that came from Cushman's Bakery. There was a spice bun and rockcakes from Newton's, the West Indian bakery across Lenox Avenue from St. Mark's School, and iced tea in a wrapped mayonnaise jar. There were sweet pickles for us and dill pickles for my father, and peaches with the fuzz still on them, individually wrapped to keep them from bruising. And, for neatness, there were piles of napkins and a little tin box with a washcloth dampened with rosewater and glycerine for wiping sticky mouths.

I wanted to eat in the dining car because I had read all about them, but my mother reminded me for the umpteenth time that dining car food always cost too much money and besides, you never could tell whose hands had been playing all over that food, nor where those same hands had been just before. My mother never mentioned that Black people were not allowed into railroad dining cars headed south in 1947. As usual, whatever my mother did not like and could not change, she ignored. Perhaps it would go away, deprived of her attention.

I learned later that Phyllis's high school senior class trip had been to Washington, but the nuns had given her back her deposit in private, explaining to her that the class, all of whom were white, except Phyllis, would be staying in a hotel where Phyllis "would not be happy," meaning, Daddy explained to her, also in private, that they did not rent rooms to Negroes. "We will take you to Washington, ourselves," my father had avowed, "and not just for an overnight in some measly fleabag hotel."

American racism was a new and crushing reality that my parents had to deal with every day of their lives once they came to this country. They handled it as a private woe. My mother and father believed that they could best protect their children from the realities of race in America and the fact of American racism by never giving them name, much less discussing their nature. We were told we must never trust white people, but *why* was never explained, nor the nature of their ill will. Like so many other vital pieces of information in my childhood, I was supposed to know without being told. It always seemed like a very strange injunction coming from my mother, who looked so much like one of those people we were never supposed to trust. But something always warned me not to ask my mother why she wasn't white, and why Auntie Lillah and Auntie Etta weren't, even though they were all that same problematic color so different from my father and me, even from my sisters, who were somewhere in-between.

In Washington, D.C., we had one large room with two double beds and an extra cot for me. It was a back-street hotel that belonged to a friend of my father's who was in real estate, and I spent the whole next day after Mass squinting up at the Lincoln Memorial where Marian Anderson had sung after the D.A.R. refused to allow her to sing in their auditorium because she was Black. Or because she was "Colored," my father said as he told us the story. Except that what he probably said was "Negro," because for his times, my father was quite progressive.

I was squinting because I was in that silent agony that characterized all of my childhood summers, from the time school let out in June to the end of July, brought about by my dilated and vulnerable eyes exposed to the summer brightness.

10   I viewed Julys through an agonizing corolla of dazzling whiteness and I always hated the Fourth of July, even before I came to realize the travesty such a celebration was for Black people in this country.

My parents did not approve of sunglasses, nor of their expense.

I spent the afternoon squinting up at monuments to freedom and past presidencies and democracy, and wondering why the light and heat were both so much stronger in Washington, D.C., than back home in New York City. Even the pavement on the streets was a shade lighter in color than back home.

Late that Washington afternoon my family and I walked back down Pennsylvania Avenue. We were a proper caravan, mother bright and father brown, the three of us girls step-standards in-between. Moved by our historical surroundings and the heat of the early evening, my father decreed yet another treat. He had a great sense of history, a flair for the quietly dramatic and the sense of specialness of an occasion and a trip.

"Shall we stop and have a little something to cool off, Lin?"

Two blocks away from our hotel, the family stopped for a dish of vanilla ice cream at a Breyer's ice cream and soda fountain. Indoors, the soda fountain was dim and fan-cooled, deliciously relieving to my scorched eyes.   15

Corded and crisp and pinafored, the five of us seated ourselves one by one at the counter. There was I between my mother and father, and my two sisters on the other side of my mother. We settled ourselves along the white mottled marble counter, and when the waitress spoke at first no one understood what she was saying, and so the five of us just sat there.

The waitress moved along the line of us closer to my father and spoke again. "I said I kin give you to take out, but you can't eat here. Sorry." Then she dropped her eyes looking very embarrassed, and suddenly we heard what it was she was saying all at the same time, loud and clear.

Straight-backed and indignant, one by one, my family and I got down from the counter stools and turned around and marched out of the store, quiet and outraged, as if we had never been Black before. No one would answer my emphatic questions with anything other than a guilty silence. "But we hadn't done anything!" This wasn't right or fair! Hadn't I written poems about Bataan and freedom and democracy for all?

My parents wouldn't speak of this injustice, not because they had contributed to it, but because they felt they should have anticipated it and avoided it. This made me even angrier. My fury was not going to be acknowledged by a like fury. Even my two sisters copied my parents' pretense that nothing unusual and anti-American had occurred. I was left to write my angry letter to the President of the United States all by myself, although my father did promise I could type it out on the office typewriter next week, after I showed it to him in my copybook diary.

The waitress was white, and the counter was white, and the ice cream I never ate in Washington, D.C., that summer I left childhood was white, and the white heat and the white pavement and the white stone monuments of my first Washington summer made me sick to my stomach for the whole rest of that trip and it wasn't much of a graduation present after all.

Re-reading/Conversations with the Text

1. Lorde begins her story by stating that "The first time I went to Washington, D.C., was on the edge of the summer when I was supposed to stop being a child." To what degree is Lorde's journey from childhood to young adulthood—marked by her graduation trip to the capital city—developed on the basis of identification and difference? With what or whom does Lorde identify? With what or whom does she establish a difference? What is the significance of these identifications and differentiations within the structure and argument of her essay?

2. Re-read Lorde's essay, looking for specific repetitions of words or images related to food. What role does food play in the essay? What is the importance of food within the context of Lorde's discussion of racial and national identity? What cultural role does food fulfill that makes it such a key issue for Lorde?

3. In discussing the racialization of whiteness, Lorde states: "[S]omething always warned me not to ask my mother why she wasn't white, and why Auntie Lillah and Auntie Etta weren't, even though they were all that same problematic color so different from my father and me, even from my sisters, who were somewhere in-between." Why is her mother's color "problematic"? What is the significance for Lorde of this recognition?

Re-seeing and Re-writing

1. Socioeconomic class is one of the major issues discussed by Lorde in her story. She begins by stating that the trip to DC was their first railroad train trip, as they had previously taken the "milk train, because it was cheaper." She also states that while she has trouble with glare hurting her eyes, her parents "did not approve of sunglasses, nor of their expense." Write an essay that traces

20

the ways in which Lorde utilizes socioeconomic class for rhetorical purposes within her story. What do you, as the reader, understand that she is trying to do by inserting these references to social class in her story? Is she successful? Why or why not?

2. Lorde's story is titled "The Fourth of July," and she states that her family takes the trip to "the fabled and famous capital of our country" within the context of the nation's independence celebration. Write an essay about how Lorde complicates her identification with other citizens of "our country" when she introduces the topic of race. Why does Lorde state that she "came to realize the travesty such a celebration was for Black people in this country"? How is national identity racialized throughout Lorde's essay? In what ways is her family's experience of July 4 in Washington, DC, marked by race? In concluding that their encounter with blatant racism is "nothing unusual," why does Lorde also state that something "anti-American had occurred"?

Intertext

Racial identification is a key issue in both Trask's "Tourist, Stay Home" and Lorde's story on her trip to DC. Re-read both essays and trace the similarities and the differences between Trask's and Lorde's discussions of racial identity. What similarities can you find between the two authors? What differences? What might be the cultural significance of your findings?

Image: *Lilo and Stitch* (movie poster)

This poster advertised the 2002 Disney movie *Lilo and Stitch.*

Lilo and Stitch poster
Walt Disney © 2002. Courtesy Everett Collection.

Re-seeing and Re-writing

1. The Disney film *Lilo and Stitch* is the story of a young Hawaiian girl who befriends a stranded extraterrestrial, in part because of their shared differences (their "outsider" status, small stature, etc.). Examine the poster for the film. How does its visual design reinforce this idea of identification between the two characters? How does it reinforce difference between the figures and the viewer?

2. *Lilo and Stitch* tackles a fairly common theme in film: two like-minded outsiders taking on a world that doesn't properly understand them. For this assignment, research other examples of this theme. Try to find promotional posters for two or three such films and assemble the images in a portfolio. (For online research, you might consult sites such as the Internet Movie Database, www.imdb.com.) Accompany your image portfolio with short analyses of how the posters use design and text to relay this theme of outsider status.

Where Do You Want to Go Today?
Cybernetic Tourism, the Internet, and Transnationality

LISA NAKAMURA

In the early days of the World Wide Web, proponents of the new communications medium welcomed it with enthusiasm; many felt that the anonymity and natural diversity of the new environment would eventually lead to the development of a truly utopian culture, one in which the power imbalances associated with difference would no longer matter. In time, academics such as *LISA NAKAMURA* came to develop a critique of this view—the rhetorics of dominance, exclusion, and Other-ing so familiar to the "real world" of Western culture were being replicated in cyberspace. Here, Nakamura examines how the idea of the exotic "Other" is employed as a consistent metaphor in the marketing campaigns of an emerging digital economy. Nakamura studies the rhetoric of digital technologies as well as postcolonial literature and critical theory. In addition to co-editing the collection *Race in Cyberspace* (2000) (from which this article is taken), Nakamura has published work on race and the Internet in *CyberReader,* *Cyberculture,* and *Reload: Rethinking Women and Cyberculture* (2002). Most recently, she has authored *Cybertypes: Race, Ethnicity, and Identity on the Internet* (2002).

There is no race. There is no gender. There is no age. There are no infirmities. There are only minds. Utopia? No, Internet.

–"Anthem," television commercial for MCI

The television commercial "Anthem" claims that on the Internet, there are no infirmities, no gender, no age, that there are only minds. This pure, democratic, cerebral form of communication is touted as a utopia, a pure no-place where human interaction can occur, as the voice-over says, "uninfluenced by the rest of it." Yet can the "rest of it" be written out as easily as the word *race* is crossed out on the chalkboard by the hand of an Indian girl in this commercial?

It is "the rest of it," the specter of racial and ethnic difference and its visual and textual representation in print and television advertise- ments that appeared in 1997 by Compaq, IBM, and Origin, that I will address in this chapter. The ads I will discuss all sell networking and communications technologies that depict racial difference, the "rest of it," as a visual marker. The spectacles of race in these advertising images are designed to stabilize contemporary anxieties that networking technology and access to cyberspace may break down ethnic and racial differences. These advertisements, which promote the glories of cyberspace, cast the viewer in the position of the tourist, and sketch out a future in which difference is either elided or put in its proper place.

The ironies in "Anthem" exist on several levels. For one, the advertisement positions MCI's commodity—"the largest Internet network in the world"—as a solution to social problems. The advertisement claims to produce a radical form of democracy that refers to and extends an "American" model of social equality and equal access. This patriotic anthem, however, is a paradoxical one: the visual images of diversity (old, young, black, white, deaf, etc.) are displayed and celebrated as spectacles of difference that the narrative simultaneously attempts to erase by claiming that MCI's product will reduce the different bodies that we see to "just minds."

The ad gestures towards a democracy founded upon disembodiment and uncontaminated by physical difference, but it must also showcase a dizzying parade of difference in order to make its point. Diversity is displayed as the sign of what the product will eradicate. Its erasure and elision can only be understood in terms of its presence; like the word "race" on the chalkboard, it can only be crossed out if it is written or displayed. This ad writes race and poses it as both a beautiful spectacle and a vexing question. Its narrative describes a "postethnic America," to use David Hollinger's phrase, where these categories will be made not to count. The supposedly liberal and progressive tone of the ad camouflages its depiction of race as something to be eliminated, or made "not to count," through technology. If computers and networks can help us to communicate without "the rest of it," that residue of difference with its power to disturb, disrupt, and challenge, then we can all exist in a world "without boundaries."

5   Another television commercial, this one by AT&T, that aired during the 1996 Olympics asks the viewer to "imagine a world without limits—AT&T believes communication can make it happen." Like "Anthem," this narrative posits a connection between networking and a demo-

cratic ethos in which differences will be elided. In addition, it resorts to a similar visual strategy—it depicts a black man in track shorts leaping over the Grand Canyon.

Like many of the ads by high tech and communications companies that aired during the Olympics, this one has an "international" or multicultural flavor that seems to celebrate national and ethnic identities. This world without limits is represented by vivid and often sublime images of displayed ethnic and racial difference in order to bracket them off as exotic and irremediably other. Images of this other as primitive, anachronistic, and picturesque decorate the landscape of these ads.

Microsoft's recent television and print media campaign markets access to personal computing and Internet connectivity by describing these activities as a form of travel. Travel and tourism, like networking technology, are commodities that define the privileged, industrialized first-world subject, and they situate him in the position of the one who looks, the one who has access, the one who communicates. Microsoft's omnipresent slogan "Where do you want to go today?" rhetorically places this consumer in the position of the user with unlimited choice; access to Microsoft's technology and networks promises the consumer a "world without limits" where he can possess an idealized mobility. Microsoft's promise to transport the user to new (cyber)spaces where desire can be fulfilled is enticing in its very vagueness, offering a seemingly open-ended invitation for travel and new experiences. A sort of technologically enabled transnationality is evoked here, but one that directly addresses the first-world user, whose position on the network will allow him to metaphorically go wherever he likes.

This dream or fantasy of ideal travel common to networking advertisements constructs a destination that can look like an African safari, a trip to the Amazonian rain forest, or a camel caravan in the Egyptian desert. The iconography of the travelogue or tourist attraction in these ads places the viewer in the position of the tourist who, in Dean MacCannell's words, "simply collects experiences of difference (different people, different places)" and "emerges as a miniature clone of the old Western philosophical subject, thinking itself unified, central, in control, etc., mastering Otherness and profiting from it" (xv). Networking ads that promise the viewer control and mastery over technology and communications discursively and visually link this power to a vision of the other which, in contrast to the mobile and networked tourist/user, isn't going anywhere. The continued presence of stable signifiers of otherness in telecommunications advertising guarantees the Western subject that his position, wherever he may choose to go today, remains privileged.

An ad from Compaq (see fig. 1) that appeared in the *Chronicle of Higher Education* reads "Introducing a world where the words 'you can't get there from here' are never

heard." It depicts a "sandstone mesa" with the inset image of a monitor from which two schoolchildren gaze curiously at the sight. The ad is selling "Compaq networked multimedia. With it, the classroom is no longer a destination, it's a starting point." Like the Microsoft and AT&T slogans, it links networks with privileged forms of travel, and reinforces the metaphor by visually depicting sights that viewers associate with tourism. The networked classroom is envisioned as a glass window from which networked users can consume the sights of travel as if they were tourists.

Another ad from the Compaq series (fig. 2) shows the same children admiring the networked rain forest from their places inside the networked classroom, signified by the frame of the monitor. The tiny box on the upper-right-hand side of the image evokes the distinctive menu bar of a Windows product, and frames the whole ad for its viewer as a window onto an "other" world.

10

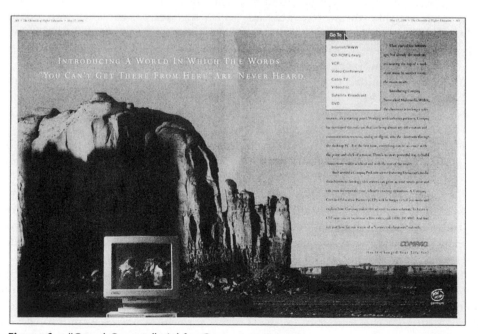

Figure 1   "Grand Canyon": Ad for Compaq computers
Courtesy of Hewlett-Packard Company.

Figure 2 "Rain Forest": Ad for Compaq computers
Courtesy of Hewlett-Packard Company.

The sublime beauty of the mesa and the lush pastoral images of the rain forest are nostalgically quoted here in order to assuage an anxiety about the environmental effects of cybertechnology. In a world where sandstone mesas and rain forests are becoming increasingly rare, partly as a result of industrialization, these ads position networking as a benign, "green" type of product that will preserve the beauty of nature, at least as an image on the screen. As John Macgregor Wise puts it, this is part of the modernist discourse that envisioned electricity as "transcendent, pure and clean," unlike mechanical technology. The same structures of metaphor that allow this ad to dub the experience of using networked communications "travel" also enables it to equate an image of a rain forest in Nature (with a capital *N*). The enraptured American schoolchildren, with their backpacks and French braids, are framed as user-travelers. With the assistance of Compaq, they have found their way to a world that seems to be without limits, one in which the images of nature are as good as or better than reality.

The virtually real rain forest and mesa participate in a postcyberspace paradox of representation—the locution "virtual reality" suggests that the line or "limit" between the authentic sight/site and its simulation has become blurred. This discourse has become familiar, and was anticipated by Jean Baudrillard pre-Internet. Familiar as it is, the Internet and its representations in media such as advertising have refigured the discourse in different contours. The ads that I discuss attempt to stabilize the slippery relationship between the virtual and the real by insisting upon the monolithic visual differences between first- and third-world landscapes and people.

This virtual field trip frames Nature as a tourist sight and figures Compaq as the educational tour guide. In this post-Internet culture of simulation in which we live, it is increasingly necessary for stable, iconic images of Nature and the Other to be evoked in the world of technology advertising. These images guarantee and gesture toward the unthreatened and unproblematic existence of a destination for travel, a place whose beauty and exoticism will somehow remain intact and attractive. If technology will indeed make everyone, everything, and every place the same, as "Anthem" claims in its ambivalent way, then where is there left to go? What is there left to see? What is the use of being asked where you want to go today if every place is just like here? Difference, in the form of exotic places or exotic people, must be demonstrated iconographically in order to shore up the Western user's identity as himself.

This idyllic image of an Arab on his camel, with the pyramids picturesquely squatting in the background, belongs in a coffee-table book (see fig. 3). The timeless quality of this image of an exotic other untouched by modernity is disrupted by the cartoon dialogue text, which reads "What do you say we head back and download the results of the equestrian finals?" This dissonant use of contemporary vernacular American techoslang is supposed to be read comically; the man is meant to look unlike anyone who would speak these words.

15   The gap between the exotic Otherness of the image and the familiarity of its American rhetoric can be read as more than an attempt at humor, however. IBM, whose slogan "solution for a small planet" is contained in an icon but-

ton in the lower left hand side of the image, is literally putting these incongruous words into the Other's mouth, thus demonstrating the hegemonic power of its "high speed information network" to make the planet smaller by causing everyone to speak the *same* language—computer-speak. His position as the exotic Other must be emphasized and foregrounded in order for this strategy to work, for the image's appeal rests upon its evocation of the exotic. The rider's classical antique "look and feel" atop his Old Testament camel guarantee that his access to a high speed network will not rob us, the tourist/viewer, of the spectacle of his difference. In the phantasmatic world of Internet advertising, he can download all the results he likes, so long as his visual appeal to us, the viewer, reassures us that we are still in the position of the tourist, the Western subject, whose privilege it is to enjoy him in all his anachronistic glory.

These ads claim a world without boundaries for us, their consumers and target audience, and by so doing they show us exactly where and what these boundaries really are. These boundaries are ethnic and racial ones. Rather than being effaced, these dividing lines are evoked over and over again. In addition, the ads sanitize and idealize their depictions of the Other and Otherness by deleting all references that might threaten their status as timeless icons. In the camel image, the sky is an untroubled blue, the pyramids have fresh, clean, sharp outlines, and there are no signs whatsoever of pollution, roadkill, litter, or fighter jets.

Including these "real life" images in the advertisement would disrupt the picture it presents us of an Other whose "unspoiled" qualities are so highly valued by tourists. Indeed, as Trinh Minh-Ha notes, even very sophisticated tourists are quick to reject experiences that challenge their received notions of authentic Otherness. Trinh writes, "the Third World representative the modern sophisticated public ideally seeks is the *unspoiled* African, Asian, or Native American, who remains more preoccupied with his/her

Figure 3 Ad for IBM: Arab and camel
Courtesy of IBM. Source: IBM Ad no. BR-96-9B, 1996.

image as the *real* native—the *truly different*—than with the issues of hegemony, feminism, and social change" (88). Great pains are taken in this ad to make the camel rider appear real, truly different from us, and "authentic" in order to build an idealized Other whose unspoiled nature shores up the tourist's sense that he is indeed seeing the "real" thing. In the post-Internet world of simulation, "real" things are fixed and preserved in images such as these in order to anchor the Western viewing subject's sense of himself as a privileged and mobile viewer.

Since the conflicts in Mogadishu, Sarajevo, and Zaire (images of which are found elsewhere in the magazines from which these ads came),

ethnic difference in the world of Internet advertising is visually "cleansed" of its divisive, problematic, tragic connotations. The ads function as corrective texts for readers deluged with images of racial conflicts and bloodshed both at home and abroad. These advertisements put the world right; their claims for better living (and better boundaries) through technology are graphically acted out in idealized images of Others who miraculously speak like "us" but still look like "them."

The Indian man (pictured in an IBM print advertisement that appeared in *Smithsonian,* January 1996) whose iconic Indian elephant gazes sidelong at the viewer as he affectionately curls his trunk around his owner's neck, has much in common with his Egyptian counterpart in the previous ad. (The ad's text tells us that his name is Sikander, making him somewhat less generic than his counterpart, but not much. Where is the last name?) The thematics of this series produced for IBM plays upon the depiction of ethnic, racial, and linguistic differences, usually all at the same time, in order to highlight the hegemonic power of IBM's technology. IBM's television ads (there were several produced and aired in this same series in 1997) were memorable because they were all subtitled vignettes of Italian nuns, Japanese surgeons, and Norwegian skiers engaged in their quaint and distinctively ethnic pursuits, but united in their use of IBM networking machines. The sounds of foreign languages being spoken in television ads had their own ability to shock and attract attention, all to the same end—the one word that was spoken in English, albeit heavily accented English, was "IBM."

20   Thus, the transnational language, the one designed to end all barriers between speakers, the speech that everyone can pronounce and that cannot be translated or incorporated into another tongue, turns out not to be Esperanto but rather IBM-speak, the language of American corporate technology. The foreignness of the Other is exploited here to remind the viewer—who may fear that IBM-speak will make the world smaller in undesirable ways (for example, that they might compete for our jobs, move into our neighborhoods, go to our schools)—that the Other is still picturesque. This classically Orientalized Other, such as the camel rider and Sikander, is marked as sufficiently different from us, the projected viewers, in order to encourage us to retain our positions as privileged tourists and users.

Sikander's cartoon-bubble, emblazoned across his face and his elephant's, asks, "How come I keep trashing my hardware every 9 months?!" This question can be read as a rhetorical example of what postcolonial theorist and novelist Salman Rushdie has termed "globalizing Coca-Colonization." Again, the language of technology, with its hacker-dude vernacular, is figured here as the transnational tongue, miraculously emerging from every mouth. Possible fears that the exoticism and heterogeneity of the Other will be siphoned off or eradicated by his use of homogeneous technospeak are eased by the visual impact of the elephant, whose trunk frames Sikander's face. Elephants, rain forests, and unspoiled mesas are all endangered markers of cultural difference that represent specific stereotyped ways of being Other to Western eyes. If we did not know that Sikander was a "real" Indian (as opposed to Indian-American, Indian-Canadian, or Indo-Anglian) the presence of his elephant, as well as the text's reference to "Nirvana," proves to us, through the power of familiar images, that he is. We are meant to assume that even after Sikander's hardware problems are solved by IBM's "consultants who consider where you are as well are where you're headed" he will still look as picturesque, as "Indian" as he did pre-IBM.

Two other ads, part of the same series produced by IBM, feature more ambiguously ethnic figures. The first one of these depicts a Latina girl who is asking her teacher, Mrs. Alvarez, how to telnet to a remote server. She wears a straw hat, which makes reference to the Southwest. Though she is only eight or ten years old, her speech has already acquired the distinctive sounds of technospeak—for example, she uses "telnet" as a verb. The man in the second advertisement, an antique-looking fellow with old fashioned glasses, a dark tunic, dark skin, and an untidy beard proclaims that "you're hosed when a virus sneaks into your hard drive." He, too, speaks the transnational vernacular—the diction of Wayne and Garth from *Wayne's World* has sneaked into *his* hard drive like a rhetorical virus. These images, like the preceding ones, enact a sort of cultural ventriloquism that demonstrates the hegemonic power of American technospeak. The identifiably ethnic faces, with their distinctive props and costumes, that utter these words, however, attest to the importance of Otherness as a marker of a difference that the ads strive to preserve.

This Origin ad appeared in *Wired* magazine, which, like *Time, Smithsonian,* the *New Yorker,* and *The Chronicle of Higher Education* directs its advertising toward upper-middle-class, mainly white readers (see fig. 4). In addition, *Wired* is read mainly by men, it has an unabashedly libertarian bias, and its stance toward technology is generally utopian. Unlike the other ads, this one directly and overtly poses ethnicity and cultural difference as part of a political and commercial dilemma that Origin networks can solve. The text reads, in part,

> [W]e believe that wiring machines is the job, but connecting people the art. Which means besides skills you also need wisdom and understanding. An understanding of how people think and communicate. And the wisdom to respect the knowledge and cultures of others. Be-

cause only then can you create systems and standards they can work with. And common goals which all involved are willing to achieve.

The image of an African boy, surrounded by his tribe, seemingly performing a *Star Trek* Vulcan mind meld with a red-haired and extremely pale boy, centrally situates the white child, whose arm is visible in an unbroken line, as the figure who is supposedly as willing to learn as he is to teach.

However, the text implies that the purpose of the white boy's encounter with an African boy and his tribe is for him to learn just enough about them to create the "systems and standards that THEY can work with." The producer of marketable knowledge, the setter of networking and software-language standards, is still defined here as the Western subject. This image, which could have come out of *National Geographic* any time in the last hundred years, participates in the familiar iconography of colonialism and its contemporary cousin, tourism. And in keeping

Figure 4　Ad for Origin: Black boy and white boy
Courtesy of Origin International Inc.

with this association, it depicts the African as unspoiled and authentic. Its appeal to travel across national and geographical borders as a means of understanding the Other, "the art of connecting people," is defined as a commodity which this ad and others produced by networking companies sell along *with* their fiber optics and consulting services.

25   The notion of the computer-enabled "global village" envisioned by Marshall McLuhan also participates in this rhetoric that links exotic travel and tourism with technology. The Origin image comments on the nature of the global village by making it quite clear to the viewer that despite technology's claims to radically and instantly level cultural and racial differences (or in a more extreme statement, such as that made by "Anthem," to literally cross them out) there will always be villages full of "real" Africans, looking just as they always have.

It is part of the business of advertising to depict utopias: ideal depictions of being that correctively reenvision the world and prescribe a solution to its ills in the form of a commodity of some sort. And like tourist pamphlets, they often propose that their products will produce, in Dean MacCannell's phrase, a "utopia of difference," such as has been pictured in many Benetton and Coca-Cola advertising campaigns.

Coca-Cola's slogan from the seventies and eighties, "I'd like to teach the world to sing," both predates and prefigures these ads by IBM, Compaq, Origin, and MCI. The Coca-Cola ads picture black, white, young, old, and so on holding hands and forming a veritable Rainbow Coalition of human diversity. These singers are united by their shared song and, most important, their consumption of bottles of Coke. The viewer, meant to infer that the beverage was the direct cause of these diverse Coke drinkers overcoming their ethnic and racial differences, was

given the same message then that many Internet-related advertisements give us today. The message is that cybertechnology, like Coke, will magically strip users down to "just minds," all singing the same corporate anthem.

And what of the "rest of it," the raced and ethnic body that cyberspace's "Anthem" claims to leave behind? It seems that the fantasy terrain of advertising is loath to leave out this marked body because it represents the exotic Other which both attracts us with its beauty and picturesqueness and reassures us of our own identities as "*not* Other." The "rest of it" is visually quoted in these images and then pointedly marginalized and established *as Other*. The iconography of these advertising images demonstrates that the corporate image factory *needs* images of the Other in order to depict its product: a technological utopia of difference. It is not, however, a utopia *for* the Other or one that includes it in any meaningful or progressive way. Rather, it proposes an ideal world of virtual social and cultural reality based on specific methods of "Othering," a project that I would term "the globalizing Coca-Colonization of cyberspace and the media complex within which it is embedded."

Acknowledgments

I would like to thank the members of the Sonoma State University Faculty Writing Group: Kathy Charmaz, Richard Senghas, Dorothy Freidel, Elaine McHugh, and Virginia Lea for their encouragement and suggestions for revision. I would also like to thank my research assistant and independent study advisee at Sonoma State, Dean Klotz, for his assistance with permissions, research, and all things cyber. And a very special thanks to Amelie Hastie and Martin Burns, who continue to provide support and advice during all stages of my work on this topic.

References

Hollinger, David. *Postethnic America: Beyond Multiculturalism.* New York: Basic Books, 1995.

McCannell, Dean. *The Tourist: A New Theory of the Leisure Class.* New York: Schocken Books, 1989.

McLuhan, Marshall. *Understanding Media: The Extensions of Man.* Cambridge: MIT Press, 1994.

Rushdie, Salman. "Damme, This Is the Oriental Scene For You!" *New Yorker,* 23 and 30 June 1997, 50–61.

Trinh Minh-ha. *Woman, Native, Other: Writing Postcoloniality and Feminism.* Bloomington: University of Indiana Press, 1989.

Wise, John Macgregor. "The Virtual Community: Politics and Affect in Cyberspace." Paper delivered at the American Studies Association Conference, Washington D.C., 1997.

Re-reading/Conversations with the Text

1. In this piece, Lisa Nakamura critiques Internet marketing techniques, claiming that they perpetuate racial stereotypes and use insensitive depictions of non-Western people that overplay their "Otherness" to the assumed Western viewer. According to Nakamura, what constitutes Otherness? Specifically, how do these advertisements construct race and ethnicity so as to make them exotic, idyllic, or romantic? Is it possible to employ race or ethnicity in advertising *without* resorting to this strategy? If so, what strategies might be used to this end? Locate examples of advertising that challenge this particular "orientalizing" gaze—what alternative values do they place upon racial and ethnic difference?

2. This assignment asks you to pay particular attention to the advertisements in Nakamura's essay, using Kenneth Burke's rhetorical concepts of identification and differentiation to analyze them. Which elements of each ad are meant to bring about identification with the viewer, and which ones point to a sense of difference? What is the overall persuasive purpose of having the viewer feel that he or she is somehow like the "Other," and why is it also important that the viewer feel simultaneously divided from the Other? How is desire for the products or services created through this interaction of identification and differentiation? Remember in your analysis to discuss not only the photographs in the ad, but also additional visual elements, including the use of text, color, overall layout, font choice, and so on.

Re-seeing and Re-writing

1. Using Nakamura's article as a starting point, explore online depictions of Otherness, and compile a list of web-based destinations to present to your

class, along with critical commentary meant to explain how Otherness is represented in each site. You might consider representations of things other than human beings—for instance, how are animals, landscapes, and even language itself made exotic? Can you discern any patterns with respect to the types of sites that are more likely to use this gaze than others—for example, in terms of their perceived legitimacy, the audience targeted by these sites, or their overall purpose?

2. One of the more effective genres of critique that exists in our society is that of satire. Spoof newspapers like *The Onion* (www.theonion.com), political cartoons gracing the op-ed page of your local newspaper, and popular television programs such as *The Simpsons* and *The Daily Show* know that the easiest, quickest route to showing an audience the problems with an issue or event is to "flip the script" on us—in other words, to act as if one is in favor of an issue or event in order to hold it up to ridicule. Visit the Adbusters Web site (www.adbusters.org) and take a look at their online gallery of spoof advertisements. As a class, discuss some of the more effective ads found on the site—what techniques, both verbal and visual, make for an effective satirical ad? Finally, working in small groups, create your own mock advertisement spoofing the ones cited in Nakamura's article. In doing this, you might ask yourselves what assumptions about racial and ethnic identity are being taken for granted in these ads, and how a spoof ad might help bring those hidden assumptions to light.

Intertext

Like Nakamura's essay on cyberspace, Kuenz's essay on Disney explores the concept of space as an artificial construction. In an analytical essay, explain the similarities and differences in how these artificial spaces are constructed, according to Kuenz and Nakamura. How do these spaces function rhetorically to persuade visitors to accept their presence as spaces? For example, how are preconceived notions about nature or culture utilized to create successful tourist parks? With what tactics are visitors persuaded to identify with such spaces? How would you characterize the discourse generated about Disney World (i.e., brochures or Web site advertisements for Disney World)? Alternately, how would you characterize the discourse generated about cyberspace? What does it suggest about the systems of value and belief to which inhabitants of cyberspace adhere? What specific sites, texts, and other artifacts of cyberspace can you find that give voice to this view?

It's a Small World After All

JANE KUENZ

Have you ever thought about Mickey Mouse as a distinctly American icon? *JANE KUENZ* has. In the pathbreaking book *Inside the Mouse: Work and Play at Disney World* (1995), Kuenz and three other scholars think about the role of Disney World in U.S. culture. This essay, excerpted from a longer chapter from the book, considers how Disney World offers visitors identifications that are powerful and pleasurable—but also limiting. Kuenz is Associate Professor of English and Women's Studies at the University of Southern Maine, where she teaches courses in American literature and popular culture.

In my family, the story goes that my sister's engagement was orchestrated by Disney. One autumn night, she and her partner placed themselves in Bistro de Paris, located somewhere in the middle of "France," one of eleven mini-countries of World Showcase circling the lagoon at Walt Disney World's EPCOT Center. Amidst its mirrored rooms and under the approving glances of both personnel and other customers, he proposed, she accepted—both foregone conclusions—as they toasted themselves on their mutual good taste. Just as they stepped out of the restaurant and onto the brick streets of "Paris," they were greeted by the music of the *1812 Overture* and the dancing lights of EPCOT's laser show, "IllumiNations." Walt Disney World had begun its nightly celebration above their heads and seemingly in their honor.

They remember this story fondly; we repeat it with affection. We don't, by the way, always do so with a straight face, though even the story's translation into farce retains something of its original intent. What we might regard as its hokeyness—especially the opportune beginning of the music and lights— becomes something else again in light of the fact that my sister and her husband, self-consciously or not, staged the scene of their engagement. His proposal was no surprise or secret. Though they had forgotten at the time that the laser show and music would begin, they certainly knew that it did so every night at that

hour, and its beginning then was only more delightful for their having forgotten it in the heat of the moment. They did not wait around for Tchaikovsky's canons and didn't need to in order to enjoy the effect; they had been there before, already knew the whole show, and could relish its resonance for them on this particular night without having actually experienced it. In effect, they chose EPCOT as the locale precisely because they knew it would structure their evening and provide for them its meaning: they had been in a "French restaurant"—in "France" no less: signs par excellence of heterosexual romance, while around them raged the lights and music reminiscent of *Love American Style*.

This vignette nicely illustrates the way people establish and affirm an identity by locating themselves within already existing social structures and the power relations they express. Disney is pretty good at providing such structures, less so at removing them. Here, the pleasure of their engagement—which, whatever else it may be, is fundamentally a pleasure of identifying oneself as heterosexual and presumably reproductive in a culture virulently approving of both—is integral to the pleasure of seeing themselves as part of the big show: music, lights, atmosphere, and the normative sexuality those elements combine to signify. It's too easy to call their experience fake; even designating it as clichéd misses the point. It wasn't false to them.

My sister, for example, remains confident that hers is a sexual identity existing prior to Disney, rather than one produced there as another of its effects, and it is through that confidence—the allocation to a prior, interior, or essential self the traits of the social—that she knows herself as real. This fact, perhaps paradoxically, confirms the validity of her sense of identity rather than compromises it. In other words, my sister's gender and sexual identities are as real to her as any she can know; that they are in large measure defined and structured in relation to the representational, political, and economic needs of social formations already out there is an insight perhaps less apparent.

I'm overstating the case, of course; Disney isn't quite the sole magnanimous purveyor of social definition it would like to be, though it does repeat and magnify the dominant social formations it finds elsewhere. Indeed, this appears to be one of its main functions. My sister's experience in EPCOT was primarily one of recognition: recognizing the experience and its meaning constructed there as versions of the same she might find and probably has found throughout her life. In this context, each retelling of her story by my family—ritualized and formative as family stories tend to be—becomes its own end, not just a reaffirmation of their commitment, nor just a reenactment of it. Every time we repeat it we participate again in a process of recognizing and confirming that ideological formation, the logic of its structures, and the pleasure that comes from locating oneself within them. Like it or not, we also recognize and affirm the penalties that come from refusing to.

5   What interests me about Disney is the way it functions in this process of recognition and identification and how out of that identification or—sometimes, though perhaps only rarely and even then unconsciously—against it, Disney produces a feeling we find pleasurable. This has required some work and a stretch of the imagination for me; I've never found Walt Disney World all that enjoyable, though living in Orlando and visiting the park has made it abundantly clear that others do. Indeed, about 13 million others do every year, visit the park, that is, and, if press releases are to be believed, enjoy that visit as well. It's worth asking, then, what we find there or, better, what we look for and how, in turn, what's found confirms for us an identity, the individuality of which is felt and made meaningful through its ties to the social and economic formations replicated in the park.

Besides the excruciatingly normative heterosexuality suggested in the above example and the strict gender roles attendant to it, Disney incites a kind of unexamined nationalism and a system of social relations based on consumption. These combine with lesser capitalist virtues conducive to "progress" to encourage the reproduction of subjects for life in what we are continually told is our future. It's important to insist that this is not a top-down process. No one is compelled at Disney to become anything, nor necessarily and definitively inscribed in one identity or another. While most of the pleasures to be had there require these identifications from us, the pleasure itself is something we produce in ourselves as we learn or recognize the nature of these roles and how to perform them adequately. This amounts to making the best of limited options, of course, because it is only through taking on these identities that we are allowed to participate at all in what Disney designates as our culture; refusing or failing to do so means being completely left out of the park's totalizing picture of "America" or the "future." The very process of acquiring these identities—consumer, national subject, heterosexual "family member"—reproduces power relations, specifically those of the dominant capitalist ideology that shaped them and made them interdependent in the first place.

In order, then, for Disney World, and especially EPCOT, to be successful—that is, for a trip there to be fun—the park's visitors must perform complex ideological maneuvers that allow them to see themselves in the representations of American life offered there, and to find those representations entertaining or, in Disney's words, instructive. As this is not a simple top-down process, neither is it necessarily a sure one. It's easy to spot those who come to Disney World just to make a point of their alienation from it. There aren't many, but they are there. What's harder to uncover is whether visitors refigure the requirements of these subject positions to fit the specifics of their own lives or evade them altogether without at the same time seeing themselves as fundamentally disqualified from the life shown in the park. I'm interested in both of these maneuvers: how the pleasure we feel at Walt Disney World is negotiated through an ongoing process of identification with and—at least in part, one hopes—evasion of the ideal subject constructed by Disney's tireless Imagineers.

According to Guy Debord, one function of the spectacle is to make a culture forget itself—forget its own history, the questions it asks of itself in order to get from here to there, even its notions of what here and there are and why we want or need to move between them. Certainly Walt Disney World participates in this process: free floating between a nostalgic past and an endless future of "progress"—though never quite touching base in the present—Walt Disney World confronts its visitors with a narrative of itself and invites us to see ourselves and our history in the workings of its own. At EPCOT, this story is epical, an ongoing tale of social advancement in which technology and its corporate sponsors are both the agent and the product of the history it writes. The rest of us are encouraged to look on, consume it visually, and take it home as such: technological power as manifest

Courtesy of Karen Klugman.

destiny whose telos radically excludes our direct participation, creativity, and control.

In this environment, whatever fantasy or desires one brings to the park get co-opted and structured immediately by what's already there. Throughout Disney World and especially at EPCOT, the various attractions showcasing what is supposed to be technology for the future tend to advertise their wares in dramatic homilies to that which is. The only potential objects for desire and fantasy in this arrangement are technology and a culture devoted to it. Each of the major attractions at Future World documents variously the same unfolding story of steady and inevitable progress from some prehistory, a.k.a. "the dawn of time," toward "a future of amazing technological creativity . . . of adventure and discovery . . . of awareness and understanding." The nominal form is not accidental; one continually hears of this future of "creativity" and "understanding" without ever hearing who will create what or what will be understood by whom. History is repeatedly read as the evolution of machines and, when unavoidable, the people whose lives are attached to them and inevitably benefited thereby. The whole experience is rather like watching the Gulf War at home, where our investment as citizens with events taking place was consistently characterized by both the military and media in terms of the performance of our weapons. As one survey conducted in the midst of the war indicated, more Americans could identify Patriot and Scud missiles than they could Sadaam Hussein. In EPCOT, it is this conversation, the sound of commodities talking to each other, that the rest of us are invited to overhear.

10   And so in "The Land" we learn that "the land is our partner" and we need to "listen to what it can teach us," the primary example of which is computerized irrigation in the service of agribusiness, Kraft specifically, whose "partnership" with various unpopulated and unspecified locales—the rain forest, "the desert," even the moon, here made equal in kind—presumably teaches it how to get along and prosper. No relationship to the land other than commercial use

by business is posited as possible or even desirable. In General Motor's "World of Motion," history follows a direct line of descent from "transportation" via empire to "freedom," assuring us that "[w]hen it comes to transportation, it's always fun to be free" and concluding, in case anyone missed the point, in an actual GM showroom with (live) sales representatives ready to show you how to buy freedom. It's too easy to pull out similar examples in other attractions: Exxon's "Universe of Energy" takes you through a prehistoric romp with the dinosaurs to some vague generality about a future void of oil spills and energy shortages somehow made possible without the use of solar power, while AT&T's "Spaceship Earth" traces the history of the world as the history of communication devices.

The conclusions to these tales of progress are always curiously left unspecified, perhaps as a sop to the "imagination" glorified throughout the park and the ostensible goal of its creation. Inevitably, though, people drop out of the picture and are replaced entirely by some technological wonder or simply the mystical speculation of it. The typical "ride"—one hesitates about what to call these—ends in some variation of total darkness, dazzling though equally blinding light, or the ubiquitous grid, all three presumably representative of a future of endless choices and possibilities in the "cityscapes" we are soon to inhabit. These are worlds where people literally cannot be represented, which is perhaps just as well since, given the direction the attractions take to that point, the sight could not be pretty: in the future everything will be done for us by technology and its purveyors, and we will dwell, no doubt, in "awareness" and "understanding" of that fact.

What we know now is that regardless of what new horizon these rides take us to, it will necessarily be "more complex" than what we have had and, consequently, "more exciting" in large part because it will provide "more choices." This, at least, is the explicit message of the Magic Kingdom's "Carousel of Progress" and the implicit message of most everything else in the park. Not only will all social relations be mediated by stuff—in "Carousel of Progress," a history of exploiting and then "freeing" women's labor is traced in the development of electrical appliances—but all of the problems facing this country and begging for its attention are seemingly solved solely by the range of goods that will be available to and for us. Because the world according to Disney is so alienating and because in its historical narratives and predictions for the future we are so thoroughly secondary, any identification with these scenes necessarily takes place on the axis of consumption and use of the technological devices we do not appear to have any say in developing. In a world where everyone is identified as consumers, fantasy is either attached to commodities (the well-being of which supposedly defines our own) or supplanted altogether by "imagination" or—its correlative in the park—technical expertise, which is not our own either.

The fantasy of the Magic Kingdom is largely not of our making but that of the robots (both Disney's famed Audio-Animatronics and the equally uncanny human guides) who perform stories already scripted or accompany us down "lost" paths toward already discovered "hidden" surprises and sights. There's no better example of this than the Magic Kingdom's "Jungle Cruise," where lions and restless natives appear on cue and just as conveniently disappear. As Louis Marin points out, Disney "reduces the dynamic organization of places" to a "univocal scheme allowing only the same redundant behavior." This is the case even on "Tom Sawyer's Island," where the winding, wooded trails and relative seclusion suggest more potential for freedom and discovery than it can actually provide: eventually all paths return you to Aunt Polly's Landing and her $1.50 glass of lemonade.

In the "hands-on" attractions of Future World's Communicore East and West, the pleasure of using new devices is offset by the fact that "use" consists mainly of momentary contact with machines created and otherwise run by someone else. The only really fun games at EPCOT are in "Journey into Imagination," and these are less "educational" or "adult" and more "for children": coloring on the wall with light, making music by stepping on different squares programmed to produce various sounds, looking through a giant kaleidoscope, conducting a computerized orchestra. Elsewhere, the computer games reproduce on a smaller scale the lessons of all the larger attractions. Though touted as educational and fun, most of them are a monumental bore: civics lessons or spiffier versions of the Home Shopping Network. At the "Fountain of Information" we're told that "the next best thing to being there is shopping there" and subsequently presented with the technology to participate in an auction by satellite. "Home Smart Home" illustrates technological devices for the home of the future, presuming, I guess, that we'll all have one. One game tests your skill in planning flight paths and schedules for a major airline. Another asks you to deal with the complexities of manufacturing by assembling a United States flag from parts moving rapidly across a screen as the machine reminds you that "getting the right parts in the right places, that's manufacturing." Since it's difficult to successfully complete either of these tasks, the effect of both games is to impress us with the skill and wherewithal of the computers normally performing them. Beyond that, the point of the computer games is apparently to dazzle us with their access to information and powers of recall. You can "Dial an Expert" for generic answers to questions you haven't asked. You can type in your birthday and receive useless information based on specious assumptions: how many hours you've slept in your life, the number of meals you've eaten, how many tons of food. A game purporting to demonstrate research technology instead provides tourist promos for all fifty U.S. states and selected individual cities, Puerto Rico, and Guam.

Many of these games suffer from the same problem: they operate from a limited menu of options from which to choose and consequently grow tiresome once you realize you can't use them as a real research tool or helpful device. 15

For example, in the game offering information on each state, it's impossible to get anything from certain areas: cities and coasts are OK; but if it's the upper Midwest you want to know about, forget it. In another, we're invited to make a music video, but rather than actually letting us do that, the screen requests choices for lead singer (white man, white woman, or black man), type of music, etc., and then constructs the finished video for us, usually to comic effect.

This is a far cry from Coney Island, where one could pay a few pennies to smash fake china and crystal in a mock-up of a typical high bourgeois Victorian parlor. The games at Coney depended in part on the thrill of doing something you otherwise couldn't but may have wanted to: express openly an alienated and hostile relationship to commodities and the frustrations associated with a life in which you maybe had fewer of them. The barker proclaimed, "If you can't break up your own home, break up ours," perhaps missing the point that at least part of the desire was for the opportunity to break up other people's homes. The games at Disney, however, are much different: rather than providing opportunities to violate social proprieties, everything in the park is designed to confirm them and make doing so fun. This is done partly by turning what is now for many people a piece of technology associated not with creativity and personal use, but with the drudgery of wage-labor—the computer terminal—into an item of fun without at the same time significantly altering their actual relationship to it: as with data entry, one simply selects from a predetermined list of options and fills in the blanks accordingly. This attempt to convert everyday items and activities into "themed" fun is made throughout Disney World, often to the point of banality. What, for example, is the "fun" or "fantasy" of GM's showroom? Elsewhere the exciting new information we're given about our world or its future is either hopelessly outdated or already available from traditional sources. As we left the introductory film at "The Living Seas" and prepared to enter "Sea Base Alpha," a prototype of an undersea research facility, one man

remarked to me only half in jest, "I could have stayed home with my *National Geographic*." Either the technology we're shown is not new at all or exposure to it does not allow anyone to take information or experience from it to their own lives and see the transformative effects therein.

Perhaps the most significant difference between Disney World and earlier amusement parks is in opportunities for direct participation in the "events" and construction of their meaning. One of the chief motivations for visiting Coney and the primary focus of attacks against it was that the place was a relatively unregulated social setting. The rides encouraged, indeed required, close physical contact, frequently between strangers, and made the spectacle of their interaction the object of entertainment for other visitors waiting to board. Part of the fun of Coney was to watch people embarrass themselves, usually in some physical way—falling onto or being jostled against each other, clothes flying up, etc.—before becoming yourself the embarrassed object of their fun. The heightened sense of sexual opportunity inherent in this situation was augmented by the feeling throughout the park and confirmed by its visitors that it was always open season for dating, casual encounters, or sexual fantasy. If fantasy is one of several "lands" in Disney World, it was the norm at Coney Island. John Kasson documents examples of young women visiting Coney Island in the guise of bourgeois ladies rather than the mundane office or factory workers they were and, once there, either pursuing relationships befitting their new station or working a bit of class privilege on the men and women with whom they would otherwise be associated.

At Walt Disney World, such contact with other people is only minimally available and not at all desirable. Most of the rides are intentionally designed to disallow seeing anyone—much less touching or talking to them—other than who you're sitting immediately next to and probably came with. (Those who visit the park alone, as I have, are typically kept separate and alone.) As Margaret King has noted, the vehicles turn on cue, focusing attention away from other people and toward whatever new screen or display is next in line. It is often impossible to see anything other than what the car's perspective affords, and the theater-like darkness reinforces the feeling that one is essentially watching a movie alone. Consistent with the park's often noted goal of using architecture and layout to control and ultimately inhibit movement, all the attractions force visitors to watch the programmed movements of Audio-Animatronic robots while remaining themselves immobilized.

This is given a new twist at the new Disney-MGM Studios, where video screens punctuate every turn in the lines and direct the attention of waiting visitors away from each other (and any possible exchanges or flirting they might engage in) and toward one "adformational" piece or another. If you're waiting in line for twenty-five minutes, you might see the same chatty narration four or five times. The people in lines at MGM resemble those in photographs of theater audiences decked in 3-D glasses. The common perspective created by the glasses and screen produces in the audience the same posture and tilt of the head: up, away, lightly out of kilter. The effect is both to limit the movement of many people and to regularize it, to take a basically stationary experience and make it even more so—everyone manages to look, perhaps paradoxically, both mass-produced and bovine. At least some people are aware of this; as we plowed our way forward in the line for "The Great Movie Ride," eyes upturned to the trusty video screen, one young man intoned in a mock-serious voice, "No mooing please, no mooing."

20   Where active audience participation is incorporated into the show, it's minor, kept out of focus, and finally beside the point. A family is selected to be Honorary Grand Marshals of one of the Magic Kingdom's parades—they wave absently from their seat at the front of a float, effectively kept from seeing the parade, which is unfortunate for them since the parades at Disney are among the best events there. In Tomorrowland Theater, members of the audience are pulled on stage, dressed in Disney shirts and Roger Rabbit ears, and then virtually ignored. The awful big dance numbers continue around them as they try to follow the steps. This would be similar to the use of other people's embarrassment as part of the ride at Coney except that nothing is really made of them by the cast; there is no fun either with them or at their expense. From the audience's perspective, it's too easy just to ignore them because they aren't integrated into the show and because it's more fun to watch Mickey, Minnie, Roger, and the rest than to watch any of the dancers, professional or otherwise. In MGM Studios, this happens again when kids from the audience are selected for a reshooting of a scene from *Honey, I Shrunk the Kids:* the actual antics of them pretending to fly on a giant bug are ignored, and everyone watches instead the omnipresent screen where their flight has been rendered realistically. What we're supposed to be watching and enjoying is not our children having fun, but the technology of film production.

This lack of genuine participation at Disney in any capacity other than viewer mirrors our lack of participation both in the future we're told is always just around the corner and in the computer games, the mechanics of which prepare us for life in it. Moreover, any erotic potential inherent in an amusement park environment is channeled at EPCOT into consumption as well, either of these images of the future and the technology required to produce it or of the merchandise actually sold in the park. If we find these attractions and games pleasurable—at least in terms of the pleasure they are courting—then we are assuming the world they present as given, which in turn requires identifying ourselves in it in the only role available: technology's beneficiary, its grateful consumer. Because failing or resisting identification as consumers results in absenting ourselves from the "future," what we're buying is time in it. Refusal to do so reveals the true horror of that future and leaves us no recourse to illusions; we either identify as consumers, or we're just left out. Any other investments we may have in ourselves, individually or collectively, have to be ignored or forgotten.

Courtesy of Karen Klugman.

Re-reading/Conversations with the Text

1. In this excerpt, Kuenz suggests that the dominant pleasures offered to Disney World's visitors are identification and recognition. Re-read the excerpt, paying careful attention to the various forms of identification and recognition Kuenz describes. Can you think of other forms she does not address here? How might these alter or supplement Kuenz's view of Disney World?

2. Re-read the second section of "It's a Small World After All." Kuenz begins this section with an idea from a prominent twentieth-century philosopher, Guy Debord: "One function of the spectacle is to make a culture forget itself." For 10 minutes, freewrite about this statement, considering what Debord means by "forget" and what the "spectacle" of Disney World allows visitors to "forget." After those 10 minutes, discuss and compare your ideas in pairs. With your partner, develop an analytical thesis based on your writing about how and what Disney World allows visitors to "forget."

3. Kuenz suggests that at Disney World, one of the only identifications available to visitors is that of the consumer: "We either identify as consumers, or we're just left out." But she also suggests that we *want* to identify as consumers; that is, we want the pleasure of being recognized as consumers, and the pleasure of belonging to a recognizable group. Re-read the essay, finding at least ten examples of how, according to Kuenz, Disney World asks us to identify as consumers. In small groups, discuss how, in each case, the visitor is able to find pleasure in consumption. Can you think of any ways in which such consumption can be experienced as *unpleasurable?* Explain.

Re-seeing and Re-writing

1. Kuenz compares and contrasts Disney World with Coney Island, a theme park constructed in the nineteenth century that, unlike Disney, "provide[d] opportunities to violate social proprieties." Keeping this in mind, spend some time perusing the photographs and other historical materials featured on The Coney Island Pages of the "Amusement Park History" Web page (history .amusement-parks.com/coneyislandpages.htm). Then, visit Disney World's official Web page (disneyworld.disney.go.com/). Based on the visual representations of each park, does Kuenz's argument seem to hold up? What other differences can you find between the two parks? Can you find any similarities between them? Develop a comparative analysis of the Web sites.

2. In this excerpt, Kuenz describes visitors to Disney World using several categories: consumer, heterosexual, family member, national subject, woman or man. She does *not,* however, address another major category of visitors: children. This assignment asks you to consider how Disney World markets to children, and whether it does so according to the categories outlined by Kuenz. You may draw upon any number of source materials in order to develop your analysis, including print or television advertisements, Disney World's Web site (disneyworld.disney.go.com/), or, if you have visited the park and you have them, the programs and brochures offered during your visit. You might use the following questions as starting points: In what way(s) does Disney World market directly to children, and in what way(s) does it market to their parents? Does it market to both simultaneously? Does Disney World imagine children as consumers? As girls or boys (gendered subjects)? As family members? As (already) heterosexual? As national subjects?

Intertext

"It's a Small World After All," like Jamaica Kincaid's "A Small Place," asks about the sources of pleasure experienced by tourists. Review both essays, noting how each author imagines touristic pleasure. What are the similarities, and what are the differences? What might account for these differences—for example, how do the geographical locations of each destination make a difference? Might some of Kincaid's observations about tourists to Antigua apply to Disney World visitors, or vice versa?

Research Prompts
TRAVELING GAZES: Shaping Mobile Identities

KEY RHETORICAL CONCEPTS

identification
difference

Option #1:

Mobile Identities and Diversity in Mainstream Television

Select two or three mainstream TV sitcoms or "reality" shows that you can watch and carefully analyze more than once. Using the key rhetorical concepts of identification and difference, consider the representational patterns of class, gender, sexuality, and/or race that each show promotes. For instance, you could look at the portrayal of young professional white women in *Friends,* the representation of gay men in *Will & Grace,* the representation of ethnic minorities in *Law and Order,* or the (re)construction of identities as depicted on extreme makeover shows or now-classic reruns such as *Survivor.* What conceptions of identity and difference characterize these shows? Are audiences made to identify with particular characters? Why? Why not? What can you glean about identity and diversity in the United States from these shows, and how might they affect the way we think about our society and our role as members of this society? What insights do your secondary sources enable you to make about these issues? How does your analysis extend, complicate, or challenge secondary readings on the subject?

Option #2:

Tourist Sites and Vacations

For this option, you will analyze how the same vacation spots are presented and represented by travel agencies, as compared to their representation in the news or alternative media. To accomplish this, you'll need to narrow your inquiry to a particular historical period. For example, you might consider how travel agencies and the New York City Department of Commerce have marketed New York City post 9/11, as compared to news media's representations of the city. To what degree does the news media support or make problematic the travel agencies' representation of identity and diversity? What does the news media highlight that the travel agencies ignore? What rhetorical patterns characterize the representation of the city in travel brochures and in the news? What insights do your secondary sources enable you to make about these rhetorical patterns? How does your analysis extend, complicate, or challenge secondary readings on the subject?

Option #3:

Seeing Differently/Cultivating Change

This prompt asks you to examine the rhetoric of a particular advocacy or activist group. You might, for example, analyze the rhetorical strategies of the anti-smoking "Truth" campaign, PETA, NRA, NAACP, NOW, ACLU, Amnesty International, anti-Sweatshop/WTO protestors, or any local or university advocacy groups. To what event(s) or issue(s) are they responding? How do they frame their approach to this event or issue? As you "read" these texts, consider the following questions: In what ways does the group seem to employ rhetorical strategies of identification or difference? Are there particular patterns that you notice? What does this reveal? Does the group use visual images as a form of persuasion? What is the relation between the visual and written texts? You might also consider how mainstream media portray these advocacy/activist groups and the implications of these representations in terms of the group's reliability, accessibility, and persuasiveness. How does your analysis extend, complicate, or challenge secondary readings on the subject?

> *Consumption is the sole end and purpose of all production; and the interest of the producer ought to be attended to, only so far as it may be necessary for promoting that of the consumer.*
>
> ADAM SMITH, *THE WEALTH OF NATIONS,* 1776

KEY RHETORICAL CONCEPTS

the appeals: *logos   pathos   ethos*

Consumer Appeal

IN THE UNITED STATES, WE CONSUME BECAUSE WE CAN. CONSUMPTION appeals to us. Representing the world's largest gross national product, we are encouraged at every turn to consume lest the economic wheels stop turning. We must be made to desire things in order to consume them; yet the desire to consume often incurs debt. Author and TV/film producer Michael Moore characterizes our desire/debt dilemma:

> The average working American earns about $24,420 a year. The average household has a yearly income of about $30,000—and carries a debt of $33,000. That's a deficit of $3,000. . . . The total consumer debt in America is just under $5 trillion—virtually the same amount as the federal debt! . . .
>
> We live in an economic system that not only encourages debt but demands it. If we weren't willing to take out loans and pay huge financing charges to banks, those institutions would go under. If we didn't have credit cards so we could go to stores and buy things we can't afford,

those stores would go under. Without us living our lives in perpetual debt, the system would collapse. Want a house? Take out a loan, go into debt! Want a car? Take out a loan, go into debt![1]

Caught between desire and debt, some of us seek to control our own consumption. One way we have done this is to take a hard look at ourselves—to gaze inward, we might say—and recognize our own identities as consumers. This informed self-identification is what long-time consumer advocate Ralph Nader has always wanted for U.S. consumers; as his biographer David Bollier explains it, Nader believes "that the consumer—active, informed, questioning—could play a critical, transforming role in making business, government and other powerful institutions more accountable to the American people."[2]

Nader's campaigns for "informed consumerism" and "consumer advocacy" attempt to create what has been called a "consumer-side economy." Such consumerism challenges the "supply-side economy," an economy that necessarily favors producers over consumers. (Nader's work is ongoing: see www.nader.org.) Nader's ideas on this subject are hardly new: This consumer-side economy is the same economy advocated by influential social theorist and economist Adam Smith—considered by many to be the father of modern capitalist economics—in his 1776 book, *The Wealth of Nations*.

As consumers, the thinking goes, we have power: the power to gaze, the power to own, the power not to consume, the power to choose. Wise use of this power, however, requires knowledge—which, ironically, requires consumption. Some of us pay, for example, for consumer reports on products and purchases we want or already have. We buy books about how to buy things better because we desire not only to consume, but to be better consumers. We can purchase credit reports of our own consumer history in order, more or less, to tell us what others (producers) already know. We pay for credit counseling—seeking ways to make our consumer profile more desirable to those who produce so that we might go on desiring, gazing, consuming. We participate in consumer opinion polls such as those on American Consumer Opinion, "a worldwide network of people who shape the future through participating in online opinions surveys" (see www.acop.com). We fill out customer satisfaction sheets even at fast food places (short forms, however, lest we linger too long).

Consumption, then, is inextricably linked with power, desire, and debt. Perhaps this is inevitable—both our right and our destiny—as history, culture, and design critic Thomas Hine suggests in a recent book, *I Want That! How We All Became Shoppers:*

> For all people, at least since Neolithic times, things have been repositories of power. Those who possessed key objects have been the rulers and wizards of their peoples. . . . But shopping is our chief exercise of the power of things. . . . It is, child psychologists have observed, one of the earliest ways in which people begin to understand the world and to develop their personalities.[3]

Born to shop? Created to consume? Certainly the producers of all we consume would like us to think so. Yet we are also encouraged at every turn to believe that we have *choice* in our consumption. And behind this choice of one product over another is rhetoric, the art of persuasion. Appeals to our logic, senses, emotions, character, and desires—and our pocketbooks—bond consumer to producer, product to consumer, desire to debt. In contemporary capitalist culture, many of these rhetorical appeals are made visually and are often circular. For even though we may have come to successfully identify ourselves as consumers and to take power in our roles as consumers, we have in doing so prompted producers to think of ever more clever, persuasive, aggressive, and sophisticated ways to appeal to our desires. In other words, we have worked to construct, manipulate, and maintain a **consumer gaze,** which we use here to refer to the rhetorical appeals (emotional, logical, ethical) that link consumers to products and often bond desire to debt.

Logic, Ethics, and Emotion in Ads

As we've seen, in his treatise on the arts of rhetoric, Aristotle outlines three kinds of arguments, which serve as the cornerstones of his theory of rhetorical practice:

- *Logos:* logical argument; an appeal to "reason"
- *Ethos:* ethical argument; an appeal based on the rhetor's (ethical) character
- *Pathos:* emotional argument; an appeal to the emotions of the audience

Consumer advertisements—which are, after all, preeminently persuasive texts—often combine all three appeals. Awareness of how these appeals work, consumer advocates would argue, is a necessary prerequisite for intelligent and responsible participation in a consumer-side economy. A nonprofit group called "AdBusters" considers such "awareness-building" one of its primary missions. Consider, for example, Figure 6.1:

Figure 6.1   Sweatshop Sneaker.
Courtesy of Adbusters.org.

Critical Frame

The point of this ad—an Adbusters' spoof of Nike ads—is not to persuade us to buy sneakers, but rather to question Nike's business and advertising practices, by using appeals to logic, ethics, and emotion:

- Logic: Why should a company like Nike charge over 300 times as much for a product as it costs to produce it?
- Ethics: Is it ethical to charge so much? More to the point, is it ethical to pay so little to the laborers in the sweatshop?
- Emotion: How do we as consumers feel about being involved in such questionable business practices? Is a "cool" sneaker worth it? (And, by the way, does the sneaker look as "cool" with the "swoosh" blacked out?)

The Nike "swoosh" is one of the primary targets of Adbusters' "Blackspot" and "Unbrand America" campaigns. In the Adbusters' campaigns, the black, unattractive "anti-sneaker" serves as their visual icon. Through the use of this anti-sneaker and a revision of other facets of the Nike image, Adbusters offers its counter-rhetoric in response to the strategies Nike itself has used in trying to establish a rhetorical community around its particular vision of "cool." Consider, for example, the counter-rhetoric in this ad (Figure 6.2) that builds upon the key concepts of *running, work,* and *being cool.*

Figure 6.2   Adbusters parody of Nike ad.

Courtesy of Adbusters.org.

The rhetoric of this ad—image and words together—employs an ethical, emotional, and logical argument against buying Nike sneakers. Of course, this argument is not limited just to the decision to buy or not to buy a pair of sneakers:

- It is about the politics of labor. (Nike products are not made in the United States and Nike's labor and employment practices in developing countries are fairly well-known as less than exemplary.)
- It is about what sports (or a sports-like image) means in U.S. society.
- It is about the recognition of the Nike brand and its "swoosh" label (the power of a successful icon), which has a rippling connotative, metaphorical force.
- It's about putting forth an already pervasive idea in our culture about fashion and its close ties to social status.
- It's about difference and identification: The viewer is asked to register the difference between the laborer shown and the active, fit person in the ad to which the Adbuster ad refers; at the same time, the viewer is encouraged to identify with the laborer, and differentiate himself/herself from the sort of person who would exploit her.

Consuming College

We consume more than just conventional, store-bought goods. An education, for example, can be thought of as a consumer item. In making the choice of which college to attend—and why and how one should (or shouldn't) attend it—we're exercising many of the same skills as the consumer choosing between two cars at a dealership. Most Americans, in fact, have come to think about "buying [their] education" rather than "earning [an] education." Consider the ways that you, and others you know, have made choices about college—

- About which one to attend in the first place.
- About which courses to take—and why and when to take them.
- About which instructors to seek out or avoid.
- About which major or career becomes your path and goal.
- About where to live while you complete (and consume) your college education.

It is quite likely that any or all of these choices have been connected to an imagined, real, or desired financial present or future for yourself. In making these choices then, you have been consuming education.

Consider what logical, ethical, or emotional appeals drew you most toward the college you're attending now. How did you inform yourself as a potential consumer of higher education about what institution might suit you? There is no shortage of guides for selecting an institution of higher education; perhaps you used some of these when you began your quest for the right college. At Peterson's online guide to colleges, for example, you can search by targeting any of the following areas: location, major, tuition, size, student/faculty (ratio, quality), GPA (average of students there; what is required for admissions), sports, religion.

What does it mean to consume a college education based on any one (or more) of these major categories? Some colleges are said to draw students based on their location primarily—a location that often helps create a certain kind of character (*ethos*). A college might also create strong appeals (whether logical, ethical, or emotional) based on the type of college it is. Gallaudet University in Washington, DC, for example, is the world's only liberal arts college for students who are deaf and hard-of-hearing. Students who are deaf and hard-of-hearing come from all over the world to attend Gallaudet, not even so much for the kind of education they will get as for the experience of learning about and participating in "Deaf culture."

The Gallaudet University Web site[4] opens with "prospective students" as the first available button. Once clicked, this button reveals a page titled "Choose Gallaudet" that lists eight reasons a student might choose Gallaudet for her or his higher education experience. The first page, for example, is entitled "The Gallaudet Experience." It opens to tell us more about "A Community of Possibilities" and the uniqueness of the world's only liberal arts college where a commitment to signed communication is the key credo for the university.

> Gallaudet is the world's only university that brings together deaf, hard of hearing, and hearing students as well as faculty in the common pursuit of education. The Gallaudet community lives by the tenets it explicitly states in its "Commitment to Sign Communication:"
>
> We have the right and responsibility to understand and be understood. Clear and well-paced visual communication is a requirement for this learning community.
>
> We will respect the sign language style of every individual and use whatever is necessary to communicate in a given situation.
>
> We will be assertive and sincere in our efforts to attain sign language proficiency so we can communicate directly with each other.
>
> There is no linguistic minority at Gallaudet. Every member of the Gallaudet community enjoys the respect and the commitment to sign.
>
> When you look back upon your years at Gallaudet, what will you remember first? Freshman hallmates? Winning the intramural volleyball championship? Taking naps on Olmsted Green on warm spring days? Finally turning in the thesis you've worked on for six months? Chatting with your friends around the Rockwell sculpture?
>
> Or maybe your favorite memory will simply be of living in a community where you could meet anyone you want, do anything you want, and become anything you want.
>
> This is your university. This is your community. Choose Gallaudet.[5]

Choice, as Adam Smith suggested, is one of the hallmarks of a capitalist economy. Here, in Gallaudet University's "credo," choice serves as a powerful standard on which to base an argument. This key page for "prospective students" at Gallaudet's Web site combines visual and verbal rhetoric to appeal to an audience of communication-conscious college consumers. The emotionally tinted uniqueness of the Gallaudet experience—"yet Gallaudet boasts a university community unlike any other"—is also blended well logically and ethically with "selling points" any prospective student might desire: the "pursuit of education," "commitment" (repeated many times over), "respect," and "community."

Morever, each of these strong bases of appeal forms the fabric for further emotional, ethical, and logical appeals. For example, the link for "The Gallaudet Experience" discusses the university's outstanding academics; its status as an "e-quipped university"; the career opportunities available for its graduates; the arts and athletics opportunities available; the university's position on celebrating diversity; and finally, its exciting location in the heart of Washington, DC.

The image in Figure 6.3 (one in a rotating series) that appeared on the Gallaudet University homepage in 2005 bolsters the textual appeals to the school's uniqueness, location, community, and communication. A Gallaudet student serving as a tour guide stands next to the famous statue of the college's founder, the Reverend Thomas Hopkins Gallaudet, with his deaf student, Alice Cogswell. Indeed, the focus of this photographic image is split between the Gallaudet/Alice statue and the sign-ing and most likely deaf student-guide. While we are connecting history with the present through this split, but shared, focus, we are also assured that the modern world is present in the form of a car whisking by on Florida Avenue, directly outside the Gallaudet campus gates. Inside the gates, however, the scene seems serene and park-like (as indicated by the bench and the cultivated, clean grounds).

A venerable history and the importance of place and (signed) communication thus flood this late afternoon "orientation" image of Gallaudet University. Further, the university's unique place in our nation's capital, Washington, DC, is presented as a positive appeal by including the blossoming cherry trees in the background. Cap-turing the familiar sight of a campus orientation tour also guides our gaze on this

Figure 6.3   Image from Gallaudet University's Web site (www.gallaudet.edu), July 2005.
Courtesy of Zhou Fang/Gallaudet University.

Critical Frame

image; we are assured that although Gallaudet University may be unique (orientation is conducted in sign language here) it is also familiar: Students (as indicated visually by their backpacks) and parents still gather together on this campus to endure the ritual of college orientation tours.

College Web sites must typically accommodate many different kinds of potential visitors (e.g., alumni, corporate sponsors, research funders, potential students, new faculty). In part, this broad appeal is why they often change so frequently as they make efforts to reach all their available audiences. Such constant change also reflects their appeal to "advancement" and being on "the cutting edge." Finally, this routine freshening of the college's website encourages constant consumption of the site in order to keep up with what's new at that U. Educational institutions must cater to many different audiences, and they must use all the available means of persuasion to connect with this varied audience.

For example, an alumnus might visit a website to see what has changed or to try looking up an old professor or former classmate. This alumnus may even be browsing the college website to see what is happening there that is worthy of a contribution—to explore what seems the best use of development dollars he or she may be thinking of donating. In this way, alumni—those who once consumed the university's education—contribute to the construction of that college as a desirable product. Similarly, businesses, corporations, and community organizations might go to a college's Web site when considering deals they might make, encourage, or sever at that institution. Finally, as in the example of the Gallaudet University site, prospective students may tour college Web sites looking for reasons to choose this institution—that is, to embrace this institution's rhetorical vision.

Thus, a college Web site encourages consumption by appealing to multiple audiences for multiple purposes and offering, as it were, multiple appeals. The site must appeal to these various shoppers and potential consumers emotionally, logically, and ethically. It must both call on memory and create memory, drawing the repeat consumer (the alumnus) back, and encouraging the potential consumer (the new student) to commit to a future there, in part by connecting to the college's memorable past. A Web site like this must, in short, tell a story, creating a narrative of place that makes its visitors want to participate.

For example, consider the visual representation of a university as a building with walls covered in ivy. This appeal employs both *ethos* and *pathos,* by communicating that the school is a venerable institution (ethos) and by drawing on the audience's emotional desire to be part of an exclusive ("ivy league") education (*pathos*). Likewise, college names and traditions, as well as their slogans, songs, and mascots, often function as metaphors or metonymic markers for things outside the college itself (see Chapter 4). Colleges often aim to create portraits of themselves as vessels of national culture, even as they present themselves as little nations—and worlds—all their own. The Washington, DC–based, cherry-blossom-covered, gated/protected, clean and well-cultivated, historic yet modern, and uniquely sign-language-centered world of Gallaudet University presented in the image above creates just such a portrait.

The Ohio State University Web site (http://www.osu.edu/) also illustrates an awareness of the multiple gazes projected by visitors to the site. The opening layout of the site[6] resembles a family album; the three key images on the main page feature people engaged in some seemingly pleasurable activity (which, although work/university-related, still seems playful). These three images carry photo-album like captions that allude to a much larger story behind the image than the image alone could capture. The three stories also feature, in randomized rotation, OSU students and faculty in close relationship to each other; in such relational depictions, the OSU Web site emotionally echoes the "family" feeling the university would like to promote.

The feature stories at the Ohio State University website include such things as stories about key community members in the central Ohio area, accomplished or award-winning alumni, important visiting scholars or speakers, and major administrative changes. In these kinds of stories, the university effectively gathers extended "family members" (an appeal to *pathos*), while it also creates a logical record of major narrative moments and key events in its history and in its present. These feature stories and images record, in effect, the significant events of the university's (family's) members and its "life."

In a more literal link to OSU's "family," images are often used to advertise or document Ohio State's commitment to women and girls via "Take a Daughter to Work Day," held on campus on the last Thursday in April. These images offer a kind of domestic mother-daughter family photo with a public educational twist. Thus, Ohio State is demonstrated as a good place for not only female faculty and staff members but also for their entire families. In fact, all nine of the Web site photos devoted to the "Take a Daughter to Work Day" in April 2002 featured young (pre-college age) girls, rapt with attention and wonder, in an Ohio State lab or classroom. The repeated intent focus of the young female learner in these images invites potential students to identify themselves here.

In choosing to represent women—particularly (academic) older women (who might be mothers)—overseeing the interests of younger women (who might be daughters), the "Take a Daughter to Work Day" image crafts a corporate *ethos* for the university that suggests that women are encouraged, looked after, and engaged in fun-but-meaningful activities at this university. What isn't shown, however, are such issues as Ohio State's long-standing lack of a maternity leave policy or flexible work schedules for mothers with young children, its relatively small university day care center, and some of its less creditable statistics with regard to women—for example, that the percentage of women as members of central administration or occupying the rank of full professor is less than 20 percent.

As we can see from the examples of Gallaudet and Ohio State, colleges create their own kind of (corporate) *ethos* as they work to assure their diverse consuming constituents—e.g., faculty, students, staff, parents, alumni, community members—that they are ethically, emotionally, and logically "good places" to invest in, spend tax and personal dollars in, get an education from, make new relationships at, develop one's (self- and community) identity at, create a career from, spend significant years of one's life at, and entrust one's child to.

As you "consume" this unit, and as you are positioned as consumers elsewhere, consider the following questions:

- Who does the text (graphic and/or written) seem to target?
- What desire(s) does the text tap into? What are the consumers expected to consume?
- Who or what does the text ask you to identify with? To distance yourself from?
- How is the product and the process of consuming made appealing?
- What emotions does the producer call upon in attempting to "sell" the product? What emotions seem located in the product or its use? What emotions seem expected of the potential consumer?
- What logic is employed in attempts to interest potential consumers in the product? What seems "logical" about getting, having, owning, using the product?
- How do the producers of the product present themselves? What kind of character do they attempt to establish? What kind of character is suggested for the consumer who might "gain" from having, owning, or using the product?

NOTES

1. Michael Moore, *Downsize This!* (New York: Crown, 1996) 137–38.
2. David Bollier, *Citizen Action and Other Big Ideas: A History of Ralph Nader and the Modern Consumer Movement,* Chapter 1, 1 Sept. 2006 <www.nader.org/history/bollier_chapter_1.html>.
3. Thomas Hine, *I Want That! How We All Became Shoppers* (New York: HarperCollins, 2002) 4.
4. This description is current as of July 2005.
5. Gallaudet University, Home page, 1 July 2005 <www.gallaudet.edu>.
6. This description is current as of July 2005.

Critical Frame

The Globetrotting Sneaker

CYNTHIA ENLOE

Activist and academic *CYNTHIA ENLOE* has long been interested in the politics of globalization and its reliance on women's work in factories. In this essay, Enloe examines the contradictory messages that sneaker companies such as Nike and Reebok give to their consumers and workers; she contrasts corporate mission statements that emphasize embracing difference, ending poverty, and promoting health with the corporations' actual business practices, including the use of sweatshops, maintenance of poor working conditions, and the exploitation of workers. Cynthia Enloe is Research Professor of Women's Studies and International Development at Clark University. She is author of *Bananas, Beaches, and Bases* (2000), an exploration of the effects of recent globalization on the lives of women.

Four years after the fall of the Berlin Wall marked the end of the Cold War, Reebok, one of the fastest growing companies in United States history, decided that the time had come to make its mark in Russia. Thus it was with considerable fanfare that Reebok's executives opened their first store in downtown Moscow in July 1993. A week after the grand opening, store managers described sales as well above expectations.

Reebok's opening in Moscow was the perfect post–Cold War scenario: commercial rivalry replacing military posturing; consumerist tastes homogenizing heretofore hostile peoples; capital and managerial expertise flowing freely across newly porous state borders. Russians suddenly had the "freedom" to spend money on U.S. cultural icons like athletic footwear, items priced above and beyond daily subsistence: at the end of 1993, the average Russian earned the equivalent of $40 a month. Shoes on display were in the $100 range. Almost 60 percent of single parents, most of whom were women, were living in poverty. Yet in Moscow and Kiev, shoe promoters had begun targeting children, persuading them to pressure their mothers to spend money on stylish, Western sneakers. And as far as strategy goes, athletic shoe giants have, you might say, a good track record. In the U.S.

many inner-city boys who see basketball as a "ticket out of the ghetto" have become convinced that certain brand-name shoes will give them an edge.

But no matter where sneakers are bought or sold, the potency of their advertising imagery has made it easy to ignore this mundane fact: Shaquille O'Neal's Reeboks are stitched by someone; Michael Jordan's Nikes are stitched by someone; so are your roommate's, so are your grandmother's. Those someones are women, mostly Asian women who are supposed to believe that their "opportunity" to make sneakers for U.S. companies is a sign of their country's progress—just as a Russian woman's chance to spend two months' salary on a pair of shoes for her child allegedly symbolizes the new Russia.

As the global economy expands, sneaker executives are looking to pay women workers less and less, even though the shoes that they produce are capturing an ever-growing share of the footwear market. By the end of 1993, sales in the U.S. alone had reached $11.6 billion. Nike, the largest supplier of athletic footwear in the world, posted a record $298 million profit for 1993—earnings that had nearly tripled in five years. And sneaker companies continue to refine their strategies for "global competitiveness"—hiring supposedly docile women to make their shoes, changing designs as quickly as we fickle customers change our tastes, and shifting factories from country to country as trade barriers rise and fall.

5   The logic of it all is really quite simple; yet trade agreements such as the North American Free Trade Agreement (NAFTA) and the General Agreement on Tariffs and Trade (GATT) are, of course, talked about in a jargon that alienates us, as if they were technical matters fit only for economists and diplomats. The bottom line is that all companies operating overseas depend on trade agreements made between their own governments and the regimes ruling the countries in which they want to make or sell their products. Korean, Indonesian, and other women workers around the world know this bet-ter than anyone. They are tackling trade politics because they have learned from hard experience that the trade deals their governments sign do little to improve the lives of workers. Guarantees of fair, healthy labor practices, of the rights to speak freely and to organize independently, will usually be left out of trade pacts—and women will suffer. The recent passage of both NAFTA and GATT ensures that a growing number of private companies will now be competing across borders without restriction. The result? Big business will step up efforts to pit working women in industrialized countries against much lower-paid working women in "developing" countries, perpetuating the misleading notion that they are inevitable rivals in the global job market.

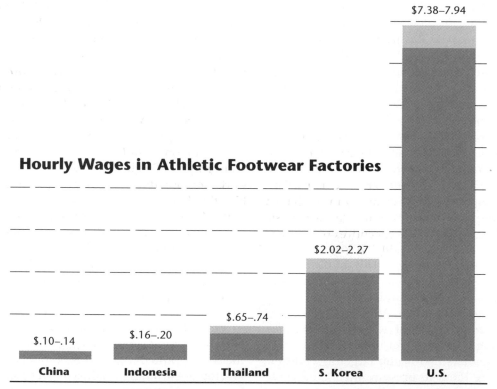

Hourly Wages in Athletic Footwear Factories

$7.38–7.94

$2.02–2.27

$.65–.74

$.10–.14 $.16–.20

China   Indonesia   Thailand   S. Korea   U.S.

Figures are estimates based on 1993 data from the International Textile, Garment, and Leather Workers foundation; International Labor Organization; and the U.S. Bureau of Labor Statistics.

All the "New World Order" really means to corporate giants like athletic shoemakers is that they now have the green light to accelerate long-standing industry practices. In the early 1980s, the field marshals commanding Reebok and Nike, which are both U.S.-based, decided to manufacture most of their sneakers in South Korea and Taiwan, hiring local women. L.A. Gear, Adidas, Fila, and Asics quickly followed their lead. In short time, the coastal city of Pusan, South Korea, became the "sneaker capital of the world." Between 1982 and 1989 the U.S. lost 58,500 footwear jobs to cities like Pusan, which attracted sneaker executives because its location facilitated international transport. More to the point, South Korea's military government had an interest in suppressing labor organizing, and it had a comfortable military alliance with the U.S. Korean women also seemed accepting of Confucian philosophy, which measured a woman's morality by her willingness to work hard for her family's well-being and to acquiesce to her father's and husband's dictates. With their sense of patriotic duty, Korean women seemed the ideal labor force for export-oriented factories.

U.S. and European sneaker company executives were also attracted by the ready supply of eager Korean male entrepreneurs with whom they could make profitable arrangements. This fact was central to Nike's strategy in particular. When they moved their production sites to Asia to lower labor costs, the executives of the Oregon-based company decided to reduce their corporate responsibilities further. Instead of owning factories outright, a more efficient strategy would be to subcontract the manufacturing to wholly foreign-owned—in this case, South Korean—companies. Let them be responsible for workers' health and safety. Let them negotiate with newly emergent unions. Nike would retain control over those parts of sneaker production that gave its officials the greatest professional satisfaction and the ultimate word on the product: design and marketing. Although Nike was following in the footsteps of garment and textile manufacturers, it set the trend for the rest of the athletic footwear industry.

But at the same time, women workers were developing their own strategies. As the South Korean pro-democracy movement grew throughout the 1980s, increasing numbers of women rejected traditional notions of feminine duty. Women began organizing in response to the dangerous working conditions, daily humiliations, and low pay built into their work. Such resistance was profoundly threatening to the government, given the fact that South Korea's emergence as an industrialized "tiger" had depended on women accepting their "role" in growing industries like sneaker manufacture. If women re-imagined their lives as daughters, as wives, as workers, as citizens, it wouldn't just rattle their employers; it would shake the very foundations of the whole political system.

At the first sign of trouble, factory managers called in government riot police to break up employees' meetings. Troops sexually assaulted women workers, stripping, fondling, and raping them "as a control mechanism for suppressing women's engagement in the labor movement," reported Jeong-Lim Nam of Hyosung Women's University in Taegu. It didn't work. It didn't work because the feminist activists in groups like the Korean Women Workers Association (KWWA) helped women understand and deal with the assaults. The KWWA held consciousness-raising sessions in which notions of feminine duty and respectability were tackled along with wages and benefits. They organized independently of the male-led labor unions to ensure that their issues would be taken seriously, in labor negotiations and in the pro-democracy movement as a whole.

The result was that women were at meetings with management, making sure that in addition to issues like long hours and low pay, sexual assault at the hands of managers and health care were on the table. Their activism paid off:

10

in addition to winning the right to organize women's unions, their earnings grew. In 1980, South Korean women in manufacturing jobs earned 45 percent of the wages of their male counterparts; by 1990, they were earning more than 50 percent. Modest though it was, the pay increase was concrete progress, given that the gap between women's and men's manufacturing wages in Japan, Singapore, and Sri Lanka actually *widened* during the 1980s. Last but certainly not least, women's organizing was credited with playing a major role in toppling the country's military regime and forcing open elections in 1987.

Without that special kind of workplace control that only an authoritarian government could offer, sneaker executives knew that it was time to move. In Nike's case, its famous advertising slogan—"Just Do It"—proved truer to its corporate philosophy than its women's "empow-

erment" ad campaign, designed to rally women's athletic (and consumer) spirit. In response to South Korean women workers' new-found activist self-confidence, the sneaker company and its subcontractors began shutting down a number of their South Korean factories in the late 1980s and early 1990s. After bargaining with government officials in nearby China and Indonesia, many Nike subcontractors set up shop in those countries, while some went to Thailand. China's government remains nominally Communist; Indonesia's ruling generals are staunchly anti-Communist. But both are governed by authoritarian regimes who share the belief that if women can be kept hard at work, low paid, and unorganized, they can serve as a magnet for foreign investors.

Where does all this leave South Korean women—or any woman who is threatened with a factory closure if she demands decent work-

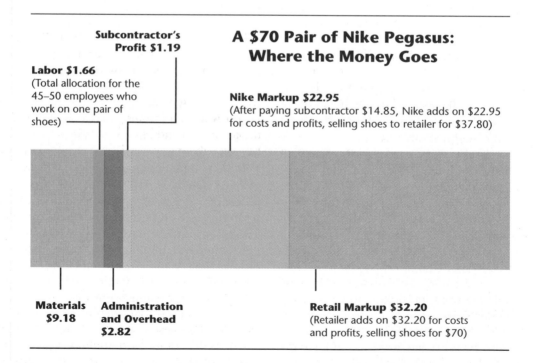

A $70 Pair of Nike Pegasus: Where the Money Goes

Subcontractor's Profit $1.19

Labor $1.66
(Total allocation for the 45–50 employees who work on one pair of shoes)

Nike Markup $22.95
(After paying subcontractor $14.85, Nike adds on $22.95 for costs and profits, selling shoes to retailer for $37.80)

Materials $9.18

Administration and Overhead $2.82

Retail Markup $32.20
(Retailer adds on $32.20 for costs and profits, selling shoes for $70)

ing conditions and a fair wage? They face the dilemma confronted by thousands of women from dozens of countries. The risk of job loss is especially acute in relatively mobile industries; it's easier for a sneaker, garment, or electronics manufacturer to pick up and move than it is for an automaker or a steel producer. In the case of South Korea, poor women had moved from rural villages into the cities searching for jobs to support not only themselves, but parents and siblings. The exodus of manufacturing jobs has forced more women into the growing "entertainment" industry. The kinds of bars and massage parlors offering sexual services that had mushroomed around U.S. military bases during the Cold War have been opening up across the country.

But the reality is that women throughout Asia are organizing, knowing full well the risks involved. Theirs is a long-term view; they are taking direct aim at companies' nomadic advantage, by building links among workers in countries targeted for "development" by multinational corporations. Through sustained grassroots efforts, women are developing the skills and confidence that will make it increasingly difficult to keep their labor cheap. Many looked to the United Nations conference on women in Beijing, China as a rare opportunity to expand their cross-border strategizing.

The Beijing conference will also provide an important opportunity to call world attention to the hypocrisy of the governments and corporations doing business in China. Numerous athletic shoe companies followed Nike in setting up manufacturing sites throughout the country. This included Reebok—a company claiming its share of responsibility for ridding the world of "injustice, poverty, and other ills that gnaw away at the social fabric," according to a statement of corporate principles.

15   Since 1988, Reebok has been giving out annual human rights awards to dissidents from around the world. But it wasn't until 1992 that the company adopted its own "human rights production standards"—after labor advocates made it known that the quality of life in factories run by its subcontractors was just as dismal as that at most other athletic shoe suppliers in Asia. Reebok's code of conduct, for example, includes a pledge to "seek" those subcontractors who respect workers' rights to organize. The only problem is that independent trade unions are banned in China. Reebok has chosen to ignore that fact, even though Chinese dissidents have been the recipients of the company's own human rights award. As for working conditions, Reebok now says it sends its own inspectors to production sites a couple of times a year. But they have easily "missed" what subcontractors are trying to hide—like 400 young women workers locked at night into an overcrowded dormitory near a Reebok-contracted factory in the town of Zhuhai, as reported last August in the *Asian Wall Street Journal Weekly.*

Nike's co-founder and CEO Philip Knight has said that he would like the world to think of Nike as "a company with a soul that recognizes the value of human beings." Nike, like Reebok, says it sends in inspectors from time to time to check up on work conditions at its factories; in Indonesia, those factories are run largely by South Korean subcontractors. But according to Donald Katz in a recent book on the company, Nike spokesman Dave Taylor told an in-house newsletter that the factories are "[the subcontractors'] business to run." For the most part, the company relies on regular reports from subcontractors regarding its "Memorandum of Understanding," which managers must sign, promising to impose "local government standards" for wages, working conditions, treatment of workers, and benefits.

The minimum wage in the Indonesian capital of Jakarta is $1.89 *a day*—among the highest in a country where the minimum wage varies by region. And managers are required to pay only

75 percent of the wage directly; the remainder can be withheld for "benefits." By now, Nike has a well-honed response to growing criticism of its low-cost labor strategy. Such wages should not be seen as exploitative, says Nike, but rather as the first rung on the ladder of economic opportunity that Nike has extended to workers with few options. Otherwise, they'd be out "harvesting coconut meat in the tropical sun," wrote Nike spokesman Dusty Kidd, in a letter to the *Utne Reader*. The all-is-relative response craftily shifts attention away from reality: Nike didn't move to Indonesia to help Indonesians; it moved to ensure that its profit margin continues to grow. And that is pretty much guaranteed in a country where "local standards" for wages rarely take a worker over the poverty line. A 1991 survey by the International Labor Organization (ILO) found that 88 percent of women working at the Jakarta minimum wage at the time—slightly less than a dollar a day—were malnourished.

A woman named Riyanti might have been among the workers surveyed by the ILO. Interviewed by *The Boston Globe* in 1991, she told the reporter who had asked about her long hours and low pay: "I'm happy working here. . . . I can make money and I can make friends." But in fact, the reporter discovered that Riyanti had already joined her coworkers in two strikes, the first to force one of Nike's Korean subcontractors to accept a new women's union and the second to compel managers to pay at least the minimum wage. That Riyanti appeared less than forthcoming about her activities isn't surprising. Many Indonesian factories have military men posted in their front offices who find no fault with managers who tape women's mouths shut to keep them from talking among themselves. They and their superiors have a political reach that extends far beyond the barracks. Indonesia has all the makings for a political explosion, especially since the gap between rich and poor is widening into a chasm. It is in this setting that the government has tried to crack down on any independent labor organizing—a policy that Nike has helped to implement. Referring to a recent strike in a Nike-contracted factory, Tony Nava, Nike representative in Indonesia, told *The Chicago Tribune* in November 1994 that the "troublemakers" had been fired. When asked about Nike policy on the issue, spokesman Keith Peters struck a conciliatory note: "If the government were to allow and encourage independent labor organizing, we would be happy to support it."

Indonesian workers' efforts to create unions independent of governmental control were a surprise to shoe companies. Although their moves from South Korea have been immensely profitable [see chart, previous page], they do not have the sort of immunity from activism that they had expected. In May 1993, the murder of a female labor activist outside Surabaya set off a storm of local and international protest. Even the U.S. State Department was forced to take note in its 1993 worldwide human rights report, describing a system similar to that which generated South Korea's boom 20 years earlier: severely restricted union organizing, security forces used to break up strikes, low wages for men, lower wages for women—complete with government rhetoric celebrating women's contribution to national development.

Yet when President Clinton visited Indonesia, he made only a token effort to address the country's human rights problem. Instead, he touted the benefits of free trade, sounding indeed more enlightened, more in tune with the spirit of the post-Cold War era than do those defenders of protectionist trading policies who coat their rhetoric with "America first" chauvinism. But "free trade" as actually being practiced today is hardly *free* for any workers—in the U.S. or abroad—who have to accept the Indonesian, Chinese, or Korean workplace model as the price of keeping their jobs.

The not-so-new plot of the international trade story has been "divide and rule." If women

20

workers and their government in one country can see that a sneaker company will pick up and leave if their labor demands prove more costly than those in a neighbor country, then women workers will tend to see their neighbors not as regional sisters, but as competitors who can steal their precarious livelihoods. Playing women off against each other is, of course, old hat. Yet it is as essential to international trade politics as is the fine print in GATT.

But women workers allied through networks like the Hong Kong–based Committee for Asian Women are developing their own post-Cold War foreign policy, which means addressing women's needs: how to convince fathers and husbands that a woman going out to organizing meetings at night is not sexually promiscuous; how to develop workplace agendas that respond to family needs; how to work with male unionists who push women's demands to the bottom of their lists; how to build a global movement.

These women refused to stand in awe of the corporate power of the Nike or Reebok or Adidas executive. Growing numbers of Asian women today have concluded that trade politics have to be understood by women on their own terms. They came to Beijing in September 1996, ready to engage with women from other regions to link the politics of consumerism with the politics of manufacturing. If women in Russia and eastern Europe can challenge Americanized consumerism, if Asian activists can solidify their alliances, and if U.S. women can join with them by taking on trade politics—the post–Cold War sneaker may be a less comfortable fit in the 1990s.

Re-reading/Conversations with the Text

1. Trade agreements such as GATT and NAFTA are misunderstood by many U.S. citizens. As Enloe notes, such trade agreements "pit working women in industrialized countries against much lower-paid working women in 'developing' countries." What does Enloe mean by this? Who do you imagine her audience to be? Can you think of examples from your own community of the working women Enloe discusses?

2. Enloe uses a mixture of facts, stories, and charts to make her argument clear. Working in groups of two, summarize Enloe's argument. Next, re-read her essay, considering what appeals (*ethos, pathos,* and/or *logos*) she uses to construct her argument. If you were to present this same data to an audience of investors, or activists, or consumers, what appeals would you use? Why?

3. Enloe describes many of the contradictory practices that sneaker companies employ to sell their shoes. What are some of these practices? Can you think of any others? When corporations give human rights awards, claim to visit sneaker factories, etc. what rhetorical appeals are they using? Who is the audience for such appeals?

Re-seeing and Re-writing

1. Enloe focuses on sneakers, but there are many other companies that have moved their manufacturing sectors overseas to take advantage of cheaper and

less restrictive labor laws. Working in small groups, research the labor practices of other apparel companies. You might consider looking to see where the clothing with your school's logo on it is made, for example. Find two or three companies' practices and then compare these practices with the mission statement expressed on the companies' corporate Web sites. Are there any contradictions? What do they say about the people who make their apparel? Next, gather your findings and put together a presentation that you will share with the rest of your class. Think about what you want them to know about your findings and remember to consider your audience. What sort of rhetorical appeals will be most persuasive to them?

2. Working in a group of about four or five people, look at the labels of all of your clothing. Make a list of where all the items were made. Next, create a map that shows where each item came from and where the headquarters of each clothing company is located. Locate another map that shows the worldwide distribution of income. Present these two maps to your class.

Intertext

This essay addresses many of the same labor issues that Duhamel, Pinsky, and Nye discuss in their poems. Using Enloe's "The Globetrotting Sneaker" as the subject, write a poem modeled after one of the "Sweatshop Poems" in this section of the textbook. Present your poem to the class along with a brief essay documenting how and why you made your rhetorical choices in writing the poem.

Images: Adbusters

The following "spoof" ads—"Aim Higher" and "Ethic-Eze"—appear on the Web site of Adbusters, a (self-described) "global network of artists, activists, writers, pranksters, students, educators and entrepreneurs who want to advance the new social activist movement of the information age" (http://www.adbusters.org/network/about_us.php).

Commercial-Free Schools
Courtesy of Adbusters.org.

Ethic-Eze!
Courtesy of Adbusters.org.

Re-reading/Conversations with the Text

These "spoof ads" from *Adbusters,* the anti-corporate website and print magazine, manipulate the language, images, and branding of popular ad campaigns in order to mock or criticize those products. Look at the ads and generate an analysis of each. What argument does each ad make to the reader/viewer? Who do you imagine might be the audience for the spoof ads? What leads you to that conclusion?

Re-seeing and Re-writing

After looking at the spoof ads in this book, visit the Adbusters website (www.adbusters.org) and view some of the others posted there. Working in groups of three, devise your own spoof ad in the style of those from Adbusters. First, pick an advertisement or ad campaign that you'd like to target. Discuss how the ad markets its product—what argument does it construct to attract customers and how might that argument be "twisted around" in order to make a spoof of it? Be sure to consider every element of the advertisement, from the text and slogans, to the graphics and layout used. Depending on what tools you have at your disposal, you might manipulate an existing ad in a graphics application such as Photoshop, manipulate print ads with scissors and markers, or create it entirely from scratch in whatever medium you wish. When you share your ad with the rest of the class, be prepared to explain the reasoning behind your finished product.

An Appeal to Walt Disney

CHARLES KERNAGHAN

CHARLES KERNAGHAN is the executive director of the National Labor Committee, an independent, nonprofit human rights and workers' rights organization. In this letter to the Walt Disney corporation, he calls for the company to recognize the social and economic rights of garment workers in Third World countries, including those of Central America and the Caribbean, who assemble Disney products for the U.S. market.

May 29, 1996

Michael Eisner
CEO Walt Disney Company
500 South Buena Vista Street
Burbank, CA 91521

Dear Mr. Eisner:

The National Labor Committee (NLC) fully supports Walt Disney's decision to source production in Haiti. The Haitian people desperately need investment and jobs, but they need jobs with dignity, under conditions which respect their basic human rights, and which pay wages that allow them and their families to survive.

The NLC would like to open a serious dialogue with Walt Disney representatives regarding working conditions and wages in Haitian factories where Disney children's clothing is currently being produced. The issues raised in this letter and the proposals which follow are the result of ongoing discussions with the workers in Haiti, as well as with concerned consumers and human rights activists across the United States and Canada . . .

Neither the NLC nor the Haitian workers we are in contact with want this attempt at dialogue, or the documentation of conditions under which Disney garments are produced, to result in Disney's pulling out of Haiti. Leaving Haiti would be a terrible mistake. Rather, in all good faith, the National Labor Committee and the coalition of religious, labor, student, human rights, and grass-roots organizations we work with, want to join the Walt Disney Company in an attempt to improve conditions in these Haitian factories.

Currently, the Walt Disney Company has licensing agreements with two U.S. apparel manufacturers, L.V. Myles and H.H. Cutler, which in turn contract production to four assembly factories in Haiti: L.V. Myles, N.S. Mart, Classic, and Gilanex. Children's clothing carrying the images of the Hunchback of Notre Dame, Pocahontas, Mickey Mouse, and the Lion King is sewn in these factories and then exported to the U.S. for sale in Wal-Mart, J.C. Penney, Kmart, and other retailers.

A shanty town where sweatshop workers live in Haiti.
Courtesy of National Labor Committee.

Living on the Edge of Misery

5   On a recent trip to Haiti in late April, I had the opportunity to visit the home of a Disney worker who lived in the Delmars neighborhood of Port-au-Prince. She worked at N.S. Mart (Plant Number 32) in the Sonapi Industrial Park where she sewed Pocahontas and Mickey Mouse shirts. Her home was typical of those of other Disney employees.

She was a single mother with four young children. They lived in a one-room windowless shack, 8 by 11 feet wide, lit by one bare light bulb and with a tin roof that leaked. The room contained: one table, three straight-backed chairs, and two small beds. This is all the room would fit. I counted four drinking glasses and three plastic plates. There was no fan, no TV, no radio, no toys, no refrigerator, no stove, no running water. She had to buy water by the bucket and carry it home. The toilet was a hole in the ground, shared with ten other families.

The children were 3½, 8, 11, and 14 years old. They were very small for their age. The mother told us that when she left for work that morning, she was only able to leave them 6 gourdes [the Haitian currency], or 30 cents U.S. The four children had to feed themselves for the day on *30 cents—7½ cents per child.* Her children had been sent home from school two and a half weeks before because she had been unable to pay their tuition. Tuition for the three older children totaled $2.63 a week, but this was more than the mother earned in a full day sewing Disney shirts.

One child had malaria, another a painful dysentery, but their mother was unable to afford the medicines, so they had to go without and simply bear it.

A Jesuit priest with whom we spoke in Haiti, who had had a similar stomach infection, told us it cost over $30 to purchase the necessary antibiotics. But this woman's salary making Pocahontas shirts was only $10.77 a week! Antibiotics for her daughter would have cost nearly three weeks' wages, which was impossible to afford.

10   Before leaving, I asked the family what they would eat that night. "*Nothing,*" they responded. There was no food. For this family, there were many days when they could not afford to eat. Instead of eating, they would just go to bed. The mother slept in one small bed, the daughters in the other, while the two boys slept on the ground under the table. No one in this home had ever seen a Disney movie.

Working at N.S. Mart Sewing Shirts for Disney

The mother had years of experience as a sewer. The production quota set at N.S. Mart is excessively high. On her assembly line, working furiously under constant pressure, she handled 375 Pocahontas shirts an hour—shirts which sell at Wal-Mart for $10.97 each. Yet her average weekly wage was only $10.77! She earned the minimum wage of 28 cents an hour.

No one can survive on 28 cent an hour wages—even in Haiti, which is not a cheap place to live. Seventy percent of what Haiti consumes is imported, including basic staples like rice, beans, and cornmeal. Food can actually be as expensive in Haiti as in the U.S. Workers producing Disney garments in Haiti are thin and tired looking. They and their families are always at the edge of hunger, sinking ever deeper into debt and misery. Far from being the exception, this woman's life and her story are typical.

The following day, we met with a large group of N.S. Mart workers . . . They told us that the majority of workers at N.S. Mart earn just 28 cents an hour, which is $2.22 for a full eight-hour day. And, they reported, at times they are shortchanged on their hours and pay.

The workers also told us the plant is hot, dusty, and poorly lit. Some complained about having trouble with their eyesight and respiratory problems. According to the workers, the production quotas and piece rates the company sets are impossible to reach. Supervisors put enormous, constant pressure on the workers to go faster. Supervisors yell, scream, threaten, and curse at the workers. Among the management, Saint Hillaire is particularly abusive. If you are young and pretty and a supervisor wants you as his mistress, you either give in to him or you are fired. Sexual harassment is common.

15   The toilets are filthy. Rats are everywhere. The holding tank for drinking water is covered only with a light piece of metal, which the rats have no trouble getting under. In the last week of April, the N.S. Mart workers told us, rats that had been poisoned were floating in the water tank.

If you dared to speak up, to complain to N.S. Mart management about these conditions or about the pay scale, you would be fired, period. Every worker we spoke with told us that if the company even suspected that they were interested in organizing to claim their rights, they would be thrown out of the factory immediately.

The most fundamental human and workers' rights of the N.S. Mart employees are being violated on a daily basis.

Payday for Disney Workers at the L.V. Myles Factory

Friday, April 26, was payday for the workers sewing Disney garments at the L.V. Myles plant (Number 30) in the Sonapi Industrial Park. A meeting with the L.V. Myles workers had been set up by our colleague and contact person in Haiti . . .

L.V. Myles management describes their factory as "*a model,*" as "*the best you will find.*" Also, Disney has had a long sourcing relationship with L.V. Myles, dating back some twenty years. Albeit a little reluctantly, one L.V. Myles officer explained to a U.S. journalist that L.V. Myles definitely pays its workers above the legal minimum wage in Haiti. When pressed, he said that L.V. Myles pays between 38 and 42 cents U.S. an hour, which would amount to weekly wages ranging from $16.72 to $18.28.

20   At 4:00 p.m., the workers began to leave the park. Soon there were forty or fifty L.V. Myles workers crowded around us . . . We had a chance to review dozens of pay stubs. We could find no workers who earned more than 30 cents U.S. an hour. We were also told that some workers in the plant, perhaps a dozen, did not even earn the minimum wage. One possible explanation for these discrepancies could be that L.V. Myles factory representatives include managers' salaries in their calculations, which would drive up the average wage paid in the plant.

The weekly earnings recorded on the pay stubs we reviewed ranged from $9.97 to $15.23, the latter including seven hours of overtime pay. L.V. Myles workers are paid biweekly. The pay stub of one woman provides an example. For two weeks of work, this woman, a sewing machine operator, earned 384.75 gourdes, or $23.67. This equates to $11.84 a week, or 28 cents an hour.

At the L.V. Myles factory, as at N.S. Mart, the daily piece-rate quota is set impossibly high. For example, in eight hours, the workers must attach 1,600 collars on Disney T-shirts or close to 1,600 shoulders, which means completing 200 pieces every hour. The work pace is relentless. If you get up to wash your face, the owner yells at you . . . "*They treat you like garbage,*" the workers said, "*they don't look at you as a human being, but as a piece of shit.*" They continued, "*The owners won't even talk to us, and if they don't like your face, or you're sick, they fire you.*" The supervisors pace the assembly lines clapping their hands and shrieking at the workers to go faster. At the end of the day, the workers are exhausted.

Crying Out in Disbelief

Prior to leaving for Haiti, I went to a Wal-Mart store on Long Island and purchased several Disney garments which had been made in Haiti. I showed these to the crowd of workers, who immediately recognized the clothing they had made. . . I asked the L.V. Myles workers if they had any idea what these shirts—the ones they had made—sell for in the U.S. I held up a size four Pocahontas T-shirt. I showed them the Wal-Mart price tag indicating $10.97. But it was only when I translated the $10.97 into the local currency—178.26 gourdes—that, all at once, in unison, the workers screamed with shock, disbelief, anger, and a mixture of pain and sadness, as their eyes remained fixed on the Pocahontas shirt . . . In a single day, they worked on hundreds of Disney shirts. Yet the sales price of just one shirt in the U.S. amounted to nearly five days of their wages! (G178.26/36 minimum daily wage = 4.95 days.) In fact, one production line of twenty workers assembles 1,000 Disney shirts in an eight-hour period. In effect, each worker assembles fifty Disney shirts in a day which, at $10.97 each, would sell for a total of $548.50 in the U.S. For her eight hours of work sewing these shirts, the L.V. Myles employee earns just $2.22! . . .

Surviving on 28 Cents an Hour

Is it possible to survive in Haiti earning 28 cents an hour?

25   The maquila factories start operating at 7:30 a.m., and demand that the workers be there at least ten to fifteen minutes early. Most factory workers get up at 5 a.m., when it is still pitch dark. They literally squeeze themselves into overcrowded tap-taps, small pickup trucks converted into buses, which crawl through the morning traffic jam to reach downtown. To get to and from work costs about 37 cents a day.

A cheap breakfast of spaghetti and coffee from food stands out in front of the factory will cost 62 cents. A modest lunch of rice, peas, and cornmeal soaking in oil, with a cup of juice, will cost the same, another 62 cents.

In total, the transportation and a small breakfast and lunch combined cost $1.61. But the factory workers only earn $2.22 for the entire day. So 73 percent of what they earn each day goes to just surviving. At the end of an eight-hour day, they have only 61 cents left over.

Since the workers have no money left over from their last paycheck, the only food they can get must be purchased on credit from the food vendors. The workers literally come to work each day to eat, but they eat only on credit. If they did not come to work, they literally would not eat.

Most workers try to, or would like to, leave $2.50 or $3.00 behind with their families when they leave for work in the morning, so that their families can eat. But that is more than a day's wages. Most families are left with only 31 cents to 62 cents a day to survive on.

30   The average rent for the typical one-room hut the workers and their families live in costs around $7.10 a week. This means that someone sewing Disney shirts must work for more than three days a week just to pay the rent.

If you have a child in school, that costs another $1.42 for tuition each week. And since the parents—given their own lack of education—cannot help their children with their lessons, they have to pay for a tutor, which costs an additional 71 cents a week.

A small can of powdered milk, which if stretched could last a week for an infant, costs $3.08, or more than the mother earns in an entire day of work. If a worker or her child are sick, a visit to the doctor costs between $3.08 and $4.62. Chloroquine pills for malaria cost 62 cents. For children suffering from diarrhea, a small bottle of medicine costs $1.54. Medicine for dysentery, which is very common, costs $4.68—over two days' wages—while a decongestant costs $2.77, and cough syrup costs $1.54.

If you or your children need glasses, you might as well forget it. Eyeglasses cost $40, or three weeks' wages!

In Haiti, in the neighborhoods the workers live in, there is no running water so you must buy your water by the bucket. To wash clothes, for example, two buckets of water and two bars of soap cost 37 cents, or more than you make in an hour.

35   No serious observer could reach any conclusion other than that the wages being paid to Haitian workers sewing Disney garments are sub-subsistence wages. No one should use the term lightly, but these are definitely starvation wages.

The Classic Apparel Factory—Again Workers Treated as Dirt

At the Classic Apparel factory, which is under contract with H.H. Cutler (the label reads "The H.H. Cutler Fun Factory"), hundreds of workers sew "Mickey's for Kids Stuff" and other children's clothing for Disney.

Are conditions at Classic any different, any better, than at N.S. Mart or L.V. Myles factories? . . .

When we inquired about conditions at the Classic factory, worker after worker responded that "*conditions are miserable.*" They continued: "*They treat us badly, like we are dirt, like we were dumb, with no respect. You can't even speak to the bosses. If you try, they fire you. The supervisors are always screaming at us to work faster. The pressure to make the quota is great. If you even try to get up to use the bathroom they scream at you.*"

The plant is very hot, we were told. It is poorly lit and dusty. The workers say the lint-filled dust gives them headaches. Rats are everywhere. The drinking water is right next to the toilet, which is filthy. Women are getting infections from the water, so the company dumps in more chlorine. Nor does the company pay sick days properly . . .

40   The production manager at Classic Apparel is John Paul Medina, who has been identified by the workers as a former member of the Fraph death squad, which killed thousands of civilians during the coup. He has told the workers that if they ask for a raise, "*the Americans will come and take the jobs to the Dominican Republic.*" However, in June 1995, when President Aristide increased the minimum wage, Medina did not hesitate to increase the daily piece-rate quota by 66 percent. Instead of sewing 720 collars on Disney garments in eight hours, now the workers must complete 1,200 pieces in order to earn the minimum wage, or a little above.

Similar to the other factories, sexual harassment is common. Also, when U.S. representatives—presumably from H.H. Cutler—tour the plant to check on production quality, they never bother to speak with the workers.

When we asked them how they were able to live on their wages, we heard the same sad story. More often than not, they and their families went to bed hungry, having no money left for food that night. They never eat meat; they cannot afford it.

When asked, they told us that their children were "*tired and weak*" and often had "*to go to school without food for lunch.*" At the time of our visit, many of their children were sick, either with malaria or stomach infections.

Like the rest of the workers we had spoken with, no one had ever heard of "Corporate Codes of Conduct" nor had Haitian Ministry of Social Affairs officials ever spoken with them. They were alone to face the working conditions in which they were trapped.

Haitian Workers Make a Proposal to Disney

45   The workers at N.S. Mart, L.V. Myles, and Classic Apparel asked the NLC to carry a message back to company representatives at Walt Disney. The Haitian workers sewing Disney clothing have several modest proposals they would like to discuss. They are as follows:

1. Primary among them is that Disney representatives come to Haiti to meet with the workers, to learn their story and see how they live. These workers want to continue sewing Disney clothing; in fact, they would like more orders. They are good at what they do and they work hard. They only want to be treated with respect.
2. They would like to work with Disney to clean up the factories, to guarantee respect for human and worker rights, including their legal right to organize. These workers want the factories to be even more productive and efficient, but they also want their rights as workers restored.
3. A very modest increase in wages from the current 28 cents an hour to 58 cents would allow the Disney workers and their families to survive. They would remain poor, very poor, but they would no longer be trapped in misery.
4. To guarantee respect for basic rights, local human rights organizations should have access to Disney's contractors' plants to monitor conditions. Such an independent monitoring agreement has already been signed with the Gap.

Not That Sort of a Trip

The NLC is aware that, following our trip to Haiti, Disney representatives did in fact visit the N.S. Mart, L.V. Myles, Classic, and Gilanex factories during the week of May 6. Before that, H.H. Cutler Company officials were also in Haiti.

However, this is not the type of meeting the workers are requesting. The workers want a meeting with Disney representatives, but in the presence of the NLC and independent local human rights organizations, away from the factory and local management, and in a secure place. The workers want to speak the truth, openly, frankly, and without the threat of being fired or retaliated against for doing so. Disney should provide their word that no harm will come to the workers for attending such a meeting and speaking truthfully.

Could the U.S. Companies Afford it?

The workers' demands seem very reasonable, perhaps even overly modest, to the NLC. The wage increase the workers are calling for would allow them to earn 58 cents an hour, which is only $4.62 a day, $25.38 a week, and $1,320 a year.

Would such a wage increase make Haiti less competitive? Available research is clear in documenting that this would not be the case. Through interviews with assembly-line workers in Haiti, the NLC is documenting production schedules and labor costs.

At the L.V. Myles Factory

50   For example, at the L.V. Myles plant in the Sonapi Industrial Park, twenty workers on a production line sew 1,000 pairs of purple Pocahontas pajamas in a single day. The

pajamas are then exported to the U.S., where they sell at Wal-Mart for $11.97. L.V. Myles claims it is paying its workers 38 cents to 42 cents an hour (which, as we have already seen, is inflated since the vast majority of sewers in the plant are actually earning between 28 cents and 30 cents). Even if we grant that the L.V. Myles Company is paying 42 cents an hour, this would mean that the twenty workers, each earning $3.32 a day (8 hours × $.42 = $3.32), collectively are earning only $66.40 for the day (20 × $3.32 = $66.40), while at the same time producing $11,970 worth of Pocahontas pajamas ($11.97 × 1,000 = $11,970). In other words, the wages the Haitian workers earn amount to just .55 percent—about one-half of one percent—of the retail price the pajamas sell for at Wal-Mart! In effect, the workers earn just 7 cents for each $11.97 pair of Pocahontas pajamas they sew.

Now, if wages were raised to 58 cents an hour—as the workers are requesting— what would be the effect?

At 58 cents an hour, or $4.64 for an eight-hour day, the Haitian sewers would earn 9 cents, instead of 7 cents for every $11.97 pair of Disney pajamas they made. The Haitian sewers would still be earning less than eight-tenths of one percent of the sales price of the garments. If the workers earned 9 cents per pajama, this would still leave Walt Disney, L.V. Myles, and Wal-Mart with over 99 percent—$11.88—of the $11.97 sales price.

At the Classic Apparel Factory

At Classic Apparel, forty workers in one production group sew 2,400 Disney Lion King children's outfits in an eight-hour day. Given the recent raise at Classic Apparel from 28 cents to 35 cents an hour, this means that forty workers earning 35 cents an hour would collectively earn $110.77 a day (8 × $.35 = 40 × $2.77 = $110.77), while producing $28,776 worth of Lion King outfits selling in the U.S. for $11.99 each (2,400 × $11.99 = $28,776) . . .

Right now, workers at Classic Apparel are earning only 5 cents for every $11.99 Disney garment they sew, their earnings amounting to only four-tenths of one percent of the sales of the Lion King garment.

55   What would happen if the Haitian workers' modest demand for 58 cents an hour was met? Instead of 5 cents for each garment they sewed, they would earn 8 cents, or six-tenths of one percent of the $11.99 retail price, leaving the U.S. companies with well over 99 percent of their share.

Not only is the 58 cent an hour wage—or higher—a desperately needed improvement for the people of Haiti, and one easily afforded by the U.S. companies, it is also good for the U.S. people. No one earning 28 cents an hour, who cannot even afford to feed his or her family, will ever purchase anything made in the U.S. You cannot trade with someone making 28 cents an hour . . .

The Haitian maquila workers are very isolated. The Haitian government's Ministry of Social Affairs, which is responsible for factory inspections and implementation of labor regulations, is not functioning. It has no budget, no money, no presence. Even the factory owners will confirm this.

On the other hand, sadly, the Haitian workers are not receiving any assistance or support from the U.S. Embassy. In a February 1996 cable to the State Department in

Washington, D.C., the U.S. Embassy in Port-au-Prince reports that in the maquila plants producing under contract for U.S. companies, the average pay is 46 cents an hour and not the 28 cents an hour (or even less) that the NLC documented. The Embassy's cable notes that a *"greater analysis of the Group's [NLC] charges will follow."*

But how did the Embassy reach its conclusions? The Embassy simply sent out a questionnaire to the maquila factory owners and waited for them to mail back their responses! This, of course, is ridiculous in a country like Haiti, where the tiny elite which controls these factories has an unparalleled record for corruption, tax evasion, cheating on bills owed to the state electrical, phone, and port agencies, and massive violations of the internationally recognized rights of their employees . . .

60   Currently the "global economy" which links the U.S. and Haiti is pitting U.S. workers against Haitian workers in a bitter race to the bottom over who will accept the lowest wages and the most miserable working conditions. Under these conditions, one of the only remaining avenues to break this destructive cycle, raise social standards, and level the playing field is to involve the U.S. consumer. Consumer pressure can move the whole system forward, as it did with the Gap, which became the first company to agree to open its contractors' plants to independent human rights monitors . . .

Disney could continue to well serve its commitment to family values by going to Haiti to meet with the workers and raising their wages to 58 cents an hour.

For its part, the National Labor Committee will go anywhere at any time to meet with Disney representatives to discuss the proposals put forth by the Haitian workers.

When we left Haiti, the people told us, "we are counting on you." It is a responsibility the National Labor Committee takes very seriously. We are committed to raising their needs with the U.S. people. Thank you.

Sincerely,

Charles Kernaghan
Director

cc:
Mr. Peter F. Nolan, Vice President, Assistant General Counsel, Walt Disney Company
Peter Levin
Chuck Champlin, Director of Communications, Disney Consumer Products

Model Letter for the Walt Disney Company

Date

Michael Eisner, CEO
Walt Disney Company
500 South Buena Vista Street
Burbank, CA 91521

Dear Mr. Eisner:

We support Walt Disney's decision to produce in Haiti. The Haitian people need jobs. However, we hope that the high level of unemployment and poverty is not used to exploit the workers.

Walt Disney Company has licensing agreements with two U.S. companies—L.V. Myles and H.H. Cutler—who in turn contract with several companies in Haiti to produce Mickey Mouse and Pocahontas pajamas. Three of these companies—Quality Garments, National Sewing Contractors, and N.S. Mart Manufacturing—are openly violating Haiti's wage laws, paying their employees as little as 12 cents per hour.

We ask the Walt Disney Company to sign the attached pledge to respect Haiti's wage and benefit laws.

We also ask that you translate Walt Disney Company's corporate code of conduct into Creole, to post it in your contractors' plants, and distribute it to the workers. We ask you to agree that independent human rights observers will have access to your contractors' plants to monitor compliance with your stated human rights concerns. Also, we know that Haitian women are being paid 7 cents for each pair of $11.97 Disney pajamas they make. This seems unjust—even criminal—to us. Is there any reason Walt Disney cannot work with your contractors to double, triple, or even quadruple the wages these women are being paid in Haiti? If you were to quadruple the wage, the women would still be earning 28 cents for every pair of $11.97 Disney pajamas they produced. Disney and the other companies involved would still keep $11.69—or 98 percent of the sales price. Couldn't the Walt Disney Company afford this? Wouldn't the $11.69 provide plenty of room for an adequate profit?

5   Lastly, can you explain to us how the U.S. people can trade with Haitian people earning 30 cents an hour? Of course, it is impossible. What do the U.S. people gain when U.S. companies pay such starvation wages in Haiti? Without fair social standards in international trade—linked to sustainable wages and human rights protections—the North American people cannot prosper, as we will be forced to compete for jobs in a race to the bottom over who will accept the lowest wages and the most miserable working conditions.

As we are sure Walt Disney Company stands by its human rights principles and has nothing to hide, we look forward to your company's promptly signing the attached Pledge. We await your response. Thank you.

Sincerely,

Attachment: Pledge

Walt Disney Company: Please Sign the Pledge

We Pledge

We, Walt Disney Company, pledge to immediately comply with all Haitian labor laws covering all employees producing goods for our company, especially:

- To pay at least the legal minimum wage of 30 cents an hour, including proper overtime rates;
- To pay all legal benefits, such as health, pension, sick days, and 7th day bonus pay;
- To end sexual harassment;
- To respect the workers' right to organize and the right to a collective contract;
- To improve working conditions and to cease arbitrary and unfair production speedups;
- To translate our code of conduct into Creole, post it in our contractors' plants, and distribute it to all employees; and
- To allow independent human rights observers to monitor our contractors' compliance with our corporate code of conduct.

Re-reading/Conversations with the Text

1. Consider the title "An Appeal to Walt Disney." What is the nature of this rhetorical appeal? Re-read the letter and consider the rhetorical appeals it applies. What are the logical or rational elements of the text? How is the argument developed and supported? How would you describe the rhetor's (Kernaghan's) character? Does the rhetor demonstrate familiarity with the topic at hand? How does the rhetor establish rapport with the audience? Finally, what emotions are generated by the text? How might these emotions enable readers to react favorably to the rhetor's purpose?

2. Kernaghan invokes a number of rhetorical commonplaces, such as comparison, in his letter. First, summarize Kernaghan's use of comparisons. Are the comparisons achieved through likeness and similarity, through changes in scale, number, or magnitude, and/or through contrast and difference? Do the comparisons advance a particular argument? If so, what are the features of this argument?

3. "An Appeal to Walt Disney" opens as a letter to the Walt Disney Company; however, the structure of the document soon moves into a first-person narration, with headings for each sub-section. Consider the structure of Kernaghan's letter. What is the rhetorical purpose of subdividing the letter into sections? How do the section titles function persuasively? What is the rhetorical effect of switching to first-person narration? Why might this shift be useful in persuading his audience?

Re-seeing and Re-writing

1. Conduct a rhetorical analysis of an anti-sweatshop campaign. You might begin by visiting the websites of organizations such as United Students Against Sweatshops, Global Exchange, or the Living Wage Campaign. What are the organization's stated goals? Consider the organization's mission statement and/or logo. How does the campaign imagine its audience? Would you consider yourself the target audience of this campaign? How would you describe the organization's *ethos* or character? How does the organization attempt to establish rapport with the audience? Does the organization appeal to the audience's self-interest? What does the organization ask of its audience? Finally, write an essay that presents the results of your rhetorical analysis.

2. In the form of a letter, write your own "appeal" to Walt Disney or another major corporation about their labor practices. Work to use all the appeals (*ethos, pathos, logos*) in your letter.

 Intertext

Compare the rhetorical strategies at work in "An Appeal to Walt Disney" and Cynthia Enloe's "The Globetrotting Sneaker." For instance, consider the use of description in both texts. What are the rhetorical functions of the descriptions of poor working conditions? Do such descriptions attempt to appeal to a reader's emotions? Are the descriptions made to function as evidence?

Coca Cola and Coco Frío (poem)

MARTÍN ESPADA

ESPADA/THE NIKE CORPORATION (LETTERS)

The *NIKE CORPORATION*'s mission, as listed on its Web site (www.nike.com), is "to bring inspiration and innovation to every athlete in the world." The word *athlete* is further illuminated in this mission statement by placing an asterisk by it and adding, "if you have a body, you are an athlete." Nike, the largest sports and fitness company in the world, is said to have begun with a partnership between University of Oregon coach Bill Bowerman and one of his former runners, Phil Knight. In 1962 Knight approached Bowerman with an idea for importing low-priced, high-tech athletic shoes from Japan in order to challenge German domination of the U.S. athletic footwear industry. The two soon founded Blue Ribbon Sports (BRS). Soon, two more business-minded runners—Jeff Johnson and Steve Prefontaine, also formerly of the University of Oregon—joined Bowerman and Knight, and Nike was born. Johnson, Nike's first full-time employee, originally sold its shoes out of the back of a van at high school track meets; Prefontaine became the first major athlete to wear Nike shoes and had a significant impact on their design.

Born in Brooklyn, New York, in 1957, *MARTÍN ESPADA* is Professor of English at the University of Massachusetts-Amherst. His newest book of poems is *Alabanza: New and Selected Poems 1982–2002* (2003), and his other books of poetry include *A Mayan Astronomer in Hell's Kitchen: Poems* (2000); *Imagine the Angels of Bread* (1996), which won an American Book Award; *City of Coughing and Dead Radiators* (1993); *Rebellion is the Circle of a Lover's Hands* (1990); and *Trumpets from the Islands of Their Eviction* (1987). He has also edited several anthologies, including *El Coro: A Chorus of Latino and Latina Poetry* (1997) and *Poetry Like Bread: Poets of the Political Imagination*. His prose collection, *Zapata's Disciple: Essays,* was published in 1998. While writing some of his earlier volumes of poetry, he was a full-time tenant lawyer and supervisor of a legal services program; much was made of the duality of his poet/lawyer roles, but Espada himself is said to have seen the two professions as united in creating "a poetry of advocacy."

Coca-Cola and Coco Frío

On his first visit to Puerto Rico,
island of family folklore,
the fat boy wandered
from table to table
5   with his mouth open.
At every table, some great-aunt
would steer him with cool spotted hands
to a glass of Coca-Cola.
One even sang to him, in all the English

10   she could remember, a Coca-Cola jingle
from the forties. He drank obediently, though
he was bored with this potion, familiar
from soda fountains in Brooklyn.

Then, at a roadside stand off the beach, the fat boy
15   opened his mouth to coco frío, a coconut
chilled, then scalped by a machete
so that a straw could inhale the clear milk.
The boy tilted the green shell overhead
and drooled coconut milk down his chin;
20   suddenly, Puerto Rico was not Coca-Cola
or Brooklyn, and neither was he.

For years afterward, the boy marveled at an island
where the people drank Coca-Cola
and sang jingles from World War II
25   in a language they did not speak,
while so many coconuts in the trees
sagged heavy with milk, swollen
and unsuckled.

Nike's Letter to Martín Espada

October 14, 1997

Mr. Martín Espada
University of Massachusetts at Amherst
Bartlett Hall Rm 251
Amherst, Massachusetts 01006

Re: Nike Poetry Slam

Dear Mr. Espada:

The enclosed package contains what we hope will be an unusual and interesting project for you.

We are developing a series of four commercials, which will be aired on national television during the 1998 Winter Olympics. Each commercial will feature an outstanding and inspiring female athlete, sponsored by our client, Nike.

We hope these short films will celebrate the poetry of competition and athletics by using your words.

Detail follows in the proposal. All poems need to be submitted, using shipping materials to be provided by November 1, 1997.

5   We are anxious to know about your participation and would like to confirm your involvement by October 22. If you have questions, please feel free to call me at _____. As well, we would like to confirm your involvement and address for delivery of video and shipping materials by October 22 with a call to the same number.

In advance, we thank you for your time to review and respond.

Sincerely,

Cindy Fluitt
Producer

Martín Espada's Reply to Nike

October 22, 1997

Cindy Fluitt, Producer
Goodby, Silverstein & Partners
720 California Street
San Francisco, CA 94108

Re: Nike Poetry Slam

Dear Ms. Fluitt:

This is a letter in response to your correspondence concerning the Nike Poetry Slam and my proposed participation.

I could reject your offer based on the fact that your deadline is ludicrous (i.e. ten days from the above date). A poem is not a pop tart.

I could reject your offer based on the fact that I would not be free to write whatever I want, nonwithstanding your assurances to the contrary, since I must "keep in mind TV network standards and practices regarding content and language." You clearly have no idea what the word "censorship" means. Where, as you put it, "the mechanics of commerce outweigh the demands of art," then de facto censorship will flourish.

I could reject your offer based on the fact that, to make this offer to me in the first place, you must be totally and insultingly ignorant of my work as a poet, which strives to stand against all that you and your client represent. Whoever referred me to you did you a grave disservice.

5   I could reject your offer based on the fact that your client, Nike, has through commercials such as these outrageously manipulated the youth market, so that even low-income adolescents are compelled to buy products they do not need at prices they cannot afford.

Ultimately, however, I am rejecting your offer as a protest against the brutal labor practices of Nike. I will not associate myself with a company that engages in the well-documented exploitation of workers in sweatshops. Please spare me the shameless dishonesty of the usual corporate response: there's no problem, and besides we're working on it. I suggest, instead, that you take the $2500 you now dangle before me and distribute that money equally among the laborers in an Asian sweatshop doing business with Nike. The funds would be much more useful to them than to me. Thank you.

Sincerely,

Martín Espada

Re-reading/Conversations with the Text

1. Divide the class into two groups: One group should focus on the "invitation" letter from Nike to Mr. Espada, while the other focuses on Espada's response to Nike. Members of each group should re-read and discuss the letter carefully, analyzing its use of rhetorical appeals. Finally, discuss, with your class as a whole, the rhetorical effectiveness of each letter.

2. Examine each of the letters carefully with an eye toward *ethos*. What can you tell about the "character" of Nike (as represented by its producer, Cindy Fluitt) and the "character" of Martín Espada from these letters? Point to specific points in each letter to make your case; profile the ethos of "corporation" and "poet" generally, but also Fluitt and Espada in particular.

3. Compare the letter written by Espada to his poem. Consider whether Espada has a primary means of persuasion (ethos, pathos, logos) common to his writing. Do you find his writing persuasive or not? Why?

Re-seeing and Re-writing

1. Continue the exchange between the Nike Poetry Slam producer, Cindy Fluitt, and poet Martín Espada for at least one more round of letters. That is, write Fluitt's response to Espada's letter of October 22; then also write Espada's next response to her further response. You might try this activity in pairs, with one of you writing the Fluitt follow-up letter and then the other penning Espada's final letter. Or, write each letter in a group together and compare your group's set of follow-up letters with other groups'.

2. Research Nike's and Coca Cola's involvement in the most recent Olympics, or research Nike's or Coke's use of any artistic "celebrities" (poets, painter, musicians, etc.) in any of their advertising campaigns. Write an analytical paper in which you discuss Nike's or Coke's corporate ethos/character as displayed through its Olympic advertising or its use of artists/authors.

Compare Espada's "Coca-Cola and Coco Frío" to Duhamel's "Oriental Barbie" poem. How do these poets represent their respective objects of consumption? What role does cultural context play in the consumption of these objects? What is the effect of the cultural references on the reader? What kinds of conclusions do the poems come to about the consumption of their respective objects? Can you find other poets who write about similar subject matter? How do those poets compare to Espada and Duhamel?

Student Activists Versus the Corporate University

LIZA FEATHERSTONE

LIZA FEATHERSTONE is a journalist who lives in New York City and has contributed to newspapers and magazines such as *The Nation, The New York Times, The Washington Post,* and *Rolling Stone.* United Students Against Sweatshops is a network of anti-sweatshop groups founded in 1998, which now has affiliates on over 200 campuses across the United States. This article focuses on the organization's challenge to the corporatization of the university.

Just about every aspect of collegiate life can be leased for corporate profit these days. Increasingly, universities outsource services they used to provide themselves; on campuses nation-wide, big capital's irresistibly cartoonish logos are becoming as ubiquitous as backpacks. Barnes & Noble has taken over the university bookstores, and Starbucks has set up shop in the student union. It's not unusual for a university to lease the rights to its own brand name: the University of Michigan, for instance, recently signed a seven-year deal, in which Nike will outfit all of the school's varsity teams and pay $1.2 million annually for the rights to the school's much-coveted logo. Many schools make such deals with apparel companies: not only does the company then own the school logo but, in Nike's case, it gets to put its own Swoosh on the clothing, or on a big flashy sign over the stadium. Universities are run increasingly like private firms, and have ever more intimate relations with private industry.

Perhaps unhappily for school administrators, this transformation has coincided with a dramatic escalation, in both numbers and militancy, in student anti-corporate activism, of which USAS has been the most effective and visible organization. That groundswell owes much to the exuberant global anti-corporate—or, outside the US, anti-capitalist—movement, made visible by carnivalesque protests from London 1999 to Porto Alegre, Quebec City and Genoa in 2001. In the US, that movement, which includes activists concerned about labor, the environment, Third World debt relief and numerous other issues, was immeasurably energized by and found expression in the historic November 1999 anti-World Trade Organization (WTO) mobilization, now referred to simply as "Seattle." Many students participated in "Seattle," but it was only a beginning. Since then, students from the University of California—Davis to the University of Vermont have held globalization teach-ins. They have urged their universities to boycott World Bank Bonds. They perform anti-WTO guerrilla theater. Many more helped shut down large portions of Washington DC in the April 2000 World Bank/International Monetary Fund protests.

With a *joie de vivre* that the American economic left has lacked since the days of Emma Goldman and John Reed, college students are harnessing their creativity, irony, and media savvy to launch a well-organized, thoughtful, and morally outraged resistance to corporate power. These activists, more than any student radicals in years, passionately denounce the wealth gap, as well as the lack of democratic accountability in a world dominated by corporations. While some attend traditionally political schools like Evergreen, Michigan, and Wisconsin, this activism does not revolve around the usual suspects: some of the most dramatic actions have taken place at campuses that have always been conservative, like the University of Pennsylvania, Virginia Commonwealth, and Johns Hopkins. This oppositional spirit is quite unlike the "don't trust anyone under 30" Oedipal crisis of baby-boomer protest. Many of the new activists have radical parents, even communist grandparents; rather than rebelling against the adults in their lives, they are following in their footsteps. Its regional diversity, too, will surprise observers of past US student protest—in addition to the Coasts, this student movement thrives in places ranging from the University of Tennessee to the University of North Dakota. Throughout 2000 and 2001, students nationwide were staging significant anti-corporate protests almost every week. It is neither too soon, nor too naively optimistic, to call it a movement.

Like other contemporary anticorporatists—those vandalizing and protesting under Golden Arches worldwide, or Charlie Kernaghan crusading against Kathie Lee and Disney—student anticorporate activists have expertly used big capital's catchy logos against it. Companies targeting a youth market are selling a brand as much as a particular product. The imagery surrounding such brands can be hypnotic, narcotic even, distracting us from the ugly social relations embedded in the manufacturing process. But as Naomi Klein observes in *No Logo: Taking Aim at the Brand Bullies,* companies trafficking in image are particularly vulnerable when those images are tarnished. Obscure information-technology companies can quietly outsource their data-entry work to Caribbean sweatshops, but companies like Gap are different: their prominence in consumers' hearts and minds makes it far easier for activists to publicize their wrongdoings. Nike has been a popular target among students, because even though exploitation pervades the industry, the sneaker behemoth's recognizable logo can help call attention to abuses. Students at Ohio State, for instance, staged a "Smash the Swoosh" demo, gleefully destroying a papier mâché Nike logo like a piñata.

5   Just like the Swoosh, "we can think of the university itself as a brand, a logo, that students consume," said anti-sweat activist Todd Pugatch,

then a student at UNC—Chapel Hill. Andrew Ross, chair of NYU's Department of American Studies and editor of the 1997 anthology *No Sweat,* agrees, pointing out that clothing bearing university names was stylish among young people even back in the 1980s, before the current romance with corporate logos. Before Fubu hats, trendy teenagers sported Notre Dame, Georgetown, or Harvard sweatshirts, whether or not they actually attended those schools. So it seems fitting that in the global youth movement to expose the exploitation concealed (as students often put it) "behind the label," a struggle over university apparel should figure so prominently. Universities, especially if they are academically prestigious, or have high-profile sports teams, depend on image as much as Nike does, and the recognizability of the University of Michigan's big yellow M, like that of McDonald's, can backfire if the logo comes to symbolize exploitation and corporate greed.

And indeed, much of students' anticorporate organizing has focused on the reality of the university as a corporate actor. During one anti-sweat occupation, for example, student activists at the University of Oregon led a campus tour of sites that illustrated the institution's numerous ties to corporations (one stop was the Knight Library, named after Nike's president and CEO). A nationwide student group called 180/Movement for Democracy and Education, based at the University of Wisconsin, articulated this problem and its connection to other issues as early as 1999, leading teach-ins on how WTO policies affect higher education.

Some of the student campaigns reveal the university as a stingy service provider (those focusing on tuition increases, for example), while others target the institution as an employer (fights over the wages of university dining hall workers, graduate student organizing and, less directly, apparel licenses). Many highlight the university's role as an investor in the global economy—those pushing to make their school's portfolios more socially responsible, for example. Others, like those who protested in solidarity with the striking students in Mexico, have strenuously objected to the worldwide privatization of public education.

A prominent feature of the corporate university is students' alienation and powerlessness; universities often treat them as anonymous consumers, rather than as members of a community who deserve a say in its policies. When administrators do that, they can expect student customers to act like politicized consumer activists. "Campus democracy" is an increasingly common rallying cry (just as, at major off-campus protests, demonstrators chant "this is what democracy looks like"). Structural complaints about current campus plutocracy and autocracy abound: the powerlessness of the committees on which students and faculty serve, the influence of private-sector donors on school policy, the impossibility of getting a meeting with the college president. Whatever the issue, indignation over students' lack of power is pervasive. Like the idealists who wrote the Port Huron Statement, students are being politicized by disappointment: academia, they believe, is supposed to provide a space in which humane values at least compete with the bottom line. Many are shocked to find out that their administrators, many of whom now like to be called CEOs, think like businesspeople.

Some protesters have responded to the university's corporatization by rejecting it outright. In snowy January 2000, at Virginia Commonwealth University, twenty students slept outside the vice-president's office for two nights to protest the university's contract with McDonald's (the school promised the fast-food behemoth a twenty-year monopoly over the Student Commons). Simply saying "no" to corporate deals has its place; student refusal warns administrators that an institution's complex relationship to the global economy is closely watched and analyzed—a grenade ready to explode at any moment into messy and embarrassing dissent.

Yet even more often—and perhaps more shrewdly—student activists are making strategic use of the university's participation in the world economy. Universities' cozy ties to large companies are, paradoxically, a boon to the global economic justice movement because they bring corporatism into students' daily lives—and, perversely, lend students power as consumers in the "academic–industrial complex." Students are learning how to use that power, just as they did in the divestment campaigns of the 1980s, when students pressured their trustees to stop holding stock in companies that did business in South Africa. After all, if the university is a corporation, it's a unique one, in that a small number of young people can complicate its daily operations enormously. Though students are seldom given a legitimate role in making university policy, they still, as protesters, have far more leverage over the university than they have over any other kind of multinational corporation. When students understand the university's corporate ties, they can put formidable pressure on the institution to do the right—or at least the somewhat better—thing.

USAS activists have been at the forefront of this strategy, but they are not alone. Campus labor activists have targeted the bad labor practices of the behemoth management companies that run universities' janitorial, laundry, and dining hall services. Others have successfully pressured their administrations to boycott notorious union buster Sodexho—Marriott, a French company that provides campus dining services and is also the largest investor in US private prisons. This campaign, which began in April 2000, has inspired protests at Arizona State, University of Texas, Xavier, Florida State, SUNY–Binghamton, Fordham and elsewhere. It has killed Sodexho contracts at American University, SUNY–Albany, Maryland's Goucher College, Evergreen State, Virginia's James Madison University, and Oberlin, and forced the company to drop its holdings in Corrections

10

Corporation of America, the largest private prison-management company in the US.

USAS activists—and the wider student movement they have so galvanized—are teaching themselves and their fellow students to question facts of social and economic life that they have been taught to take for granted all of their lives. "We are training an entire generation to think differently about [*pause*] capitalism," says Laurie Kimmington of Yale's Student Labor Action Committee. She glances at a reporter's notebook and giggles cheerfully. "Oops, maybe I shouldn't say that."

As Kimmington's good-natured hesitation makes clear, US students are far more readily anticorporate than anticapitalist. Yet, at times, anticorporatism seems too limiting a language. One student activist, interviewed shortly after Sodexho—Marriott's divestment from CCA, said she and her colleagues were still trying to kick the food service corporation off campus. Asked why—given the campaign's recent victory—she said, "It's a big corporation. We'd rather have some small local company make our food."

At such moments, one wonders whether anticorporatism is really about social justice, or simply an aesthetic objection to bigness. It has, among middle-class white people, become the dominant idiom of resistance in the US—even penetrating national electoral politics via Ralph Nader's Green presidential campaign—and in many ways it's a useful one. As the villains everyone loves to hate, corporate power and greed lend coherence to a global youth movement that's too often viewed as diffuse and lacking focus. Anticorporatism translates admirably into union solidarity and, like "globalization," a term whose evasions journalist Doug Henwood soundly thrashes in *A New Economy?*, corporations provide a convenient euphemism for capitalism, which few Americans want to talk about—after all, who wants to be taken for a glassy-eyed sectarian-newspaper pusher?

15   Students are well aware of the problem. "We need to develop a new rhetoric that connects sweatshops—*and* living wage *and* the right to organize—to the global economy," says the University of Michigan's Jackie Bray. Liana Molina of Santa Clara University, who doesn't shy away from the c-word, agrees: "I think our economic system determines everything!" But about USAS's somewhat vague ideology she has mixed feelings. "It's good to be ambiguous and inclusive," so as not to alienate more conservative, newer, or less politicized members, she says. "But I also think a class analysis is needed. Then again, that gets shady, because people are like, 'Well, what are you *for*, socialism? What?'"

Outside of the United States, massive protests against the predations of capital are called anticapitalist, even by the press. But in this country, capitalism is generally treated as an irrevocable given, even by activists with no great fondness for it. Corporations, on the other hand, arouse tremendous resentment and ire. Even relatively conservative Americans can identify with Jimmy Stewart in *It's a Wonderful Life* defending the small business and small town way of life against the Bad Mr. Potter, the corrupt embodiment of big $$. Or his modern-day analogues—Russell Crowe fighting big tobacco, or Julia Roberts and her breasts taking on the chemical companies.

As an enemy, the corporation would seem to have some unifying power; few people actually head companies, so in theory almost everyone could be an anticorporatist. And the movement has done a commendable job of expanding its analysis beyond institutions like the IMF/World Bank to a more expansive opposition to capital itself. But as many students realize, building a social movement to fight poverty may require a broader vision. Many people of color and poor people in the United States say that anticorporatism fails to describe adequately their experiences of everyday inequality and injustice. (This, of course, is part of the reason Nader's presidential campaign had more support among the upscale than among the poor.) Addressing USAS's summer 2000 national conference, Maria Cordera of the Third Eye Movement, a San Francisco Bay Area youth organization that fights police brutality and the prison industry, observed that poor people and people of color weren't so concerned about globalization. "That's not our bread and butter issue," she said. "We're worried about how we are going to feed our kids."

Complaints about "corporations" and "globalization" may not be adequate stand-ins for what old-fashioned radicals might call class struggle. For example, confronted with the problem of massive over-incarceration in the United States, student anticorporatists focus on those aspects of the prison industry that enrich private corporations, like private prisons or prison labor. Antisweat activists at California schools, for example, wishing to make common cause with antiprison activists, have been "redefining prisons as sweatshops," because some prisons lease inmate labor for corporate profit. This idea has been commendably effective in building multiracial coalitions between anticorporatists and young people fighting a racist criminal justice system. Yet the profiteering aspects of prisons are relatively peripheral, compared to the horror of prison itself, and to the injustice of sentencing policies. As Christian Parenti points out in his recent book *Lockdown America,* prison labor isn't as widespread as many activists claim, and, contrary to student and youth activist rhetoric, the lure of profits, whether through prison labor or privatization, does not motivate incarceration policy. Rather, Parenti argues, incarcerating large numbers of people is, "intentionally or otherwise, a way to manage rising in-equality and surplus populations."

Another problem with anticorporatism is that it makes no demands on the state. Unlike European activists, who envision a clear role for the government in correcting injustice, US anticorporatists, especially young people, are wary of state power, and skeptical about government solutions. That skepticism is well-founded, and offers a valuable counter to a left-liberalism that has often been too dependent on a state that has, as Pierre Bourdieu observes in *Acts of Resistance,* largely abandoned its left-wing (social welfare, education) functions in favor of its right-wing ones (law enforcement, social control). Although we shouldn't hold our breath on this, the movement's anarchist tendencies may at some point help it to produce a coherent critique of the state's role in perpetuating inequality. They might also help the American left develop some brand of autonomous politics, an anarcho-socialism that completely rejects nations, states, and national borders altogether.

But although that's a delightful long-term vision, it is, for USAS, becoming impossible to ignore the role of laissez-faire governments in perpetuating sweatshops. And the lives of poor and working-class people in the United States, at least in the short run, aren't likely to be radically improved by a movement that eschews state solutions. In the United States, in a time of ebbing government services and worsening economic equality, to simply repudiate—or, like most anti-corporate activists, completely ignore—the state is to write the majority of poor and working people right out of a movement.

The ending of what Bill Clinton called "welfare as we know it," for example, has wrought suffering on a par with sweatshop exploitation, and has only just begun to get any attention from the overwhelmingly white and middle-class US youth movement. Some USAS activists, beginning to move beyond anticorporatism, have been figuring out how to make common cause with welfare rights activists, helping the Kensington Welfare Rights Union, a welfare rights direct action group, fundraise for its Poor People's Conference in November 2000. In a similar confrontation with state negligence, throughout the summer of 2001, USAS activists, working with the Campaign for Labor Rights, visited twenty-five Mexican consulates to urge

20

the Mexican government to enforce its own labor laws in a dispute at a garment factory in Puebla.

In addition, students fighting poverty in the United States must confront culprits more complicated—and closer to home—than corporate greed: class interests and an appalling collective indifference to suffering. This past spring, Dave Snyder, a Johns Hopkins student who helped organize a spring 2000 sit-in over campus laundry workers' wages, led a USAS delegation to Kensington, the desperately poor Philadelphia community in which the welfare rights group is based. The residents "kept talking about the people who live in this nearby middle-class neighborhood, people who ignore them and shut them out," Snyder remembers. "I felt this rage against those middle-class people, trying to imagine what kind of horrible people they must be. Then we [the students] went to that neighborhood because someone's parents lived there, and I realized, this is my middle-class neighborhood; my parents would live here. I could live here."

Of course, such class inequality is what's wrong with America—and the world—and the corporation is just one of many instruments through which that inequality is maintained. In the same way, what's wrong with the university isn't the presence of Nike logos—unsightly though they may be—or even the fact of the institution's participation in the global economy. It's the meaning of these logos and deals—they signify that the institution is not run in the public interest, but to reap profits for the rich, and produce white-collar worker-cogs for the machine (or foot soldiers for the ruling class, depending on the prestige of the institution). As students are realizing, talk of "corporate control" becomes meaningless without some acknowledgement of class power. Indeed, if the public owned and democratically controlled corporations, and workers controlled their labor, the sight of a Nike logo would cause little distress.

"Smash the Swoosh!"

Pulling into Columbus, Ohio, at 1 a.m. on the morning of a big action, we might have expected to find the lead organizers trying to get some sleep. But the house was hopping when we got there—Alice Chen, Matt Teaman, Zakiyyah Jackson and other OSU radicals were bopping to music, joking around, painting huge banners ("OSU and Nike: Schools and Sweatshops Hand in Hand") and putting the finishing touches to a 10-foot-long papier mâché and chicken-wire Swoosh.

At the end of last semester a broad coalition of student groups at OSU came together for a sit-in in support of striking CWA workers that lasted twenty-eight days. Buoyed by the momentum from that sit-in, its organizers are starting an ambitious anti-sweatshop campaign in the fall aimed at getting OSU to join the Worker Rights Consortium. Revenue from OSU merchandise is among the highest of any school in the nation, and most OSU apparel is manufactured by Nike. Needless to say, the Nike Truth pilgrims were excited about the Columbus stop.

Early-afternoon rain cleared up just in time for our group of fifty or so students and local labor activists to set up a moving picket in front of Campus Expressions, a store which sells Nike-licensed OSU apparel. "Everybody wants to have a living wage. Everybody wants to be able to take care of themselves and their family. Everybody wants to retire and feel good, enjoy life. Breathe. Live. Eat. You know, the regular shit. We're not asking for nothing extra special," said second-year OSU graduate student Sheri Davis at the rally.

"Expose Nike! Smash the Swoosh!" we yelled as the aforementioned orange construction was torn apart at the end of the rally. From the hollow insides of the giant effigy spilled words describing Nike's business practices—"Poverty Wages," "Exploitation," and "Child Labor."

Chris McCallum

Re-reading/Conversations with the Text

1. Featherstone writes, "A prominent feature of the corporate university is students' alienation and powerlessness; universities often treat them as anonymous consumers." To whom do you think this essay, and more particularly this passage, is addressed? Is this an accurate description of you? Are students positioned by universities as consumers? Is this a role with which you are comfortable? Why or why not? To what degree do students willingly adopt this role?

2. Featherstone makes sophisticated connections among sweatshop workers, welfare recipients, low-wage workers, and the middle class. Draw a visual map of these connections/this argument. Next, consider what rhetorical appeals she uses to make these connections.

3. According to anti-sweatshop activist Todd Pugatch, then a student at UNC-Chapel Hill, "the university itself [can be considered] a brand, a logo, that students consume" (quoted in Featherstone). To what degree might your university or college be considered a corporation? Look at your college or university's website. How does the university or college present itself? What are the logical or rational appeals of the website or particular web pages? How is the argument for the school developed and supported? In other words, what are the sources for evidence? How would you describe the college or university's character? What emotional appeals does it use?

Re-seeing and Re-writing

In this essay, Liza Featherstone highlights the corporatization of universities and colleges across the nation, with examples such as the buyout of university bookstores by Barnes and Noble and the proliferation of Starbucks coffeehouses on campuses. Tour your own campus and consider the extent to which corporations have infiltrated your university or college. What businesses did they replace? What have been the benefits or consequences of such developments? Interview staff workers on your campus and/or students affiliated with the United Students Against Sweatshops campaign on your campus. What issues has the local campaign addressed and with what consequences?

Intertext

In "Student Activists . . . ," Liza Featherstone discusses the ways that college students in the United States have recently organized to speak and stand out against U.S. corporations' involvement—and in some cases, their own college's involvement via association with those corporations—in sweatshop labor. With this essay in mind, do one of the following:

a. Examine your own college catalog (or the catalog/index created on its Web site) or, even better, examine the composite of media texts your college produces (alumni newsletters, the official student newspaper, the college Web site, special newspapers created by student organizations, etc.) and consider these texts together as a consumer "catalogue" of your institution. What image(s) are being produced from these texts? Consider the way your own college's "labels" are produced, marketed, consumed.

b. Look into your college's affiliation and association with certain corporations (like Coca-Cola), and, taking your cues from Featherstone's journalistic style, write an article detailing your college's practices, and offering either censure or praise for them.

Images: Child Labor

LEWIS WICKES HINE is known as a pioneer of documentary-style photography. As a major activist during the Progressive era and a reformer employed by the National Child Labor Commission, Hine documented children working in U.S. factories, mills, farms, and on urban streets. His most influential photographs were taken between 1908 and 1921. Although child labor was common in the eighteenth and nineteenth centuries, and laboring children of ethnic families were widely visible as servants, farm workers, factory workers, etc., Hine's photographs alarmed many Americans.

Certain representational patterns characterize documentary photographs of child labor of this period: Among the most common are images of working children as isolated figures against the backdrop of their workplaces (Images 1 and 2); secularized versions of the Madonna and child (as in Image 3); and images of disability and loss (Image 4).

Girl Worker in Carolina Cotton Mill, 1908.
Photographer: Lewis Hine. Courtesy of George Eastman House.

Mississippi cannery, Shrimp picker, 5 years old, 1911.
Photographer: Lewis Hines. Courtesy of George Eastman House.

Little Mother in the Steel District, Pittsburgh 1909.
Photographer: Lewis Hine. Courtesy of George Eastman House.

Boy Lost Arm Running Saw in Box Factory, ca. 1909.
Photographer: Lewis Hine. Courtesy of George Eastman House.

Re-reading/Conversations with the Text

1. Take a moment to look closely at the historical images by Lewis Hines reproduced above. Think about their rhetorical appeal. What stories do they tell? Do the images elicit a sympathetic gaze? In what ways do they appeal to your emotions (*pathos*) or to reason (*logos*)? Do these images seem to dignify poverty and/or child labor? Can you imagine any of these images in an anti-child labor campaign? Why or why not?

2. Now consider the set of images below of child labor taken in the late twentieth and early twenty-first centuries. Choose two images that seem particularly compelling or interesting to you. Jot down five or so observations of each photograph. What, despite their different geographical and historical locations, do the images have in common? Imagine the two images in a contemporary anti-child labor campaign. Do you think they would be successful? Why or why not?

3. Once you have described in some detail the images themselves and highlighted significant visual patterns among them, it's time to learn a little more about the historical contexts, social conditions, and laws that enable or restrict child labor. You might begin by checking out several human rights campaigns on child labor, such as Human Rights Watch, International Initiative to End Child Labor, Behind the Label, and UNICEF (especially its *State of the World's Children* 2006 report). Write an essay or create a website, PowerPoint presentation, or pamphlet that highlights the situation of child labor today and that is also informed by and draws on representations of child labor of past centuries.

Re-seeing and Re-writing

One could argue that images such as these, when presented as part of anti-child labor campaigns, aim to move their audience to action. Imagine you, too, are moved to stop child labor. Your task, as an expert rhetorician, is to convince your skeptical friends that this is a worthy cause with which to be involved. Create a website, PowerPoint presentation, or pamphlet that integrates all or some of these images with text that attempts to persuade others to join the campaign.

Opium Production in Afghanistan.
© Shaul Schwartz/CORBIS All Rights Reserved.

Hands of Child Sweatshop Worker, India.
© Karem Kasmauski/CORBIS All Rights Reserved.

Underage Indian Carpet Weavers.

An 11-year-old boy picking red chiles in the early morning hours, New Mexico, 1997.

SWEATSHOP POEMS

DENISE DUHAMEL, ROBERT PINSKY, NAOMI SHIHAB NYE

DENISE DUHAMEL was born in Woonsocket, Rhode Island, in 1961 and currently teaches creative writing and literature at Florida International University. Her most recent book of poems is *Queen for a Day: Selected and New Poems* (2001), and others include: *The Star-Spangled Banner* (1991), winner of the Crab Orchard Poetry Prize; *Exquisite Politics* (with Maureen Seaton) (1997); *Kinky* (1993); *Girl Soldier* (1996); and *How the Sky Fell* (1996). Duhamel's poetry has been widely anthologized and appears in four volumes of *The Best American Poetry.* She is noted for using irony and outright humor in her poems, and she has claimed that "For me, humor is a way to temper rage in writing, as well as in life. Being funny is a way for me to deal with material that would otherwise be too painful. Some of my poems would be extremely maudlin or depressing or self-indulgent without humor." As you read her poem "Manifest Destiny," listen for that rage mixed with irony and humor.

Born in New Jersey in 1940, **ROBERT PINSKY** has authored six volumes of poetry, two translations, and four books of criticism, while also garnering numerous significant awards: the American Academy of Arts and Letters award, the William Carlos Williams Award, a Guggenheim Foundation fellowship, and appointment as the 1997 United States Poet Laureate and Consultant in Poetry to the Library of Congress. In a 1997 interview with *The Paris Review,* Pinsky was asked about his "affection for the language of trade." Pinsky replied, "I grew up with respect for the skills and the knowledge of people who knew how to do things." Pinsky himself has mentioned jazz, sixteenth-century poetry, and "voice"—how a poem actually sounds when it is read aloud—as strong influences on his poetry. Be sure to read his poem "Shirt" aloud and listen carefully for historical detail, "the language of trade," jazz influences, and references to any sixteenth-century poetry you might know.

NAOMI SHIHAB NYE was born in St. Louis, Missouri, in 1952, to a Palestinian father and an American-born mother. She received her B.A. from Trinity University in San Antonio, Texas, where she still lives. She is the author of numerous books of poems, including *19 Varieties of Gazelle: Poems of the Middle East* (2002); *Fuel* (1998); *Red Suitcase* (1994); and *Hugging the Jukebox* (1984). She has also written books for children and edited several anthologies of prose. She has twice traveled to the Middle East and Asia for the United States Information Agency, promoting international goodwill through the arts. Nye has gained a reputation for poetry that shows ordinary events, people and objects from a new perspective. She says, "For me the primary source of poetry has always been local life, random characters met on the streets, our own ancestry sifting down to us through small essential daily tasks" (http://voices.cla.umn.edu/authors/NYEnaomishihab.html). In "Catalogue Army," she focuses on such "small essential daily tasks" as sorting the day's mail and dealing with the onslaught of consumer catalogues.

Manifest Destiny

DENISE DUHAMEL

In the Philippines
women workers in fashion doll factories
are given cash incentives
for sterilization. Body parts roll
5   too fast on conveyor belts.
It's not like the famous episode
in which Lucy and Ethel
try a day of work, boxing chocolates
on an assembly line in the U.S. They stuff
10   most of the quick-coming candy
into their mouths, laugh brown drool
when they are fired because it doesn't really matter—
Ricky and Fred have good jobs.
To prove they're the ones
15   who belong at work, the men on TV
make a mess in Lucy's kitchen,
a pot of rice exploding
like a white volcano. The women
in the Philippines and elsewhere ponder
20   big business, the benefits
of discontinuing its own children. In dreams
these women package Toys "Я" Us uteruses
while a sterile Barbie, her hair tucked up
inside her Lucite helmet, plants
25   a flag for Mattel on the cheesiest moon.

Shirt

ROBERT PINSKY

The back, the yoke, the yardage. Lapped seams,
The nearly invisible stitches along the collar
Turned in a sweatshop by Koreans or Malaysians

Gossiping over tea and noodles on their break
5   Or talking money or politics while one fitted
This armpiece with its overseam to the band

Of cuff I button at my wrist. The presser, the cutter,
The wringer, the mangle. The needle, the union,
The treadle, the bobbin. The code. The infamous blaze

10   At the Triangle Factory in nineteen-eleven.
One hundred and forty-six died in the flames
On the ninth floor, no hydrants, no fire escapes—

The witness in a building across the street
Who watched how a young man helped a girl to step
15   Up to the window sill, then held her out

Away from the masonry wall and let her drop.
And then another. As if he were helping them up
To enter a streetcar, and not eternity.

A third before he dropped her put her arms
20   Around his neck and kissed him. Then he held
Her into space, and dropped her. Almost at once

He stepped to the sill himself, his jacket flared
And fluttered up from his shirt as he came down,
Air filling up the legs of his gray trousers—

25   Like Hart Crane's Bedlamite, "shrill shirt ballooning."
Wonderful how the pattern matches perfectly
Across the placket and over the twin bar-tacked

Corners of both pockets, like a strict rhyme
Or a major chord. Prints, plaids, checks,
30   Houndstooth, Tattersall, Madras. The clan tartans

Invented by mill-owners inspired by the hoax of Ossian,
To control their savage Scottish workers, tamed
By a fabricated heraldry: MacGregor,

Bailey, MacMartin. The kilt, devised for workers
35   To wear among the dusty clattering looms.
Weavers, carders, spinners. The loader,

The docker, the navvy. The planter, the picker, the sorter
Sweating at her machine in a litter of cotton
As slaves in calico headrags sweated in fields:

40   George Herbert, your descendant is a Black
Lady in South Carolina, her name is Irma
And she inspected my shirt. Its color and fit

And feel and its clean smell have satisfied
Both her and me. We have culled its cost and quality
45   Down to the buttons of simulated bone,

The buttonholes, the sizing, the facing, the characters
Printed in black on neckband and tail. The shape,
The label, the labor, the color, the shade. The shirt.

Catalogue Army

NAOMI SHIHAB NYE

Something has happened to my name.
It now appears on catalogues
for towels and hiking equipment,
dresses spun in India,
5   hand-colored prints of parrots and eggs.
Fifty tulips are on their way
if I will open the door.
Dishrags from North Carolina
unstack themselves in the Smoky Mountains
10   and make a beeline for my sink.

I write a postcard to my cousin:
This is what it is like to live in America.
Individual tartlet pans congregate
in the kitchen, chiming my name.
15   Porcelain fruit boxes float above tables,
sterling silver ice cream cone holders
twirl upside-down on the cat's dozing head.

For years I developed radar against malls.
So what is it that secretly applauds
20   this army of catalogues marching upon my house?
I could be in the bosom of poverty, still they arrive.
I could be dead, picked apart by vultures,
still they would tell me
what socks to wear in my climbing boots.
25   Stay true, catalogues, protect me
from the wasteland where whimsy and impulse
never camp.
Be my companion on this journey between dusts,
between vacancy and that smiling stare
30   that is citizen of every climate
but customer to nothing,
even air.

Re-reading/Conversations with the Text

1. Consider how these three poems draw attention to gender relationships and identities. Chart all the ways that men/women show up in these three poems and map their historical, political, personal, and economic relationships. For example, Pinsky's "Shirt" includes an unknown young man who "freed" girls from the Triangle Factory fire in 1911, a Hart Crane story character, Scottish kilt wearers, dockyard workers, plantation workers, and George Herbert. Imagine and chart how all of these male figures relate to the women who make his shirt.

2. Two poems ("Manifest Destiny" and "Catalogue Army") describe contemporary consumer culture, while the other ("Shirt") features historical settings. How do these three poems differ in writing about sweatshops and consumer culture? How do they employ rhetorical appeals (*logos, pathos, ethos*)?

3. The "subjects" of the poems are dolls, a shirt, and catalogues. How do the different subjects affect the tone, details, narrative perspective, and rhetorical appeals of the three poems?

Re-seeing and Re-writing

1. With a group of three to five of your peers, come up with a list of four or five consumer items you and your peers all buy. Next, research the corporate identity and labor practices behind each of them. Create a website or research report that addresses the elements of those items' production, marketing, and sale.

2. Pinsky's "Shirt" invites historical reflection. Research the history of production and consumption of a common consumer item in your life (e.g., your glasses, your computer, your favorite shampoo), and write an analytical paper in which you trace the historical development of that product. How have appeals to logic, emotions, and ethics/character been a part of the production, marketing, and sale of this item?

Intertext

Like Barbara Ehrenreich's essay "Maid to Order," these poems are in part about socioeconomic markers that reveal themselves even in everyday items (like shirts, catalogues, or dolls/toys). These texts are also about racial/ethnic/gender differences among those who produce or merely "observe" the items, and those who can actually have or consume them. For this assignment, do one of the following: Try turning one of the poems into an essay, using "Maid to Order" as your model or pattern; or try making "Maid to Order" into a poem, using one of the poems as your model.

Maid to Order

BARBARA EHRENREICH

BARBARA EHRENREICH is a political essayist and social critic. She is the author or co-author of twelve books, including *Fear of Falling: The Inner Life of the Middle Class* (1989), *Nickled and Dimed: On (Not) Getting By in America* (2002), and, most recently, *Bait and Switch: The (Futile) Pursuit of the American Dream* (2005). "Maid to Order" was first published in the collection *Global Women* (2002), in which Ehrenreich and other authors explore how women live on the wages paid for unskilled labor. Ehrenreich's essay focuses on women forced into the job market by welfare reform and investigates how they survive on the $6- to $7-an-hour jobs generally available to them.

As class polarization grows, the classic posture of submission makes a stealthy comeback. "We scrub your floors the old-fashioned way," boasts the brochure from Merry Maids, the largest of the residential cleaning services that have sprung up in the last two decades, "on our hands and knees." This is not a posture that independent "cleaning ladies" willingly assume—preferring, like most people who clean their own homes, the sponge mop wielded from a standing position. In her comprehensive guide to homemaking, Cheryl Mendelson warns, "Never ask hired housecleaners to clean your floors on their hands and knees; the request is likely to be regarded as degrading."

But in a society where 40 percent of the wealth is owned by 1 percent of households, while the bottom 20 percent reports negative assets, the degradation of others is readily purchased. Kneepads entered American political discourse as a tool of the sexually subservient, but employees of Merry Maids, The Maids International, and other new corporate-run cleaning services spend hours every day on these kinky devices, wiping up the drippings of the affluent.

I spent three weeks in September 1999 as an employee of The Maids International in a New England city, cleaning, along with my fellow team members, approximately sixty houses containing a total of about 250 scrubbable floors—bathrooms, kitchens, and entryways requiring the hands-and-knees treatment. It's a different world down there below knee level, one that few adults voluntarily enter. Here you find elaborate dust structures held together by a scaffolding of dog hairs; dried bits of pasta glued to the floor by their sauce; the congealed remains of gravies, jellies, contraceptive creams, vomit, and urine. Sometimes too you encounter some fragment of a human being: a child's legs, stamping by in disgust because the maids are still present when he gets home from school, or, more commonly, the Joan and David-clad feet and electrolyzed calves of the female homeowner. Look up and you may find this person staring at you, arms folded, in anticipation of an overlooked stain. In rare instances, she may try to help in some vague, symbolic way, by moving the cockatoo's cage, for example, or apologizing for the leaves shed by a miniature indoor tree. Mostly though, she will not see you at all, and may even sit down with her mail at a table in the very room you are cleaning, where she will remain completely unaware of your existence—unless you were to crawl under that table and start gnawing away at her ankles.

Housework, as you may recall from the feminist theories of the 1960s and 1970s, was supposed to be the great equalizer of women. Whatever else women did—jobs, school, child care—we also did housework, and if there were some women who hired others to do it for them, they seemed too privileged and rare to include in the theoretical calculus. All women were workers, and the home was their workplace—unpaid and unsupervised to be sure, but a workplace no less than the offices and factories men repaired to every morning. If men thought of the home as a site of leisure and recreation—a "haven in a heartless world"—this was to ignore the invisible female proletariat that kept it cozy and humming. We were on the march then, or so we imagined, united against a society that devalued our labor even as it waxed mawkish over "the family" and "the home." Shoulder to shoulder and arm in arm, women were finally getting up off the floor.

5   In the most eye-catching elaboration of the home-as-workplace theme, in 1972 Marxist feminists Maria Rosa Dallacosta and Selma James proposed that the home was in fact an economically productive and significant workplace, an extension of the actual factory, since housework served to "reproduce the labor power" of others, particularly men. The male worker would hardly be in shape to punch in for his shift, after all, if some woman had not fed him, laundered his clothes, and cared for the children who were his contribution to the next generation of workers. If the home was a quasi-industrial workplace staffed by women for the ultimate benefit of the capitalists, then "wages for housework" was the obvious demand.

But when most American feminists, Marxist or otherwise, asked the Marxist question *Cui bono?* they tended to come up with a far simpler answer: men. If women were the domestic proletariat, then men made up the class of domestic exploiters, free to lounge while their mates scrubbed. In consciousness-raising groups, we railed over husbands and boyfriends who refused to pick up after themselves, who were unaware of housework at all, unless of course it hadn't been done. The "dropped socks," left by a man for a woman to gather up and launder,

joined lipstick and spike heels as emblems of gender oppression. When, somewhere, a man dropped a sock with the calm expectation that his wife would retrieve it, it was a sock heard round the world. Wherever second-wave feminism took root, battles broke out between lovers or spouses over sticky countertops, piled-up laundry, and whose turn it was to do the dishes.

The radical new idea was that housework was not only a relationship between a woman and a dust bunny or an unmade bed; it also defined a relationship between human beings, typically husbands and wives. This marked a departure from the more conservative views of Betty Friedan, who, in *The Feminine Mystique,* never thought to enter men into the equation, either as part of the housework problem or part of an eventual solution. She raged against a society that consigned its educated women to what she saw as essentially janitorial chores, beneath "the abilities of a woman of average or normal intelligence" and, according to unidentified studies she cited, "peculiarly suited to the capacities of feebleminded girls." But men are virtually exempt from housework in *The Feminine Mystique*—why drag them down too? At one point she even disparaged a "Mrs. G.," who "somehow couldn't get her housework done before her husband came home at night and was so tired then that he had to do it." Educated women would just have to become more efficient so that housework could no longer "expand to fill the time available."

Or they could hire other women to do it—an option Friedan approved in *The Feminine Mystique.* So did the National Organization for Women, which Friedan helped launch: at the 1973 congressional hearings on whether to extend the Fair Labor Standards Act to household workers, NOW testified to the affirmative, arguing that improved wages and working conditions would attract more women to the field, and that "the demand for household help inside the home will continue to increase as more women seek occupations outside the home." One young NOW member added, on a personal note, "Like many young women today, I am in school in order to develop a rewarding career for myself. I also have a home to run and can fully conceive of the need for household help as my free time at home becomes more and more restricted. Women know [that] housework is dirty, tedious work, and they are willing to pay to have it done." On the aspirations of the women paid to do it, assuming at least some of them were bright enough to entertain a few, neither Friedan nor these members of NOW had, at the time, a word to say.

So the insight that distinguished the more radical, post-Friedan cohort of feminists was that when we talked about housework, we were really talking, yet again, about power. Housework was not degrading because it was manual labor, as Friedan thought, but because it was embedded in degrading relationships and inevitably served to reinforce them. To make a mess that another person will have to deal with—the dropped socks, the toothpaste sprayed on the bathroom mirror, the dirty dishes left from a late-night snack—is to exert domination in one of its more silent and intimate forms. One person's arrogance—or indifference, or hurry—becomes another person's occasion for toil. And when the person who is cleaned up after is consistently male, while the person who cleans up is consistently female, you have a formula for reproducing male domination from one generation to the next.

10   Hence the feminist perception of housework as one more way by which men exploit women or, more neutrally stated, as "a symbolic enactment of gender relations." An early German women's-liberation cartoon depicted a woman scrubbing on her hands and knees while her husband, apparently excited by this pose, approaches from behind, unzipping his fly. Hence, too, the second-wave feminists' revulsion at the hiring of maids, especially when they were women of color. At a feminist conference I attended in 1980, the poet Audre Lorde

chose to insult the all-too-white audience by accusing them of being present only because they had black housekeepers to look after their children at home. She had the wrong crowd; most of the assembled radical feminists would no sooner have employed a black maid than they would have attached Confederate flag stickers to the rear windows of their cars. But accusations like hers, repeated in countless conferences and meetings, reinforced our rejection of the servant option. There already were at least two able-bodied adults in the average home—a man and a woman—and the hope was that, after a few initial skirmishes, they would learn to share the housework graciously.

A couple of decades later, however, the average household still falls far short of that goal. True, women do less housework than they did before the feminist revolution and the rise of the two-income family: down from an average of 30 hours per week in 1965 to 17.5 hours in 1995, according to a July 1999 study from the University of Maryland. Some of that decline reflects a relaxation of standards rather than a redistribution of chores; women still do two-thirds of whatever housework—including bill paying, pet care, tidying, and lawn maintenance—gets done. The inequity is sharpest for the most despised of household chores: cleaning. Between 1965 and 1995, men increased the time they spent scrubbing, vacuuming, and sweeping by 240 percent—all the way up to 1.7 hours per week—while women decreased their cleaning time by only 7 percent, to 6.7 hours per week. The averages conceal a variety of arrangements, of course, from minutely negotiated sharing to the most clichéd division of labor, as described by one woman to the *Washington Post:* "I take care of the inside, he takes care of the outside." But perhaps the most disturbing finding is that almost all the increase in male participation took place between the 1970s and the mid-1980s. Fifteen years after the apparent cessation of hostilities, it is probably not too soon to call the question: in the "chore wars" of the 1970s and 1980s, women gained a little ground, but overall, and after a few strategic concessions, men won.

Enter then, the cleaning lady as dea ex machina, restoring tranquillity as well as order to the home. Marriage counselors recommend hiring them as an alternative to squabbling, as do many within the residential cleaning industry itself. A Chicago cleaning woman quotes one of her clients as saying that if she were to give up the service, "My husband and I will be divorced in six months." Managers of the new corporate cleaning services, such as the one I worked for, attribute their success not only to the influx of women into the workforce but to the tensions over housework that arose in its wake. When the trend toward hiring out was just beginning to take off, in 1988, the owner of a Merry Maids franchise in Arlington, Massachusetts, told the *Christian Science Monitor,* "I kid some women. I say, 'We even save marriages.' In this new eighties period, you expect more from the male partner, but very often you don't get the cooperation you would like to have. The alternative is to pay somebody to come in." Another Merry Maids franchise owner has learned to capitalize more directly on housework-related spats: he closes 30 to 35 percent of his sales by making follow-up calls on Saturday mornings, the "prime time for arguing over the fact that the house is a mess." The microdefeat of feminism in the household opened a new door for women, only this time it was the servants' entrance.

In 1999, somewhere between 14 and 18 percent of households employed outsiders to do their cleaning, and the numbers have been rising dramatically since. Mediamark Research reports a 53 percent increase, between 1995 and 1999, in the number of households using a hired cleaner or service once a month or more, and Maritz finds that 30 percent of the people who hired help in 1999 did so for the first time that year. Among my middle-class, professional women friends and acquaintances, including

some who made important contributions to the early feminist analysis of housework two and a half decades ago, the employment of a cleaning person is now nearly universal. The home, or at least the affluent home, is finally becoming what radical feminists in the 1970s only imagined it was— a "workplace" for women and a tiny, though increasingly visible, part of the capitalist economy. The question is this: As your home becomes a workplace for someone else, is it still a place where you want to live?

Strangely, or perhaps not so strangely at all, no one talks about the "politics of housework" anymore. The demand for "wages for housework" no longer has the power to polarize feminist conferences; it has sunk to the status of a curio, along with the consciousness-raising groups in which women once rallied support in their struggles with messy men. In the academy, according to the feminist sociologists I interviewed, housework has lost much of its former cachet—in part, I suspect, because fewer sociologists actually do it. Most Americans, more than 80 percent, still clean their homes, but the minority who do not include a sizeable fraction of the nation's opinion makers and culture producers: professors, writers, editors, media decision makers, political figures, talking heads and celebrities of all sorts. In their homes, the politics of housework is becoming a politics not only of gender but also of race and class, and these are subjects that the opinion-making elite, if not most Americans, generally prefer to avoid.

Even the number of paid household workers is hard to pin down. The Census Bureau reports that there were 549,000 domestic workers in 1998, up 9 percent since 1996, but this may be a considerable underestimate, since so much of the servant economy is still underground. In 1993, for example, the year when Zoë Baird lost her chance to be attorney general for paying her undocumented immigrant nanny off the books, the *Los Angeles Times* reported that fewer than 10 percent of those Americans who paid a

15

housecleaner reported these payments to the IRS. Sociologist Mary Romero, one of the few academics who retains an active interest in housework and the women who do it for pay, offers an example of how severe the undercounting can be. The 1980 census found only 1,063 "private household workers" in El Paso, Texas, although at the same time, that city's Department of Planning, Research and Development estimated these workers' numbers at 13,400, and local bus drivers estimated that half of the 28,300 daily bus trips were taken by maids going to and returning from work. The honesty of employers has increased since the Baird scandal, but most experts believe that household workers remain, in large part, uncounted and invisible to the larger economy.

One thing you can say with certainty about the population of household workers is that they are disproportionately women of color: "lower" kinds of people for a "lower" kind of work. Of the "private household cleaners and servants" it managed to locate in 1998, the Bureau of Labor Statistics reports that 36.8 percent were Hispanic, 15.8 percent black, and 2.7 percent "other." Certainly the association between housecleaning and minority status is well established in the psyches of the white employing class. When my daughter, Rosa, was introduced to the wealthy father of a Harvard classmate, he ventured that she must have been named for a favorite maid. And Audre Lorde can perhaps be forgiven for her intemperate accusation at the feminist conference mentioned above when we consider an experience she had in 1967: "I wheel my two-year-old daughter in a shopping cart through a supermarket . . . and a little white girl riding past in her mother's cart calls out excitedly, 'Oh look, Mommy, a baby maid.' "

The composition of the household workforce is hardly fixed, and it has changed with the life chances of the different ethnic groups. In the late nineteenth century, Irish and German immigrants served the urban upper and middle classes, then left for the factories as soon as they could. Black women replaced them, accounting for 60 percent of all domestics in the 1940s and dominating the field until other occupations opened to them. Similarly, West Coast maids were disproportionately Japanese-American until that group found more congenial options. Today, the color of the hand that pushes the sponge varies from region to region: Chicanas in the Southwest, Caribbeans in New York, native Hawaiians in Hawaii, native whites, many of recent rural extraction, in the New England city where I briefly worked.

The great majority—although again, no one knows the exact numbers—of paid housekeepers are freelancers, or "independents," who find their clients through agencies or networks of already employed friends and relatives. To my acquaintances in the employing class, the freelance housekeeper seems to be a fairly privileged and prosperous type of worker, sometimes paid $15 an hour or more and usually said to be viewed as a friend or even as "one of the family." But the shifting ethnic composition of the workforce tells another story: many women have been trapped in this kind of work, whether by racism, imperfect English skills, immigration status, or lack of education. Few happily choose it. Interviews with independent maids collected by Romero and by sociologist Judith Rollins, who herself worked as a maid in the Boston area in the early eighties, confirm the undesirability of the work to those who perform it. Even when the pay is deemed acceptable, the hours may be long and unpredictable; there is no job security; there are usually no health benefits; and if the employer has failed to pay Social Security taxes (in some cases because the maid herself prefers to be paid off the books), there are no retirement benefits. And the pay is often far from acceptable. The BLS found full-time "private household workers and servants" earning a median income of $223 a week in 1998, which is $23 a week below the poverty level for a family of three. Recall that in 1993 Zoë Baird paid her undocumented household workers $5 an hour out of her earnings of $507,000 a year.

At the most lurid extreme there is slavery. A few cases of captivity and forced labor pop up in the press every year, most recently involving undocumented women held in servitude by high-ranking staff members of the United Nations, the World Bank, and the International Monetary Fund. Consider the charges brought by Elizabeth Senghor, a Senegalese woman who told the court that her Manhattan employers forced her to work fourteen-hour days without any regular pay and with no accommodations beyond a pullout bed in her employers' living room. Hers is not a particularly startling instance of domestic slavery; no beatings or sexual assaults were charged, and Ms. Senghor was apparently fed. What gives this case a certain rueful poignancy is that her employer, former U.N. employee Marie Angelique Savane, is one of Senegal's leading women's-rights advocates, and had told the *Christian Science Monitor* in 1986 about her efforts to get the Senegalese to "realize that being a woman can mean other things than simply having children, taking care of the house."

20   Mostly though, independent maids and their employers complain about the peculiar intimacy of the employer-employee relationship. Domestic service is an occupation that predates the refreshing impersonality of capitalism by several thousand years, conditions of work being still largely defined by the idiosyncrasies of the employers. Some of them seek friendship and even what their maids describe as "therapy," though they are usually quick to redraw the lines once the maid is perceived as overstepping. Others demand deference bordering on servility, while an increasing portion of the nouveau riche is simply out of control. In August 1999, the *New York Times* reported on the growing problem of dinner parties in upscale homes

being disrupted by hostesses screaming at their help. To the verbal abuse, add published reports of sexual and physical assaults—the teenage son of an employer, for example, kicking a live-in nanny for refusing to make sandwiches for him and his friends after school.

For better or worse, capitalist rationality is finally making some headway into this preindustrial back-water. Nationwide and even international cleaning services like Merry Maids, Molly Maids, and The Maids International, all of which have arisen since the 1970s, now control 20 to 25 percent of the $1.4 billion housecleaning business, and perhaps their greatest innovation has been to abolish the mistress-maid relationship, with all its quirks and dependencies.

The customer hires the service, not the maid, who has been replaced anyway by a team of two to four uniformed people, only one of whom, the team leader, is usually authorized to speak to the customer about the work at hand. The maids' wages, their Social Security taxes, their green cards, backaches, and child-care problems are the sole concern of the company, meaning the local franchise owner. If there are complaints on either side, they are addressed to the franchise owner; the customer and the actual workers need never interact. Since the franchise owner is usually a middle-class white person, cleaning services are the ideal solution for anyone still sensitive enough to find the traditional employer-maid relationship morally vexing. In a 1997 article about Merry Maids, *Franchise Times* reported tersely that the "category is booming, [and the] niche is hot too, as Americans look to outsource work even at home."

Not all cleaning services do well. There is a high rate of failure among the informal, mom-and-pop services, like one I applied to by phone that did not even require a cursory interview; all I would have had to do was show up at seven the next morning. The "boom" is concentrated among the national and international chains—outfits like Merry Maids, Molly Maids, Mini

Maids, Maid Brigade, and The Maids International—all named, curiously enough, to highlight the more antique aspects of the industry, although the "maid" may occasionally be male. In 1996, Merry Maids claimed to be growing at 15 to 20 percent a year, while spokespersons for Molly Maids and The Maids International each told me that their firms' sales are growing by 25 percent a year. Local franchisers are equally bullish. My boss at The Maids confided to me that he could double his business overnight, if only he could find enough reliable employees.

To this end, The Maids offers a week of paid vacation, health insurance after ninety days, and a free breakfast every morning, consisting, at least where I worked, of coffee, doughnuts, bagels, and bananas. Some franchises have dealt with the tight labor market by participating in welfare-to-work projects that not only funnel them employees but often subsidize their paychecks with public money, at least for the first few months of work (which doesn't mean that the newly minted maid earns more, only that the company has to pay her less). The Merry Maids franchise in the city where I worked is conveniently located a block away from the city's welfare office.

25 Among the women I worked with at The Maids, only one said she had previously worked as an independent, and she professed to be pleased with her new status as a cleaning-service employee. She no longer needed a car to get her from house to house, and she could take a day off—unpaid, of course—to stay home with a sick child without risking the loss of a customer. Cleaning services are an especially appealing option for recent immigrants, who are unlikely to have cars or the contacts they would need to work as independents; large services, like The Maids, have videotapes used for training new hires in Spanish as well as English. I myself could see the advantage of not having to deal directly with the customers, who were sometimes at home while we worked and eager to make use of their supervisory skills. Criticisms of our methods, as well as demands that we perform unscheduled tasks, could simply be referred to the team leader or, beyond her, to the franchise owner.

But workers inevitably face losses when an industry moves from the entrepreneurial to the industrial phase—most strikingly, in this case, in the matter of pay. At Merry Maids, I was promised $200 for a forty-hour week, with the manager hastening to add that "you can't calculate it in dollars per hour," since the forty hours includes all the time spent traveling from house to house—up to five houses a day—which is unpaid. The Maids International, with its straightforward starting rate of $6.63 an hour, seemed preferable, although this rate was conditional on perfect attendance. Miss one day and your wage dropped to $6 an hour for two weeks, a rule that weighed particularly heavily on those who had young children. In addition, I soon learned that management had ways of shaving off nearly an hour's worth of wages a day. We were told to arrive at 7:30 in the morning, but our billable hours began only after we had been teamed up, given our list of houses for the day, and packed off in the company car at around 8:00. At the end of the day, we were no longer paid from the moment we left the car, although as much as fifteen minutes of work—sorting through the rags dirtied in the course of the day, refilling cleaning-fluid bottles, and the like—remained to be done in the office. So for a standard nine-hour day, the actual pay amounted to about $6.06 an hour, unless you were still being punished for an absence, in which case it came out to $5.48 an hour.

Nor are cleaning-service employees likely to receive any of the perks or tips familiar to independents—free lunches and coffee, cast-off clothing, or a Christmas gift of cash. When I asked, only one of my coworkers could recall ever receiving a tip, and that was a voucher for a free meal at a downtown restaurant owned by a customer. More than a year later, she still hadn't used it, probably because she would have to eat alone, the $20 or so for a companion's meal being out of the question. The customers of cleaning services are probably no stingier than the employers of independents; they just don't know their cleaning people and probably wouldn't recognize them on the street. They may even get a different crew each visit. Besides, customers probably assume that the fee they pay the service—$25 per person-hour in the case of my franchise of The Maids—goes largely to the workers who do the actual cleaning.

The most interesting feature of the cleaning-service chains, at least from an abstract, historical perspective, is that they are finally transforming the home into a fully capitalist-style workplace, and in ways that the old wages-for-housework advocates could never have imagined. A house is an innately difficult workplace to control, especially a house with ten or more rooms, like so many of those we cleaned; workers may remain out of one another's sight for many minutes, as much as an hour at a time. For independents, the ungovernable nature of the home workplace means a certain amount of autonomy. They can take breaks (though this is probably ill-advised if the home owner is on the premises); they can ease the monotony by listening to the radio or television while they work. But cleaning services lay down rules meant to enforce a factorylike—or even conventlike—discipline on their far-flung employees. At The Maids, there were no breaks except for a daily ten-minute stop at a convenience store for coffee or "lunch," meaning something like a slice of pizza. Otherwise, the time spent driving between houses was considered our "break" and was the only chance to eat, drink, or (although this was also officially forbidden) smoke a cigarette. When the houses were spaced well apart, I could eat the sandwich I packed each day in one sitting; otherwise it

would have to be divided into as many as three separate, hasty snacks.

Within a customer's house, nothing was to touch our lips at all—not even water. On hot days, I sometimes broke that rule by drinking from a bathroom faucet. Televisions and radios were off-limits, and we were never, ever to curse out loud, even in an ostensibly deserted house. There might be a home owner secreted in some locked room, we were told, ear pressed to the door, or, more likely, a tape recorder or video camera running. At the time, I dismissed this as a scare story, but I have since come across ads for concealable video cameras, like the Tech 7 "incredible coin-sized camera," designed to "get a visual record of your babysitter's actions" and "watch employees to prevent theft." It was the threat or rumor of hidden recording devices, set up by customers to catch one of us stealing, that provided the final capitalist-industrial touch: supervision.

But what makes the work most factory-like is 30 the intense Taylorization imposed by the companies. An independent, or a person cleaning his or her own home, chooses where she will start and, within each room, probably tackles the most egregious dirt first. Or she may plan her work more or less ergonomically, first doing whatever can be done from a standing position and then squatting or crouching to reach the lower levels. But with the special "systems" devised by the cleaning services and imparted to employees through training videos, there are no such decisions to make. In The Maids' "healthy-touch" system, which is similar to what I saw of the Merry Maids' system on the training tape I was shown during my interview, all cleaning is divided into four task areas—dusting, vacuuming, kitchens, and bathrooms—which are in turn divided among the team members. For each task area other than vacuuming, there is a bucket containing rags and the appropriate cleaning fluids, so the biggest decision an employee has to make is which fluid and scrubbing instrument (rag, brush, or Dobie-brand plastic scouring pad) to deploy on which kind of surface; almost everything else has been choreographed in advance. When vacuuming, you begin with the master bedroom; when dusting, with the first room off the kitchen, then you move through the rooms going left to right. When entering each room, you proceed from left to right and top to bottom, and the same with each surface—left to right, top to bottom. Deviations are subject to rebuke, as I discovered when a team leader caught me moving my arm from right to left, then left to right, while wiping Windex over a French door.

It's not easy for anyone with extensive cleaning experience—and I include myself in this category—to accept this loss of autonomy over her movements from minute to minute. But I came to love the system: first, because if you hadn't always been traveling rigorously from left to right, it would have been easy to lose your way in some of the larger houses and to omit or redo a room. Second, many of our houses were already clean when we started, at least by any normal standards, thanks probably to a housekeeper who kept things up between our visits; but the absence of visible dirt did not mean there was less work to do, for no surface could ever be neglected, so it was important to have "the system" to remind you of where you had been and what you had already "cleaned." No doubt the biggest advantage of the system, though, is that it helps you achieve the speed demanded by the company, which allots only so many minutes per domicile (from about forty-five for a smallish apartment up to several hours per house). After a week or two on the job, I found myself moving robotlike from surface to surface, grateful to have been relieved of the thinking-process.

Even ritual work, however, takes its toll on those assigned to perform it. Turnover is dizzyingly high in the cleaning-service industry, and not only because of the usual challenges that confront the working poor, including child-care problems, unreliable transportation, evictions, and prior health conditions. As my longwinded interviewer at Merry Maids warned me, and as my coworkers at The Maids confirmed, this is a physically punishing occupation, something to tide you over for a few months, not year after year. The hands-and-knees posture damages knees, with or without pads; vacuuming strains the back; constant wiping and scrubbing invite repetitive-stress injuries even in the very young. In my three weeks as a maid, I suffered nothing more than a persistent muscle spasm in the right forearm—from scrubbing, I suppose—but the damage would have been far worse if I'd had to go home every day to my own housework and children, as most of my coworkers did, instead of returning to my motel and indulging in a daily after-work regimen of ice packs and stretches. Chores that seem effortless at home, even almost recreational when undertaken at will for twenty minutes or so at a time, quickly turn nasty when performed hour after hour, with few or no breaks and under relentless time pressure.

So far, the independent, entrepreneurial house cleaner is holding her own, but there are reasons to think that corporate cleaning services will eventually dominate the industry. New users often prefer the impersonal, standardized service offered by the chains, and in a fast-growing industry, new users make up a sizable chunk of the total clientele. Government regulation also favors the corporate chains, whose spokesmen speak gratefully of the "Zoë Baird effect," referring to customers' worries about being caught employing an undocumented immigrant. But the future of housecleaning may depend on the entry of even bigger players into the industry. Merry Maids, the largest of the chains, has the advantage of being a unit within the $6.4 billion ServiceMaster conglomerate, which includes such related businesses as Tru-Green ChemLawn, Terminix, Rescue Rooter, and Furniture Medic. A few other large firms are testing, or have tested, the water: Johnson Wax acquired Molly Maid in 1987–88, then abandoned it, according to a Molly Maid spokesperson, because the wax people were too "product oriented" for the "relational" culture of a service-providing company. Swisher International, best known as an industrial toilet-cleaning service, is operating Swisher Maids in Georgia and North Carolina; and Sears may be feeling its way into the business too. If large multinational firms establish a foothold in the industry, the mobile customers sociologist Saskia Sassen calls the "new transnational professionals" will be able to find the same branded and standardized product wherever they relocate. For the actual workers, the change will, in all likelihood, mean a more standardized and speeded-up approach to the work, with less freedom of motion and fewer chances to pause.

The trend toward outsourcing the work of the home seems, at the moment, unstoppable. Two hundred years ago, women manufactured soap, candles, cloth, and clothing in their own homes, and the complaints of some women at the turn of the twentieth century that they had been "robbed . . . by the removal of *creative* work" from the home sound pointlessly reactionary today. Not only have the skilled crafts, like sewing and cooking from scratch, left the home, but many of the "white-collar" tasks are on their way out too. For a fee, new firms like San Francisco–based Les Concierges and Cross It Off Your List in Manhattan will pick up dry cleaning, baby-sit pets, buy groceries, deliver dinner, even do the Christmas shopping. With other firms and individuals offering to buy your clothes, organize your financial files, straighten our your closets and drawers, and wait around in your home for the plumber to show up, why would anyone want to hold on to the toilet cleaning?

35   Absent a long-term souring of the economy, there is every reason to think that Americans will become increasingly reliant on paid housekeepers and that this reliance will extend ever further into the middle class. For one thing, there is no reason to expect that men will voluntarily take on a greater share of the burden, and much of the need for paid help arises from their abdication. As for children, once a handy source of household help: they are now off at soccer practice or SAT-prep classes, and Grandmother has relocated to warmer weather or taken up a second career. Furthermore, despite the fact that people spend less time at home than ever, the square footage of new homes swelled by 39 percent between 1971 and 1996, to include family rooms, home-entertainment rooms, home offices, bedrooms, and often a bathroom for each family member. By the second quarter of 1999, 17 percent of new homes were larger than three thousand square feet, which is usually considered the size threshold for household help, or the point at which a house becomes unmanageable to the people who live in it.

One more trend impels people to hire outside help, according to cleaning expert Cheryl Mendelson: fewer Americans know how to clean or even to "straighten up." I hear this from professional women defending their decision to hire a maid: "I'm just not very good at it myself " or "I wouldn't really know where to begin." Since most of us learn to clean from our parents (usually our mothers), any diminution of cleaning skills is transmitted from one generation to the next, like a gene that can, in the appropriate environment, turn out to be lethal or disabling. Upper-middle-class children raised in the servant economy of the early twenty-first century are bound to grow up as domestically incompetent as their parents, and no less dependent on others to clean up after them. Mendelson sees this as a metaphysical loss, a "matter of no longer being physically centered in your environment." Having cleaned the rooms of many overprivileged teenagers during my stint with The Maids, I think the problem is a little more urgent than that. The American overclass is raising a generation of young people who will, without constant assistance, suffocate in their own detritus.

If there are moral losses, too, as Americans increase their reliance on paid household help, no one has been tactless enough to raise them. Almost everything we buy, after all, is the product of some other person's suffering and miserably underpaid labor. I clean my own house, but I can hardly claim purity in any other area of consumption. I buy my jeans at the Gap, which is reputed to subcontract to sweatshops. I tend to favor decorative objects no doubt ripped off, by their purveyors, from scantily paid Third World craftspersons. Like everyone else, I eat salad greens picked by migrant farm-workers, some of them possibly children. And so on. We can try to minimize the pain that goes into feeding, clothing, and otherwise provisioning ourselves—by observing boycotts, checking for a union label, and so on—but there is no way to avoid it altogether without living in the wilderness on berries. Why should housework, among all the goods and services we consume, arouse any special angst?

Yet it does, as I have found in conversations with liberal-minded employers of maids, perhaps because we all sense that there are ways in which housework is different from other products and services. First is its inevitable proximity to the activities that constitute "private" life. The home that becomes a workplace for other people remains a home, even when that workplace is minutely regulated by the corporate cleaning chains. Someone who has no qualms about purchasing rugs woven by child-slaves in India, or coffee picked by ruined peasants in Guatemala, might still hesitate to tell dinner guests that, surprisingly enough, his or her lovely home doubles as a sweatshop during the day. You can eschew the chain cleaning services of course, hire an independent cleaner at a generous hourly wage, and even encourage, at least in spirit, the unionization of the housecleaning industry—and of course you should do all these things if you are an employer of household help. But none of this will change the fact that someone is working in your home at a job she would almost certainly never have chosen for herself—if she'd had a college education, for example, or was a native-born American with good English skills—or that the place where she works, however enthusiastically or resentfully, is the same as the place where you sleep.

It is also the place where your children are raised, and what they learn pretty quickly is that some people are less worthy than others. Even better wages and working conditions won't erase the hierarchy between an employer and his or her domestic help, since the help is usually there only because the employer has "something better" to do with her time, as one report on the growth of cleaning services puts it, not noticing the obvious implication that the cleaning person herself has *nothing* better to do with her time. In a merely middle-class home, the message may be reinforced by a warning to the children that that's what they'll end up doing if they don't try harder in school. Housework, as radical feminists once proposed, defines a human relationship and, when unequally divided among the social groups, reinforces preexisting inequalities. Dirt, in other words, tends to attach to the people who remove it—"garbagemen" and "cleaning ladies." Or, as cleaning entrepreneur Don Aslett told me with some bitterness—and this is a successful man, the chairman of the board of an industrial cleaning service and a frequent television guest—"The whole mentality out there is that if you clean, you're a scumball."

Increasingly often, the house cleaner is a 40 woman of color and a recent arrival from the Third World, so that the implicit lesson for the household's children is that anyone female with dark skin and broken English is a person of inferior status—someone who has "nothing better" to do. What we risk as domestic work is taken over by immigrant workers is reproducing, within our own homes, the global inequalities that so painfully divide the world.

There is another lesson the servant economy teaches its beneficiaries and, most troublingly, the children among them. To be cleaned up after is to achieve a certain magical weightlessness and immateriality. Almost everyone complains about violent video games, but paid housecleaning has the same consequence-abolishing effect: you blast the villain into a mist of blood droplets and move right along; you drop the socks knowing they will eventually levitate, laundered and folded, back to their normal dwelling place. The result is a kind of virtual existence, in which the trail of litter that follows you seems to evaporate all by itself. Spill syrup on the floor and the cleaning person will scrub it off when she comes on Wednesday. Leave the *Wall Street Journal* scattered around your airplane seat and the flight attendants will deal with it after you've deplaned. Spray toxins into the atmosphere from your factory's smokestacks and they will be filtered out eventually by the lungs of the breathing public. A servant economy may provide opportunities, however limited, for poor and immigrant women. But it also breeds callousness and solipsism in the served, and it does so all the more effectively when the service is performed close up and routinely in the place where they live and reproduce.

Individual situations vary, of course, in ways that elude blanket judgment. Some people—the elderly and disabled, parents of new babies, asthmatics who require an allergen-free environment—may well need help performing what nursing-home staffers call the ADLs, or activities of daily living, and no shame should be attached to their dependency. In a more generous social order, housekeeping services would be subsidized for those who have health-related reasons to need them—a measure that would generate a surfeit of jobs for the entry-level workers who now clean the homes of the affluent. And in a less gender-divided social order, husbands and boyfriends would more readily do their share of the chores. The growing servant economy, with all the quandaries it generates, is largely a result of men's continuing abdication from their domestic responsibilities.

However we resolve the issue in our individual homes, the moral challenge is, put simply, to make work visible again: not only the scrubbing and vacuuming, but all the hoeing, stacking, hammering, drilling, bending, and lifting that goes into creating and maintaining a livable habitat. In an ever more economically unequal world, where so many of the affluent devote their lives to ghostly pursuits like stock trading, image making, and opinion polling, real work, in the old-fashioned sense of labor that engages hand as well as eye, that tires the body and directly alters the physical world tends to vanish from sight. The feminists of my generation tried to bring some of it into the light of day, but, like busy professional women fleeing the house in the morning, they left the project unfinished, the debate broken off in mid-sentence, the noble intentions unfulfilled. Sooner or later, someone else will have to finish the job.

Re-reading/Conversations with the Text

1. Barbara Ehrenreich's essay discusses gender, race, and class identities, particularly as they relate to the evolution of the role of the house-worker over time. Consider the ways in which gender, race, and class figure into a consumer relationship that allows one party to buy human labor and the other to be bought. Who is most likely to buy such services? Who is most likely to perform them? According to Ehrenreich, what are the larger social implications of these rela-

tionships? To what extent can these gendered, raced, and classed relationships in the housecleaning industry affect larger social relationships?

2. In order to educate the reader on the politics of the maid service industry, Ehrenreich incorporates the following into her essay: personal experiences, quotes, statistics, and other forms of discourse. Working in groups of two, paraphrase Ehrenreich's primary claims. Next, re-read her essay, considering what appeals (*ethos, pathos,* and/or *logos*) she uses to construct her argument. What appeals would you use if you were to present this data on different days to an audience of potential investors for the maid corporations; to labor activists; and to consumers (people wanting to hire a maid for their home)? How would these be similar to and/or different from Ehrenreich's appeals? Why?

3. Ehrenreich uses rich descriptive language to show her audience both the labor performed by the maids and the ways companies and customers behave towards the maids. Look back through the essay for passages where Ehrenreich has used vivid description: How does she describe the labor of the maids? How does she describe their experiences with maid services and customers? How does she describe the ways maids see their employers and customers, and how does she describe how the customers and employers see (or don't see) the maids themselves? Next, consider how these descriptions serve the larger argument Ehrenreich makes in the essay about maid services. In what ways might these descriptions help persuade viewers to accept Ehrenreich's claims? How persuasive would this essay be without its rich descriptive details?

Re-seeing and Re-writing

1. As Ehrenreich makes clear throughout her essay, wages for maid services are often very low. This assignment asks you to research and to document both the minimum wage requirements for your state and the average cost of housing for your area. Consider, on average, how much money a family of four must make to subsist (i.e., adequate housing, food, utilities, healthcare costs, etc.) in your area and whether minimum wage jobs can sustain the average family. Your ultimate task is to craft a realistic proposal that addresses minimum wage requirements, housing subsidies, or food prices (for example). You might visit your state or local government's Web site to see recent legislative proposals and to get a better sense of the audience, purpose, rhetorical appeals, and tone of the text. Remember: Your audience is both government officials and the general public, so you will want to consider ways to reach both audiences.

2. Ehrenreich spends a lot of time discussing how maid services persuade customers to purchase their services and how they persuade employees to take jobs as maids. For example, she says the maid services encourage customers to purchase their services because the consumer has "'something better to do'. . . not noticing the obvious implication that the cleaning person herself

has *nothing* better to do with her time." For this assignment, research the persuasive strategies used by local or national maid services in sales materials such as newspaper or magazine ads, brochures, or company Web sites. What specific appeals do these sales materials use? What aspects of the service, such as pay and the labor involved, are made visible to customers, and which aspects are downplayed or made invisible? How are potential customers encouraged to see the maids who perform the labor or the companies that provide such services? In what way(s) do the sales materials help consumers justify the need for a housecleaning service? Now consider similar questions for job ads designed to recruit maids: In what ways are the persuasive strategies used similar and/or different?

Intertext

In Charles Kernaghan's letter "An Appeal to Walt Disney," he explains that corporations that choose to manufacture in third world countries such as Haiti pit U.S. workers against those who will provide cheaper labor overseas. Although the workers Ehrenreich describes are not living in abject poverty like those who work in Disney's sweatshops in Haiti, there are some similarities between these groups of workers. Consider the relationship between low-wage workers in the United States and those in third-world countries. To demonstrate this relationship, create a visual text, using Photoshop, Flash, or other tools of your choice. Be prepared to present your image(s) to your classmates and explain the choices you have made in your representation(s).

New York City, 1989

PAM SPAULDING

PAM SPAULDING is a photographer for *The Courier-Journal* in Louisville, Kentucky. Spaulding has gained recognition for her freelance photography, including her work on a project exposing the long-term effects of toxic solvents on railroad workers in Louisville. The photograph below features a young Mexican girl playing with a Barbie doll at Ellis Island, formerly the primary immigration station for the United States.

Pam Spaulding, "New York City, 1989."
Courtesy of Pam Spaulding.

Re-reading/Conversations with the Text

1. This is an image of a young Mexican girl on Ellis Island, the chief U.S. immigration station (now a museum) through which more than 12 million people passed between 1892 and 1954. What story does this image tell about the United States as a nation? What story does the image tell about immigration or migration? What does the image say about the fluidity of U.S. identity? To what does the image appeal in its depiction of American-ness? Does the image appeal to logical thinking (*logos*), to the emotions (*pathos*), to particular values or beliefs (*ethos*), or to a combination of these?

2. Are we as viewers invited to look *with* or *at* the young Mexican girl and the cultural differences she represents? Do the various angles of vision, including the mirror image, move viewers toward identification with or distance from the young girl?

3. How might this image be read as an example of the intersection of the national and consumer gazes? For example, what image of American-ness does the Barbie doll emphasize? What question(s) does the photograph raise about gender and national identity? How does the photographer use camera angles and reflection to convey this connection?

Re-seeing and Re-writing

1. Think about your own residence in the United States. Does your family have an immigration/migration story? If so, in what ways has your family represented this story? Or, if your family owns multiple residences, and therefore multiple national identities, how has your family negotiated this movement across national borders?

2. Tour the Ellis Island Immigration Museum Web site (www.ellisisland.com) to learn more about the history of immigration. What stories of immigration are highlighted on the Web site? Browse the museum's photographs. What stories do these images convey? Do the photographs appeal to logical thinking (*logos*), to the emotions (*pathos*), to particular values or beliefs (*ethos*), or to some combination of these?

ON BARBIE

HEID E. ERDRICH, SUSAN DEER CLOUD, DENISE DUHAMEL, RABBI SUSAN SCHNUR

One of the most popular icons in U.S. society and much of the world, Mattel's Barbie doll has been revamped numerous times in order to keep her image fresh and in tune with the fashions and styles of the time.

HEID E. ERDRICH is the author of a volume of poems, *Fishing for Myth* (1997) and co-editor (with Laura Tohe) of *Sister Nations* (2002), a volume of Native American poetry and prose; her poem "Butter Maiden and Maize Girl Survive Death Leap" appears in that volume. She teaches creative writing and Native American Literature at the University of St. Thomas in St. Paul, Minnesota. She is both of German ancestry and a member of the Turtle Mountain band of Ojibwe; she was raised in Wahpeton, North Dakota, where her parents taught at the Indian school. In describing her own writing for a review of *Fishing for Myth,* Erdrich has said: "When events or memories seem impossible or inexplicable, I listen for the voice that tells how they came to be—the story voice, the mythteller. These poems are the result of that listening." Pay attention to the mixing of myths in her "Butter Maiden and Maize Girl" poem.

SUSAN DEER CLOUD is an adjunct professor in the creative writing program at Binghamton University, New York. She contributed two poems to *Sister Nations* (2002), a volume of Native American poetry and prose. "Her Pocahontas" is one of those poems.

DENISE DUHAMEL was born in Woonsocket, Rhode Island, in 1961 and currently teaches creative writing and literature at Florida International University. Her most recent book of poems is *Queen for a Day: Selected and New Poems* (2001), and others include: *The Star-Spangled Banner* (1991), winner of the Crab Orchard Poetry Prize; *Exquisite Politics* (with Maureen Seaton) (1997); *Kinky* (1993); *Girl Soldier* (1996); and *How the Sky Fell* (1996). *Kinky* contains several poems about Barbie, two of which are reprinted here. Duhamel's poetry has been widely anthologized and appears in four volumes of *The Best American Poetry.* She is noted for using irony and outright humor in her poems, and she has claimed that "For me, humor is a way to temper rage in writing, as well as in life. Being funny is a way for me to deal with material that would otherwise be too painful. Some of my poems would be extremely maudlin or depressing or self-indulgent without humor."

RABBI SUSAN SCHNUR is the current editor of *Lilith* magazine, an independent Jewish women's magazine that aims to chart "Jewish women's lives with exuberance, rigor, affection, subversion and style" and features "award-winning investigative reports, new rituals and celebrations, first-person accounts both contemporary and historical, entertainment reviews, fiction and poetry, art and photography" (http://www.lilith.org/). Schnur is also a clinical psychologist at Princeton University. "Barbie Does Yom Kippur" makes interesting connections among women's/girl's desires to control their bodies, consumer culture, and religious tradition.

Butter Maiden and Maize Girl
Survive Death Leap

HEID E. ERDRICH

Even now, Native American Barbie gets only so many roles:
Indian Princess, Pocahontas, or, in these parts, Winona—
maiden who leapt for brave love from the rock
that overlooks that river town where eagles mate.

5   In my day, she might have been asked to play
Minnehaha, laughing waters, or the lovely one
in the T.V. corn oil ads: "We call it maize . . ."
Or even Captain Hook's strangely Asian Tiger Lily.

Oh, what I would have done for a Chippewa Barbie!
10 My mother refused to buy tourist souvenir princesses
in brown felt dresses belted with beads, stamped Made in China.
"They're stunted," Mom would say. Her lips in that line

that meant she'd said the last word. She was right, those dolls'
legs were stubby as toddlers, though they wore sexy women's
15 clothes. They were brown as Hershey bars and, Mom pointed out,
clothed in bandanas and aprons when sold as "Southern Gals."

Most confusing was the feather that sprouted at the crown
of each doll's braided hair. "Do they grow there?"
a playmate once asked, showing me the doll her father
20 bought her at Mount Rushmore. I recall she gazed at my

own brown locks then stated, "Your mother was an Indian Princess."
My denial came in an instant. My mother had warned me:
"Tell them that our tribe didn't have any royalty."
But there was a problem of believability, you see.

25 Turns out Mom had floated in the town parade
in feathers, raven wig and braids, when crowned "Maiden"
to the college "Brave" in the year before she married.
Oh, Mom . . . you made it hard on us, what you did at eighteen,

and worse, the local rumor that it was *you* on the butter box
30 from the Land O'Lakes that graced most tables in our tiny town.
You on their toast each morning, you the object of the joke,
the trick boys learned of folding the fawn-like Butter Maiden's

naked knees up to her chest to make a pair of breasts!
I cannot count the times I argued for Mom's humble status.
35 How many times I insisted she was no princess, though a beauty
who just happened to have played along in woodland drag one day.

I wonder, did my sisters have to answer for the princess? Did you?
Couldn't we all have used a real doll, a round, brown, or freckled,
jeans and shawl-wearing pow-wow teen queen? A lifelike Native Barbie—
40 better yet, two who take the plunge off lover's leap in tandem and survive.

Her Pocahontas

SUSAN DEER CLOUD

"Why will you take by force
    what you may have quietly by love?"

POWHATAN, FATHER OF POCAHONTAS

Her Pocahontas was a doll given to her by her mother.
Her Pocahontas was an earth-skinned, dark-haired, amber-eyed baby
pressed into her three-year-old arms starting to reach past infancy
and innocence. "This doll's name is Pocahontas," her mother said.
5 "This doll is Indian like me. This doll is Indian like you.
Take good care of her. Hold her close to your heart."

Her Pocahontas was the most her mother ever said about being Indian.
It was the 1950s. People had secrets. People kept silent.
No one talked about it, and the children didn't know why.
10 Her Pocahontas was a soft, sad darkness who couldn't cry,
whose eyes never closed, who had an invisible tongue.
Her Pocahontas liked to be sung to deep in the forest.

Her Pocahontas was nothing like the dolls the other girls had.
Their dolls were Christmas presents with blue eyes, curly blonde hair,
15   petite plastic noses. Their dolls would never need nose jobs or smell
fear. Their dolls had eyes that shut so they wouldn't have to take
everything in. Their dolls cried fake tears. They made an awful
whining sound if you turned them upside-down.

Her Pocahontas was Indian. The other girls played house with dolls
20   that had skin like refined sugar for baking cakes. They expected
their dolls to grow up, to be like the actresses they worshipped
on vast movie screens—blonde, pug-nosed Doris Day always
"holding out," golden, pout-lipped Marilyn hinting with winks
she "put out." Her Pocahontas had technicolor visions in the woods.

25   Her Pocahontas was a doll with a short life expectancy.
Her Pocahontas was a baby who knew better than to cry. No one
talked about it, but there was an unspoken memory of soldiers
and death. Her Pocahontas had a body dark as night, undomesticated
as stars, naked as dreams. The other girls hated her Pocahontas.
30   They had their own Pocahontas, a confection of lies.

Their Pocahontas had two white Johns and became white herself.
Their Pocahontas was a fantasy that popped up on medicine bottles,
cigar lids and butter boxes. Their Pocahontas was a film star, first
a squaw saving the White Man in bad cowboy-and-Indian movies, last
35   a buckskin-Barbie disguised by Disney as politically correct.
Any girl could be one. Her Pocahontas knew the truth
but couldn't speak.

When her mother died too young, her eldest brother asked her
after the funeral, "Whatever happened to that doll Ma gave you—
40   Pocahontas?" She stood there in the whirling snow, cradling
darkness close to her heart, and couldn't remember.
"Maybe," she told him, "she died of smallpox, of arms and legs
broken for trying to bring back the old dances, of a tongue
slit for speaking her own language."

45   Her Pocahontas was a doll given to her by her dead mother.

Oriental Barbie

DENISE DUHAMEL

She could be from Japan, Hong Kong, China,
the Philippines, Vietnam, Thailand, or Korea.
The little girl who plays with her can decide.
The south, the north, a nebulous
5   province. It's all the same, according to Mattel, who says
this Barbie still has "round eyes,"
but "a smaller mouth and a smaller bust"
than her U.S. sister. Girls, like some grown men,
like variety, as long as it's pretty, as long
10   as there's long hair to play with.
On a late-night Manhattan Cable commercial,
one escort service sells Geishas to Go,
girls from "the Orient, where men are kings . . ."
White Ken lies on his stomach
15   while an Oriental Barbie walks on his back.
Or is it a real woman stepping on Ken?
Or Oriental Barbie stepping on a real man?
You have to travel to Japan
to buy this particular Barbie doll. A geisha girl
20   can be at the door of your New York apartment
in less than an hour. Of course,
there is no Oriental Ken.
Those who study the delicate balance
of American commerce and trade understand.

Buddhist Barbie

DENISE DUHAMEL

for Nick

In the 5th century B.C.
an Indian philosopher Gautama
teaches "All is emptiness"
and "There is no self."
5   In the 20th century A.D.
Barbie agrees, but wonders how a man
with such a belly could pose,
smiling, and without a shirt.

Barbie Does Yom Kippur

RABBI SUSAN SCHNUR

Some years ago, when I was fresh out of seminary and installed in my first pulpit, I nourished a number of stupid ideas about synagogue life—not the least of which was the idea that kids should do whatever they want during religious services. That's right, *whatever they want*. I based this ridiculous notion on my own childhood congregational experience—years and years of weekly shulgoing, during which time I never so much as *once* cracked open a prayerbook. What I did do, however, *religiously*—what a whole loose-knit bunch of us kids did every Sabbath at synagogue, *religiously*, was smash each other with the sanctuary's swinging doors, hold shrieking matches in the stairwells, toss all the fur coats in the cloakroom into one huge pile and bury ourselves, crawl under and over bathroom stalls in strict monastic sequences, terrify each other in the industrial kitchen's enormous walk-in freezer, and play checkers on the parquet floor of the elegant shul vestibule with *yahrtzeit* glasses purloined from the custodial closet.

Years after these anarchic Sabbaths, when, as a grown-up, I would occasionally bump into an old shul-crony, we would immediately rush into blabbing contentedly about those long-ago long-shadowed tumbleweed Saturdays—orthodox, of course, in their own scrupulous fashion—and we'd marvel about how our luxurious *Shabbos* antics had translated for us, for all of us—effortlessly, cozily—into a bedrock love of religion.

Thus it was with complete confidence that I headed into my first Yom Kippur as a full-fledged rabbi, inviting children to bring whatever they wanted to the season's long penitential services: Barbies, Lotto, He-Men, comic books, *Pat the Bunny*. That year's haunting Kol Nidre service, I remember, felt particularly spiritual and introspective: lights low, Torahs held aloft by ancient *zeidehs* (grandpas)

whose davvening (praying) was mood-alteringly Yiddish-inflected, the feel in the sanctuary lean, the medieval chant spellbinding, almost primevally genetic . . . when *kaboom!!!*, an ear-splitting volley of machine-gun fire hit the room, and I wheeled around to see my own rotten child, age four, gunning down all the Jews in the sanctuary with his man-sized, Toys "Я" Us weapon. My husband yanked the kid out the door, and the room became abruptly, tensely silent. There *is* historic precedent, after all, for Jews being shot, burned, beaten, raped, starved, frozen, et cetera, in locked Ashkenazy shuls during the Days of Awe. Why wasn't this kid playing red-light, green-light in his fuzzy-wuzzy socks on the wall-to-wall Berber like a *good* little recreant? What happened to checkers?

But heavy-duty weaponry, it turned out, was not the only arsenal being built up that Yom Kippur. While the boys stockpiled their counterphobic fantasy objects—that is, those items of play that children gravitate toward in order to master their anxieties about someday being full grown-ups who run the world, who win—the girls were amassing theirs, in the form of Barbies, those beautiful women with "female power" who the girls hoped one day to become. By the next morning at shul, there were dozens of Barbies in attendance; leggy Trojan horses in the High Holiday wings, they were virginal, masochistic, eager to offer themselves sacrificially on the Yom Kippur altar.

Barbie's formal religious debut, however, did not occur until the near-end of the holy day, at the twilight—at which dust-motey hour the sanctuary is no longer a roomful of individuals praying but rather a single fossil organism that breathes, a palliation of survivors, a lump of gatekeepers against the silence of the universe, glazed guardians of the human promise to *be* in

5

this world. Those of us who lasted twenty-five hours had stood, sat, bowed, chanted, ritually beaten our breasts with our fists, and intoned hour after endless hour—tired, thirsty, very bored, hungry, irritable, malodorous—until finally dusk began to hint at our reward: Catharsis, Renewal, Virtue, Serenity, Purity, Love.

Suddenly, though, as we lugubriously cranked out the final "Our Father, our King, we have sinned before Thee," dragging the syllables so that our crowning prayer would coincide with the achingly slow filibuster of the dying sun, we heard a stampeding racket above our heads, painfully reminiscent of the awfulness of the previous night's shrill gunfire. Wasting not a second, I ran out the door, up the Hebrew-school steps, and there, in flagrante delicto, I caught sight of dozens of girls, little girls, very little girls— the oldest, maybe eleven—barreling up and down the hall holding Barbies. They were racing, up and back, up and back, clutching Barbies.

"Let me guess," I said to the girls breathlessly, hushing them and gathering them around. "Barbie's exercising." They nodded. "Why?" I continued rhetorically, still panting. "Because, let me guess, she fasted for Yom Kippur." They nodded again.

"Barbie is exercising off some last-minute pounds before she breaks the fast by bingeing on all the food they're setting up downstairs. You smell it?" They nodded. "Am I right?" "Yeah." *Our rabbi knows everything!* I imagined them thinking. I considered, in my own head, the nature of epiphany. Was my discernment of the meaning of the girls' play a theosophical insight sent to me by the Lord God Himself, King of the Bathroom Scales, deeply male Ruler of the Universe, Who loves virgins and nonvirgins alike, so long as they all stand naked before Him, genuflecting to better read the little numbers, praying for the miracle of the lost half pound, surrendering themselves before His all-critical Power? This God, I thought problematically, *loves* complicitous girls who are preoc-

cupied by self-loathing and utterly stupid tiny meaningless things. No, I think, my quick take on the meaning of Barbie's weight-reduction marathon was not a religious epiphany at all, but rather a reflexive lurch toward warped bulimic logic, derived from a combination, in this circumstance, of the previous night's gendered shoot-out and my own plummeting heart. Downstairs we were fasting for moral redemption, and upstairs we were fasting for Ken.

Suddenly, the girls started a spontaneous chant—Barbie's Kol Nidre, I guess—holding the dolls, modern iconic war goddesses, at flat chest-height, and militarily marching them down the hall: "I/Lost/the *Most*/Weight. I/Lost/the *Most*/Weight. . . ."

"Look," I said to them in summary, crouching to their level to impart a final piece of resigned rabbinic wisdom. "If you're going to run around, take off your shoes."

As I headed back down to the chapel in my white *kittel,* the special garment that is the color of mercy, worn only on the Day of Atonement, I heard a precocious five-year-old avouch nasally, "My Barbie *wins.*"

It was this kid—*this kid*—who I credit finally with ruining my entire spiritual year.

There are many ways to understand the role Barbie played that Day of Atonement, but what struck me then was that *my* childhood synagogue impieties felt worlds apart from that of these kids'. *Our* actings-out had to do with the absolute safety and all-encompassing coherence of our religious, liberal, white, middle-class, American, 1950s lives—exemplified by the Sabbath but present *every* day. On *Shabbos,* parking our parents (and their parents, and virtually every grown-up we knew) with God as babysitter, we had the *preconditions* for running amok, for our unruly intoxications at the margins. Our palimpsest was *simpler* than met the eye; Barbie's, though, is more complicated.

Barbie, Toys "Я" Us machine guns—these are "charged objects," contaminative; they

10

represent the dog-eat-dog world, the obsessively competitive culture that synagogues and mosques and churches strive to keep *out*. Barbie expresses the dilemmas of our desires, the sustained dissonance in our lives between the spiritual and the materialistic, the emotional gridlock inherent in our culture of relentless individualism. Barbie is a concretization of what the critic Walter Lippmann called, as far back as 1929, "the acids of modernity"; she strands us in narcissism, self-esteem struggles, the empty victories of consumerism. The kiddy-instigated pollutions at my latter-day shul (not my childhood one) involved gendered mastery exercises around the dialectical themes of domination/control, violence/beauty, sexuality/power, love/envy, aggression toward the self and toward the other.

15   In my childhood shul, our developmental task felt quite different: We kids used the synagogue the way babies use parents' laps: to be rocked, soothed, reassured, to be filled up with love and emotional security, to be steeped in the predictable *because* it is developmentally empowering.

Then again, these interpretations are all, perhaps, beside the point. I could as easily say that the theme of Yom Kippur *is* "the acids of modernity," *is* contamination, since the liturgy is all about the construction of contrasts: pure vs. impure, obedience vs. rebellion, order vs. disorder, Life vs. Death. To quote the seminal High Holiday prayer,

> On Rosh Hashana the decree is inscribed and on Yom Kippur it is sealed, who shall live and who shall die, who shall perish by fire and who by water, who by sword and who by beast, who by hunger and who by thirst, who shall have rest and who shall go wandering, who shall be tranquil and who shall be disturbed. . . .

The penitential season is one of purification, a realigning of everything that is out of whack, a killing off of what's "bad." This is why the Israelite priests took the famous ur-scapegoat and drove it into the wilderness with all the people's sins on its head, to chase out all that was impure, to cleanse. The word *kippur* itself means "purge"—to purge ourselves of anxieties and dissatisfactions, to choose a new course in life, to purify. Maybe even binge and purge—one of Barbie's specialties.

Perhaps the girls running laps with their Barbies at synagogue, exercising addictively, fasting, were pointing out the hypocrisies of religious life—that our penance doesn't really change us, that our "fasts" are feel-good catharses that fail to generalize into our real lives, that fasts only set up binges, penitence only sets up the next reactive round of guilty indulgences.

It could be that we need *more* Barbies and war toys at our religious services in order to mock our prayers, to shove into our faces the entrenched hear-no-evil/see-no-evil ethos that religious life secretly sanctions. As we read (on Yom Kippur) from the prophet Isaiah, "Is such the fast I desire, a day for people to starve their bodies? No. *This* is the fast I desire: to loose the fetters of injustice." Or maybe, if I had been speedier of mind at Barbie's anorectic Yom Kippur debut, I could have gathered up all the dolls and all the plastic weapons, put all our community's sins upon them, and driven them into the wilderness with great ceremony, or burned them, or thrown them off a cliff, or put them in the recycling bin and thought about that. How to restore Eden. Next year in Jerusalem. All that stuff.

20   As I sit at my desk finishing up this essay, my son, now tall and sixteen, reads over my shoulder. "I think you have it wrong, Ma," he concludes. "You know that Chassidic story about the illiterate shepherd boy who comes to synagogue on Yom Kippur but he doesn't know how to pray? Finally, he just takes out his shepherd's flute in synagogue and blows it as hard as he can, and the people freak out because it's forbidden to play instruments on the most holy day of the year. But the rabbi

says, 'This boy's prayer, more than ours, will *certainly* reach Heaven, because he prays from the gut.'

"I remember that incident in shul when I was four," he continues, "and Dad came from nowhere and yanked me out to the parking lot. Maybe I was praying with that machine gun. Maybe we pray with our violence; we pray with our anorexia. We pray." He shrugs.

"That's lovely," I say to my wonderful son who once gunned down a roomful of worshipers. And I put it in my essay.

Re-reading/Conversations with the Text

1. Consider the relationship dynamics established around/through the Barbie or doll figure in each of these pieces. All deal with the relationship of the central character(s)/subject(s) of the pieces to "others." First, determine who you think the central character or subject in each piece is. Then establish whom that person is mostly in relationship with in the piece: mothers, men, society at large, peers? Now consider how the doll figures in that relationship.

2. Does it matter who is narrating? Consider the point of view (he, she, you, we) and the narrative perspective (distant, involved, omniscient and outside the scene, emotional, judgmental, objective, etc.) of each poem. How does the point of view affect the logical, emotional, and ethical appeals that are made upon you as the reader? What would happen if you changed the point of view or narrative position in each poem?

3. Make a list of the metaphors and similes (figurative language) used in the poems. What kinds of things is the girl-doll being compared to? How is she described? How do the metaphors, similes, and descriptions in the poems convey logical, emotional, or ethical appeals?

Re-seeing and Re-writing

1. Explore the world of Barbie (and Ken, too, if you like). What alternatives to Barbie exist? Which ones are (still) missing? For this assignment you have two options:

   a. Create a new Barbie (or Ken) with a different identity, and then create a poem/short prose piece about her or him using one of these four poems as a model.

   b. Write a poem/short prose piece about an alternative "Barbie" that already exists, using any or all four of these poems as a model.

   If you are at all artistically inclined, try representing your Barbie in an illustration as well.

2. Research and write a paper on a certain kind of doll (e.g., G.I. Joe figures, American Girl dolls, Disney princess dolls, generic baby dolls) or on Barbie

dolls. Your paper should focus on the consumption of *identity* as conveyed by these dolls. Be sure to consider all of the following in writing your paper:

a. Facts and figures concerning the creation, production, marketing, and consumption of your doll.

b. Who the intended audience seems to be for this kind of doll (and how you know).

c. The kind(s) of logical, emotional, and ethical appeals used in producing, marketing, and selling this doll.

d. The corporate identity of the company that makes this doll, and how it relates to the identity conveyed through the doll.

Intertext

In "Maid to Order," Barbara Ehrenreich focuses on various strategies that house cleaning services employ to sell their "product." Compare the strategies these businesses engage in with those used in marketing Barbie. Your analysis might take one of several forms:

• An academic comparison/contrast paper, based on research.

• A business memo that documents the similarities and differences in strategies in order to help the company you work for to increase its own sales.

• A poem about a house cleaning service modeled on one (or all) of the Barbie pieces.

• A poem or short fictional piece or news report about Barbie going to work as a maid.

"OM" Hinduism in American Pop Culture: Global Strategy or Sacrilegious Mistake

S A R A L A   N A G A L A

Born in 1983 in North Dakota, *SARALA NAGALA* is currently studying public policy at Stanford University. She is a recipient of the Eben Tisdale Fellowship, which enables students to visit Washington, DC, to study public policy issues related to technology and the economy. Her article focuses on the possibilities and problems associated with pop culture and the appropriation of Hindu iconography and traditions in Western media.

As the stage is illuminated, the colorful backdrop decorated with depictions of the Hindu deities Krishna and Shiva appears. Then the focus shifts to the woman dressed in the ephemeral, shimmering black dress. Her forehead is adorned with tilaka markings, which symbolize devotion in the Hindu religion; her hands are bedecked in traditional Indian mehendi hand paint. The song she performs is "Shanti," with lyrics written entirely in Sanskrit. This seemingly religious scene is instantly transformed when, for her next number, American pop singer Madonna changes into a see-through tank top and launches into a provocative dance with guitarist Lenny Kravitz. Though the background images were gone, Madonna remained in the Indian makeup, juxtaposing two cultures in a way that has not become uncommon in America. This performance is only one instance of the burgeoning trend of borrowing Hindu religious and cultural symbols for use in mainstream American pop culture. Several other celebrities have also integrated Hindu symbols into their dress, behavior, and art. Trying to emulate America's entertainment elite, young people are flocking to fashion boutiques to purchase various manifestations of this cultural borrowing. Shirts, shoes, and accessories have been screen-printed with such images as India's elephant god. Ganesha, and the word comparable to Christianity's "amen," Om.

Conflicting opinions about this apparent exploitation have prompted a heated debate. On one side are some Hindus who consider the images, in this context, sacrilegious to what they perceive as an already tolerant religion. On the other are those who believe that utilizing such symbolism allows for freedom of artistic expression and, furthermore, draws attention to an Eastern culture often neglected in a predominantly Eurocentric worldview. Therefore, the question must be posed: Is the emergence of Hindu symbols in Western popular culture inappropriate or simply an innocent side effect of evolving fashion trends? To answer this question effectively, we must elucidate the underpinnings of Hinduism, the manner in which these images are portrayed, the motivations behind those who use and purchase the images, and the broader conceptions of Hinduism in America. Acknowledging that various definitions of Hinduism lead to both positive and negative interpretations of Hindu images, it can be hypothesized that the positive, harmless fashion examples are most pervasive in mainstream society.

Before examining America's escalating use of Hindu symbols, it is important to review some basic aspects of Hinduism. Although the exact numbers are uncertain, Stanford University Professor of Cultural and Social Anthropology Akhil Gupta estimates that over 850 million people in India and significant diasporas in the Caribbean, Africa, South America, the Pacific Islands, and North America identify themselves as members of the Hindu religion (Interview). In the United States alone, there are 1.4 million Hindus in the last census count, a ten-fold increase since 1990 ("New Study"). Due to this immense world-wide following, Hinduism, a pantheistic religion, has evolved quite differently in disparate regions. Anantanand Rambachan, Hindu scholar and author of *The Hindu Vision,* explains: "The term 'Hindu' was used originally to describe a geographical entity rather than uniform religious culture. Today, it refers to a multiplicity of beliefs and practices" (*1*). Hinduism differs from Western religions in that it lacks a single identifiable founder, specific theological system, or a central religious organization. Over the centuries, various sects of the religion have developed and, due to this variation, beliefs and rituals of worship are not uniform across the whole religion. The diversity that exists within this religion prompts the foregrounding of certain beliefs by a sect that another group may consider inconsequential. Because priorities are skewed among different deities, beliefs, and practices, the reactions of Hindus to the use of their symbols in Western fashion greatly vary.

Various experts have attempted to define Hinduism, and they have failed to agree on a solid characterization. India's first prime minister, Jawaharlal Nehru, expressed both his views and those of Mahatma Gandhi, who led India to independence through his campaign of non-violence:

> Hinduism, as a faith, is vague, amorphous, many-sided, all things to all men . . . In its present form, and even in the past, it embraces many beliefs and practices, from the highest to the lowest, often opposed to contradicting each other.

. . . Mahatma Gandhi has attempted to define it: "If I were asked to define the Hindu creed, I should simply say: A man may not believe in God and still call himself a Hindu. Hinduism is a relentless pursuit after truth. . . . Hinduism is the religion of truth. Truth is God." (75)

This hazy, indistinct picture given of Hinduism by two of India's premier leaders is testament to the religion's lack of a clear-cut definition. Stanford's Professor Akhil Gupta goes so far as to claim that "there is no such thing as 'Hinduism,' per se" and also notes that Hinduism as a classification emerged only during the parallel construction of a Muslim community in nineteenth century colonial India. The ancient roots of Hinduism have evolved greatly over time. Because of the paucity of dogmatic principles laying out precisely what "is" and "is not" Hinduism, the religion has formed a metaphorical umbrella, accepting various—and often contradicting—viewpoints as doctrine. The lack of an accepted overarching definition of Hinduism accentuates the role of the individual in determining his or her own personal depiction of the religion. This room for individual interpretation is central to the debate over the use of Hindu symbols in American popular culture, as some Hindus consider it innocuous while others are strongly offended.

This disparity provokes the question: What are these symbols and how are they being used? India has been called the "land of 33 million gods," and "individual Hindus might worship any of thousands of different deities" (KRON-TV). Several of these deities are prevalent in Western fashion designs: Ganesha, depicted as an elephant, is seen as the remover of obstacles; Goddess Laksmi, often decked in beautiful clothing and sitting on a lotus flower, represents prosperity; Shiva, the destroyer of evil, is also the lord of art and dance: and many other deities represent complex combinations of different traits (see Figure 1). Moreover, many American women have taken to wearing bindi and mehendi, markings of cultural importance

5

Figure 1   T-Shirt Depicting Hindu Deity.

Courtesy of Todd Gipstein/National Geographic Image Collection.

to Indians. Generally, America's entertainment industry has been the foremost propagator of Hindu symbols. Use within the entertainment industry itself can be divided into three categories: Those entertainers who use the symbols with an understanding of their significance to Hindu culture; those people who adopt the symbols simply as a fashion trend; and those artists who, deliberately or inadvertently, use symbols of Hinduism in a derogatory manner.

First we shall address the inquisitive individuals who have learned about the cultural significance of the images they use. One such figure is American pop singer Madonna. Although her performance at the 1998 MTV Music Awards described earlier forced the issue of cultural borrowing to the surface, she has been known to embrace many aspects of Hinduism (see Figure 2). Shibani Patnaik, a college student who performed classical Indian dance with Madonna in that controversial performance, extols Madonna's respect for and knowledge of Hinduism. Patnaik states: "Madonna knows everything about the deities—her baby daughter even has a statue of Krishna. She is very aware of Hindu practices and traditions, incorporating some of them into her own wedding. She also practices yoga

Figure 2   Madonna at the 1998 MTV Music Awards.
Courtesy of Kevork Djansezian/AP Wide World Photos.

and studies Sanskrit" (Interview). This demonstrated interest in Hinduism is testament to Madonna's appreciation of multiculturalism. Because of her earnestness, a watchdog group named American Hindus Against Defamation (AHAD) had to concede that her actions at the MTV performance were sincere and therefore warranted forgiveness ("Hindus React"). Other entertainers who have expressed genuine appreciation for Hindu culture are such singers as Sting and the late George Harrison, a member of the Beatles. Sting has incorporated typical Indian melodies into his songs. Harrison's interest began when the Beatles traveled to India. After meeting an Indian swami in London, the Beatles were exposed to Hindu philosophy and music. In fact, "During the 1960s many Hindu ideas and practices came to the West and had a large impact upon the counterculture then developing. Dominant figures in popular culture—pop stars such as the Beatles—promoted Hindu ideas and gurus" (Flood

271). While these ideas mushroomed in the 1960s and 1970s, their popularity receded until the late 1990s when they began to appear again in the entertainment industry.

Though entertainers such as Madonna and Sting have set trends of embracing Hinduism, there are those who get swept up in the trend and use the images without understanding their cultural importance. In the entertainment industry, this paradigmatic "I do it because it's cool" view is represented by Gwen Stefani, the lead singer of the band No Doubt. She has integrated Indian jewelry and traditional adornment into her wardrobe, and she has been photographed numerous times wearing a bindi, the dot between the eyebrows on the lower part of the forehead (see Figure 3). To Indian women, this mark has a significant meaning. It

Figure 3   Gwen Stefani, Lead Singer of No Doubt, Wearing Bindi.
Courtesy of Frank Trapper/Corbis/Sygma.

represents a symbolic third eye that "promotes prosperity and festivity within a person" (Mangla). Stefani's use of the bindi can be deemed superficial because she typically wears it when dressed in Western outfits. Her marginalization of a single Hindu symbol leads to the conclusion that Stefani's interest is spurious. In contrast, Madonna tends to incorporate several Hindu features such as dress, bindi, and mehendi at once, therefore demonstrating multifaceted interest rather than borrowing simply for fashion's sake. However, Stefani has not received universal criticism for her utilization of the bindi, as the prevailing sentiment is that her method is relatively harmless and not disparaging to Hinduism.

Nevertheless, her actions, and those of others in Hollywood who use the images purely for their fashion appeal, have had far-reaching effects. Their somewhat flippant attitude has filtered down to mainstream American popular culture and is partially the reason that stores like Dharma, a fashion boutique in San Francisco's trendy Upper Haight district, have noticed a dramatic increase in sales of shirts, bags, and other accessories emblazoned with Hindu insignia. Jackie Wilson, longtime owner of Dharma, states that her most popular items have been apparel with Hindu deities Ganesha, described earlier; Krishna, a blue-bodied deity whom Hindus worship as an incarnation of the universe's creator, Vishnu; Rama and Sita, where Rama is another form of Vishnu and Sita his ideal wife; and images of the Tibetan Buddha. "In the last couple of years we have sold hundreds of these shirts and now we have the wrap skirts with the same deities," says Wilson (Interview). Among those designers who use these deities in their contemporary fashion lines are Donatella Versace, Christian Dior, and Indian designers Ravi Chawla and Rohini Khosla (Verma). Surprisingly, these designers are not being criticized for producing the clothes that instigate controversy. One may infer that where demand exists, products will be

supplied. Designers are simply acting as these suppliers. While most of the patterns are for women's clothing, some are emerging for men as well. This trend is quickly engulfing the nation, as apparel and accessories with Hindu symbols are becoming ubiquitous in cosmopolitan America. This evidence prompts curiosity about why this fascination with all things Hindu has blossomed so rapidly in recent years.

It is difficult to pinpoint one main motivation for those who purchase these images; rather, an intricate combination of factors has catalyzed this trend. These reasons are key because they help to explain the trend's popularity. In general, the American public seems to perceive Eastern culture as mystical and mysterious, compared to the mundane, ordinary life of the United States. Linda Hess, a religious scholar, explains: "Hinduism has fantastically rich mythic/religious imagery, and the American market has an insatiable appetite for novel and vivid images to sell" (qtd. in KRON-TV). Americans are attracted to the perceived exoticism of India and its images. They desire an element of exoticism in their own lives and feel that by wearing Ganesha or Om, they can embody the mysticism of both the deity and the religion as a whole. Added to this fascination is the visual appeal of the symbols. Hess also attributes the images' appeal to their colorfulness and beautiful detail, calling them "arresting" (qtd. in KRON-TV). Professor Gupta of Stanford agrees, asserting that while the interest in Hinduism in the 1960s was steeped more in such aspects as Indian philosophy, yoga, and incense, contemporary society has developed into a "visual culture" more concerned with physical images than philosophical roots. This tendency away from deeper understanding toward superficial appropriation is also the reason Gupta considers this fashion trend a fleeting fad that will likely die out when the fashion market evolves to other styles (Interview). However, there is no evidence that this transformation will come any time soon because consumer

10

demand for these products is not ebbing. Due to this enormous fixation, the entertainment industry has tried to sell Hindu culture—sometimes going too far.

While most of Hollywood uses symbols of Hinduism in a respectful manner, there are those instances where the entertainment industry has, in a twisted attempt to quench the public's thirst for Hindu imagery, used the images in a way considered disparaging and disrespectful to the religion. However, negative depictions have been so quickly retaliated against that, other than negative publicity toward the images' producers, they have had no significant effect on mainstream popular culture.

Take, for example, the April 1999 issue of *Vanity Fair* magazine, which featured a two-page spread of Mike Myers, star of the *Wayne's World* and *Austin Powers* films, with a partially shaved hairstyle, saffron-colored silk robes, traditional mehendi body paint, and a jeweled bindi on his forehead. An accompanying photo showed Myers seated in the lotus position with an elongated tongue like the Hindu goddess Kali and surrounded by naked, blue-skinned models and an odd "monkey" god (Johnson 6). Myers also has the phrase "Call my agent" henna-painted on his hand and poses holding a Palm Pilot that reads "Om" on its screen. American Hindus Against Defamation (AHAD) encouraged the deluge of incensed letters *Vanity Fair* received in response to the photographs. Those who protested felt that the depictions violated the religious sanctity of Hindu imagery. "What bothers me is the ease with which religious symbols important to a peripheral group can be appropriated and used in this manner," said one distraught Hindu (qtd. in *Newsweek* March 22, 1999). The photographer, David LaChapelle, later apologized on the South Asian Journalists Association Web site. The important distinction here is the egregious nature of the images: There is little argument that the photos were inappropriate. Whereas American teenagers might try to dress or act

like Madonna because of her positive use of Hindu symbols, Myers' depiction crosses an invisible boundary into a realm that is vulgar, disrespectful, and clearly derogatory.

Several other instances have been judged disparaging as well, and, consequently, shunned by mainstream America. For example, AHAD was initially formed to protest the 1997 release of the Aerosmith album "Nine Lives," of which the cover featured a traditional depiction of Lord Krishna, but with a cat's face and female breasts. After Sony Music was inundated with over 20,000 e-mails, it agreed to redesign the cover ("Hollywood Hinduism"). In another incident, Stanley Kubrick's 1999 film *Eyes Wide Shut,* starring Tom Cruise and Nicole Kidman, was supposed to include chanted verses from the Bhagavad Gita, the holy text of Hinduism, during a sexually explicit scene. AHAD called its inclusion "utterly tasteless and insensitive" (qtd. in KRON-TV) and the scene was eventually deleted. Furthermore, in July 2001, a Los Angeles shoe company was forced to discontinue production of shoes decorated with the Hindu goddess Laksmi. The shoe protest illuminates how an interest in Hindu imagery can backfire. First, Hindus will not stand for anything representative of the religion to be printed on leather, because cows are seen as sacred in the religion and are not killed under any circumstance. Second, Hindus consider the feet unclean and wearing shoes that bear the image of God means tracking that image through dirt, which is considered sacrilegious. Organized resistance stopped these items in the production stage, therefore not allowing them to become part of the fashion trend. For if they did, outrage from Hindus would be swift. This evidence supports the conclusion that, due to appropriate protests and awareness of what is in good taste, most Americans are exposed to the positive Hindu imagery perpetuated by the entertainment industry.

These positive uses have larger implications in society. Viewed from a different perspective, the entertainment industry's usage of Hindu symbols actually encourages multicultural understanding and appreciation. For one, it has drawn attention to a southeastern Asian culture that has remained predominantly unrecognized in America. Amazingly, a 2001 study commissioned by the Hindu Leaders Forum found that 96 percent of Americans do not know what Hinduism is, despite the fact that the 1.4 million American Hindus contribute $20 billion to the United States economy ("New Study"). Professor Gupta reinforces this statistic, saying that "most people don't have a clue about what Hinduism is" (Interview). However, apparel decorated with Hindu images gives both the wearer and the observer a link to Hinduism, if only in recognizing that the images are derived from Hinduism rather than another religion. This realization is only the first step, though. The purchasers and observers will begin to inquire about which deity the shirt depicts and then what that deity represents in Hinduism. This cycle, now initiated by the existence of Hindu symbols in American popular culture, will lift Hinduism from its obscure position into one of more prominence. Thomas Wendell, author of *Hinduism Invades America,* speaks of America's potential: "As oriental countries in the recent past furnished good soil for the sowing of Western culture because of their material helplessness and subjection, so America today offers good soil for the sowing of Eastern culture because of its growing liberalism" (244). This "growing liberalism" also precipitates greater multicultural awareness in the United States. Prior to this recent emergence of Hindu imagery, Indians were represented by such characters as *The Simpsons'* Apu Nahasapeemapetilon, whose Indian movie characters babble nonsensically and whose idol of a six-armed God was displayed at the Kwik-E-Mart where he worked (Mangla). Although this image persists today, the other more positive,

or, at the least, harmless fashions perpetuated by Madonna, Sting, and even Gwen Stefani have permeated American culture and have encouraged young men and women to wear Ganesha, Krishna, Om, and bindi. As Americans aim to build a stronger multicultural society, deviation from archetypal American fashion styles to more international designs exposes us to new ideas. This novelty undoubtedly has benefits, one of which is augmented appreciation and understanding of different cultures.

Based on this perspective, it is important to realize that while there are some negative portrayals of Hinduism by the entertainment industry, these are carefully patrolled by watchdog groups such as AHAD and are also spurned by the American public's good judgment. Rather, America accepts the vibrant, colorful depictions perpetuated by sincere stars like Madonna that are ultimately innocuous. This warm reception has effects which leave the individual sphere, having instead the potential to change America's global awareness. And as for those Hindus who still take offense to the images, refer to Gotham Chopra, son of Indian new-age philosopher Deepak Chopra: "The principal problem with any faith is when the followers begin to take themselves too seriously" ("All the Raj"). Although their concerns are well-intentioned, these followers are misplaced in the changing tides of both American fashion and culture. 15

The true beauty of Hindu imagery is that it stands to shrink the globe and bridge cultural divides. As Gavin Flood, author of *An Introduction to Hinduism,* states, "Global Hinduism has a sense of India as its point of reference, but has transcended national boundaries" (265). It is just this essence of transformation which we have to endorse, encourage, and embrace if we are to see beyond the images to the underlying message of multiculturalism. It is the first step to a coalescence of continents and a smaller, more tightly-knit global community.

WORKS CITED

"All the Raj." Editor's note. *Vanity Fair* June 1999.

"A Vanity Fair Controversy." March 3, 2002. <*http://www.saja.org/vfdetail.html*>.

Flood, Gavin. *An Introduction to Hinduism.* Cambridge: Cambridge University Press, 1996.

Gupta, Akhil. Personal interview. February 21, 2002.

"Hindus React to Madonna's MTV Show." *Hinduism Today* January 1999, 50.

"Hollywood Hinduism: Art Vs. Morality." July 30, 2000, February 3, 2002. <*http://hinduism.about.com/library/weekly/aa073000a.htm*>.

Johnson, Richard, and Jeane MacIntosh. "Star's Photo Stunt Enrages Hindus." *New York Post* March 16, 1999: 6.

KRON-TV. "Krishna Culture" (story synopsis). January 21 2001. *ACF News Source.* <*http://www.acfnewsource.org/general/filesheet_religion.html*>.

"Losing Their Religion." *Newsweek* March 22, 1999.

Mangla, Marla. "Indianism: The New American Fad." *360 Degrees.* 2000-01. Vol. 3, No. 1. Feburary 27, 2002 <*http://students.syr.edu/360/winter/indianism.html*>.

Mehta, Monica. "Express Yourself." *Little India.* February 20, 2002 <http://206.20.14.67/achal/archive/Oct98/express.htm>.

Nehru, Jawaharlal. *The Discovery of India.* Calcutta: The Signet Press, 1946.

"New Study Reveals Hindu Myths and Misconceptions." *U.S. Newswire* national desk, August 15, 2001.

Patnaik, Shibani. Personal interview. February 5, 2002. (http://206.20.14.67/achal/archive/Oct98/express.htm).

Rambachan, Anantanand. *The Hindu Vision.* Delhi: Motilal Banarsidass Publishers Private Limited, 1992.

Verma, Neharika. "Ram On Your Bust!" IndiaBytes Bureau, *Sify Entertainment.* February 3, 2002. <http://www.entertainment.sify.com/content/weekendstory.asp?news_code_num=236&lang_code=Fashion>.

Wendell, Thomas. *Hinduism Invades America.* New York City: The Beacon Press, Inc., 1930.

Wilson, Jackie. Telephone interview. February 26, 2002.

Re-reading/Conversations with the Text

1. Consider Nagala's central question: "Is the emergence of Hindu symbols in Western popular culture inappropriate or simply an innocent side effect of evolving fashion trends?" Ask yourself what Nagala deems as inappropriate, or (alternatively) as innocent. Trace the (inappropriate/innocent) binary as it evolves through her essay. Which aspects of the essay reinforce this binary? When (if ever) does the binary break down?

2. Nagala uses statistics, examples of Hindu symbols in popular culture, and quotations from a variety of people. Working in groups of two, re-write Nagala's argument in your own words. Next, re-read her essay considering the rhetorical appeals (*ethos, pathos, logos*) that she uses to construct her argument. For instance, when Madonna or Mike Myers use Hindu symbols, are they employing them in order to bolster their own image (*ethos*), or perhaps to evoke an emotional connection with their audience (*pathos*)?

3. Nagala's essay explores juxtapositions between Western popular culture and Hindu symbolism. List her examples of such juxtapositions. Can you think of other examples of the juxtaposition of Hindu symbolism and Western popular culture? Nagala focuses on the use of Hindu symbols on/as products or *commodities* (in music, ads, and fashion items). What are the implications of symbols of a culture being bought and sold by another culture?

Re-seeing and Re-writing

1. Working in a small group, locate examples of symbols of Christianity, Judaism, or other religions used in popular culture in the United States or elsewhere. What would Nagala's analytical framework suggest about the trends you have noticed? Present your findings to the class using PowerPoint or some other visual medium.

2. Research the use of Hindu symbolism in one of its many Western permutations (fashion, music, art, etc.). Consider what company is producing the material you are considering. Where are the headquarters located? Who/where are their primary consumers? Design a map showing the flow of production and distribution of these products, and then construct a map displaying the dominant religion(s) in these areas. Present these maps and findings to the class.

Intertext

In her article "Los Intersticios: Recasting Moving Selves," Evelyn Alsultany discusses how her identity "fractures as [she] experience[s] differing dislocations in multiple contexts." Nagala talks about the problems and possibilities associated with the use of Hindu symbols in varying cultural contexts. Read one essay against the other. Would Nagala argue that Hinduism "fractures" as it is appropriated in different contexts? Does Alsultany's argument about identity apply to a religion or other element of culture, as it might to an individual's identity?

KEY RHETORICAL CONCEPTS

rhetorical
appeals:
logos
ethos
pathos

Research Prompts
CONSUMER GAZES: Made in the USA?

Option #1:

The Appeal of Advertising Lifestyles

This option invites you to focus on consumer culture by drawing attention to the sub-text within advertising strategies that aim to sell not only a product, but a lifestyle as well. Your task is to decipher what lifestyle is being sold, to whom, and what it reveals about a particular cultural and historical moment. What is the product's relationship to the buying public? What type(s) of images and words are repeated? Are the advertising strategies primarily ethical, emotional, and/or logical (i.e., do they employ *ethos, pathos, logos*), or are they a combination? You might consider one of the following approaches:

a. **Gender/Sexuality:** Gender and sexuality often play defining roles in a product's relationship to its buying public. What types of gender roles are being "sold"? To what degree are these depictions normative (i.e., representing "good" gender performance versus "bad" gender performance)? To what audience(s) might these roles appeal, and why? How does your analysis extend, complicate, or challenge secondary readings on the subject?

b. **Race/Ethnicity:** Examine a commodified ethnic product (e.g., food products such as Taco Bell tacos or Uno's Pizza; Native American casinos; Chinese fireworks), and analyze the degree of cultural filtration involved, and what it reveals. To whom is the product being marketed? What visual cues suggest this? To what degree do the products rely upon racial/ethnic stereotypes? Which stereotypes do they employ? Why? In what ways do the products claim cultural authority or "authenticity"? Are the ad campaigns based primarily on logical (*logos*), authoritative and ethical (*ethos*), or emotional (*pathos*) appeals? How does your analysis extend, complicate, or challenge secondary readings on the subject?

Option #2:

Controversy and the Consumer Industry

This option invites you to examine a number of public controversies concerning the consumer industry (FDA regulations, migrant/third-world worker exploitation, animal exploitation, globalization, etc). Your task is to examine the public discourse (pamphlets, websites, media accounts, court records, government documents) surrounding the issue and to analyze the rhetorical strategies of the particular parties involved.

a. **Consumer Advocacy/Activism:** Analyze the rhetorical strategies of one of the following: the anti-smoking "Truth" campaign; PETA; anti-World Trade Organization protestors; the "National Do Not Call Registry"; or *Supersize Me* by filmmaker Morgan Spurlock. Are the rhetorical strategies primarily authoritative,

Research Prompts

emotional, or logical (*ethos, pathos, logos*)? What is higlighted? What is ignored? How are these groups/individuals portrayed by other media? What similarities or difference do you notice between the organizations'/individuals' representations of themselves and their representations in other media? What cultural, historical, or political factors contribute to the visibility or viability (acceptance) of certain representations? How does your analysis extend, complicate, or challenge secondary readings on the subject?

b. **Consumer Industry Leaders:** Either independently or in conjunction with an opposing organization, analyze the rhetoric employed by businesses or organizations under public scrutiny, such as cigarette manufacturer Phillip-Morris (now Altrice), Nike, or some other product or company. Are the rhetorical strategies the organizations use to defend themselves primarily authoritative, emotional, or logical (*ethos, pathos, logos*)? How are these groups/individuals portrayed by the media? What similarities or differences do you notice between the organizations' representations of themselves and their representation in other media? What cultural, historical, or political factors contribute to the visibility or viability (acceptance) of certain representations? How does your analysis extend, complicate, or challenge secondary readings on the subject?

An 80-year-old woman, one of few remaining ethnic Russians living in the basement of her bombed-out Chechen home.
Photographer: Thomas Dworzak (Magnum).

imagine

(all the people living life in peace)

Imagine a worldwide movement working to protect the dignity and rights of all people. And imagine it works.
For 40 years, Amnesty International members have saved countless lives – people unjustly imprisoned, tortured,
or persecuted for their beliefs. Make a difference. Take action. Join us. And the world will live as one.

www.amnestyusa.org

Truth and meaning: the two are likely to be equated with one another. Yet what is put forth as truth is often nothing more than a meaning.

TRINH T. MINH-HA: *THE TOTALIZING QUEST OF MEANING*

genre *kairos*

Understanding (the) Genre

MANY OF US HAVE SEEN DOCUMENTARY FILMS THAT HAVE BEEN PRO-duced recently on diverse topics such as national spelling bees, the migration of birds, and gun violence. Have you ever wondered "Why this topic?" or "Why tell the story now?" These questions get to the heart of the primary rhetorical functions of documentaries: to preserve historical evidence, to instruct audiences, and to enact change through persuasion. The etymological root of the word **documentary** includes the Latin term *docere*, which means to instruct or to advocate a cause. In the eighteenth century, the term *document* developed associations with written records and proof (such as deeds, legal artifacts, insurance polices, etc.). While the goals of instructing and recording are important, the primary focus of this unit is the persuasive purpose of documentary. Documentary, *genre*, and *kairos* constitute key rhetorical concepts for this unit, which examines how documentary films and other texts represent history.

Critical Frame

When we talk about documentary, we are talking about a type of film, or a genre. **Genre** is a French term for a kind, literary type, or class; we often use it to describe types of literature or other works of art. Classical genres of literature, for example, include the epic, tragedy, lyric, comedy, and satire, which have been joined in latter centuries by the novel and realist genres such as autobiography and biography. Genres, however, are not simply static labels. They also create and respond to audience expectations. For example, if you are reading a science fiction novel, you expect to come across a story about people's relationship with technology and space; you might also expect a utopian or dystopian plot. Those expectations about science fiction influence how you read and understand the novel.

Just as the science fiction genre has its own characteristics, so too does the documentary genre. Film scholar Michael Renov has identified four purposes of film documentaries (summarized below), which also apply to other kinds of documentary texts and images, including documentary photography and video.

Purposes of documentary

1. **To record, reveal, or preserve:** A common expectation of documentary forms is that they will directly record, preserve, or otherwise replicate historical reality. But as the concept of the rhetorical triangle illustrates (see pp. 2–6), meaning is created as a result of the interaction of rhetor, audience, and text. There are, for example, always issues of selection to consider (the filmmaker chooses particular content, and a particular way of presenting it); these choices are further mediated through editing and other processes of development; and the meaning of the final product is interpreted by the audience. For all of these reasons, the relationship between film and the historical event to which it refers is somewhat fragile: Documentary images can never purely reflect the historical events to which they refer. Ken Burns' Civil War series is an example of the effective use of documentary techniques: Burns's judicious use of selection, editing, and voice-over presentation of letters and documents captured a large popular audience, resurrecting historical events more than 200 years after they took place. As with all other forms of documentary, however, the reality (the soldiers' experience of the Civil War) and the representation of it (Burns's film) must be understood as two very different things.

2. **To persuade or promote:** Documentary forms of representation persuade through ethical, emotional, and logical means; in other words, we might be persuaded by the ethical status of the filmmaker or subject of the film, by sentimental appeals, or by rational arguments. Political campaign ads and Michael Moore's controversial film *Fahrenheit 911* (2004) offer vivid examples of how documentary materials (interviews, archival research, campaign or debate footage, for example) can be shaped in attempts to persuade audiences.

3. **To analyze or interrogate:** Given that documentaries claim a link to "truth," we must always ask, "How much of a hand does the filmmaker have in interpreting events?" Michael Moore's documentary films are designed to interrogate commonplace truths and assumptions. *Bowling for Columbine,* for instance, challenges mainstream assumptions about the links between violence and the sale of guns.

Moore twists this assumption back on itself when he reveals that Canada has more guns than the United States, but less violence. In drawing our attention to "commonsense" assumptions and how they shape political arguments, Moore reveals that he is not just recording data, but also directing viewers' understanding of that data.

4. **To express:** The aesthetic, or expressive, function of documentary is often undervalued because of the genre's association with nonfiction and the related idea that images simply record, rather than frame and interpret, reality. However, the aesthetic nature of a documentary such as *Winged Migration,* about the migration of birds, is precisely what allows that film to speak to an audience beyond birdwatchers—to be called, in fact, "beautiful," "magnificent," and even "humbling" in numerous critical reviews. And, too, such things as point of view, tone, editing style, narrative rhythm, photographic style, use of intertitles/other text, and musical accompaniment can play an important role in achieving documentary's other functions (particularly persuasion). As we've seen before, the content of a text (in this case, a documentary) is intimately bound up with its form, and vice versa. A call to action boringly presented will likely fail; a stirring presentation of the same case will call thousands to the barricades.[1]

But what exactly do documentary images ask us to remember, change, promote, or analyze? Why are certain documentary images or films popular at particular historical and cultural moments? What cultural or political forces and events contribute to the public's readiness for such images and texts? For whom and in what contexts are certain images and texts persuasive?

To analyze why an image or text is persuasive, or why it has a sense of urgency at a particular historical moment, is to examine its *kairos*. **Kairos** [KY rōs] is a Greek term that refers to cultural climate—to the historical and cultural moment in which an argument or image appears, and to the views of an audience at that particular time and place. The concept was illustrated in classical rhetoric by the figure known as Opportunity (Figure 7.1), usually depicted balancing precariously on a pole while holding a set of scales on a knife or razor.

Balance in a rhetorical text is achieved and sustained to the extent that its *kairos* can anticipate the needs and values of imagined or intended audiences at any given time and place.

Documentary Images at War

Consider the aerial photograph (Figure 7.2) taken by a U.S. fighter jet during Operation Desert Storm (part of the 1991 Gulf War). To what extent does the image make moral or emotional demands on viewers? As a viewer, how do you feel you are positioned? As a passive by-stander? As an ally of the fighter pilot? As something (or someone) else?

The image sets up a simple narrative: A building is targeted; a bomb is dropped on it; the building explodes. The "story" is brief and contains no characters. As

Figure 7.1   *Kairos,* god of opportunity. First-century carved stone relief of Greek origins.

Courtesy of Zbirka Umjetnina Kairos, Church of St. Nicholas, Trogir, Croatia/Lucio Rossi/Dorling Kindersley.

important as what is seen in these images, however, is what's not seen. Although we know soldiers—people—must be involved, none are visible. Our point of view from far above (the viewpoint of the jet dropping the bomb) doesn't permit us to see any individuals who might have been affected. However, the Department of Defense now acknowledges that nerve-agent-filled rockets were stored in Bunker 73.[2] No precautions were taken to protect army personnel from the potentially lethal chemical agents released; ongoing investigations have yet to determine conclusively whether and to what extent this incident has contributed to reportedly high rates of illness among Gulf War veterans.

War images have clear rhetorical purposes and characteristics. The aerial photograph discussed above creates a sense of psychological and moral distance from the suffering of individual people caused by acts of war. Similar images saturated the American media coverage of the Gulf War in the early 1990s, dulling the public's emotional response to the war. The images' composition helped to facilitate national denial, enabling us to avoid troubling, unsettling ideas—like recognizing the human casualties of war.

We can find numerous additional instances of similarly spectacular, yet distancing, images of suffering in wartime. Consider, for example, the iconic image of the

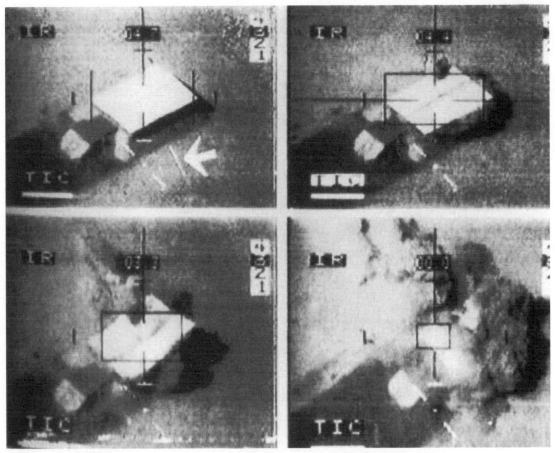

Figure 7.2   An aerial photograph taken in March 1991 of the Khamisiyah Ammunition Storage Complex in Southern Iraq showing Bunker 73, which was destroyed by U.S. Army engineers.

Courtesy of US Department of Defense.

"mushroom cloud" resulting from atomic bombs dropped on Japan during World War II (Figure 7.3).

As with the aerial footage from Operation Desert Storm, the photograph of the bomb over Nagasaki leaves something out—namely, the bodies of the injured, dying, and the dead.

Documentary images of war often reflect particular national rhetorical visions or gazes. As we saw in Chapter 4, the **national gaze** refers to how images create a sense of national identity and national power. Such images can be, but need not necessarily be, government-sponsored. State-sponsored documents and other forms of communication importantly shaped public response to World War I and World War II, for example. Public service announcements, government news bulletins, recruitment

AND **WRITING**

genre

Imagine yourself walking into your local video store. Notice the organized display of movies and videos, with separate aisles for documentary, drama, action, mystery, and romance. These different classifications are called **genres.** Works of literature, films, video games, and television programs can all be organized in genres. Television shows might be classified, for instance, as sitcoms, reality shows, game shows, or dramas. Video games can also be classified by genre—consider Shoot 'Em Up games, or games based on the principles of the Maze, Escape, Adventure, or the Chase. Likewise, literary works are organized and marketed by genre: poetry, fiction, drama, autobiography, and so on.

Genres are changeable and can also overlap. Consider, for example, hybrid genres such docu-drama, mock-umentary, or autobiographical fiction. Moreover, genres are always in flux; new genres continually appear. Marilyn Gardner, for instance, recently identified the emergent genre of "Matron Lit," which focuses on women in their 60s who begin new lives and which might be seen as an extension of "Chick Lit" (literature for young women). Reality TV constitutes a new media genre that intermixes several other TV show genres: adventure, game show, romance, home or self-improvement shows, for example, are often blended in "reality TV."

In order to identify a particular text as a certain genre, you need to examine its form (is it in verse? prose? is it structured into acts?), its content (is it about love and romance? a real historical event?), and the rhetorical relationship that the text sets up with its audience(s) (does it aim to make you cry? to inspire you to take action? are you supposed to believe it is a true story?). Genres respond to—and establish—audience expectations. In fact, it can be argued that these shared expectations are what turns a text into a genre. For instance, when reading an autobiography, readers assume that the narrative represents a true story, something that actually happened to the author. Similar expectations accompany the genre of documentary, which is also associated with truth-telling. A crucial question to ask about genre, then, is how a given text seeks to affect its audience.

Examples ∎∎∎

❶ In "The Stories We Tell: Television and Humanitarian Aid," Michael Ignatieff identifies a genre within the mass media that he calls *moral stories.* Moral stories focus on injustices and suffering. Ignatieff argues that "moral stories usually tell us what we want to hear: that we are decent folk trying to do our best and that we can make good the harms of the world." These narratives, he argues, "turn strangers into neighbors, aliens into kin. They also suggest some idea of reciprocal obligation: if we do not help them, these stories imply, they will not help us when our turn with adversity comes around."

② In "Conveying Atrocity in Image," Barbie Zelizer discusses the characteristics of *atrocity photographs* as tools of documentation. Zelizer identifies patterns in placement, the number of people represented, and the types of gaze at work that are characteristic of the genre. At the opening of the excerpt included in this section, Zelizer writes, "Using images to bear witness to atrocity required a different type of representation than did words. Images helped record the horror in memory after its concrete signs had disappeared, and they did so in a way that told a larger story of Nazi atrocity." She concludes with the following claim, which likewise indicates that atrocity photographs framed historical events in particular ways for viewers:

> Playing to the symbolic dimensions of these images had an important effect on publics, not only because they may have been the most effective and least uncomfortable way to comprehend the tragedies of Nazi Europe, but also because they framed events in such a way that all who saw the photos could bear witness to the atrocities. Within that frame, the exact details of the atrocities mattered less than the response of bearing witness.

Exercises ■ ■ ■

❶ Fake News

As a long-standing genre, satire has historically functioned to demystify a society's common myths, values, and beliefs. Consider news satire such as *The Daily Show* or *The Onion* (the online version of this newspaper can be found at http://www.theonion .com/). How does this genre complicate, demystify, or shed light on "real" news reporting? What techniques do these satirists employ in making their critiques and their counter-arguments? Finally, using a "straight" news report as a source text, construct your own satire based on these techniques. In small groups, revise and re-script your chosen news report and present it to the rest of the class.

❷ Music Genres

Create a list of music genres. You might start with some of your favorite forms of music. What qualities and characteristics determine each genre? (Be sure to consider form, content, and audience.) Are certain genres bound to particular historical periods? What performers and bands have challenged or re-created certain genres? What are some of the emergent genres on the scene today? Compare your list with those of your classmates.

Figure 7.3 Mushroom cloud over Nagasaki, Japan, following a second nuclear attack by the United States on August 9, 1945.

Courtesy of Bettmann/Corbis Images.

materials, calls for volunteers/patriotic efforts, and many other texts used various strategies, including stereotypical depictions of the enemy, to shape desired responses. After the bombing of Pearl Harbor, for example, countless stereotypical images of the Japanese and even of Japanese Americans appeared in U.S. government propaganda (see Figure 7.4).

Coverage of war in the popular media often reflects official government viewpoints. For example, during the recent U.S. war with Iraq, anti-war demonstrations, as well as the flag-draped coffins of U.S. soldiers, were more often than not excluded from national news coverage. A cursory search on the Internet and in newspapers for images of the Iraq war led us to mostly patriotic images of government officials, U.S. generals, U.S. soldiers, and families at home waiting for their loved ones to return (Figure 7.5). These patriotic images celebrate U.S. military power, the nation, and

Figure 7.4 Poster for Thirteenth Naval District, United States Navy. Created for the Works Project Administration (WPA) Art Project by Edward T. Grigware between 1941 and 1943.

Courtesy of the Library of Congress.

the family, and they promote certain national narratives and not others. Such images are an easier "sell" for news organizations faced with a public by and large eager for good news about the state of the war and the state of the nation.

Of course, not all documentary images of war reflect the official viewpoint. For example, Errol Morris's 2003 documentary *The Fog of War: Eleven Lessons from the Life of Robert S. McNamara* challenges prominent national narratives of World War II and Vietnam. In the film, McNamara, who served as Secretary of Defense under presidents Kennedy and Johnson and as a bombing statistician during World War II, suggests that the firebombings of Japan constituted war crimes. "Lemay [the military leader of the firebombings] said, 'If we'd lost the war, we'd all have been prosecuted as war criminals.' And I think he's right. He, and I'd say I, were behaving as war criminals. . . . What makes it immoral if you lose and not immoral if you win?"

Figure 7.5 Yokosuka, Japan, U.S. Naval base, May 6, 2003. Combat Systems Chief Petty Officer Demeyer Christopher hugs his daughter while disembarking USS Kitty Hawk after its tour in the Persian Gulf.

Courtesy of Koichi Kamoshida/Getty Images.

Even such counter-conventional perspectives are, however, just that—perspectives. Documentary modes of representation privilege certain stories over others and always tell only partial histories. In short, while notions of neutrality and objectivity are commonly associated with the genre, documentary images do not simply portray facts. Instead, documentary film and photography create particular stories and capture particular viewpoints to the exclusion of others. Documentary forms of representation are therefore rhetorical, in the sense that they are laden with particular gazes, purposes, and perspectives, including the gazes of the filmmaker or photographer and the subjects within the image.

Interventionist and Humane Gazes

The aerial images of war with which we opened this chapter contrast with those that define the campaigns of human rights and humanitarian organizations such as Amnesty International. Humanitarian images privilege *interventionist* and *humane*

Figure 7.6   Amnesty International
Advertisement

"IMAGINE" by John Lennon © 1971, 1999 Lenono
Music (admin. by EMI Blackwood Music Inc.).
Courtesy of Amnesty International/Magnum
Photos, Inc.

documentary gazes in their appeal to the audience's emotions and in their call for a
moral response and political action. Consider, for instance, the Amnesty International campaign image of a Chechen woman in her bombed house (see Figure 7.6).
At first glance, the use of the tagline "Imagine," associated in many of our minds
with the lyrics of the John Lennon song about peace, seems dourly ironic—the
image is anything but an image of peace, or, in fact, of anything we'd commonly like
to "imagine."

Yet the image is not without hope. A bright blue sky with large white clouds shines
through the one remaining window of the bombed house, perhaps suggesting that it
is possible to respond to violence through an act of imaginative substitution
(weapons and war for a limitless blue sky). The ad has the same imperative tone of
John Lennon's song, which, as a call to serious creativity for serious problems,
demands that the listener (re)imagine the world.

As a human rights organization, Amnesty International represents the oppressed
and suffering of the world; simply representing this suffering can be ineffective at

Research Prompts

genre kairos

AND **WRITING**

kairos

Kairos [KY rōs] refers to timeliness. This "timeliness" for an argument or moment of persuasion typically requires sensitivity to the cultural climate and to the audience to whom the text or speech is targeted. To analyze why an image, speech, or other text is persuasive at a particular time and for a particular audience within a particular place or culture is to examine its *kairos*.

Paying attention to *kairos* as we write means accounting for an audience's needs and expectations, as well as understanding how our own stance on an issue is shaped by the particularity of cultural, historical, and rhetorical moments.

Example ■ ■ ■

● In Paul Fischer's interview, "Moore's Lore Re-evaluates U.S. Gun Culture," Michael Moore comments on the timeliness—the *kairos*—of his film *Bowling for Columbine:* "After Columbine, I'd just kind of had it. It seemed like back then there was like a school shooting a week, and I just thought: Oh, geez! I've got to do something with this!" This quote suggests that Moore's documentary film, *Bowling for*

influencing viewers, however, because of information overload and desensitization—what some psychologists refer to as *compassion fatigue,* and others, like sociologist Stanley Cohen, refer to (more specifically) as *media fatigue*—which are the result of a cynical media's endless proliferation of images of suffering, based on the assumption that such images sell. In this instance, Amnesty International uses strategies borrowed from advertising in order to engage viewers' attention and challenge them to rethink their commitment to change.

More and more international human rights organizations have turned to innovative forms of visual communication to bring local stories of injustice to a broader public audience. For instance, Witness—a non-governmental human rights organization launched in 1992 and backed by musician Peter Gabriel—distributes video cameras to human rights observers across the globe. These observers create documentary videos that Witness then uses in grassroots campaigns and news broadcasts and as evidence before the United Nations, courts, and tribunals. Such documentary evidence is meant to counter official denial of atrocities and to persuade audiences to take action concerning subjects such as the incarceration of minority youth, refugees'

Columbine, was largely a response to these school shootings; these tragic events provided an occasion for him to investigate school violence and, more generally, gun culture in the United States.

Exercises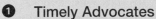

❶ Timely Advocates

Consider how advocacy groups and political campaigns attempt to persuade audiences by appearing timely. Look, for example, at the web pages of nongovernmental organizations that respond to natural disasters or the tragedies of war, such as Amnesty International, the Red Cross, Doctors without Borders, or any local or university advocacy group in your community. What images, captions, or headlines appear on their home pages that suggest they are responding to a particular current event or crisis? What rhetorical techniques do the organizations employ to persuade readers that their cause is important and requires immediate (timely) action or response?

❷ Join Us

Be creative: Design a poster for a campus organization to which you belong, or for one that you believe should exist. Make the focus of your poster/flyer the timeliness of your organization/cause. Think about how you might persuade other students to join the organization. To what social or academic issues does the organization respond? Why is it crucial that the organization seek members now?

rights, women's and children's rights, the sweatshop industry, and the death penalty.

Documentary as Advocacy

Documentary films, as mentioned earlier, can have many functions. Their primary purpose may be to record or preserve the past, but they can also persuade or promote certain political positions and agendas, therefore becoming forms of advocacy. Consider, for instance, the award-winning documentary film *Supersize Me*, in which Morgan Spurlock, producer, director, and main character, goes on a McDiet, eating only McDonald's foods for each and every meal for an entire month. Before he starts the McDiet, Morgan gets a thorough medical physical, and he is deemed by three doctors to be in excellent health (he is within normal weight range, has low cholesterol, and so on). After several weeks on the McDiet, however, he becomes overweight, tired, and depressed; his cholesterol levels soar; and his liver function is compromised.

Supersize Me establishes reliability through its documentary footage of Morgan as he consumes McDonald's products, interviews consumers across the United States about their eating habits, and undergoes medical exams, in which three doctors monitor his health using established medical procedures. Thus a good part of the film's credibility rests on the results of background research integrated into the film, and the careful description of the presumably sound experiment in diet. Part, however, also comes from the seemingly "unedited," rough appearance of the documentary, which suggests that the filmmaker has nothing to hide; no veneer of professional "slickness" distances him from his viewers. Part of the film's credibility undoubtedly comes, too, from the likablity/seeming trustworthiness of Spurlock (his *ethos*). After release of the film, Spurlock achieved minor "folk hero" status, as a modern-day David taking on the Goliath of the fast food industry.

Soon after the 2004 release of *Supersize Me,* an embarrassed (and embattled) McDonald's responded with a series of ads and public statements to counter the film's negative portrayal of its food. "No one eats McDonald's food three times a day, every day, and no one should," said Guy Russo, the chief executive of McDonald's Australia. Clearly, in *Supersize Me,* Spurlock exceeds most people's fast-food eating habits; nevertheless, the film attempts to convey a "truth." The crisis to which the film responds—its *kairos*—is the declining support from the U.S. government for health and physical education in our nation's schools and the increase in the number of overweight and obese U.S. children and adults. (Within the United States, 37 percent of children and adolescents are overweight; nearly 60 percent of adults are overweight or obese.) Furthermore, the film was released at a time when a lawsuit was pending against McDonald's in the United States for allegedly making two adolescent girls obese. Therefore, the film responds not only to the physical consequences of the U.S. desire for and reliance upon fast food, but to the financial and legal costs as well.

Supersize Me fulfills general audience expectations for the genre of documentary. But not all forms of representation (including documentary films) follow the "laws of genre." Representations that break a genre's "laws" and challenge audience expectations are characterized as **outlaw genres.**

Documentary Outlaws: Challenging Audience Expectations

Thus far, we have focused on documentary films and images that presume a close correspondence between what is seen and what actually happened—or at least one interpretation of it. But, as you know, seeing is not always believing. Consider, for instance, the controversial and provocative work of performance artists Coco Fusco and Guillermo Gomez-Peña. In one of their most famous collaborations, *Two Undiscovered Amer-Indians Visit the West* (Figure 7.7), Fusco and Gomez-Peña presented themselves as indigenous Amer-Indians from the fictional tribe Guatinaui, allegedly from an island in the Gulf of Mexico. Fusco and Gomez-Peña appeared in a cage that

Figure 7.7   "Two Undiscovered Amerindians Visit Madrid": Coco Fusco and Guillermo Gomez-Peña from *The Couple in the Cage,* 1992.

Courtesy of Nancy Lytle.

contained pseudo-primitive "artifacts" from their make-believe homeland. Fusco appeared in a leopard skin print bikini top and long grass skirt, and Gomez-Peña wore a studded black collar and a Mexican wrestling mask. The cage also contained a television and tourist kitsch, such as plastic sunglasses and a souvenir tablecloth. The performance was staged in various public spaces around the world.

These performances often took place in historical and art museums, either outside or in actual exhibit spaces. The location is significant because museums are associated with documentation and therefore promote expectations of truthfulness in representation: A museum exhibit is not supposed to be fake or make-believe. In part and no doubt as a result of this context, their performance, intended as a satire of popular nineteenth-century cultural expositions, was taken literally by some audiences.

"Realistic" museum depictions of "primitive" cultures have traditionally been staged as static displays, with backdrops characteristic of the period and location. Fusco and Gomez-Peña's performance violated these conventions of documentation—the "laws of genre"—in a number of ways. The performance broke out of the frame of genre by presenting live figures instead of mannequins; by substituting

myth and stereotype for reality; and by drawing attention to the questionable practice of putting the lifestyles of foreign and exotic "Others" on display for purposes of
edu-tainment. The performance urged viewers to consider how museums, as documentary spaces, have privileged certain gazes over others and facilitated the consumption of the cultural or national "Other."

Both the performance *Two Amer-Indians Visit the West* and *The Couple in the Cage,* a
video made from it, might be described as belonging to an outlaw genre, in that they
challenge audience's expectations about documentary and the uses to which it is put.
More specifically, they reveal the power dynamics and value judgments involved in
the creation of documentary evidence and its reception by audiences. Understanding the concept of outlaw genres, and thinking about how rhetors challenge the conventions and audience expectations of genre, can help us better "read" documentary
images and analyze how they attempt to persuade.

NOTES

1. Michael Renov, "Toward a Poetics of Documentary," *Theorizing Documentary,* ed.,
   Michael Renov (New York: Routledge, 1993) 12–36.
2. See, e.g., Persian Gulf War Illness Task Force, "Khamisiyah: A Historical Perspective
   on Related Intelligence," 9 April 1997, 13 Sept. 2006 <http://www.fas.org/
   irp/gulf/cia/970409/cia_wp.html>.

The Stories We Tell: Television and Humanitarian Aid

MICHAEL IGNATIEFF

There is a long-standing debate in our society about journalism's capacity to be objective—that is, to give its audience the unadulterated facts on the events and issues it covers. Critics of this belief wonder if true objectivity can ever be achieved when subjective human beings report on events. In "The Stories We Tell," *MICHAEL IGNATIEFF* critiques television news media, particularly for how they help to create a common perspective on humanitarian aid through a group of similar stories—what he calls a "grand metanarrative." According to Ignatieff, this narrative is supported by a number of deep-seated biases that affect how the news is reported. A professor of human rights at Harvard University, Ignatieff's work includes such books as *The Warrior's Honor: Ethnic War and the Modern Conscience* (1998), *Virtual War: Kosovo and Beyond* (2000), and *The Rights Revolution: Human Rights as Politics and Identity* (2000).

There are strict limits to human empathy. We make some people's troubles our business while we ignore the troubles of others. We are more likely to care about kin than about strangers, to feel closest to those connected to us by bonds of history, tradition, creed, ethnicity, and race. Indeed, because moral impingement is always a burden, we may use these differences as an excuse to avoid or evade obligation.

It is disagreeable to admit that instincts play a relatively small role in our moral reactions. We would prefer to suppose that the mere sight of suffering victims on television would be enough to rouse us to pity. In fact, there is nothing instinctive about the emotions stirred in us by television pictures of atrocity or suffering. Our pity is structured by history and culture.

The idea, for example, that we owe an obligation to all human beings by simple virtue of the fact that they are human is a modern conception. We still encounter tribal cultures in the world in which such an idea seems nonsensical. Universality comes late in the moral history of humankind, once Judeo-Christian monotheism and natural law have done their work. Even when these traditions have established themselves, people go on finding ingenious ways to evade their implications.

When we do make the misfortunes, miseries, or injustices suffered by others into our business, some narrative is telling us why these strangers and their problems matter to us. These narratives—political, historical, ethical—turn strangers into neighbors, aliens into kin. They also suggest some idea of reciprocal obligation: if we do not help them, these stories imply, they will not help us when our turn with adversity comes around.

Storytelling gives up pleasure, and the pleasures of moral stories are just as suspect as or at least as complex as the pleasures of, say, a dirty joke. Our moral stories usually tell us what we want to hear: that we are decent folk trying to do our best and that we can make good the harms of the world. We would hardly tell these stories if they did not make us feel better, and they make us feel better even when they make us feel guilty, because guilt endows us with capacity—it suggests that we have the power to make a difference and are failing to do so. The truth might be grimmer, after all: that we have less power than we suppose; far from being able to save others, we may be barely able to save ourselves.

Thus, if moral activity always involves the imagination, it is as much about imagining "us" as it is about imagining "them"; the stories we create always place us as their chief subject, and to the degree that this is so, our imagination is always susceptible to moral narcissism. The stories we tell lead us to think better of ourselves than we deserve.

Beside moral stories linking us and them, there are metastories governing the larger relationship between zones of safety and zones of danger. In the nineteenth century there were the stories of empire: the nexus of interest, economic, geopolitical, religious, and ideological, which bound the metropolis to the periphery. The imperial narrative—bringing civilization to the world of savagery—gave the media a metanarrative, a grand story into which each local event could be fitted and given its meaning.[1]

With the passage of the nineteenth-century empires and the creation of the postwar Soviet and American hegemony, the story that linked the two zones was the superpower rivalry for power and influence. What brought television to the war zones of these areas was the prospect of witnessing the proxy wars in which the world balance of power would be shifted. Now the superpower rivalry is over; "we" are no longer there, because "they" are no longer there, either. The proxy wars are no longer fed from Washington and Moscow, and while they continue—as in Angola—their salience and interest to the developed world has diminished. As for the parallel narrative of decolonization, some ex-colonies have made a successful transition to genuine independence and some degree of economic development, whereas others have foundered into tribalism, oligarchy, or civil war. Either way, there is no simple narrative to tell anymore. Instead, the narrative that has become most pervasive and persuasive has been the "chaos narrative," the widely held belief, only reinforced by the end of direct colonialism, that large sections of the globe, especially in central Africa and the fiery southern edges of the former Soviet empire, have collapsed into a meaningless disorder, upon which no coherent pattern can be discerned.[2] The "chaos narrative" demotivates: it is an anti-narrative, a story that claims there is no story to tell and therefore no reason to get involved. Since the end of the Cold War, television has simply reproduced the chaos narrative. As it does so, it undermines even its own limited engagement in zones of danger.

These demotivating elements are reinforced by the collapse of two other narratives. In the first of these, liberals were interested in Africa and Asia because the narrative of colonial nations achieving freedom and independence after years of struggle seemed to confirm the liberal story of progress. Now that a generation or two has passed and many of these societies have either achieved independence or thrown away its advantages, the story has lost its moral gleam. There are few partisans of African and Asian independence left, and more than a few who are overtly nostalgic for the return of colonial rule.

Another metanarrative that sustained interest in the third world after World War II was socialist internationalism, the faith that newly independent states were a test bed for the possibilities of a socialist economy and way of life. Generations of Western leftists were lured to Cuba, Vietnam, and other places in the hopes of finding their dreams confirmed. The collapse of the Marxist and socialist project has ended this metanarrative of hope, and as it does, disillusioned and demotivated socialists turn away from developing societies altogether.

No new sinews of economic interdependence have been created to link zones of safety and zones of danger together. In the heyday of empire, there was at least ivory and copper, gold and timber. As the developed world entered the phase of permanent postindustrial revolution, based in knowledge and computers, it appears to stand in less need of the raw materials of the developing world. Large sectors of the world's population are not being drawn into globalized commerce but banished backward into sustained underdevelopment. The developed

10

world is tied in ever-tighter linkage—the Internet, twenty-four-hour global trading, jet travel, global hotels, resorts, credit card networks, and so on—while sections of central Africa, Asia, Latin America, since they no longer even supply vital raw materials, cease to be of either economic or strategic concern.

This leaves only one metanarrative drawing zones of safety and zones of danger together: the humanitarian narrative. We are in one world; we must shoulder each other's fate; the value of life is indivisible. What happens to the starving in Africa and the homeless in Asia must concern us all because we belong to one species. This narrative, with its charter document—the Universal Declaration of Human Rights—and its agencies of diffusion—the nongovernmental humanitarian agencies and the U.N. system— puts a strong priority on moral linkages over economic and strategic ones. The question is how television mediates this moral linkage.

We should consider the possibility, first, that the media change little at all. Our best stories— from King Lear to Peter Pan—seem to survive any number of retellings. Why *should* the technology of storytelling change the story? We should beware of technological determinism in thinking about the moral impact of media. The claim that global media globalizes the conscience might be an example of technological determinism at work. It is certainly true that modern real-time television news-gathering technology has shortened both the time and the distance separating zones of safety—the small number of liberal capitalist democracies that possess power, influence, and wealth— from the zones of danger—the small number of collapsing states in Africa, Asia, Eastern Europe, and Latin America—where refugees and war victims stand in need of aid and assistance.

But it does not follow that media technology has reduced the "moral distance" between these zones. Real and moral distance are not the same. Real distance is abolished by technology; moral distance is only abolished by a persuasive story. Technology enables us to tell stories dif-

ferently, but it does not necessarily change the story we want to tell. Indeed, one could say that the media follow where the moral story leads. To the extent that television takes any notice whatever of zones of danger, it does so in terms of a moral narrative of concern that antedates the arrival of television by several centuries. This narrative: that we are our brothers' keeper; that human beings belong to one species; that if we "can" help, we "must" help—all of this emerges out of the Judeo-Christian idea of human universality secularized in European natural law beginning in the sixteenth century. At best television merely allows us to tell this old moral story more efficiently. The medium is just a medium. The modern conscience had written its moral charter—the Universal Declaration of Human Rights—before television had even entered most of our living rooms. Television would not be in Kosovo or Kabul at all, if it were not for these antecedent moral narratives.

It may be the case that television cannot *create* any moral relationship between audience and victim where none exists already. If television's moral gaze is partial and promiscuous, it is because ours is no less so. The TV crews go where we were already looking. We intervene morally where we already can tell a story about a place. To care about one place is necessarily to cast another into shadow. There is no morally adequate reply to the charge that Europeans and North Americans, to the degree that they cared at all, cared more about Bosnia than Rwanda. The sources of our partiality were only too obvious. One was in Europe, the other in Africa; one was a frequent holiday destination, the other was off most people's map. For most white Europeans and North Americans this partiality was transparently a function of race, history, and tradition. But how can it be otherwise? Our knowledge is partial and incomplete; our narratives of engagement are bound to be inconsistent and biased. To lament this point is understandable, except when it is supposed that we *should* be capable of moral omniscience. We cannot be. It is simply unrealistic to expect that

15

each of us should feel connection to every place in the world where victims are in danger. We are bound to care more about places and people we already know something about. It is certainly invidious to believe that white victims matter more than black ones, that coreligionists are more naturally a matter of our concern than nonbelievers; and we can counteract these biases where we can, but at the end of the day, we will care more about what we know something about, and if this is Bosnia, so be it. The media will simply reflect the biases intrinsic to their own audience: their coverage may indeed exacerbate them, but in itself, they are not responsible for them. Indeed, television coverage can do relatively little to counteract the inherent moral biases of its viewers. It follows where it and other media lead.

What is more to the point is that media ownership concentrates media power in mostly white European and North American hands, and their angle of vision determines the focus of world media coverage. For these reasons, natural partiality is grossly magnified, and the world's majority—nonwhite, non–North American, non-European—is forced to take the minority's moral priorities. This bias cannot be corrected by well-meaning gestures. It will only change as the majority takes economic power into its own hands and creates media institutions that reflect its own moral priorities. This is already occurring across southeast Asia, and there is no reason to suppose that it cannot happen eventually in Africa and Latin America.

The fact that television reflects but does not create moral relationships does not exclude the possibility that it may also distort these relationships. Three possible distortions are evident. First, television turns moral narratives into entertainment; second, television turns political narratives into humanitarian drama; third, television individualizes—it takes the part for the whole. All three forms of bias are interrelated yet distinct. Television news is an entertainment medium. It derives its revenue and

influence from its capacity to make the delivery of information pleasurable. Pleasurable story lines are generally simple, gripping, and easy to understand. Now all moral life requires simplification, and all forms of moral identification proceeds by way of fictions. In framing up our moral world, we all seek for good guys and bad guys, innocent victims and evil perpetrators. Nothing is intrinsically wrong about this resort to fictions and simplifications. It is also puritanical to suppose that moral problems should never be mixed with entertainment values. Moral drama is always compelling, and television can be easily forgiven for seeking to build revenue and ratings on the production of moral drama out of news.

Dramatization only becomes problematic when the actors in our moral dramas stop playing the roles on which our identification with them depends. For moral roles frequently reverse: innocent victims turn perpetrators; perpetrators turn victims. In such circumstances, it may become difficult to alter the story line in the public mind. Serbs who were perpetrators of ethnic cleansing in Bosnia in 1993 turned out to be victims of ethnic cleansing in Croatia in 1995. But their demonization in 1993 foreclosed the possibility of empathy—and the assistance that rightly follows empathy—in 1995.

The distorting bias here is sentimentalization, because sentimental art, by definition, sacrifices nuance, ambivalence, and complexity in favor of strong emotion. Hence, it is art that prefers identification over truth. To the degree that television is an art form whose revenue stream depends on creating strong identifications, it is axiomatic that it will occasionally sacrifice moral truth. Occasionally, but not always: there are times when the sentimental is true, when we identify strongly with a story that happens to have got its facts straight.

The second distortion flows from the visual bias of the medium. Television is better at focusing on the consequences of political decisions than the rationale for the decisions themselves:

20

hence on the thunder of the guns rather than the battle plans; the corpses in the ditch rather than the strategic goals of the ethnic cleansers. The visual bias of television has certain obvious advantages; it enables any viewer to measure the guilt that separates intentions from consequences; it allows a viewer to move, shot by shot, from the prevarications of politicians to the grimy realities these prevarications attempt to conceal. But the very intensity of the visual impact of television pictures obscures its limitations as a medium for telling stories. Every picture is *not* worth a thousand words. Pictures without words are meaningless. Even when pictures are accompanied by words, they can only tell certain stories. Television is relatively incoherent when it comes to establishing the political and diplomatic context in which humanitarian disaster, war crime, or famine take shape. It has a tendency to turn these into examples of man's inhumanity to man; it turns them from political into natural disasters, and in doing so, it actively obscures the context responsible for their occurrence. Its natural bias, therefore, is to create sentimental stories that by making viewers feel pity also, and not accidentally, makes them feel better about themselves.

Thus, television pictures from the Ethiopian famine in 1984 focused naturally on the pathos of the victims, not on the machinations of the elites who manufactured famine as a instrument of ethnic oppression or other long-term failures of the African economy or ecology. It did so simply because it chooses identification over insight, and it did so because television depends for revenue and influence on the heightened drama of this visual mimesis of one-to-one contact between the watching spectator and the suffering victim.

The third related difficulty is that television, like all forms of journalism, makes up its stories by means of *synecdoche,* by taking the part for the whole. Journalism is closer to fiction than to social science: its stories focus on exemplary individuals and makes large and usually tacit assumptions about their typicality. This is synecdoche: the starving widow and her suffering children who stand for the whole famished community of Somalia; the mute victim behind the barbed wire at Tranopole who stands for the suffering of the Bosnian people as a whole. Given that victims are numberless, it is natural that identification should proceed by means of focusing on single individuals. Synecdoche has the virtues of making the abstractions of exile, expulsion, starvation, and other forms of suffering into an experience sufficiently concrete and real to make empathy possible. But there are evident dangers. First, is the individual typical? Notoriously, television chooses exemplary victims, ones whose sufferings are spectacular and whose articulacy remains undiminished. Viewers trust experienced reporters to make these exemplary choices, but when viewers begin to question the typicality of the witness, they also begin to question the terms of their identification. When they feel that human suffering has been turned into entertainment cliché, they begin to feel manipulated: the ward full of abandoned orphans; the star-crossed Romeos and Juliets who loved each other across the ethnic divide and whose love shows up the folly of ethnic hatred; the plucky journalists who keep on publishing right through the shelling; the war-torn child whom the journalist adopts and spirits back to safety and endless interviews.[3] These forms of synecdoche forfeit any kind of complex identification with the whole panorama they are supposed to evoke.

The identification that synecdoche creates is intense but shallow. We feel for a particular victim, without understanding why or how he or she has come to be a victim; and empathy without understanding is bound to fritter away when the next plausible victim makes his or her appearance on our screen or when we learn something that apparently contradicts the image of simple innocence that the structure of synecdoche invited us to expect.

It may be, therefore, that television itself has something to do with the shallowness of forms of identification between victims and donors in zones of safety. Television personalizes, humanizes, but also depoliticizes moral relations, and in so doing, it weakens the understanding on which sustained empathy—and moral commitment—depend. The visual biases of television thus deserve some place in our explanation of "compassion fatigue" and "donor fatigue"— growing reluctance by rich and well-fed publics to give to humanitarian charities or support governmental foreign aid. Real distance has been drastically shortened by visual technology, but moral distance remains undiminished. If we are fatigued, it is because we feel assailed by heterodox and promiscuous visual claims and appeals for help coming from all corners of the world. Moral narratives have been banalized by repetition and in repetition have lost their impact and force.

25   Aid agencies, such as the International Committee of the Red Cross (ICRC), are waking up to the erosion of the narratives of moral engagement on which they depend to sustain both the morale of their field staff and the political support of donor governments. For aid agencies are moral storytellers: they tell stories to mediate and motivate, and they typically use television to get these stories and messages to pass from the zones of danger back to the zones of safety.

Typically the stories aid agencies tell are different from the ones television journalists tell, and these differences illustrate the moral dilemmas aid agencies characteristically encounter. Unlike journalists, aid agencies cannot point the finger of blame. They can name victims, but they cannot identify perpetrators, or if they do so, they must be careful not to do so in such a way as to jeopardize their access to victims. This limitation is especially the case for the ICRC, which has made moral neutrality its touchstone; but even groups such as Médecins sans Frontières (MSF), that have explicitly contested

moral neutrality have learned that if they do engage in blame, they may gain credibility among victims, but they lose it among perpetrators and consequently lose the capacity to work in the field. If tables are turned, and victims become perpetrators and perpetrators victims, aid agencies that have told a blame-heavy story may find it impossible to change their line of response to the disaster.

Yet, if aid agencies refuse to tell a political story—one that attributes causation and consequences for the disaster they are helping to relieve—they risk falling back on a narrative of simple victimhood, empty of context and meaning. This disempowers the agencies when they appeal to governments and ordinary people for support. For purely sentimental, purely humanitarian stories create shallow identifications in the audiences they are intended to sway; such stories deny the audience the deeper understanding—bitter, contradictory, political, complex—on which a durable commitment depends. In the recourse to the pure humanitarian narrative of support for innocent victims, the aid agencies actively contribute to the compassion fatigue they purport to deplore.

Getting out of this contradiction is not easy. The pure humanitarian narrative preserves neutrality, and with it the agencies' autonomy and capacity to act. A political narrative commits the agency to a point of view that compromises its credibility with the group it has accused.

Aid agencies such as the ICRC have responded to this dilemma, in effect, by telling two moral stories, one in public, the other in private. The one reserved for public consumption preserves the neutrality of the organization and avoids attributing political responsibility for the disaster, war, or conflict in which it is intervening. The private message is more political: it is directed to governments, donors, and sympathetic journalists and does point the finger of blame. In the former Yugoslavia, the ICRC's public story offered emotionally charged but ethnically neutral descriptions of humanitarian tragedy, whereas the private back-channel story, told by its delegates and high officials, did not hesitate to attribute blame and responsibility and recommend political action. Its public statements about the Serbian camps in central Bosnia in 1992 preserved ethical neutrality; the private messages of its delegates on the ground did not mince words.[4]

30   Organizations that split their message in this way risk appearing duplicitous and hypocritical. The objective may be laudable: to preserve sufficient credit with perpetrators that access to victims can be preserved. But inevitably a certain credit is lost with victims and those who side with victims, notably journalists.

Faced with these challenges to their moral integrity, some agencies have tried to harmonize both public and private storytelling. Médecins sans Frontières has been most explicit: refusing to be even-handed as between perpetrator and victim; refusing to offer humanitarian assistance when the political conditions are unacceptable; denouncing both perpetrators and outside powers when they obstruct humanitarian efforts. In Afghanistan, likewise, Oxfam and UNICEF have refused to split their messages about Taliban treatment of women, publicly denouncing Taliban attitudes toward women. There are risks in this outspokenness—not merely that the Taliban may shut these agencies out but that these agencies themselves become more enamored of the politics of moral gesture than of reaching and assisting female victims themselves. So if the ICRC runs the moral risk of duplicity and hypocrisy by sharply distinguishing between what it says in public and what it says in private, agencies that refuse this distinction run the risk of moral narcissism: doing what feels right in preference to what makes a genuine difference.[5]

But these are not the only dilemmas that occur when aid agencies try to tell moral stories. Their humanitarian action is frequently exploited as a moral alibi. Aid agencies become victim of a certain moral synecdoche of their own. Thus, the fact that the ICRC has been doing humanitarian work in Afghanistan for a decade is taken, by the watching world, as a sign that "at least" "we" are doing something about the human misery there. The "we" in question is the moral audience of the civilized world, and this "we" has proven adept at taking moral credit for humanitarian interventions in which it has strictly no right to take credit at all. For there is no "we"; the so-called civilized world has no such moral unity, no such concentrated vision, and if politicians who represent its concerns claim credit for the humanitarian work of agencies in the field, they do so illegitimately.

Anyone engaged in humanitarian action in the field is indignantly aware of the extent to which his or her individual efforts are incorporated by the watching moral audience on television as proof of the West's unfailing moral benevolence. For television does not like to depict misery without also showing that someone is doing something about it. We cannot have misery without aid workers. They conjure away the horror by suggesting that help is at hand. This is synecdoche at its most deceiving, for if help is getting through in this instance, it may not be getting through in others, and sometimes help may actually make a bad situation worse—for example, if food assistance falls into the hands of combatants and enables them to continue a civil war. Television coverage of humanitarian assistance allows the West the illusion that it is doing something; in this way, coverage becomes an alternative to more serious political engagement. The Afghan civil war cannot be stopped by humanitarian assistance; in many ways, humanitarian assistance prolongs the war by sustaining the populations who submit to its horrors. Only active political intervention by the Great Powers forcing the regional powers bordering Afghanistan to shut off their assistance to the factions is likely to end the war. Aid workers in the region indignantly believe—and with reason—that their humanitarian presence allows the West the moral alibi to abstain from serious political engagement with the problem.

Thus, when humanitarian agencies bring television to a conflict site, they may not get what they bargained for. They may have wanted to generate stories that would focus the attention of policy makers on the need for substantive diplomatic or political intervention; what they get instead is the production of moral drama: sentimental tales of suffering, using a poor country as a backdrop, which, by stimulating exercises in generosity, simply reinforces donors' sensation of moral superiority.

35   This idea certainly goes against the received wisdom about the impact of television on foreign policy and humanitarian intervention. It has been generally supposed that television coverage drives policy and intervention alike, the pictures creating a demand that "something must be done." We have already questioned the technological determinism implicit in these assumptions, by arguing that it is not the pictures that have the impact but the particular story—moral or otherwise—that we happen to tell about these pictures. Where stories are wanting, television cannot supply them. Those who have examined the impact of television coverage on the propensity of governments to intervene in zones of danger would take this argument still further. After closely studying cases such as the Somalia, Haiti, and Bosnia interventions, most analysts come away with a marked degree of skepticism about the efficacy of the so-called "CNN effect."[6] Policy makers insist that they decide whether to commit their countries to action not according to what they see on the screen but according to whether it is in the stable, long-term national interest of their countries. According to these studies, three years of drastic and sometimes ghastly television footage did little to move European

policy makers away from their reluctance to commit troops and planes to bring the Bosnian war to an end. At most, the television images stimulated a humanitarian response: aid agencies moved in, donations flowed, and some of the misery on the screen was alleviated. But television did little or nothing to drive the Bosnia policy of Whitehall or the White House. Here the determinant factor against intervention was Vietnam-bred caution about sinking into a quagmire. No amount of sentimental coverage of humanitarian disaster was able to shift the policy makers' and military analysts' basic perception that this was a "lose-lose" situation.

Both the victims themselves and the humanitarian agencies in Bosnia supposed that getting the cameras there would help trigger decisive military and political action. Both were angrily disillusioned when this action was not forthcoming. It was as if both believed that misery tells its own story, that pictures inevitably suggest the moral conclusions to be drawn from them. But, as I have argued, pictures do not tell their own story, and misery does not motivate on its own.

Yet skeptics go too far when they claim that television pictures had no impact on the foreign policy of states or the conscience of a watching public. Policy makers and military planners have an institutional stake in denying that they are at the mercy of television images and public pressure. It is essential to their *amour propre* and professional detachment to believe that they make policy on grounds of rational interest rather than on the basis of inflammatory and sentimental television reports. Yet their disclaimers on this score are not entirely to be believed. What the pictures from Bosnia undoubtedly did engage was a small but vocal constituency of people who felt disgust and shame and were roused to put pressure on the politicians who stood by and did nothing. It was not the pictures themselves that made the difference but the small political constituency in favor of intervention that they helped to call into being. Television itself did not create this constituency; rather, the images helped the constituency widen its basis of support; it could point to these images and draw in others who felt the same outrage and disgust as they did.

The numbers who care about foreign issues will always be much smaller than for domestic ones, but their influence is out of all proportion to their numbers. Most of them—in the press, the humanitarian agencies, the think tanks—have the power to create and mold public opinion.[7] For three years, a small constituency pounded away at the shame of Bosnia, and in the end their campaign worked—not, I hasten to add, because political leaders themselves felt any great shame but because, in time, they were made to feel that they were failing to exercise "leadership." Once a political leader feels his or her legitimacy and authority are put under sustained moral question, he or she is bound to act sooner or later. Added to this, in the Bosnian case, was the undoubted fact that prolonged inaction was beginning to erode the cohesiveness of the NATO alliance and open up important splits between Europe and America. In the end, the Clinton administration intervened and set the Dayton process in motion, not because it had been shamed by television but because it felt, with good reason, that at last an overriding political interest was at stake in Bosnia: the coherence of the alliance structure and the continued hegemony of America in European affairs. In other words, humanitarian pressure, in the form of outraged editorials and gruesome television footage, set up a train of consequences that only three years later eventually helped to generate a national interest basis for intervention. This national interest drove policy, but it does not follow that the intervention was motivated solely by national interest considerations. The humanitarian, moral pressure was integral to the process by which a reason for intervention was eventually discerned and acted on.

All of this suggests that the moral stories we tell through television are less influential than their visual impact would suggest, but they are not as unimportant as skeptics would imply; and that they do play a continuing role in structuring the interventions, humanitarian and otherwise, through which the zones of safety attempt to regulate and assist the zones of danger.

As humanitarian agencies confront the question of how to use television more effectively to sustain engagement, by donors and governments, and to counter "donor fatigue," they need to address the general breakdown of metanarratives linking the developed and developing worlds. We have two metanarratives on offer, globalization and the chaos narrative: economic integration and collapsing time and distance constraints for the wealthy few in the northern world; state fragmentation, ethnic war, and economic disintegration for the unfortunate citizens of as many as twenty-five nations in Africa, Asia, and Latin America. The rhetoric of globalization—and especially the globalization of media—altogether conceals the fact that this promise is withheld from the majority of the world's population. Indeed, as the developed world integrates still further, it is reducing, not extending, its contacts with the worlds of danger. Highly mediatized relief operations, such as Somalia, Goma, and Afghanistan, conceal the shrinking percentages of national income devoted to foreign aid, just as highly mediatized charitable campaigns such as Live Aid conceal the shrinkage of private donations to international humanitarian charities. The metanarrative—the big story—is one of disengagement, while the moral lullaby we allow our humanitarian consciences to sing is that we are coming closer and closer.

Notes

1. See my *Warrior's Honour: Ethnic War and the Modern Conscience* (New York: Henry Holt, 1998), chap. 4.
2. See Robert D. Kaplan, *The Ends of the Earth* (New York: Vintage Books, 1996).
3. Gilbert Holleufer, "Images of Humanitarian Crises: Ethical Implications," *International Review of the Red Cross* (November–December 1996): 609–13.
4. See Roy Gutman, *Witness to Genocide* (Middleton, Wisc.: Lisa Drew, 1993).
5. Michael Keating, "The Reality Gap," *Geographical Magazine*, September 1996, 23–24; also M. Keating, "Painting It Black: Who's to Blame?" *Crosslines* 18–19 (December 1995): 21–22.
6. Nik Gowing, "Real-Time Television Coverage of Armed Conflicts and Diplomatic Crises: Does It Pressure or Distort Foreign Policy Decisions?" Joan Shorenstein Center, Kennedy School of Government, Harvard University, occasional paper, June 1994; see also Steven Livingston, "Clarifying the CNN Effect: An Examination of Media Effects According to Type of Military Intervention," Joan Shorenstein Center, Harvard University, occasional paper, June 1997; see also Nik Gowing "Media Coverage: Help or Hindrance in Conflict Prevention?" report for the Carnegie Commission on Preventing Deadly Conflict, New York, 1997.
7. Larry Minear, Colin Scott, and Thomas G. Weiss, *The News Media, Civil War and Humanitarian Action* (Boulder, Col.: Lynne Rienner, 1996).

Re-reading/Conversations with the Text

1. In making his argument that journalism supports an uncomplicated, even shallow, narrative of humanitarianism when it reports on events in other parts of the world, Michael Ignatieff focuses primarily on television. Does he offer a reason for choosing this particular medium to critique? If so, what is his rationale? Do you see this narrative at work in other news media like print and radio? Are these media able to frame or shape the narrative in a manner different from television? If so, how would you characterize the difference?

2. Do you agree with Ignatieff's claim that the only metanarrative used in television news that "draw[s] zones of safety and zones of danger together" is the humanitarian narrative? In other words, have the grand narratives he points out in paragraphs 7 through 10 really been left in the past, or do they still exist today alongside the humanitarian myth? Can you identify newly emerging myths that create a different narrative of world affairs? If so, provide examples.

3. How does genre affect the messages given in these television news reports? More specifically, how do the generic elements of a television newscast (e.g., length, use of editing, specialized diction or jargon, use of light and sound, costuming, setting, and so on) contribute to the telling of a particular story or

event? How might the telling of that story change if it were told within another genre—say, a half-hour sitcom or a talk show?

Re-seeing and Re-writing

1. Ignatieff lists "three possible distortions" of moral relationships that might occur when television reports stories of conflict abroad: "First, television turns moral narratives into entertainment; second, television turns political narratives into humanitarian drama; third, television individualizes—it takes the part for the whole." For this assignment, record footage of a television news report on a current international conflict and play it for your class. As you play it, provide running commentary, pointing out examples of the kinds of distortion that Ignatieff lists. Afterward, lead the class in a follow-up discussion in which you debate the overall rhetorical effectiveness of the report.

2. As a long-standing genre, satire has historically functioned to demystify common myths, values, and beliefs of a society. This assignment asks you to look specifically at news satire such as *The Daily Show, The Colbert Report,* or *The Onion* (the online version of this newspaper can be found at *http://www .theonion.com*). How does this genre complicate, demystify, or shed light on what Ignatieff says is often hidden bias in "real" news reporting? What techniques do these satirists employ? Finally, using a "straight" news report as a source text, construct your own satire. In small groups, revise, re-script, and re-shoot your chosen news report and present it to the rest of the class.

How does Barbie Zelizer's "Conveying Atrocity in Image" complicate or extend Ignatieff's claims in "The Stories We Tell"? Conversely, how does "The Stories We Tell" complicate Zelizer's claims in "Conveying Atrocity in Image"?

Conveying Atrocity in Image

BARBIE ZELIZER

In this essay, BARBIE ZELIZER asks us to consider the role images play in perpetu-ating the memory of atrocities. As you read the essay, think about the capacity and/or limitations of images to perpetuate the memory of atrocities such as the Holocaust, recent wars, famines, and other mass trauma. Barbie Zelizer teaches at the Annenberg School of Communication at the University of Pennsylvania. She is the author of numerous publications, including Covering the Body: The Kennedy Assassination, the Media, and the Shaping of Collective Memory. *The essay below is an excerpt from one of her chapters in* Remembering to Forget: Holocaust Memory through the Camera's Eyes *(University of Chicago Press, 1998).*

Using images to bear witness to atrocity required a different type of representation than did words. Images helped record the horror in memory after its concrete signs had disap-peared, and they did so in a way that told a larger story of Nazi atrocity. As the U.S. trade journal *Editor and Publisher* proclaimed, "the peoples of Europe, long subjected to floods of propaganda, no longer believe the written word. Only factual photographs will be accepted."[1]

While words produced a concrete and grounded chronicle of the camp's liberation, photographs were so instrumental to the broader aim of enlightening the world about Nazi actions that when Eisenhower proclaimed, "Let the world see," he implicitly called upon photogra-phy's aura of realism to help accomplish that aim. Through its dual function as carrier of truth-value and symbol, photography thus helped the world bear witness by providing a context for events at the same time as it displayed them.

Atrocity Photos as Tools of Documentation

The photographs that became available on the liberation of the western camps were too numerous and varied to be published together by any one U.S. or British publication. This was because scores of photographers in different capacities—professional, semiprofessional, and amateur photographers as well as soldiers bear-ing cameras—accompanied the liberating forces into the camps, and most were placed immediately under the aegis of the U.S. Signal Corps, the British Army Film and Photographic Unit, and other military units. Making available numerous atrocity photos already in the first days after the camps' liberation, these photog-raphers displayed horror so wide-ranging and incomprehensible that it enhanced the need to bear witness, forcing an assumption of public responsibility for the brutality being depicted.

How did photographers record the scenes of barbarism that they encountered? Like reporters, photographers accompanying the lib-erating forces received few instructions con-cerning which camps they were entering or what they should do once they arrived; they were given even fewer guidelines about which shots to take or how to take them. This meant that for many the so-called professional response to the event was simply one of "mak-ing do," an improvisory reaction to often faulty equipment, bad weather, and uneven training and experience. As one photographer with the British Army Film and Photographic Unit said simply, "we did what [we] saw at the time."[2]

The atrocity photos played a complex role in recording the atrocities. Like words, the images

5

were of limited representativeness, providing only a partial picture of the consequences of years of forced torture, harassment, and eventual death—not the Holocaust per se but a partial depiction of its final phase. As British M.P. Mavis Tate commented, "you can photograph results of suffering but never suffering itself." But photography also offered graphic representations of atrocity that were more difficult to deny than with words. Photographers, one reporter claimed, sent pictures bearing such "irrefutable evidence of Nazi degradation and brutality" that were "so horrible that no newspaper normally would use them, but they were less horrible than the reality." Photographs thus pushed the authenticity of unbelievable camp scenes by pitching depictions closely to the

events being described at the same time as they signaled a broader story of Nazi atrocity. It is no surprise, then, that photographs flourished for the press as an effective mode of documenting what was happening.[3] [. . .]

Practices of Composition: Placement, Number, and Gaze

Though numerous and wide-ranging in their depictions of horror, the atrocity photos were somewhat unusual due to the repetitive scenes reproduced by different photographers, regardless of their degree of professional training. While varying the depiction—by changing the camera position, camera angle, focal length of the lens, light, and length of exposure—might have lent an individualized signature to the

Figure 1   General Eisenhower and other officers examine corpses at Ohrdruf, April 12, 1945.

Courtesy of the NARA (National Archives and Records Administration).

photos, this was generally not characteristic of these photos. Instead, near identical images arrived over the wires within hours and days of each other, differing only slightly in focus, distance, exposure, and perspective.

Placement   The decision of where to place evidence of atrocity in a photo created a layering between the atrocity photos' foreground and background, for the two often communicated different levels of specificity about what was being depicted. Witnesses and bodies were depicted in many of the images, and one was used as context for the other.

Evidence of atrocity usually meant pictures of corpses, and it often alternated with witnesses in either the shot's foreground or background. One widely circulated image portrayed General Eisenhower and other ranking generals at Ohrdruf viewing corpses strewn across the

camp's forecourt [Figure 1]. Eisenhower and company faced the camera from the back of the shot while they overlooked the dead bodies in its foreground that spilled into the camera. Taken by an unidentified photographer, the photograph appeared in the *Washington Post* on April 16 and resurfaced frequently over the next two weeks. It played in the *Illustrated London News* as a full front-page photo whose legend told readers that "the usually genial General Eisenhower shows by his grim aspect his horror of German brutality." The photo not only heightened the role of the American GI as witness to atrocity but juxtaposed the reader with the GI across the space of the bodies. It was impossible to contemplate the GI's act of witnessing without first contemplating the corpses.[4]

Elsewhere the foreground and background were switched, with the corpses positioned in the back of the shot. The British *News Chronicle*

Figure 2   German civilians view corpses at Buchenwald, April 16, 1945.
Courtesy of the NARA.

ran a front-page picture of Belsen that showed women cooking and peeling potatoes in the foreground and heaps of dead bodies in the background. Another frequently circulated triangular shot of the Buchenwald courtyard depicted a visual confrontation juxtaposing U.S. soldiers, a stack of dead bodies on a wagon, and the backs of German civilians [Figure 2]. The bodies occupied the back right-hand corner of the shot, soldiers the back left-hand corner, and civilians the foreground. In viewing the shot, the reader had to look over the shoulders of the German civilians in order to see the bodies, creating a layering between the shot's foreground (where the Germans were standing) and the background (where the victims and liberators stood). The effect was magnified by the middle of the shot, where a seemingly impassable white space kept the groups at a distance

from each other. That aesthetic was reproduced in other atrocity photos.[5]

Number A second practice of composition had to do with the numbers of people who were depicted in atrocity photos. The photos oscillated between pictures of the many and pictures of the few. Pictures of the many portrayed mass graves, where bodies had been thrown together so indiscriminately that it was difficult, if not impossible, to discern which appendage belonged to which body; pictures of the few portrayed single individual bodies frozen in particularly horrific poses—a starved man stretched out in rigor mortis on the grounds of one of the camps. Taken together, the images portrayed both individual agony and the far-reaching nature of mass atrocity, suggesting that the depiction of each individual instance of horror represented thousands

10

Figure 3 Corpses of civilians killed at Buchenwald, April–May 1945.

Courtesy of the NARA.

more who had met the same fate. The photos functioned not only referentially but as symbolic markers of atrocity in its broadest form.[6]

On the whole, the press presented collective images of atrocity more frequently than it did those of individuals. Perhaps because the group shots suggested a collective status that helped offset public disbelief, group shots appeared frequently regardless of the type of collective represented—groups of victims, survivors, or witnesses. Group images tended to be less graphic than those of individuals, partly because the rarely visible eyes and faces worked against the possibility of identifying the victims being depicted. Foremost here was a famous shot by Margaret Bourke-White, captioned simply "Victims of the Buchenwald Concentration Camp." Unaccredited at the time it originally appeared, the photo portrayed piles of human feet and heads angled away from the camera; the pile gave viewers the impression that it was about to spill over onto the photographer, and

that it was barred from doing so only by a length of chain at the bottom of the picture [Figure 3]. Other photographs, less renowned than Bourke-White's, showed the same pile of bodies from a long shot, a perspective that revealed them to be stacked atop a wagon in the camp's courtyard. That same wagon, portrayed from an even further distance, was featured in the aforementioned triangular shot of the Buchenwald courtyard [Figure 2].[7]

Images of other kinds of groups—survivors, German civilians, German perpetrators, and official witnesses—also proliferated, each displayed with repeated visual characteristics. Groups of witnesses were nearly always portrayed at one side of the frame, looking sideways at corpses that were either inside or outside the field of the camera. Groups of German perpetrators, for instance, were almost always portrayed at harsh angles to the camera and in rigid and upright postures [Figure 4]. These individuals looked angry and cruel,

Figure 4   Women SS guards at Belsen, April 17, 1945.
Courtesy of The Imperial War Museum, London.

almost maniacal. That perception was upheld in the captions that accompanied images of this type, as when the *Illustrated London News* labeled a group of perpetrators "The Female Fiends."[8]

Often the shots depicted confrontations between groups—German civilians and victims or news editors and survivors. One image— which circulated under the caption "Slave Laborer Points Finger of Guilt"—depicted a survivor of an unidentified camp pointing at a German guard [Figure 5]. The guard stood at the right-hand corner of the image, his contorted face twisting away from both the camera lens and the accusing, outstretched finger of the former prisoner. Although the prisoner was portrayed sideways to the camera, the photographer's empathy with him was clear.[9] Behind the two figures stood other officials, one of whom was witnessing the confrontation.

Thus, in each case framing the depiction as an act of collective, not individual, contemplation reflected a need to collectively address and

understand the atrocities. While the emphasis on collective representation may have worked against a recognition of the individual tragedies that lay underneath each photo, the emphasis on groups fit more effectively than did an individual focus on Eisenhower's aim to use the photos as persuasive tools for the war effort. Groups, more than individuals, lent the war effort urgency. Understanding the scope and magnitude of atrocity, in this sense, was equally important to recognizing its individual cases.

Gaze   Yet a third compositional practice had to   15 do with the gaze of those being depicted. The gaze of emaciated, near-dead survivors, whose eyes seemed not to comprehend the target of vision, tended to be frontal and appeared to signify frankness—though, as one British Army Film and Photographic Unit photographer of Belsen recalled, many of the same people were "incapable of coherent thought. . . . It was a very quiet, silent business. They sat about, very little

Figure 5   Russian survivor identifies former camp guard at Buchenwald, April 14, 1945.

Courtesy of the NARA.

movement. Some of them were too far gone to move." The survivors were almost always represented in frontal gazes that stared directly at the camera or at a short distance behind the photographer [see Figure 6].[10] In a sense, atrocity survivors appeared to see without seeing. One such photo, which appeared in *PM*, depicted two young adult women in a close shot that echoed their hollowed cheekbones and vacant eyes [Figure 7]. "Here's How Nazis Treat Their Captives . . . ," read the caption to the photo, as it implored readers to look at the "faces of these women."[11] [. . .]

German perpetrators generally were depicted in side views or three-quarter gazes, their eyes averted and narrowed [Figure 8]. Often they were depicted looking sideways at a survivor or soldier, who nearly always stared either directly at them or toward the camera. One such widely circulated image was that of

Belsen commander Josef Kramer. It portrayed him walking in Belsen, his mouth pursed and features tight, under a guard's watchful eye, who stared at him intently from the right-hand corner of the photograph. The same figures were portrayed from a greater distance in the *Daily Mail*, where Kramer was shown to be accompanied on his stroll not only by a soldier at his side but by another soldier prodding a rifle into his back.[12]

Conclusion

In composition, then, the published photos depicted a level of horror that went beyond one specific instance of brutality so as to present it as a representative incident. The combination of corpses and witnesses in the photos facilitated both the display of a particular act of barbarism and its more general context of atrocity; the

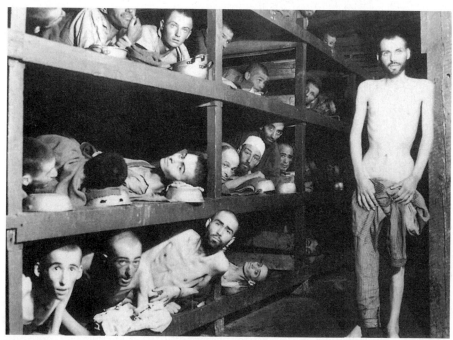

Figure 6 Former prisoners of Buchenwald, April 16, 1945.
Courtesy of the NARA.

Figure 7   Two survivors in Bergen-Belsen, April 30, 1945.
Courtesy of The Imperial War Museum, London.

number of individuals depicted in atrocity photos facilitated an emphasis on the collectives involved in atrocity—either as victims, survivors, perpetrators, or witnesses; and the gaze of those associated with atrocity opened the photographic document to the act of bearing witness in different configurations for victims, survivors, and perpetrators. In each case, on the level of composition photographs offered more than just the referential depiction of one specific event, action, or camp. Compositional practices suggested a broader level of the story that went beyond the concrete target of photographic depiction. [. . .]

All of this suggests that by capitalizing on the symbolic dimensions of images, the press set in place a broader interpretive scheme for comprehending and explaining the atrocities. Playing to the symbolic dimensions of these images had an important effect on publics, not only because they may have been the most effective and least uncomfortable way to comprehend the tragedies of Nazi Europe, but also because they framed events in such a way that all who saw the photos could bear witness to the atrocities. Within that frame, the exact details of the atrocities mattered less than the response of bearing witness. For those inundated with a guilt that came from not having responded earlier, this was no small aim.

Figure 8   Former women guards at Bergen-Belsen, April 1945.
Courtesy of The Imperial War Museum, London.

NOTES

1. Jack Price, "'Doormat' Label Develops Ire of Cameramen," *Editor and Publisher,* March 10, 1945, p. 44.

2. Interview with Sgt. W. Lawrie, Department of Sound Records, IWM; cited in Martin Caiger-Smith, *The Face of the Enemy: British Photographers in Germany, 1944–1952* (Berlin: Nishen, 1988), p. 11.

3. "Europe's Problem: What M.P.s Say of the Nazi Horror Camps," *Picture Post,* May 12, 1945, p. 25; Edward R. Murrow, "Despatch by Ed Murrow—CBS," transcription, April 15, 1945, p. 2 (Templeton Peck Papers, Box 1, HIA).

4. Picture captioned "'Ike' at Scene of Atrocity," *Washington Post,* April 16, 1945, p. 4, picture appended to "German Atrocities."

5. "There Was Fuel in Plenty," *News Chronicle,* April 21, 1945, p. 1. The British photographer who snapped this shot later wrote home of the difficulties he experienced in doing so. "There were hundreds of bodies lying about, in many cases piled 5 or 6 high," he wrote. "Amongst them sat women peeling potatoes and cooking scraps of food. They were quite unconcerned when I lifted my camera to photograph them. They even smiled" (letter from Sgt. Midgley, IWM, cited in Caiger-Smith, *Face of the Enemy*, p. 14). The triangular shot of Buchenwald, taken on April 16, appeared in numerous newspapers, including a picture captioned "At Buchenwald," *London Times*, April 19, 1945, p. 6, and a picture captioned "German Civilians See Truckload of Bodies," *Boston Globe*, April 25, 1945, p. 13.

6. Such pictures were typical of a two-page pictorial spread entitled "When You Hear Talk of a Soft Peace for the Germans—Remember These Pictures," *PM*, April 26, 1945, pp. 12–13. The journal displayed an additional page of atrocity photos the next day.

7. Picture appended to "This Was Nazi Germany—Blood, Starvation, the Stench of Death," *Stars and Stripes*, April 23, 1945, pp. 4–5. A long shot of the same wagon was used by photographers to depict the witnessing activities of different groups, such as Weimar civilians facing Allied troops in the aforementioned triangular shot of Buchenwald or official delegations inspecting the bodies. See "Nazi Barbarism," *Philadelphia Inquirer*, April 26, 1945, p. 14, and "Penna. Congressman Sees Evidence of Foe's Cruelty," *Philadelphia Inquirer*, April 26, 1945, p. 14.

8. Shot captioned "Study in Evil: The S.S. Women of Belsen," *Daily Mail*, April 23, 1945, p. 3; picture appended to a set of pictures entitled "Like a Doré Drawing of Dante's Inferno: Scenes in Belsen," *Illustrated London News*, April 28, 1945, supplement, p. iii.

9. Picture captioned "Slave Laborer Points Finger of Guilt," *Washington Post*, April 26, 1945, p. 9.

10. "Dachau—a Grisly Spectacle," *Washington Post*, May 2, 1945, p. 3. The image was taken on April 16 (Document #208AA-206K-31, file "German Concentration Camps—Buchenwald and Dachau," NA) and appeared as "Crowded Bunks in the Prison Camp at Buchenwald," *New York Times Magazine*, May 6, 1945, p. 42. One exception to the anonymity rule was a Dachau survivor named Margit Schwartz, who insisted on being photographed in the same upright pose she had assumed in her only prewar possession—a photograph of herself standing. Despite the protestations of those around her, she dragged herself to her feet and prodded the photographer to take her image. British Official Photo (Document #208-AA-129G-3, file "Atrocities–Germany–Belsen," NA).

11. Interview with Sgt. M. Lawrie, cited in Caiger–Smith, *Face of the Enemy*, p. 11; picture appended to "Here's How Nazis Treat Their Captives . . . ," *PM*, May 1, 1945, p. 8.

12. Picture appended to Peter Furst, "Anti-Nazi Bavarians Helped to Seize Munich," *PM*, May 1, 1945, p. 12, and to Hibbs, "Journey to Shattered World," p. 21; *Lest We Forget: Horrors of Nazi Concentraton Camps Revealed for All Time in the Most Terrible Photographs Ever Published* (London: Daily Mail, 1945), p. 73.

Re-reading/Conversations with the Text

1. In the introduction to this section, we discuss the fact that all documentary forms are selective, or partial. In what ways did the photographs of the liberation of the Western camps reflect a partial depiction of the suffering of Jews during the Nazi regime? If photographs represent only partial visions, upon what form(s) of historical evidence can we rely?

2. According to Zelizer, what is the pedagogical role of photography in educating the masses? What are the ranges and types of responses or stances that photographic images call for from viewers?

3. Summarize Zelizer's discussion of the compositional elements of images of atrocity. According to Zelizer, what is the rhetorical function of repetition in scenes, the placement of witnesses and victims, the number of people depicted, and the gaze? Why were "collective images of atrocity" published more frequently than "images of individual victims"? To what extent might images of atrocity constitute a distinct *genre?*

Re-seeing and Re-writing

1. In "Conveying Atrocity in Image," Zelizer describes depictions of Nazi atrocities as "an act of collective, not individual, contemplation." She argues that this emphasis on the collective representation of the corpses of civilians killed at Buchenwald, for example, "lent the war effort urgency" and enabled viewers to understand "the scope and magnitude of atrocity." This assignment invites you to consider images of the aftermath of the attacks on the World Trade Center on September 11, 2001. What rhetorical features characterize images of "Ground Zero"? Consider, for instance, visual patterns and repetitions. Who is represented? Victims? Witnesses? What type of documentary gaze is depicted? Do you see similar compositional patterns between representations of "Ground Zero" and the concentration camps? After you have analyzed the images, consider whether your analysis can support the claim that the images constitute a subgenre within the larger genre of atrocity images. If so, what conventions or structures of meaning define this subgenre?

2. Zelizer claims that photographs of atrocities function as tools of historical documentation. When Eisenhower proclaimed, "Let the world see," Zelizer argues, "he called upon photography's aura of realism" to enlighten the world about the Nazis' actions. This writing prompt asks you consider the function of the images in Zelizer's essay. In what ways do these images function as a form of documentation or support for Zelizer's analytical claims and observations? To what extent do the images do more than simply document? How would you describe Zelizer's scholarly gaze at these images? How would you describe your own gaze?

 Intertext

Write an essay in which you analyze and compare the essays of Zelizer and Coles. Apply the rhetorical triangle to both essays. How does each author imagine his or her audience? What is the author's main purpose? What is the subject of each text? Does the author rely upon certain rhetorical strategies or genre conventions to make his/her subject and claims palatable to readers? What do you think the authors hope to accomplish? How might particular contexts alter interpretations of these two works?

The Tradition: Fact and Fiction

ROBERT COLES

ROBERT COLES is an essayist, poet, and child psychologist. Early in his career, Robert Coles observed workers who migrated north of Florida as part of the research for his book *Migrants, Sharecroppers, Mountaineers* (1971). *Migrants* was the second volume of Coles' Pulitzer Prize–winning series *Children of Crisis*. The excerpt that follows is from Coles' book *Doing Documentary Work* (1997). Coles is the author of over fifty books, including *The Call of Stories: Teaching and the Moral Imagination* (1989) and *The Call of Service: A Witness to Idealism* (1993). Coles is currently the James Agee Professor of Social Ethics at Harvard University and founder of the Center for Documentary Studies at Duke University.

The heart of the matter for someone doing documentary work is the pursuit of what James Agee called "human actuality"—rendering and representing for others what has been witnessed, heard, overheard, or sensed. Fact is "the quality of being actual," hence Agee's concern with actuality. All documentation, however, is put together by a particular mind whose capacities, interests, values, conjectures, suppositions and presuppositions, whose memories, and, not least, whose talents will come to bear directly or indirectly on what is, finally presented to the world in the form of words, pictures, or even music or artifacts of one kind or another. In shaping an article or a book, the writer can add factors and variables in two directions: social and cultural and historical on the one hand, individual or idiosyncratic on the other. As Agee reminds us in his long "country letter," his aria: "All that each person is, and experiences, and shall ever experience, in body and in mind, all these things are differing expressions of himself and of one root, and are identical: and not one of these things nor one of these persons is ever quite to be duplicated, nor replaced, nor has it ever quite had precedent: but each is a new and incommunicably tender life, wounded in every breath, and almost as hardly killed as easily

wounded: sustaining, for a while, without defense, the enormous assaults of the universe."

Such an emphasis on human particularity would include the ups and downs of a life, even events (both internal and external) in that life that would seem to have nothing to do with the objectivity of, say, the world of central Alabama, but everything to do with the world of the writer or the photographer who will notice, ignore, take seriously, or find irrelevant Alabama's various moments, happenings, acts and deeds and comments, scenes. Events are filtered through a person's awareness, itself not uninfluenced by a history of private experience, by all sorts of aspirations, frustrations, and yearnings, by those elusive, significant "moods" as they can affect and even sway what we deem of interest or importance, not to mention how we assemble what we have learned into something to present to others—to editors, museum curators first of all, whose personal attitudes, not to mention the nature of their jobs or the values and desires of *their* bosses, all help shape their editorial or curatorial judgment. The web of one kind of human complexity (that of life in Hale County, Alabama) connects with, is influenced by, the web of another kind of human complexity (Agee and

Evans and all that informs not only their lives but those of their magazine and book editors).

So often in our discussion of documentary work my students echo Agee, emphasize the "actuality" of the work—its responsibility to fact. They commonly pose for themselves the familiar alternative of fiction, as though we were dealing in clear-cut opposites: if not the true as against the false, at least the real as against the imaginary. But such opposites or alternatives don't quite do justice either conceptually or pragmatically to the aspect of "human actuality" that has to do with the vocational life of writers, photographers, folklorists, musicologists, and filmmakers, those who are trying to engage with people's words, their music, gestures, movements, and overall appearance and then let others know what they have learned. No one going anywhere, on a journalistic trip, on a documentary assignment, for social-science research, or to soak up the atmosphere of a place to aid in the writing of a story or a novel, will claim to be able to see and hear everything, or even claim to be able to notice all that truly matters. Who we are, to some variable extent, determines what we notice and, at another level of intellectual activity, what we regard as worthy of notice, what we find significant. Nor will technology help us all that decisively. I can arrive in America's Alabama or England's Yorkshire, I can find my way to a South Seas island or to central Africa, I can go visit a nearby suburban mall with the best tape recorder in the world, with cameras that take superb pictures, and even with a clear idea of what I am to do, and still I face the matter of looking *and* overlooking, paying instant heed *and* letting something slip by; and I face the matter of sorting out what I *have* noticed, of arranging it for emphasis—the matter, really, of *composition,* be it verbal or visual, the matter of re-presenting; and here that all-important word *narrative* enters. Stories heard or seen now have to turn into stories put together with some guiding intelligence and

discrimination: I must select *what* ought to be present; decide on the *tone* of that presentation, its *atmosphere* or *mood*. These words can be as elusive as they are compelling to an essay, an exhibition of pictures, or a film.

Even if the strict limits of oral history are never suspended (*only* the taped interviews with informants are used in a given article or book, or any comments from the practitioner of oral history are confined to an introduction or to explanatory footnotes) there still remains that challenge of selection, with its implications for the narrative: which portions of which tapes are to be used, and with what assertive or clarifying or instructional agenda in mind (in the hope, for instance, of what popular or academic nod of comprehension or applause). How does one organize one's "material," with what topics in mind, what broader themes? How does one deal with the mix of factuality and emotionality that any taped interview presents, never mind a stock of them, and how does one arrange and unfold the events, the incidents: a story's pace, its plot, its coherence, its character development and portrayal, its suggestiveness, its degree of inwardness, its degree of connection to external action, and, all in all, its dramatic power, not to mention its moral authority?

The above words and phrases are summoned all the time by writers and teachers of fiction. Fictional devices, that is, inform the construction of nonfiction, and of course, fiction, conversely, draws upon the actual, the "real-life." A novelist uses his or her lived experience and the observations he or she has made and is making in the course of living a life as elements of a writing life. I remember William Carlos Williams pausing, after a home visit, to write down not only medical notes but a writer's notes: words heard; a revealing moment remembered; the appearance of a room on a particular day, or of a face brimming with surprise or happiness, a head lowered in dismay, a look of anticipation or alarm or dread, fear on

5

a child's face, those details of life, of language, of appearance, of occurrence for which novelists are known, but which the rest of us also crave or require, as readers, of course, but also in our working lives: we all survive and prevail through a mastery of certain details, or fail by letting them slip through our fingers. [. . .]

Documentary work, then, ultimately becomes, for most of us, documentary writing, documentary photographs, a film, a taped series of folk songs, a collection of children's drawings and paintings: reports of what was encountered for the ears and eyes of others. Here we weed and choose from so very much accumulated. Here we connect ourselves critically with those we have come to know—we arrange and direct their debut on the stage, and we encourage and discourage by selecting some segments and eliminating others. Moreover, to repeat, some of us add our own two cents (or more); we work what others have become to *us* into *our* narrative—the titles we give to photographs, the introductions we write for exhibitions, the statements we make with films. Even if our work is presented as only about *them,* we have been at work for weeks, for months, discarding and thereby concentrating what we retain: its significance mightily enhanced because so much else has been taken away.

It is not unfair, therefore, for an Oscar Lewis or a Studs Terkel or a Fred Wiseman to be known as the one who is "responsible" for what are supposedly documentary reports about all those others who were interviewed or filmed. Those others, in a certain way, have become "creations" of Lewis, Terkel, Wiseman—even if we have no explanatory comments from any of them about what they have done, and how, and with what purpose in mind. The stories such documentarians tell us are, in a way, the surviving remnants of so very much that has been left aside. We who cut, weave, edit, splice, crop, sequence, interpolate, interject, connect, pan, come up with our captions and comments, have

our say (whenever and wherever and however) have thereby linked our lives to those we have attempted to document, creating a joint presentation for an audience that may or may not have been asked to consider all that has gone into what they are reading, hearing, or viewing.

I remember, a wonderfully enlightening afternoon spent with labor economist Paul Taylor in 1972, while I was working on a biographical study of Dorothea Lange. Jane and I sat in Taylor's spacious, comfortable Berkeley home, the one he and Dorothea Lange occupied together until her death of cancer in 1965. He took me, step by step, through their work together, the work that culminated in *American Exodus* (1939). We examined many of Lange's photographs, some of them prints that were never published or shown. We were looking at an artist's sensibility, as it informed the selections she had made—which picture really worked, really got across what the photographer intended for us to contemplate.

I studied her iconic "migrant mother," a picture known throughout the world, a visual rallying ground of sorts for those who want to be reminded and remind others of jeopardy's pensive life [Figure 1]. There she sits, her right hand touching her lower right cheek, the lady of Nipoma, caught gazing, in March of 1936, one of her children to her left, one to her right, head turned away from us, disinclined to look at the camera and, through it, the legions of viewers with whom it connects. The three figures seem so close, so "tight," it would be said in the South, yet each seems lost to the others: the children lost in the private world they secure by hiding their eyes, the mother lost in a look that is seemingly directed at no one and everyone, a look that is inward and yet that engages with us who look at her, and maybe with her, or through her, at the kind of life she has been living. But only minutes before Lange took that famous picture, she had taken others. At furthest remove [Figure 2] we are shown the

Figure 1

same mother and her children in the makeshift tent that is their home; two others, a bit closer, show her with another child who has just been suckling at her breast and now has settled into a sleep. In one picture [Figure 3] the mother is alone with that child; in the next, [Figure 4] another of her children has come to her side, its face on her left shoulder. I return to the picture Lange has selected: now the older children are alongside their mother, but her appearance commands our attention—her hair lightly combed, her strong nose and broad forehead and wide mouth giving her face authority, her informally layered plainclothes, her worker's arms and fingers telling us that this is someone who every day has to take life on with no conviction of success around any corner.

Dorothea Lange has, in a sense, removed that woman from the very world she is meant, as

10

Figure 2

Figure 3

Figure 4

a Farm Security Administration (FSA) photographer, to document. The tent is gone, and the land on which it is pitched, and the utensils. The children, in a way, are gone, their backs turned to us, their backs a sort of screen upon which we may project our sense of what is happening to them, what they feel. But one child's head is slightly lowered, and the other has covered her face with her right arm—and so a feeling of their sadness, become the viewer's

sadness, has surely seized so many of us who have stared and stared at that woman, who is herself staring, and maybe, as in a Rodin sculpture, doing some serious thinking: struggling for a vision, dealing with an apprehension, experiencing a premonition or a nightmarish moment of foreboding. We are told by Lange that she is a "migrant mother," because otherwise she could be quite another kind of working (or nonworking) mother, yet she has been at

Figure 5

least somewhat separated from sociological clues, and so she becomes psychologically more available to us, kin to us. A photographer has edited and cropped her work in order to make it more accessible to her anticipated viewers. As a documentarian, Lange snapped away with her camera, came back with a series of pictures that narrate a kind of white migrant life in the mid-1930s—and then, looking for one picture that would make the particular universal, that would bring us within a person's world rather than keep us out (as pitying onlookers), she decided upon a photograph that allows us to move from well-meant compassion to a sense of respect, even awe: we see a stoic dignity, a thoughtful-

ness whose compelling survival under such circumstances is itself something to ponder, something to find arresting, even miraculous.

Another well-known Lange picture that Paul Taylor and I studied was "Ditched, Stalled, and Stranded," taken in California's San Joaquin Valley in 1935. Taylor first showed me the uncropped version of that picture [Figure 5], with a man seated at the steering wheel of a car, his wife beside him. He has a wool cap on, of a kind today more commonly worn in Europe than here. He has a long face with a sturdy nose, and with wide eyes he stares past his wife (the right car door open) toward the viewer. The woman's right hand is in the pocket of her coat, which has

Figure 6

a fur collar, and she is looking at an angle to the viewer. She has a round face, and seems to be of ample size. A bit of her dress and her right leg appear beyond the bottom limit of the coat. My dad, politically conservative, had seen that version of the picture years ago, and had pointed out to me that he was not impressed by Lange's title: here, after all, in the middle of the 1930s, at the height of the Great Depression, a worldwide phenomenon, were a couple who seemed well-clothed, well-fed—and who had a car. Did I realize, he wondered, how few people in the entire world, even in America, could be so described at

that time? An automobile and a fur-collared coat to him meant something other than being "ditched, stalled, and stranded."

Lange chose to crop that photograph for presentation in various exhibitions and books [Figure 6]. She removed the woman, save a touch of her coat (the cloth part), so the driver looks directly at us. Like the migrant mother, his gaze connects with our gaze, and we wonder who this man is, and where he wants to go, or is headed, and why he is described by the photographer as so thoroughly at an impasse. The photographer, in turn, tries to provide an answer.

The man's left hand holds lightly onto the steering mechanism just below the wheel, and he seems almost an extension of that wheel, the two of them, along with the title given them, a metaphor for a troubled nation gone badly awry: whither his direction, and will he even be able to get going again, to arrive where he would like to be? Once more, Lange turns a photograph into a melancholy statement that embraces more than the population of a California agricultural region. She does so by cropping (editing) her work, by denying us the possibility of a married couple in which one spouse seems reasonably contented, by reducing a scene to a driver who is readily seen as forlorn, and also as deeply introspective, eager for us, his fellow citizens, to return the intensity of his (moral) introspection.

I remember Paul Taylor gazing intently at the migrant mother and the man who was "ditched, stalled, and stranded"—a return on his part to a 1930s world, but also a moment's opportunity to reflect upon an entire documentary tradition, in which *American Exodus* figures importantly. No question, Paul and Jane reminded me, social observers and journalists have been journeying into poor neighborhoods, rural and urban, for generations, and in so doing have connected their written reports to a visual effort of one kind or another. Henry Mayhew's sensitively rendered *London Labour and the London Poor*, which describes nineteenth-century London, was accompanied by the drawings of Cruikshank, the well-known English illustrator—an inquiry that included a pictorial response. When George Orwell's *The Road to Wigan Pier* was first published in 1937, its text was supplemented by photographs, poorly reproduced, their maker unacknowledged—yet surely some who read Orwell's provocative and suggestive text were grateful for a glimpse of the world this great essayist had visited.

By the 1930s, under the auspices of the Farm Security Administration, and especially Roy Stryker, who had a keen sense of the relationship between politics and public awareness, a number of photographers were roaming the American land eager to catch sight of, and then, through their cameras, catch hold of a country struggling mightily with the consequences of the Great Depression—in the words of President Franklin Delano Roosevelt (1937) "one-third of a nation ill-housed, ill-clad, ill-nourished." So it is that Russell Lee and Ben Shahn and Arthur Rothstein and Walker Evans and Marion Post Wolcott, and, not least, Dorothea Lange became part of a significant photographic and cultural moment—the camera as an instrument of social awareness, of political ferment.

Though some photographers place great 15 store by the titles they attach to their pictures, or write comments that help locate the viewer, help give him or her a sense of where the scene is or even provide a bit of context (how the person taking the picture happened to be at a particular place at a particular time), most photographers are content to let their work stand on its own, a silent confrontation of us all-too-wordy folk, for whom language (in the form of abstractions and recitations) can sometimes become an obstacle rather than a pathway to the lived truth of various lives. But Dorothea Lange's work in the 1930s, quite able, of course, to stand on its own, became part of something quite unique and important; and that connection (her photographs and the statements of some of the men and women whose pictures she took, joined to text written by Paul Taylor) would become a major achievement in the annals of fieldwork, of social-science research, of public information as rendered by a photographer and an academic (who in this case happened to be husband and wife).

It is possible to take much for granted as one goes through the pages of the 1939 edition of *American Exodus* (it was re-issued in 1969 with a foreword by Paul Taylor). The pictures are still powerful, even haunting, and some of them have become absorbed in an American iconography of sorts—the one titled "U.S. 54 in Southern New Mexico" for instance, or the one taken in the Texas Panhandle in 1938 that shows a woman in profile, her right hand raised to her brow, her left to her neck: a portrait of perplexity, if not desperation That woman is quoted as saying "If you die, you're dead—that's all," and we, over half a century later, are apt to forget that in the 1930s there was no solid tradition of interviewing the subjects of a photographic study, linking what someone has to say to her or his evident circumstances as rendered by the camera. Again and again Dorothea Lange asked questions, wrote down what she heard (or overheard). Her sharp ears were a match for her shrewd and attentive eyes, and she knew to let both those aspects of her humanity connect with the people she had tried to understand.

Meanwhile, her husband was daring to do an original kind of explorative social science. As he accompanied her, he learned about the individuals, the locales she was photographing: how much workers got paid for picking crops, how much they paid for living in a migratory labor camp, and, more broadly, what had happened in the history of American agriculture from the earliest years of this century to the late 1930s. This was a study, after all, of a nation's fast-changing relationship to its land, of a major shift both in land usage and population: from the old South and the Plains states to California and Arizona, and from small farms or relatively genteel plantations to so-called factory-farms that now utterly dominate our grain and food (and animal) production. A combination of the economic collapse of the 1930s and the disastrous drought of that same time dislodged hundreds of thousands of Americans, some of whom sought jobs in cities, but many of whom embarked on the great trek westward, the last of the major migrations in that direction. For Paul Taylor, such an economic disaster was also a human one, and he knew how to do justice to

both aspects of what was truly a crisis for humble small-farm owners or sharecroppers or tenant farmers or field hands. Taylor wanted to let his fellow citizens know the broader social and economic and historical facts and trends that had culminated in the 1930s "exodus"; Lange wanted us to see both the world being left and the world being sought, and to attend the words of the participants in a tragedy (for some) and an opportunity (for others).

Although these two observers and researchers concentrated on the largely white families that departed the plains because a once enormously fertile expanse had become scorched earth, we are also asked to remember the Delta of the South, parts of Mississippi and Louisiana and Arkansas, and, by implication, the especially burdensome life of blacks, whose situation in the 1930s, even for progressives, was of far less concern than it would become a generation later, in the 1960s. The New Deal, it must be remembered, was very much sustained, politically, by the (white) powers-that-be of the South, and black folk, then, as now, on the very bottom of the ladder, were not even voters. Nevertheless, Lange and Taylor paid them heed, and did so prophetically—took us with them to the cities, to Memphis, to show us another exodus, that of millions of such people from the old rural South to its urban centers, or, more commonly, to those up North.

Also prophetically, these two original-minded social surveyors were at pains to attend what we today call the environment—what happens to the land, the water, that human beings can so cavalierly, so insistently take for granted. In picture after picture, we see not only human erosion—people becoming worn and vulnerable—but the erosion of the American land: farmland devastated by the bad luck of a serious drought, but also by years and years of use that become abuse. It was as if the prodigal land had been deemed beyond injury or misfortune. But suddenly the parched land said no to a people, to a nation, and suddenly the roads that covered that land bore an unprecedented kind of traffic: human travail on the move.

20   But Lange and Taylor go further, give us more to think about than the tragedy of the dust bowl [having] become a major event in a nation already reeling from the collapse of its entire (manufacturing, banking) economy. Some of the pictures of California (the promised land!) tell us that new misfortunes, even catastrophes would soon enough follow what had taken place in Oklahoma and Texas and Kansas and Nebraska and the Dakotas. The lush Imperial Valley, where thousands came in hope of using their hands, their harvesting savvy, to pick crops and make a living, was already in the 1930s becoming a scene of litter, a place where the land had to bear a different kind of assault than that of a succession of plantings that aren't rotated, aren't planned in advance with consideration of what the earth needs as well as what it can enable. The debris, the junk that covers some of the California terrain was no doubt shown to us by Lange so that we could see how disorganized and bewildered and impoverished these would-be agricultural workers had become, see their down-and-out, even homeless lives: the bare earth all they had in the way of a place to settle, to be as families, at least for a while. Yet today we know how common such sights are across the nation—how those who live under far more comfortable, even affluent circumstances have their own ways of destroying one or another landscape, defacing fields, hills, and valleys that might otherwise be attractive to the eye, an aspect of nature untarnished.

These pictures remind us, yet again, that tragedies have a way of becoming contagious, that one of them can set in motion another, that the temptation to solve a problem quickly (let those people cross the country fast, and find much-needed work fast) can sometimes be costly indeed. There is something ever so desolate about the California of Lange's pictures—even though that state welcomed the people who flocked to it by providing jobs, and the hope that goes with work. Environmental problems to this day plague parts of the western states, problems that have to do with the way both land and water are used. Half a century ago, Lange and Taylor more than hinted at those problems, just as when they followed some of the South's black tenant farmers into the ghettos of a major city, Memphis, they gave us a peek at the urban crisis we would be having in a decade or two.

Also prophetic and important was the manner in which this project was done: informally, unpretentiously, inexpensively, with clear, lucid language and strong, direct, compelling photographs its instruments. For some of us, who still aim to learn from people out there in that so-called field, this particular piece of research stands out as a milestone: it offers us a guiding sense of what was (and presumably still is) possible—direct observation by people interested in learning firsthand from other people, without the mediation of statistics, theory, and endless elaborations of so-called methodology. Here were a man and a woman, a husband and a wife, who drove across our nation with paper, pen, and camera; who had no computers or questionnaires or "coding devices," no tape recorders, or movie cameras, no army of research assistants "trained" to obtain "data." Here were two individuals who would scorn that all-too-commonly upheld tenet of today's social-science research, the claim to be "value-free." They were, rather, a man and a woman of unashamed moral passion, of vigorous and proudly upheld subjectivity, anxious not to quantify or submit what they saw to conceptual assertion but to notice, to see and hear, and in so doing, to feel, then render so that others, too, would know in their hearts as well as their heads what it was that happened at a moment in American history, at a place on the American subcontinent. Here in Lange's photos, finally, the camera came into its own as a means of social and even economic and historical reflection. These pictures, in their powerfully unfolding drama, in their manner of arrangement and presentation and sequencing, in their narrative cogency and fluency, tell us so very much, offer us a gripping sense of where a social tragedy took place and how it shaped the lives of its victims. This is documentary study at its revelatory best—pictures and words joined together in a kind of nurturing interdependence that illus-

trates the old aphorism that the whole is greater than the sum of its parts.

American Exodus was not only a wonderfully sensitive, compellingly engaging documentary study; it challenged others to follow suit, to do their share in taking the measure, for good and bad, of our nation's twentieth-century fate. Dorothea Lange was an energetic ambitious photographer, but she also was a moral pilgrim of sorts, ever ready to give us a record of human experience that truly matters: our day-to-day struggles as members of a family, of a neighbor-

Figure 7

Figure 8

hood, of a nation to make do, to take on life as best we can, no matter the obstacles we face. And so with Paul Taylor, a social scientist who dared pay a pastoral regard to his ordinary fellow citizens, even as he mobilized a broader kind of inquiry into the forces at work on them and on their nation. We can do no better these days than to look at their book, over half a century after it appeared, not only as an aspect of the past (a remarkable social record, an instance of careful collaborative inquiry), but as a summons to what might be done in the years ahead, what very much needs to be done: a humane and literate kind of social inquiry.

Speaking of such inquiry, Paul Taylor was quick to mention *Let Us Now Praise Famous Men* to Jane and me. He reminded us of Walker Evans's genius for careful, sometimes provocative cropping and editing of particular photographs—his ability to sequence his prints, look at their narrative momentum, and choose particular ones for presentation: the exactly memorable, summoning, kindling moments.

Taylor made reference to Evans's photograph in *Let Us Now Praise Famous Men* that introduces one of the tenant farmers, a young man in overalls, his head slightly tilted to his right, his eyes (set in an unshaven face topped by curly hair) confronting the viewer head-on with an almost eerie combination of strength and pride on the one hand, and an unavoidable vulnerability on the other, as so many of us have felt [Figure 7]. That picture, now on the cover of the latest (1988) paperback edition of the book, signals to us the very point of the title, of the entire text as Agee conceived it: an ode to those hitherto unacknowledged, a salute to this man and others like him, this man whose fame has awaited a moral awakening of the kind this book hopes to inspire in us, just as the writer and photographer themselves were stirred from a certain slumber by all they witnessed during that Alabama time of theirs.

In the picture of this "famous man," as with certain of Lange's pictures, the viewer is given no room to wander, to be distracted. This is

25

Figure 9

eye-to-eye engagement, a contrast to other possibilities available to Evans of the same man sitting at the same time in the same position. That farmer's daughter was actually sitting in a chair beside her father; one negative gives us a full-length portrait of him and her both, with the door and part of the side of their house and a portion of the porch also visible [Figure 8]. But Evans is struggling for an interiority, that of his subject and that of his subject's future

viewer/visitor: let us not only praise this man, lift him to the ranks of the famous, but consider what might be going on within him, and let us, through the motions of our moral imagination, enter his life, try to understand it, and return with that understanding to our own, which is thereby altered. This is a tall order for a single picture, but then Evans and Agee were ambitious, as evidenced by their constant citation of the inadequacy of their project (vividly

Figure 10

restless dreamers fearing the cold light of a morning).

Taylor also wanted us to look at a sequence of Evans's photographs of a tenant's daughter, bonneted, at work picking cotton. We who know the book remember her slouched, bent over the crops [Figure 9]. We don't see her face, don't really see any of *her;* she *is* her clothes, as if they were perched on an invisible person who is beyond our human approximations, who is of no apparent age or race. She is huddled over the fertile, flowering land to the point where she seems part of it, only barely above it, a lone assertion of our species and, too, a reminder of our incontestable dependence on the surrounding, the enveloping world of plants and shrubs. Yet, other negatives taken of that same scene at that same time reveal the girl standing upright, looking in profile at the surrounding terrain [Figure 10], or hunched over a part of it

Figure 11

that hasn't the abundance of crops that we see in the picture Evans chose to show us [Figure 11]. There is one photograph, taken from above [Figure 12], that shows only the girl's straw hat, immersed in the foliage—an "arty" picture, an "interesting" one, a pretty image. With the circularity of straw (another crop!) imposed, so to speak, on the cotton field, the girl becomes a mere bearer of that hat (only a hump of her is evident).

Evans resists the aesthetic temptations of that last picture and of others in the series; he picks and chooses his way through a narrative sequence that might be titled in various ways: Alabama child labor; a young harvester; a girl at work picking cotton; or, drawing on Rupert

Figure 12

Vance's wonderfully literate 1930s work at the University of North Carolina, an instance of a white child's connection to the "cotton culture." A photographer is carving out his own declaration based on his own survey research. He wants us, finally, to face facelessness, to see a child who isn't looking at us or at the nearby terrain (despite the fact that he had pictures of the girl doing both), but whose eyes were watching a row of plants, and whose body, whose very being, seems scarcely above them, tied to them, merging with them.

There is, to be sure, an appealing beauty to the picture Evans selected from this sequence for the book: a graceful curve to the body, an elegance, a consequence of a learned, relaxed capability to pick and pick, as I saw in a migrant worker I once knew, who tried to teach me how to harvest celery. As I watched him look carefully, then make this cut, then the next one with his knife—swiftly, adroitly, with seeming ease and authority and exactitude—I caught myself thinking of his dignity, his full knowledge of a particular scene, while at the same time I worried that I was being a romantic: I was struggling with my own obvious lack of skill by ennobling his hard, tough, ill-paid labor (as, arguably, Orwell did when he went down into those mines in 1936). And so, perhaps, with this picture of Evans: we attempt to contemplate people's strenuous exertions even as we try to rescue them, at least partially, from those exertions. A miner can have his nobility, or be seen in a noble light by an observer, and that migrant can exact from his terribly burdened life moments of great, knowing competence, and this girl whom Evans noticed so painstakingly can also have her times of agility, balance, suppleness, the mystery of a lithe, enshrouded form as it "works on a row." Or are we to think of her only as an example of exploited child labor? When, that is, does our empathy and compassion ironically rob those whom we want so hard to understand of their loveliness, however tough the circumstances of their life? (I recognize the serious dangers, here, of an aesthetic that becomes a moral escape, a shameful avoidance of a grim actuality, a viewer's flight of willful blindness—hence, I think, Evans's refusal to let us dote on that hat, with its "interesting" setting.)

Walker Evans, in his own way, addressed the broader question of documentary expression in a lecture at Yale on March 11, 1964. He was sixty-one then; he had spent a lifetime traveling with his camera, planning and then executing various photographic expeditions. At Yale he said this: "My thought is that the term 'documentary' is inexact, vague, and even grammatically weak, as used to describe a style in photography which happens to be my style. Further, that what I believe is really good in the so-called documentary approach in photography is the addition of lyricism. Further, that the lyric

is usually produced unconsciously and even unintentionally and accidentally by the cameraman—and with certain exceptions. Further, that when the photographer presses for the heightened documentary, he more often than not misses it. . . . The real thing that I'm talking about has purity and a certain severity, rigor, simplicity, directness, clarity, and it is without artistic pretension in a self-conscious sense of the word. That's the base of it."

So much there to applaud, especially the descriptive words "inexact" and "vague" and "grammatically weak": the difficulty we have in doing justice to the range and variation of writing and photography and film that a given tradition embraces. The word "documentary" is indeed difficult to pin down; is intended, really, as mentioned earlier, to fill a large space abutted on all sides by more precise and established and powerful traditions: that of journalism or reportage, those of certain academic disciplines (sociology and anthropology in particular), and of late, a well-organized, structured approach to folklore and filmmaking (as opposed to an "unconscious" or "unintentional" or "accidental" approach)—university departments of "film studies" and "folklore studies." Evans's three adjectives are themselves meant to be scattershot, if not "inexact" and "vague"—a means of indicating a style, a manner of approach, or, in his friend Agee's phrase, "a way of seeing," and also a way of doing: the one who attempts documentary work as the willing, even eager beneficiary of luck and chance, the contingent that in a second can open the doors of a craftsman's imaginative life. Academics have their well-defined, carefully established, and ever so highly sanctioned (and supported) routines, procedures, requirements, "methodologies," their set language. Journalists are tied to the news closely or loosely. Nonfiction writing deals with the consideration of ideas and concepts, with ruminations and reflections of importance to a

30

particular writer and his or her readers. Certain photographs follow suit, address *their* ideas and concepts: light, forms, the spatial arrangements of objects—lines, say, rather than lives. In contrast, even the word *documentarian* (never mind the nature of the work done) may be imprecise, hard to pin down, at times misleading—in fact, no "documents" need be gathered in the name of authenticity, in the name of moving from a suspect (to some) "oral history" to a history of affidavits and wills and letters, the older the better. But that is the way it goes—and there are advantages: no deadline of tomorrow for the morning edition, or three or four days for the Sunday one; no doctoral committee to drive one crazy with nit-picking scrutiny of a language already sanitized and watered-down and submitted to the test of departmental politics, a phenomenon that is surely a twentieth-century manifestation of original sin.

Instead, as Evans suggested, the doer of documentary work is out there in this world of five billion people, free (at least by the nature of his or her chosen manner of approach to people, places, events) to buckle down, to try to find a congenial, even inspiring take on things. Evans celebrates a lyricism, and defines aspects of it nicely: a directness and a lack of pretentiousness, a cleanness of presentation that he dares call severe and pure. It is a lyricism, be it noted, that proved worthy (in its expression by Evans) of companionship with Hart Crane's *The Bridge*, a lyricism that in general bridges the observer, the observed, and the third party, as it were, who is the second observer—a lyricism, Dr. Williams would insist, of "things," a broad rubric for him that included human beings, and a rubric meant to exclude only the rarefied, the insistently abstract. The document in mind (mind you) can for a while be hungrily, ecstatically abstract—the dreaming, the planning, the thinking out of a project—but down the line, somehow, in some way, we have to get to "the thing itself."

Here is Evans being ambitiously abstract, as well as impressively industrious, aspiring, enterprising: "Projects: New York Society in the 1930s. 1. national groups 2. types of the time (b. and wh.) 3. children in streets 4. chalk drawings 5. air views of the city 6. subway 7. ship reporter (this project get police cards)." He continues, "the art audience at galleries, people at bars, set of movie ticket takers, set of news-stand dealers, set of shop windows, the props of upper class set, public schools faces and life." Those notes were, appropriately enough, scribbled on the reverse side of a Bank of Manhattan blank check in New York City during 1934–35. Another series of notes: "the trades, the backyards of N.Y., Harlem, bartenders, interiors of all sorts—to be filed and classified." A letter to Roy Stryker of the FSA in 1934: "Still photography, of general sociological nature." The point was to dream, to wander from topic to topic, and then, finally, to find the specific place and time, so that the eyes were free to follow the reasons of heart and mind both: a lyrical sociology; a journalism of the muse; a dramatic storytelling adventure that attends a scene in order to capture its evident life, probe its secrets, and turn it over as whole and complicated and concrete and elusive as it has been found to those of us who care to be interested. [. . .]

To be less exhortative, more declarative, they are of many "sorts and conditions," documentarians (if that is what they want to be called—and we oughtn't be surprised if lots of people decline, say no to that word, maybe any word, any combination of words: "not the letter, but the spirit"). I think of writers or photographers or filmmakers, of musicologists who spend their time enraptured up Appalachian hollows or in Mississippi's Delta, of folklorists (Zora Neale Hurston was one) crazy for wonderfully wild stories told in odd and loony ways. I think of documentary work that is investigative or reportorial; that is muckraking; that is appreciative or faultfinding; that is pastoral or contemplative; that is prophetic or admonitory; that reaches for humor and irony, or is glad to be strictly dead-pan and factually exuberant; that knows exactly where it is going and aims to take the rest of us along, or wants only to make an impression—with each of us defining its nature or intent. In a way, Orwell, in *Wigan Pier,* showed us the range of possibilities as he documented the life of the Brookers (and blasted them sky-high) and documented the life of certain miners (and put them on a tall pedestal), and, in between, wondered about the rest of us, himself and his buddies included: wondered about the way a study of others comes home to roost. In a way, as well, Williams was being more enlightening and helpful than a young listener of his comprehended when he jokingly referred to the documentary side of his prowling, roaming New Jersey patrol, and when he posed for me a consideration of how a clinician ought to think of the documentary work he is trying to do—home and school visits in which he talks with children who are of interest not because they have medical "problems," but because they are part of one or another larger (social or racial or national or economic) "problem." Journalists cover those children in their way; a documentarian will need to put in more time, and have a perspective at once broader and more detailed, one that is, maybe, a follow-up to the first, difficult, sometimes brave (and costly) forays of journalists.

How well, in that regard, I recall conversations with Ralph McGill of the Atlanta *Constitution* during the early years of the civil-rights struggle (1961–63). He had no small interest in the fate of the nine black students who initiated (high school) desegregation in Georgia's capital city during the autumn of 1961, even as my wife, Jane, and I were getting to know those black youths and their white classmates (Atlanta had managed to prevent the kind of riots that had plagued other Southern cities, such as Little Rock and New Orleans). The three of us would meet and talk, and from him, through his great storytelling generosity,

Jane and I learned so very much. Often we discussed what Mr. McGill referred to as "the limits of journalism." He would remind us that "news" is the "commodity" his reporters go everywhere to pursue, their words worked into the "product" that gets sold on the streets and delivered to stores and homes. But those reporters (and photojournalists) are also great documentary teachers and scholars: they know so very well how to go meet people, talk with them, take pictures of them, right away take their measure, decide when and how to go further, look for others to question. They know how to make those utterly necessary first steps (find contacts, use them) that the rest of us can be slow in realizing will make all the difference in whether a particular project will unfold. They know, many of them, and they know well, how to pose the toughest, most demanding and scrutinizing questions, at times utterly necessary questions, and ones that naïfs such as I have certainly shirked entertaining, let alone asking. "How did you learn to do your work?" students ask me all the time. I reply: from the great reporters I was lucky to meet and observe, from Pat Watters of the *Atlanta Journal,* from Claude Sitton, the Southern correspondent of the *New York Times,* from the ubiquitous and sometimes riotous Maggie Long, who edited the *New South,* but called herself "an old newspaper hand," and from Dorothy Day, who edited the *Catholic Worker* when I first met her, but who had worked on journalistic assignments for newspapers for years (in the 1920s) before she turned her life so radically around upon her conversion to Catholicism, and who, as she often reminded us, was the daughter of a newspaperman and the sister of two of them.

Yet, as Mr. McGill sadly had to aver: "At a certain point we have to stop"—meaning that a documentary inquiry ends, in favor of the requirements of another documentary initiative. It is then, he explained, that "the magazine boys take over"—his way of referring to the greater amount of space magazines allow, but

35

also, of course, to the more leisurely way of exercising Evans's "documentary style." We never got into specifics, but because of his comparison, I began to think of the essays I read in various magazines (including those published by newspapers) in a different way: began to see the relative degree to which the author turns to people other than himself or herself as fellow bearers of a story's burden, and the degree, as well, to which such people are allowed (encouraged) to teach us by giving of themselves. Today, I think of Truman Capote's *In Cold Blood,* of Ian Frazier's pieces, short and long, of Alec Wilkinson's efforts with migrants in Florida, of his remarkable *A Violent Act;* and I remember *The New Yorker* of William Shawn as very much, at times, given to a "documentary style." Among photographers we can go back to Matthew Brady and the devastation of war that he made a lasting part of our knowledge, if we care to remember; to Lewis Hine and those children through whose condition he aroused our moral sensibility (again, if we care to take notice); to, of course, the FSA men and women; and today, Wendy Ewald, with her many brilliantly ingenious, spiritual explorations of childhood, aided by the children to whom she gives cameras, and whose photographs and words she shares with us. Photographers Alex Harris and Eugene Richards and Susan Meiselas and Gilles Peress and Danny Lyon and Robert Frank and Thomas Roma and Helen Levitt and Lee Friedlander; filmmakers Robert Flaherty and Pare Lorentz and Fred Wiseman and Robert Young and Michael Roemer and Ken Burns and Buddy Squires—all of these men and women are deservedly famous in the way Agee and Evans meant to signify for their Alabama teachers, known to the world as tenant farmers: humble by various criteria, but learned in ways any documentary tradition worth its name would aim to detail, to corroborate.

At a certain point in his research on Gandhi's life, Erik H. Erikson became dissatisfied. He had read many books and had spent a long time talking with a variety of scholars, historians, and political scientists, not to mention his psychoanalytic colleagues. He had obtained access to various library collections; he had attended a number of conferences; he had reviewed, courtesy of microfilm, journalistic accounts of Gandhi's various deeds and evaluations of the significance of his life. Nevertheless, this would-be biographer felt himself at an impasse. Why? I had no answer, despite the fact that I was teaching in his course then, helping him run a seminar, and trying to write about him, even as he was "struggling" with Gandhi (the phrase he often used)—almost as if the two were personally at odds, I sometimes thought.

We are sitting in Erikson's Widener study and I am interested, at the moment, in his work on Luther (my favorite of all his writings). He doesn't want to talk about that; he wants to talk about Gandhi's moral virtues, and, just as important, his flaws, if not vices: "I don't know whether I can proceed without in some way having it out with him [Gandhi]—how he fasted so honorably, risked his life for a just and merciful and fair political settlement, how he developed a decent and civilized manner of protest [nonviolence], and yet how he behaved as a husband and a father." Eventually, Erikson would write his well-known "letter," a breakthrough moment both in *Gandhi's Truth* and in psychoanalytic and historical thinking generally: a direct confrontation, a "having it out" with the spirit (the psychological "remains") of a figure who has left the living yet will endure through the ages. I listen, nod, try to steer us back to the fifteenth century, to *Luther*'s contradictions—it is, after all, *my* interview that we are conducting! Few of my attempted subtleties miss my teacher's notice. Why am I now so interested in *Luther?* Well, Erik, why are *you* now so interested in Gandhi? That is the "line" of our reasoning together: mutual irritation expressed through a reductionist assault, by implication, on one another's motives, all under the dubious protection our shared profession provides. Finally,

Erikson tells me, in annoyance at someone *else*, what he'd recently heard said by a distinguished cultural critic (and political philosopher)—that his *Young Man Luther* was a "marvelous novel"! I am taken aback; I keep silent; I worry about what my face wants to do, smile; I worry about what my voice wants to say (that such words are a high compliment), for I feel sure he wouldn't agree. He can sense, though, that I don't share his apparent chagrin. He puts this to me: "What do *you* think?" Lord, *that* question, the endlessly recurrent one of the late-twentieth-century, psychoanalyzed American *haute bourgeoisie!* I gulp. I feel my lips holding on tight to one another. I feel the inquiring openness of those wide blue eyes of this almost awesome figure. I find myself glancing at that shock of white hair flowing backward. I plunge: "Erik, it's a high compliment." I pause. I know I need to amplify, but I'm not prepared to, I'm afraid to. I settle for two more words, "the highest." He stares back at me. His face is immobile. I plead silently for the descent of compassionate understanding upon both of us. Continued silence; seconds become hours. I'm ready to speak, though I don't really know what I'll say—a dangerous situation, people like Erikson and me have long known: random conversational thoughts are a grist for an all-too-familiar (these days) mill, a gradual presentation by the unconscious of various unsettling thoughts.

But suddenly, amid a still persisting silence, the great one's face yields a broad smile. I immediately return it without having any prior thought that I should or would. He ribs me: "I know why you said that." I then pour out my explanation: that "novel" is not a pejorative word, certainly. I then make a statement about the revelatory nature of stories, not unlike the one I have tried to write here and elsewhere. I remind him that no one can know for *sure* what "young man Luther" thought and felt; that his story has to do with speculations, with informed guesses as well as facts, all told persuasively if not

convincingly; that imagination is at work in such an effort; and that sometimes, in those "gray areas" or moments, the imagination appeals to or invokes the imaginary—a Luther who becomes more in a writer's mind than he can possibly be with respect to anyone's records, recollections, or reports. I tell him about a question I once heard William Shawn ask of an about-to-be *New Yorker* writer: how would you like us to present this piece? What did Shawn mean? As a factual piece, a profile, or a short story? But, the writer said, it's about someone who was real, who lived! Yes, it certainly is, the distinguished, knowing editor acknowledges, but he could imagine it being presented, with a few narrative changes, as a *story*, with that "someone" as a character in it. Erikson now goes beyond smiles; he laughs heartily and tells me that I seem to be "enjoying all this," and he goes further: "Now, you see why I want to go to India and interview those people who knew Gandhi and worked with him! You see why I want you to show me how you use your tape recorder!"

He stops; it is my turn to laugh. I tell him he'll become a "field worker." He gets irritated, and justifiably so; he reminds me of his expeditions to Indian reservations (the Sioux, the Yurok) in the 1930s and 1940s, trips I well know to have been brave and resourceful (and, yes, imaginative) actions, given the prevailing psychoanalytic orthodoxy then settling in on his generation in the United States. I apologize. He tells me he isn't asking that of me; he wants us, rather, to discuss the nature of those trips, of his forthcoming "visit" to the Indian subcontinent. I call them, cautiously (following his lead), "field trips." He wonders about the adjectival addition of "anthropological." I demur. I say that these days any conversation with a child or adult on one of our Indian reservations gets connected to the discipline of anthropology—an outcome that needs its own kind of historical inquiry, because conversations by Erikson or anyone else (who isn't an anthropologist) in this country ought not be so reflexively regarded. We sit quietly thinking—one of the joys, always, with him: a capacity, a willingness to put aside mere chatter, to endure those lulls which, after all, sometimes fall for a good reason. Finally, he smiles, asks me this: "What would your friend Agee call those 'trips'—or the one I'm going on?"

40   I have been teaching Agee in my weekly section of Erikson's course, and I have introduced the professor to some of the more compelling passages of *Let Us Now Praise Famous Men*. I smile; we banter. I observe that I don't know what Agee would say, because he's so hard to pin down on such matters, even in connection with his own Alabama trip, but Erikson asks me to surmise. I reply that whatever Agee would say, it would be long, constantly modified, and perhaps hard to fathom without a good deal of effort. Erikson laughs, and tells me that I need to learn to "speak on behalf of Agee," whom I admire and whose values and work and thoughts interest me. No way, I say.

Now I feel him headed toward his own research, toward our earlier discussion, and we get there with the help of his jesting self-criticism, meant also to put more bluntly on the record a perception of mine, maybe even a felt criticism of mine with respect to his work: "You don't seem to want to do with Agee what I may do with Gandhi, and did with Luther: try to figure out what was more or less likely to have happened in someone's life, and then say it—with the knowledge on your part, and [on that of] your readers, that we're not talking about letters or diaries or conversations recalled by someone, but that it's someone today doing the best he can with what *is* available." I think and think, let his words sink in. I take a stab: I say yes, maybe so. But then I try to embrace what I've hitherto kept at arm's length. I use the word *documentary,* and say that in the 1930s that word had a common usage among certain photographers and filmmakers, including Agee's friend Walker Evans. Perhaps, I suggest, Agee, were he to be "sent back" here by his Maker, might oblige us with that word—might allow Erikson's search for a firsthand *documentary* exposure to Indians here, and now Indians abroad, in the hope that what he saw and heard and then described would, in sum, be informative.

He likes the word *documentary*. I've seen him savor English words before, he who spoke German as his native language for over two decades, and who learned to speak such excellent English and write a beautifully flowing, even graceful and spirited English prose. He looks the word up in his much-used Oxford dictionary. I tell him that a dictionary "doesn't always help." Quickly he replies, "What does?" I'm slow in replying: "A word can gradually emerge in its meaning—can fill a gap." "What gap?" We're on to an extended discussion now, one that anticipates by a long three decades these lectures, this book. We speak, especially, about "seeing for oneself," as he keeps putting it—the importance of "making a record that you the writer can believe, before you ask someone else to believe it." I remember that way of saying it, will keep going back to those words, will regard them as helpful, as greatly "clarifying" (a word Erik loved to use): the documentary tradition as a continually developing "record" that is made in so many ways, with different voices and visions, intents and concerns, and with each contributor, finally, needing to meet a personal test, the hurdle of *you,* the would-be narrator, trying to ascertain what you truly believe *is,* though needing to do so with an awareness of the confines of your particular capability—that is, of your warts and wants, your various limits, and, too, the limits imposed upon you by the world around you, the time allotted you (and the historical time fate has given you) for your life to unfold.

When Erikson returned from that voyage to India, he was full of new energy, excited by what he'd been told, what he'd witnessed. He loved being back in his Widener study, but as often happens to us when we have gone on a long and important and memorable journey, he was finding it hard to "settle down." He was full of memories of what he'd experienced; he was trying to do justice to those memories; and he was recounting them, fitting them into a narrative, one the rest of us would soon read; he was speaking of his "colleagues," now not professors in a big-shot university, but rather hitherto (for him) nameless, faceless fellow human beings who would soon become (for us readers) developed characters with something to put on "record." He was, indeed, doing documentary work. And so it goes, then—doing documentary work is a journey, and is a little more, too, a passage across boundaries (disciplines, occupational constraints, definitions, conventions all too influentially closed for traffic), a passage that can become a quest, even a pilgrimage, a movement toward the sacred truth enshrined not only on tablets of stone, but in the living hearts of those others whom we can hear, see, and get to understand. Thereby, we hope to be confirmed in our own humanity—the creature on this earth whose very nature it is to make just that kind of connection with others during the brief stay we are permitted here.

Re-reading/Conversations with the Text

1. How does Coles characterize the genre of documentary? What, in his view, is the relationship between fiction and documentary? In what ways is the process of writing fiction similar to or different from documentary work?

2. Coles describes the interpretative aspects of documentary-making: "I must select *what* ought to be present; decide on the *tone* of that presentation, its *atmosphere* or *mood*." First, why do you think Coles italicized particular words in this passage? Why italicize *what, tone, atmosphere,* and *mood* rather than *select* and *decide?* Second, if documentary representations (like all representations) are partial, in that they reflect "human particularity," what then is their historical value?

3. What is the rhetorical function of the photographs in Coles's essay? Do the photographs seem to function as evidence and support for his analytical claims? In what ways might Coles's analysis of them be said to represent a partial view? What doesn't Coles account for? In what ways might Coles's reading of these images reflect the *kairos*—timeliness—of interpretation?

Re-seeing and Re-writing

1. Coles suggests that Dorothea Lange's cropping of her famous "Migrant Mother" photograph dissociates the image of the woman from "sociological clues, and so she [the migrant mother] becomes psychologically more available to us, kin to us." First, re-read Coles's essay, paying particular attention to the rhetorical decisions he claims that Lange made in order to connect with certain audiences. Then, consider the rhetorical concept of *kairos,* introduced in the critical frame to this unit. In what ways might Lange's gaze be understood as a function of *kairos?* In what ways might Coles' analysis of Lange's

photographs be said to represent his own partial, and historically located, view? Finally, consider how your own position and the timeliness of your own response to these images alter their meaning.

2. This assignment invites you to gather a series of recent documentary representations of poverty. Who is represented? Whose stories are told? Who is the projected audience? Are certain groups depicted as victims and others as heroes or villains? How are national, cultural, religious, ethnic, or racial differences represented? Do these images represent a humanitarian documentary gaze? An interventionist documentary gaze? A helpless documentary gaze? What role do these images seem to create for or expect of viewers? After you have analyzed and compared the images, consider how these representations might be shaped by "human particularity" (Coles's concept) and the historical and cultural moment they seek to depict.

This assignment asks you to re-read Coles's essay through the lens of Michael Ignatieff. First, read (or reread) Ignatieff's essay "The Stories We Tell: Television and Humanitarian Aid," paying particular attention to his discussion of the motives for representing the suffering of others. Compare Ignatieff's discussion of humanitarian stories to Coles's claim that in representations of the poor, "we attempt to contemplate people's strenuous exertions even as we try to rescue them, at least partially, from those exertions" and his assertion that, at times, "empathy and compassion ironically rob those whom we want so hard to understand of their loveliness, however tough the circumstances of their life." What is similar or different about Coles's and Ignatieff's analyses and their assessments of the documentation of human suffering and injustice?

Moore's Lore Re-evaluates U.S. Gun Culture

PAUL FISCHER

The provocative documentaries of filmmaker Michael Moore present audiences with decisive opinions on a variety of issues: the inequities of corporate welfare, the injustice of our government's policies toward poverty, and, in the Oscar-winning *Bowling for Columbine,* the media-fueled epidemic of gun-related violence in the United States. In *PAUL FISCHER*'s 2002 interview of Moore, we get a glimpse into how, during the course of producing *Bowling for Columbine,* the opinion of the filmmaker shifted with respect to gun laws and America's historical propensity toward violence. This interview originally appeared in the British online film e-zine *io (Inside Out) Film* (http://www.iofilm.co.uk/).

> *Michael Moore, the burly corporation-basher from Flint, Michigan, is madder than ever on the subject of gun control in award-winning documentary* Bowling for Columbine. *Interview by Paul Fischer.*

"After Columbine, I'd just kind of had it. It seemed like back then there was like a school shooting a week, and I just thought: Oh, gees! I've got to do something with this!"

Thus bombastic, talkative 48-year-old Michael Moore started his investigation into America's dangerous obsession with guns.

Moore, who reveals in the feature-length documentary that he is a card-carrying member of the NRA, recalls starting off "with a sort of typical liberal view point, in that if only we had less guns and more gun control laws, we'd have less violence."

Change of View

That changed once he started making the film he began to see things differently. "It became clear to me that that wasn't the answer and especially once coming to Canada, you know, and going to the office of Canadian statistics where they've got seven million registered guns in this country.

5   "Ten million households, right, seven million guns. I thought that's a hell of a lot of guns to have lying around. Even though the majority of them are shotguns and rifles, you know, they don't have oozies here, no hand gun in the night table, you know. But, if you want to get a gun in Canada you can. You got to go through a lot of hoops, you can't be a wife-beater or anything like that, but you know, if you wait a month you can get a gun."

But the Canadians don't have the monopoly over the ease of gun ownership. The opening sequence of Moore's startling film has him being able to get a gun by merely opening a bank account in one town. Hilarious and absurd on the one hand, disturbing on the other. "I was so nervous about that very issue, that I did not say the city it was in because I was just afraid," Moore chuckles.

"When the teller says that there were 500 guns in the vault, this is not something that I should be advertising exactly where this is."

Of course Moore's vision, as often startling as it is, is by no means parochially American or Canadian. Sold internationally at record levels, clearly *Bowling for Columbine* is designed to take an American tragedy and broaden its ramifications internationally.

The reason is simple, he says. "People from other countries are afraid that you may be becoming more like us," says Moore with a quieter tone.

10   "Americans in Cannes, when the film sold so well internationally, had the attitude that, "It's because you guys hate Americans," "You love to laugh at Americans," "Goofy Americans," or whatever. But the truth was—because I saw it with the international audiences in Cannes—the feeling coming out of there was, 'Whatever we do we have to stop going down this road.' "

What's the Solution?

Moore is unapologetic about his Leftist stance, but with school shootings on the rise and recent sniper attacks bombarding the airwaves, he believes that most Americans, at any rate are on his side. He may be right, and what he wants, is for this so-called Christian country to live up to its Judaic-Christian doctrine. No kidding.

"Americans need to be a little more Christian. What would Jesus do? Would Jesus beat up on the poor? No really, I wonder how we come off calling ourselves Christians or a Christian country when the whole message of this guy was 'blessed are the poor.' That was the first thing out of his mouth on that mountain, right?"

But to Moore, the problems that lead to excessive gun ownership go beyond a lack of Christian values. "We are in an economic system that is set up to benefit the few at the expense of the many, which is wrong. Now I don't know what the solution is to it. I'm not saying that Communism or Socialism or whatever are the answers; I've never read anything by Marx, I am not that educated even though I know I look like a smart guy," quips Moore.

The 48-year-old filmmaker from Flint, Michigan, is best known for his confrontational style, which resulted in acclaimed films such as *Roger & Me* and television shows such as *The Awful Truth*. He also wrote the hit book *Stupid White Men. Bowling for Columbine,* which was a smash sensation at the Cannes Film Festival in May, has the potential to be his most popular film ever, and argues "that it's the kind of movie I like to see. It's funny, poignant and interesting, your perfect Saturday night out," says Moore.

"I set out first of all to make a film that I   15 would want to go see on a Friday night so my first audience is me, and I trust that there is at least a million or two million people like me, you know, 270 million that like to see the same movie. I don't set out to try and please some audience or demographic."

Here's the Good News

While Moore's vision in this film is often tough-minded and deals with some thorny issues, he says that after seeing his film, it should be evident that at heart, he remains an optimist.

"Things get better. Slavery ends, Hitler dies. Things get better and the bad guys usually do lose in the end. That is the truth. And in the end, things do improve and, so you have a lot of the humour in these films, because the humour is there as a part of release of the pressure," says Moore striking a more upbeat note.

"If you leave the theatre depressed, you are paralysed by the despair. I don't want you to go have a beer and go, 'Let's just forget about that' and 'So the world sucks.' I want you to leave the theatre angry, and feeling like you'd better do something. I am kind of pushing your citizen button, to activate it to say, 'This is a democracy! This is not a spectator sport! And this is a participatory event!' If the people don't participate, it doesn't exist."

Re-reading/Conversations with the Text

1. Paul Fischer's interview with filmmaker Michael Moore was originally intended for a readership primarily from the United Kingdom. Re-read the interview, pinpointing evidence that this particular audience is invoked. What specific questions, topics, or responses might suggest a non-American audience? How might this article be structured differently if it were written for an American publication?

2. Near the end of the interview, Moore says that when making his films, "I don't set out to try and please some audience or demographic." How does Moore characterize the audience he imagines when he creates his films? How do you think this affects the ways that the audience reacts to his films?

3. The first section of this interview, subtitled "Change of View," charts the changes in Moore's opinion on the subject of gun control as he filmed *Bowling for Columbine.* This shift in thinking might be characterized as dialectical: that is, Moore originally held a tentative thesis on the issue, but the evidence he gathered along the way ended up being antithetical to his thesis, so he was persuaded to revise his position. Describe Moore's "change of view." Do you find it surprising? Why or why not?

Re-seeing and Re-writing

1. For this assignment, watch *Bowling for Columbine.* Consider how the film functions rhetorically as a documentary film. What elements and techniques make it a documentary? How do these elements enhance or detract from the film's ability to persuade its viewers? How might a different cinematic approach—say, a fictional film dealing with the complexities of gun violence—work differently to persuade viewers?

2. One of the Key Rhetorical Terms for this section is *kairos,* the ancient Greek concept of appropriateness and timeliness. A central tension in Moore's *Bowling for Columbine* hinges on a disagreement over the *kairos* of particular rhetorical events—namely, Charlton Heston's NRA rallies in cities affected by gun violence involving children, often done within days of the violent event. For this assignment, compare how Moore and Heston differ in their opinions of whether the NRA rallies are appropriate given the circumstances. How does each man differently interpret the *kairos* of the situation?

Intertext

Write an analysis of Michael Ignatieff's essay and Moore's *Bowling for Columbine* in which you decide how each text depicts the *kairos,* or timeliness, of the issues under consideration. For this assignment, you should provide a detailed definition of the concept of *kairos,* and show how each text succeeds in or fails to meet the criteria established by your definition.

Dream Museum: Blindness, Language and Visual Art

GEORGINA KLEEGE

The passage of the Americans with Disabilities Act (ADA) in 1990, now almost two decades old, helped secure the rights of people with disabilities to access educational and public (government-funded) places. As a blind person, a writer, and a college teacher, *GEORGINA KLEEGE* asks us to consider: Whom are museums, especially art museums, for? In positing the experience of a blind visitor to such places, Kleege also educates us about what "blindness" is and isn't, chipping away at long-standing cultural stereotypes about blind people. Finally, Kleege performs a sophisticated, albeit imaginary, "visual analysis" of a photograph or painting even as she teaches us about the art of "audio description," a form of assistive and access technology that is now sometimes used by blind and vision-impaired people in "viewing" films, TV, art, etc. The author of a novel, *Home for the Summer*, and a collection of personal essays, *Sight Unseen*, Kleege also teaches creative writing and disability studies classes at the University of California, Berkeley.

For several years I have been working on a book about Helen Keller, the American deaf-blind writer and activist. One night I had a dream in which I went to an exhibition at a New York gallery of photographs of Keller by Margaret Bourke White. Somehow I knew a good deal about the exhibition; perhaps I had read an article or announcement somewhere. I was particularly interested in a group of pictures where Keller was posed on a high ledge of the Chrysler building, with the skyline 1930s' Manhattan behind and below her.

I should point out that as far as I know, Margaret Bourke White never photographed Helen Keller. In fact, she was not known as a portrait photographer. She had photographed the Chrysler building, however. And she was a pioneer and an innovator so it seemed only natural—at least according to the logic of my dream—that she would have wanted to photograph another pioneer and innovator.

In my waking life at the time I was thinking a lot about Helen Keller and photography. I had begun to speculate that Keller may have been the most photographed woman of the twentieth century, in part because she lived to the age of eighty-eight, and spent most of her life in the public eye. She was photographed with all the celebrities of her day: movie stars, politicians, intellectuals, and artists—and was extremely photogenic. Although she had been totally blind since the age of nineteen months and had no first-hand experience of photography, she seemed to understand from an early age that she could use her image to communicate with a public that was at once fascinated and horrified by her disability. She was adept at striking natural poses for the camera, and knew how to aim her eyes, prosthetic as they were. Directly at the lens.

But back to my dream. In the dream I presented myself at the gallery right at its opening hour. There were two women at the front counter, who told me politely but firmly, that the labels for the photographs were not available in Braille or large print or audio recording, and there was as yet no catalogue that I could buy to read, or have read to me at home. I said that I could return later with a companion who could read me the labels and describe the images, but still they declined. They expected a large crowd and the time I would take before each photo would impede the flow of patrons through the gallery. I insisted that I am quite nimble, and have a good sense of when someone near me wants me to move out of the way. And as everyone who reads to me knows, I am a very fast listener. I routinely set my computer's synthesized voice at the fastest possible speed. I promised, trying hard not to plead, that my presence in the gallery would in no way affect the enjoyment of other visitors. But nothing I could say changed their minds. All the while they remained calm, polite but mostly a little perplexed at my request, while I became more and more frantic, trying with a stream of reasonable arguments flowing from my lips to keep them from speaking the words I knew were on their mind: "What do you expect? This is no place for a blind person."

5   In my real life as a museum goer I have never been denied access in this way. But anyone who enters a museum or art gallery carrying a white cane or using a service dog is familiar with the stir our presence causes. Did we take a wrong turn and end up there by accident? What can the visual arts possibly mean to someone who cannot see? Nevertheless, museums around the world have begun to address this very question. In the last decade and more a good many other conferences and symposia have been held, as well as articles and books published, internships and training programs established, organizations and consumer groups founded. For the most part, however, the access that is available tends to occur in special by-appointment-only tours or else to segregate blind visitors to special collections, frequently consisting of replicas and models of art works. As valuable as these programs are, they do not answer the needs of visually impaired patrons who already know something about art and art history, or who may be seeking access to an exhibition that has not been previously designated as of interest to the blind.

This then is what we are here to explore, today and tomorrow: how to move access

beyond simple art appreciation to accommodate greater numbers of blind people. We need to start from the premise that the blind museum visitor is not necessarily a child and is not in need of charity or special favors. The most reductive and destructive of all the stereotypes about blindness is that our experience and consciousness are so far from whatever is considered normal that we might as well have come from another planet. In fact, blind museum visitors have much in common with sighted visitors. For one thing, most of us used to be sighted, some until quite recently. And even those of us who were born blind grew up and attended school with sighted people. We read books written by and about sighted people and visual matters. We watch movies and TV shows featuring sighted characters. We speak languages replete with visual idioms and metaphors and can use these terms with as much skill as sighted speakers. In other words, the average blind person knows more about what it means to be sighted than the average sighted person knows about what it means to be blind.

I am using the word blind to encompass the widest possible range of visual impairments, including people born without any light or form perception to those who retain some residual vision, to those who had average sight throughout most of their life but have recently begun to lose some degree of acuity. Many will dispute this use of the word, and will want to make distinctions between the early and late blind, the partially sighted and totally sightless. Many will consider the very topic of this conference—blind access to visual art—to be insensitive, even offensive to people who are totally, congenitally blind. It may be useful to a museum docent leading a tour for blind people to know something about what those visitors can or once could see, or to know, for instance, that people who become blind late in life are less likely to read Braille than those who have been blind since childhood. Once we make all the fine distinctions about degrees of impairments and age of onset, however, there is too much of a risk that some subset of the group gets shortchanged. Aids and assistance designed for people who have been totally sightless from birth can also be useful to people who retain some residual vision. As we have learned in the organized blind movement and the disability rights movement generally, there is a danger in creating a hierarchy of the deserving and less deserving blind.

And speaking of objections, others will object that the topic of this conference is trivial when we take into account that the vast majority of blind Americans, including those with residual sight, are undereducated and unemployed. Only about 45 percent of people with severe visual impairments or blindness graduate high school compared to 80 percent of their sighted peers. Unemployment among working-age blind Americans still hovers around 70 percent. I am not arguing that access to the visual arts will improve these disturbing statistics, but I believe that social change needs to happen on many fronts at once. If we as a society can enlarge our understanding of what blind people can do, we can perhaps raise the low expectations among the people who educate and rehabilitate the blind.

In addition to considering degrees of impairment, we need to include the widest possible range of visual interest or knowledge. I will not presume that people who are totally blind will have no interest in the visual arts. In fact, many of the people I know who are most articulate about visual matters have impaired sight. They do not take vision for granted and are accustomed to interpreting incomplete or imperfect visual experience, and the conscious mental effort they employ to draw from visual memories or to make sense of what they see makes it easier for them to communicate it. By the same token, I will not assume that all people with a visual acuity of 20/20 will want to spend their leisure time in art museums.

10   There is then, an element of self-selection in all this. I do not propose that we drag unwilling blind people into art museums with some abstract notion that it will be good for them, any more than I would propose rounding up hoards of unwilling sighted people. Determining why sighted people might avoid art museums is a problem for someone else. When blind people, with or without residual vision or visual memory, show up at an art museum, it is likely that they have some expectations about what they will find there and are willing to employ a good deal of effort to get something out of the experience. Our goal is to find ways to make that experience easier and more rewarding. To use myself as an example, I lost most of my sight at the age of eleven. I now see about 5 to 10 percent of what's considered normal. This does not mean that there is a massive blank spot before my eyes, blotting out 90 percent of the visual field. I can perceive light, color, and motion with some degree of accuracy. But forms are amorphous, mutable, and without distinct details. I sometimes say that I see Impressionistically, suggesting that my vision is something like an Impressionist painting, where fine detail is subordinated to a more general sense of light, movement, and color. But also when I look at an object, I may be under the impression that it is a teacup or a turtle, but to know for sure, I must employ some other means to determine what it is. My visual perception is often entertaining and sometimes aesthetically pleasing, but it is notoriously unreliable, so in my ordinary life I use a number of nonvisual tools and techniques to find objects, to move through space, to read, to write, and to perform other routine tasks. At the same time, however, I know a good deal about vision and the visual arts. Both my parents were visual artists. From my earliest childhood I was familiar with the materials and techniques of oil painting and various forms of sculpture. I spent a lot of time in artists' studios and in galleries and museums and heard the talk of artists, critics, and art historians.

Many will argue however, that what I know about art I know by hearsay—literally what I have heard said, or heard read about it. I have no first-hand experience of art, except of course for those works that I have been allowed to touch. This points to a fundamental problem. At least since the Enlightenment, philosophers have defined human knowledge as coming to us through the senses. And since vision is understood to be overwhelmingly the dominant sense in humans, knowledge therefore must be primarily made up of visual experience. For this reason, seeing is synonymous with knowing as in such idioms as "I see what you mean," while blindness is synonymous with ignorance and obliviousness as in such idioms as: blind rage, blind lust, blind drunk, blind alley, blind chance, blind fool, and so forth. I have observed, however, albeit imperfectly since I cannot see what I'm talking about, that many sighted people claim knowledge of things they have not actually seen. Do you need to go to the desert to know that it's dry?

I will not deny that there are aspects of the visual arts that I simply do not "get." I can understand linear perspective intellectually and know that artist use precise formulae to draw lines at the correct angles to create the illusion of three-dimensional depth on a two-dimensional surface, but I cannot say that I have ever experienced the illusion. Similarly, I know that some artists are so expert at these effects that they can make tromp l'oeil—an illusion so powerful that viewers believe they are seeing rough texture on a smooth surface, or protrusions and recessions where there are none. My question is this: Are these viewers truly duped, or is there a willing suspension of disbelief? Have I so internalized the notion of the preeminence of sight that I cannot believe that the eye could ever truly be tricked?

Hearsay or not, I carry the knowledge I have about art with me when I enter a museum. And while I habitually disregard my flawed visual perceptions in ordinary situations, in a museum I make the most of them. To do this, I must

stand as close to the canvases as the guards can tolerate, often at an odd angle and move my gaze over the surface of the painting to catch fragmentary glimpses of its parts. I usually have a companion with me to read me the labels and correct or enhance whatever I may be able to see. This may involve a good deal of pointing and gesturing, which can farther alarm the guards. Certain media, pen and ink drawing, and black and white photography for instance, are almost impossible for me to see, so I tend to skip those works. Since, as I say, I see impressionistically, I often feel most comfortable viewing art where the distortions I experience as part of my impairment are a part of the image on the canvas. I naturally gravitate toward abstraction where there is no need to identify represented objects, and I instead can take pleasure in color, texture, and energy. Still, I can never predict in advance what I may or may not see in an unfamiliar situation. Lighting, the weather, my own levels of concentration or fatigue can be factors.

Recently, I have begun to avail myself of touch tours, a relatively new innovation at some museums where blind visitors are allowed to touch certain works of sculpture. This can be immensely satisfying, especially when one is allowed to touch the actual works themselves rather than plaster casts. It is so gratifying, in fact, I wish the option was available to all visitors, even those with sight, since there are aspects of the materials and techniques of sculpture that are not necessarily apparent to the naked eye. This is the sort of comment that will send art conservators screaming from the room, because even the most durable materials that can withstand the tactile examination of a few blind connoisseurs would quickly deteriorate under the touch of the throngs of visitors who would like to get their hands on them. I have also made use of tactile diagrams of two-dimensional works. These are also valuable, but seemed based on wishful thinking; the idea that touch in the blind is an absolute equivalent for sight in the seeing. A tactile drawing can help explain concepts such as composition or perspective, but cannot do full justice to other features or other types of images.

15   I have also used audio tours even though, until recently, these have been produced primarily for sighted auditors. The commentary usually includes enough description to give me at least a sketchy notion of the work before me. Audio description for blind visitors is increasingly on offer at art museums around the world. Originally conceived for live theater, film, and television, audio description holds out the greatest hope that blind art lovers can access the widest range of art works, independently and without damage to museum collections. New playback equipment allows producers to add tracks designed for blind users to those produced for the sighted. But will audio description allow me and others like me to simulate the ideal experience of the sighted viewer. What is that ideal?

In the ideal, the art viewer stands before the work of art, to contemplate it alone and in silence. With the advent of linear perspective, the viewer even obtained an optimum viewing position—an exact location before the painting where the illusion of depth painters strove to achieve would have its maximum effect. The viewer might be an artist, there seeking inspiration or to pick up technical tips. Occasionally, the viewer may have a companion to murmur a few words of appreciation or criticism. This companion might even be the artist, giving a private showing to a potential buyer or patron, or hoping to show up a rival. But conversation is kept at a minimum. The viewer has an encyclopedic knowledge of the history of world art and so can instantly recognize influences and innovations that have shaped the creation of the work. Between the viewer and the art work there is a silent and unmediated rapport, a wordless communion of perfect mutual understanding. The viewer's experience is at once emotional and intellectual, ephemeral and tenacious, ineffable and sublime.

Like most idealized representations, this one has at best a minimal corollary in the real world. For one thing, real-life museums today are too crowded and noisy to allow these viewing practices. The proliferation of wall texts and audio tours reflect the expectation that even sighted viewers need guidance and information. Still, there is an expectation that a sighted viewer placed before a work of art can experience the perfect wordless communion of the ideal. And because that communion is perfectly wordless unmediated by another's interpretation, people resist the idea that it can be communicated to anyone who cannot see. A picture may be worth a thousand words, but the assumption seems to be that those thousand words—or even a million words—will not do full justice to the picture. This belief persists despite the fact that *ekphrasis,* or poetry that describes visual art, has been around at least since Homer. Consider Keats on the Grecian urn, or Wallace Stevens on Picasso. It can be argued of course, that these poems are meditations launched by the works of art rather than true descriptions, and that the poets assumed readers would be able to see the works in question, even while the poet, as in the case of Homer, might be blind.

So the question becomes: Is it possible to translate the viewer's experience and make it comprehensible to people who have not had it themselves? Is it possible to describe a work of art with complete objectivity? Let us pretend that there is a painting here that I can see and you cannot. Since this is a fantasy, feel free to imagine that this is any painting, by any artist, from any public or private collection in the world. I insist on imagining a painting rather than a slide, first because I do not want to enter the controversy about digital versus film. More importantly, I believe that looking at a painting is different in every way from looking at a photograph of a painting. For one thing there is the issue of the size, relative to the viewer. Standing before a very large canvas one has the sense of it looming overhead, which can produce a feeling of awe. A smaller canvas can feel more intimate. In addition to the issue of size, there's the matter of paint, the very materiality of paint, its texture and dimensionality that is impossible to capture in even the highest resolution photograph. And I suspect that for me to tell you about this painting I will eventually, inevitably have to talk about the paint: how it appears to have been applied, how its thickness or thinness contributes or detracts from what it is used to depict, how well or poorly its surface has been preserved since the time it was first applied. To better illustrate my point, I would even invite you up here to touch the paint (remember this is a fantasy) because I believe this would give you a better feel for anything I have to say about the artists "hand"—the brush work, or handling of the paint.

So we have our painting here. What would be the best way for me to describe it to you? Should I do it systematically, from left to right and top to bottom as I would read a text? Or should I begin with what's central to the painting, recognizing that this might not be at the precise center of the canvas, and work outward to the less significant periphery? Is the periphery always less significant, or is it necessary to provide context and therefore meaning to the whole? Note that there is already an act of interpretation here, a distinction that makes a hierarchy, sorting out what's most valuable or meaningful in opposition to what's merely secondary.

20   If, for instance, there are any eyes in the painting, perhaps I should start there. We know that artists have many techniques to create images of eyes that look convincingly like real eyes, looking back from the painted surface, perhaps even appearing to meet the viewer's gaze, and follow the viewer's movements around the room. Are the eyes meant to be a focal point, the central point of interest? Is the viewer drawn in through those eyes like a strand of thread drawn through the eye of a needle? Once drawn in, drawn through, where are we?

And what exactly am I looking at here? Is it a window, through which I view the artist, a hand suspended in the act of creation, a brush poised somewhere around the eyes, in an attempt to capture an ephemeral vision of the world? To describe this painting then, should I describe the painter I glimpse through the window of the art work? And what do I really know of this artist? Is he or she, if not a figment of my imagination, then at least a compilation of information I have derived from reading biographies, reviews, and criticism, and other material secondary to the painting before me? The painting then becomes not a window, but a screen onto which I project not only what I may know about this artist, but also what I know about other artists of the same time period and the generations of artists that came before. Is the painting then a mirror in which I see my own perceptions, intuitions, knowledge, and beliefs about this artist and art in general?

Perhaps we need to abandon the ideal of the objective, unmediated description, and embrace instead the very subjectivity of the whole enterprise. Whatever I find to say about this painting will be different, perhaps in every respect, from what another viewer might say. Multiple, even contradictory perspectives can add richness to my description. Are there any poems about this painting? And what about the artist? Should I quote what the artist has said or written about this painting and his or her artistic practices and philosophy? But having assembled all these words will I have brought you any closer to the painting we are contemplating?

Let us return to my dream for a moment and consider a question that many sighted people find intriguing—what are blind dreams like? For me, my dream as I experienced it, as in memory, is not essentially visual. There were, however, some visual elements in the dream.

There was a certain quality of light that I associate with New York, and perhaps particularly New York art galleries of a certain kind. The light suggested a space a floor or two above street level, perhaps on Madison Avenue, on the east side of the street: bluish winter sunlight filtered through gauzy shades over clean plate glass. There was also the pleasing quality of softly polished surfaces: the pale wood floors and the muted gray counter of some sort of faux stone where the two women sat. The two women were the least visible elements in the dream scene, not so much distinct forms, as sleek auras and a whiff of what I knew to be pricey fragrance. On top of the general atmosphere of a posh art gallery there was my excitement. I did not expect to be able to see the photographs, since as I say, black and white photography is inaccessible to me. And in my dreams I never see more than I can see in waking life. Rather, what I wanted to find there was information around those images. I wanted some narrative about the meeting of these two formidable women. What did they say to each other? What did Bourke-White hope to achieve posing Keller out on that ledge? What did Keller make of the idea? Did she go out there willingly, or did she need a lot of cajoling. Was there a brisk wind blowing? Did they use a safety net?

If any of my words evoke a mental image—of Helen Keller, of Margaret Bourke-White's photography, of the Chrysler Building, of New York art galleries—let me ask you this: What is that Image made of? What is its substance? Where does it come from? Does it come to you unbidden? Can you control and manipulate it? Could you communicate it to someone else through words or other media? Could you draw me a picture of my dream?

25 If we can answer these questions, pinpoint the location of the mental image in the case of those of us who have one, I think we are getting closer to our goal. The task of translating a work of visual art into language may be a daunting one, but not so daunting that we should throw up our hands in despair. We need to remember that the people receiving these words also have imagination, knowledge, memory, and curiosity, whether or not they have perfect vision.

I would like to turn briefly to the second aspect of our topic. While we are concerned with the issue of providing access to museum visitors who are blind, we also want to consider the challenges faced by blind artists who wish to gain access to mainstream museums and galleries. Throughout the history of art, the artist's vision has always been assumed to be perfect. In fact, artistic vision is always represented as somehow superior to that of the average sighted person. Of course, we know that many artists have had varying degrees of visual impairments. Artists' eyes, like those of all human beings, are prey to injuries, illness, and aging. Some experts have speculated about possible vision impairments from features of an artist's work, in effect diagnosing vision problems from the art work left behind when the literal eyes are no longer available to examine. In more recent history, there are well documented cases of artists who developed significant impairments in their later lives—Degas and Monet to name two familiar examples. We accept the fact that an established artist may lose vision late in life, and this will affect the way he or she works or thinks about the work. But after a lifetime of work, are those artists dependent on their eyes alone, or do they make use of images in their mind's eyes—images made up of observation, memory, intellect, and desire? And what happens when the artist relies on assistants for visual tasks? Is this different from the assistance artists have always employed for mechanical tasks of their work—painting in backgrounds, making casts of sculptures, or prints of photographs?

Do blind artists who announce their disability limit their audience? Is there a risk that their work will be seen as a version of a freak show display, with only charitable or scientific interest? Do they automatically fall victim to the prejudice that a person with low vision cannot produce high art? Would it be better to let the art speak for itself without the messy details of the artist's biography? Or should these artists invite the scrutiny and allow the work to engage in dialogue with work by sighted artists? And what about those artists? In what ways does the work of a blind artist or a blind viewer alter other artists' goals and practices? Should we rule out the possibility of artists born blind, or assume that they would choose sculpture rather than painting or photography or some other medium or combination of media yet to be named? And how does any of this art affect the ways it should be displayed and viewed?

I will leave these questions to the panel of artists who follow and conclude by adding fantasy to my dream about the Helen Keller photographs. Can I imagine a happy ending to my dream, an ideal museum that would be accessible to me and others like me? In this dream the women at the reception desk would greet me without surprise. It would seem only natural to them that I should want to visit this exhibit; they would tell me that they could offer me large print, Braille, or audio descriptions of the photos. There would be an easy to operate portable audio device with a menu of tracks to choose from. In addition to descriptions of each of the photos, there might be a reading of Keller's own account of the photo shoot, a recorded interview with Bourke-White recalling the event, and some commentary by photography critics. There might also be some sort of tactile diagram of at least some of the photos highlighting compositional features, or other aspects unique to Bourke-White's work. There might even be a scale model of the Chrysler building. These would be as interesting to sighted visitors as to the blind. The gallery would be crowded, because in my dream, such an exhibit would attract a large audience. But there would be space enough for me and others to approach the photographs without raising an alarm. There might be music in the gallery, to evoke the time period or the personalities of the two women, though I cannot think what this should be. Better perhaps would be a sound piece involving a recording from the top of the Chrysler building, with the sound of the whistling wind at ear level, and the hum of traffic way down on the street below.

Among the other visitors there may well be a young artist. She may well be blind. But she has studied art history and visited museums with services designed to enhance that study. She may have encountered art by blind people and derived inspiration from it. She may also, as young artists are prone to do, reject its premises and practices in favor of innovations, new media, and techniques of her own devising. I sense her presence near me, leaning in to peer at a print, holding her breath to keep from fogging up the glass. She leans back. Perhaps she smiles, perhaps she frowns. Perhaps her free hand opens and closes in an unmistakable gesture of making something. In her mind, an idea takes shape. The idea may have visual elements, or sound, or words, or palpable forms. After another minute, she turns and leaves the gallery, returning the audio device she's been using to the front desk. She does not speak, wary of disturbing the idea in her head with words. Then she takes the idea home with her where she will begin to work.

Re-reading/Conversations with the Text

1. Consider the various rhetorical strategies Kleege employs in her "eye-catching" introduction. For example, why do you think she opens her essay with mentions of Helen Keller and Margaret Bourke-White? What do they have to do with Kleege's essay and her argument? (You might try looking up more about either or both of these important figures in order to gain a better contextual understanding of Kleege's use of them in her introduction.) Why do you think Kleege opens with "a dream"? What does the content of the dream (as a kind of genre) tell us that might have been told or conveyed differently if it weren't in a dream?

2. Several American and European cities now have restaurants that are known as "blind cafés." In West Hollywood, for example, "Opaque" recently opened (see: *http://opaque-events.com/*); Paris, Zurich, Berlin, and London have such cafés as well. In a May 22, 2005 article in the British *Sunday Times,* Edouard de Broglie, the founder of the first such café in Paris, claimed that: "The preconception of what food tastes like because of how it looks is gone. . . . All your other senses are abruptly awoken and you taste the food like you have never tasted it before. It makes you rethink everything. You become blind and the blind waiters become your guide." Using this quotation as your starting point, devise an outline for an essay, "Blind at the Café." Following the model of Kleege's essay, sketch out some of the examples, elements, and persuasive moves of such an essay. What "dream scene" could the essay use? Could Helen Keller still be used effectively? How so? Who might be substituted for Margaret Bourke-White? How might you otherwise conduct a visual-centered analysis of a dining experience?

3. Kleege points to the use of stereotypes surrounding "blind" that riddle our language (and thus, our ways of thinking about blindness and blind people as well). She writes:

   > For this reason, seeing is synonymous with knowing as in such idioms as "I see what you mean," while blindness is synonymous with ignorance and obliviousness as in such idioms as *blind rage, blind lust, blind drunk, blind alley, blind chance, blind fool,* and so forth. I have observed, however, albeit imperfectly since I cannot see what I'm talking about, that many sighted people claim knowledge of things they have not actually seen. Do you need to go to the desert to know that it is dry?

   Continuing in Kleege's vein of thought, compile a list of stereotypes and phrases in our language that present disability in certain ways (consider deafness, mental disabilities and disorders, developmental disabilities, physical disabilities, etc.) Once you have such a list, go on to discuss the last part of the quotation from Kleege: What do such stereotypes and phrases suggest that a person with x, y, z kind of disability is, does, can be, thinks?

Re-seeing and Re-writing

1. Kleege gave this piece first as a public lecture at "Blind at the Museum," an exhibit she helped organize at the Berkeley Art Museum in 2004. The Web site for that exhibit opens with the following paragraph:

   > An art museum would seem to be no place for the blind. Yet art objects can address all of the senses—sight, touch, hearing, scent, taste—and thus offer an opportunity to reconsider the process of "viewing" or responding to art. Visual artists often think about the very nature of vision: What does it mean to "see"? How does an artwork address the viewer? What are the behaviors of looking? And what are the limits, or the liabilities, of the gaze? (http://www.bampfa.berkeley.edu/exhibits/blind/)

   This paragraph contains six major statements (four in the form of questions). Form six small groups, with each group taking one of the six statements/questions; within each group, generate either some examples for the statement or answers for the question. Share your examples/answers with the rest of the class.

2. Write a preliminary script or script notes for the production, filming, and marketing of a documentary on being "blind at the museum." As you sketch your plans, you might consider the following:

   - What (kind of) museum(s), and what kind of artifacts, might be featured in the documentary?
   - What would be the "plot line" of the documentary? Its argument or purpose?
   - Would it contain only blind people?
   - Would blind people only be visitors to these museum spaces, or would they also be curators, directors, security guards, etc.?
   - How would you market it (and to whom)?
   - How would you build "access" into the filming, marketing, and screening of the documentary?
   - How would this documentary be like other documentaries? How would it be different?

Intertext

In his essay, Coles describes the documentary-making process as a "matter of looking *and* overlooking, paying instant heed *and* letting something slip by . . . sorting out what I *have* noticed, of arranging it for emphasis." He continues, "I must select *what* ought to be present; decide on the *tone* of that presentation, its *atmosphere* or *mood*." Write a brief critical paper in which you compare and contrast Kleege's discussion of "audio description" and her sample "visual analysis" of an imagined piece of art with Coles's description of documentary interpretation.

The Politics of Staring: Visual Rhetorics of Disability in Popular Photography

ROSEMARIE GARLAND-THOMSON

A professor of Women's Studies at Emory University, *GARLAND-THOMSON* is one of the leading scholars in disability studies. Combining her interest in "freakery" and "the extraordinary body" with her interest in nineteenth- and twentieth-century African American and women's literature, Garland-Thomson has produced several books, including *Extraordinary Bodies: Figuring Disability in American Culture and Literature; Freakery: Cultural Spectacles of the Extraordinary Body;* and *Disability Studies: Enabling the Humanities.* As both an academic and disability rights activist, Garland-Thomson took a leading role in the campaign to have a wheelchair included in the representation of Franklin Delano Roosevelt at the FDR Memorial in Washington, DC. In the essay below, she outlines a visual-rhetorical approach to the photographic representations of people with disabilities.

The history of disabled people in the Western world is in part the history of being on display, of being visually conspicuous while politically and socially erased. The earliest record of disabled people is of their exhibition as prodigies, monsters, omens from the gods, and indexes of the natural or divine world. From the New Testament to the miracles at Lourdes, the lame, the halt, and the blind provide the spectacle for the story of bodily rehabilitation as spiritual redemption that is so essential to Christianity. From antiquity through modernity, the bodies of disabled people considered to be freaks and monsters have been displayed by the likes of medieval kings and P. T. Barnum for entertainment and profit in courts, street fairs, dime museums, and sideshows.[1] Moreover, medicine has from its beginnings exhibited the disabled body as what Michel Foucault calls the "case," in medical theaters and other clinical settings, in order to pathologize the exceptional and to normalize the ordinary (*Birth of the Clinic* 29). Disabled people have variously been objects of awe, scorn, terror, delight, inspiration, pity, laughter, or fascination—but they have always been stared at.

Staring at disability choreographs a visual relation between a spectator and a spectacle. A more intense form of looking than glancing, glimpsing, scanning, surveying, gazing, and other forms of casual or uninterested looking, staring registers the perception of difference and gives meaning to impairment by marking it as aberrant. By intensely telescoping looking toward the physical signifier for disability, staring creates an awkward partnership that estranges and discomforts both viewer and viewed. Starers gawk with abandon at the prosthetic hook, the empty sleeve, the scarred flesh, the unfocused eye, the twitching limb, but seldom does looking broaden to envelop the whole body of the person with a disability. Even supposedly invisible disabilities always threaten to disclose some stigma, however subtle, that disrupts the social order by its presence and attenuates the bond between equal members of the human community. Because staring at disability is considered illicit looking, the disabled body is at once the to-be-looked-at and not-to-be-looked-at, further dramatizing the staring encounter by making viewers furtive and the viewed defensive. Staring thus creates disability as a state of absolute difference rather than simply one more variation in human form. At the same time, staring constitutes disability identity by manifesting the power relations between the subject positions of disabled and able-bodied.

The rapid flourishing of photography after 1839 provided a new way to stare at disability. In our ocularcentric era, images mediate our desires and the ways we imagine ourselves.[2] Among the myriad, often conflicting, and never indifferent images modernity offers us, the picture of ourselves as disabled is an image fraught with a tangle of anxiety, distance, and identification. As a culture, we are at once obsessed with and intensely conflicted about the disabled body. We fear, deify, disavow, avoid, abstract, revere, conceal, and reconstruct disability—perhaps because it is one of the most universal, fundamental of human experiences. After all, we will all become disabled if we live long enough. Nonetheless, in representing disability in modernity, we have made the familiar seem strange, the human seem inhuman, the pervasive seem exceptional. By the beginning of the twentieth century, for example, public displays of disabled people became inappropriate in the same way that public executions and torture came to be considered offensive. Disabled people were sequestered from public view in institutions and the private sphere as middle-class decorum pronounced it impolite to stare. Photography, however, has enabled the social ritual of staring at disability to persist in an alternate form.

———————————

Photographs seem to be transparent windows onto reality that ensnare truth. But like all representations, photographs organize our perceptions, shaping the objects as they depict them by using conventions of presentation that invoke cultural ideas and expectations. Photographs evoke the familiar only to make it seem strange, eliciting a response Alan Trachtenberg describes as "astonishment mingling with recog-

nition" (*Reading* 4). Because disability has such potent cultural resonances, our capitalist democracy has enlisted its imagery to manipulate viewers for a wide range of purposes. Popular photography catapults disability into the public sphere as a highly mediated image shorn from interactions with actual people with disabilities. Photography's immediacy, claim to truth, and wide circulation calcifies the interpretations of disability embedded in the images, at once shaping and registering the public perception of disability.

Photography authorizes staring. Photos are made to be looked at. With the actual disabled body absent, photography stylizes staring, exaggerating and fixing the conventions of display and eliminating the possibility for interaction or spontaneity between viewer and viewed. Photos absolve viewers of responsibility to the objects of their stares at the same time that they permit a more intense form of staring than an actual social interchange might support. Disability photography thus offers the spectator the pleasure of unaccountable, uninhibited, insistent looking. This license to stare becomes a powerful rhetorical device that can be mobilized to manipulate viewers. By exploring some of the purposes to which popular photography's "dialectic of strange and familiar" has been put, I aim here to suggest how modern America imagines disability and disabled people (Trachtenberg, *Reading* 4).[3]

To look at the way we look at disability, I elaborate a taxonomy of four primary visual rhetorics of disability. They are the wondrous, the sentimental, the exotic, and the realistic. This template of visual rhetorics complicates the often restrictive notion of images as being either positive or negative, as communicating either the truth of disability or perpetuating some oppressive stereotype. Thus, I analyze more than evaluate. These visualizations of disabled people act as powerful rhetorical figures that elicit responses or persuade viewers to think or act in certain ways. The wondrous, the sentimental, the exotic, and the realistic converge and inflect one another in individual pictures as well as across all genres of disability photography. These visual rhetorics seldom occur discretely; rather, the photographs blend together in individual photographs. They wax and wane, shift and combine over time as they respond to the purposes for which the photographs are produced. Moreover, these rhetorics constitute part of the context into which all representations of disabled people enter. Not only do these representational modes configure public perception of disability, but all images of disabled people either inadvertently or deliberately summon these visual rhetorics and their accompanying cultural narratives. None of these rhetorical modes operates in the service of actual disabled people, however. Indeed, almost all of them appropriate the disabled body for the purposes of constructing, instructing, or assuring some aspect of a putatively nondisabled viewer.

The first visual rhetoric is the wondrous. The oldest mode of representing disability, the wondrous continues to find a place in modernity's framing of disability. This genre capitalizes on physical differences in order to elicit amazement and admiration. The antecedents of the wondrous disabled figures are the monsters of antiquity, who inspired awe, foretold the future, or bore divine signs, and freaks, who were the celebrities in nineteenth-century dime museums and sideshows (Garland-Thomson, "From Wonder"). The rhetoric of the wondrous springs from a premodern interpretation of disability as either augury or marks of distinction, whether representing good or evil. Oedipus, Teiresias, monsters, giants—even Shakespeare's Richard III—were imposing if ominous disabled figures.

A nineteenth-century example is Charles Tripp, the famous Armless Wonder (fig. 1), pictured eating with his toes in a carte de visite,

one of the exceedingly popular photographic portraits commonly sold to augment and promote live appearances. This carefully choreographed portrait includes samples of his calligraphic skills, paper figures he's cut out, as well as the pen and scissors he used to accomplish such remarkable tasks. The silver tea set in the picture refers to other photos of him drinking from a cup with his toes. The composition is a visual résumé documenting Tripp's supposedly amazing accomplishments. The spectacle tries to elicit awe from the viewers, whose sense of their own clumsy toes makes Tripp's feet feat seem wondrous.

Photography introduced into the rhetoric of wonder the illusion of fusing the ordinary with the extraordinary. This picture invites a relation of identification and differentiation between Tripp and his viewer, making him seem simultaneously strange and familiar. Viewers see a typical man engaged in the quotidian acts of writing, eating, or drinking tea, but—to those with arms—he does this in a most extraordinary manner. Only the single detail of eating with feet rather than hands marks this scene as distinctive. Disability operates visually by juxtaposing the singular (therefore strange) mark of impairment in a surrounding context of the expected (therefore familiar). By telescoping the viewer's eye to the mark of impairment, the picture instructs viewers to stare and coaches them to understand impairment as the exception rather than the rule. Orchestrated and provoked by the photo, staring creates a particular relation between the viewer and the viewed that gives meaning to impairment.

Modernity secularized wonder into the stereotype of the supercrip, who amazes and inspires the viewer by performing feats that the nondisabled viewer cannot imagine doing. Contemporary wonder rhetoric emphasizes admiration rather than amazement, in part because bourgeois respectability now deems it inappropriate to delight in staring at disabled people. One example is a recent ad for adventure tours

10

Figure 1   Surrounded here by the products of his agile feet, the famous nineteenth-century freak show entertainer, Charles Tripp, one of the many "armless wonders," is presented as amazing and yet ordinary.

Courtesy of the Robert Bogdan Collection, Syracuse, NY.

that features a rock climber using a wheelchair (fig. 2). Here the photographic composition literally positions the viewer as looking up in awe at the climber dangling in her wheelchair. By making the disabled figure exceptional rather than ordinary, the wondrous can estrange viewer from viewed and attenuate the correspondence that equality requires.

Sentimentality has inflected the wonder model, producing the convention of the courageous overcomer, contemporary America's favorite figure of disability. Even though armless

Figure 2   This photograph for adventure vacations invokes wonder by inviting the viewer to look up in admiration and awe at the person who can scale rocks while using a wheelchair.

Courtesy of Wilderness Inquiry, www.wildernessinquiry.com.

calligraphers are no longer an acceptable form of middle-class entertainment, photos of disabled people who have adapted tasks to fit their bodies still ask their viewers to feel a sense of wonder. An advertisement for Habitat for Humanity, for example, pictures a disabled volunteer worker building a house (fig. 3). Like Tripp, this man is portrayed as entirely ordinary except for the detail of the fingerless hands holding the hammer, which occupies the center of interest, at once inviting and authorizing the stare. As is typical in disability photography, the text instructs the viewer how to respond to the picture, with a headline that says, "Extraordinary Volunteer, Unstoppable Spirit." The picture thus combines the narrative of admiration for overcoming disability with the narrative of empowerment characteristic of a post-disability rights movement consciousness. By making disabled subjects masters of ordinary activities such as climbing rocks, drinking tea, or using hammers, these photos create a visual context that elicits adulation for their accomplishing what the normalized viewer takes to be a superhuman feat.

The second visual rhetoric is the sentimental. Whereas the wondrous elevates and enlarges, the sentimental diminishes. The sentimental produces the sympathetic victim or helpless sufferer needing protection or succor and invoking pity, inspiration, and frequent contributions. The sentimental disabled figure developed as a part of the larger nineteenth-century bourgeois culture of fine feelings.[4] The pathetic, the impotent, and the suffering confirmed the Victorian bourgeoisie by arousing

Figure 3   This photograph of a volunteer worker for Habitat for Humanity, an organization that builds homes for the needy, utilizes the narrative of overcoming to elicit admiration for working despite having a disability.

Courtesy of *Habitat World.*

their finest sentiments. As the increasingly empowered middle class imagined itself capable of capitalizing the world, it began to see itself as responsible for the world as well, a stewardship that launched humanitarian and reform movements to which today's telethons are heir. This discourse of middle-class noblesse oblige operates on a model of paternalism, often trafficking in children and alluding to the cute, the plucky, the long-suffering, and the courageous.

The rhetoric of sentiment found an effective home in the photographic conventions of the poster child of mid-twentieth-century charity campaigns. The 1946 March of Dimes poster child (fig. 4) echoes the spunky cuteness of freak figures such as General Tom Thumb. But where Tom Thumb delighted with his miniature adulthood, this poster child breaks hearts as he is propped vulnerably up in a corner of his crib in the before-and-after format. In order to catalyze the adult, to whom the photo addresses itself, this March of Dimes poster presents disability to the middle-class spectator as a problem to solve, an obstacle to eliminate, a challenge to meet. In such appeals, impairment becomes the stigma of suffering, transforming disability into a project that morally enables a nondisabled rescuer. The viewer's dimes, the poster suggests, will literally catapult the unhappy little fellow trapped in braces in his crib into a smiling and spirited tyke, striding with determination and gratitude toward the viewer. Sentimentality makes of disabled people occasions for the viewers' own narratives of progress, improvement, or heroic deliverance and contains disability's

Figure 4 The March of Dimes 1946 poster boy appeals to the rhetoric of sentiment, which often employs pathetic, courageous, or cute children to elicit the viewers' sympathy and money.

Donald Anderson, 1946 March of Dimes poster. Reprinted by permission of the March of Dimes Birth Defects Foundation.

Figure 5   Sentimental cuteness and high fashion come together in this public relations brochure's presentation of a developmentally disabled child in a school supported and outfitted by Benetton clothing stores. Concept: O. Toscani.

© Benetton Group S.p.A. 1998—Photo: Oliviero Toscani.

threat in the sympathetic, helpless child for whom the viewer is empowered to act. Whereas earlier sentimental literature accentuates suffering to mobilize readers for humanitarian, reform, or religious ends, the poster boy's suffering is only the background to his restoration to normalcy that results from "your dimes." The optimism of cure thus replaces the intensity of sympathy, testifying to an increasing faith in clinical treatment and scientific progress as modernity increasingly medicalizes and rationalizes the body.

The rhetoric of sentiment has migrated from charity to retail in late capitalism's scramble to capture markets. For example, the cover of a 1998 Benetton public relations brochure (fig. 5) distributed in stores employs a chic sentimentality in documenting a school for developmentally disabled children Benetton supports and outfits. This cover girl with both Down syndrome[5] and a stylish Benetton hat fuses sentimental cuteness with high fashion to produce the conviction in the viewer-shopper that Benetton is humanitarian rather than solely commercial. In anticipation of its patron's skepticism, the brochure instructs its viewers that Benetton launched this campaign as social commentary, although people are apt to see it as "cynical advertising." Benetton devotes a whole introductory page to assuring its customers that this brochure is about "the gift of love" (United Colors 3). So while commercial fashion marketing demands a certain sophistication and sleekness that precludes the gushy sentiment of the 1940s poster child, Benetton still assures its viewers of their tolerance and allows them to fantasize rescuing this child from the stigma of being disabled by dressing her smartly and supporting her school.

———————

15   The third visual rhetoric is the exotic. The rhetoric of sentiment domesticates the disability figure, making it familiar and comforting. In contrast, the visual rhetoric of the exotic presents disabled figures as alien, distant, often sensationalized, eroticized, or entertaining in their difference. The exotic reproduces an ethnographic model of viewing characterized by curiosity or uninvolved objectification and informed by the proliferation of popular ethnographic photography that accompanied the era of Western imperialism. For example, nineteenth-century freak photography often transformed disabled people into "wild men" or other exotic "savages," whose impairments were translated into marks of alien ethnicity (Garland-Thomson, "From Wonder" 5). The exotic demedicalizes, fascinates, and seduces with exaggeration, creating a sensationalized, embellished alien.

The introduction of disabled models has exploded the contemporary fashion world in the last several years, returning the rhetoric of the exotic into disability photography. Where the sentimental makes the disabled figure small and vulnerable in order to be rescued by a benevolent agent, the exotic makes the disabled figure large, strange, and unlike the viewer. Ever straining for novelty and capitalizing on titillation, the fashion arm of the advertising world was sure to discover the power of disabled figures to provoke responses from viewers. Advertising has learned that disability sells in two ways. One is by making consumers feel good about buying from a company that is charitable toward the supposedly disadvantaged,

which is the Benetton brochure's pitch. The other is to capture the disability market, which is 54 million people and growing fast as the baby boomers age and as their spending power is estimated to reach the trillion-dollar mark in 2000 (J. Williams 29).

The exotic serves this commercial aim by upsetting the earnest, asexual, vulnerable, courageous image of disability that charity rhetoric has so firmly implanted. One image advertising wheelchairs presents a tattooed biker figure brandishing a hockey stick (fig. 6). The image alludes at once to the strong men and tattoo kings of the sideshows and then inflects it with a hyperphallic sexuality, completely rewriting the cultural script of the emasculated invalid and the male who becomes feminized by disability. As is typical with much popular disability photography, the text instructs the viewer on how to read this photo. The exaggeration characteristic of exoticization here marshals ironic hyperbole to mount a brazen, sensational parody, provocatively challenging the viewer by lewdly commanding. "Lick this!" Such representations preclude even a trace of the sentimental or the wondrous, insisting instead on the empowerment of the transgressive, even at the expense of distancing the spectator from the spectacle.

Another venue for disability as the exotic is emerging in the high-fashion market, which is always desperate to keep its edge. These advertisements and magazine features present disabled models in a dual attempt to capture a market and to novelize high fashion by introducing bodies that at once depart from and conform to the exhausted image of the high-fashion body. Alexander McQueen, known in England as the bad boy of fashion design, recently collaborated with other designers and the fashion photographer Nick Knight for a shoot called "Accessible," featuring eight disabled models. Knight's shots fold the models' impairments into a context of exoticism that extends to the entire frame, as in the shot of

Figure 6   The rhetoric of the exotic in this ad for wheelchairs "with an attitude" employs the tattooed biker-jock figure to create a transgressive, hypermasculine image for the wheelchair user.

Courtesy of Colours Wheelchairs, www.colourswheelchair.com.

Aimee Mullins, the double-amputee celebrity cover girl, rendered as a kind of high-tech bionic mannequin (fig. 7). No attempt is made to disguise her cosmetic prosthetic legs—so she can pass for nondisabled; rather, the entire photo thematically echoes her prostheses and renders the whole image chic. As a gorgeous amputee, Mullins becomes an embodied contradiction. Her prosthetic legs parody, indeed proudly mock, the very idea of the perfect body that has been the mark of fashion until now, even while the rest of her body conforms precisely to fashion's impossible standards. Rather than conceal, normalize, or erase disability, these photos use the hyperbole and stigma traditionally associated with disability to quench postmodernity's perpetual search for the new and arresting image. These transgressive juxtapositions of disability and high fashion, such as the macho chair user and the athletic but leg-

Figure 7   The high-fashion layout of the model, sports star, and double amputee Aimee Mullins emphasizes rather than conceals her prosthetic legs, exploiting the exotic mode to make disability seem chic.

Image by Nick Knight. "Fashion-able." Aimee Mullins, "Dazed & Confused, September 1998."

less Mullins, produce a fresh, attention-grabbing brand of exotic radical chic that redefines disabled identity for the disabled consumer.

————————

The fourth visual rhetoric is the realistic. Where the exotic mode cultivates estrangement, realism minimizes distance and difference by establishing a relation of contiguity between viewer and viewed. The wondrous, sentimental, and exotic modes of representation tend to exaggerate the difference of disability to confer exceptionality on the object in the picture. The rhetoric of the realistic, however, trades in verisimilitude, regularizing the disabled figure in order to avoid differentiation and arouse identification, often normalizing and sometimes minimizing the visual mark of disability. Realism domesticates disability. Realist disability photography is the rhetoric of equality, most often turned utilitarian. The use of realism can be commercial or journalistic, and it can also urge the viewer to political or social action.[6]

Realism emerged as a property of portraiture, documentary, and medical photography of the nineteenth century. Documentary

20

photography such as that made famous by Lewis Hine and Jacob Riis aimed photographic realism at the progressive obsession with social reform.[7] Documentary and journalistic photographies differ from charity and commercial photographies in that they do not solicit the exchange of money so directly but rather aim to democratically disseminate information intended to shape the viewers' actions and opinions. Hine and Riis recorded the fabric of the American underclass, exposing the supposed truth of the conditions in which it struggled. Hine photographed wounded workers whose disabilities robbed them of the male privilege and duty of work (fig. 8), and he featured children whose disabilities he felt stole their childhood. The caption below an amputee worker reads, "When a man's hand is mutilated, he keeps it out of sight" (Stange 60). The implied message is that the social mandate to hide disability precludes entry into the workplace. Hine enlists disability in documentary photos ultimately to tell a cautionary tale: disability is a scourge that can and should be avoided in a world that works right. In spite of the political support and social acceptance the

AN ARM GONE AT TWENTY
This young brakeman when last seen was studying telegraphy in order to stay in the service

Photo by Hine

THE WOUNDS OF WORK
When a man's hand is mutilated he keeps it out of sight

Figure 8 Lewis Hine documented wounded workers in 1907–08 by using the rhetoric of realism as a form of social protest against excluding disabled men from the privileges of labor.

picture confers, the photograph nevertheless marks this worker as a person the viewer does not want to be.

A more sensationalized use of realism recently provoked controversy and roused political protests over what constitutes unacceptable looking at women's breasts. The Breast Cancer Fund, a San Francisco–based nonprofit organization dedicated to education about and funding of breast cancer research, mounted a public awareness campaign in January 2000 called Obsessed with Breasts, featuring three posters showing women boldly displaying mastectomy scars. The posters parodied a Victoria's Secret catalog (fig. 9), a *Cosmopolitan* cover, and a Calvin Klein perfume ad, all of which typically parade women's breasts in soft-porn modes that have become an unremarkable staple of commercial magazine advertising. The posters disrupt the visual convention of the female breast

Figure 9   This controversial 2000 Breast Cancer Fund poster employs the sensationalism often characteristic of realism to protest inadequate breast cancer research and to expose the cultural effacement of mastectomies.

Courtesy of the Breast Cancer Fund, www.breastcancerfund.org.

as sexualized object for male appropriation and pleasure by replacing the now normative, eroticized breast with the proscribed image of the amputated breast. The powerful visual violation produced by exchanging the spectacle of the eroticized breast, which has been desensationalized by its endless circulation, with the medicalized image of the scarred breast, which has been concealed from public view, was so shocking to viewers that many demanded that the images be removed. Of course, the censuring and censoring of images that demand a recognition of the reality of breast cancer ignited a vibrant controversy. The images intensify this forbidden version of the disabled breast by ironically juxtaposing it with the commonplace but virulently sexist eroticization of the breast. The posters thus advance a potent feminist challenge not only to sexism in medical research and the treatment for breast cancer but also to the oppressive representational practices that make erotic spectacles of women's breasts an everyday thing while erasing the fact of the amputation that one woman in eight will have. By mocking the tired sensationalism of pornography, these pictures protest against the refusal of contemporary America to literally and figuratively look at breast cancer.

The visual rhetoric of the ordinary has emerged in a climate of integration and diversity created by the disability rights movement and resulting legislation such as the Americans with Disabilities Act of 1990 (ADA). While the post-ADA era is not without resistance and backlash to the integration of people with disabilities, the social environment is filling with disability in the popular press. Disability not only appears in the sensationalist underbelly of the press, where it always has, but also is tucked with various degrees of conspicuousness into the fabric of common visual culture. Department store and catalog advertising, for instance, has adopted the rhetoric of the ordinary both to appeal to disabled people as a market and to suggest an ethic of inclusion. L. L. Bean pro-

motes a wheelchair backpack in its catalog; Walmart and many other stores feature disabled models and mannequins in everything from frumpy jog suits to evening gowns. Toy lines like Barbie and the upscale American Girl have wheelchair-using dolls. Such routinization of disability imagery not only brings disability as a human experience out of the closet, it also enables people with disabilities—especially those who acquire impairments as adults—to imagine themselves as a part of the ordinary world rather than belonging to a special class of untouchables and unviewables. Images of disability as a familiar, even mundane, experience in the lives of seemingly successful, happy, well-adjusted people can reduce the identifying against oneself that is the overwhelming effect of oppressive and discriminatory attitudes toward people with disabilities.

The most radical reimagining of disability offered by the realist mode is, ironically, the least visually vivid of the images discussed here, perhaps because it is the only mode with no commercial purpose. The genre of disability photography I conclude with is the official portrait, exemplified by the Department of Education's simple photographic portrait of Judith E. Heumann, assistant secretary of education during the Clinton administration (fig. 10). The conventions that govern such pictures strive for the effect of the everyday, inflected with enough dignity and authority to communicate the importance of the position but not enough to separate the official from the constituency. In a democracy, official portraits depict public servants, after all, in no-nonsense black and white, with standard costuming and poses, and flanked unpretentiously by flags. Unlike commercial photographs, these portrayals are neither generalized nor stylized; rather, they are particularized. The photo suggests that here is a real, recognizable person responsible for certain official duties. The radical aspect of this common visual rhetoric is that part of this woman's particularization is the wheelchair that

Figure 10 The contrast between this official portrait of Assistant Secretary Judith E. Heumann sitting in her wheelchair and the many photos of FDR that hid the wheelchair he used daily during his presidency marks the difference between a pre- and post–civil rights era.

Courtesy of United States Department of Education.

is clearly an aspect of her identity, an integral element of who and what the photograph says she is. The glimpse of her chair is descriptive, as fundamental to her image as the shape of her chin, the cut of her hair, or the tint of her skin. In its ordinariness, the photograph discourages staring without prohibiting it. Indeed, it encourages forms of looking such as glancing, if the viewer is not very interested in the secretary, or perhaps beholding, if the viewer is interested in her. By depicting Secretary Heumann as an ordinary person who has a position of official status in the society, the portrait encourages both viewers who consider themselves disabled and those who consider themselves nondisabled to identify with her. The photograph suggests neither that her accomplishments are superhuman nor that she has triumphantly overcome anything. She thus becomes more familiar than strange. Most important is the picture's message that a woman with a disability can occupy such a position.

Secretary Heumann's picture sits in bold historical opposition to the many now-controversial official photos of President Franklin D. Roosevelt that hide the wheelchair he used daily.[8] Authorized by the cultural changes the civil rights movements wrought, Heumann's official portrait exemplifies one of several genres in contemporary photography that familiarize disability rather than defamiliarize it. Indeed, such representations banish the strange and cultivate the ordinary, radically reimagining disability by installing people with disabilities in the realm of human commonality and dismantling the assumption that disability precludes accomplishment.

———

This taxonomy of four primary visual rhetorics of disability provides a way to see the way we see disability. These pictures choreograph a social dynamic of looking, suggesting that disability is not simply a natural state of bodily inferiority and inadequacy. Rather, it is a culturally fabricated narrative of the body, similar to what we understand as the fictions of race and gender. Disability, then, is a system that produces subjects by differentiating and marking bodies. Furthermore, this comparison of bodies legitimates the distribution of resources, status, and power in a biased social and architectural environment. As such, disability has four aspects: first, it is a system for interpreting bodily variations; second, it is a relation between bodies and their environments; third, it is a set of

25

practices that produce both the able-bodied and the disabled; fourth, it is a way of describing the inherent instability of the embodied self. The category of disability exists as a way to exclude the kinds of bodily forms, functions, impairments, changes, or ambiguities that call into question our cultural fantasy of the body as a neutral, compliant instrument of some transcendent will. Moreover, *disability* is a broad term in which cluster ideological categories as varied as sick, deformed, ugly, old, crazy, maimed, afflicted, abnormal, or debilitated—all of which disadvantage people by devaluing bodies that do not conform to cultural standards. Thus *disability* functions to preserve and validate such privileged designations as beautiful, healthy, normal, fit, competent, intelli-

gent—all of which provide cultural capital to those who can claim such status, who can reside within these subject positions. Thus, the various interactions between bodies and world make disability from the raw material of human variation and precariousness.

All visualizations of disability are mediations that shape the world in which people who have or do not have disabilities inhabit and negotiate together. The point is that all representations have social and political consequences. Understanding how images create or dispel disability as a system of exclusions and prejudices is a move toward the process of dismantling the institutional, attitudinal, legislative, economic, and architectural barriers that keep people with disabilities from full participation in society.

Notes

1. For a historical account of the display of disabled people as monsters and freaks, see Altick; Bogdan; Dennett; Garland-Thomson, "From Wonder"; and D. Wilson.
2. For an account of the ocularcentric in Western culture, see Barthes; Crary; Debord; and Jay.
3. I am not including medical or artistic photography here, although both genres inform the visual construction of disability. I am limiting this analysis to popular photography, which I take to be the primary register and shaper of public consciousness. For an analysis of images of insanity, see Gilman.
4. For a discussion of the development of middle-class feeling as a form of distinguishing respectability, see Halttunen; for a discussion of how sentimentality uses disabled figures, see Garland-Thomson, "Crippled Little Girls."
5. The term "Down syndrome" is now preferred over "Down's syndrome" by more politicized parents and guardians looking to mark some distance from the English physician John Langdon Down, who first described the syndrome's characteristic features (i.e., they are challenging his "ownership" of Down syndrome). See, for example, Richards.
6. To use the term *realistic* does not suggest that this visual rhetoric is more truthful, accurate, or real than the other modes discussed here. Realism's function is to create the illusion of reality, not to reproduce or capture reality's elusive and complex substance. Although more subtle perhaps, the rhetoric of realism is just as constructed and convention-bound as the rhetorics of the wondrous, sentimental, or exotic.
7. For further discussion of Hine, see Rosenblum, Rosenblum, and Trachtenberg.
8. For a discussion of Franklin Roosevelt's disability, see H. Gallagher.

Re-reading/Conversations with the Text

1. Garland-Thomson develops her claims about how disabled people have been stared at (and represented) in photography by foregrounding the dual attention to both the familiar and the strange that such photography (and documentary) often asks of us:

   > Photographs seem to be transparent windows onto reality that ensnare truth. But like all representations, photographs organize our perceptions, shaping the objects as they depict them by using conventions of presentation that invoke cultural ideas and expectations. Photographs evoke the familiar only to make it seem strange. . . .

   Scan each of the ten images in Garland-Thomson's essay and then, working with a classmate, construct notes and commentary for each of the images based on the way the image draws our attention to both the familiar and the strange. Share your commentary on any one image with your classmates.

   Finally, as a class, discuss how much the familiarity and the strangeness of the images are a factor of *kairos*. How much, in other words, does the context of an era matter in our perspective on an image of a person with a disability?

2. Garland-Thomson tells us at the beginning of her essay that "staring at disability choreographs a visual relation between a spectator and a spectacle." Further, she claims that "photography authorizes staring . . . eliminating the possibility for interaction or spontaneity between viewer and viewed." In a short essay, consider the following: How are disability and/or bodily/mental/physical/sensory difference documented through the act of staring in our culture? What are our "rules" for staring? Who can/can't be stared at—by whom, in what settings and circumstances? In the frozen relationship of spectator-spectacle, how does *stigma* appear? How might staring constitute a genre of "documentation" in and of itself?

3. Discuss each of the four visual rhetorics Garland-Thomson details in this essay by also considering how each visual rhetoric she names constitutes a genre of looking/staring. Can you expand these genres of looking/staring beyond disability? Why or why not?

Re-writing and Re-seeing

1. Outline this essay by creating a context for each of the four visual rhetorics that Garland-Thomson discusses. To create this context, divide your class into four groups, with each group focusing on one particular form of visual rhetoric and constructing one context. Some things you might consider in constructing your context(s):

   - Draw a map or diagram of this particular form of visual rhetoric and its relationship(s) between viewed and viewer.

- Supplement or surround your map—fill in your context—with examples of this form of visual rhetoric. Examples might come from this textbook or from a wider search you conduct through various media sources.
- What context(s) does this visual rhetoric typically appear in—that is, where do such images typically appear (or not appear)? For example, is this visual rhetoric often screened on TV, in films, in advertisements, in public settings, in family albums, in newspaper stories?
- What kinds of narratives typically accompany this kind of visual rhetoric?
- What is often documented in this particular form of visual rhetoric? What does *not* appear in the documentation/documentary and how and why is its absence created?

2. Gather popular magazines—e.g., fashion, sports, entertainment, hobbies/lifestyles, news magazines—for this exercise. In groups of three to four, look for any images that you might analyze using Garland-Thomson's visual rhetorics. (The images need not necessarily include people with disabilities, although if they do, your analysis might arguably be easier for this exercise.) Present some of your findings to the rest of your class. Then, individually, write a focused critical analysis of the visual rhetoric(s) at work in any one magazine image your group discovered.

Intertext

Applying Garland-Thomson's visual rhetorics and Cole's approach to the "tradition" of "fact and fiction" in (documentary) photography, write an extended critical analysis—complete with images—of how another group of people has been photographed and gazed/stared at (documented) through the camera's "eye." You might choose, for example, images of women in general or in any particular period or region or setting; images of teenagers or images of children (again from possible particular periods or regions or settings); images of citizens from countries that the United States is currently not in strong positive relations with; images of (fallen or rising) celebrities; images of animals in general or a certain species of animal; images of "others" (as defined by those behind the camera); images of members of any ethnic group; images of a socioeconomic class ("the poor," "the middle class," "the wealthy"); images of "tourists"; or images of people in certain professions (police officers, firefighters, coal miners, military personnel, business people, medical professionals, teachers, etc.).

Photographs from S-21

CATHERINE FILLOUX

CATHERINE FILLOUX is a playwright living in New York City. In 2001, she went to Phnom Penh, Cambodia, on a Playwright's Residency grant from the Asian Cultural Council. Filloux's play "Photographs from S-21" draws its inspiration from a 1997 exhibit at the Museum of Modern Art in New York that displayed photographs from the Tuol Sleng archive in Cambodia.

Tuol Sleng—or S-21, as the Khmer Rouge referred to it—was a detention, torture, and execution center used by the Khmer Rouge regime in Cambodia. In the 1970s, the Khmer Rouge killed at least 1 million people in Cambodia out of a population of 7.3 million. All prisoners brought to the Tuol Sleng center were photographed upon their arrival. Tuol Sleng was discovered by Vietnamese soldiers in 1979. Eventually, the center was converted into the Tuol Sleng Museum of Genocide. A nonprofit organization called the Photo Archive Group began to clean and catalogue the photographs in 1993.

"Photographs from S-21" has been produced around the United States and the world. A finalist for the 1999 Heideman Award at the Actors Theatre of Louisville, the play is published in *HB Playwrights Short Play Festival 1998: The Museum Plays.*

> *A young woman and a young man pose, frozen, in the huge lifesize frames of their black and white photos, facing each other. They both wear black pajamas and ID tags. The young woman's ID is a long number, with some Cambodian handwriting and a date. The young man's is simply a tag with the number 3. They both stare at the camera the moment after blindfolds were taken from their eyes. There is a light shining at the bottom of the woman's frame. The woman lets out a soft wail.*

YOUNG WOMAN: I can't go on.

YOUNG MAN: . . . What did you say?

YOUNG WOMAN: I don't know where I am.

YOUNG MAN: Me neither . . .

5   YOUNG WOMAN: Who are you? All day long I listen to voices. I understand nothing, but I understand you.

YOUNG MAN: I am across from you. On the wall. Look, can you see me?

YOUNG WOMAN: No, my eyes are weak. They blindfolded me for a long time. Then suddenly they took off the blindfold and took my photo.

10   YOUNG MAN: Yes, the same with me. But I can see you.

YOUNG WOMAN: Who are you?

YOUNG MAN: A photograph, on the wall, like you.

YOUNG WOMAN: It is unbearable. During the day the people pass. They stare into my eyes. At night, there is no air. Like the inside of a cushion.

(A beat).

15   YOUNG MAN: Would you like to move from where you are and meet me at the center of the room? There is a bench. Then you could see *me.*

YOUNG WOMAN: I can't move.

YOUNG MAN: Try and I will try.

20   YOUNG WOMAN: I don't know who you are.

YOUNG MAN: I speak your language.

YOUNG WOMAN: They spoke my language.

YOUNG MAN: Who?

YOUNG WOMAN: The Khmer Rouge.

25   YOUNG MAN: I'm not Khmer Rouge.

(He breaks out of the photo to show her.)

YOUNG MAN: Look, no red scarf. That's why I'm here. I ran away.

(A beat.)

YOUNG MAN: Would you like me to describe you? So that you know I can see you.

YOUNG WOMAN: No . . . I am ashamed.

YOUNG MAN: Why?

30   YOUNG WOMAN: My black pajamas.

YOUNG MAN: I wear the same.

YOUNG WOMAN: The number they pinned on me.

YOUNG MAN: I am Number Three.

YOUNG WOMAN: My number is much longer.

35   YOUNG MAN: Yes. There is also a date for your identification . . . It says, "Seventeen, Five, Seventy-eight."

YOUNG WOMAN: You must have very good eyesight.

YOUNG MAN: Thank you. I have been staring at you for a long time. You are always there, except when the crowds become big and block you, or the
40   guard turns off the light . . . I see so many things in you, now . . . fear, determination, beauty, surprise . . . your eyes are like water in a lake that reflects the passing seasons . . . I have begun to see you like that . . .

YOUNG WOMAN: The date on my identification is May 17, 1978.

(He moves toward her.)

45   YOUNG MAN: There is something strange at the bottom of your picture. It is blurred . . . I cannot make it out . . .

YOUNG WOMAN: *No.*

YOUNG MAN: . . . I see it. Something just inside the frame, moving skyward . . .

YOUNG WOMAN: No, there is nothing. *(A beat.)* My husband *cried* when they killed his mother.

50   YOUNG MAN: They killed you if you cried.

YOUNG WOMAN: I know. In the labor camp. They cracked her skull with a shovel because she was too slow working. We could not even bury her. So now she is *kmauit*—a restless ghost . . .

(The Young Man moves to the bench.)

55   YOUNG MAN: I always envy the visitors who sit here. Sometimes they sit in groups. Families. They read the books that are here. They write in a book too.

YOUNG WOMAN: Sometimes the people come like a parade. They walk in and out. Like a stream, staring into my eyes. Their eyes are all different colors. Blue. Green. Yellow. Like lights.

60   YOUNG MAN: It's nice to find someone who speaks the same language.

(He stretches out on the bench.)

YOUNG MAN: Are you sure you don't want to stretch your legs? . . . You know we aren't the only ones on the wall. There are twenty-two of us. Cambodians. Or at least that's what I think I see. All being posed for photos at "S-21."

65   YOUNG WOMAN: S-21 used to have another name . . . "Tuol Sleng."

(He looks through the guest book on the table and reads.)

YOUNG MAN: Someone's written something here in our language! Listen. "*Do not forget.*" Signed, "Sovindara Hun. New York City." *(A beat.)* We're in America . . .

(The woman moves from her photograph very stiffly.)

YOUNG MAN: Hey, you did it! . . . Please, come sit down. This is comfortable.

70   YOUNG WOMAN: No. Let me stand for a moment. I'm dizzy.

YOUNG MAN: You want me to coin you?

YOUNG WOMAN: No, no, no.

YOUNG MAN: I have a coin! *(He rolls up the cuff of his pajama pants and feels in the lining.)* I sewed this little pocket, when I returned from the labor

75   camp to my grandmother's. I'd heard she was dying and they gave me
        permission to go see her. I asked her for a needle and thread and I
        made a secret pocket. I hid some gold she gave me and some coins. My
        lighter. A lot of good it did me. *(He takes out the coin.)* Come on, sit
        down. Here, give me your arm. I'm sorry, I don't have any oil . . .

        (She sits and he starts to rub her arm forcefully with the coin.)

80   YOUNG MAN: How does it feel?

     YOUNG WOMAN: *(In awe.)* I do not believe it.

     YOUNG MAN: What do you mean?

     YOUNG WOMAN: I am in a dream.

     YOUNG MAN: No, you're in America . . .

85   YOUNG WOMAN: America?

     YOUNG MAN: You know, rich people, lots of cars. Willie Nelson.

     YOUNG WOMAN: Oh, yes . . . Is that why they sent you to S-21? Because they
        found the gold?

     YOUNG MAN: No, they never got the gold! *(He quickly takes a piece of gold out
90   of the secret pocket and shows her, delighted.)* Look, it's right here. I tricked
        them! *(He puts it back in his pocket.)* Here give me your other arm.

        *(He touches one of her hands, which is always clenched in a fist. She pulls
        away.)*

     YOUNG MAN: You're shaking.

     YOUNG WOMAN: I'm always cold. Shaking with fright.

     YOUNG MAN: They're not here.

        (She looks at her uniform and ID tag.)

95   YOUNG WOMAN: They can't be far away . . .

        (He puts his arm around her.)

     YOUNG MAN: Here, let me warm you, darling.

     YOUNG WOMAN: Why do you call me that?

     YOUNG MAN: I called my sister that . . . We're dead, so you don't have to be
        scared . . . I mean, that is the truth . . . I wish we had something to
100   eat . . . What kind of food do you wish for, if you could have anything?

     YOUNG WOMAN: But we are *here*, Number Three.

     YOUNG MAN: Don't call me that. I have a name.

     YOUNG WOMAN: Who knows it now?

     YOUNG MAN: You. *(He puts his palms together and bows.)* "Vuthy."

        (She puts her palm and fist together, bowing back.)

105   YOUNG WOMAN: Tuol Sleng was a school, Vuthy. As a girl I went there to
               learn to read and write. That's where they took me on May 17, 1978. I
               walked in and remembered forming my letters so carefully, reading the
               words . . . *They* killed you if you could read and write . . .

       YOUNG MAN: I know. *(He points to the frame.)* It's strange to be here now.

110   YOUNG WOMAN: America.

       YOUNG MAN: I don't know if we're really here.

       YOUNG WOMAN: We feel real.

               (He resumes his position in the frame.)

       YOUNG MAN: Maybe it's because we're in the photographs. And people pass
               by. And every time their eyes touch ours we're back there again.

115   YOUNG WOMAN: They look at me so strange. Like they are asking me a question.

       YOUNG MAN: Yes.

       YOUNG WOMAN: I can never turn away.

       YOUNG MAN: Caught.

       YOUNG WOMAN: Who are they, who look?

120   YOUNG MAN: Ghosts, maybe . . . Ghosts of the Khmer Rouge.

       YOUNG WOMAN: But they do not look the same.

       YOUNG MAN: Why else would they come back again and again to see us? To
               check on us?

       YOUNG WOMAN: Perhaps you are right, Vuthy. Perhaps they are the enemy,
125   disguised . . .

               (The Young Man moves away.)

       YOUNG WOMAN: *(Urgently.)* Where are you going? Please don't leave me here.
               You don't know what can happen.

       YOUNG MAN: I just want to see what is nearby. The people always seem to be
               passing on their way to something called "Picasso."

               (He exits and she follows, but stops.)

130   YOUNG WOMAN: Vuthy, come back! . . .

               (She stands alone. She reenters her frame and starts to take her position.)

       YOUNG WOMAN: No, no, no, no. *(She leans down.)* No, no, no . . .

               (The Young Man hurries back in.)

       YOUNG MAN: Darling, what's happened? What's wrong?

               (The Young Woman stares into space, totally lost.)

       YOUNG MAN: Darling, tell me what happened. Please tell me what hap-
               pened to you.

(She says nothing at all.)

135   YOUNG MAN: There, there.

(He takes out the gold.)

YOUNG MAN: Why don't you take this piece of gold?

(She takes it, absently.)

YOUNG MAN: Isn't it beautiful? Hold it to the light.

(She doesn't.)

YOUNG MAN: Well, I'll tell you what I saw, next door. More photographs. Of horses, of flowers, of bananas, just bananas. A boy swimming, a girl
140   dancing, cars—we're in America—dirt, there were photos of dirt, yes. Hills. Houses, square houses with windows, airplanes, old people with lots of wrinkles, a little girl with a short dress, a bicycle, a woman with a hat—smoking a cigarette, a city with many lights. Walls and walls of this, I stopped when I heard your screaming, but it went on and on . . . I
145   want to show you. It's easy. Just follow me. We'll go past the photographs, find a door . . . Or perhaps we don't need doors, since we're ghosts . . .

YOUNG WOMAN: How can I be dead and feel like this?

(The Young Man has no answer.)

YOUNG WOMAN: What happened to you?

150   YOUNG MAN: Shocked me with an electric current, starved me, shackled me to the other men, made me sleep in my own . . .

YOUNG WOMAN: Why did they send you to S-21?

YOUNG MAN: I ran away from the camp. I ate insects and rats, slept underwater . . . You want to know my real crime? I stayed alive.

155   YOUNG WOMAN: And after they took off your blindfold?

YOUNG MAN: . . . My blood joined the blood of others on the floor . . .

YOUNG WOMAN: . . . Vuthy?

YOUNG MAN: Yes?

YOUNG WOMAN: You saw right.

(He looks at her, waiting.)

160   YOUNG WOMAN: There was something at the bottom of my photo . . . A child's hand . . .

YOUNG MAN: *(Softly.)* Oh, yes, I looked at it for so long . . .

YOUNG WOMAN: They took off the blindfold. My daughter reached up to me. *I did not move. (Softly.)* Did not move . . . They shot her first . . . I did
165   not protect her.

(She reaches down to take the hand of the imaginary child.)

Young Woman: She reached up her hand . . .

(He takes her hand.)

Young Man: Come, we don't want to be ghosts, haunting people at night, making them afraid to fall asleep . . .

Young Woman: I have no one left to haunt. All my family is gone.

170   Young Man: We must have some peace, darling. A proper funeral for us.

Young Woman: . . . I don't deserve peace . . .

(He takes her hand and they begin to leave. They are captured in a shaft of light during their odyssey outside.)

Young Woman: Are we outside?

Young Man: Yes. The cement feels strange on my feet.

Young Woman: Rough. It is raining?

175   Young Man: No, it is a fountain. A proper funeral or we will remain ghosts. Come, stand in the water. *(He leads her into the fountain.)* Close your eyes.

(He caresses her.)

Young Man: Shhshhh . . .

(He takes incense from his pocket and lights it with his lighter. He bows before her. She holds out her clenched fist to him.)

Young Woman: When I am newly born in my next life, I will still remember the Khmer Rouge.

(She opens her hand and he takes a child's ribbon from her palm. Blackout. The young woman and man reappear in their frames. A flash and the click of a shutter.)

Re-reading/Conversations with the Text

1. In Filloux's play, the photographs break out of their frames and speak for themselves. What is the significance of the fact that they speak? You might read the play aloud or have two classmates perform the play. As you read, listen for the voices' efforts to establish common experiences. In what ways might the fact that the photographs speak counter the murder of Cambodians by the Khmer Rouge?

2. Consider how the play introduces its own context. When, for example, do you first recognize that the play takes place in a museum? What effect might the suspension of this knowledge bring to your experience of the play? Consider the line spoken by the young man at the onset of the play: "I have been staring at you for a long time." What do this line and the following lines suggest

about the power of images? About how viewers project emotions or identifications onto others?

3. Describe each character individually, and then consider their relationship to each other. What do you come to understand by the end of the play about the significance of this relationship? What do you come to understand about the significance of the exhibition?

Re-seeing and Re-writing

1. Which aspects of the play offer an argument about the documentation and exhibition of the past? Consider how the context of the museum shapes not only what the characters say, but also a particular relationship of viewing and listening. What gaze does such a context invite from you as reader? Are you positioned as an accidental witness? A museum goer? Something/one else? How might current issues and the cultural or national climate (*kairos*) shape your interpretations? Write an essay in which you explore the role that context plays in framing our understanding of the past.

2. "Photographs from S-21" falls into the larger genre of drama. How would you characterize this play and the rhetorical situation it sets up between the characters and its audience? Is the rhetorical situation ceremonial in nature? Political? One of mourning?

3. Review the introduction to this section of your text. Then go to the Web site at Yale University's Cambodian Genocide Project (http://www.yale.edu/cgp). How does the website frame the photographs from Tuol Sleng? Is the website documentary in nature? What is its stated mission? How does it imagine its primary audience?

In "Photographs from S-21" there seems to be a tension between surveillance and witnessing. On the one hand, these photographs are the documents of the torturers, and it is through their gaze that we see the victims. Yet, on the other hand, these photographs are displayed in a museum, which casts them as documentary and *aesthetic* objects. Re-read the play in conversation with Zelizer's essay "Conveying Atrocity in Image," paying particular attention to these and other tensions inherent in the representation of historical atrocity. Then write an essay in which you explore these tensions and their significance.

Research Prompts
DOCUMENTARY GAZES:
Representing History

KEY RHETORICAL CONCEPTS

genre
kairos

Just Advocacy?

Analyze the rhetorical strategies of an organization such as PETA, NRA, NAACP, NOW, ACLU, Amnesty International, anti-Sweatshop/WTO protestors, or any local or university advocacy groups. What is the group's primary mission? How does it frame this mission? Are the rhetorical strategies the group employs primarily authoritative, emotional, or logical (*ethos, pathos, logos*)? How does it use these strategies and to what end? What binary constructions are employed? What is ignored? How does the media portray the group? What are the implications of said representations and for whom? How does your analysis extend, complicate, or challenge secondary readings on the subject?

Writing and Social Change

Choose a group of speeches and/or popular writings written on a specific theme (e.g., human or civil rights since 9/11; environmentalism since the last presidential election; ethnic/racial profiling since 9/11). What is at issue? How do the texts interpret the issue? To what degree do they commemorate or seek to suppress important or infamous occurrences in our past? How do they support or challenge binary categories and ways of thinking? What are the implications of such binaries? What do they ignore? Are there other rhetorical patterns that characterize these texts? If so, what are these patterns and how do they complicate, extend, or enhance our understanding of the events that the authors are discussing?

Just Stories?

Many of the readings in this section discuss the ways in which attempts to document a culture, place, issue, or event produce "stories" or narratives about our relationship to these issues or events. For this option, "flip the script" and examine *fictional* representations of a culture, place, issue, or event, and discuss how these fictional representations might also "document" them. What do we learn from these stories?

Whether she was a grandmother, stout, thick, old, didn't make any difference. I was running ahead of him with my Leica looking back over my shoulder . . . Then suddenly, in a flash, I saw something white being grabbed. I turned around and clicked the moment the sailor kissed the nurse.

—ALFRED EISENSTAEDT

MOST RHETORICAL CRITICS BEGIN THEIR OWN WRITING BY ANALYZING written texts or images that are important to their research question, but they usually don't stop there. Thoughtful critics typically move on to discover what others have said about the texts. They do so not only to find others who support their own views, but also to find others whose views diverge from their own. In fact, no one can have much confidence in his or her conclusions until they have been tested against alternatives. We can think of the research process as coming upon a conversation about a subject that interests us, listening to what others are saying, and then—as our own conclusions take shape—putting in our own "two cents' worth."

The research project described in this chapter provides an opportunity for you to develop a rhetorical analysis of a selection of textual materials (primary sources) and to consider your analysis in relation to the

Courtesy of Rod Gonzalez.

insights of others (secondary sources). You should use all of the key rhetorical concepts (KRCs) to extend your study of the primary sources. Three key rhetorical concepts, however, are central to this project: representation, genre, and *kairos.*

The term **representation** refers here to the ways in which ideas and concepts are mediated through texts. For example, in Tommy Hilfiger advertisements, an array of models represent youth, wealth, and diversity, but this message is complicated by their physical arrangement, in which people of color are often placed on the margins (see photo). In contemporary advertising, it is possible to locate a number of images whose composition is similar to that of the Hilfiger ads. We use the term **representational trend** to refer to this recurrence—that is, to refer to patterns that occur with frequency at particular cultural or historical moments. (These patterns can be visual or verbal; this chapter uses the example of a paper focused on a visual representational trend.)

To consider such patterns, we must take into account textual and cultural conventions such as genre. **Genre** is a term that refers broadly to types or kinds and, more specifically, to kinds of texts. Classical genres of literature included the epic, tragedy, lyric, comedy, and satire; more contemporary forms include the novel, autobiography, and biography. We can also group other kinds of texts, such as film, video games, and television programs, in terms of genres; television shows, for instance, could be divided into sitcoms, reality shows, game shows, and dramas. Genres can overlap, as in hybrid genres such as docu-drama or autobiographical fiction. Genres are also always in flux; in other words, genres are not static literary or cultural classifications.

The research project described in this chapter also asks that you consider *why* a particular representation or genre is popular at a particular historical and cultural moment. ***Kairos*** is a term that refers to the cultural climate of rhetorical situations. For instance, to consider why "reality" television shows (e.g., *Survivor*) have been so popular among certain audiences is to examine their *kairos*. It is important as a researcher to understand why a particular trend is important within a particular historical and cultural climate.

Representational trends are not limited to particular genres; trends occur across genres. For example, our culture's fascination with cosmetic surgery can be seen in genres as disparate as reality television programs like *Extreme Makeover* and *The Swan;* television dramas like *Nip/Tuck;* and countless nonfiction books such as *Beauty Junkies.* We can imagine research papers that are comparative in nature, that compare one genre (say, reality television) to another (television drama). Given the amount of time that most of you will have to spend on the research paper, however, we suggest that you stick to one genre. You might consider questions such as the following:

- Why are such programs so successful?
- To whom do they appeal?
- What is it about our current climate that might account for the popularity of these shows?
- And, importantly, what have others said about this trend?

This research project will ask you to answer these questions through your analysis of the representational trend (your primary sources), aided by secondary sources that help to contextualize the trend in its cultural and historical moment. For example, a paper on reality shows that focus on cosmetic surgery would treat the shows themselves as primary sources, but it might include research on the history of reality television, the rise of cosmetic surgery as a medical field, and more general articles about the representation of women and beauty on television. The secondary sources you select should help you test and challenge your ideas.

The academic research paper has traditionally been seen as a project of collection, organization, and dissemination of the ideas and arguments of experts. *Rhetorical Visions* challenges one central convention of this genre. The research paper we propose here features *you*, the student writer, and your analysis of primary and secondary texts. By putting your own analyses and arguments in conversation with the arguments of others, this research project asks you to join a conversation among an academic community of scholars.

Selection and Analysis of Primary Texts

This research project will take you through several steps of selection, analysis, research, and writing, but you should remember that you may not necessarily go through each of these steps one at a time, or in this exact order. Writing, much like map-making, is far messier than that. Much about your process through these various steps will depend on your topic, your available tools (primary and secondary sources, methods of analysis), and your own writing skills and preferences.

As we go through these steps, we will apply them to three images (our primary texts) in order to illustrate how an initial idea develops into an argument about a representational trend, and then how that argument develops into a full research paper.

For our example, we are going to look at images of a very simple and universal human behavior: kissing. Why kissing? First, just because it is so common; kissing will almost certainly generate a wide selection of images from which we may choose. Second, kissing is deeply significant and highly sensitive to cultural context. A kiss doesn't mean the same thing everywhere and at all times, so it seems likely that as culture or historical/situational context changes, images of kissing and the function of these images within a specific culture or context would change as well. Third, kissing can be connected to the texts and topics of any of the five major sections in this book: Kissing occurs in family relationships, as well as on the national stage; it is often consumed, most significantly in advertising and the popular media; it certainly crosses cultures; and it is both amply documented and itself a form of documentation in public and private ceremony.

The following steps will help us (a) identify a series of images of kissing, (b) identify to what genre these images belong, (c) consider how the meaning of these images is shaped by particular historical and cultural moments (*kairos*); and (d) analyze a representational trend.

1. Collect a set of primary sources (images and/or texts) and begin taking notes.

In order to identify a representational trend, you will first need to select a series of primary texts (sources) that you intend to analyze. These sources—and the subject of your representational trend—may contain visual elements (e.g., images, charts, graphs, page design, font style, images) as well as text, and may come from a range of genres (e.g., print texts, advertisements, websites, photographs, television programs, film). Primary sources might also include public speeches, various forms of journalism, music lyrics, performances, literary texts, and so on. Your initial research questions and working thesis will emerge from your preliminary analysis of these primary texts.

The number of primary sources you choose to work with will depend upon the length and level of detail in the source (a single image, for example, can be reviewed more quickly than a film) and the amount of time and space you have for the project (a ten-page paper can obviously consider more sources than a three-page paper). However, in general, it is better to analyze few sources in more detail than it is to analyze many sources only superficially.

For our sample research project, our first task will be to collect scenes and images of kissing that we might want to write about. Where might we go to find such images? Let's suppose that you were intrigued by an image that you saw on the cover of your local newspaper of an embrace by soldiers returning home from Afghanistan or Iraq. Let's suppose that you wanted to explore further the appeal of such images and pos-

WRITE

Selecting Sources

1. Keep a running list of the primary sources that you are considering for your project: Note title, author, publication information or source, date, and other relevant information (Web address, etc). You will need enough information so that others who read about the source will be able to locate it based on your bibliographic entry for it. (Your instructor may require you to use a citation format such as MLA or Chicago style for your entries. We discuss these guides more in the section on secondary sources and annotation below.) As you eliminate sources and add others, simply cross out and add onto your list, so that you can keep track of your progress.

2. Generate brief notes (perhaps a notebook page or computer file) for each source that you consider. What is (in) the source? What details do you notice? Where did you find it or where does it appear? Who is it aimed at or who would observe it? Why do you find it interesting? What about this source brought it to your attention? These details may be important later as you develop a thesis and read secondary sources about your representational trend. Even sources that you decide eventually to discard may hold clues to the representational trend that you are working to explain and interpret.

sible links between images of kissing and concepts of national identity. You might begin by quickly brainstorming the kinds of sources that would be likely to contain such images: posters advertising war movies, book covers, photography collections, advertisements, or clip art. You can, of course, use a search engine such as Google to help with brainstorming. Be forewarned, though: If you simply do an image search on "kissing," you'll likely wind up with too many hits; instead, you might "Google" something more specific, like *kissing+national*.

We have selected for our initial analysis the following three images: an image of the Pope kissing the Koran (Figure 8.3), an image of George Bush kissing Condoleezza Rice (Figure 8.1), and a widely known photograph by Alfred Eisenstaedt of a soldier kissing a nurse in Times Square on V-J Day—that is, August 14, 1945, the date of Japan's surrender to Allied forces at the end of World War II (Figure 8.2).

Taken in November 2004, Figure 8.1 shows President Bush kissing Condoleezza Rice, in the Roosevelt Room of the White House, after announcing that she was his nominee for Secretary of State. Because the photo was originally taken by Agence France-Presse, an international news agency, this image appeared in numerous periodicals, including *USA Today* (where we found it).

Figure 8.1   "Read These Lips: Bush Gets Quite Continental," *USA Today Online,*
November 18, 2004.

Courtesy of Pablo Martinez Monsivais/AP Wide World Photos.

With a few context notes recorded, we begin then to study this image more carefully and jot down some brief initial observations and questions.

Positive "rhetorical vision"

- American flag in the background—unites Bush and Rice
- Flag: patriotism and U.S. democracy (*ethos* and *pathos*)
- Bush's red tie links him to flag (*ethos*)
- Do we identify Bush, Rice, and the ceremony with the flag's positive, "all-
  American" values?
- Suggestion of diversity—inclusion of African Americans, women, in
  government?
- Do we identify with Bush? Rice? Neither? Does the "intimacy" of Bush's
  gesture convince us?

Complicating factors

- Gender, Race, and Sexuality: Rice, female and African American; Bush, white male. Does he kiss all his appointees? Heterosexual norms frame the kiss and its appropriateness.
- Bush wears a conservative, black suit; Rice wears ivory edged with black— negatives of each other?
- Awkwardness: Bush leans in, but Rice's shoulders look stiff.
- Why can't we see his face? What kind of expression does his position hide? Is he whispering something to her? How do we describe the expression on her face?

We could (and should) continue this brief note-taking process for each of the other images we have gathered thus far.

2. Select analytical tools to guide your analysis of these sources.

Once you have a selection of primary sources, you will need to decide on which analytical tools to use. You'll probably want to focus on one or two key rhetorical concepts (KRCs) and a few specific features of your source texts (e.g., composition,

WRITE

Reviewing Key Rhetorical Concepts

1. Review the KRCs listed as part of the critical frames for each of the five units in this book. Also review the checklist "Reading Rhetorically: The Rhetorical Triangle" on page 7. List any of these concepts or approaches that you feel will be useful to you and briefly note why. What do the key rhetorical term(s) you have selected and/or "reading rhetorically" questions help you to see and to say about the images you have found? What features of the image(s) or texts do they bring into focus?
2. Go through your list of likely KRCs and questions one at a time, while looking at your sources; take notes on what that term or question helps you to notice about the image. When you are finished with these preliminary notes, select those terms that seemed to be most generative in helping you write about your sources.

| W R I T E |

Brainstorming

1. *Listing:* You may want to begin simply by listing, in no particular order, all the elements of the texts that seem important, interesting, or puzzling. A color scheme, a facial expression or gesture, a movement, the proximity of two figures: Any detail is worth recording. The checklist on the inside covers of your book should come in handy here.

2. *Clustering:* You may try a "clustering" approach: Take a large sheet of paper and jot down your observations on the page as they occur, using lines, arrows, or some other scheme to suggest relationships, patterns, oppositions, or connections, and placing these observations spatially in relationship to each other. Perhaps you place the most important features at the center of your page and more doubtful or minor details further out. Perhaps, through your clustering, you notice a binary or triangulated relationship among images or elements.

color, emotional tone, action). In our discussion of the red state/blue state political maps in Chapter 2, for example, we used the KRCs of *metaphor* and *identification,* while we focused on color, centrality, and depth to guide our analysis. Your analysis is not limited to what you can say with the analytical terms or concepts that you select, of course, any more than something you built would be limited by the tools you owned before you started a project. You might need to add, substitute, or even invent new terms and concepts to help you understand and articulate how, why, and for whom the representational trend works.

For the Bush–Rice image, we found that two of the most important rhetorical terms were *ethos* and *pathos,* or the ethical and emotional appeal of the image. Our preliminary notetaking on the image suggested to us that the image's emotional power was linked to the ethical appeal of the flag as a symbol of national identity, which designates the ceremony as an important event and places national value on the unifying kiss as an indicator of equal opportunity. We also found *identification* and *difference* useful for analyzing the photograph in greater detail. For example, which elements of the photo resemble each other? Which elements seem to stand in contrast? How do we as audience relate to them? How do these relationships contribute to the meaning we derive from the image?

3. Analyze your primary sources using established "standards."

You are ready now to begin analyzing your texts in detail. At this stage, it is better to produce too much material than too little, better to record details that turn out to be unimportant than to overlook details that may be highly significant. Keeping your KRCs and questions in mind, begin to record the details that you notice in the sources that you have selected. Whatever sources you choose, and whatever representational trend you uncover, your overall task will be to discover how the texts work, what they say about the time and place from which they emerge, and how/whether they encourage a certain way of thinking and acting in their audience(s).

Our use of the key rhetorical terms *ethos, pathos,* and *identification* have led us to focus on certain aspects of the photograph of President Bush kissing Condoleezza Rice (Figure 8.1). In further preliminary analysis we might compare this to Eisenstadt's famous photo of a sailor and a nurse kissing in Times Square on V-J Day at the end of World War II (Figure 8.2).

The V-J Day photograph, like the Bush–Rice image, portrays a kiss, signaling positive emotions to its audience, but, in both photos, the stiffness of the postures seems to undermine the notion that the kisses are purely joyful, or spontaneous, or (perhaps) authentic. The Eisenstaedt photo signals joy and perhaps relief at the end of the war, but it captures an awkward posture: The man's left elbow and fist seem stiffly and unnaturally held; the woman's back is bent at what seems an uncomfortable angle, and her hand clutches at her dress.

The concepts of identification and difference we used in making notes on the Bush–Rice photo might also help us here; the man and the woman are both in uniform (a sailor and a nurse), which encourages us to see them as a unit. Yet, the awkwardness of the pose and seeming aggression in the man's stance—at best, he seems to have caught the woman unawares—seem to speak for a distance between them. The photographer spotted the sailor "running along the street grabbing any and every girl in sight," he explained. "Whether she was a grandmother, stout, thick, old, didn't make any difference. I was running ahead of him with my Leica looking back over my shoulder. . . . Then suddenly, in a flash, I saw something white being grabbed. I turned around and clicked the moment the sailor kissed the nurse" (www.life.com/Life/special/ kiss03.html). There are also interesting differences and similarities in the relationship between the images and their audience(s): The couple in the V-J Day photo is caught in a private act in a public space—in a sense they're completely unaware of and separate from us, though the act is performed in public. Bush and Rice, on the other hand, while engaged in what we often think of as a private act, are very conscious of themselves as actors in a public ceremony.

We should also step outside the frame of each of these images in order to consider historical and cultural context. The Times Square kiss marks an important occasion: victory in war. The kiss, therefore, might be thought to signal not the love between a man and a woman (who were, according to most accounts, complete strangers), but the joy and relief of a nation as a devastating war comes to a close. Rather than as lovers, we might identify with the figures as people caught up in a

Figure 8.2   "The Smack Heard Round the World."

Courtesy of Alfred Eisenstaedt, V-J Day: Sailor Kissing Girl (1945). Life Magazine. © 1945 TimePix..

frenzy of relief, excitement, jubilation. The Bush and Rice photo similarly depicts a celebratory moment—we're being asked to identify with two public officials announcing an important appointment, and at the same time with the values they represent, including, but not limited to, the endorsement of diversity in the United States. Context, then (another KRC), is also an important element in analyzing images of "the kiss." We use the term context to refer to the history, time, space, location, and situation in which a piece of writing, speech, or image is created, as well as the context in which it is interpreted.

4. Identify a representational trend based on your analysis of the sources.

After selecting a set of sources and collecting notes on them, you will gradually begin to see a "trend" or a pattern that will provide the basis for your thesis. Your next task will be to work on articulating this trend in a way that reflects what you see in your sources. It will be important to keep an open mind about the trend or pattern that you notice and what you want to say about it. Be ready and willing to revise, restate, reject, and reinvent these conclusions as you look more deeply into your primary and secondary sources. Your goal is not to settle upon the first thing that you notice, but to find the most interesting, the most provocative, the most powerful thing that you notice—and this kind of discovery often means rejecting your early conclusions for more interesting ones that come later. Often, asking others what they see or notice and comparing that to your own notes will be helpful.

For the kissing images, we have begun to notice a trend that we might describe as the "ceremonial" kiss. Both the Bush–Rice image and the Eisenstaedt image depict kisses that mark special occasions usually connected with joy—a celebratory ceremony and the end of war. Yet interestingly enough, the images convey signs of tension, rigidity, and awkwardness that complicate our understanding of the images as strictly celebratory. These two representations of kissing are unlike more private images of kisses as tender and romantic. The specter of power relations and the suggestion of performance (with, by implication, a hint of "acting" and "pretending"—hence, inauthenticity) seep in to our analysis of what is often thought of as the simplest and most natural of gestures.

| WRITE |

Identifying a Trend

Based on your notes, describe the general pattern or trend that you see emerging and working across your images. Try describing this trend in several different ways.

- How does it shape our view of reality, our understanding of ourselves, our relationships, our abilities, our worth, or our world?
- How and why do these types of images appeal to various audiences? What exceptions do you notice in this trend?
- Where and when does the trend appear? Where and when does it disappear?
- Why has the trend gained cultural acceptance or achieved cultural prominence at this particular time (*kairos*)? In other words, what cultural or historical factors contribute to the visibility and acceptance of such representations at this point in time?

Figure 8.3   Pope John Paul II kisses the Koran (Qu'ran), May 14, 1999.

At this point, we decide to shift focus and concentrate on official, political, ceremonial kisses—a category where the V-J day photograph doesn't comfortably fit. Now we may look for further political and ceremonial kisses, perhaps in films, paintings, photography, or advertisements. In our original search for ceremonial images of kissing, we recall one that portrays the Pope kissing the Koran in 1999 (Figure 8.3).* Pope John Paul II's gesture was repeatedly shown on Iraqi television. The context of the image remains especially significant, as the photo was taken in 1999, while Iraq was under the dictatorship of Saddam Hussein and before the September 11, 2001, terrorist attacks on the United States and the subsequent "war on terror."

*There is some question about the authenticity of this photograph. According to *Catholic World News*, Patriarch Raphael I Bidawid claimed in an interview with *Fides*, a Vatican-sponsored site, that he was present when the photo was taken (http://www.cwnews.com/news/viewstory.cfm?recnum=10415). Though the image appears on many Internet sites, we have not been able to find verification of the story/photograph in any reputable publication apart from *Catholic News*.

WRITE

Drafting a Key Analytical Claim

At the top of one sheet of paper or a new file, write your central argument. What do you think is going on with this representational trend? What does it reveal? How does it work? To whom does it appeal and why? What does it suggest about the cultural moment in which it occurs?

Below this central claim (eventually, it will become your thesis), list all the reasons for making this claim, including the details and patterns that you discovered in your primary source.

Here, as in other ceremonial kisses, we see the romantic notion of the kiss replaced by something else—a demonstration of reverence for a holy book, and, by extension, for a religion. Our analysis of the image using KRCs lead us to conclude that the photo is inundated with *metonymic* figures. (Recall that *metonymy* refers to the process wherein an image or object stands in for a larger concept. For more on metonymy, see p. 162.) The Pope stands in for Catholicism and the Western world, while the Koran and the Iraqi minister of religion signify the Muslim religion and the non-Western world. The Iraqi ministry official watches the Pope's gesture; non-Muslim viewers are asked to identify with him (as fellow onlookers), but also to recognize differences, with his garments signalling another religion and another culture. Similarly, Christians are encouraged to identify with the Pope, as a Westerner, but also to recognize the obvious differences that separate them from this elaborately garbed, elderly white male. The meaning of this image as one of tolerance, acceptance, and respect for religious differences is based upon the recognition of such identifications and differences.

The two images—Bush–Rice and the Pope with the Koran—feature kisses as an element of public performance. In using the kiss as a public display, these images turn away from private moments. Such images—carefully staged to deliver a certain message—bring an act associated with private life (the life of love and intimacy) into the public and political arena.

We can formulate our thoughts as a question to help us move closer to an argument: What is the importance of a trend that represents kissing in public lives/spaces? What are we to make of the "ritual kiss" or "ceremonial kiss" that mimics love, but is in fact part of a cultural and political performance? This tension, we realize, is what made us interested in these images in the first place; the seemingly paradoxical mixture of emotion and formality, and sincerity and posturing. How far does this trend extend?

5. Develop a preliminary argument (claims and reasons) about this trend.

With the notes based on your primary sources and a preliminary statement about the trend that you notice, you are ready to begin formulating the claims and reasons that will constitute your central argument.

We are now ready to hazard an initial trial at our central argument. Here is what we came up with as a preliminary thesis/support:

Preliminary Central Argument

Images of ceremonial kissing are often used by newspapers, Web sites, and magazines because they are performances that are intended to deliver a positive message. For instance, images of kissing are used to symbolize reconciliation/resolution of conflict, in the face of national and international tensions (political, racial, gender-based, and religious).

Support:

1. Bush–Rice photo:

    a. The American flag symbolizes patriotism and national unity.
        i. The stripes and the stars within the flag depict unity of states that form a larger nation.
        ii. Traditional American colors of red, white, and blue are often used to designate things "down-home" or "authentic"—and are mimicked in Bush's red tie.
    b. The kiss between Bush and Rice symbolizes the establishment's acceptance of diversity, and, more specifically, the inclusion of African American females in places of power.
        i. Civil rights is still an issue within U.S. society.
        ii. Bush and Rice are presented as colleagues, friends, and equals.
        iii. The embrace symbolizes a mutual affirmation of progress in race relations.
    c. At the same time, the kiss signals that racial and gender inequality still exist in U.S. society.
        i. The need to present the kiss implies that there's still a problem.
        ii. Rice's shoulders are stiff or rigid.
        iii. Bush's face is hidden, and Rice's face is turned away from him.
        iv. Opposite colors (negatives of each other?) show distance/difference between the couple despite kiss/attempt to establish identification.

2. Pope–Koran photo:

    a. The Pope and the Iraqi religious minister, as well as the Koran itself, function *metonymically* as stand-ins for the West and Catholicism/Christianity, and the Middle East and the Muslim faith, respectively.
    b. The kiss expresses reverence on the part of the Pope for the Muslim faith, and hope for world peace/unity.

      i. We can identify and feel distance from both the Pope (in his ceremonial garb) and the Iraqi minister—we can accept or reject the message depending on our identification/lack of identification.

      ii. The context of the photo is important (and is different now from the time the photo was originally published, in 1999). Hussein was in power in 1999; now, he's on trial, and we're engaged in warfare in Iraq.

  c. As with the Bush–Rice photo, certain elements of the photo contradict its seeming claim of harmony.

      i. The Iraqi minister's face is mostly hidden from us; from what we can see, he's caught in the act of speaking. There's no smile or indication of approval.

      ii. The need to perform the kiss publicly undermines the public statement of peace/unity.

3. These images become public—used in websites, magazines, and newspapers—to depict important ceremonies or historical events that often are new beginnings or endings.

  a. Ceremonial kisses are given and received to express positive developments.

  b. While they retain overtones of the romantic kiss (because that's prevalent in our culture), ceremonial kisses complicate and challenge the notion of the kiss and the message it sends.

We aren't completely happy with this as our central argument yet, and we have to remind ourselves that this argument is still just a preliminary one. At this point, it serves as a guide to help us focus further research and analysis. But we feel ready now to take a look at what others have said about the social and cultural role of kissing in general and of these images in particular. As mentioned earlier, we need to pay attention to how representational trends anticipate or respond to the perceived needs and values of imagined or intended audiences at particular historical moments. To analyze why an image or text is persuasive at a particular historical moment is to examine its *kairos*. Therefore, we might ask the following questions as we proceed with our research: Through what venues have these two images entered the public sphere? What was the public reaction to them? Has either image become part of a larger political campaign or been the subject of controversy? Our preliminary analysis suggests that there is something more going on here than meets the eye, a pattern of representation that reveals something larger about our culture, our time, and we'd like to find out more about it.

Remember that every thesis worth its salt needs to make a claim that is neither completely obvious (if no one would dispute it, why bother arguing for it?) nor unbelievable (you have to be able to give reasons for supporting it). You should clearly have some commitment to, and interest in, your preliminary argument in order to make your developing research and analysis more effective. Of course, you may still find that further shaping, re-articulation, or even a significant shift in your central claim may be necessary as you move further into both primary and secondary sources and begin to develop warrants (supporting evidence and examples) for your claim.

Research and Annotation

After you have spent some time with your sources, articulated a representational trend, and developed a preliminary argument about that trend based on your analysis, it is time to engage the expertise of others who are interested in the same topic. As we argue throughout this book, your work of analyzing texts has placed you within a community of critics who are interested in the same texts and/or the same representational trend. You share with them a common rhetorical vision, and you can now call upon this larger community to check your analysis and your tentative arguments. Finding critics who disagree with your analysis or who seem to be saying something different entirely doesn't mean that you are wrong, but it does mean that you should go back to your sources and your argument to see what, if anything, needs to be changed. Below are some suggestions for getting started.

1. Search library databases and Web sites for relevant keywords or headings.

Once you have defined a representational trend, you will need to generate a list of search terms to use as keywords or subject terms for secondary sources. Using the wrong search term can mean coming up empty-handed. Every database and bibliography uses a list of terms as subject headings; the most common in the U.S. is the Library of Congress subject heading list. Many online databases include a thesaurus to help you locate the proper term, and even a desk thesaurus can be useful to generate a list of synonyms that you can use while searching. For example, articles for plastic surgery may appear under "cosmetic surgery" or "facelift," "liposculpture," or "arthroplasty."

Next, you'll need to access one or more **research databases,** which are lists of books and/or journal articles arranged by title, author, subject, and keyword. **Periodical indexes** list the contents of magazines, journals, or newspapers. For example, the *Social Sciences Abstracts* present **abstracts**—brief summaries—of articles from about 350 journals all in the social sciences (in fields like anthropology, economics, geography, psychology, sociology, and urban studies). Some indexes are specific to a particular field, region, or time period: The online index *Contemporary Women's Issues* is an index that covers just what its title says. This database happens to be a **full-text** database, which means that it will link you to the actual article, book chapter, or essay, rather than simply providing its bibliographic information or summary. Some indexes, such as the *New York Times Index*, collect material from only one source. Other indexes are quite broad and inclusive—*Academic Search Premier,* for example, collects material from over 3,430 sources in a wide range of fields.

For our "kissing" research, we used the combined terms "kiss" and "public" to search *Academic Search Premier,* which yielded sources from such diverse publications as *The New York Times, USA Today, Sports Illustrated, The Advocate, The Economist, The Lesbian News,* and *Rolling Stone.* And we also tried "kiss" and "photography" and found references and journal and magazine articles on such things as images of kissing in Japanese photography; "the goodbye kiss"; the "wedding kiss"; and "when does a kiss become a kiss-off?"

In addition to these databases, you will also likely have access to your school's library catalog, which lists the titles of books that may have material relevant to your topic. For example, a search through our university library catalog revealed *The Kiss in History,* a book that looks perfect for our project, but that was published so recently that the library has not yet received a copy. Darn. Another source we found, *The Kissing,* turns out to be a collection of short stories—not what we are looking for. Other finds include a book called *The Kiss Sacred and Profane* on kissing in Christian history and an art photography book called *The Kiss.*

2. Evaluate the quality and relevance of sources you find.

Once you have found a list of possible sources and retrieved those sources, either in digital or hard copies, you will be ready to evaluate the sources for their relevance to your topic. In fact, much of this weeding out occurs as you are looking through indexes. Titles and abstracts, if available, are the best clue to the relevance and readability of a source. Not all of the sources that you find will be equally useful or relevant to your topic. If the index you are searching abstracts its sources, rely on the abstracts to point you to the most promising of them.

Once you have located the actual articles, there are a few ways to quickly assess their value. Ideally, you should locate approximately twice as many sources as you will eventually use. This way, when sources turn out to be less relevant or more difficult that you thought (or are not available in your library), you will have others that you can fall back on. If you retrieve more than you need, these setbacks will not slow you down much (or send you back to the beginning of the search process).

Genre

Journal articles and scholarly books from university presses are your most reliable sources, largely because they are "refereed." This means that a group of specialists in a field have read the article or book before it was published to assess its value and accuracy. If the specialists find problems with it, it doesn't get published; thus, there is a sort of quality control to what you find in these kinds of sources.

Major *newspapers and magazines* like the *Wall Street Journal* or *National Geographic* also stake their reputation on the quality and value of their work, but they often still have to print retractions for errors. Also, be aware that every source has biases that will impact what gets printed. Multiple sources for one story or topic can help you to see how a topic or story gets told from different perspectives.

Trade books (the kind sold to the general public and printed by nonscholarly presses) rely less on reputations for accuracy than on the name recognition of their authors and titles. They don't ordinarily print retractions for errors, nor do they always independently check the accuracy of the information contained in the books they publish.

Most problematic are *Web sites,* which are much easier to "publish" than journal articles or books. Anyone with a computer, Web access, and adequate technical skills—but not necessarily expert knowledge on the site's topic—can create a professional-looking site, so even the Web sites of official-sounding organizations can be unreliable and full of error. For this reason, while there is no doubt an abundance of excellent information accessible on the Web—and many of us find ourselves relying on it more and more for research—careful evaluation is necessary. Double-check what you find on Web sites against other sources, and place little confidence in individually authored or unattributed sites. Also check the date of the source: depending on your topic, an older source may no longer be useful.

Subheadings and Text Features

Glance over the chapters, subheadings, or section headings of your source. Are they understandable? Do they sound useful and relevant? Look for other text features. Some sources may include a valuable bibliography at the end, a glossary of important terms, or other useful features (charts, appendices, etc). Finally, read beginning and ending paragraphs (or chapters), where the overall argument of the source may be summarized. When you have finished, select those that you plan to use, and shelve the others (for now).

For our project, we've decided to use the book *The Kiss Sacred and Profane* only briefly, to discuss the importance of the kiss in European Christianity (the focus of the book). The book *Ritual and Symbol in Peacebuilding* offers far greater possibilities, especially the chapters "Understanding Ritual and Symbolic Acts," "Designing the Stage: Peacebuilding Spaces," and "Peacebuilding Pantomime: Negotiating Without Words."

3. Read and take notes on these sources for points of contact with your argument.

With your selection of secondary sources now established, you are ready to begin reading and taking notes. We refer to this as "active reading" because you are not simply reading the article to see what it says, but rather you are actively searching for material that answers your question or comments on your topic. As you read each source, look for places where it seems to speak to the representational trend you are writing about and the preliminary argument you have drafted. You might ask yourself the following questions:

- Do your secondary sources agree with your claims about this trend?
- What do they see differently?
- Do they use similar texts that reinforce, complicate, or challenge your arguments?
- What historical, cultural, or situational information do they bring to bear upon your images that change your reading of them?
- What questions do they ask that might influence your own process of analysis and argument?

The more you mark up and take notes on your sources (as though you are talking back to and with them), the better you will remember and understand them. While it can help your note-taking some, <u>underlining</u> or highlighting/outlining passages that seem relevant and important is still largely a passive reading exercise. More valuable and active reading is accomplished by *writing brief notes in the margin*, summarizing a point, explaining its importance, or comparing a point to another source. (Don't write in the original source if you don't own it, of course, only on your photocopy or e-copy.) Perhaps the most useful kind of notetaking for a research project or paper comes from taking notes in your own notebook. Keep track of page numbers of the original sources as you take your notes.

More research using *Academic Search Premier* yielded a newspaper article called "President's Papal Kiss Sparks Controversy in Mexico." In this short article, the author describes the controversy that arose on Pope John Paul II's visit to Mexico, when Mexican President Vincente Fox greeted the Pope by kneeling and kissing his ring (Figure 8.4). Typically, when a churchgoer kisses the Pope's ring, it is considered a sign of veneration. But in this case, the gesture generated a church–state controversy. Mexico has historically struggled to find an appropriate role for the Catholic Church and to maintain a segregation of church and state. The church's public role was restricted until recent years, and the President's gesture of veneration was seen as a sign of the church's growing power. When viewed within Mexico's historical and cultural context, then, tensions are quickly revealed, as public figures and their actions take on symbolic meanings beyond themselves. We'll need to think about whether we want to include the controversy surrounding this event in our paper, but it has

Figure 8.4   Mexican President Vicente Fox greeted Pope John Paul II when the Pope visited Mexico and canonized the Americas' first indigenous saint. July 31, 2002, *CBS News Online.*
Courtesy of Getty Images, Inc.

already provided an example of how secondary research can enrich your thinking on any question or subject. Moreover, the response to the President's gesture prompts us to consider the rhetorical function of kissing as a gesture that serves to advance, support, or refute certain cultural and national positions or arguments.

Drafting and Revision

You have been taking notes and writing down ideas and sources throughout your process of reading and analysis with primary and secondary sources. Now it is time to move from these preliminary notes to an essay draft. We suggest you do so in three distinct stages, generating first an annotated bibliography, then the research prospectus, and finally, the final paper.

1. The Annotated Bibliography

a. Bibliographic Entry

The purpose of the bibliographic entry is to allow you, or others, to reliably locate the source to follow up on your work. Bibliographic entries follow one of a number of standard formats established by scholarly organizations (MLA, APA, and Chicago style are common ones). These entries typically include at least the name of the source, the author, the publisher, and the date of publication. In MLA format, the bibliographic entry to one of our sources would look like this:

Schirch, Lisa. *Ritual and Symbol in Peacebuilding.* Bloomfield: Kumarian P, 2005.

b. Annotation: Summary

You will need to recount the following in order to compose a brief summary of your source:

1. The central argument or "point" of the source. You should look at chapters, section headings, subheadings, and introductory and concluding paragraphs for clues about the central argument or line of reasoning in the source.
2. The primary evidence, details, or reasons that this source uses to support its argument.
3. Enough of the context surrounding the source to help understand its significance. For example, what difference does the author, publication venue (with its intended audience), and date of publication make with regard to the argument the source makes?

c. Evaluation

In addition to a summary of your research sources, you will need to provide some review of the importance or value of this source to your particular research question or topic. How will it help you to pursue your argument or answer your question? What does it bring to the project? Describe the relevance of this source for your project as well as any special features of the source (like illustrations, a bibliography, section or chapter titles) that demonstrate its value. For example, the book, *The Kiss Sacred and Profane: An Interpretative History of Kiss Symbolism and Related Religio-erotic Themes,* will be useful in helping to contextualize kissing as a religious act through history. The book shows that kissing was associated with Christian greetings and symbolized the peace and unity of all believers (the kiss of peace, the holy kiss) as well as being a sign of grace, as when bishops kissed newly converted Christians to symbolize the infusion of the Holy Spirit into them.

2. The Research Prospectus

a. Situating Your Topic: Background and Context

Your research prospectus should describe your proposed research, approach, and thesis in relation to the context (historical, disciplinary, topic-related), and in relation to research already done in this area by others.

Your first goal in preparing a prospectus is to describe the context for your study. Consider answering these key questions: What is it about? How did you come to this as a topic? What field is it situated in? What have others said about this topic? What cultural or historical background will help your audience to understand your topic? In trying to answer these important questions, you may find secondary (or primary) sources useful in establishing some background information.

b. Situating the Problem: *Kairos,* or Exigency

Research should carry with it a sense of *kairos,* the ancient rhetorical concept for "timeliness" or exigency; research should demonstrate the *here and now* importance of the angle, thesis, and approach being offered.

- Why is your topic/issue important or significant? Why is it important now?
- In what way is the work on this topic by others incomplete or incorrect? What needs to be added or corrected?
- What are we now understanding incorrectly, or incompletely, or not thinking enough about, and why is this a problem?

Describe the issue, question, or problem that you see arising out of the context of your research and working thesis. Try to state your topic/thesis as a question or issue that could be answered in several different ways—and that also might be answered by researching and analyzing visual images. Don't ask questions too large in scope. And don't ask questions that require the kinds of information to which you will not have access. For example, a question about the meaning of kissing in different cultures will not be appropriate to an analysis of a few images from European or American origin. Nor would a question about the history of the representational trend, if all your sources are contemporary.

c. Situating Your Audience: Significance

Research should carry with it a sense of the potential significance (importance) for your intended audience. How does your topic, your approach, and your particular thesis fit for your intended audience? Who should care? Why should they care?

Further questions to consider in order to guide your articulation of the significance of your own research, project, and thesis are these:

- Why is the question you pose or the problem you introduce interesting or valuable to examine in the context of this cultural or historical background?
- What makes this study appropriate given this context?
- What do we often misunderstand, or overlook, or think about incorrectly concerning this topic? How will your study deepen, expand, or complicate our thinking about this issue?

d. Situating Your Authority: *Ethos*

Finally, research should also carry a sense of the researcher's own authority and strength in carrying out this particular project. It is important to explain how you will address the question or issue that you posed. What sources will you look at to help you answer this question, and why? This is your opportunity to demonstrate that you know your topic, that you have done your homework, and that you have something interesting to say about it. Refer to both primary and secondary sources here to demonstrate both what you know and how you will proceed.

Also give some consideration to your stance (distant, familiar, humble, etc.) in relation to both your topic/subject/thesis and your audience. How will you develop your own character and authority—your *ethos*—in relation to your topic and your argument? What makes you worth listening to on this topic?

For our project on images of kissing, we would need to think about why this topic is important (now)—its exigency—and how to establish it as an issue or problem. Kissing is normally not a hot topic in the news, so we'll have to be creative to generate interest in this topic as a representational trend and to argue for its significance. In our research, we came across several interesting articles and essays about homosexual kissing in public—we remember, too, the buzz that accompanied the onstage kiss between Madonna and Britney Spears a few years back. Maybe this is one way to introduce the topic of public kissing (in general) as a significant current issue, especially in light of the possible intersections between our "public ceremony" focus, the debates over public recognition of homosexual unions in marriage, and church/state issues generally. In fact, given our level of time and energy, this line of inquiry *could* lead to a substantial revision of our thesis and to the focus of our paper. On the other hand, it could just as well serve to pique our audience's interest in the topic we've developed so far.

3. The (Draft) Research Paper

Okay. We've done some preliminary analysis and we have our secondary sources; we've also taken notes, annotated, and prepared a prospectus. Now we're ready to draft the paper.

Some people like to begin by planning the sections or paragraphs of their paper first. Others prefer simply to begin writing and go where their thoughts take them. Some need to start in the middle, with the analysis, and work outward toward beginning and end. Some have to have the perfect title or they can't really begin, while others need a good idea of where and how they will conclude before they even start. In other words, everyone writes differently—and that's fine. As long as the result is a coherent, persuasive analytical text, the precise process you adopt is unimportant. However you write, keep your thesis in sight, but remember that it is still preliminary: You should expect to continue revising it right up until the end. If you don't revise your thesis at all throughout the writing process, you probably haven't learned anything new.

While we originally, reflexively, thought of kissing as a private expression of love, we now realize that it can take many forms, including public, political forms, and that it can elicit diverse responses. George W. Bush and Condoleezza Rice are metonymic of the United States, American values, and democracy; their public kiss seems to speak to issues of diversity and power. The Pope and the Koran likewise are metonymic for their respective religions and cultures. The Pope's kiss, therefore, is not just a kiss; it symbolizes a hoped-for reconciliation between warring religious/political/cultural entities.

Revised Thesis Statement:

Ceremonial kisses between public figures are performed to establish unity or reconciliation between different political, religious, and cultural entities. They bear some resemblance to conventional kisses expressing love or romance in that they suggest positive associations; unlike romantic kisses, however, they call these associations into question, because they exist within the context of, and as a response to, larger cultural and political tensions.

Describe and analyze primary sources.

Several paragraphs or sections of your paper should be devoted to the analysis of your primary sources. What details about these primary sources will you focus on? Describe the texts you are working with, attending most to those elements that will contribute to your overall argument and thereby support the claims that make up your thesis.

Introduce secondary sources.

Your paper should also respond to the material you've gathered from your secondary sources. As you look over your notes, arrange or mark them up to indicate where you think you will use these sources. Perhaps one source is useful for the introduction, others to support your thesis, and another as the perfect point to bolster your conclusion. You could cut your handwritten notes into strips; if you took notes on the computer, cut and paste the ones you'll use in the order that you'll use them. Whatever system you use, be prepared for the fact that this usage and order will likely change as you begin actually drafting your paper.

Refine and complicate your initial thesis.

Finally, as you draft your paper, you may want to return to the thesis and rethink it. Does it still describe the paper as it is turning out? If not, revise the thesis to fit what the paper is now doing. Your thesis will come either very early in the paper (after a brief contextualizing introduction) or at the end (as the conclusion to all your analysis and argument). When in doubt, go with your gut sense of what is interesting rather than what you imagine the instructor (or other students) want to hear. If you are excited and interested in your subject, that interest and excitement will come through in your writing.

As we've noted, plans often change between the prospectus stage and the actual completion of the project. If our project were to evolve into a discussion of images of public kissing that call into question the boundary between socially approved (adult heterosexual, ceremonial, or religious) and prohibited (homosexual) forms of love, then we will need to include images of "prohibited" kissing, such as two men or two women kissing, perhaps one in a religious context and the other not. Indeed, our research piqued our interest in the political uses of and responses to kissing images. We became more interested in these tensions—boundaries—and how they are exploited and/or reframed in the context of particular political campaigns or advocacy. This interest led to further research and additional primary texts for analysis.

At first, we searched for *kissing campaigns* on the Internet, and we found several interesting sources. One source highlighted the gestures of shaking hands and kissing babies in political campaigns and elections in the United States; another referred to the controversial Bennetton ad of a priest and nun kissing, and another focused on the "Kissing Doesn't Kill" art project and campaign (Figure 8.5). We chose the art project because of its use of kissing images to contest traditional boundaries, and because of the campaign's reliance upon common advertising strategies.

In the mid-to-late 1980s, gay activists focused on government negligence and media indifference to the AIDS crisis. Gran Fury, a collective of AIDS activists, created the "Kissing Doesn't Kill" image of three kissing couples of mixed race and same sex as part of a larger campaign. (Among other public projects that emerged during this period, and to which Gran Fury campaign might be compared, were the SILENCE-DEATH Project [1986], the Red Ribbon Project [1989], and the AIDS Memorial Quilt [1985]).

The Gran Fury campaign consisted of two parts. The first part of the campaign featured the mass mailing of a postcard version of the image. On the back of the postcard, the following message appeared: "Corporate Greed, Government Inaction and Public Indifference Make AIDS a Political Crisis." The second part of the campaign involved making a 12′ × 3′ full-color poster of the image, which was later mounted on New York City buses in 1989. The project traveled the country, but not

Figure 8.5   Gran Fury billboard, 1989, photo by Aldo Hernandez.

Courtesy of Gran Fury Records, Manuscripts and Archives Division, The New York Public Library, Astor, Lenox and Tilden Foundations.

all cities were willing to display this image via public transportation. For instance, the Chicago Transit Authority did not allow the "Kissing Doesn't Kill" project to run in its city. Among Gran Fury's most inflammatory work was its infamous "Pope Piece," which criticized the Pope's anti-safe-sex rhetoric. The "Kissing Doesn't Kill" posters and art campaign used visual texts and public transportation venues to reach a broader audience and to provoke action. Mulling over all these issues led us to the following thoughts, which we present here in outline form:

1. "Kissing Doesn't Kill" image and campaign
   a. The kiss symbolizes tolerance and understanding across differences.
      i. Repetition of kissing gesture and postures.
      ii. Mixed races and same-sex couples kissing.
   b. At the same time, the kissing campaign and image testify to the cultural indifference to and invisibility of the AIDS crisis in the late 1980s.
      i. Logical appeal of "Kissing Doesn't Kill: Greed and Indifference Do."
      ii. AIDS is a misunderstood issue within U.S. society.
      iii. Invisibility of AIDS requires the mounting of a public campaign that would appeal to a broad and diverse audience—passers-by.

We now have an additional primary text and observations that both complement and complicate our original thesis. For instance, we might generate the following claim based on our initial observations and analysis above:

> Advocacy groups have used images of mixed race and same-sex couples kissing to educate audiences, to provoke action, and to respond to cultural indifference.

Some writers might decide to reshape their initial thesis to include this new claim. But it is also possible, and perhaps preferable, to introduce this campaign and analytical claims later in the paper as a way of complicating our original argument and providing alternative perspectives. Either way, further research is needed to explicate this image as part of a larger representational trend.

More research using our library's main search engine yielded several relevant books, the one closest to our topic being *A Leap in the Dark: AIDS, Art and Contemporary Cultures,* edited by Allan Klusacek and Ken Morrison in 1992. There is a section in this book focusing on public art on AIDS that looks very promising because it provides further context for understanding the urgency and timeliness of these campaigns.

Arranging the Research Paper Draft

- **Organize analytical claims and support.** What major claims will you make? What texts will you analyze in detail? Will you discuss each text separately, or will you consider all the texts together as you make each point in your argument? What order do you want to consider them in? Rhetorical theory has traditionally said to use the strongest arguments at the beginning and end of the body of your paper, with the weakest in the middle. Even if you take this advice, you need to decide just what your strongest arguments are and why.
- **Generate and place revised thesis.** As your draft proceeds, you should gain some sense of where you want to state your thesis and how it needs to be revised to fit into the draft. The final draft of your thesis should suggest the major argument of your paper and all its parts, and it should lead your audience to anticipate it. As you move from paragraph to paragraph and from section to section, you'll want to provide "signposts" for readers to remind them of the thesis and where you are in its development.
- **Consider introductions.** For many writers, drafting the introduction doesn't come until near the end of the project, when you know how the paper looks. Think about what your audience already knows about kissing, about why they might be interested in kissing, and what might make them think this a topic worth reading more about. One way to start your research paper might be by describing one of your images and then linking that description to your working thesis.
- **Consider conclusions.** Finally, the conclusion. What are the historical, political, and/or cultural implications of the representational trend you have identified? Why should we concern ourselves with this trend at this point in time? What's at stake and for whom? What do you want your audience to remember? What final image do you want to leave them with?

Finishing the Paper

One word: revise. Remember that everything you've done so far is still in the draft stage. Expect to share drafts with your instructor and peers in class, and prepare to go back to your primary texts to gather more evidence for your claims. As you generate additional claims and evidence, remember to revise your initial thesis or to sequence your analytical claims throughout the paper to demonstrate the development and refinement of your thesis. Finally, expect to go over your paper again to revise for style, grammar, transitions, and the like.

Conversations Across Sections

Assignment Sequences

These assignment sequences are thematically driven. Each sequence draws together assignments from two or more sections of the textbook. If you haven't done so already, you should plan to read the critical frames for the sections represented. The assignments are intended to build on each other and to encourage you to read one essay through the lens of another.

Assignment Sequence 1
Private Publics/Family Albums

Sections: Familial Gazes and National Gazes

Maxine Hong Kingston, "Photograph of My Parents"
bell hooks, "In Our Glory: Photography and Black Life"
Mark Jeffreys, "The Visible Cripple (Scars and Other Disfiguring Displays Included)"
Marianne Hirsch, "Reframing the Human Family Romance"
Marita Sturken, "The Image as Memorial"
Jeff Wolin, "Written in Memory" (photographs)

Essay 1: Reworking the Family Album

Option 1: Photo Definitions
Readings: Hirsch, hooks, Kingston
Preparation: Read Critical Frame for Familial Gazes

This sequence invites you develop an interpretation of the role of visual culture, particularly photography, in defining familial and national ideals and values. For this assignment, choose one family photograph, a series of related photographs, or a home video. The questions you should be concerned with as you develop your interpretation are these:

- Are the photographs you have chosen part of an unofficial history of your family?
- In what ways are the family album, snapshots, or video a way to represent the family members' everyday lives?
- More specifically, does the photograph represent an idealized image of your family, yourself, or particular family members? Like the essays by hooks, Kingston, and Jeffreys, your essay should:

  1. Move among descriptions of the family photograph(s)/other artifact(s) and the family's interpretation of them.
  2. Demonstrate a cultural analysis of both the photograph(s)/artifact(s) and their surrounding narratives.
  3. Reveal the complexity of the role of photography in constructing a sense of familial history and identity.

Try to remember key emotional, social, or economic events that link up to the years you are dealing with in the photographs. Following are additional questions that you might consider in developing your analysis of the visual arguments put forth and the narratives that surround their interpretation:

- How did these events shape the family's image of itself?
- In what ways do these photographs prompt you to reconsider your "self-history"?
- What is missing from the photograph? What pictures might have been taken but never were? What events or people were not recorded? What might it have been impossible to represent?
- What scenarios are seen as possible subject matter for the family album? In other words, what remains invisible within family archives?
- What do these photographs tell you about the ways in which particular people in your family are positioned in the family and/or world?
- What social and cultural values and ideas shape the family's visual representation of itself?
- What does the artifact(s) tell you about power relationships within the family?
- Does the artifact represent power struggles between men and women or between adults and children?

Option 2: An Album of You
Reading: Jeffreys
Preparation: Read Critical Frame for Familial Gazes

Much of Mark Jeffreys' essay relies on key photographs from his family—and especially of his brother Jim—to build his analysis of how the "invisible cripple" is constructed in our culture. Explore your own family album or any family/self pictures you have and first build a collage—or narrative—of *you* from these photos. Use five to ten photos. (Note how a collage of photos will probably be different from a narrative collection of photos.) Organize and arrange them as you see fit. Now write an essay that approaches your collage/narrative in multiple ways:

a. By offering a brief *caption* beneath each picture.

b. By offering a more extended *description* of the pictures somewhere in your essay (you can decide where it best goes).

c. By offering a *narrative* of what the collage or sequence tells about you.

d. By *analyzing* such issues as why the photo was taken; who took it and what he or she seemed to want to represent of you; how it conflicts with, compromises, or carries out a seamless portrait of you overall; what is erased, left out, made invisible in this series or collage; what is enhanced, illuminated, brought to the foreground in this series or collage; what someone else—someone who doesn't know you at all—might *interpret* about you from this series or collage; and any other relevant analytical frames you can think of.

Essay 2: Familial Ideals and the Nation

Readings: Hirsch, Wolin
Preparation: Read Critical Frame for Familial Gazes *and* National Gazes

Rhetoric about the family often imagines the "family" to be an ideal, safe space away from the hardships of the public world. Moreover, images of families abound in popular culture, demonstrating the permeable boundaries between public and private spheres. Ideals of family have changed considerably over the course of the twentieth century, making a good argument for the need to read images of families within the contexts in which they were produced and later viewed.

The second essay assignment in this sequence asks you to select a sequence of photos, either the Wolin images or others included in this book, or elsewhere (you may work with images from the mass media, museums, art galleries, Internet sites, etc.), and to consider the following question: Does the photographer challenge or reproduce certain notions of the family and/or nation?

For this assignment, you might review the theoretical frameworks, concepts, and essays introduced in the *National Gazes* chapter and consider how certain essays, such as Kozol's, might help you describe and analyze the familial gaze and its relation to national identity. Questions you might consider:

- If the family is the central focus in the photograph, do different members of the family embody or challenge ideals of gender, race, ethnicity, sexuality, family, or national identity?

- What specific visual elements (such as composition, gaze, lighting) in the photographs support or challenge dominant (or mainstream) beliefs about families?

- Family images often catch our attention because they look both familiar and unfamiliar at the same time. How does the photo essay you selected handle the tensions between normative values and the differences that specific families embody?

- Do the photographs represent or silence trauma or conflict in the family portrait? What are the implications of the presence or absence of trauma in shaping perceptions about families in contemporary society?

Essay 3: National and Community Archives

Readings: Hirsch, Sturken, Taylor
Preparation: Read Critical Frames for Familial Gazes *and* National Gazes

The last assignment in this sequence asks you to consider the functions of institutional archives (historical societies, museums, national archives, etc.) and how they shape, and perhaps limit, our understandings of visual culture, the family, and national identity. First, you'll need to locate a national or community archive. Try to identify an archive that includes images of the family and/or particular communities as part of the story it tells. Consider whose memories are archived by such an exhibit. Do images of the family play a particular role in this archive? For instance, how do certain portraits of the family establish particular notions of community? If you do not have access to a national archive, you might visit your local historical society, church archives, or local museums. Do particular essays in the *Familial* and *National Gazes* sections help you analyze the images and their function in this archive? Why or why not? Possible topics that you might consider:

a. The U.S. Holocaust Museum includes as part of its exhibition a wall of family photographs. In what ways does this collection of family photographs of Holocaust victims and their families reconfigure the role of family photographs as public documents?

b. Sturken's essay discusses how personal images have been incorporated into public memorials to create a "collective memory" that both offers a testimony to those lost and affirms the trauma of war, AIDS, and violence against children. The Internet has provided a new public venue for individuals and groups to participate in cultural memory and testimony. Find a site that uses photographs of individuals as part of its public message and discuss how it supports or negates Sturken's interpretation of "participatory interaction" with public events. You can find some good examples at the Smithsonian American Memory site (http://memory.loc.gov), or you can look for a more recent example of your own to analyze.

c. According to Sturken, many things besides photographs are left at the Vietnam memorial and incorporated into the AIDS quilt, including letters, teddy bears, wedding rings, and articles of clothing. For example, a Harley-Davidson motorcycle was left at the Vietnam Memorial, perhaps a tribute to a passionate enthusiast. These objects frequently exemplify aspects of culture that we value—childhood, relationships, work, hobbies—and that are "perceived as a testimony not to death but to lives lived." Imagine that you have an opportunity to leave a small collection of photographs and objects about yourself in a public place, a testimony to a "life being lived." What would you choose, and why? How would you say these objects reflect U.S. cultural values? In what ways might they resist or oppose mainstream values and beliefs, and why?

d. If you are interested in the construction of community memorials in New York City post–9/11, you might go to the "Witness and Response" Web site of the Library of Congress (http://www.loc.gov/exhibit/911//911-docphotos.html). What patterns do you notice among the memorials? Do certain icons or symbols appear more than others? To what objects are the memorializers drawn? With what images do you identify and why? What do particular objects symbolize and what is their rhetorical impact? In what ways do these memorials transform or appropriate pre–9/11 notions and symbols of the city?

e. If you are interested in the designing process and debates over the national memorial on the site of the former World Trade towers, you might consult reports from the past two years in *The New York Times* or other newspapers and magazines. What characterizes these debates over the location and design of the national memorial? Are certain positions adopted by particular groups, such as victims' families, residents, builders, government workers, or artists? How would you characterize these various positions? Do certain groups or individuals identify with particular symbols or aspects of the city? What rhetorical techniques do they use to rationalize their views and/or designs? Which designs or arguments do you find the most persuasive or compelling and why? Finally, illustrate your stance with a visual argument or alternative memorial.

Assignment Sequence 2
Racing the Nation/Documenting Discrimination

Sections: National Gazes and Documentary Gazes

Dinitia Smith, "Slave Site for a Symbol of Freedom"
Marita Sturken, "The Image as Memorial"
Diana Taylor, "Lost in the Field of Vision"
Barbie Zelizer, "Conveying Atrocity in Image"

Essay 1: Visualizing Civil Rights: Struggles and Achievements

Readings: Sturken, Taylor
Preparation: Read Critical Frame for National Gazes

This assignment asks you to locate a national or community memory site that represents struggles and achievements in the United States with regard to discrimination based on gender, race, class, sexuality, national identity, or ability. You might consider, for example, the Civil Rights Memorial that Maya Lin created for the Southern Poverty Law Center or the Memorial proposed for Ground Zero, among others. Consider the stories and images of struggle and achievement depicted. Find out all you can about the production (design, creation, financial backing, etc.) of the memory site and its reception (the public's response). To complete this assignment, you will need to do some library and perhaps archival research on your chosen memory site and the public response at the time of its initial construction or display. How was the memory site described in local newspapers? Has the memory site received local and/or national attention? Why or why not? Have particular disputes arisen with regard to the memory site? If so, what positions characterize the disputes? If not, why do you think the public was/has been so eager to accept the memory or narrative the site offers? Did/do particular social, political, or economic factors shape the public's response? How might past reactions contrast with contemporary viewers' reactions? What historical or political factors might account for these different responses?

Essay 2: Slavery as a Site of Memory

Reading: Smith
Preparation: Read Critical Frame for National Gazes

The New York Times article "Slave Site for a Symbol of Freedom" highlights the disputes over the plans of the National Park Service to showcase the Liberty Bell. Local residents and scholars argued that the site is an inappropriate memorial to freedom precisely because it is housed on a site where George Washington once lived and where slaves labored. This assignment asks you to research memory sites that commemorate the emancipation of slaves or that portray slavery as an institution in the United States. We define memory sites in the introduction to the National Gazes section to refer to *public* spaces for collective grieving or national memory. For this assignment, feel free to expand the definition of memory sites to include literary texts that rely upon the visualization of the trauma of slavery. (For example, you might consider novels such as Toni Morrison's *Beloved,* slave narratives such as Harriet Jacob's *Incidents in the Life of a Slave Girl,* and poems about the legacy of slavery, among others.) You might also consider visual prints of slaves from the nineteenth century or national memorials such as the Freedmen's Memorial to Abraham Lincoln (see, e.g., http://www.cr.nps.gov/nr/travel/wash/dc87.htm).

First, analyze the visual argument that the memorial or visual image presents. If you are working with a literary text, think about how the author creates visual images or memories of the trauma of slavery. What is the primary rhetorical function of the visual image? For example, is the memorial or image meant to persuade viewers (or readers, as the case may be) to remember certain historical events and forget others? Does it convey a particular character's or subject's experience? What power relationships are configured through the visual placement of particular subjects or objects? Who is gazing at whom? If you are working with a public memorial, consider how its location and geographical context shapes its meaning. How does the memorial imagine its audience? Does the memorial invite a particular sensory response? What roles does the memorial or image assume of its viewers or readers?

Essay 3: The Work of Memory

Option 1: Memorial Functions
Readings: Sturken, FDR Images, Garland-Thomson
Preparation: Read Critical Frame for National Gazes

In focusing on the FDR memorial and the controversy over FDR's representation, Garland-Thomson (see Documentary Gazes) makes many statements about what memorials generally do and represent in our culture. She argues, for example, that "Memorials are inherently controversial." She also differentiates between the "old" and "new" kinds of memorials. She notes that "the FDR memorial follows [Maya] Lin's transformation of memorials from classic, often phallic, edifices that suggest ancient sites of worship to a more decentered and interactive public space. These new memorials are experiential and democratic rather than monumental and hierarchical . . ." ("The FDR Memorial: Who Speaks from the Wheelchair?," *Chronicle of Higher Education,* 26 Jan. 2001). This assignment asks you to think about the function of memorials in our culture at large and to examine the form and function of a local memorial. Look for one on your campus or in your town. And then write about it in these terms:

- What kind of memory function does it serve?
- What is it attempting to represent?
- Is it using any of the key memory-representation tropes (metaphor, metonymy, synecdoche, paradox, irony)?
- What function does it seem to be serving? Who would go there and why? What kind of feeling or action would they be expected to leave with?
- Who or what is to be remembered?
- Who or what is to be doing the remembrance?
- What is supposed to be the relationship between the remembered and the rememberer?
- Would you characterize it as an "old" or "new" style of memorial? Why?

Option 2: The Trauma of Representation
Readings: Zelizer, Ignatieff
Preparation: Read Critical Frame to Documentary Gazes

This assignment invites you to gather a series of atrocity images, namely footage of governmental, international, or national crises, such as wars, or visual archives of atrocities such as those documented by the Cambodian Genocide Project (http://www.yale.edu/cgp/img.html) or the Holocaust Cybrary (http://www.remember.org). In keeping with the theme of this assignment sequence, consider the ways in which cultural, religious, ethnical, or racial differences are represented. Analyze a series of images with the four primary compositional elements of atrocity images articulated by Zelizer in mind. Consider, for instance: What visual patterns and repetitions appear? Who is represented? Victims? Witnesses? What type of documentary gaze is depicted? After you have analyzed the images, consider whether your analysis can support the claim that the images constitute a subgenre within the larger genre of atrocity images. If so, what conventions or structures of meaning define this subgenre? Finally, consider Ignatieff's claims about the rhetorical appeal of images of suffering and the extent to which the media has shaped our memory of the event conveyed.

Assignment Sequence 3
Under Western Eyes

Sections: Consumer Gazes and Traveling Gazes

Catherine Lutz and Jane Collins, "The Photograph as an Intersection of Gazes"
Audre Lorde, "The Fourth of July"
Jamaica Kincaid, "A Small Place"
Cynthia Enloe, "The Globetrotting Sneaker"
Charles Kernaghan, "An Appeal to Walt Disney"
Lisa Nakumura, "Where Do You Want to Go Today? Cybernetic Tourism, the Internet, and Transnationality"

Essay 1: Magazine Tours

Reading: Lutz and Collins
Preparation: Read Critical Frame to Traveling Gazes

Lutz and Collins quote Susan Sontag, who describes the photographer as the "super-tourist, an extension of the anthropologist, visiting natives and bringing back their exotic doings and strange gear" as a means to combat boredom and keep readers "fascinated." This assignment asks you to collect a variety of magazines and examine the ways in which we are invited to tour another's identity or experience. Consider the magazine's audience and contemplate how this targeted audience might inform the way the magazine depicts identity and difference. Are there certain compositional elements at work throughout all the photos? Are particular subjects or objects positioned at the center of the image or on the margins? Who looks at whom? What sort of gaze do the photographs elicit?

Essay 2: Seeing and Being Seen

Readings: Lorde, Kincaid
Preparation: Read Critical Frame to Traveling Gazes

Both Audre Lorde and Jamaica Kincaid use "seeing" and "being seen" as tropes through which to demonstrate the power of looking. Kincaid emphasizes the power of looking that the tourist to Antigua has by using direct address to her readers: e.g., "You will see . . . ," "You will look. . . ." However, she complicates this looking by also noting what the tourist will not see and suggesting that the native Antiguans retain significant power to look back. Lorde talks about how visible racial differences shaped her history and her family's visit to Washington, DC. How do these ways of seeing and being seen—of looking, looking away, looking back—provide examples of *identification* and *difference,* as these items are explained in the Introduction and in the critical frame for *Traveling Gazes*? In what ways do they defy a simple connection with these terms?

Essay 3: Made in the USA?

Readings: Enloe, Kernaghan
Preparation: Read Critical Frame to Consumer Gazes

Option 1: Corporate Images

While Enloe focuses on sneakers, many other items of consumer apparel are also now made abroad, where there are cheaper and less restrictive labor laws. This assignment asks you to research the labor practices of other apparel companies. You might consider looking to see where the clothing with your school's logo on it is made. Find out about three or more companies' practices and then compare these practices with the companies' corporate Web sites. Are there any contradictions? What does each site say about the people who make its apparel? Gather your findings and put together a presentation that you will share with the rest of your class. Remember to consider your audience's needs; what sort of rhetorical appeals will be most persuasive to them?

Option 2: Mapping Your Clothes

Working in a group of four or five people, look at the labels of all of your clothing. Make a list of where all the items were made. Next, create a map that shows where each item came from and where the headquarters of each clothing company is located. Locate another map that shows the worldwide distribution of wealth, or create your own map after researching online this distribution. Present these two maps to your class. Alternatively, you might map your clothes as follows:

- Map/create an illustration of how the particular clothes are designed, manufactured, and so on.
- Create a map of where you buy these clothes.
- Map who is involved from start to finish in the production of the clothing item and also consider its recycling, if relevant.

Assignment Sequence 4
Examining the Normalizing Gaze

Sections: Familial, Traveling, and Documentary Gazes

Mark Jeffreys, "The Visible Cripple (Scars and Other Disfiguring Displays Included)"
John Hockenberry, "Walking with the Kurds"
Rosemarie Garland-Thomson, "The Politics of Staring: Visual Rhetorics of Disability in Popular Photography"
Georgina Kleege, "Dream Museum: Blindness, Language, and Visual Art"
Aimee Mullins images

Essay 1: Cultural Representations of Disability

Our culture produces numerous artifacts that are widely disseminated in the public sphere: movies, television shows, music videos, advertisements, cartoons, paintings, magnets, bumper stickers, etc. These artifacts often make powerful visual arguments, working to persuade us to believe or act in a certain way.

Disability, like gender, is a historical, cultural, and social construction that is often represented in various cultural artifacts; how disability is constructed (or visually represented, in this case) can influence attitudes toward and treatment of disabled people.

Reading: Garland-Thomson
Preparation: Read Critical Frame for Documentary Gazes

For this assignment, choose a cultural artifact: a documentary film about or a series of images of disability or disabled people. In your essay, you should analyze the artifact and its representation of disability using the rhetorical concepts introduced in the critical frame for this unit.

- Describe the artifact in detail for your audience.
- What argument does the artifact make about disability and/or disabled people?
- Connect your artifact to Rosemarie Garland-Thomson's "The Politics of Staring." Consider which of Garland-Thomson's categories for the "visual rhetorics of disability" your artifact fits into. How can this categorization help you with your analysis?
- What genre does the artifact belong to? (Is it a film, an advertisement, a bumper sticker, etc.?) What are audience expectations for this genre? How do audience expectations for this artifact influence audience interpretation of it?
- Consider *kairos* (the "timeliness" and context) in your analysis of the artifact. What is the cultural and historical climate in which the artifact appears? How might this "timeliness" have influenced the creation of the artifact? How does it influence its reception by the audience?

Essay 2: Familial Representations of Disability, Ability, and Normalcy

Families often create and project their image based on cultural representations and expectations. For this essay, you will be asked to analyze familial representations of disability/normalcy. Mark Jeffreys contrasts the photos of his brother's disability to a wedding photo of his family that hides their disabilities. He poignantly describes this cultural habit aimed at concealing difference: "At the seam where body joins culture, every construction of the body begins and ends. On the efforts of cultures to hide that seam, every oppression depends." For this essay, you will consider representations of family that create illusions of "normalcy" and distort, conceal, or disguise reality, giving in to culturally created ideal images of family.

Reading: Jeffreys
Preparation: Read Critical Frame for Familial Gazes

For this paper, you should analyze one or two family photos (yours or another that you are familiar with) that create an illusion of normalcy or the absence of disability, much like the wedding photo Jeffreys describes in his essay. Address the following in your paper:

- Describe the image(s).
- Describe the narrative that the photo or photos tell.
- Now interpret the photo(s).
  - What image of the family is the photograph(s) intended to create?
  - How can you "prove" these intentions? (What evidence can you use from the photograph itself?)
- Discuss how the photograph(s) create this illusion or "hide the seam"—veiling the physical or emotional reality. What's being hidden? What's being emphasized? Why?
- Discuss why this family would be interested in veiling its reality. Consider the context in which the photo(s) were created. How did the social, cultural, and historical context of the photo(s) influence their creation? Their reception by an audience? You may want to examine wider images of the family produced by and perpetuated by popular media (television, film, magazines, etc.) at the time. How might these images have contributed to the creation of an illusion of normalcy in the photo(s) you are examining?

Essay 3: Public Space, Disability, and Mobility

In this essay, you will consider the representation of disability, public space, and access. Without a disability, many of us fail to recognize the obstacles those with disabilities face when they enter the public sphere.

Readings: Hockenberry, Kleege
Preparation: Read Critical Frames for Traveling Gazes
and Documentary Gazes

Both Hockenberry and Kleege address the entrance of disabled people into public spaces. For this paper, you should analyze a public space you are familiar with that requires disabled people to enlist assistance in order to be, perform, enter, or participate in that space.

- Describe the public space you have chosen.
- Describe the assistance required for disabled people. What would it take to make this space accessible?
- Analyze the lack or existence of accommodation that this public space provides. If "accommodations" exist, are they added on (retrofitted) to the space or do they appear to be "naturalized" in the general design and purpose of the space?

- Consider how access and accommodations in this public space may benefit (or hamper) other kinds of people (those who do not necessarily have a disability).
- Consider the *kairos* (the "timeliness" and context) of the public space. How might the social, cultural, and historical context of the space enhance your disability-focused analysis of it?

CREDITS

Dorothy and Thomas Hoobler, "La Familia," from *The Mexican American Family Album* by Dorothy Hoobler and Thomas Hoobler, pp. 78–83. © 1994 by Dorothy and Thomas Hoobler. Used by permission of Oxford University Press.

Tomás Rivera, "The Portrait," is reprinted with permission from the publisher of *Sandia . . . And the Earth Did Not Devour Him,* by Tomás Rivera. Translation by Evangelina Vigil-Pinon (Houston: Arte Publico Press-University of Houston © 1987).

Marianne Hirsch, "Reframing the Human Family Romance," reprinted by permission of the publisher from *Family Frames: Photography, Narrative and Postmemory,* by Marianne Hirsch, pp. 41–43, 46–58, 63–67, 69–71. © 1997 by the President and Fellows of Harvard College.

Sharon Olds, "Looking at Them Asleep" and "I Go Back to May 1937," from *The Gold Cell,* by Sharon Olds. © 1987 by Sharon Olds. Used by permission of Alfred A. Knopf, a division of Random House, Inc.

Dinitia Smith, "Slave Site for a Symbol of Freedom," © 2002 by The New York Times. Reprinted with permission.

Marita Sturken, "The Image as Memorial," from Marianne Hirsch, ed. *The Familial Gaze.* Hanover, NH: University Press of New England, 1999, pp. 178–195.

Diana Taylor, "Lost in the Field of Vision: Witnessing September 11, including images taken by Diana Taylor," in *The Archive and Repertoire,* pp. 237–265. Copyright © 2003, Duke University Press. All rights reserved. Used by permission of the publisher.

Wendy Kozol, "'The Kind of People Who Make Good Americans': Nationalism and *Life*'s Family Ideal," Chapter 3 from Wendy Kozol, <u>*Life's America: Family and Nation in Postwar Photojournalism.*</u> © 1994 Temple University Press.

Aurora Levins Morales, "Child of the Americas," from Aurora Levins Morales and Rosario Morales, *Getting Home Alive.* Milford, CT: Firebrand Books, 1986, p. 636.

Robert Kaplan, "The Rusted Iron Curtain," originally appeared in *Altantic Monthly.* © Robert Kaplan. Reprinted by permission.

Maya Angelou, "Champion of the World," from *I Know Why the Caged Bird Sings* by Maya Angelou, copyright © 1969 and renewed 1997 by Maya Angelou, pp. 566–568. Used by permission of Random House, Inc.

Elizabeth Bishop, "Questions of Travel," from *The Complete Poems 1927–1979* by Elizabeth Bishop. Copyright © 1979, 1983 by Alice Helen Methfessel. Reprinted by permission of Farrar, Straus and Giroux, LLC.

Adrienne Rich, Part XII "What homage will be paid to a beauty built to last," from "An Atlas of the Difficult World," from *An Atlas of The Difficult World: Poems 1988–1991* by Adrienne Rich. Copyright © 1991 by Adrienne Rich. Used by permission of the author and W.W. Norton & Company, Inc.

Catherine Lutz and Jane Collins, "The Photograph as an Intersection of Gazes," Chapter 7 of Catherine A. Lutz & Jane L. Collins, *Reading National Geographic.* © 1993 University of Chicago Press. Reprinted by permission.

INDEX